EXPLORATIONS
IN CRISIS

EXPLORATIONS
IN CRISIS

PAPERS ON INTERNATIONAL HISTORY

William L. Langer

Edited by Carl E. Schorske and Elizabeth Schorske

THE BELKNAP PRESS OF
HARVARD UNIVERSITY PRESS
CAMBRIDGE, MASSACHUSETTS
1969

Prefatory Note

Many of William Langer's students have from time to time contemplated a *Festschrift* of essays in traditional tribute to him as one of America's great teachers of history. Such projects have always foundered on the same rock, the generous good sense of Langer himself. He has stoutly maintained that the *Festschrift* form has become outdated. In an era when even the specialist has difficulty locating the relevant material in his field, an anthology of diverse articles no longer suits the conditions of scholarly work. Originally intended as a monument to the achievement of the master, the *Festschrift* has become today a tomb for the work of his students. Their articles, catalogued under their teacher's name, are all too often placed beyond the reach of future scholars. In the case of Professor Langer, this problem looms even larger than usual. He has trained students whose areas of interest range from Denmark to Ethiopia, from Turkey to Japan, and whose approaches vary from economic to intellectual history, from the sociological to the diplomatic. Langer's very success in cultivating the diverse interests of his students has made his objections to the pluralism of a *Festschrift* not just cogent but compelling in his own case.

Inverting the usual procedure, we are honoring Professor Langer by presenting to a wider public a collection of his own papers. This volume makes available some essays not previously published, and rescues others already in print from that inaccessibility which the teacher had solicitously feared for the labors of his students.

Many have shared in the idea of this volume—too many to be separately thanked for their encouragement. Professors Ronald Coons and Harry Marks were about to launch a similarly conceived project when they discovered that this one was in progress. For suggestions and advice in the preparation of the introduction, the editors owe particular debts of gratitude to Roderic H. Davison, Felix Gilbert, Arno Mayer, Jeanne Peterson, and Robert Lee Wolff. Cyril Black assisted with problems of Russian transliteration, John Masson Smith with

v

Turkish and Arabic ones. Mrs. William Langer gave not only warm encouragement but indispensable assistance.

Professor Langer has spared no pains to provide the materials, especially those in manuscript, that have made this volume possible. The editors alone are responsible for the selection and arrangement of the papers. While the collection is not complete (see Chronological List of Publications, page 497), we have omitted only those few writings which either seemed too ephemeral to reveal a dimension of the author's work or which duplicated too fully the content of the essays included. We have not enlarged or emended the author's original scholarly apparatus, confining our efforts to modernizing and clarifying the footnotes to make the sources cited more readily accessible.

The Introduction aims to situate the several papers in Professor Langer's intellectual development and in the persistent world crisis which has been his life-long concern as scholar and public servant. Where the interpretations of the Introduction are affected by political views divergent from his own, the editors count on the intellectual force of the papers themselves to enable the reader to form that independent judgment which William Langer has always prized.

Carl E. Schorske
Elizabeth Schorske

Berkeley, California
September, 1968

Contents

Contents

Introduction by Carl E. Schorske

In his massive studies of international history William Langer characteristically writes no introductions. To embark upon one of these engrossing works is like setting out on a canoe trip in strange waters with a seasoned guide. No concessions to the greenhorn, no charts or maps handed out before the voyage; they can be broken out enroute if we need them. The traveller simply takes his place in the bow. The guide in the stern, with a single deft stroke, drives the canoe out into the current. Thus Langer propels his reader into the stream of history, making him at once a participant observer. Having to use his eyes, to watch like a bowsman for eddies, snags, and rocks, the reader learns by direct encounter the contours of the valley of the river of time. As direct observation brings security to the voyager, a sense of orientation, of meaning, even wonder awakens in him too.

The Diplomacy of Imperialism opens in this way. Only its first sentence is interpretive, separating, as it were, one stretch of river from another: "Bismarck's fall from power in March 1890 was the great dividing point that separated the Franco-German War from the great conflict of 1914." By the very next sentence we are in midstream with the men of 1890: "News of the event [Bismarck's dismissal] struck Europe like a thunderbolt, and for some time the diplomatic world could hardly find its bearings." [1] How the diplomatic world found—or failed to find—those bearings is what the book is all about. By identification with the events as they unfold, with the men as they define themselves in action, the reader absorbs the shock of their strange immediacy and learns to comprehend them as meaningful elements in a larger landscape. Neither drama, as for Thucydides, nor a painted triptych, as for Burckhardt, provides the structural model for Langer's mode of historical presentation. He simply associates his reader with him as

[1] William L. Langer, *The Diplomacy of Imperialism, 1890–1902* (New York and London, 1935), I, 3.

ix

apprentice explorer. Introduction and "background" about what's gone before, up-river, are not necessary.

In presenting this collection of his papers, the editors would have preferred to respect Langer's method, to let the reader simply embark without benefit of maps or charts. We are dealing, however, not with a single enterprise, but with a whole series of discrete explorations undertaken over fifty years. The connections among them are not immediately apparent, for they are part of a lifetime of scholarly and political experience. To illuminate their unity in terms of the historian's longer intellectual voyage, some guidance to the reader seems desirable.

The papers in this volume range widely in purpose, style, and substance—from research articles to addresses on public issues designed for a general audience. Despite their varied character, however, they fall quite naturally into four groups, representing distinct phases in Langer's intellectual evolution. They reflect his involvement not ony in historical scholarship but also in political life, whether as citizen, as public educator, or as state official. The essays make clear that, for Langer, historical understanding and contemporary politics illuminate and enrich each other. A historiography impervious to reassessment in the light of present experience is dead; a politics uninformed by consideration of past experience is blind. In the four periods into which the author's intellectual development may be divided, past and present always appear in a kind of polyphonic union. In some, the voice of the past rings the stronger; in others, the voice of the present; neither wholly dominates. In relation to his major works, the minor writings represent now preludes, adumbrating themes to be developed later in larger forms; now postludes, recasting old themes for new times.

In the 1920's, the young historian developed his scholarly powers as an analyst both of political events and of the wider systematic implications of diplomatic history. If international politics in the Era of Good Feeling color Langer's treatment of the disintegrating European states system before 1914, they do not determine his questions. Part I, "Systems, Games, and Players," probes the weaknesses of the international system of the past for an audience of professional historians.

The majority of the essays in Part II, "Imperialism Old and New," were composed for a wider public in the face of the fascist menace. Truly essays, not scholarly articles, they are the product of a new, self-conscious effort on the part of the historian to bring the past to bear upon his contemporaries' understanding of a terrifying present. The involvement of America in World War II brought a second shift in Langer's focus, reflected in the pieces which comprise Part III, "The United States as a World Power." While placing his expertise at the disposal of his government during the war and postwar years, the historian of Europe turned from his earlier interests to consider the changing place of the United States in the international scene. If the concerns of present policy predominated now, they opened up new questions about the past.

After completing in the early 1950's his two great volumes on the United States' entry into World War II, Langer returned to European history once more. Part IV, "Explorations in New Terrain," offers a wealth of new problems and perspectives which reach beyond the confines of diplomatic history. In his fourth period, as in his first, Langer addresses his work largely to a professional audience. But both the historical issues and his modes of approaching them reveal the impact of a world more troubled and complex than the one young Langer had set out to master as historian in the 1920's. Each group of essays sheds its own light on this story of five decades.

I

The problem of the origins of World War I inevitably dominated the historiography of Europe during the twenties and the early thirties. Historians in the European countries, their national passions still enflamed by the war and its legacy of hate, treated the problem of the origins of war essentially as a problem of guilt. American scholars, their traditional suspicions of European power politics reinforced by Wilson's ideals and their collapse, developed a somewhat different approach. They introduced into their study of prewar international relations an evenhandedness and comprehensiveness virtually unknown to their European contemporaries. It has been plausibly argued that American historiography of Europe came of age through these independent researches into the origins of World War I.[2] With Bernadotte Schmitt, Sidney Fay, and others, Langer participated in the great inquest. But in one respect, his work was distinguished from the rest. What he said of the purposes of his *European Alliances and Alignments* in 1931 held true for his other work of the twenties and early thirties

[2] John Higham, Leonard Krieger, and Felix Gilbert, *History* (Englewood Cliffs, New Jersey, 1965), pp. 357–361.

as well: "I have written this book not with the outbreak of the World War especially in mind, but as a study of the evolution of the European states system." [3] He focussed on the system and its operations. This led Langer to ignore deliberately many of the events of diplomatic history, stressing only those which affected the configurations and power groupings as they evolved. At the same time, it enabled him to identify himself strongly with the statesmen who operated within the system, regardless of what states they served. Langer's historical realism rested on "scrupulously avoiding the injection of postwar notions into the discussion," in the conviction that "a just appreciation of the past can be gained only if the events of the past are viewed with the eyes of the actors." [4] Thus he analyzed the system of international relations essentially as the product of men playing a game whose rules were known, but whose stakes became fully apparent only with the unfolding of events.

If the prewar system had a justification, Langer felt that Bismarck provided it. By his exemplary utilization of tensions, he created a multisided equilibrium, one that could absorb new pressures into an old order. Yet Langer's work makes clear that genius itself probably could not have adapted this system to the dynamic unleashed by imperialism. The game could no longer contain the chaotic energies of the participants. Where most historians of his generation approached international relations before World War I with the question, "Who played foul?" Langer raised a deeper question: "What has happened to this game, that it should destroy its players?"

In the book-length studies which occupied him throughout the twenties, Langer examined the development of the European system from its Bismarckian apogee. The publication of *The Franco-Russian Alliance* (1929) brought to a close eight years of research into the initial steps in the dismantling of the Bismarckian system. While analyzing the removal of the keystone from the edifice of peace reared by the "master-builder of the Wilhelmsstrasse," [5] Langer was led in two directions, back to the period before the Franco-Russian Alliance, and forward to the decades 1894–1914. The first exploration resulted in *European Alliances and Alignments* (1931), a comprehensive study of

[3] William L. Langer, *European Alliances and Alignments* (New York, 1931), p. vii.
[4] William L. Langer, *The Franco-Russian Alliance, 1890–1894* (Cambridge, Mass., 1929), pp. vii–viii.
[5] *Ibid.*, p. 3.

the European system at the height of its effectiveness. Surely this is a classic monument to Bismarck as European and to the positive potentialities of a statesmanship of disciplined national interest. For Langer, the Bismarckian system, however precarious, represented a kind of Eden, a model against which later international behavior could be assessed, though its reality could never be recaptured. But even as he explored its achievements, Langer turned to the dynamics of the breakdown, dynamics that lay outside and beyond the division of Europe into two camps in the chaos of imperialistic world politics.

To the confusions which this extra-European expansion produced in the workings of the European system, Langer devoted several shorter studies in the twenties. The first of these concerned great power conflicts over Tunis, which arose within the Bismarckian era and could still be accommodated within the Bismarckian system.[6] In a subsequent block of four articles Langer pursued his broader interest of the 1920's in systems, games, and players in international politics. In these pieces, which constitute the bulk of Part I of this collection, Langer leapt even beyond the period he would deal with in *The Diplomacy of Imperialism* to consider the workings of the state system in the last decade before World War I. By focussing on the policies of Tsarist Russia, the weakest yet perhaps the brashest of the imperialist powers, he analyzed international behavior after 1904, revealing first in Asia the uncontrollable potential for destruction which imperialist politics could unleash, then in Europe the almost imperceptible ease with which the time-honored diplomatic minuet could slip into a *danse macabre*.

The first essay in this series, "The Origin of the Russo-Japanese War," was published in 1926. It reveals the powerful moral impulse that smouldered beneath the hard surface of young Langer's historical realism. One senses Wilson here more strongly than Bismarck. The tone and focus of the article, while it was Langer's own, may have been influenced by the policies of *Europäische Gespräche*, the periodical which commissioned it. As its title suggests, *Europäische Gespräche* was a journal designed to promote international dialogue among Europeans. Its editor, Albrecht Mendelssohn-Bartholdy, devoted himself especially to breaking through the narrow nationalist limits within

---

[6] William L. Langer, "The European Powers and the Occupation of Tunis, 1878–1881," *American Historical Review*, XXXI, 55–79, 251–265 (October 1925 and January 1926). The substance of this series was absorbed into *European Alliances and Alignments*, chap. 7.

which the problems of war and war-guilt were being discussed in Germany after Versailles. As part of his political effort, Mendelssohn launched in 1924 a series probing into the causes and consequences of wars in the past century. Langer's article on the Russo-Japanese War was commissioned as the third in the series. Young Langer must have found the approach of *Europäische Gespräche* to international affairs congenial. Using a method partly historical, partly theoretical, Mendelssohn and his collaborators proceeded in a spirit of cosmopolitan liberalism to analyze the shortcomings not of a given state, but of the whole modern system of power politics.[7]

In his contribution, Langer treated the Russo-Japanese War as "a classic example of a conflict waged purely for imperialistic motives" on both sides. Unlike earlier European national wars, "there was no sentiment or tradition involved." Hence there were also no checks, no consideration for the interests of others, to inhibit "the predatory tactics [of the great powers] which had gained tremendous momentum during the second half of the nineteenth century." The issue between Russia and Japan was at bottom "merely a question of which nation should victimize the moribund Korean and Chinese Empires." Imperialist war appeared quite simply here as the warfare of the predatory powers among each other for the control of the moribund.

Langer specifically abjures as "not properly the work of the historian . . . the attempt to assess the responsibility for this or that war," which has, he sadly notes, become "quite the fashion nowadays." Yet his analysis of the Russo-Japanese War breathes a kind of total disgust with imperialism at work. Young Langer's sympathy is wholly with the "hapless peoples," the Chinese and Koreans. "When all is said and done, the aggressions of the strong states against China and the other weak states of the Orient fill one of the blackest pages in the history of modern civilization." Langer very nearly transforms his sympathy for the victims into a principle of explanation when he identifies as the "underlying root" of the Russo-Japanese War "the inability of China and Korea to resist the aggressions of the European states."

---

[7] For the purposes and principles governing the series, and the inspiration its editor drew from the example of the English internationalist Arthur Ponsonby, see Albrecht Mendelssohn-Bartholdy, "Der Krieg: Ursachen and Anlässe, Zielen and Folgen. I. Der Krimkrieg," *Europäische Gespräche*, II (1924), 417–419. See also the strong indictment of U.S. imperialism in the second article of the series, Alfred Vagts, "Der spanisch-amerikanische Krieg," *Europäische Gespräche*, III (1925), 626–650.

Langer does not, of course, pursue the sources of Asian weakness by an analysis of Asian society as an international historian would have to do today. Asian civilization and its fate provide him only with moral perspective for the analysis of European power politics, not with dynamic constituents in the historical process as a whole. In Western eyes, Russia and Japan alone provided the action in this phase of the imperialist drama. If the formation and interaction of their policies remained the center of Langer's concern, he nevertheless pressed in this early work toward the internal political springs of external aggression. His story shows how, in the high councils of both powers, moderate expansionists in effect laid out a course which gave the most irrational military groups their opportunity. Count Witte's policy of peaceful economic penetration of China led his domestic opponents, "the aggressive group in St. Petersburg, to hatch more extensive projects" for controlling Korea. Making extensive use of the Soviets' new studies and documentary publications on the old régime, Langer penetrated Witte's justifications of his dovish course to show his contributions to the hawks who superceded him. Similarly Prince Ito's moderate promotion of Japanese economic interests in Korea and China created the premises for his being swept away by the military expansionists. Langer confined his domestic analysis of the dynamic of imperialist policy to the level of court and bureaucracy. But by placing internal policy-formation in its international context, he showed how the imminent tendency toward the transformation of economic penetration into military expansion in one country reinforced a similar tendency in the other. Within both governments international tension strengthened the hands of the domestic champions of aggression, the more brutal players in the game, in a dialectic that found its natural outcome in war.

In the evenhanded spirit of *Europäische Gespräche,* Langer did not end his account with a mere icy judgment on the two belligerents. He was interested not only in the growing aggressiveness of Russia and Japan as the dirtier players gained the upper hand in each country, but also in the influence of the whole group of powers that played the imperialist game. The other powers, according to the rules of that game, did much to encourage and nothing to prevent the war. Langer professes to leave the reader free "to formulate his own opinion of the ethics" of British and American policy; in fact, he describes the policy in such a way that the reader can only recoil in as much shock at the cold-bloodedness of the nonbelligerents as at the aggressiveness of the antagonists. In the opening years of our century, international politics in Asia seemed reduced to rapacity stripped clean of all pretense, for "those who held the ring"—Britain and the United States—as much as for those who fought in it.

Severely weakened by military defeat and domestic revolution, the Tsarist régime temporarily put aside its imperialist ambitions in Asia in favor of a pacific policy in Europe. How Russia's somewhat bizarre attempts to strengthen her security contributed to Europe's instability after 1905 constitutes the matter of the next three articles (Nos. 2–4) of Part I. Each piece concentrates on one of the crises that brought Europe to the brink: the Straits, the Bosnian annexation, and the Balkan Wars.

When he wrote these articles in the years 1928 and 1929, Langer had not yet developed fully the sympathetic attitude toward prewar states-manship which he shows in *European Alliances and Alignments*. He is hard on players who ruin the game. It is difficult to imagine a sterner, more rigorously founded arraignment than that of Russian foreign min-ister Alexander Isvolski, the central figure in two of the articles: "Men-dacious to the last degree, high-strung and emotional, he was constantly engaged in selfish projects which were based on ruthless lack of consid-eration for others, friends as well as foes." Langer pursues Isvolski un-sparingly through his attempts to win for Russia the right to send her warships through the Straits. Though the indictment is personal in focus, it acquires its real import from the international context. At the personal level, Langer demonstrates that Isvolski neither understood the domestic and foreign political forces with which he had to work, nor had the minimal stability and candor necessary to create confidence in his intentions even when they were good. Despite his adroit com-mand of courtship routines and the other aristocratically-tinted conven-tions of diplomacy, Russia's foreign minister nevertheless painted him-self into a corner. His excess of cleverness led him into international bargains which his government could not honor and his allies could not respect. Langer's story of Isvolski and the powers reads like a bitter satyr-play performed after the classic tragedy of Bismarck. The differ-ence between the two men lay not only in their characters, but in the context of their operations. In their aims one could find similarities. Like Bismarck after 1871, Isvolski after 1905 eschewed adventurism. Like Bismarck, he sought his nation's security in a European orientation and through understandings with *all* the great powers. But the openness of international relations, which enabled Bismarck's diplomacy to articulate Europe's tensions into a flexible network of international balances, had been superseded. The Franco-Russian Alliance had begun a rigid dualism in power alignments which made all attempts at crossing the line between the two alliance systems dangerous. Hence the irony that Isvolski should have succeeded in advancing Russia's aims better with her foes than with her friends; or that, as Langer shows, his very failures in the eyes of his government and his English ally made it necessary to retain him as foreign minister. If Isvolski, like many of his associates, fell "victim to the intrigue, jealousy, and diversity of views which were so characteristic of the old régime," that too was partly a product of the post-Bismarckian international system. Though his policy was rejected, "he had to be held and he had to be supported, because Europe, in 1908 as in 1914, was divided into two hostile camps, each of which dreaded disruption and humiliation and in each of which members had to be prepared to fight on an issue in which they had no direct interest."

Langer drew no general theoretical conclusions about the state of the international system in the years covered by his Russian series. But his account leaves the reader in no doubt that the system was both decadent and dangerous. It was still an age of diplomatic virtuosity— "the players of the other side were scarcely less adroit than Isvolski"— but technical skill had become actually dangerous to political stability. It was as though, in the years that lay between Bismarck's Ptolemaic mastery of the political universe and Wilson's Copernican revolution, the game favored only those players whose virtuosity was most deadly. And these players, whose psychological security had come to lodge in the flamboyant assertion of their manliness, seemed incapable of imagining the actual consequences of their own bravado. "'Either we shall make Serbia a huge cemetery, or we shall make Greater Serbia.'" Thus a Belgrade newspaper demanded compensation for the annexation of Bosnia and Herzegovina. Foreign Minister Milanovic of Serbia beautifully synthesized the traditional attitudes of diplomatic problem-solving with the most uninhibited death-fantasy: "'Ah, yes, if at the same time as the liquidation of Turkey the disintegration of Austria could take place, the solution would be greatly simplified.'" The politics of risk was "realistic" enough when it elevated real-estate transactions into life-and-death questions. Its realism failed abysmally, however, when it came to visualizing the faces of war and death. That was the reality which a balance of power based on two alliance systems brought closer, by favoring the most daring and irresponsible players in the game, the Isvolskis and the Aehrentals, the Sazanovs and Conrads.

Langer builds this case from the viewpoint of the participants as the dynamic unfolds rather than from the perspective so fashionable in the twenties. His approach preserves the naiveté as well as the blindness, the valuations as well as the virtuosity of the makers of the politics of decadence, and stresses the complexity of possibility rather than the arbitrary simplicity of the single "road to war." Perhaps it was unfair of Langer to have chosen moribund Tsarist Russia as the particular vehicle for his inquest into the last years of the old order. But since Europe's stability before 1914 had come to rest on the policies of its most erratic members rather than on those of its sturdier ones, the behavior of neurotic Russia offered as reliable an indicator of the health of the whole as could be had.

In the 1960's, well after he had put aside diplomatic history for other concerns, Langer returned to Bismarck once more. The two papers (Nos. 5 and 6) which conclude Part I of this collection do not, however, bear the full stamp of the Langer of the sixties. They had their origin in his student days, in a paper on Bismarck and the outbreak of the Franco-Prussian War, and are cast in a frame of analysis less ambitious than the Russian articles of the late twenties. In them Langer pursues one of the most elementary yet pleasurable aspects of the historian's craft: the task of penetrating the actor's recollections of the past to set the record straight. Not Bismarck the champion of international stability, but Bismarck the brilliant master of political provocation is the focus of "Bismarck as a Dramatist" (No. 5). In a careful critique of Bismarck's account of his handling of the Ems telegram, Langer cuts a cubit off the statesman's stature. He does not exploit the opportunity for psychoanalytic explanation offered by Bismarck's *distortio veri;* nor does he examine the political circumstances which may have conditioned Bismarck's retrospective self-magnification as provocative manipulator of France. He simply corrects the story and rests his case: the Chancellor's love of the good yarn and his all-too-human tendency toward self-dramatization must suffice as motive.

"Red Rag and Gallic Bull" (No. 6) takes up the episode of the Ems dispatch from the French end. Again the treatment is deflationary. The Ems episode had little formative force on the policy of the French government, where the hawks already ruled the roost in cabinet and chambers. Langer suggests that Bismarck might have been inspired to create his own legend of the Ems dispatch by seeing the use that the French hawks made of it. In public and parliamentary debates, they gave it "greater significance than he intended or could have foreseen." The reason for the bellicosity of the French political community is little explored. Langer simply wants to show that Bismarck's "red rag" was not as dazzling as he painted it, and that the "Gallic bull" would have charged without it. Bismarck emerges more mendacious as autobiographer and less provocative as statesman; Gramont and the French, less gullible and more bellicose. Langer's reconstruction is direct and simple, lacking in analytic pretension. It is an exhibition of the historian's first and fundamental obligation—to straighten out the record under the ordinance of time. It was an obligation which Langer fulfilled to the delight of generations of undergraduates in his fast-paced lectures, and inculcated as a cardinal virtue in his graduate seminars. Only when the story was straight could one begin the quest for meaning: this premise finds clear reflection in the essays that stem from Langer's student years. In the late twenties arose his graver concern for the weaknesses of the states system exemplified in the Russian articles. And beyond these lay years of deeper search and methodological doubt, occasioned as much by the unsettling impact of the living present as by the scholarly effort to comprehend the past.

II

During the six years between 1929 and 1935, Langer had neither time nor inclination for article-length studies. He was immersed in producing the works that will doubtless stand as his greatest contributions: *European Alliances and Alignments* (1931) and *The Diplomacy of Imperialism* (1935). In them Langer carried to their highest perfection the traditional methods of Rankean diplomatic historiography. In them he revealed his masterful capacity to compress the almost insuperable volume of documentary and secondary materials that confronts the modern historian into a faithful distillate of the actions, attitudes, and reciprocal relations of the policy-makers. But more, he offered a luminous structural clarification of the Ptolemaic world of inter-governmental relationships in an era when they had reached bewildering complexity. In *The Diplomacy of Imperialism* Langer could still treat the interactions of states as part of an international *system*, despite the fact that the multiplication of friction points outside

Europe now prevented that system from achieving any real equilibrium.

Sustained involvement with the problems of the policy-makers of the past had its effect on the historian. Langer became more tolerant of the prewar statesmen than he had been in his articles of the twenties. "In the course of my researches," he wrote in 1931, "I have been drawn further and further away from the . . . arraignments of the 'old diplomacy' which are so much in vogue in the present day. I have become less and less willing to believe that men in that day were more wicked, more unscrupulous and more evil-minded than in our own or any other day." [8] The Rankean method of reconstructing the outlook of a historical actor from the documents in which the actor expressed himself naturally engenders in the historian a sympathy for the human predicament of his subjects. Yet even as he developed this sympathy, Langer began to show dissatisfaction with the limitations of the method he was using so successfully. "The study of diplomacy," he wrote in the preface to *European Alliances and Alignments*, "if it is to lead to anything worthwhile, must go beyond the mere digest or analysis of documents and negotiations." The statesmen seemed now, for good or for ill, to be less free as makers of history. They "were confronted by the rapidly growing complexity of modern life." They were borne on "broad currents" of economic and military development, "tides" of national sentiment, and the irresistible "surge of mass feeling." [9] The imagery here is oceanic, with all its threatening fluidity and force.

What were these forces that drove the European system toward destruction? In *The Diplomacy of Imperialism* Langer made his first systematic attempt to sound the depths and chart the currents of imperialism as a social force. He confined the inquest to England, the classic land of imperialism in the nineties, and proceeded rather to describe the ingredients of the phenomenon than to analyze its dynamic. Moreover, the examination remained a kind of experiment, isolated in a chapter of its own (chapter 3). While it provided a backdrop against which developing international tensions could be viewed, the analysis of imperialism, with its social, economic, or ideational constituents, rarely penetrated the political narrative.

Was Langer's intellectual disquiet with the methods of diplomatic history reinforced by the world politics of the living present? We cannot answer with certainty, but the shock effect of the rise of fascism

[8] Langer, *Alliances and Alignments,* p. vii.
[9] *Ibid.,* pp. vii–viii, 4–7.

is dramatically reflected in his shorter studies of the thirties. In March 1935, Langer had penned the final lines of *The Diplomacy of Imperialism* convinced that imperialism was dead:

> One cannot study this period without marvelling at the exuberance and optimism which went hand in hand with recklessness and confidence in the conduct of foreign affairs. It was taken for granted that the world was marked out by Providence for exploitation by the European white man . . . The rise of Japan, the Adua disaster, the Boxer rising, none of these epoch-making events really opened the eyes of Europe. Even Lord Salisbury could see in the world nothing but a few virile nations and a large number of dying nations. The basic problem of international relations was who should cut up the victims. In our own day we have learned otherwise and all this now seems long ago.[10]

It was now the historian's turn, Langer likes to recall, to have his optimism and confidence jolted. "Almost before the ink was dry on the pages, Mussolini embarked on the conquest of Ethiopia," to be followed by Japan's invasion of northern China and soon by Hitler's series of aggressions.[11] In the face of renewed imperialism, unexpected to him as to so many of his contemporaries, Langer turned to explore the relationship between past and present, between the imperialism of the late nineteenth century and that of the era of burgeoning fascism.

The essays of Part II, "Imperialism Old and New," are devoted to this theme. All but the last were written in the years 1935–1938, when the fascist powers were at the height of their career of expansion-by-blackmail. Whereas most of the articles of Part I were addressed to professional historians, these, tackling current issues in historical perspective, were aimed at the educated public. *Foreign Affairs*, organ of the conservative-internationalist Council on Foreign Relations, offered a fitting vehicle for Langer's reflections on current developments.

In "The Critique of Imperialism" (No. 7), Langer tackled once more the thorny problem of the nature of imperialism, using a reissue of Hobson's classic analysis of the subject as a point of departure. While criticizing Hobson and his Marxist followers for the inadequacy of their economic prophecies, Langer nevertheless accepted the idea that imperialism was "closely connected with the great changes in the social structure of the western world." Yet no theoretical categories seemed

[10] Langer, *Diplomacy of Imperialism*, II, 797.
[11] William L. Langer, "The Revival of Imperialism in the 19th Century," unpublished address delivered at Brown University, Oct. 8, 1947.

to account for the Protean nature of aggressive expansionism. In his attempt to escape what William James termed "the spectral dance of bloodless categories," [12] Langer insisted that the new imperialism of Italy, Japan and Germany was simply atavistic and irrational, "bound up with conscious or subconscious ideas of force, of brutality, of ruthlessness." Langer's later interest in psychoanalysis seems adumbrated here, arising naturally out of the threatening, oceanic forces of the new, fascist imperialism. In 1935, Langer still spoke with the confidence that the atavism of imperialism, whatever its basic cause, would not last. In an era when, as Hobson had rightly predicted, Asia, Africa, and Latin America were kicking back at the great powers with Western ideas and Western weapons, Japan and Italy could only fail in their attempts to turn back the clock by reviving the aims and methods employed at the turn of the century.

In four successive articles (Nos. 8–11) Langer examined the actual points of international tension between the Axis and the Western powers. Here, however, he returned to his traditional categories of analysis. Examining the events of current international politics as reflected in the stream of history, he found little to cheer and much to fear. In "The Struggle for the Nile" (No. 8), Langer traced the continuity of British policy in the eastern Mediterranean. If Great Britain had recently "taken her stand with the angels" by working through the League in the first phases of the Ethiopian affair, that was only to pursue by other means the same aim she pursued in the Fashoda crisis: protection of the headwaters of the Nile. Langer warned that Britain might, like Laval, "yield to the temptation and allow her imperialism to get the better of her internationalism." Beneath the Wilsonian forms Langer thus again discerned national interest, concretized in specific territories (in this case Lake Tana), as the real substance of international politics.

To be sure, there was a brief moment of hope in January 1936, when it seemed as if the legacies of Bismarck and Wilson might converge to roll back Italian aggression. In "Alliance System and League" (No. 9), an article which shows his *Gestalt*-making capacity at its finest, Langer watched France's early efforts to check Italy through her alliances while Britain worked through the League. "What we have," Langer observed, "is the astonishing situation in which both the revived alliance systems of olden days and the League system of postwar origin are working

[12] *Ibid.*

together in the interest of peace and security." A beautiful vision, too good to last! It was shattered by the failure of both systems to place an effective brake on the Fascist juggernaut in Ethiopia.

With "The Revival of Imperialism," (No. 10) written for a Harvard student periodical in 1937, Langer's pessimism expressed the failure. Wilsonianism comes to the surface, but so does a tendency toward appeasement which often overcame American liberal internationalists in 1937 and 1938. Langer sees the Italian conquest of Ethiopia as a turning point. It has done more than "deliver the coup de grâce to the system of collective international action" of the League of Nations; it has "called to life all of the latent energy, blind discontent, and animal bellicosity of a congested and restless Europe." Writing for undergraduate readers, Langer gave vent to a more uninhibited and direct expression of political opinion than was his wont. Mussolini's misbehavior, having gone unpunished, has left "the whole [European] family . . . demoralized." As Mussolini has broken up the League, so Hitler is tearing up the rest of the treaties. Though seeing "the new surge of imperialism" as arising out of "deeply rooted social problems" which "the removal of a few symptoms will not do much to cure," Langer suggested only a symptomatic remedy: that the Germans be given back some colonial territory. It was a reaction shared by many in every political camp when the historical anticipations of the Era of Good Feeling suddenly dissolved under the threat of fascist expansionism.

In "Tribulations of Empire" (No. 11), Langer analyzed even the Spanish Civil War in the perspective of older imperialist international relations. To those accustomed to thinking of the Spanish upheaval as an international social war, with Russia and the Axis fighting it out while the Western powers let the Spanish Republic die of starvation, Langer's approach will come as a surprise. Writing in early 1937, he cast the Spanish problem in the framework of a struggle for strategic and economic control of the Mediterranean. The Mediterranean agreements of 1887, which stabilized and neutralized the Mediterranean, provided the ideal basis for the analysis; the conflicts and alignments of the nineties provided its real political referent. With Mussolini adding to his conquest of Ethiopia a foothold at the other end of the sea in Spain, he threatened the strategic and commercial lifelines of Britain and France to their Asian and African possessions. The integrity of the old empires was thus again theatened by the new. If it seems strange to the modern reader to find the Spanish crisis analyzed without reference to either Russia or Communism, it should remind us that the world reacts to events quite differently from the way in which it remembers them. Langer's analysis was closer to the kind of concerns that governed the making of Western foreign policies in the early phases of the Spanish crisis than were the ideological and social attitudes which in the end led the democracies to let Spain fall into the grip of Franco. Whatever fears were held of her, the Soviet Union was not, in those days, regarded as a member of the club which could play imperialist games. Langer made it clear in this article that the dependence of both France and England on overseas territories—for oil, airways, and military manpower—increased rather than declined over the years. Though the age of expansion might be over, the interests of both France and Britain in the Mediterranean as lifeline "had grown enormously." It was in this context of persistent imperialism—aggressive in Italy, defensive in the West—that Langer interpreted the significance of the Spanish Civil War for a European states system once again spinning out of orbit.

By 1938, it no longer seemed adequate to assess the nature and intentions of the new imperialism as a politics of interest. In "When German Dreams Come True" (No. 12), Langer sought to illuminate the contemporary international situation from a different historical perspective, the ideological one. He treated the Nazi will-to-conquest as a product of pan-German traditions, both North German and Austrian. This dual ideological background helped explain Hitler and *Mein Kampf*. Through it Langer enlarged the scope of conventional power analysis with intellectual history. He warned his contemporaries to judge Hitler's intentions not by German ideology alone, but also by the opportunity which the international constellation would give him. Painting the gloomiest picture of Nazi intentions and capabilities, Langer had completely overcome the fleeting temptation to buy off the Germans with a colonial concession. Anticipating the early seizure of Czechoslovakia (the article, published in July 1938, must have been written in the preceding winter), Langer held out almost no hope for resistance to Hitler's continued expansion. His assessments have historical interest today, even—or especially—when the predictions are faulty, as they necessarily are at times. They show the depth of despair into which an informed observer could fall as the whole great power system revealed, for the second time, its total bankruptcy.

The domestic and social dimensions of this collapse Langer touched only rarely. Like the other articles of Part II, "When German Dreams Come True" was conceived against an ideal background of European collective containment of aggression, half Bismarckian, half Wilsonian —an ideal which the several powers were prevented by their narrow and partial definitions of their national interest from realizing. The ideologically fortified neo-imperialism of the Nazis, viewed in the perspective of the past, revealed to Europe only the wretchedness of its own impotence. Britain, upon whom all others depended, was the most wretched of all. "Living in a fool's paradise," believing that she could keep her empire by sacrificing the continent, Britain, so Langer predicted, would be Hitler's major victim "when German dreams came true."

It was the last article which Langer wrote on imperialism before the war broke, in its dark prophecy a fitting end to the series. The private scholar who since 1935 had sought to enlighten the political public by bringing his historical work to bear on contemporary imperialist politics had by 1938 become a grim public warner. Current history had led Langer from concerned reflection toward a felt need for action: from the generalities of "A Critique of Imperialism," through the increasingly concrete examination of new power conflicts in Ethiopia and Spain, to describing the bankruptcy of the great powers in the face of the German menace. As historian of Europe he had tried to explicate the change; as American public official he would soon work to stem it.

The essay, "Farewell to Empire" (No. 13), which brings Part II to a close, appeared nearly thirty years after "A Critique of Imperialism." Yet it constitutes a kind of companion piece to that earlier essay. Once more Langer probed the elusive nature of imperialism. With his felt need for theory always tempered by empirical suspicions of it, he had returned to the subject again and again, never exhausting it to his satisfaction.[13] For us, the chief interest in this latest attempt lies in the author's reassessment of the vitality of imperialism in 1962. Conceived in an era of détente after the long night of the Cold War, the essay reflects an almost irenic wisdom, striking in its contrast to the anxious observations on reawakened atavism in the essay of 1935. The reader may appreciate "Farewell to Empire" most fully not only in the light

[13] First posed in *The Diplomacy of Imperialism*, chap. 3, the problem appears not only in the two essays reprinted here, but in several unpublished addresses: "The Revival of Imperialism in the 19th Century," Brown University, Oct. 8, 1947; "The Eclipse of Imperialism," U.S. Military Academy (West Point), Jan. 22, 1954; and, less directly, in "Floodtide of Nationalism," Mills College, June 5, 1960.

of "A Critique of Imperialism," but also in relation to the development of Langer's ideas on American foreign policy contained in the essays of Part III.

Whether America's resumption of the imperialistic course in its Vietnam adventure would lead Langer to reconsider his finding of 1962 once more we cannot say. But one may point to an underlying conception to which Langer adhered throughout, whether he deplored or defended specific acts of imperialist powers: that imperialism, even while it extended European power, disrupted the European state system and created the premises for the self-development of non-European peoples. In 1962, he saw this clearly as a benefit to all mankind: "Imperialism's one great achievement was to open up the world and to set all humanity on the high road to eventual association and collaboration." The sufferings of the "hapless victims of the predatory powers" with which the young historian had sympathized in 1925 seemed to the older scholar to have become meaningful in a larger economy of history. But what a cruel economy it was!

III

The inexorable pressures of the fascist threat had turned Langer's attention in the thirties from the world politics of the past to those of the present. Then as before, his interest had centered on the European international system. The American position in relation to it, though it colored his outlook, had not yet claimed his particular attention.

Nineteen-forty changed all that. With the fall of France, Langer became an advocate of American intervention on behalf of the embattled democracies. In August 1941 he moved from advocacy to action and entered government service. Participating in the founding of the Research and Analysis Branch of the Office of Strategic Services, Langer began a virtual second career as intelligence adviser and administrator in Washington, a career which was to continue intermittently with the State Department and the Central Intelligence Agency deep into the postwar years.

Langer accomplished more easily than most the change in role from politically concerned scholar to governmental expert. Yet engagement in the official life of the country undoubtedly affected both his interests and his historical outlook. Before World War II, Langer had treated international politics in a universal perspective, with an eye always trained on the international system. During World War II, he developed a more national perspective, devoting his attention to the assumption and exercise of world power by the United States. In the process, his lifelong scholarly search for the conditions of international stability became inextricably linked with the American interest as seen from Washington. The historian of European imperialism became a scholar of emergent imperial America, chronicling, explaining, and often justifying his country's sudden rise to primacy.

The papers of Part III, "The United States as a World Power," span the wide arc of Langer's intellectual development as political actor and scholarly interpreter of America's international position (1941–1956). It must be emphasized that of the six papers in this section, four were composed as public addresses. They bear the mark of informality appropriate to their genre. They also show, more sharply than would articles written for publication, the clear stamp of the contemporary situation. To do them justice one should read them today less as scholarly contributions than as sources for the evolving outlook of an American historian engaged in the public life of our swiftly changing nation.

The first essay, "The Faith of Woodrow Wilson" (No. 14), stands out from Langer's writings for its anguished eloquence. Written in western Europe's darkest hour (May 1941), it sounded a ringing reminder to America of the moral, almost missionary, strand in her foreign policy tradition. Langer showed how Wilson's "intense and unswerving faith in democracy" led him not only to espouse its cause with military power, but above all to throw America's weight into the balance in order to reconstruct international relations on a wholly new basis. "He had a vision and he had a message." By rejecting the President's call to join the League of Nations, America had betrayed herself and the world. Would America do so again in the forties? "We who thought once more to wash our hands of responsibility and to stand aloof from the European mess may well in these cataclysmic days return to Woodrow Wilson," Langer wrote. He urged Americans to "shoulder the burden" to save a "mankind once more in jeopardy." In this plea Langer clearly subsumed America's national interest under the moral conception of building the new world order which Wilson had failed to realize. "The League is dead; long live the League!" Thus, on the eve of America's entry into the war, the cosmopolitan idealism which informed Langer's work of the twenties broke forth anew in full untrammeled vigor. Fifteen years later, he would return to Woodrow Wilson, his faith and his failure, in a more sober and reflective article. "Woodrow

Wilson: His Education in World Affairs" (No. 19). In the difference between the two, one can discern the impact of practical government experience and of America's wars hot and cold on Langer's attitude toward America as a world power.

Meanwhile the arduous years of wartime intelligence work virtually precluded any historical research. As the war drew to a close, however, with that prodigious energy that has ever characterized him, Langer produced his first monograph on American foreign policy. *Our Vichy Gamble* (1947) stands as one of his most vivid narrative histories. Politically charged as it is, it will doubtless also remain his most controversial major work. Undertaken at the request of Secretary of State Cordell Hull, *Our Vichy Gamble* offered a vindication of the administration's much contested policy of wooing away Hitler's French collaborators. At a time when political intentions and military objectives were becoming increasingly difficult to hold apart, Langer justified America's Vichy policy on grounds of military expediency alone. The "only real arguments against our Vichy gamble," he wrote, were "arguments of a sentimental or ideological character," and these could carry no weight with a government with a war to win.[14] "Real national interests" must take precedence over all else. But by whom were these interests to be defined? As historian, Langer turned to the sources which contained and reflected the ideas of the men who hammered out the policy. Historical objectivity and political fidelity here converged in a neo-Rankean realism, wherein the values of the policy-makers provided both the coordinates of historical analysis and the norms of political judgment. Thus the tensions which had enriched Langer's earlier works—between Wilsonian and Bismarckian values, between the obscure dynamic forces of world politics and the acts of statesmen responding to them within the rules of their game—were lifted in favor of a cohesive but essentially short-term doctrine of national interest and military expediency. *Our Vichy Gamble,* for all its verve and empathetic power, reflected the hardening effect of war not only on American foreign policy but on Langer's thinking as historian and citizen.

Though it is obviously impossible to compare writings of such radically different scale and purpose as "The Faith of Woodrow Wilson" and *Our Vichy Gamble,* the little article and the substantial monograph represent in sharpest form the two poles of Langer's thinking: international idealism and *Realpolitik.* Each principle might be invoked to the

14 William L. Langer, *Our Vichy Gamble* (New York, 1947), p. 398.

exclusion of the other in a specific political context, but neither alone could provide an understanding of America's complex behavior on the world scene. Langer did not rest with either, once his imagination stirred to the larger problem of America's new international role. The historian's question: "How had she come to assume it?" and the policy-maker's question: "What should she do with it?" interacted in his mind throughout the postwar decade as he sought for America the kind of reciprocal illumination of past and present he had pursued in the thirties for Europe.

With Everett Gleason, Langer tackled the historian's question on a major scale in the two massive works on the making of America's decision to enter World War II: *The Challenge to Isolation* (1952) and *The Undeclared War* (1953). As in *Our Vichy Gamble*, the evolving consciousness of the United States policy-makers gave the authors the core of their story, but they examined it in a broader international and domestic context. These works concentrated only on the few years between 1937 and 1941, during which America overcame her own resistance to entering the fray. What were the fundamental historical factors in America's international experience that conditioned the form of her response to the world crisis of the thirties? With his distaste for long introductions, Langer did not take up that question in the book itself. He incorporated the fruits of his research and reflection into a series of three lectures in 1948, "The American Attitude toward Europe: an Historical Approach" (No. 15). Although prepared for a British audience, these hitherto unpublished lectures might well be read as an introduction to *The Challenge to Isolation*.

Langer's interpretation of the American attitude toward Europe is particularly interesting for its articulation of the relationship of universal ideal and national power. He shows that the basic experience of Americans in the eighteenth century, when the colonies were hapless victims of European power conflicts, was traumatization. Isolationism—or, more accurately, "continentalism"—implied both more and less than an attempt to avoid entanglement in European affairs. To avoid European intrusion into their affairs was the real aim, and to realize it Americans willingly paid the price of continental confinement of their political principles. Thus, despite their conviction of the universal applicability of their political system, Americans refused to take risks in support of their co-believers in Europe.

When the United States finally made her first serious forays into dures governing the making of our foreign policy.[15] In order to overcome the tension between the executive and legislative branches, Langer suggested the creation of a standing foreign policy committee or cabinet, under the president or secretary of state and comprising ranking members of the foreign affairs committees of both houses of Congress.[16] This would constitute a kind of institutional parallel to and extension of political bipartisanship in foreign policy, which Langer, like many others, expected to be a lasting feature of the national scene. For an America resolved to exercise power in the deeply split postwar world and to maintain a state of permanent military and political maneuverability to that end, it was only logical to reduce traditional American checks and balances in favor of the kind of administrative-legislative integration that Langer proposed. The implications of such consolidation for the democratic process and for the legitimacy of criticism in foreign policy formation did not command attention as a mighty yet anxious America searched for national consensus and governmental effectiveness to fortify herself for permanent international crisis.

In "Scholarship and the Intelligence Problem" (No. 17) Langer urged the importance of scholarly analysis to foreign policy and its operation in "any nation which, whether it likes it or not, is called upon to play a major part in world affairs." Here again, as in the case of bipartisanship in foreign policy, wartime improvisation was to be retained and expanded into a permanent feature of the peacetime establishment. Langer's suggestions for government support to universities to train specialists, some of whom could become intelligence analysts, have been largely realized.

In 1952, Langer addressed himself directly to the broad aims of United States policy. "American Objectives" (No. 18), a lecture prepared for the Naval War College Global Strategy Discussions reflects the clear stamp of the harshest phase of Russo-American antagonism. The historian opened his address by associating himself with George Kennan's call to Americans to abandon "the habit of attaching ourselves to abstract moral principles, such as freedom and justice, and looking to the orderly processes of international law to protect our interests and assure our security." Using an incisive prose appropriate to his logic, Langer pleaded that the country "get down to brass tacks."

[15] William L. Langer, "The Mechanism of American Foreign Policy," *International Affairs*, XXIV (July 1948), 319–328.
[16] *Ibid.*, pp. 328, 324.

In the "great clash of ideas and cultures," wherein the antagonists were "acting on incompatible principles and not even speaking the same language of international relations," he said, "I see no alternative to armament and more armament, at all cost short of national ruin." Langer dismissed as mistaken the notion that American aid "is a matter of generosity, if not charity, and that Europe alone is on the receiving end. Actually the vital issue is to hold western Europe in line . . ." Preventive war, to be sure, would be no answer; indeed, any war "might well prepare the ground for the spread of the very social revolution we are intent on combatting." Short of that, Langer advocated the extension of American power by every practical means so that one might engage the enemy, if engage one must, "as far away as possible from one's own frontiers."

The reader will not easily find a more candid or unvarnished statement of America's policy in the Truman-Eisenhower era than this. Cant was never a part of Langer's makeup; if his espousal of America's determination to be arbiter of the world's destiny in 1952 was complete, he presented it in the language that fit the case: the language of pure self-interest.

"American Objectives," while indicative of the degree to which Langer could canalize his analyses of world affairs into sharply formulated recommendations for public policy, cannot be read as his lasting assessment of America's position or proper posture. When the crisis of the two worlds began to recede after Stalin's death, Langer turned from immediate policy questions to historical reflection. He then expressed a wider and more modulated view of America's character and prospects as a world power.

It was fitting that, in looking back to assess the larger meaning of America's experience of international affairs over his own lifetime, Langer should have turned once more to Woodrow Wilson. For the third time in fifteen years, he examined that enigmatic statesman, who embodied in his person and his fate so many of his country's glories and failings as it whip-sawed its way to the front rank of power. In 1956, the hundredth anniversary of Wilson's birth, Langer prepared no less than three addresses on him.[17] Of these the paper reprinted here, "Woodrow Wilson: His Education in World Affairs" (No. 19), is the

---

[17] Besides the one included in this volume, they are "From Isolation to Mediation" and "Peace and the New World Order," in *Woodrow Wilson and the World Today*, ed. Arthur P. Dudden (Philadelphia, 1957), pp. 22–46, 67–96.

most personal; it is also the one most charged with general significance for the evolution of the United States as a world power.

Is one justified in discerning some biographical component in Langer's fascination with Wilson? It was under that austere, idealistic president that Langer saw his first war service. In his first history, that of his company in the First Gas Regiment, young Langer captured and recorded in 1919 the innocent patriotism which he shared with his fellow doughboys. The mature historian, reminiscing in 1965, found it hard to believe that a bloody and disastrous war, "the source of so many woes of the twentieth century world," could have been embraced with such an unalloyed sense of high adventure as he himself had shared. The absence of politics in his company history reflected the outlook of the fighting men, he wrote in retrospect. "Possibly we already felt that, in the American interest, Western democracy must not be allowed to go under. But I doubt it. I can hardly remember a single instance of a serious discussion of American policy or of larger war issues." [18] The naiveté of this America was a characteristic which Wilson, at another, more lofty level, both shared and had to overcome. Wilson understood the realities of war and of world politics little better than his America did. Both had to "fight free of illusion," both had to learn the same lessons from bitter experience. "But Wilson was forced by circumstances and by the requirements of his own personality to apprehend in three years what it took most Americans thirty years to grasp."

"He had a vision and he had a message"—that luminous sentence, which Langer had written of Wilson in his summons to America in 1941 burned bright once more for him as America groped for a way out of the deadlock of nuclear confrontation in 1956. In an essay without peer in this collection for the subtle rigor of its structure, Langer traced the vicissitudes of Wilson's reputation in America as the nation fought its way over the years toward the President's painful realization that he must deal with the world, but deal with it as it was, abandoning his abortive attempts to engineer peace on American terms. "Only a peace between equals can last," Langer quoted from Wilson: "Only a peace the very principle of which is equality and a common participation in a common benefit." Surely what held for the lesson of peace-making in 1918, held for the world in 1956. If the American people had once

[18] William L. Langer, *Gas and Flame in World War I* (New York, 1945), especially the retrospective introduction, pp. xxv, xviii, and *passim*.

relegated "peace and the new world order to the world of dreams," they had come to adopt Wilson's principles now. "If the world today," Langer observed, "instead of living in peace and harmony, is racked by cold war and plagued by the nightmare of atomic annihilation, the explanation is clearly not to be sought in too much, but rather in too little Wilsonism."

Had the historian, looking upon the United States as a world power in 1956, returned to the pure exaltation of Wilsonism which had informed his call to arms in 1941? Yes and no. Here Wilson's *own* failure —that innocence, that excess of ideological zeal which had blinded him in coping with foreign and domestic political reality—remained from Langer's more critical evaluation of 1948 as part of his historical assessment. But now Langer stressed the fact that America had to recapitulate Wilson's "education." This process meant, on the one hand, the recognition of the hard realities that the interests of nations and cultures other than our own create; on the other, the necessity of an ideal of international comity as a central, practical ingredient in the exercise of world power.

Can one discern in this ingenious projection of Woodrow Wilson's education in world affairs the lineaments of Langer's own development as the United States ran the swift and bitter course from victory in war to the deadlocked terror of an unstable peace? Had not the defeat of American hopes at the close of World War II led him to a commitment to an armed *Pax Americana,* and to an overextension of American power in a world grown fearful of it? Langer does not address himself to these questions, but his three Wilsons suggest the line of development. The first Wilson, the epic hero who bravely embodied idealistic values in the face of a perverse reality was gone now; so too the second Wilson, the stiff-necked crusader of "The American Attitude." Langer's third, new and complex Wilson was a tragic hero, whose dream of making the world safe for democracy had to be transmuted through his own defeat into the less ambitious but no less noble aim of making the world safe for diversity.

The conclusion of the essay suggests both a moral and a social-psychological finding to which the long experience of Langer the political actor must have led Langer the historian. It was a finding which Woodrow Wilson was too much of a democrat to admit to himself, but which America would finally have to accept if she were not to imperil herself and the world.

The common man may by instinct favor what is good and noble, but one can hardly escape the conviction that modern, total war involves such an effort and requires such aggressive impulses and hostile sentiments that in the hour of victory it is hardly possible to create a climate in which a just and reasonable settlement would find popular support. If indeed Mr. Wilson could never bring himself to acknowledge that lesson, it is nonetheless essential that mankind understand that modern war, from its very nature, precludes any improvement in international relationships. On the contrary, its legacy promises to be the heightening of old and the creation of new antagonisms.

In this statement, which brings to a close his writings on the United States as a world power, Langer adumbrated a new conception for America's role not present in his earlier essays. Its premise seemed to be the end of both isolation and ideology; three decades of experience had demonstrated that both were unrealistic and divisive. Where he had earlier steered a middle course between Bismarck and Wilson under the narrow pennant of "national interest," in his new conception Langer synthesized the sober realism of the first and the organizational vision of the second in a pluralistic world order that knew its greatest enemy to be war. Langer was not and would never be a pacifist, any more than he could ever be a militarist. But his realism drove him in a new direction as he examined Wilson for the third time. Langer returned neither to his 1941 adulation of the idealist Wilson nor to his 1948 criticism of the rigid missionary, but lifted the assessment to a new level. He recalled what Wilson had said of Burke: " 'He went on from the wisdom of today to the wisdom of tomorrow to the wisdom of all mankind,' and it was impossible for ordinary mortals to follow him so far." Perhaps through his own political experience, Langer had discovered in Wilson what Wilson found in Burke: a wisdom for all time. Thanks to the harsh realities of modern war, however, this wisdom had begun to look like the necessary wisdom for tomorrow to the historian reflecting on America's rise to world power in a revolutionary age.

IV

When, in his presidential address of 1957 to the American Historical Association, Langer urged the utility of psychoanalysis for historical understanding, many of his auditors were astonished. How extraordinary that the master of diplomatic historiography, the most established branch of the historian's craft, should step forth as champion of methodological radicalism! The surprise was the greater by virtue of the fact that, to illustrate his case, Langer chose the impact of plague on society, a problem far removed from his previous concerns.

Those who knew Langer as a teacher might have been surprised by the particular area of his newest exploration but hardly by the fact of exploration itself. Catholicity of interest and comprehensiveness of view were the hallmarks of his Harvard lectures on modern European history. Langer employed the comparative international approach to that field well before it became the foundation-supported fashion that it is today. In graduate seminars and in the supervision of doctoral candidates Langer encouraged the opening up of problems outside conventional political and diplomatic history, revealing his wide knowledge in fields not technically in his speciality. In fact, Langer never thought of himself as a specialist at all, but as a historian in the broad, etymological sense of the word: an "inquirer." To a true inquirer, no area could fail to yield historical understanding. No point of view, however foreign to his own, could fail to open a new vista when controlled by a critical employment of empirical evidence.

In his work as editor no less than as teacher, Langer demonstrated his commitment to a holistic view of history. In *The Rise of Modern Europe,* the multi-volume series he launched in 1934, Langer insisted that the authors treat *all* aspects of social life—not merely the political ones—in an international framework. Each author was left free to find his own principles to make European evolution comprehensible in a given era, but he was committed to treat Europe as a differentiated whole. When he edited *An Encyclopedia of World History* (Boston, 1940), Langer personally took on the research into those remoter areas of history in which no suitable scholarly collaborator could be found, and delighted in acquiring such new "specialities" as medieval Africa, an area in which the white world had as yet developed no interest.

Part IV, "Explorations in New Terrain," comprises a series of Langer's forays into areas outside modern international history. As in Part I, the articles are addressed to a scholarly audience rather than to the broader public.[19]

Langer made the first of his excursions into a new field in the 1920's. His comprehensive bibliographical article of 1929, "Recent Books on

[19] On those occasions when Langer wrote for a non-professional audience on the topics of Part IV, the articles duplicated closely the principal content of the essays included and hence have not been reproduced here.

the Near East," showed several characteristic features of his approach.[20] While deploring the tendency of contemporary political concerns to debase the quality of most works on Near Eastern history, Langer gave high praise to those who, like certain Soviet and Turkish historians, whatever their politics, helped to "pave the way for a juster interpretation of the Ottoman Empire" by a serious utilization of sources. Langer did not terminate his discussion with works already produced; he pointed beyond these to "the next assignment," to the kind of studies that were needed to develop a proper understanding of the area's history.

Langer typically defined his ventures into new areas as assessments of the state of a field which would lead others to go on to further specific tasks. In 1932, however, when he was at the height of his productivity as diplomatic historian, Langer undertook one of the most far-ranging of these tasks himself. With some assistance in Eastern language materials from his colleague, Professor Robert P. Blake, Langer explored the obscure and thorny problem of "The Rise of the Ottoman Turks" (No. 20). Having acquired his conversance with the subject through teaching the course in Ottoman history created by Archibald Cary Coolidge, Langer developed new views on the basis of a careful assessment of the state of the problem in the literature. Inevitably some of his conclusions have been challenged, particularly by G. G. Arnakis in *'Oi Protoi Othomanoi* (Athens, 1947). Langer's article nevertheless remains recognized as a valuable contribution to its field, and continues to offer English readers a good starting point for the study of Ottoman origins. On some of the questions which Langer raised, scholarly disagreement still bubbles. The article demonstrates Langer's capacity to break through even the unusually wide bounds of his modern historical expertise to work as a true *érudit* in a distant province of learning.

Although Langer continued through the years to develop in teaching and editing a variety of interests beyond diplomatic history, the pressures of world politics and government service exercised a prior claim upon his scholarly energies until the 1950's. Then, as he gradually disengaged himself from official responsibilities, and as he completed his historical studies of American foreign policy, Langer turned his full attention to exploring new terrain.

"The Historian and the Present" (No. 21), an address delivered to

[20] William L. Langer, "Recent Books on the History of the Near East," *Journal of Modern History,* I (September 1929), 420–441.

the Modern European History section of the American Historical Association, suggests why Langer felt it necessary to subject recent history in particular to quite new kinds of analysis. Here, as in the crisis of neo-imperialism in the thirties, the living present had imposed new demands upon those who would deal with the past. In the fifties, however, Langer concluded that the crisis of the twentieth century was so severe that the ordinary canons of political history could not make it comprehensible. Not only had recent technological developments "altered completely the conditions of life," but they had been accompanied by an intellectual revolution "so extensive and far-reaching as to have called in question just about all the previously accepted values of our civilization." Two great wars and the revolutions which followed them had in fact "rocked civilization to its foundations." There is ontic bite in Langer's description of the present condition of the Western world. Optimism has no place in it:

> If out of all this turmoil there were emerging a new philosophy, a new religion, a new political or social doctrine, or a new style, we might at least be able to get our bearings and catch the light at the end of the tunnel. But the trends and movements that we see and sense about us all suggest disruption if not total destruction of our society.

The crisis of "uncertainty, confusion, and blind groping for security" was perhaps not unrelated to Langer's political concern with the threat of Communism. Somehow, the "schemers of the Kremlin" seemed to possess a psychological security lacking to the West, and only waited to take advantage of a "Western society that had lost its moorings." The hard line American foreign policy which Langer propounded to a naval audience in the same year in "American Objectives" (No. 18) can perhaps be better understood in the light of these deeply pessimistic reflections to his colleagues in "The Historian and the Present." As a professional speaking to his own kind, he stressed the need for coming to grips with the crisis intellectually, for "a broader conception and profounder treatment" of recent history.

Once again, as in his work on imperialism, Langer was moved by his sense of the oceanic, the larger forces at work beneath the surface of historical development. In the thirties, his questioning of previous methods was primarily cognitive; now it was more existential, the product of a deep sense of traumatization in our culture as a whole. Quoting Alfred Weber, Langer called for an inquest into that "universal psychic wave . . . a collective supra-personal force, chained and hidden" until recently, which broke loose and "swept away values . . . held to be unshakeable." One could not deal with so deep a crisis of culture with the methods of the intellectual historian alone. Langer suggested, among other approaches, those of social psychology, demography, and the history of the arts.

On its surface a slight and somewhat loosely structured address, "The Historian and the Present" in fact adumbrated the principal new directions which Langer's subsequent work would take, and sketched in the boldest terms the way in which the crisis of contemporary society must itself open up new kinds of historical exploration. In the everchanging relationship between history and politics, politics seemed to have come to the end of its wisdom, and history would have to recast its questions in a more comprehensive form if it were to clarify the grave condition of the contemporary world.

Each of the three papers which bring this volume to a close, though dealing with periods remote from our own, explores a new method in order to illuminate an issue of relevance to our society. "The Next Assignment" (No. 22) has been generally received by historians as an injunction to exploit depth psychology for historical purposes. The particular field in which Langer chose to illustrate the potentialities of the method has been less frequently noted: namely, the social consequences of mass death, the effects of a "shattering experience" upon a culture. Many years before he turned to Freud, Langer had developed an interest in the Black Death and in "the repercussions—economic, social, spiritual—of so massive an experience of dying." [21] The original interest was as much demographic as cultural. Later, Freud and other depth psychologists made it possible to conduct a theoretical exploration of the general consequences of the mass phenomenon of plague. What Freud added, according to Langer, was an analysis of guilt feelings, which enables us to understand the strengthened sense of sin, the explosion of hedonistic abandon, and the unleashed aggression characteristic of a mass encounter with disaster and death. It is worth observing that Langer cites in this connection Freud's *Thoughts for the Times*

[21] William L. Langer, "Population in the Perspective of History," *Harvard Public Health Bulletin*, XXII (January 1965), Supplement, p. 6. For a separate treatment of the great plague, see William L. Langer, "The Black Death," *Scientific American*, CCX (February 1964), 114–121. It has not been reprinted here because "The Next Assignment" includes most of its material. Designed for a general audience, it is less oriented toward problems of method.

on War and Death, an essay written by Freud in 1915 out of deep despair that a civilization whose science had conquered the divine scourge, plague, seemed powerless to control the human one, war. In the light of the description of the anxiety of cultural dissolution in modern Western society in "The Historian and the Present," Langer's exploration of the cultural consequences of mass dying in late medieval Europe has the ring of relevance. Perhaps for Langer, as for Thucydides and Camus, the impact of plague on culture afforded intellectual access by analogy to the effects of protracted war and revolution.

In "Europe's Initial Population Explosion" (No. 23), Langer turned, as the title suggests, to another problem of great contemporary interest. As he had entered the realm of social psychology in search of the larger forces conditioning historical development, so now he sought in the area of agricultural technology for explanations of the pressures that made for social crisis. Here again Langer began with a historical problem of dislocation: What produced the increasingly severe social crises that finally issued in the explosion of 1848? It was a problem of central concern for the volume on the era from 1832 to 1850 which he has been preparing for his series, *The Rise of Modern Europe.* Langer became impressed initially by the extraordinary and often shocking methods of population control in the early nineteenth century—the crypto-infanticide of foster-parenthood, alcoholism, orphanages. Why should such practices develop within a pattern of population expansion? With an economic base strong enough to permit a high birthrate, Europe nevertheless seemed incapable of sustaining the number of people added to the population. Langer found the answer to the dislocation in the spread of the potato. By a combination of statistical analysis and empirical description, he showed that the potato made new life possible, but not bearable. He advanced his hypothesis with the caution appropriate to the complexity of the problem. By colligating a variety of aspects of social behavior hitherto held separate, he invited historians through his own suggestive exploration "to pay greater attention to the evolution of the human diet and its social consequences." Here too, though he did not labor the point, was a personal venture into new terrain which, by its example, might define a "next assignment" in bio-history to match the call to psycho-history.

Where in the previous two papers Langer searched out fundamental factors making for social change, in "The Pattern of Urban Revolution in 1848" (No. 24) he examined the means by which the rulers attempted to contain social change when it assumed threatening form. The point of view in this essay is essentially governmental: revolution is simply unjustified. It is also avoidable. Accordingly, Langer examines the revolutions of 1848 in terms of the effectiveness of governments in containing the explosive masses. He assumes that "chronic social tensions" prevailed in Europe's cities before 1848, but maintains that these nowhere produced a political leadership or an organizational strength sufficient to "make" a revolution. The decisive factor was whether the forces of law and order moved with sufficient firmness and skill. On these premises, Langer offers a comparative study in domestic counterinsurgency. He finds the British and the Russian governments the only ones who practiced successfully the "systematic repression" necessary to prevent insurrection. What Tsar Nicholas achieved by cossack sabre charges, the British achieved by developing, for a society more sensitive to civil rights, a civil police force trained in the tactics of riot control and deterrence of opposition leaders through clearly defining the limits of popular demonstrations.

To explain why revolution came to Paris, Vienna, and Berlin, and not to England or Russia, Langer maintains, "stress should be laid on the failure of the monarchy, rather than on the forces of revolution." Although he accepts the traditional liberal interpretation that the rulers failed because they did not make concessions to the liberal opposition, he goes beyond it. The more concrete failure of the governments was in the area of planning and enforcing crowd control to prevent aimless and innocuous demonstrations from turning into insurrection. In England, crowds were prevented from assembling; in the continental capitals, they were allowed to mill about until they became dangerous. The continental authorities, lacking well-trained police, used unreliable troops who precipitated full-scale revolution. The psychological insecurity of rulers filled with the nameless terror of revolt made them fail to respond "promptly and energetically" as the situation required.

Langer's historical analysis of ways of confronting domestic social crisis may suggest to the reader the "law and order" approach to America's recent wave of urban unrest and protest against racial oppression and the Vietnam War. I believe it would be mistaken to construe "The Pattern of Urban Revolution in 1848" as intended as a lesson of history for American cities in 1968. Although civil unrest had begun when the essay was written, "law and order" had not yet appeared on the horizon as a political slogan. On the other hand, Langer's preoccupation with contemporary American foreign policy may well have conditioned his approach to the problem of order in 1848. Having treated America's contemporary international problem from the point of view of policy-makers who saw America's task as one of exercising military power prophylactically against revolutionary states and their insurgent allies, Langer could understandably transfer the same perspective to the history of nineteenth century domestic revolutions. Whatever contemporary politics may have contributed to his analysis, Langer's fresh and original treatment of 1848 has opened up challenging questions which those concerned with revolutionary process in the nineteenth century will have to take into account.

The papers of Part IV, which date from the fourth and fifth decades of Langer's productive life, stand out for their intellectual boldness. Never had he pressed more vigorously into the largest and most elusive problems that historians can confront: the emotional components of man's response to his historical experience, the technological and demographic sources of social change, and the nature of attempts to contain revolutionary pressures. Yet even these bold ventures had their deep affinities to Langer's earlier work. From his beginnings in diplomatic history, he had been an explorer of crisis, even of breakdown. His interest came to focus where men confronted historical forces which, with or without their knowledge, threatened the structures that gave their lives coherence. First came the breakdown of the Bismarckian states system. In the articles of Part I Langer showed how imperialism altered the political constellation within the system without producing new forms to canalize its explosive energies. Again in the essays on inter-war international relations that dominate Part II, Langer charted the failures of both the old and the new international systems to contain the irrational force of fascism on the march. In Part III, Langer traced America's response as the premises of her continental isolation were eroded by a pressingly insistent world of power politics that drew her, willing or not, into its orbit. Finally in the papers of Part IV, he showed us men responding to the traumatic experiences of plague, social dislocation, and revolution.

In all these crises of breakdown, Langer tended to concentrate less on the forces of movement or the self-proclaimed protagonists of change, than on those who had to deal with the change, whether by espousal, by adaptation, or by resistance. This stress on men—usually men in power—encountering history imparts to Langer's writing a sense of immediacy, of actuality. His fidelity to the historical experience as a response to unforeseen complexities and unexpected situations led Langer, especially in his younger years, to concentrate on the story, on events. Taken as seriously as Langer takes it, the sense of encounter may have served as the source of his inexhaustible and ever-increasing desire to penetrate beneath the events, where the mystery screened from the historical actor might become accessible to the historian. What, this historian so wary of change asks ever more insistently as he grows older, what are the driving forces with which history compels its actors to deal?

Langer's sense for the importance of the undisclosed wellsprings of change shimmers through even his earliest work, coming clearly to the surface in *The Diplomacy of Imperialism*. Does it perhaps link his tendency toward political conservatism, his sympathy for those who have to confront profound and disconcerting change not of their own making, with his growing intellectual radicalism? Do not his explorations of the last fifteen years—in some ways the youngest in spirit of all his works—bespeak a new awareness that international crisis is but part of a continuing crisis of civilization deeper than the young author of "The Origin of the Russo-Japanese War" could have dreamt of? [22] Few historians have the capacity to assimilate the experience of living history and turn it to account for the enlargement of man's understanding of his past. These papers demonstrate that William Langer must be counted among their number.

[22] In "The Wellspring of Our Discontents" (No. 25), received too late for consideration in the Introduction, Langer analyzes World War I as an event which "helped substantially to undermine the foundations on which our civilization so precariously rests." Langer brings together the rich intellectual concerns of a lifetime in his sweeping, multidimensional interpretation of the war: the crisis of international systems, imperialism and its collapse, the psychological impact of mass dying, Wilson's ill-starred efforts for a new world order, and the effect of the Communist revolutions on peacemaking at Versailles and subsequent international history.

PART I

Systems, Games, and Players

1

The Origin of the Russo-Japanese War

1926

Although in point of magnitude and extent the Russo-Japanese War has been overshadowed by the cataclysm of 1914–1918, its intrinsic importance can hardly be exaggerated. Not only is the question of dominance in the Far East as acute today as ever, but it promises to become more and more crucial as time goes on. Besides, the Russo-Japanese War still remains the classic example of a conflict waged for purely imperialistic motives. There was no sentiment, no tradition involved. The Japanese and the Russians were equally disliked by the populations of the territories which they desired to control. At bottom it was merely a question of which nation should victimize the moribund Korean and Chinese Empires.

The underlying root of the struggle was, of course, the inability of China and Korea to resist the aggressions of the European states whose predatory tactics had gained tremendous momentum during the second half of the nineteenth century. And, looked at in its larger aspect, the Russo-Japanese conflict was not merely due to rivalry in Korea and Manchuria. The question at issue was really that of the mastery of the Chinese Empire and the whole Far East.[1]

It would be impossible in a single article to review the whole course of developments in the Far East from 1895, or even earlier, to the outbreak of hostilities in 1904. Such has been the conventional approach, and reliable as well as readable accounts are now available in all languages.[2] The purpose of this article is rather to utilize the extensive new

Note: This article first appeared as "Der Russisch-Japanische Krieg," in *Europäische Gespräche: Hamburger Monatshefte für Auswärtige Politik,* IV (1926), 279–322.

[1] The idea is developed by René Pinon, *La Guerre russo-japonaise* (Paris, 1906), p. 12, and by numerous later writers.

[2] K. Asakawa, *The Russo-Japanese Conflict* (Boston and New York, 1904), utilizing Japanese sources; O. Franke, *Die Grossmächte in Ostasien* (Braunschweig, 1923); Hans Rohde, *Der Kampf um Ostasien* (Stuttgart, 1926); the works of René Pinon, Victor Bérard, and André Chéradame; and the older books by Henri Cordier (*Histoire des relations de la Chine avec les puissances occidentales,* 3 vols. [Paris, 1901–02]), and H. B. Morse (*International Relations of the Chinese Empire,* 3 vols. [New York, 1910, 1918]), to mention only a few.

source material now at our disposal, in an attempt to determine the ultimate aims of the contestants, the methods employed in realizing these aims, and the part played by the other powers in precipitating the conflict.

It should be remarked at the outset that there is no occasion for criticizing the traditional view of Japanese policy. Excepting only the memoirs of Count Hayashi no source material of significance has appeared, at least not in Western languages. What information can be gleaned indirectly from other sources seems only to strengthen the accepted version of Japanese aims and actions.

It is well-known that the claims of Japan to a voice in Korean affairs go back to the dim period of legend and mythology. In the sixteenth century the country was overrun by the Japanese and compelled to acknowledge Japanese suzerainty. The problem was bound to become more acute in the latter part of the nineteenth century, when the rapid increase of the Japanese population and the gradual industrialization brought the need for new areas for colonization, new markets for goods, and new sources of food supply to the fore as the dominating factor in Japanese politics.[3] It may well be questioned whether this problem was sufficiently acute in 1894 to justify the war with China, and even so, the thesis that one nation has the right to victimize another in order to satisfy its own needs is at least debatable.[4] The Japanese, to be sure, avowedly fought the war in order to assure the independence of Korea from China, but no one can be under any illusions as to what this involved. In any case, it would be difficult to justify the Japanese policy in demanding the cession of the Liao-tung Peninsula after the war. It has been said that the purpose of this action was to secure Korea strategically against further Chinese encroachment, but it would certainly be nearer the truth to maintain that the more moderate Japanese statesmen of the Ito type were swept away by the pressure of the aggressive military group.[5]

[3] The classic formulation of this doctrine may be found in Asakawa's introductory chapter, where abundant statistical material is adduced. See also Tyler Dennett, *Roosevelt and the Russo-Japanese War* (New York, 1925), pp. 97–98; Arthur D. Brown, *The Mastery of the Far East* (New York, 1919), p. 119.

[4] According to H. Plehn, *Nach dem englisch-japanischen Bündnis* (Berlin, 1907), p. 35, there was no appreciable emigration from Japan prior to 1904, in which year there were only some 300,000 Japanese abroad.

[5] The Japanese view in Asakawa, *The Russo-Japanese Conflict,* p. 70, quoting the semi-official *Tokushu Joyaku.* On the whole subject of the Sino-Japanese War and the intervention after Shimonoseki the fundamental account is that of O. Franke, *Die Grossmächte in Ostasien,* pp. 31–105.

It is impossible to prove that the Japanese action in 1894 was designed primarily to check the advance of Russia upon China and Korea, but on the other hand, it is quite clear that the Japanese statesmen even in 1894 were distinctly alarmed by the forward march of the Russian colossus. This anxiety can be traced back to the eighteenth century, and in 1873, the Iwakura mission to Europe reported that the Russian advance to the south was "the chief peril for Japan." [6] Russia, after living on peaceful terms with China for over two hundred years, had begun her forward movement in the 1850's under the leadership of Muraviev-Amurski. She had attempted to cross the Amur and had actually acquired the Maritime Province with Vladivostok, and a frontier contiguous to that of Korea. It was largely the policy of Muraviev personally, carried out, like so many of Russia's conquests in Central Asia, without instructions from St. Petersburg. Indeed, there was no reason for the Russian advance. There was no need for new areas for colonization, because Siberia was as yet practically untouched. There was no need for an open port, so long as the hinterland was undeveloped. There was no need for a market for Russian goods, for Russia had none to sell, and the tea and silk bought in China had been going the overland route through Mongolia for centuries. In brief, it may be said that Russia's action was that of a predatory state—expansion for its own sake under the leadership of a governor who tried to serve his tsar too well. [7]

The history of Russia furnishes countless examples of the way in which one conquest leads to another. The new territory must be protected, it must be developed, it must be linked up with the homeland. Hardly had the Maritime Province and Northern Sakhalin been acquired than Russia began to send out her tentacles towards Korea and northern China. Her activities in Korea in the 1880's were so extensive that the English, at that time masters of the Far East, deemed it neces-

[6] Plehn, *Nach dem englisch-japanischen Bündnis,* p. 17; Robert K. Douglas, *Europe and the Far East* (Cambridge, 1913), pp. 191–192. G. Trubetzkoi, *Russland als Grossmacht* (Stuttgart and Berlin, 1913), pp. 45–46, states that prior to 1894, the Japanese considered joining the Franco-Russian alliance because they felt menaced by Russia. André Chéradame, *Le Monde et la guerre russo-japonaise* (Paris, 1906), p. 81, quotes an extremely interesting letter of a French diplomat written in 1881 and reporting the official Japanese press as declaring "Que le gouvernement du Mikado, dût-il y périr, devrait engager jusqu'à son dernier homme et son dernier bâtiment, plutôt que de laisser s'accomplir l'absorption de la Corée par la Russie."

[7] The idea is developed in T. W. Overlach, *Foreign Financial Control in China* (New York, 1919), p. 70; Chéradame, *Le Monde et la guerre,* pp. 393 ff.; E. J. Dillon, *The Eclipse of Russia* (London, 1918).

sary to intervene.[8] It is said that as early as 1894 the Russians proposed to the Japanese a partition of Korea, and attempts were made by Japan to effect an understanding with England, in order to erect a barrier to the Russian advance.[9] The Trans-Siberian railway, the construction of which had been discussed as far back as the 1850's, was begun in 1891 and was even then regarded as a convenient instrument for the extension of Russian influence, political as well as economic.[10]

It would be absurd, then, to say that the conflict between Russian and Japanese interests in the Far East dates from 1895. It merely entered upon the acute phase at that time, the Russian interests having become so far-reaching that even a moderate statesman like Count Witte regarded intervention as absolutely necessary in order to force the retrocession of the Liaotung Peninsula by Japan. Even at that time the two powers were confirmed enemies. The Russians were determined to go the length of an armed conflict and the Russian admiral would have "Copenhagened" the Japanese squadron had his French colleague been willing to cooperate.[11] As for the Japanese, it is quite evident that they

[8] For early Russian policy in Korea and the opposition of the English, see Franke, *Die Grossmächte in Ostasien*, p. 25; Brown, *Mastery of the Far East*, p. 134; and especially Tyler Dennett, *The Americans in Eastern Asia* (New York, 1922), chaps. 23–27; Plehn, *Nach dem englisch-japanischen Bündnis*, pp. 18–19; A. M. Pooley, ed., *The Secret Memoirs of Count Hayashi* (New York, 1915), pp. 45–46; S. A. Korff, "Russia in the Far East," *American Journal of International Law*, XVII (1923), p. 260; A. S. Hershey, *International Law and Diplomacy of the Russo-Japanese War* (New York, 1906), pp. 6, 42.

[9] Chéradame, *Le Monde et la guerre*, p. 83, who gives no authority. Roman Rosen, *Forty Years of Diplomacy* (New York, 1920), II, 134, mentions attempts made to reach an agreement with England. Charles Dilke, *Europe in 1887* (London, 1887), p. 175, advocated an alliance with China or even with Japan, in order to check the Russians. A Japanese writer, Manjiro Inagaki, *Japan and the Pacific* (New York, 1890), p. 40, in 1890 predicted the Russian advance to Liao-Tung and pointed out the necessity of an Anglo-Chinese-Japanese understanding to meet this danger. The Russian views are clearly expressed by A. Ia. Maksimov, *Nashi Zadachi po Tikhom Okeanie* (St. Petersburg, 1894): "The protectorate over Korea is the ultimate goal of Russian diplomacy in the Far East." (Quoted by Constantin von Zepelin, *Der ferne Osten* [Berlin, 1907], p. 29.)

[10] Chéradame, *Le Monde et la guerre*, pp. 393 ff. The authoritative account of the origins of the Siberian railway is in B. B. Glinskii, "Prolog Russko-Iaponskoi Voiny," a series of twelve articles in *Istoricheski Vestnik*, vols. CXXXV–CXXXVIII (January–December 1914), reprinted in 1916 under the same title. Glinskii's work is based largely upon material from the Witte archives. With the exception of certain sections dealing with the Yalu concession, it was translated into French and published as the work of Pierre Marc, *Quelques Années de politique internationale: Antécédents de la guerre russo-japonaise*, Etudes sur l'histoire de l'Europe orientale, vol. II (Leipzig, 1914).

[11] Glinskii, *Vest.*, CXXXV, 205 (Marc, *Quelques Années*, p. 2). The naval incident was first recounted by Felix Martin, *Le Japon vrai* (Paris, 1898), pp. 174 ff.,

too would have sought a decision on the field of battle had they been adequately prepared and had Russia not been supported by France and Germany.[12]

The immediate result of the Sino-Japanese War was that Korea was at least detached from China. The Celestial Empire was no longer a factor in the Korean problem. Curiously enough the Russians made no great effort to take its place,[13] and the Japanese had a fairly free hand until the abominable murder of the Korean queen in the autumn of 1895 and the flight of the king to the Russian legation ruined their position at the Korean court.[14] All the Japanese could hope to do for the time being was to hold their own. They made desperate efforts to buy off the Russians, and during the coronation festivities at Moscow in May 1896, Yamagata offered to partition Korea, leaving Russia the larger northern part, with the harbors of both the west and the east coasts, and retaining for Japan the southern part with Seoul.[15] This offer the Russians refused, on the theory that they had recognized the independence of Korea, and in the end the Japanese had to content themselves with the very meagre concessions laid down in the Lobanov-Yamagata agreement of June 1896.[16]

Had the Russians concentrated on Korea in the period immediately

and was corroborated by Chéradame, *Le Monde et la guerre,* pp. 325, 525; see also Eugène de Guichen, "La Politique extérieure du Japon," *Revue d'histoire diplomatique,* XXIII (January, 1909), 89–107; John W. Foster, *Diplomatic Memoirs* (Boston and New York, 1909), II, 51. [*Copenhagen:* to subject a fleet to a surprise attack; derived from the British assault on the Danish fleet (allied with Napoleon) in Copenhagen harbor, April 2, 1801.—Ed.]

[12] Asakawa, *The Russo-Japanese Conflict,* p. 76; A. Gérard, *Ma Mission en Chine* (Paris, 1918), pp. 45–48.

[13] Although in September 1895 there were rumors of Russia's intention of seizing some point on the Korean coast. See Johannes Lepsius, Albrecht Mendelssohn-Bartholdy, and Friedrich Thimme, eds., *Die grosse Politik der europäischen Kabinette, 1871–1914* (Berlin, 1922–26), XIV, 12. (Hereafter cited as *G.P.*).

[14] Brown, *The Mastery of the Far East,* pp. 135 ff., and numerous others.

[15] *Der russisch-japanische Krieg: Amtliche Darstellung des russischen Generalstabs,* German trans. by Eberhard von Tettau (Berlin, 1911–12), I, 6. (Hereafter cited as *Amtliche Darstellung*). This account has been little used by historians, although the chapter on the origins of the war is an abstract of a three-volume history, *Diplomaticheskiia Snosheniia Rossii i Iaponii ot Nachala etikh Snosheniia do Russko-Iaponskoi Voiny* written in part by P. Simanski with all documents at his disposal and not censored by the Russian Foreign Office. The larger account was never published, but the abstract in the official history is full of interesting material. (See the article by Simanski in *Na Chuzhoi Storonie,* no. 11 [1925].)

[16] On the Lobanov-Yamagata agreement, see Glinskii, *Vest.,* CXXXV, 637 (Marc, *Quelques Années,* p. 34); Trubetzkoi, *Russland als Grossmacht,* p. 51; Sergei Witte, *Memoirs of Count Witte,* trans. and ed. A. Yarmolinsky (New York, 1921), p. 97.

following, they might have gained control of the state. They had the king under their thumb, and the Japanese were not a serious obstacle. It seems that the Tsar did assume a rather informal protectorate over Korea, and it is obvious that the naval men were intent on securing a base on the Korean coast, but Witte was still all-powerful in St. Petersburg and insisted that Russia's efforts be confined to peaceful penetration. His policy is reflected in the Russian attempts to get control of the financial and military matters of Korea in the period from 1896 to 1898.[17] The Japanese, of course, protested, arguing that such procedure was contrary at least to the spirit of existing agreements, but their remonstrances were ignored by the Russians. Japan was in no position to fight, at least not without allies. But the Russian policy, not sufficiently vigorous to solve the question in her own sense, was yet sufficiently active to enrage and alarm the Japanese, who from this time onward began serious military and diplomatic preparations for a conflict which they regarded as inevitable.[18]

The weakness of Russian action in Korea after 1896 was partially due to failure in determining a consistent policy, but perhaps even more to the fact that the Russian statesmen had become fascinated with the prospects opened up in China, where, at one stroke, Russia had displaced the English influence and secured the first place in the confidence of the Chinese statesmen.[19] In China the Russian policy was at

[17] Rosen, *Forty Years of Diplomacy*, II, 125, feels sure that the Tsar promised to protect Korea, without consulting his ministers on the subject. In the extremely important serialized article by Van Larlarsky [V. M. Vonliarliarski], "Why Russia Went to War with Japan," *Fortnightly Review* (May and June 1910), the statement is twice made (pp. 819, 821) that Korea asked for protection, but that the request was refused. As for the question of a naval base in Korea, it appears that Li Hung Chang advised the Tsar in May 1896 to seize a port, though at that time the Tsar refused (*G.P.*, XIV, 31). Rosen, *Forty Years of Diplomacy*, II, 141, says the naval authorities had their eyes fixed on Masampo in 1896, and it is evident from the German documents that in August 1896 and again in the autumn of 1897 extensive plans were on foot, and that the seizure of Phyong-Yang was being contemplated to provide a terminus for the Manchurian railway (*G.P.*, XIV, 31, 77, 79; also Van Larlarsky, *Fortnightly Review* [May 1910], p. 819). The military instructors and financial advisers were sent at the request of the Korean government (*Amtliche Darstellung*, I, 7; Glinskii, *Vest.*, CXXXV, 636 ff. [Marc, *Quelques Années*, p. 34]; Van Larlarsky, *Fortnightly Review* [May 1910], p. 821). For the extensive scheme of reorganizing the Korean army, see Rosen, *Forty Years of Diplomacy*, II, 140. The Russians also secured numerous concessions of an economic nature. (See Brown, *The Mastery of the Far East*, p. 142.)

[18] See Rosen's warnings in *Forty Years of Diplomacy*, II, 144.

[19] Franke, *Die Grossmächte in Ostasien*, p. 104; Chéradame, *Le Monde et la guerre*, p. 523, quotes a remarkable letter written by de Fleurac, the French

first not aggressive territorially speaking. Witte, who still played the decisive role at St. Petersburg, was the advocate of a policy of peaceful penetration. He was willing to respect the political independence and integrity of the Chinese Empire, but was intent on getting control of her economic life. Witte was clever enough to flood the world with apologies in later years, and took care to represent his policy as perfectly innocent and justifiable, wholly devoid of the danger of international complications. As a matter of fact, it was as justifiable as that of the other European powers and no more. As for the danger involved, it should be remembered that Witte's policy extended to Korea as well as to northern China, and it is by no means certain that it in itself would not have led to war.[20]

Witte, having secured a hold upon the Chinese government by the intervention after the war with Japan and by supplying the loan with which China was enabled to pay off the indemnity, was now able to obtain the permit to run the Trans-Siberian Railway through northern Manchuria.[21] The Chinese were by no means blind to the possible implications of such concessions, but they were not in a position to resist and Li Hung Chang himself seems to have been convinced that without Russian friendship the empire would be doomed. After almost interminable negotiations the Chinese statesman allowed himself to be persuaded to sign the Moscow Convention (May 22, 1896), by which the two contracting powers promised each other assistance in warding off a Japanese attack upon China or Korea. Russia, acting through the Russo-Chinese Bank, received at the same time permission to construct the Eastern Chinese Railway "in order to facilitate the expedition of help to China in case of need." [22]

---

attaché in Peking, on March 16, 1895, in which he forecasts almost all the developments arising from the intervention at Shimonoseki.

[20] Witte's policy is ably set forth in his *Memoirs*, p. 83. Of the apologies one need only mention XXX [evidently Witte himself], "Origines exactes de la guerre russo-japonaise," *Revue de Paris*, XII (July 15, 1905); also, Sergei Witte, *La Guerre avec le Japon* (Paris, 1911); the articles by Glinskii; and Dillon, *The Eclipse of Russia*. Able criticisms of the policy may be found in A. Kuropatkin, *The Russian Army and the Japanese War* (New York, 1909); and especially in B. A. Romanov, "Kontsessiia na Yalu," *Russkoe Proshloe*, I (1923), 87–108.

[21] The project of running the railway through northern Manchuria was suggested in the 1880's and discussed in 1887. Glinskii, *Vest.*, CXXXV, 210 ff. (Marc, *Quelques Années*, pp. 8–9); *G.P.*, XIV, 18; Matignon, "Li Hung Chang," *Nouvelle Revue* (Aug. 1 and 15, 1925).

[22] On the negotiations see Glinskii, *Vest.*, CXXXV, 210 ff. (Marc, *Quelques Années*, pp. 11 ff.); Trubetzkoi, *Russland als Grossmacht*, pp. 55–57; Witte, *Memoirs*,

The great objection to Witte's policy in the matter of the railway is that it tended to involve Russia more and more deeply in the Far East. The railroad itself would perhaps never have led to war and the concession in itself was no better and no worse than countless others extorted from the Chinese government. But, on the other hand, the railroad formed the opening wedge and encouraged the aggressive group in St. Petersburg to hatch more extensive projects. At the same time, the Japanese could not help looking at it askance and taking precautions to meet the great strengthening of Russian influence which necessarily followed from the concession.

Witte's policy was not long to remain unchallenged at St. Petersburg. The German occupation of Kiao-chow raised the question of whether Russia should not secure her naval position in the Far East in a similar manner. Witte immediately recognized the implications of such a policy and saw that it would result in Japanese aggression on Korea.[23] But at the council held to discuss the matter, he was unable to make his view prevail. The Tsar considered himself duped by the Kaiser, and followed Muraviev in seeing the matter through, in spite of all difficulties.[24]

No step taken by Russia was so decisive as the lease of Port Arthur. Not only did it involve the abandonment of the principle of Chinese integrity and the loss of China's friendship and confidence,[25] it also led to

---

pp. 88–95. The treaty was not first revealed by Li's son in the *Daily Telegraph*, Feb. 15, 1910, as stated by J. V. A. MacMurray, *Treaties with and Concerning China* (New York, 1921), I, 81. The substance is correctly given by XXX [presumably Witte], *Revue de Paris*, XII (July 15, 1905), 226.

[23] *G.P.*, XVI, 104. Glinskii, *Vest.*, CXXXV, 621 ff. (Marc, *Quelques Années*, p. 20).

[24] For a brief statement see E. Brandenburg, *Von Bismarck zum Weltkrieg* (Berlin, 1924), pp. 84 ff. See further Witte, *Memoirs*, pp. 99–100, 103; Dillon, *The Eclipse of Russia*, p. 249; Rosen, *Forty Years of Diplomacy*, II, 156; Alexander Isvolski, *Memoirs of an Ambassador* (New York, 1921), pp. 119–120; and XXX, *Revue de Paris* (July 15, 1905), where the story of the conference is first told. The subject is fully considered by Romanov, *Russkoe Proshloe*, I, 91 ff., and by Glinskii, *Vest.*, CXXXV, 621 ff. (Marc, *Quelques Années*, pp. 20–21) where it is pointed out that in the treaty of 1896 Russia promised China aid only in the case of aggression by Japan. On the other hand, it must be remembered that in 1895 Russia had intervened against Japan in behalf of China's integrity. Glinskii also makes the interesting statement that Port Arthur had at an earlier date been found unsatisfactory. At the council held to discuss the matter Admiral Tyrtov had been opposed to the lease. He would have preferred Masampo!

[25] The Chinese had appealed to the Russians for aid against the Germans, but in the end the Russians refused to take action, this attitude being easily explainable in view of the peculiar Russo-German relations in the matter. See Glinskii, *Vest.*, CXXXV, 616 (Marc, *Quelques Années*, pp. 18, 21); Trubetzkoi, *Russland als Grossmacht*, p. 58; Witte, *Memoirs*, p. 98; Romanov, *Russkoe Proshloe*, I, 92.

increased hostility on the part of the Japanese, from whom the selfsame base had been taken away in 1895 on the plea that it would give the power possessing it control of the Gulf of Pechili and therewith of the Chinese capital. But there were other less obvious but equally important results of the Port Arthur adventure. By the projected railway from Harbin to Port Arthur the Russians would invade the thickly populated area of southern Manchuria. The hostility of the inhabitants would require elaborate measures of protection and lead inevitably to the outright annexation of Manchuria.[26] In such a case the Russians would undoubtedly find themselves opposed by other European powers, to say nothing of the United States. As a matter of fact, the Russian action in Liaotung not only led to a general scramble for "leases" and to the Boxer troubles with their fateful consequences,[27] it had the further effect of setting Korea in a new position in respect to Russia. The Land of the Morning Calm now appeared as a high rock on both sides of which the Russian glacier descended.[28] To ensure connections both by land and by sea between Port Arthur and Vladivostok, Korea must be subjugated before it became a base for hostile forces.[29]

The Japanese were certainly justified in regarding their position in Korea as more menaced than ever after the Russian occupation of Port Arthur. It was not the Russian advance in Manchuria itself, but rather the danger therefrom to Korea that precipitated the conflict.[30] The Chinese appealed to the Japanese for aid, and a naval demonstration was staged in January 1898.[31] The English, already greatly excited by the establishment of the Russo-Korean Bank in the autumn of 1897 and by the attempt made to replace the Englishman Brown by the Russian Alexeiev as Inspector of Customs in Korea, and further estranged by the dispute with Russia as to the construction of the Peking-Shanhaikwan railroad, were evidently ready to assist China and Japan. An alliance

[26] The point is developed in Romanov, *Russkoe Proshloe*, I, 95.

[27] There is no evidence that the German action at Kiao-chow would have led to the scramble. Germany's responsibility lies in the sole fact that her action provoked that of Russia.

[28] The figure is from Pinon, *La Guerre russo-japonaise*, p. 16.

[29] Brown, *The Mastery of the Far East*, p. 123.

[30] This comes out most clearly in the negotiations for the Anglo-Japanese Alliance (see Pooley, *Hayashi Memoirs*, especially p. 130). Note also the categorical statement to this effect by Kogoro Takahira, "Why Japan Resists Russia," *North American Review* (March 1904), pp. 321–327.

[31] For China's appeal to Japan, see Glinskii, *Vest.*, CXXXV, 628 ff. (Marc, *Quelques Années*, p. 56). It is not clear whether this preceded the Japanese demonstration. On this see *G.P.*, XIV, 149.

with Japan had been discussed in the press since 1895, and in March 1898 Chamberlain made definite advances to Baron Kato.[32] The Japanese rejected the offer, partly because they felt inadequately prepared and partly because they evidently feared that France and Germany would once again stand by Russia.[33] They consequently determined to make another attempt to settle the conflict of interests by compromise. In March 1898 they approached the Russians with a proposal that amounted to an offer of a free hand in Manchuria in return for similar freedom in Korea. Japan demanded the sole right to give Korea advice and assistance, but was willing in return to declare Manchuria and its coast as in every respect outside the sphere of Japanese interests.[34] This offer the Russians felt unable to accept. Indeed, since the occupation of Port Arthur they could not help feeling as much menaced by the Japanese in Korea as the Japanese felt endangered by the Russian position in Manchuria. Russia, however, was no more prepared for war at the moment than was Japan. She had already voluntarily withdrawn the Russian military instructors from Korea and was only too glad to shelve the whole question by a makeshift agreement. By the Rosen-Nissi Convention of April, a condominium was set up for Korea, Russia giving Japan a free hand economically in the country.[35] Official Russia thereby suspended her activity in Korea, apparently until such time as the Trans-Siberian railroad should be completed.[36]

It would be interesting to trace the development of both the Russian and the Japanese policies after 1898, but this would lead us too far afield. Suffice it to say that the Japanese threw themselves with redoubled vigor into extensive military and naval preparations so costly

[32] On the Russian-English tension just before and during the Port Arthur crisis see above all Glinskii, *Vest.*, CXXXV, 639 ff. (Marc, *Quelques Années*, pp. 34 ff.). Hayashi had urged the necessity for an alliance with England in 1895 (Pooley, *Hayashi Memoirs*, especially p. 114), and similar suggestions were made in the English press (Franke, *Die Grossmächte in Ostasien*, p. 67). For English advances to China see Glinskii, *Vest.*, CXXXV, 1031 (Marc, *Quelques Années*, p. 50). The English offers to Japan are recounted in Pooley, *Hayashi Memoirs*, p. 89; see also *G.P.*, XIV, 150, 159, 160 and especially 198.

[33] *G.P.*, XIV, 160 note.

[34] Rosen, *Forty Years of Diplomacy*, II, 157–158; Trubetzkoi, *Russland als Grossmacht*, p. 59.

[35] On the withdrawal of the Russian instructors see *Amtliche Darstellung*, I, 7; on the Rosen-Nissi Agreement, see Glinskii, *Vest.*, CXXXV, 640 ff. (Marc, *Quelques Années*, pp. 36 ff.); Rosen, *Forty Years of Diplomacy*, II, 159; Asakawa, *The Russo-Japanese Conflict*, p. 27.

[36] Van Larlarsky, *Fortnightly Review* (May 1910), p. 821; it is quite evident that Muraviev meant to secure Russian communications between Port Arthur and Vladivostok by a connecting railroad (*G.P.*, XIV, 159).

that it seemed doubtful whether the finances would stand the strain.[37] Meanwhile, taking advantage of the agreement with Russia, Japanese traders flocked to Korea by the thousand, secured one concession after the other from the helpless government and economically subjugated the country.[38] At the same time the Japanese devoted their attention to China and strained every nerve to secure over the government that influence which the Russians had so wantonly sacrificed. Evidently they even then had hopes of a coalition of the yellow race against the intruder. The yellow peril was not entirely a phantasy sprung from the minds of irresponsible alarmists.[39]

The outstanding characteristic of the Japanese policy was the singleness of its aims. With the Russians the situation was exactly the reverse. The Port Arthur affair had dealt Witte's policy a serious blow, had forced a partial withdrawal from Korea and had led to recriminations between the Tsar and his minister. Witte, to be sure, continued on the path he had chosen and made the best of the matter. Millions of roubles were spent in Manchuria; Dalny sprang up overnight, and work on the railroad was pressed forward.

But Witte no longer possessed the confidence of the Tsar, at least not so far as Far Eastern affairs were concerned. He had characterized the seizure of Port Arthur as "childish" and "premature" and pointed out that it involved partial withdrawal from Korea to say the least. But the whole action had been largely the work of the Tsar himself, and he was ready to listen to those who could propose methods for the reconstitution of the Russian position. Prince Uktomski, who had accompanied the Tsar on his trip to the Far East in 1890, advocated the peaceful conquest of China through the medium of the Buddhist priesthood. His influence may be traced in the development of Russian policy in Tibet and in the attempts to cultivate the friendship of the Dalai Lama.[40]

---

[37] Japanese military expenditures increased tenfold between 1894 and 1898 (Plehn, *Nach dem englisch-japanischen Bündnis*, p. 15). The Russians expected a financial crash in Japan, and hence did not hasten their own armaments (Rosen, *Forty Years of Diplomacy*, II, 204). Full statistics in Asakawa, *The Russo-Japanese Conflict*, p. 80.

[38] See especially *Amtliche Darstellung*, I, 8; Brown, *The Mastery of the Far East*, pp. 150 ff., Chéradame, *Le Monde et la guerre*, pp. 104 ff.

[39] The fullest account in Glinskii, *Vest.*, CXXXV, 1036 ff. (Marc, *Quelques Années*, pp. 56 ff.); Pinon, *La Guerre russo-japonaise*, pp. 58–59, 116 ff.; C. E. Maître in the excellent *Bulletin de l'école française d'extrême orient*, IV (January to June 1904), 499–522.

[40] On Uktomski see Heinrich Friedjung, *Das Zeitalter des Imperialismus* (Berlin, 1919), I, 146; Uktomski's views were laid down in the introduction of his great

But of Uktomski, we know comparatively little. More important was the Bezobrazov group, which presented plans for the gradual absorption of northern China and Korea by means of a great trading company, modelled on the East India Company of earlier days.

Much has been written of the activity of this group and of the so-called "Yalu Concession" in 1903, but no consideration has been given to the earlier history of "Bezobrazovism," which is absolutely indispensable to an understanding of Russian policy.[41] A Russian merchant named Brinner had in 1896 secured from the Korean government a concession to exploit the timber tracts along the Tumen and Yalu rivers. As a result of the Russian withdrawal from activity in this region he decided to sell it to international interests, specifically to Rothstein, director of the International Bank and one of the directors of the Russo-Chinese Bank, a son-in-law of one of the Rothschilds. News of this leaked out and a small group composed of Matiunin, just appointed Russian minister to Seoul, Vonliarliarski, a well-known developer, and later Bezobrazov, a retired officer and councillor, decided to save the project and utilize it for the expansion of Russian interests which official Russia was giving up. In February 1898 after an unsuccessful attempt to interest Muraviev, this group turned to the Tsar himself, and proposed establishing an East Asiatic Company to serve as a political institution "guided by the august will of the Russian Emperor." The enterprise required a number of stockholders "who would not demand immediate dividends" and who would be prepared to "render a service to the Tsar." The promoters claimed that the enterprise would soon enable Russia to obtain complete control of Korea, and it was planned to have representatives of the company enter the Korean service. Vorontsev and the Grand Duke Alexander Michailovich were interested, and in March a memorandum was submitted to the Tsar in which the necessity of Russia's establishing her influence in Korea was stressed.

---

account of the journey of the Tsarevich to the Far East and in the articles which appeared in the *Moskovskiia Viedomosti,* of which he was editor. For Russian policy in Tibet, see among others Pinon, *La Guerre russo-japonaise,* pp. 55–56, 86–87; Lovat Fraser, *India under Lord Curzon and After* (London, 1911), chap. 17.

[41] The fundamental treatment of the whole subject is the rare article by Romanov, *Russkoe Proshloe,* I, 87–108. This is based on the original documents and on earlier accounts drawn up at the command of the Tsar but never published. The most important of these is Vonliarliarski's account, twenty-one pages of which were published by Vonliarliarski in his book on the Chukhotsk Peninsula in 1913. Even Romanov does not seem to be aware that the whole first part of Vonliarliarski's account had appeared earlier in the *Fortnightly Review* for May and June 1910. These carry the story to 1900, when the publication was abruptly stopped.

The project was quite feasible, and American and other capital could be taken in to act as a screen. A conflict with Japan could be avoided by "granting her certain material advantages in Korea with the help of the company." Above all, on the area covered by the concession could be deployed "our fighting vanguard, up to 20,000 men, disguised as lumbermen."

The Tsar was impressed by the possibility of saving Korea for Russia and in this way making good the blunder involved in the seizure of Port Arthur. It was decided to acquire the concession from Brinner, Privy Councillor Neporoshnev acting as dummy. The Grand Duke and Vorontsev were to be in charge, while Bezobrazov and Vonliarliarski were to do the actual managing. Furthermore, a large sum of money was set aside from the Imperial Cabinet funds to finance an expedition to northern Korea. This expedition set out in June 1898, armed with instructions from Baron Fredericks, who had been ordered to participate "in a private way, as the Emperor's man of confidence." The War Department sent along an officer to make surveys, and Muraviev was told frankly that the expedition was pursuing "political aims." Neporoshnev was in command, and all but succeeded in getting from the Emperor of Korea a concession to exploit the Cabinet lands and the mineral resources of Korea. The story of the expedition is a long and complicated one. Here it is necessary only to mention the work it accomplished. It drew up a description of Northern Korea from the military, economic, and climatic viewpoints; it surveyed large areas; it studied the river conditions; it made surveys for a railway from Port Arthur to Vladivostok; it studied carefully Port Shestakov on the east coast of Korea, to which a railroad was to be built from Girin through Kapsan; it made certain that the population was not hostile and that the Japanese had not yet arrived on the scene.[42]

In spite of this auspicious beginning the enterprise had to be postponed. Witte was not even informed of the undertaking in this early stage, but even Muraviev objected to spending money on the mineral concession and so the project was dropped. Pending a more favorable opportunity the concession was transferred in May 1899 to Matiunin and Albert, who gave an express promise to hand it back to Fredericks, or to anyone designated by Fredericks, whenever asked to do so. They

[42] As aforesaid, I am relying here entirely on Vonliarliarski's story and on the briefer exposition of Romanov. Glinskii's account (*Vest.*, CXXXVI, 242 ff.) is incorrect in several particulars.

declared further that all rights under the concession belonged to them only nominally. It was hoped that the company could be organized as a private concern, but those who were approached apparently feared the opposition of Witte. An attempt was then made to set up the Volunteer Fleet as a separate administration which might act as a cover for the company, but to this the naval authorities objected. As a matter of fact they were pursuing their own schemes in the Far East, and in the winter of 1899–1900 made desperate efforts to secure a footing at Masampo, which were frustrated by the Japanese. So tense had the situation become by March 1900 that war did not seem at all improbable, and Kuropatkin spoke of the necessity of depriving Japan of the right to maintain a fleet.[43]

It is possible then, to distinguish three different aspects of the Russian policy in the years 1898–1900. The naval men, working through Muraviev almost precipitated war by their attempts to acquire a base at Masampo. At the same time the Bezobrazov group continued its efforts to develop Russian interests in Korea. Witte himself was approached for support, but wrote characteristically to Vonliarliarski: "Let those who started the idea carry it out." A new attack was then launched on Nicholas himself as the "standard-bearer." The Tsar promised to submit the matter to the Council of Ministers, but Fredericks, evidently in collusion with Witte, now objected, on the theory that the participation of the court could not be kept a secret and would arouse distrust against Russia. The Tsar, therefore, once more postponed action and Bezobrazov was ordered to "await circumstances" and the "psychological moment." [44]

The third policy was that of Witte. It was confined to Manchuria and northern China, and though its methods were pacific, like those of the Bezobrazovists, the aims were no less extensive. The suggestion for a railway to Port Shestakov was ignored, and, instead, the railway to Port Arthur was pushed. But Witte's plans did not end there. The Russian claims in China extended over all Mongolia and in fact as far south as the Hoang-ho. A Russian memorandum of January 1, 1898, defined the

---

[43] Witte, *La Guerre avec le Japon*, p. 30. The Masampo affair is well-known, and it is not necessary to go into details. See Rosen, *Forty Years of Diplomacy*, II, 161; Trubetzkoi, *Russland als Grossmacht*, pp. 60–61; Asakawa, *The Russo-Japanese Conflict*, pp. 274, 278; Brown, *The Mastery of the Far East*, pp. 142 ff.; Bernard Schwertfeger, ed., *Zur europäischen Politik, 1897–1914* (Berlin, 1919), I, 57–58.

[44] Romanov, *Russkoe Proshloe*, I, 99–100.

sphere of "Russia's exclusive influence" as including "the provinces of northern China, with the whole of Manchuria, the province of Chi-li, Chinese Turkestan," in which territories Russia could not admit any foreign political influence.[45]

The schemes of Witte necessarily aroused the interest and alarm of the other powers. The Germans, who were well posted, were ready to recognize the Russian claims, provided the Russian government recognized Germany's predominant interests in Shantung and the valley of the Hoang-ho.[46] The English on the other hand felt particularly menaced by the Russian advance in China, just as the Japanese felt endangered by the Muscovite intrigues in Korea. English policy in the Far East had been unusually passive since 1895. The mistaken calculations of the Foreign Office during the Sino-Japanese War had apparently upset the English statesmen, and shortly after they became embroiled in the South African affair.[47] As a result they had not been able to offer much resistance to Russia. In 1897, during the dispute about the Shanhaikwan railroad, they evidently tried to reach some sort of agreement, but nothing seems to have come of the negotiations. England was therefore obliged to look elsewhere for support. The German occupation of Kiao-chow was fully approved and the Japanese were encouraged to act during the Port Arthur crisis.[48] But the Japanese refused to act and the English contented themselves with the occupation of Wei-hai-wei, which, together with Port Arthur, commands the entrance to the Gulf of Pechili. When the Russians proposed a railroad agreement in the summer of 1898 the English were only too willing to accept. The important convention of April 1899 involved an engagement by England not to seek railroad concessions in the territory north of the Great Wall, while the Russians made a similar engagement in regard to the Yangtse Valley. This agreement did not prevent the Russians from cooperating with the Belgian interests on the Peking-Hankow railroad, nor did it prevent the Russians from immediately demanding from the Chinese

[45] *G.P.*, XIV, 134.

[46] *Ibid.*, 115, 136, 139. The Kaiser, however, thought the Russian claims to Chi-li with Tientsin and Peking "ein starker Bissen."

[47] On English policy, see Franke, *Die Grossmächte in Ostasien*, pp. 33–40. It has been suggested that in the 1880's the English encouraged the active policy of the Chinese in Korea, in order to check the Russians (Dennett, *The Americans in Eastern Asia*, pp. 471 ff.).

[48] On English negotiations with Russia in 1897 see *G.P.*, XIV, 250; Tyler Dennett, *Roosevelt and the Russo-Japanese War*, pp. 53–54. On the approval of German policy see *G.P.*, XIV, 147.

the concession for a railroad from the Manchurian line to Peking, but it was, nevertheless, tantamount to the abandonment of Manchuria by the English, a step which the Japanese had already offered to take and which the Germans had actually taken.[49]

The situation, then, was sufficiently critical when the Boxer troubles of 1900 broke out. In a sense the whole affair signified a defeat for the pro-Japanese reforming party in China, and the Japanese were eager to play a prominent role in suppressing the movement.[50] The English supported the Japanese,[51] but the Russians objected. As a matter of fact, the period of the Boxer rising simply marks a further development of the conflict in St. Petersburg. Witte, and the new foreign minister, Lamsdorff, were in favor of total abstention, hoping in this way to regain the confidence and gratitude of the Chinese court. Hence Russia officially urged moderation. They were the first to withdraw from Peking and the first to accept Li Hung Chang as a negotiator.[52] But the success of Witte was by no means complete. From the first he was challenged by Bezobrazov, who urged the Tsar to take advantage of the golden opportunity offered by the general confusion. "We are suffering," he wrote in July, "not from the Chinese big fist, but from that of St. Petersburg . . . Witte has created a system which, even in times of peace, weighed heavily upon the productive forces of the country, and has given us a mass of disaffected and impoverished people; but in times of war it causes fears of the state's bankruptcy . . . Instead of working through our best forces, we have left the work to Jews and Poles, whom Witte has charged with the task of bearing our standard . . . The active forces in the Far East have been the Russo-Chinese Bank and the Manchurian builders, but this Polish-Jewish clique gave us no timely information and did no real business." He asks the question: "Shall we rise

[49] As early as April 1898, Chamberlain regarded it as too late to check the Russian advance in Manchuria and spoke of abandoning this territory and concentrating on attempts to prevent a further expansion of Russian influence to the south (*G.P.,* XIV, 203, 215 and especially 222). On the Anglo-Russian railroad agreement, see Marc, *Quelques Années,* p. 52. The significance of this convention has not been sufficiently emphasized. Li Hung Chang called it the "partition of China." On the Peking-Hankow project see Overlach, *Foreign Financial Control in China,* p. 92.

[50] Pinon, *La Guerre russo-japonaise,* p. 65 and *passim.*

[51] *G.P.,* XVI, 16.

[52] On Witte's policy see his *Memoirs,* p. 108; Dillon, *The Eclipse of Russia,* p. 267; Glinskii, *Vest.,* CXXXVI, 226 ff. (Marc, *Quelques Années,* pp. 68 ff.); *G.P.,* XVI, 38 ff.; Alfred Waldersee, *Denkwürdigkeiten* (Stuttgart and Berlin, 1923), III, 24; Matignon, *Nouvelle Revue* (Aug. 15, 1925). It was only by mistake that the Russians took part in the expedition to Peking at all.

to the occasion and consolidate the Russian cause politically and economically, or shall we fall into the hands of the Jewish Kahal and the machinations of European diplomacy?" Bezobrazov followed up this assault by "Concrete Proposals for the Desirable Utilization of our Successes," in which he urged the necessity of Russia's securing sole influence in Manchuria and northern China. Other foreign influences must move further south. This policy demands Russia's dominant military position on the spot and a continental European agreement based upon "a partition of British interests in China." In this way the Celestial Empire could be freed of the "insatiable British leech." With sufficient forces in the Far East, Russia could accomplish her ends by mere "mimicry." But in spite of this eloquent appeal Witte, supported by Fredericks, succeeded in dissuading the Tsar, and in the summer of 1901, Bezobrazov, filled with "grief over the fate of our national interests," was forced to tell the Tsar that the whole matter would have to be dropped until "we have a new Minister of Finances." [53]

But Witte's policy of abstention was challenged from another quarter. Kuropatkin, the war minister, had been for intervention in Manchuria from the first. When the news of the Boxer rising reached St. Petersburg, he is reported to have said: "I am very glad; this will give us an excuse for seizing Manchuria . . . We will turn Manchuria into a second Bokhara." [54] He furthermore argued that in order to get control of China, one must get control of the Queen Dowager, and hence he insisted on the despatch of troops to Chi-li. The outbreaks in Manchuria, which were not by any means entirely Boxer in their nature and which seem to have been instigated by the Chinese government in revenge for the perfidious policy of the Russians since 1898, gave an added opportunity for intervention. Even Witte was compelled to ask for forces to protect the railway.[55] In this way the military men suddenly found themselves in the ascendancy, and they went so far as to dispute the possession of the Peking-Shanhaikwan railway with the English.[56] The

---

[53] Romanov, *Russkoe Proshloe*, I, 100 ff.

[54] Witte, *Memoirs*, p. 107. On Kuropatkin's policy, see further Glinskii, *Vest.*, CXXXVI, 226 ff. (Marc, *Quelques Années*, pp. 68 ff.); Dillon, *The Eclipse of Russia*, p. 267; *G.P.*, XVI, 24, 35, 40.

[55] On the rising in Manchuria, see Witte, *Memoirs*, pp. 109–110; Glinskii, *Vest.*, CXXXV, 1017 ff. (Marc, *Quelques Années*, pp. 40 ff.); *Amtliche Darstellung*, p. 9; Romanov, *Russkoe Proshloe*, I, 100.

[56] See especially *G.P.*, XVI, 235 ff., 259–260, and Waldersee, *Denkwürdigkeiten*, III, 25 ff., from which it becomes perfectly obvious that the railway was meant by the military men as an entering wedge for the domination of Chi-li. The same

two rivals almost came to blows in Tientsin, and it was only then that the Russians drew back. They had, in the meanwhile, however, scored a resounding victory over the English in Tibet.

One can easily understand the feelings of the English during the crisis. Involved in the South African War, menaced by the Russians in central Asia, they of necessity tried every method to check the Muscovite advance in China. This was the crucial point, for the break up of China was regarded as inevitable by most of the powers. The Germans were anxious to rescue Chi-fu and the Hoang-ho Valley from the debris, and the English themselves made desperate efforts to reserve the Yangtse Valley.[57] They had no hopes of keeping the Russians out of Manchuria, but they were anxious to keep them out of Chi-li, and, besides, there was a prospect of finding allies to oppose the enemy in this focal region. In the end the Russian advance in central Asia might be checked by a defeat in northern China.[58]

The original object of the so-called Yangtse Agreement concluded between England and Germany in 1900 was to build up opposition to Russia, and the Japanese immediately adhered to it. But the English were forced to admit that it was a failure when the Germans made it clear that they could not consent to the inclusion of Manchuria in the sphere of the treaty.[59]

---

sources throw light on the crisis in Tientsin. See further Asakawa, *The Russo-Japanese Conflict*, p. 156, and the Gr. Br., F. O., Correspondence respecting the affairs of China (*British Blue Books: China*), no. I (1898); no. I (1899); no. II (1904).

[57] The English hopes become perfectly obvious from a reading of the documentary material. For the Kaiser's desires, see especially Waldersee, *Denkwürdigkeiten*, III, 6, 57.

[58] For the fears of the English of a further advance by the Russians, see *G.P.*, XVII, 88–89. From Trubetzkoi, *Russland als Grossmacht*, p. 28; Chéradame, *Le Monde et la guerre*, p. 498; and Valentine Chirol, *The Middle Eastern Question* (London, 1903), it is clear that the English were concerned chiefly by events in central Asia. Compare also Pooley in the introduction to the *Hayashi Memoirs*, p. 68: "When the first alliance was signed (with Japan) its honest *ultima ratio*, so far as England was concerned, was fear of Russian aggression in India and Constantinople."

[59] In January 1901 the Germans actually told the Russians that they could go as far as they liked in Manchuria (*G.P.*, XVI, 311 note). On the Yangtse Agreement, see especially, *G.P.*, XVI, 224 ff., and particularly Salisbury's remark on p. 233: "I confess that since you have altered it to make it agreeable to Russia, I am not very much in love with this agreement." A similar remark by Devonshire in Hermann Eckardstein, *Lebenserinnerungen und politische Denkwürdigkeiten* (Leipzig, 1919–1921), II, 202. A good general account of the whole affair may be found in Brandenburg, *Von Bismarck zum Weltkrieg*, pp. 126 ff.

The Russians had, from the beginning, declared their intention of evacuating Manchuria as soon as circumstances should permit.[60] But this was only the official view, that of Witte and his friend Lamsdorff. Kuropatkin and the military men about the Tsar never intended to give up Manchuria now that they had their hands upon it.[61] But it should not be forgotten that while Witte urged evacuation, he nevertheless set on foot schemes of a far-reaching nature. The proposals submitted to the Chinese in the winter of 1900–1901 are the most eloquent proof of this. It was Witte who inserted the demands for a railway "in the direction of Peking" and asked that the Chinese government engage not to accord to any foreigners, without the consent of Russia, concessions for railroads, mines, or other industrial enterprises in Manchuria, in Mongolia, and in the whole of Eastern Chinese Turkestan (Tarbagatai, Ili, Kashgaria, Yarkand, Khotan Keriya), representing a Russian advance on Tibet.[62] It was not the Russian occupation of Manchuria, but these demands that led to the acute international crisis of February and March 1901. Here was a flagrant violation of the "open door" and it was with comparatively little difficulty that the United States, itself protected by a high tariff wall, was persuaded to drop its rather Russophil attitude and join England and Japan in protesting against the conclusion of the Russo-Chinese agreement.[63] The representations of the powers were so outspoken that the Russians were compelled to drop the negotiations, and besides were forced to give up their claims to the Shanhai-kwan railroad. It appears that an attempt was made to reach a separate agreement with England on the basis of a free hand in the Yangtse Ba-

[60] See especially the Russian note of August 1900 (Asakawa, *The Russo-Japanese Conflict*, p. 151), and the declarations of Lamsdorff to the German Ambassador at the same time: "Nicht einen Fussbreit chinesischen Territoriums wolle Russland annektieren." (*G.P.*, XVI, 102, 108).

[61] Witte, *La Guerre avec le Japon*, pp. 42, 45. The Germans put the Russians' declarations on a par with the English promises in regard to Egypt (*G.P.*, XVI, 104–105). See also Romanov, *Russkoe Proshloe*, I, 94.

[62] On the negotiations with China see especially Glinskii, *Vest.*, CXXXVI, 600 ff. (Marc, *Quelques Années*, pp. 99 ff.); Asakawa, *The Russo-Japanese Conflict*, pp. 166 ff., 173 ff.; *G.P.*, XVI, 314; Waldersee, *Denkwürdigkeiten*, III, 91, ascribed to the Russians the plan not only of controlling the Peking-Shankaikwan railroad, but of building a line from Peking to Hankow.

[63] For a sharp criticism of American policy see Chéradame, *Le Monde et la guerre*, pp. 151 ff. America was still getting its Far Eastern news largely from London, and was convinced that the Japanese were the champions of the open door (De Guichen, *Revue d'histoire diplomatique*, XXIII [January 1909], 89 ff.; Dennett, *Roosevelt and the Russo-Japanese War*, p. 29). See further M. T. Bau, *The Open Door* (New York, 1923).

sin in return for a similar free hand in northern China.[64] But evidently the English refused. The Russian pretensions were too far-reaching, and, besides, the tide had begun to turn in favor of the English. Witte's policy as expressed in the negotiations with China had ended in a total debacle. The ranks of the powers in opposition had begun to close, and in St. Petersburg the military men were for the moment triumphant.

In a discussion of the origins of the war, the crisis of February 1901 can hardly be overemphasized. The English were evidently determined to proceed to extremes and had hopes of consummating an alliance including Japan, Germany, and perhaps the United States, and directed against Russia.[65] It is not possible entirely to separate the negotiations opened with Germany and those conducted with Japan in the course of 1901. The object of both was to enlist aid against Russia, the difference being that those with Germany failed while those with Japan culminated in the alliance of January 1902. The Germans were unwilling to be made the catspaw of England, and their interests in the Far East they considered secondary. It is conceivable that a defensive agreement might have been concluded if England had been willing to assume the same obligations in respect to Germany's allies as she asked Germany to assume in regard to India and China.[66]

As for the Japanese, their interests were more directly involved. They had not stopped short of menaces in protesting against the proposed Russo-Chinese agreement.[67] But with real statesmanship they considered all the difficulties. War was generally regarded as inevitable, and the Japanese were ready to act in case Russia made a move to establish herself in Korea, provided England and Germany would remain neutral. On the other hand they were determined not to act against Russia in the Manchurian question unless England actually gave assistance and

---

[64] *G.P.*, XVI, 304; Eckardstein, *Lebenserinnerungen*, II, 277–278. The Russians reduced their demands under pressure of the first protest and restricted the sphere of their exclusive interest to Manchuria, but even this the Chinese refused, being supported by the powers (Glinskii, *Vest.*, CXXXVI, 609 ff. [Marc, *Quelques Années*, pp. 105 ff.]).

[65] The Kaiser later maintained that during his visit to England in January 1901 Lansdowne had told him that England would join the Japanese (*G.P.*, XVII, 96). The idea of a quadruple alliance against Russia appears as early as March 1899 (*G.P.*, XIV, 184).

[66] It is unnecessary to go into details here. See especially *G.P.*, XVII, chap. 109; Eckardstein, *Lebenserinnerungen*, II, chap. 15, and the excellent accounts in Brandenburg, chap. 7 and in Eugen Fischer, *Holstein's grosses Nein* (Berlin, 1925).

[67] The Japanese threatened war on China if she accepted the Russian terms, but promised her support if she resisted. See *Amtliche Darstellung*, I, 14; Glinskii, *Vest.*, CXXXVI, 609 (Marc, *Quelques Années*, p. 105).

22

Germany remained neutral. As a matter of fact they never expected actual military aid from England and were willing to abandon Manchuria to the Russians, provided the latter respected the treaty rights of the other powers.[68] The English tried to get the Germans to promise, in case of war, to warn the French to remain neutral, but this the Berlin government refused to do. The negotiations between England and Japan therefore lagged through the summer of 1901.[69]

In the meanwhile the Russians reopened negotiations with the Chinese, looking to the evacuation of Manchuria. Witte and Lamsdorff urged the necessity for such a step, arguing that failure to evacuate would lead to complications with Japan and other powers. Kuropatkin favored the abandonment of southern Manchuria and the annexation of northern Manchuria outright, a procedure which would give Russia a more defensible frontier. Apparently Witte kept the upper hand, and the Chinese were offered rather favorable terms of evacuation. But the offer was accompanied by a new demand of Witte's, and this time the economic proposals were kept separate from the military ones in order to avoid interference by foreign powers. China was to promise not to give concessions to other foreign interests in Manchuria without first offering them to the Russo-Chinese Bank. Though these conditions were much more lenient than those of February, the Chinese still objected, chiefly to the economic clauses. They undoubtedly realized that in this way they could mobilize support abroad, and they apparently kept the Japanese informed, and perhaps also the English. The negotiations dragged on through the autumn and winter.[70]

News of the resumption of pourparlers between China and Russia hastened the discussions between England and Japan. Hayashi made it plain that Japan's interests in Manchuria were only indirect, and the negotiations really turned not upon Manchuria, but upon the question of Japanese support of English interests in India and the extent to which Korea should be abandoned to the Japanese.[71] The difficulties

[68] See especially the important utterances of Hayashi in *G.P.*, XVI, 324, 338; XVII, 136; Eckardstein, *Lebenserinnerungen*, II, 339.

[69] *G.P.*, XVI, 341–342; XVII, 40–42; Eckardstein, *Lebenserinnerungen*, II, 279.

[70] On the Russo-Chinese discussions see above all, Glinskii, *Vest.*, CXXXVI, 640 ff. (Marc, *Quelques Années*, pp. 135 ff.); also Asakawa, *The Russo-Japanese Conflict*, pp. 189 ff., and Gr. Br., F. O., *Blue Book: China*, no. II (1904). On Kuropatkin's views see Witte, *La Guerre avec le Japon*, p. 47.

[71] On the negotiations for the Anglo-Japanese Alliance, see Pooley, *Hayashi Memoirs*, pp. 123 ff., especially p. 130: "In my opinion the interests of Japan in Manchuria are only indirect," and p. 134: "My country considers as its first and

arising on these points strengthened the hands of those Japanese statesmen who, like Count Ito, desired to avoid war if possible. Hayashi's
memoirs certainly do not give an accurate picture of the significance of
Ito's visit to St. Petersburg in November 1901. In the first place it should
be pointed out that Ito was not opposed to an alliance with England,
but simply took the stand that this alliance should have nothing to do
with the Korean question. He was convinced that this problem could
best be settled by a special arrangement concluded between Russia
and Japan, and he believed that the Tsar, Witte, and Lamsdorff favored
a settlement of this question. In Ito's opinion the Korean question
should be gotten out of the way before the negotiations with England
were brought to a close.[72]

In support of his contentions the Japanese statesman could point to
the fact that in February and again in July 1901 Witte had suggested an
agreement on the following basis: the Japanese to recognize Russia's
preponderant interests in Manchuria, Korea to be neutralized, but Japan to have the right to supply administrative and financial advisers and
to control the police.[73] Here at least was a suitable basis for discussions. Ito and his followers could not know that Witte's suggestions
were not entirely bona fide, and that he merely meant to give up Korea until Russia's position was so strong in the Far East that Russia
could threaten Japan more effectively and perhaps seize Korea.[74] The
negotiations seem to have been begun in September 1901, and the Ito
mission was simply the last phase. Ito began by suggesting a return to
the Nissi proposal of 1898: a free hand in Manchuria in return for a
free hand in Korea. But Lamsdorff was unwilling to give up all Russian
claims in Korea. Japan might establish strategical bases in Korea and
in this way obstruct Russian communications between Vladivostok and
Port Arthur. Ito replied that Japan would be willing to give "the most
solemn promise" that the harbors of southern Korea would never be
fortified and that Russian communications would not be interfered

---

last wish the protection of its interests in Korea and the prevention of interference
by any other country in Korea." A good summary in A. L. P. Dennis, *The Anglo-
Japanese Alliance* (Berkeley, California, 1923).

72 *G.P.*, XVI, 338; Pooley, *Hayashi Memoirs*, p. 157.

73 Such was the Russian suggestion of July 1901 (*G.P.*, XVII, 143); the February suggestion evidently provided simply for the neutralization of Korea, and was
rejected by the Japanese (*ibid.*, XVI, 338).

74 See Witte, *Memoirs*, p. 117, where he quotes a letter of November 28, 1901;
then see, in Glinskii, *Vest.*, CXXXVI, 1029 ff. (Marc, *Quelques Années*, pp. 149 ff.);
the same letter with the parts omitted by Witte in his memoirs.

with. The fear of the Japanese, he said, was that the Russians were attempting to seize a base in Korea. If Russia were willing to set the Japanese at rest on this point, "she might in future do as she liked in China without meeting with any opposition from Japan." He drew up the following draft of an agreement: a reciprocal guarantee of the independence of Korea; reciprocal obligation not to employ any part of Korean territory for strategic purposes; or to take military measures upon the coast of Korea which would hamper the freedom of passage in the Gulf of Korea; Russia to recognize Japan's liberty of action in Korea from the political, industrial, and commercial points of view; and Japan's exclusive right to aid Korea with advice and assistance in the execution of engagements which devolve upon every well-organized government, and to send forces to quell risings or other disorders likely to violate the pacific relations between Japan and Korea.[75] Witte urged an agreement, even if it meant complete renunciation of Korea, subject, to be sure, to the mental reservation already mentioned. He furthermore demanded that Japan recognize the rights of Russia in all the territories contiguous to the Russian frontier and that Japan leave Russia full liberty of action in these countries. On this point Ito would not have made any objections, but his conversation with Lamsdorff on December 4 was not wholly satisfactory, and he left abruptly for Berlin. The Russian counterproposals were sent after him. In them Lamsdorff asked that Japan promise in certain cases to send only the necessary troops to Korea and not to allow them to cross a section of northern Korea which was to be neutralized. The Japanese troops were to be withdrawn as soon as their presence was no longer necessary. Japan was not only to recognize Russia's interests in all Chinese territories contiguous to her frontier and to give Russia freedom of action therein, but the right of Japan to "advise" Korea was to be made conditional on a previous understanding with Russia in each case. These terms were a distinct restriction of the earlier proposals, but Ito was evidently still optimistic and promised to send a definite reply when he returned to Tokyo.[76]

As a matter of fact a council before the throne in Tokyo on December 7 decided to drop the negotiations with Russia and to proceed to the conclusion of the alliance with England. It appears from Hayashi's

---

[75] Glinskii, *Vest.*, CXXXVI, 1029 ff. (Marc, *Quelques Années*, p. 149 ff.); Trubetzkoi, *Russland als Grossmacht*, pp. 68–69; Pooley, *Hayashi Memoirs*, pp. 169 ff., 201 ff.

[76] *Amtliche Darstellung*, I, 16.

memoirs that the majority of the Japanese statesmen had not supported Ito from the beginning, and they cannot be defended against the accusation that they willfully rejected an offer which so prominent a statesman as Ito regarded as a basis for a settlement.[77] It is the one point that is questionable in the Japanese policy, but one should not forget that in point of fact they were justified in distrusting Russia.

The Japanese government had intended the Ito mission as a measure to bring pressure upon England. Indeed the English could not afford to let the Japanese go, and they were sufficiently frightened to accept practically all of the Japanese demands, so that the alliance was concluded in January 1902.[78]

The failure of the Ito negotiations and the publication of the Anglo-Japanese Alliance in many respects mark a turning point in the history of the origins of the war. In the first place the Russians were soon to learn how isolated they were. They attempted to persuade the Germans to join in a counter-declaration, but the Germans were not so foolhardy.[79] The Kaiser had for years been encouraging the Russians to persist in a forward policy promising to guard the Russian rear in case of complications. It was in the German interest to divert Russia from Europe to the Far East.[80] It was also to Germany's interest that both Japan and Russia should be weakened, and consequently the Japanese were encouraged to resist the Russian advance and were promised Germany's benevolent neutrality.[81] As for the French, they had looked askance at the dissipation of Russian power in the Far East, but they were powerless to stop it. They joined Russia in a declaration which appeared like an extension of the Franco-Russian Alliance to the Far

[77] Pooley, *Hayashi Memoirs*, pp. 161 ff.

[78] As early as August 1901 Sir Frank Lascelles admitted to the Kaiser that England could no longer hold her own without the aid of Japan (*G.P.*, XVII, 97); see also Pooley, *Hayashi Memoirs*, p. 159, from which it is evident that the Japanese realized England's position and were determined to exploit it.

[79] On the surprise of the Russians, see *G.P.*, XVII, 155; Schwertfeger, *Zur europäischen Politik*, I, 96. On the attempt to draw Germany into a counter-declaration see *G.P.*, XVII, 157 ff.

[80] The policy was initiated by Bismarck and was clearly expressed in the Kuldja incident (Chéradame, *Le Monde et la guerre*, pp. 68 ff.). For the Kaiser's encouragement of the Russians, see Wilhelm II, *The Kaiser's Letters to the Tsar* [the Willy-Nicky correspondence] (London, 1920), especially pp. 10, 11, 13, 27; and *G.P.*, XIX, 4 note. After the war had broken out the Kaiser boasted of his policy to his friends. See Robert Zedlitz-Trützschler, *Zwölf Jahre am deutschen Kaiserhof* (Stuttgart, 1923), p. 71.

[81] The Germans hinted to the Japanese that they would remain neutral as early as December 1897. Definite assurances were given in February 1901 and in June 1901. *G.P.*, XIV, 120; XVI, 337 ff., 343–345; XVII, 139.

East, but Delcassé, anxious not to estrange England, took care to make it perfectly clear that the declaration amounted to no more than mere words.[82]

In view of the general situation the Russians were in no position to insist on the demands made upon China. The negotiations looking to a Russian monopoly of concessions in Manchuria were dropped in February 1902 as a result of a new protest by the powers, and in the agreement of April 8, 1902, the Russians promised to evacuate Manchuria in eighteen months. This would appear as a victory of the moderate party in St. Petersburg, but the agreement was concluded only under pressure of the threatening international complications, and it should be noted that the Russian evacuation was still made conditional on the restoration of order in Manchuria and the abstention of foreign powers from interference.[83]

Had the Russians lived up to the April Convention and carried out the evacuation of Manchuria systematically there would have been no war. Not a single major power concerned would have disputed the Russian influence.[84] In April 1903 when the situation had already been acute, Lord Balfour suggested an imaginary dividing line between the English and the Russian spheres of influence, to run from Alexandretta to the mouth of the Yangtse, and as late as July 1903 the English were willing to recognize Russia's special interests in that part of China contiguous to her frontiers, provided that Russia make similar concessions to England in other parts of China.[85] The American attitude was not much different. "We are not in any attitude of hostility towards Russia in Manchuria. On the contrary, we recognize her exceptional position in northern China," wrote Hay to Roosevelt on May 1, 1902.[86] "We regard Manchuria as lost and as outside the sphere of influence of the other powers, but we demand absolute maintenance of the open door

[82] Cf. *G.P.*, XVII, 179; André Tardieu, *France and the Alliances* (New York, 1908), pp. 18 ff.

[83] This had been the Russian stand from the very beginning.

[84] Much is made of this fact in a letter from Balashev, the Tsar's agent in the Far East, to his master, March 25, 1902. Mikhail Pokrovskii, ed., *Russko-Iaponskaia Voina* (Leningrad, 1925), pp. 133–134.

[85] On the Balfour suggestion see *G.P.*, XVII, 537. Cf. also the remarks of Sir Arthur Hardinge, *ibid.*, p. 538; Landsdowne's stand in Gr. Br., F. O., *Blue Book: China*, no. II (1904), nos. 138, 139; Lord Cranborne further specified in his speech to the Commons on July 23, 1903: "We have recognized Russia's special position in Manchuria since the Railway Agreement of 1899; if Russia is willing to consider our treaty rights and commercial interests, she will not find us intransigent."

[86] Dennett, *Roosevelt and the Russo-Japanese War*, pp. 135–136.

in the regions ruled by Russia," remarked Roosevelt to the German ambassador in the presence of Hay, in November 1902.[87] But it is clear that both the English and the American attitudes were conditional on the preservation of the open door in Manchuria. In the case of Japan the situation was somewhat different. She, of course, also desired the open door, but she also felt menaced by the military occupation of Manchuria by the Russians, because this constituted a threat to her own position in Korea. Realizing that the support of England and the United States could not be reckoned on to oppose the occupation of Manchuria unless the Russians closed the door there, the Japanese government in August 1902 once more suggested to the Russians an amicable agreement. Both sides were to recognize the independence and territorial integrity of both China and Korea, and both were to agree not to use any part of Korea for military purposes. Japan was to have exclusive rights in Korea, and in return was to recognize the Russian lease of Kwantung and the right of Russia to take measures for the protection of her railways and other interests in Manchuria. This proposal, in a way, foreshadowed the Japanese note of August 1903 and was, to be sure, less generous than the previous offers. Still, it was as broad as Russia could expect.[88]

The Russians treated the Japanese suggestions in a dilatory manner. The fact was that they could hardly afford to accept them. Russia had, even at this time, reached an impasse. The seizure of Port Arthur had necessitated measures of protection, and had in a way made the occupation of Manchuria logical. On the other hand the lease of Port Arthur had been accepted by Witte and his group and the economic possibilities arising from it had been exploited to the full. Russia had spent hundreds of millions on Manchuria and as yet had secured no return. The Russians consequently felt as much unable to give up their military position in the Far East to please Japan as to resign their economic policy to please England and the United States.[89] Even at this time war was regarded as inevitable in high Russian circles. The Tsar himself re-

[87] *G.P.*, XVI, 490.

[88] The terms of the Japanese offer in *Amtliche Darstellung*, I, 19; cf. also Glinskii, V*est.*, CXXXVI, 1031 (Marc, *Quelques Années*, p. 154). There was nothing disloyal to England in this policy. See the statement of Spring-Rice on a later occasion, *G.P.*, XIX, 17–18.

[89] It should be remembered that the Russian demands for economic concessions had been dropped in February 1902 only because of foreign protests and because of the conclusion of the Anglo-Japanese pact.

marked to Prince Henry of Prussia in October 1901 that he did not really want Manchuria, but that he did not want anyone else to have it. In the same way he declared: "I do not want Korea myself, but in no case can I permit the Japanese to get a firm footing there. If they try it, that would be a *casus belli* for Russia. A Japanese occupation of Korea would be like creating a new Bosporus question in the Far East. Russia can in no case permit that." [90] Of course, the war which Nicholas regarded as inevitable did not seem to him a very serious matter. Colonel Vannovski, the military attaché at Tokyo since 1900, was sending the most sarcastic reports about the Japanese military machine. It would take perhaps hundreds of years for the Japanese army to acquire the moral foundation necessary to put it on a par with even the weakest European force. Against such an army a strong cavalry regiment equipped with artillery could win a certain and decisive victory if it acted reasonably quickly and energetically. Another observer reported that the Japanese forces were like an "army of sucklings," while a third was convinced that "the Japanese army cannot be compared to any of the major European armies, least of all to ours." [91]

The Russians, then, were not in a very conciliatory mood. The April Convention was a mere makeshift and there was no unity of opinion as to what the next step should be. The general perplexity supplied the "psychological moment" for which Bezobrazov and his friends had been waiting. Their enemy, Witte, had failed to secure the necessary guarantees and they now had some basis for a concerted attack upon him. Hardly had the agreement with China been signed than they began to bombard Nicholas with memoranda characterizing the convention as a confession of weakness, as an abandonment of Russian interests and as a menace to Russia's position not only at Port Arthur, but in the whole Far East.[92] The new minister of the interior, von Plehve, evidently had his eye upon Witte's position and expounded the theory of the "little victorious war" as a corrective for domestic unrest. He therefore identified himself with the Bezobrazov group, and his support was probably

---

[90] *G.P.*, XVIII, 35. In the summer of 1901, the Tsar told the Kaiser that Russia was preparing for the conflict and that it would probably break out in 1904. *G.P.*, XVII, 144–145 marginalia; Wilhelm II, *Vergleichende Geschichtstabellen* (Leipzig, 1921).

[91] *Amtliche Darstellung*, I, 163 ff.

[92] Romanov, *Russkoe Proshloe*, I, 192 ff.; *Amtliche Darstellung*, I, 20 ff. In a remarkable letter to the Tsar, March 25, 1902, Balashev urges the annexation of Manchuria and opens up further vistas. See Pokrovskii, ed., *Russko-Iaponskaia Voina*, pp. 133 ff.

decisive.[93] Rumors of a Sino-Japanese *rapprochement* played further into the hands of this group, which urged the necessity of vigorous and immediate action to save the Russian position.[94] When Witte returned from a visit to the Far East in the late autumn of 1902 and submitted a long and able memorandum exposing the unpardonable high-handedness of the Russian authorities in Manchuria and urging not only the observance of the April Convention but an agreement with Japan on Korea, he was entirely ignored.[95]

The Russian evacuation of the southwestern part of Mukden province and the return of the Shanhaikwan-Sinmintin line in October 1902 precipitated matters in St. Petersburg. At a ministerial conference, it was openly stated that the eventual annexation of Manchuria was inevitable.[96] A general demand for guarantees from China and for promises not to open the evacuated territory to foreigners made itself heard, and it was argued that the very elasticity of the April Convention supplied adequate excuses for repudiating it. Witte took the stand that the safest policy would be to observe existing arrangements and to rely upon the friendship of China to secure Russia's interests in an unobtrusive way.[97] The military men insisted upon demands to protect the railway and Russia's strategic position, so that a compromise between the conflicting viewpoints seemed impossible.

The opportunity had come for Bezobrazov to step forward. He, at least, had an all-embracing plan. The trouble with Russian policy, as he saw it, was that it lacked unity of purpose and of direction. The minister of war is so engrossed in European problems that he is unwilling to devote sufficient attention to the Far East. Russia should strive to effect an understanding with Germany and thus bring together the Dual and Triple Alliances. The continental powers would then be able to reduce expenditures for land armaments. Germany could throw greater weight on naval construction while Russia could strengthen her

[93] Romanov, *Russkoe Proshloe*, I, 192 ff.; Witte, *Memoirs*, p. 124; A. N. Kuropatkin, "Prolog Manshurskoi Tragedii," printed in Pokrovskii, ed., *Russko-Iaponskaia Voina*, p. 41. (Cited hereafter as Kuropatkin, "Prolog.")

[94] *G.P.*, XVIII, 64; XIX, 8.

[95] Glinskii, *Vest.*, CXXXVI, 1031 ff. (Marc, *Quelques Années*, pp. 154 ff.); Romanov, *Russkoe Proshloe*, pp. 102 ff. Witte had been formally invited to visit Japan, but was not given permission to do so.

[96] Witte, *La Guerre avec le Japon*, pp. 53–54; Glinskii, *Vest.*, CXXXVII, 608 ff. (Marc, *Quelques Années*, pp. 178 ff.).

[97] The Witte propaganda has entirely obscured the fact that the minister of finance was the "Father of Russian Imperialism" and that he agitated in behalf of military evacuation, not of economic capitulation.

forces in the Far East. Together they could work in the Orient against England and prevent her from utilizing Japan as a tool to bring pressure on Russia. Japan supported only by England will be helpless and can be put off with some minor concessions, possibly the southern part of Korea, which she already possesses in an economic way. Meanwhile Russia must show energy and determination. Far from evacuating Manchuria the Russians should make it clear that this question concerns no one but Russia and China and that it cannot be made the subject of an international debate. Russia must greatly strengthen her forces in the Far East in order to silence the opposition. She must build up a screen on the Yalu in order to protect her Manchurian flank from a possible Japanese attack and in order to threaten the Japanese if they make trouble. Furthermore, Russia must give up the timid policy of Witte, which has led only to difficulties. She must create real economic interests in the Far East. On the Yalu this might be done through the East Asiatic Industrial Corporation based upon the Brinner concession. Other concessions might be obtained in Korea, and an attempt should be made to associate American capital, in order to deprive the Japanese of American support and draw American sympathy and interest to the Russian side. As for Manchuria an attempt should be made to gain control of the major economic undertakings. In order to satisfy the Americans and other malcontents the doors might be thrown open to foreigners, but the effect of this could be wiped out by an alliance between the Russians and the Manchurian brigands, the Hung-hu-tzu, who would make the ground so hot for both Chinese and foreigners that the Russians would soon find themselves in complete and undisputed control.[98]

Bezobrazov's plans appealed to the imagination of the Tsar, and when the former volunteered to go to the Far East to reorganize and consolidate the activities of the Russians, he went not only with the blessing of Nicholas, but with 2,000,000 roubles appropriated by the ministry of finance "for purposes known to His Imperial Majesty." [99]

[98] The idea of Bezobrazov and the "Koreans," as they came to be known, may be studied in his memoranda to the Tsar. See Glinskii, *Vest.*, CXXXVII, 598 ff., 619 ff.; *Amtliche Darstellung*, p. 24; Romanov, *Russkoe Proshloe*, I, 87 ff.; and above all the invaluable correspondence between Bezobrazov and the Tsar published in Pokrovskii, ed., *Russo-Iaponskaia Voina*, especially pp. 151 ff., where the larger aspects of the scheme are worked out in detail. From this time on Bezobrazov's chief collaborator was his cousin, Rear Admiral Abaza.

[99] Another 200,000 roubles was appropriated for the use of Bezobrazov's chancellery. Full details in Romanov, *Russkoe Proshloe*, I, 102–103, 107; cf. also A. N. Kuropatkin, "'Dnevik," *Krasnyi Arkhiv*, II (1922) 81, (hereafter Kuropatkin,

He was apparently also released from the obligation to "keep silent about his main support," and at any rate made no secret of the fact that he took his orders only from headquarters. He carried letters recommending him to Admiral Alexiev, who was in command at Port Arthur.[100]

With feverish haste Bezobrazov began to establish "real Russian interests." Offices of the East Asiatic Industrial Corporation were opened at Port Arthur and at Seoul. His agents had already secured from the governor of Mukden a short term permit to cut lumber on the Manchurian side of the Yalu, but this was regarded as inadequate, and Bezobrazov started negotiations to secure a twenty-five year monopoly on this business. Meanwhile lumbering activities were begun in dead earnest on the Korean side, and a small force of reserve officers was sent to act as a skeleton for a larger number of Hung-hu-tzu in the service of the Russians.[101] Similar activity was developed in Seoul. Waeber, the former Russian agent, was sent back to his post, and Baron Ginsburg, an agent of the Bezobrazov group (Jews were not scorned for business purposes), approached the Korean government for a concession for a railroad from Seoul to Wiju on the Yalu.[102] When Bezobrazov returned to St. Petersburg things were well under way.

In view of the fact that the star of the "Koreans" was in the zenith, the half-hearted attempts made by his opponents have little more than academic interest. Witte was practically beaten when he was forced to appropriate money for the development of Bezobrazov's schemes, but Kuropatkin, who was himself a favorite of the Tsar, put up a struggle. Together with Lamsdorff, Witte and Kuropatkin formed the "ministerial triple alliance," as Bezobrazov termed it, and for nine months the bat-

---

"Diaries") and Vladimir Burtsev, *Tsar i Vnieshniaia Politika* (Berlin, 1910), p. 15.

[100] On Besobrazov's trip see Romanov, *Russkoe Proshloe*, I, 102; and particularly Glinskii, V*est.*, CXXXVII, 250 ff., 598 ff., based in large part on the revelations of "Nemo" in the newspaper *Vladivostok* in 1905. This material is omitted in Marc. See also Kuropatkin, "Diaries," pp. 11–12; *Amtliche Darstellung*, I, 22.

[101] Glinskii, V*est.*, CXXXVI, 258; Kuropatkin, "Prolog," p. 7; *idem*, "Diaries," p. 12.

[102] For the activity of the Russians in Korea, see among others Maître, *Bulletin de l'école française d'extrême orient* (January to June 1904), p. 503; Gustav Krahmer, *Die Beziehungen Russlands zu Japan, mit besonderer Berücksichtigung Koreas* (Leipzig, 1904), p. 212; L. Putnam Weale [pseud. of Benton Lenox Simpson], *The Reshaping of the Far East* (New York, 1905), II, 47 ff.; Kuropatkin, "Prolog," p. 41 says that Bezobrazov's idea was to control the projected railways of northern Korea as far south as Gensan.

tle royal was waged for the control of Russia's policy.[103] Bezobrazov, who had long before recognized the danger from the bureaucrats, continued to urge the establishment of a separate administration for Far Eastern affairs, and was finally victorious over "the enemy." His opponents tried to crush him by sheer weight of numbers, and no less than three conferences were held at St. Petersburg and one at Port Arthur between January and July 1903 to discuss the merits of the case and to outline the course of procedure. They one and all of them recognized the dangers of possible complications arising from Russian activity in Korea, urged the withdrawal of the troops on the Yalu and the reduction of the project to a strictly commercial and, if possible, to a private basis, and advised a resumption of negotiations with Japan for the settlement of the Korean problem.[104] But on the Manchurian question the views were widely divergent. Kuropatkin and the military men demanded guarantees prior to evacuation and urged the retention of control over northern Manchuria. In this they were supported by the "Koreans," who, however, demanded further economic reservations and objected to evacuation under any conditions. The result of the conferences, therefore, was that they drew up various lists of demands to be submitted to China and lengthy reports to the Tsar.[105]

Nicholas no longer had any taste for longwinded conference reports. His mind was filled with visions of the acquisition of half of Asia, and he found the flowery and exuberant epistles of Bezobrazov more palatable.[106] It was apparently due entirely to Bezobrazov's influence that the evacuation period of March 1903 was allowed to pass without any-

[103] Cf. Alexander Ular, *Russia from Within* (New York, 1905), and particularly the Bezobrazov correspondence in Pokrovskii, *Russko-Iaponskaia Voina;* cf. also Romanov, *Russkoe Proshloe,* I, 87–108, *passim.*

[104] On these conferences see the detailed discussions in Glinskii, *Vest.,* CXXXVII, 241 ff., 609 ff., 618 ff., 962 ff. (Marc, *Quelques Années,* pp. 167 ff., 180 ff., 186 ff.); Witte, *La Guerre avec le Japon,* pp. 54–55, 63 ff., 70 ff.; Kuropatkin, *The Russian Army,* I, 163, 173 ff., 180 ff.; *idem,* "Prolog," pp. 6, 9, 16, 22, 28–32; *idem,* "Diaries," p. 21; *Amtliche Darstellung,* I, 23–24; the Bezobrazov correspondence in Pokrovskii, *Russko-Iaponskaia Voina,* which is very illuminating.

[105] Bezobrazov at Port Arthur in July demanded not only more troops and Hung-hu-Tzu for the Yalu, but advocated the concentration of 75,000 men in southern Manchuria, to "throw the Japanese into the sea." Kuropatkin, *The Russian Army,* I, 132, 173; Glinskii, *Vest.,* CXXXVIII, 563 ff.

[106] See Romanov, *Russkoe Proshloe,* I, 98 ff. for an excellent characterization of Bezobrazov's mode of attack. On the Tsar's dreams, see Kuropatkin, "Diaries," p. 31, according to which the Tsar hoped "to take for Russia Manchuria; to proceed to annex Korea; to take under his rule Tibet and Persia, and to seize not only the Bosporus but also the Dardanelles." (February 1903).

thing being done.[107] To the reports submitted by the ministers condemning the plans of the favorite, Nicholas replied by appointing him secretary of state without portfolio. By eloquence and by somewhat questionable methods of procedure Bezobrazov won the Tsar over completely. Nicholas was not perturbed by the prospect of war, and was convinced that a crisis could be avoided if a policy of firmness were adopted and consistently carried out.[108]

Meanwhile the policy of the "new course" had once more raised the question of Manchuria to an international status. The demands presented to China involved the exclusion of foreigners from Manchuria, and the secure locking of the door.[109] At the same time the Russians had broken their promise, given to the powers, to evacuate Niuchwang, the only treaty port in Manchuria. Their failure to carry out the evacuation of the southern provinces as provided for in the April Convention was taken as further evidence of the Russian plans. The result was the formation of what amounted to a triple alliance of England, the United States, and Japan. They not only induced the Chinese to reject the Russian demands but began to bombard the Russians themselves with inquiries and admonitions.

The Russians now found themselves in a position analogous to that into which they had placed the Japanese in 1895. They were as though caught in a trap; no matter what course they decided on they were bound to lose; they simply had to make concessions. In the last six months before the outbreak of hostilities they came down from their demands one by one. They declared themselves unopposed to the opening of new treaty ports in Manchuria; they accepted the opening of four ports in the Chinese commercial treaties signed with the United States and Japan in October 1903; they notified the powers that they were ready to recognize treaty rights acquired by other nations as they applied to Manchuria. Similarly they were compelled to reduce the demands made on China, until in the end there was very little left.[110]

107 Kuropatkin, *The Russian Army*, II, 309; *idem*, "Prolog," p. 7; Burtsev, *Tsar i Vnieshniaia Politika*, p. 12.

108 Kuropatkin, "Prolog," p. 9. The Tsar was still indulging in contemptuous remarks about the Japanese and their Mikado. See Kuropatkin, "Diaries," p. 41.

109 On the Russo-Chinese negotiations, see Glinskii, *Vest.*, CXXXVII, 618 ff.; *Amtliche Darstellung*, I, 23 ff.; Asakawa, *The Russo-Japanese Conflict*, pp. 241 ff.; and the excellent account by Francis Rey, *Revue générale de droit international public*, XII (1905), 215–319, based on British and American documents.

110 Glinskii, *Vest.*, CXXXVIII, 938 ff. For the demands of the powers and the Russian replies, the reader is referred to the numerous general treatises on the Far Eastern question.

But while these concessions might conceivably have satisfied the English and the Americans, they could not content the Japanese, who were interested not only in the economic aspect of the Manchurian question, but also in the strategic considerations, to say nothing of Korea. Very likely the Japanese would have hesitated about going to war on account of Manchuria alone.[111] But the developments in Korea were such that in the view of the Japanese they alone justified vigorous action. On the Yalu a veritable warfare was going on between the Russians and the Japanese timbermen, and the struggle found its counterpart in Seoul, where the Russians were demanding permission to build a railroad from Wiju to the capital and were exerting themselves to the utmost to secure a lease of Yongampo at the mouth of the Yalu. Only the vigorous protests of the Japanese representative, who practically submitted an ultimatum to the Korean government, frustrated the Russian plans. The situation had become extremely critical even before negotiations were opened between the two countries.[112]

In view of the growing tension the Tsar decided in June 1903 to open negotiations with the Japanese. Apparently this was due to the alarming reports sent by Rosen and by Kuropatkin from Japan.[113] In any case Abaza, representing the "Koreans," approved of this new move, in the absence of Bezobrazov. What it amounted to was this: the Russians were to abandon Korea unconditionally to the Japanese, with the exception of the northern quarter, included in the Yalu-Tumen basins where the timber company was attempting to establish itself.[114] Abaza

[111] This was the conclusion to which Kuropatkin came after his visit to Japan. See Kuropatkin, *The Russian Army*, I, 175, 187; see also Chéradame, *Le Monde et la guerre*, pp. 126 ff.

[112] For the Russian activities on the Yalu, see especially Glinskii, *Vest.*, CXXXVII, 265 ff., 960 ff.; CXXXVIII, 227 ff. So critical had the situation become by September 1903 that Balashev, who was in charge, advocated the transfer of the company headquarters to Masampo, from which the Japanese coast could be more easily bombarded! See further, Weale, *The Reshaping of the Far East*, II, 47 ff.; Asakawa, *The Russo-Japanese Conflict*, pp. 282 ff.; Maître, *Bulletin de l'école française d'extrême orient* (January to June 1904), p. 503.

[113] Kuropatkin, "Prolog," p. 29; *idem, The Russian Army*, I, 176; *Amtliche Darstellung*, I, 168.

[114] *Russian Orange Book*, no. 1. Abaza to Bezobrazov, June 11/24, 1903. This collection of documents (thirty-seven in all) was published in June 1905 under the title: *Dokumenti po Peregovoram s Iaponiei, 1903–1904. Khraniashchiesia v Kantseliarii Osobago Komiteta Dalniavo Vostoka*. It was published by the Committee on the Far East as an apology for its actions, but was almost immediately called in because of Lamsdorff's protests. The Russian government officially repudiated it, but though it was only circulated in the highest circles, a good deal of it leaked out. Parts of it were printed in *The Times* (London) of June 3, 12, 15, and 16,

drew up and submitted to the Tsar a memorandum entitled *Bases of our Future Relations with Japan* (June 27), which has practically the form of an official note. The striking passage reads as follows: "Provided that Japan shows a sincere desire to maintain good relations with us, Russia will be prepared to recognize unconditionally the establishment of Japan in Korea. The boundaries of Japanese Korea might be defined as the watershed of the Tumen-Ula basin to the north and the watershed of the Yalu basin to the west. The northern and western slopes of these watersheds enter into the confines of the Russian concessions, where the Russians have already begun to manifest their activity, and consequently these regions must remain in Russian hands. Under so broad a recognition of Japan's ambitions on the part of Russia there should be established perfect concord between the two nations, and fortifications of the Korean shores by the Japanese should serve against the common foes of Russia and Japan. They should, therefore, be constructed only by mutual agreement." Abaza urged that the Russians should openly seize Manchuria before making the offer to Japan, while Lamsdorff advised giving up Korea before the Japanese demanded it.[115] The whole matter is an extremely obscure one, and it would seem that the Russian action was delayed chiefly because of disagreement as to what should be done with Manchuria. As it was, the Russians made no advances to the Japanese before the latter opened negotiations.

The first Japanese note was presented on August 12, 1903, and coincided exactly with the final victory of the "Koreans" at St. Petersburg. It was at this time that the Viceroyalty of the Far East was created, followed soon after by the Committee for the Far East, sitting in the capital. Therewith Bezobrazov and his friends at last freed themselves from the domination of the ministers and found themselves in a position to

---

1905, and others in the Russian liberal organ, *Osvobodenie* (Stuttgart) on August 10, 1905 (reprinted in Kuropatkin, *The Russian Army*, II, app. I). With some important omissions the collection was reprinted by Burtsev (*Tsar i Vnieshniaia Politika*) who also prints Lamsdorff's objections. Some of the documents are utilized in *Amtliche Darstellung*, and others are quoted in full in Kuropatkin, "Prolog." On the entire subject of these important documents, see Simanski's essay on the Kuropatkin Diaries in *Na Chuzhoi Storonie*, XI (Prague, 1925).

[115] The Abaza Memorandum is printed in *Russko-Iaponskaia Voina*, pp. 145–146 and is dated June 14/27. The documents on pages 144 and 148 also bear on this subject. Bezobrazov was probably not enthusiastic for this policy, judging from his letter of August 7 (*ibid.*, p. 154).

put their theories into practice. Witte's resignation in September was merely the logical conclusion of this chapter.[116]

It seems hardly necessary to discuss in detail the negotiations between Russia and Japan, which have been examined so many times by other writers.[117] The Japanese felt seriously menaced by the Russian activities in Korea. They could not wait for matters to develop further, for within a short time the Russians would equal them in a military way, and it would be possible for reinforcements to be sent over the new railways.[118] Besides, the international situation was more favorable than could have been hoped for, because the Manchurian question could be utilized as a bond of common interest to enlist the support and sympathy of England and America. There was always danger that the Russians might satisfy the powers on this point and leave the Japanese in the lurch. It is worth remembering that the English and the Americans were kept fully posted by the Japanese, and that there was the fullest cooperation between the three powers.[119]

The chief feature of the Japanese proposals was the insertion of the Manchurian question. The Japanese demanded freedom of action for themselves in Korea and at the same time attempted to subject the Russian policy in Manchuria to restrictions similar to those under which Japan had labored in respect to Korea. Furthermore, the Japanese demanded freedom of trade and industry in Manchuria and the recognition of the independence and territorial integrity of China. In this way the Japanese made themselves the champions of the open door and at the same time created a basis for bargaining. They could give up claims in Manchuria in order to secure all that they desired in Korea.

[116] It appears from Kuropatkin's "Diaries," p. 47, that the Tsar had considered the Viceroyalty for the previous eighteen months. The inside story of the agitation in this direction appears from the Bezobrazov correspondence (Pokrovskii, *Russko-Iaponskaia Voina*). See further Glinskii, *Vest.*, CXXXVIII, 941 ff.; *Amtliche Darstellung*, p. 24. Lamsdorff and Kuropatkin both offered to resign soon after, but their request was not granted.

[117] The Japanese documents were published under the title "Correspondence regarding the Negotiations between Japan and Russia, 1903–1904" (Japan, F. O. [Washington? 1904?]). A full discussion from the Japanese standpoint may be found in Asakawa, *The Russo-Japanese Conflict*, while the Russian viewpoint is set forth in *Amtliche Darstellung*, pp. 25 ff.

[118] In July 1903 the Russians had sent two brigades over the railway to try it out. It is said that in August 1903 the Japanese learned through the treason of a Russian agent that 300,000 troops were to be sent to the Far East as soon as possible. In any case the Japanese were well served by their intelligence officers.

[119] See especially *Foreign Relations of the United States for 1903* (Washington, 1904), pp. 615–621.

On the Russian side the view taken was that Manchuria was a question concerning only Russia and China, a sort of *noli me tangere*.[120] In order to force the admission of this view the Russians insisted on attaching conditions to the Japanese claims respecting Korea. In the first place they never meant to give up northern Korea, and besides they demanded guarantees against the use of Korea for strategic purposes. It may be safely said, I think, that the Russian determination not to yield northern Korea made an agreement impossible from the start.[121]

[120] *G.P.*, XIX, 20. As late as January 1904 the Tsar spoke of the Japanese demand that Russia recognize the territorial rights of China in Manchuria as "insolent." See Kuropatkin, "Diaries," p. 101.

[121] Kencho Suyematsu, *The Risen Sun* (London, 1905), p. 30, terms the Russian demand for a neutral zone in northern Korea "outrageous" and says it "evoked in Japan a perfect storm of indignation and protest." On the other hand, one can readily see that the Japanese counter-proposal to extend the neutral zone on both sides of the Yalu could not satisfy the Russian desires. See *Amtliche Darstellung*, II, 34–35.

In the *Russian Orange Book*, there is a document dated August 16/29, 1903, which was not reprinted by Burtsev. So far as I know it has been published in only two places, in Glinskii, *Vest.*, CXXXVIII, 938, and in the Bezobrazov correspondence (Pokrovskii, *Russko-Iaponskaia Voina*, pp. 159–160). According to Simanski it contains the terms suggested by Bezobrazov as a reply to the first Japanese note, and according to Kuropatkin ("Prolog," p. 47), it was approved by the Tsar. Simanski maintains that it was dropped because of Lamsdorff's opposition. I confess I cannot understand or explain this document, which, to say the least, is not in consonance with the views expressed by Bezobrazov on other occasions. Here is the text with the preamble:

"As Japan is bound by an agreement with England, Russia is compelled to adhere strictly to existing treaties and conventions. A definite, amicable agreement with Japan, highly desirable from the Russian point of view, is possible only if Japan will restore her own freedom of action, for in this case only would it be possible to base an agreement upon the actual needs of the two powers. Supposing Japan accepted these conditions, Russia suggests the following points for an agreement: (1) Mutual undertaking to respect the independence and territorial integrity of the Chinese and Korean Empires; (2) Mutual recognition of existing analogous interests—of Japan in Korea and of Russia in Manchuria; (3) Mutual guarantees on the part of Russia and Japan not to obstruct the development of such commercial and industrial enterprises as do not conflict with point 1 of the present agreement; (4) The recognition, on the part of Russia, of Japan's right to give instructions and advice in the inauguration of reforms and the establishment of a good administration in Korea; (5) The present agreement is a confirmation of all preceding agreements concluded between Russia and Japan."

The only possible interpretation of this extraordinary document that I can see is that it was meant as a bait to wean Japan from the alliance with England, which was a bugbear to Bezobrazov. Had it been submitted to Japan and accepted, there is no doubt that Bezobrazov later would have demanded the repudiation of the obligations assumed by Russia. Only just before, in a letter of August 2, he remarked: "As for treaties and conventions, they must no longer be allowed to prevent us from realizing our historic problem in the Far East." See Glinskii, *Vest.*, CXXXVII, 259 (Marc, *Quelques Années*, p. 178).

The actual negotiations were far more complex than one would be led to believe from a perusal of the *Japanese White Book*. At Peking the Russians were attempting to force an agreement on China in order thus to rule out the Manchurian question. At Seoul they were pressing for concessions which were evidently to be used for bargaining purposes. The Japanese, on the other hand, seconded by the Americans, not only stiffened the resistance of the Chinese but also succeeded in opening new treaty ports in Manchuria and in northern Korea (Wiju).

Meanwhile the Russians were dragging out the negotiations. They did not believe that Japan really meant war and were convinced that the Japanese were merely playing a game of bluff.[122] Besides, they were certain of the superiority of their fleet and felt equally certain of eventual victory on land. Admiral Withoft, chief of Alexiev's naval staff, declared in October 1903: "I, personally, cannot admit the possibility of the annihilation of the Russian fleet by the Japanese." [123] General Kuropatkin himself assured the Tsar in August that Russia had less cause for uneasiness than she had two years before. He was certain that a war would end with a Russian invasion of Japan, and just after hostilities began he drew a vivid picture of the Russian advance, following an initial defensive. The Russians would drive the Japanese from Manchuria and then from Korea. The further steps in this triumphant feat of arms would be: "landing in Japan, annihilation of the Japanese territorial army, suppression of the national rising, capture of the Mikado." [124] In the same way *Novoie Vremia* declared in July: "A war by Japan against us would be like committing suicide. It would be the shipwreck of all her hopes. The armies of Napoleon were of no avail against the power of the Russian giant, and after that experience no enemies hold any terror for Russia." Alexiev, in whose hands the negotiations lay, never tired in his attacks on the insolence and presumption of the Japanese and continued to urge a policy of firmness. Any other procedure would inevitably lead to "an inglorious Sebastopol." [125]

Nothing could have been more mistaken than the Tsar's idea that the

[122] Kuropatkin, *The Russian Army*, I, 194; *idem*, "Prolog," p. 5; *Amtliche Darstellung*, I, 59; the letter of Spring-Rice in Dennett, *Roosevelt and the Russo-Japanese War*, p. 151; Chéradame, *Le Monde et la guerre*, p. 125.

[123] *Amtliche Darstellung*, I, 90, 102–103; Kuropatkin, "Prolog," p. 10.

[124] *Amtliche Darstellung*, I, 102–103, 120; Witte, *La Guerre avec le Japon*, pp. 32–33; *G.P.*, XIX, 53.

[125] Alexiev's criticisms of the Japanese notes were in the *Russian Orange Book* and are reprinted by Burtsev and in *Amtliche Darstellung*.

preservation of peace depended solely upon his own will.[126] The Japanese could not afford to wait until the Russians had increased their forces. They were just as certain of victory as the Russians were. The population was unanimous for war and the statesmen simply had to reach a decision or else forever give up their pretensions.[127] It seems probable that by December they had practically decided that war was the only way out.[128] All the later negotiations were hardly more than camouflage, and very likely it was hoped that they would fail.[129] The English were kept fully posted and, by the demonstration in the Persian Gulf and the expedition to Tibet in November, had already begun to bring pressure to bear on Russia. It is almost certain that they secured an assurance from France that she would remain neutral, and after that the English did nothing to prevent the conflict. If anything, they encouraged it.[130] The Americans, as aforesaid, continued to stand shoulder to shoulder with the Japanese, and the Russian concessions in Manchuria came too late to assuage American indignation. In January they promised Japan neutrality, and Roosevelt even went so far as to warn Germany and France that the United States would intervene on behalf of the Japanese if either of the two European powers took the side of Russia.[131]

[126] "Ein grober, unfassbarer Irrtum," the Kaiser termed it (*G.P.*, XIX, 53). Nothing shows the Tsar's attitude more clearly than his remarks to Kurino at the New Year's reception in January, when he reminded the Japanese representative that Russia covered a large part of the world's surface and that there was an end to her patience.

[127] On public opinion in Japan see, among others, Maître, *Bulletin de l'ecole française d'extrême orient*, IV (January to June 1904), 505 ff., 516 ff.; Chéradame, *Le Monde et la guerre*, pp. 148–149. The financial condition of the country evidently also made early action necessary.

[128] On December 24 Hayashi was expecting war to break out in six weeks (Eckardstein, *Lebenserinnerungen*, III, 58–60). Cf. also Nagao Ariga, *La Guerre russo-japonaise* (Paris, 1908), pp. 27–28; Maître, *Bulletin de l'école française d'extrême orient*, IV (January to June 1904), 518.

[129] Apparently the Japanese were merely anxious not to appear as the aggressors and were waiting for two cruisers bought in Genoa to pass Suez (Eckardstein, *Lebenserinnerungen*, III, 187–189).

[130] The Japanese memorandum handed to the English on December 21 practically announced the coming war (*G.P.*, XIX, 39–40). For further evidence of England's knowledge and of the certainty of French neutrality, see *G.P.*, XIX, 20–21; Eckardstein, *Lebenserinnerungen*, III, 58–60; H. W. Steed, *Through Thirty Years* (New York, 1924), I, 211.

[131] Dennett, *Roosevelt and the Russo-Japanese War*, p. 2; Eckardstein, *Lebenserinnerungen*, III, 189. For Roosevelt's opinion of the Russians, see Dennett, p. 5; and *Selections from the Correspondence of Theodore Roosevelt and H. C. Lodge* (New York, 1925), II, 133–134. As a matter of fact, France meant to remain neutral even if England entered the war, provided only that Russia were not attacked in Europe (*G.P.*, XIX, 26).

By January the Russians had awaked to the dangers of the situation. They yielded almost every point of an economic nature respecting Manchuria, and only the strictly Russian-Japanese question of Korea remained.[132] While Kurino was urging an early reply to the fourth Japanese note and hinting rather broadly at the dangers involved in further delay, a conference at Tsarskoi Selo on January 28, 1904, attempted to decide what concessions should be made in regard to Korea. Lamsdorff advocated the abandonment of the demand for a neutral zone and urged that Russia should content herself with assurances that Korea would not be used for strategic purposes. Abaza, on the other hand, urged the opposite point of view. Even to the very end he objected to the abandonment of the Yalu scheme. What was more he expounded this view to Kurino on the morning of January 30. Kurino assumed that the word of Abaza was worth more than that of the foreign minister, and it was apparently on the basis of his report that the Japanese statesmen decided on the rupture of relations and the initiation of hostilities (evening of February 4). Meanwhile, Lamsdorff was putting off the official Russian reply. It was not until the evening of February 4 that he informed Kurino that the Russian note had been sent to Alexiev. Kurino's telegram announcing this fact did not reach Tokyo until after instructions to break off relations had been sent to him.[133]

The Japanese government never received the last Russian note, which the Russian government later claimed was very conciliatory. As a matter of fact the text of the Russian reply shows that the Russians still refused to recognize the territorial integrity of China. The demand for a neutral zone had been dropped, though the demand for guarantees regarding the use of Korea for strategic purposes was retained. But not only had Abaza indicated to Kurino that the Russians meant to reserve northern Korea; Lamsdorff did the same in speaking to Kurino on the evening of the fourth. There is no getting around the fact that he gave the Japanese minister a thoroughly mistaken idea of the Russian reply. The reason is obvious. Lamsdorff knew that at bottom the Russians were making mental reservations, and we know it from the Tsar's correspondence with Alexiev. On January 26, Alexiev had been in-

---

[132] The official Russian account of the outbreak of the war and the Japanese rejoinder are reprinted in Chéradame, *Le Monde et la guerre*, pp. 113 ff. See also Ariga, *La Guerre russo-japonaise*, chap. 1.

[133] Abaza's talk with Kurino he reported to the Tsar on January 31 (*Russian Orange Book*, no. 31). On this all-important episode see Burtsev, *Tsar i Vnieshniaia Politika*, pp. 18 ff., based on the Lamsdorff memorandum.

structed to resist a Japanese landing in Korea north of the latitude of Chemulpo, and as late as February 8 the Tsar wired him to oppose a Japanese landing north of Gensan on the East and latitude 38 on the West.[134] However we may look at it, the oft-repeated statement that the last Russian reply was a complete surrender is a pure myth.[135]

It has been claimed that the Japanese purposely delayed the Russian reply so that it did not reach Rosen until February 7, that is, after diplomatic relations had already been broken off. In regard to this point, it will suffice to say that there is no convincing evidence. Kurino was not told by Lamsdorff whether the Russian note was sent to Alexiev on February 3 or 4, though Lamsdorff did indicate that the viceroy might make some changes and thereby delay it further. Neither did he say that it was being sent to Rosen at the same time. The assertion that the note was sent to Alexiev on the third, and to Rosen on the fourth, and by Alexiev to Rosen on the fifth appears only in later Russian statements. It should also be pointed out that in the earliest Russian communiqués on the matter, it was stated that the note reached Rosen on the fifth, not on the seventh, as maintained by the Russians later.[136]

The rupture of relations took the Russians completely by surprise, and it was only then that they appealed to the English for mediation, offering to yield on all the Japanese demands. But the English turned a deaf ear to the appeals both of the Russians and of the French, and before anything more could be done hostilities had broken out.[137]

It has become quite the fashion nowadays to attempt to assess the responsibility for the outbreak of this or that war. This is not properly the work of the historian, but a few words by way of general conclu-

---

[134] The Russian reply is printed in *Amtliche Darstellung*, I, 48, and in Kuropatkin, "Prolog," pp. 51–52. It should be pointed out that the Russians also failed in it to declare Korea outside the sphere of Russian influence. Cf. Lamsdorff's remarks to Kurino in the *Japanese White Book*, no. 50. The instructions to Alexiev are in the *Russian Orange Book*, also reprinted in Kuropatkin, "Prolog," pp. 45–51, with added details. See also *Amtliche Darstellung*, I, 116–118.

[135] There is absolutely nothing to substantiate Simanski's statement that the Russian reply was communicated to Lansdowne who declared that it removed all cause for war, or that Hayashi thereupon telegraphed his Government to hold up the Russian reply.

[136] This whole matter is exhaustively dealt with by Rey, *Revue générale de droit international public*, XIII (1906), 621 ff.; see also *Amtliche Darstellung*, I, 50 ff.

[137] On the surprise of the Russians see *G.P.*, XIX, 44; Kuropatkin, "Diaries," p. 97. The Tsar went to the theater regularly in the last critical days and learned of the attack on Port Arthur as he was returning from the performance. See Nicholas II, *Tagebuch des letzten Tsaren* (Berlin, 1923), p. 186. On the appeal for mediation and the Russian offer of complete surrender see *G.P.*, XIX, 58. The appeal was made on February 7.

sion may not be out of place. Curiously enough, there is no consensus of opinion even now in regard to the responsibility for the Russo-Japanese War. This is, perhaps, due to the fact that the material has hitherto been so inadequate. But with the sources we now have at our disposal, I think it is fairly clear that, in the first place, the war on the whole was as sordid as any from which humanity has suffered. At bottom there was little to choose between the Japanese ambitions and the plans of the Russians. Both were intent upon victimizing helpless peoples and in subjecting populations which disliked and even hated them. About all one can say by way of extenuation is that in this respect the two powers concerned were no better and no worse than most of the other great powers. When all is said and done the aggressions of the strong states against China and the other weak states of the Orient in the last years of the past century and the first years of the present fill one of the blackest pages in the history of modern civilization.

Brushing generalities aside, it can at least be said for Japan that her policy was based upon a real need. The argument for self-preservation is in her favor. However great or small her need for Korea was at the time, it is easy to see that she could not afford to allow the peninsula to fall into the hands of some power which would seal it hermetically against Japanese colonization or trade. With the Russians the case was entirely different. If they are honest with themselves they admit, like Kuropatkin, that Russia had no need of expansion in the Far East. It is only too characteristic that men like Bezobrazov should have thought it necessary to "create" real interests for Russia by main force, for in spite of all the expenditures and all the efforts Russia had no real interests, even in 1904, unless we mean an interest in not losing money foolishly invested. The fact was that the predatory tendency of the Russian autocracy had led to expansion, in many cases senseless expansion, in the Far East as in the Middle East. The more she had the more she wanted, and had Russia had her way she would have gulped down half of China before she had even begun to digest what she already had in Siberia. The acquisition of the Maritime Province made a railway desirable. The needs of the railway demanded a foothold in northern Manchuria, and also an ice-free port. Fortunes were poured into developments which were to make the railway pay, and once the money had been invested it had to be protected. It is hard to assess the blame in a process like this. In the end Witte must be held just as responsible for later events as the military men and the "Koreans" of the Bezobrazov type. It was his policy of peaceful penetration that created the background for the activities of the others, and it was his policy that alarmed the powers as much as the military occupation of Manchuria did. War could be avoided only if Russia changed her tactics, and that was improbable, to say the least.

Japan has often been accused of having prepared for war after 1895 and of having worked incessantly in that direction. This is very true, but it should also be remembered that time and time again the Japanese extended their hand for an amicable arrangement. It is patently unjust to judge their conduct in the prewar years by their conduct later, under entirely different circumstances. The evidence would all go to show that almost till the very end the Japanese would have been content with Korea, and it is not saying too much to assert that the war was at bottom a war for Korea, not for Manchuria. The Russians, however, had created a situation from which they could not extricate themselves without making sacrifices, and there is very little to show that they were ever sincerely thinking of turning back. On the contrary, the Tsar, at least, allowed himself to be drawn on by phantoms more and more. The situation that developed in St. Petersburg after the seizure of Port Arthur is a condemnation of the whole régime in Russia. Almost any policy would have been better than the conflict of policies, the back-biting and intrigue which characterized the last year before the war. No wonder that the Japanese became desperate and that the conflicting views and statements made by the Russians gave them the reputation of being wholly unreliable and totally dishonest. In the end the Japanese lost all confidence in what they said, and came to feel that the word of the Russians was worse than useless.

If this essay shows anything, it shows that on numerous occasions the Japanese offered to settle the differences between the countries in an amicable way. It was by this method that the conflicts between the other great powers in the Far East were straightened out. But the Russians never showed a real willingness to compromise. In part this was due to the fact that in any settlement they were bound to lose, bound to give up some of the ideas which had become a part of them. In part, however, it was due to disagreement among the competent authorities. Here again, it is useless to attempt to assess responsibility. Bezobrazov was no statesman, but in the long run the military policy he advocated was not so far from that of the military circles, and the economic policy he urged may have been different in methods from that of Witte, but was not so different in substance. The trouble with the Russians in 1903 was that the men who knew something of international affairs were ruled out of the discussion of the Far Eastern question, while those who decided the Russian policy in the Far East knew little or nothing of the general political scene. It was in this way that Russia came into conflict not only with Japan, but with the United States and England as well. It follows from this that the Japanese, who had long since lost confidence in the Russians, should take the opportunity to exploit the general conflict regarding Manchuria to secure their own ends in Korea. Not to do so would have been evidence of poor statesmanship. But in closing one can hardly refrain from a condemnation of the attitude of the powers. They were, after all, largely responsible for the actual outbreak of the war. If France actually gave England assurances that she would remain neutral, she was, in a way, betraying her ally, even though technically the alliance may not have extended to the Far East. As for England, she was apparently glad to see Russia whipped, and so solve her own problem at the expense of others. Germany was no better. It would be difficult to find words sufficiently strong to condemn the manner in which she egged on Russia and at the same time encouraged Japan by assurances of neutrality. And finally there was the United States, the policy of which would stand a good deal of elucidation. Mr. Dennett, whose opinion on the matter is as good as any, to say the least, believes that if the United States had taken a still stronger stand the Russians would have backed down in time. As it was, the United States and England together kept the ring while the fight was on. They literally sent Japan into the fire, chiefly in order to remove the Russian menace, but also, no doubt, in the hope that the struggle would weaken the Japanese as well as the enemy. The reader may be left to formulate his own opinion as to the ethics of such a policy.

2

Russia, the Straits Question, and the European Powers, 1904–1908

1929

During the reign of Tsar Alexander III (1881–94) European statesmen and diplomats were generally agreed that the ultimate aim of the Russian autocrat was to secure possession of Constantinople.[1] So firmly rooted was this conviction that one might almost say that the policies of the powers centered about this time-honored problem. Bismarck, certainly, exploited it to the full, and succeeded in maintaining the traditional connection between the Russian and German governments by freely offering his neighbors the 'key to their house'.[2] At the same time, however, he played upon the apprehensions of the other powers, Austria-Hungary, Italy, and England, and encouraged, if he did not actually engineer, the Mediterranean Agreements of 1887 which sealed the opposition of these states to any Russian designs in the Near East.[3] France was effectively isolated, and European peace was the more firmly secured, so Bismarck thought, because it seemed extremely unlikely that France, the ally of England in the Crimean War, would ever acquiesce in the Russian Near Eastern policy.[4]

With the abandonment of the Reinsurance Treaty of 1890 the situation was abruptly changed, for Russia, left alone in the face of several potential enemies, was obliged to find an ally in order to safeguard her-

Note: Reprinted from *English Historical Review*, *XLIV* (January 1929), 59–85.

[1] Johannes Lepsius, Albrecht Mendelssohn-Bartholdy, and Friedrich Thimme, eds., *Die Grosse Politik der europäischen Kabinette, 1871–1914* (Berlin, 1922–26), V, 47, 74, 213; VII, chap. 55 *passim;* see also the writer's articles on the origins of the Franco-Russian Alliance in the *Slavonic Review*, III (March 1925) and IV (June 1925).

[2] For example, his remarks to Shuvalov in 1887: "L'Allemagne n'aurait rien à redire en vous voyant maîtres des détroits, possesseurs de l'entrée du Bosphore et de Constantinople même." *Krasnyi Arkhiv*, I, 96.

[3] Among more recent references see William N. Medlicott, "The Mediterranean Agreements," *Slavonic Review*, V (June 1926).

[4] C. von Hohenlohe-Schillingsfürst, *Denkwürdigkeiten* (Stuttgart, 1907), II, 461; *Krasnyi Arkhiv*, I, 68; *G.P.*, VI, 101, 102, 105, 121, 313, 342.

self in the event of attack. With great reluctance the Tsar finally concluded the alliance with France, and therewith the whole international order was revolutionized.[5] As a matter of fact the agreement was entirely defensive, and France was no more prepared to support the Russian designs in the Near East than Russia was to assist in the reconquest of the lost provinces.[6] But of course there was no way of knowing the provisions of the pact, and during the last years of Alexander's reign the European world was in a state of sustained apprehension, constantly expecting a Russian advance on the Turkish capital or the Bosphorus.[7] Had the French been willing to countenance the Russian aspirations in the Near East it might well have been possible for the Russians to emerge from the Black Sea, and then the English squadrons, caught between the French at Toulon and the Russians in the eastern Mediterranean, would probably have been compelled to evacuate the Mediterranean and abandon Egypt.[8]

The position of the English government was not an enviable one. In the days of Disraeli it had been the champion of the Turk, and had taken the lead in the action directed against Russia after the treaty of San Stefano. But even at that time there had been men of influence in England who questioned the wisdom of opposing Russia for the sake of the Turk. Rumors of a coming understanding been England and Russia recurred with monotonous regularity in the 1880's and 1890's, especially after the occupation of Egypt had weakened the position of England in Constantinople and had exposed the British government to the hostility of France as well as Russia. But suspicion of Russian designs had been deeply rooted in the mind of the average Englishman ever since the Crimean War, and public opinion would almost certainly have rejected the suggestion that concessions should be made to the

[5] See the writer's articles on the origins of the Franco-Russian Alliance in the *Slavonic Review*, III and IV.

[6] Hanotaux was particularly opposed to making concessions to Russia in regard to the Straits: "La question des détroits nous touche de trop près et j'espère toujours que la Russie n'y touchera pas, car cela pourrait devenir trop gros pour nous." *G.P.*, XI, [document] no. 2676; XII, no. 2916.

[7] I am relying here largely upon unpublished reports of the years 1893 and 1894 in the Vienna archives, of which I am making use in a monograph on the origins of the Franco-Russian Alliance; but see also *G.P.*, IX, chap. 55 *passim*.

[8] *G.P.*, VIII, no. 1857; X, no. 2372; Sidney Lee, *King Edward VII* (London, 1925), I, 658; Thomas Brassey, *Papers and Addresses* (London, 1894), II, 331–339; Admiral P. H. Colomb, in Brassey's *Naval Annual, 1894* (New York), chap. 7; S. Wilkinson, *The Command of the Sea* (Westminster, 1894), pp. 77–78; and the typical articles published by W. L. Clowes and others in *The Nineteenth Century* in December 1893 and from September 1894 to May 1895.

eastern colossus. So the English muddled along, contenting themselves unenthusiastically with the accepted policy, maintaining close relations with the Triple Alliance and depending more or less upon Austria's taking the lead in combating any move by Russia in the Near East. It was a thoroughly unsatisfactory arrangement, and it may well be doubted whether even the Mediterranean Agreement would have functioned in a crisis. After the visit of the Russian squadron to Toulon in 1893 an attempt was made to provide more effectively for the contingency of combined French and Russian action in the Mediterranean; but Austria refused to take the lead and England would not go beyond general promises, so that no plan of action could be drawn. The future was left to the fates.[9]

The critical years of the Armenian massacres, which entirely discredited the Turks in the eyes of the English, made it even more difficult to stand by the policy of 1878. Salisbury, indeed, seems to have considered for a moment sending the English fleet through the Dardanelles, but the cabinet voted down the proposal, in view of the hostility of France and the almost certain opposition of the Russians. The English minister was condemned, from the very nature of things, to a policy of vacillation. At times he even talked of relinquishing the spoils to his antagonist.[10] Attempts made by the Austrians to have the Mediterranean Agreement revised in the direction of greater clarity and more specific obligation were rejected. The statesmen in Vienna were in despair and the Germans, themselves not directly interested, resented such velleities, which involved the desertion, by the English, of Germany's allies.[11]

That the apprehensions of the powers were not entirely unfounded is shown by the characteristic scheme for a Russian *coup de main* against the Bosphorus advanced by Nelidov, the ambassador at Constantinople, towards the end of 1896. It is unnecessary to enter into details, for nothing came of the project, partly because the Russians were not

[9] See the unpublished material mentioned above, note 7. Cf. also *G.P.*, IX, chap. 55; and X, chap. 62.

[10] On Salisbury's readiness to act see M. Lozé, *La Question des détroits* (Paris, 1908), pp. 77–78; *G.P.*, XII (pt. 1), no. 2918. Salisbury had begun to waver in his attitude as early as 1892. See *G.P.*, IX, nos. 2127, 2128. In regard to the Straits he would undoubtedly have preferred to have them opened to all nations. On his general attitude during the Armenian crisis see *G.P.*, X, nos. 2381, 2387, 2392, 2463, 2573; XI, no. 2664; XII (pt. 1), nos. 2918, 2919; XVIII (pt. 1), nos. 5640, 5642.

[11] On the attitude of the Austrians and Germans see *G.P.*, X, nos. 2495, 2497; XI, no. 2670; XII (pt. 1), nos. 2931, 3114. Francis Joseph and Golochowski were agreed on this question, but the Germans were anxious not to be drawn into war.

adequately prepared and partly, no doubt, because the French refused to entertain the suggestion.[12] Furthermore, the Russians had already embarked upon their Far Eastern adventure. The powerful minister of finance, Witte, had induced the rejection of the Nelidov plan, and diverted the energies of the empire to Asia. The Balkans were "put on ice" for a time and the opposing powers were temporarily relieved of anxiety without any exertion on their part. In the well-known Austro-Russian Agreement of May 1897 it was stated that the questions of Constantinople and the adjacent territory and of the Straits were eminently European in character and could not be made the subject of a separate agreement. Count Muraviev, the Russian foreign minister, declared that, far from desiring a modification of the existing situation, the Russian government was intent upon the maintenance of the arrangements, "which gave full and complete satisfaction to Russia." To this declaration the Austrian government heartily subscribed.[13]

While they were engaged in the Far East it was very important for the Russians that the principle of the closure of the Straits to foreign warships, as laid down in the treaties, should be scrupulously observed. For Russia it obviated the necessity of maintaining a large fleet in the Black Sea. Men like Witte actually considered it the best possible arrangement.[14] It had been provided for in the Treaties of the Three Emperors in 1881 and 1884, and in 1885 it had actually saved Russia from an English attack. The only shortcoming of the existing regulations from the Russian point of view was that they were humiliating, and that in time of war they made it impossible for the Russians to make use of their Black Sea squadron elsewhere. On several occasions the Russians denied their own past and attempted to send ships through the Straits, adopting for the moment the view taken by Lord Salisbury at the Berlin Congress that England's obligations were to the Sultan

---

[12] For details of this episode see the documents printed in *Krasnyi Arkhiv*, I (some of them translated in *Die Kriegsschuldfrage*, IV [March 1926], 175–181). See also *G.P.*, XII (pt. 1), nos. 2929 ff., 3090. A fairly accurate account of the matter was published by Amateur, "A Diplomatic Reminiscence," *National Review* (February 1909), pp. 908–918. See also E. J. Dillon, *The Eclipse of Russia* (London, 1918), chap. 13; Sergei Witte, *The Memoirs of Count Witte* (Garden City, 1921), pp. 186 ff.; Roman Rosen, *Forty Years of Diplomacy* (New York, 1922), I, chap. 14; G. N. Trubetzkoi, *Russland als Grossmacht* (Stuttgart, 1913), pp. 161–162.

[13] The text of the agreement in A. F. Přibram, *The Secret Treaties of Austria-Hungary* (Cambridge, 1920), I, 184 ff.; see also *G.P.*, XII (pt. 1), no. 3126.

[14] *G.P.*, XII (pt. 1), no. 2941; similarly Count Kapnist in no. 3118. Cf. also Gr. Br., F.O., *British Documents on the Origins of the War*, ed. G. P. Gooch and Harold Temperly (London, 1927–1938), no. 367.

and not to the powers generally. In order to meet the situation the English, at such times, went over to the traditional Russian view, urging the European nature of the existing agreements and protesting against concessions made by the Sultan to any one of the signatory powers.[15] There was no deeper significance in all this beyond the fact that it illustrated the lack of precision in the existing treaties and the desirability of revision.

For the English, opposition on the Straits question was becoming progressively more difficult. Embroiled in South Africa, at odds with the French in the Sudan, and confronted with the hostility of the Russians in the Far East and in Middle Asia, they were constantly faced with the possibility of a dangerous coalition or even war. Germany refused an alliance, and the English statesmen were forced to consider the possibility of an arrangement with their bitterest enemies.[16] So strong was the antipathy of France after Fashoda that an understanding with Russia for the time promised great prospects of success. Numerous articles appeared in the English press urging a settlement of outstanding disputes between the two powers, especially in Central Asia and on the Indian frontier.[17] But these efforts were somewhat premature, for no satisfactory liquidation of the existing rivalries was possible so long as the Far Eastern problem had not been solved. The Anglo-Japanese Alliance of January 1902 was the logical first step in this direction. Meanwhile the English were agreeably surprised by the offer of an entente with France. They accepted with alacrity, and the treaties of April 1904, by putting an end to the dispute in regard to

15 *G.P.*, XVIII (pt. 1), nos. 5654, 5656, 5659, 5664. On the conflicting interpretations and the reversal of the English and Russian positions in 1902 see Lozé, *La Question des détroits*, pp. 82 ff.; R. Pinon, "La Mer Noire et la question des détroits," *Revue des deux mondes* (Oct. 15, 1905); J. B. Espéret, *La Condition internationale des détroits du Bosphore et des Dardanélles* (Toulouse, 1907), pp. 132 ff.; and especially N. Dascovici, *La Question du Bosphore et des Dardanelles* (Geneva, 1915), pp. 254–268.

16 *British Documents*, I, 8, shows that as early as January–March 1898 Salisbury was ready for an understanding on all points, and ready to recognize that Russia had a greater interest than England in that part of the Ottoman Empire "which drains into the Black Sea or the sea as far as the beginning of the Aegean Sea."

17 Some of the writers did not hesitate to suggest the sacrifice of England's traditional policy in the Near East as well. For example, Sir Rowland Blennerhassett, "England and Russia," *National Review* (March 1901), pp. 21–32; A,B,C, etc., "British Foreign Policy," *National Review* (September 1901), pp. 343–358; similarly Calchas, "Russia and Her Problem," *Fortnightly Review* (August 1901).

Egypt, removed the most dangerous basis of an eventual conflict in the Mediterranean.

Of course France's position as the ally of Russia and the friend of England was, to say the least, an anomalous one, and Delcassé's idea from the very beginning had been to associate Russia in the new combination. There was much talk of an Anglo-Russian entente at the time of the signature of the agreement between England and France, though little could be hoped for until the conflict in the Far East had been brought to a close.[18]

English statesmen generally seem to have regarded the idea with sympathy. The entente with France would never be of real value so long as the loyalty of France was divided between Russia and England. There was no longer any danger of French and Russian action in the Mediterranean, and with their control of Egypt secure the English had less to fear from the presence of the Russians at Constantinople. As a matter of fact there was little likelihood that the Russians would make much progress in that direction, for Germany had gradually acquired a dominant position at the Porte. The Baghdad railway scheme had become much more of a menace to England's position in the Near East than Russian designs on the Straits. In fact common apprehension in respect to German policy might very well become the basis for an entente.

King Edward had long since become converted to the idea of an Anglo-Russian understanding, and had made no secret of his predilections.[19] In the spring of 1904, while the King was on a visit to Copenhagen, the French minister, M. Crozier, introduced him to his Russian colleague, Alexander Isvolski.[20] Isvolski had grown up in the Slavophil tradition, like most of his contemporaries, but had, in large measure, emancipated himself. The intense patriotism still remained, but otherwise he had become a westerner. For him the ideal system of government was the constitutional monarchy as it existed in England. So

[18] *G.P.*, XIX (pt. 1), no. 5945; XX (pt. 1), no. 6381. On Declassé's attitude see especially *British Documents*, I, nos. 198, 262 (September 1898). "He had always regarded as eminently desirable a cordial understanding between England, France, and Russia."

[19] Lee, *King Edward VII*, I, chap. 36. In the last months of 1903 both sides had expressed willingness to consider a settlement (*ibid.*, II, 280–281; *British Documents*, II, nos. 250, 258, 262).

[20] Philippe Crozier, "L'Autriche et l'avant-guerre," *Revue de France* (Apr. 1, 1921), pp. 275–276.

Anglophil had he become that he even went so far as to say that he would have preferred an alliance with England to the alliance with France, because of the slighter diversity in political outlook.[21] Beyond having a distinct leaning towards the English connection Isvolski was a firm adherent of the European orientation of Russian policy. He had been minister at Belgrade, and while representing his country at Tokyo had warned and protested so loudly against the Far Eastern adventure that he had been recalled and sent to Copenhagen, half in disgrace.[22]

Isvolski's great ambition for Russia was to have the Straits opened to her warships. It appears to have been almost an obsession with him, and he seems to have talked about it to anyone who would listen. As a patriot he regarded the existing arrangement as humiliating as well as detrimental. During the war with Japan, the Black Sea fleet was bottled up and entirely useless when it might have proved decisive in the Far East.[23] Besides, the Straits were becoming more and more important for Russia commercially. Some 10,000 ships entered and cleared Constantinople annually, the great majority engaged in the through trade to the Black Sea, and a very large percentage of these called at Russian ports. In fact, almost all of Russia's export trade went through the Straits, and the shipments of cereals, the chief item in the outgoing trade, went almost entirely from ports like Odessa, Rostov, Nicolaiev, Mariopol, Berdiansk, and Kherson.[24] To be sure, the Straits were technically open to all merchantmen in time of peace and in time of war, but this arrangement could be depended on only so long as the all-important passage, second only to Suez and Gibraltar, was in the control of a weak Turkey or of Russia herself. And yet Turkey was falling more and more under the influence of the Germans, who might conceivably induce the Porte to close the Straits at the crucial moment.

[21] Alexander Isvolski, *Recollections of a Foreign Minister* (Garden City, 1921), p. 91. Curiously enough in 1898 Delcassé remarked that he would have preferred an Anglo-French to a Franco-Russian Alliance (*British Documents*, I, no. 1980). See also Crozier, *Revue de France* (Apr. 1, 1921), pp. 275–276, and on pp. 186–187, the sympathetic character sketch of Isvolski.

[22] For the development of Russia's Asian policy, see "The Origin of the Russo-Japanese War." [Part I, Number 1, of this volume.]

[23] Crozier, *Revue de France* (Apr. 1, 1921), pp. 275–276, 186–187.

[24] Shipping figures vary greatly, depending upon whether small coasting craft are included or not. The tonnage through the Straits rose from about 10,000,000 in 1891 to 15,000,000 in 1904, that through Suez being greater. See the *Statesman's Yearbook* (London, 1864 to date), *passim*, and L. Jurowsky, *Der russische Getreideexport* (Stuttgart, 1910), p. 22; A. Raffalovich, *Russia, Its Trade and Commerce* (London, 1918); O. Friebel, *Der Handelshafen Odessa* (Berlin, 1921); and M. S. Miller, *The Economic Development of Russia, 1905–14* (London, 1926).

Isvolski may have regarded the possession of Constantinople as a religious dream, the realization of which was becoming more and more hopeless. But the Straits were another matter, and in his opinion a revision of the treaties in Russia's interest was absolutely necessary for political, strategical, and economic reasons.

King Edward and Alexander Isvolski were quite obviously men who could see eye to eye. When informed of the King's views by his French colleague, Isvolski entered upon the discussion of an Anglo-Russian entente with the greatest enthusiasm. Asiatic problems, he declared, would not be an obstacle, for Asia was large enough for all.[25] A meeting was arranged and the Russian diplomat immediately raised the question of the Straits. The King admitted that the principle of closure was not an absolute or eternal one. It was quite possible to conceive of a situation in which it might be possible for England and advantageous for everybody to open the Straits. But, for the moment, English public opinion was, he declared, absolutely hostile and therefore nothing could be done. The two men parted, very well impressed with each other and undoubtedly hopeful of the future.[26]

Isvolski's report of his conversation with the King was apparently ignored at St. Petersburg.[27] Feeling against England was running too high, and before long the Dogger Bank incident brought the two countries to the very verge of war. There was not the slightest prospect of an agreement, and the English government on more than one occasion made it clear that it would oppose any attempt to send the Russian Black Sea fleet through the Straits.[28]

[25] Crozier, *Revue de France* (Apr. 1, 1921), pp. 275–276.

[26] *Ibid.*, which adds that the Empress Dowager was so well impressed with Isvolski's ideas that she did her utmost to secure his appointment as foreign minister. See also Edward's letter to Nicholas, lauding Isvolski (Lee, *King Edward VII*, II, 289). Cf. also Isvolski, *Recollections*, p. 4, and on these Copenhagen conversations *G.P.*, XIX (pt. 1), no. 6038. Wilhelm von Schoen, *Erlebtes* (Berlin, 1921), p. 76, says that Isvolski discussed the Straits problem with him too while he was German minister to Denmark.

[27] *G.P.*, XIX (pt. 1), no. 0000, quoting King Edward. See the account in Lee, *King Edward VII*, II, 284 ff. No mention is there made of the Straits, nor is this problem referred to in Isvolski's report, which is printed. The reason is obvious, and Isvolski himself says the report is "un résumé fort succinct et certainement très incomplet."

[28] *G.P.*, XVIII (pt. 1), nos. 5654–64; XIX (pt. 1), nos. 6058, 6063, 6068, 6070; Lozé, *La Question des détroits*, pp. 84 ff.; and the very detailed account in Espéret, *La Condition internationale des détroits*, chaps. 6–8. Lansdowne was very firm on this matter (see *British Documents*, II, no. 285, and especially the dispatch on p. 401, envisaging a collision between England and Russia). Neither King Edward nor Hardinge agreed (Lee, *King Edward VII*, II, 289–290).

But as soon as the war was over the road once more became clear. The ink was hardly dry on the Treaty of Portsmouth when the subject was broached in the press of both countries. There was a distinct sentiment in favor of a settlement on both sides. The *Spectator*, an English independent Conservative organ which had urged friendship between the two nations for a decade back, showed no hesitancy in speaking out:

> The English [it argued on August 26, 1905] have long since recognized that in 1854 they, to repeat Lord Salisbury's phrase, "put their money on the wrong horse," and with the Nile Valley in their own hands, they are now inclined to regard with calmness the expulsion of the Turks from Europe and to recognise the truth that no great people can be permanently refused access to the open water. In our opinion [it continued on September 16, 1905] we should tell the Russians plainly that we have ceased to consider the maintenance of the integrity and independence of the Ottoman Empire an essential British interest and that, though we could not view with indifference the destruction of the independent kingdoms of the Balkan Peninsula, we should not regard the presence of the Russians on the Bosphorus as injurious to us, nor resent the absorption of those portions of Asia Minor which naturally go with the possession of Constantinople. [Russia would, of course, have to settle up with the other powers, but Austria might be given Salonica and the territory necessary to connect the port with Bosnia, France might have Syria, and Italy could be pacified with Tripoli.] [29]

The *Novoie Vremia*, a leading Russian organ, replied rather cynically that England was offering what was not hers, but on the whole took a favorable attitude. Russia did not want or need Constantinople, but desired a free passage through the Straits for her warships.[30] Before long the subject was being discussed throughout Europe, and from that time onwards the Anglo-Russian entente was in the air.[31] Lansdowne seized the opportunity to suggest an agreement on Persia, Afghanistan, and Tibet, but it does not appear that negotiations were seriously entered upon at this time. When Witte reached Paris on his return journey from Portsmouth, he found Poklevski, the secretary of the London embassy,

[29] *Spectator*, Aug. 26, 1905; Sept. 16, 1905. Cf. also the article in the number of Oct. 7, 1905.

[30] *Spectator*, Sept. 23, 1905; André Tardieu, *France and the Alliances* (New York, 1908), p. 240; *G.P.*, XIX (pt. 2), no. 6358; "Episodes of the Month," *National Review* (October and November 1905).

[31] *The Times* (London), Oct. 9, 1905; *G.P.*, XIX (pt. 2), no. 6359.

awaiting him with proposals which, he wrongly claimed, had been approved by King Edward and by the British foreign office. Witte was opposed to an alliance and may, in part at least, have been responsible for the postponement of the matter. In any case the revolution in Russia left no time for far-reaching projects of foreign policy.[32]

Sir Edward Grey, who took over the foreign office in December 1905, was, if anything, more strongly convinced than his predecessor of the desirability of an entente with England's traditional enemy. During the election he had declared, in a speech before the London United Liberal Association on October 20, 1905, that

> if Russia accepts, cordially and whole-heartedly, our intention to preserve the peaceable possession of our Asiatic possessions, then I am quite sure that in this country no government will make it its business to thwart or obstruct Russia's policy in Europe. On the contrary, it is urgently desirable that Russia's position and influence be reestablished in the councils of Europe.[33]

It is well known that the problem was again discussed during the Algeciras Conference by the Russian and English representatives, Count Cassini, Sir Arthur Nicolson, and Sir Donald MacKenzie Wallace.[34] The appointment of Isvolski as Russian foreign minister in May 1906 promised well for the future. Already in March 1906 he had gone over the projected entente with Nelidov, Benckendorff, and Muraviev, the ambassadors at Paris, London, and Rome, all of whom heartily sub-

---

[32] Erich Brandenburg, *Von Bismarck zum Weltkrieg* (Berlin, 1924), p. 220; *The Times* (London), Oct. 23, 1905; B. Schwertfeger, ed., *Zur europäischen Politik* (Berlin, 1919), II, nos. 22, 23, 38. Benckendorff denied that the suggestion of a free hand for England in Middle Asia in return for a free hand for Russia in Constantinople and Asia Minor had been made to him by responsible persons, but admitted that it had been raised in political circles. *G.P.*, XIX (pt. 2), no. 6360. On the Poklevski mission and Witte's attitude see Dillon, *The Eclipse of Russia*, pp. 350 ff.; Witte, *Memoirs*, pp. 432–433; Lee, *King Edward VII*, II, 307. According to Nelidov (letter to Lamsdorff, Oct. 5, 1905) Witte recognized the necessity for an understanding with England, though he was opposed to an alliance (*Krasnyi Arkhiv*, V, 32). In May 1905 Lamsdorff had expressed himself in favor of an agreement, and in January 1906 the Tsar did likewise (Lee, *King Edward VII*, II, 306, 310).

[33] *The Times* (London), Oct. 21, 1905; cf. also the *National Review* chronicle for December 1905: "Every thoughtful and patriotic Englishman must share the earnest desire of all pacific elements in Europe that Russia may speedily resume her position as a leading member of the European concert . . . Russia is an absolute necessity to Europe."

[34] André Tardieu, *La Conférence d'Algésiras* (Paris, 1908), pp. 78–79, 461. The French continued their efforts to bring their two friends together (A. Zaiontchkovsky, "Rélations franco-russes avant la guerre de 1914," in *Les Alliés contre la Russie* (Paris, 1926), pp. 17–18, 42–43.

scribed.[35] Negotiations were almost immediately opened, but progress was slow. It was felt in London that, if the revolution in Russia were completely crushed, English public opinion would not react favorably to an understanding with a ruthless autocracy. In Russia the reactionary court circles appear to have blocked an arrangement as long as possible.[36] Isvolski and his friends, however, were very eager and offered such large concessions in Central Asia that the English government was more than astounded. Grey was constantly expecting demands for concessions in the Near East in compensation for sacrifices to be made in Asia. He doubted whether a permanent settlement would be possible unless the Near East, where the original causes of hostility lay, were included. But naturally enough he felt that it was for the Russians to take the initiative; he wrote to Nicolson:

> It is not for us to propose changes with regard to the treaty conditions of the Dardanelles. I think some change in the direction desired by Russia would be admissable and we should be prepared to discuss the question if Russia introduces it.[37]

Finally, in the spring of 1907, Isvolski did raise the question. The discussion was carried on in London through Count Benckendorff. Of the details we know almost nothing, but the suggestion appears to have been made that Russia should have free egress from the Black Sea through the Straits, while other powers should have the right to send their vessels of War into the Straits without going into the Black Sea. There seems also to have been some talk of Russia's occupying the Bosphorus and England the Dardanelles, after which the Straits might be opened to other warships as well.[38] Nothing came of the negotiations, though the reasons for their being dropped are somewhat obscure. In England the committee of imperial defence had just decided that in any case an attempt upon the Dardanelles would be too risky and should,

[35] Isvolski, *Recollections*, pp. 21–22, 73. Nelidov's attitude is further illustrated by his letters to Lamsdorff, quoted by Zaiontchkovsky.

[36] *G.P.*, XXV (pt. 1), chap. 83 *passim;* Schwertfeger, *Zur europäischen Politik,* II, nos. 39, 43 ff.

[37] Edward Grey, *Twenty-five Years* (London, 1925), I, 155 ff. Cf. also Dillon, *The Eclipse of Russia,* pp. 350 ff.

[38] Grey, *Twenty-five Years,* I, 179; *G.P.*, XXII, no. 7383 note; XXVI (pt. 1), nos. 9005, 9075 note. Isvolski also refers to these negotiations in a letter of October 12, 1911 (René Marchand, ed., *Un Livre noir* [Paris, n.d.], I, 148; F. Stieve, ed., *Der diplomatische Schriftwechsel Isvolskis* [Berlin, 1924], I, no. 141). In Lee, *King Edward VII,* II, 570, there is only a veiled reference to the discussion of the problem, describing Grey as uncertain on this point.

if possible, be avoided.[39] Grey himself seems to have been opposed to a one-sided agreement in favor of Russia and to have preferred to wait until English opinion had become accustomed to the idea of cooperation with Russia.

Evidently Isvolski did not press the point. Not that he was indifferent. But there was great difference of opinion among the military and naval authorities in Russia. A joint commission, after sitting for weeks, was unable to agree, but the prevalent view was that the opening of the Straits would require a great increase of the Black Sea fleet and considerable strengthening of the coast defences. For this Russia had neither time nor money.[40] Isvolski was once more obliged to shelve the problem, and there was no mention of it in the Anglo-Russian agreement of August 31, 1907.

One of the difficulties in the way of Isvolski was the fact that the Russians themselves did not know what they wanted and could not decide whether the existing arrangements were better or worse than some other. No doubt they would have been glad to see the Straits opened to Russian warships and closed to all others, but that was too much to hope for. Even the English showed no inclination to make such a concession, and besides there were all the other powers. Russia had repeatedly recognized the international character of the problem, and had again and again defended this view as against the English.[41] Isvolski decided to prepare the way by discussion with the other powers, evidently in the hope that, if he had their consent to making the Black Sea a mare clausum for the Russians, not even the English would be able to withhold their approval.

No effort had been spared by Isvolski to convince the central powers that the agreement with England did not involve hostility to other nations, and soon afterward he set out on one of his numerous visits to the West.[42] It was, above all, necessary to sound the Austrians, for, next to the English, they had most consistently opposed the Russian designs.[43] The two governments had for years been on comparatively

[39] William Robertson, *Soldiers and Statesmen* (London, 1926), I, 77–79; Grey, *Twenty-five Years*, I, 158–159.

[40] *G.P.*, XXVI (pt. 1), no. 9005.

[41] The fatal disagreement among Russians themselves is well set forth by Gabriel Hanotaux, *La Politique de l'équilibre* (Paris, 1914), pp. 277–280.

[42] Isvolski's assurances in Brandenburg, *Von Bismarck zum Weltkrieg*, pp. 221, 224–225.

[43] *G.P.*, X, nos. 2488, 2497; XI, nos. 2670, 2680; XII (pt. 1), nos. 2931, 3114; XVIII (pt. 1), no. 5644.

friendly terms and had been cooperating in the work of Macedonian reform. Aehrenthal, the new Austrian foreign minister, was regarded as a friend of Russia.[44] The two men met in the last days of September 1907 at Vienna. Isvolski raised the question of the Straits, but only in an academic way, in connection with general Near Eastern problems.

> Russia [he said] had lost Manchuria and Port Arthur and there-with her access to the Eastern Seas. The centre of Russian naval de-velopment henceforth lay in the Black Sea. Russia must secure access to the Mediterranean.[45]

Aehrenthal had for some time been anxious about the Anglo-Russian agreement and may have suspected that there was a secret clause con-ceding the Russian desires in this question.[46] He therefore contented himself with pointing out the seriousness of the problem and reserving judgement.[47] Meanwhile he communicated with the German govern-ment. It was felt by both allies that it would be dangerous to allow Isvolski to get what he wanted from England and France and then pre-sent the central powers with a *fait accompli*.[48] Neither power was pleased with the prospect of having so thorny a question put before them, but resistance was out of the question since England had joined the opposing camp, and it was decided that the best and safest course would be to sell approval as dearly as possible. Conrad von Hötzen-dorf urged upon the Austrian foreign minister a scheme by which Russia might be given a free hand in the Straits question in return for recognition of Austrian annexation of Bosnia and Herzegovina.[49]

An arrangement along these lines might easily have been made, for the welfare of the Southern Slav states was not of primary concern to Isvolski. But Aehrenthal's Sanjak railway project introduced dissension between the two powers. Isvolski had been informed of it beforehand, but the scheme had nevertheless come as a shock.[50] The Austrian min-

---

[44] Crozier, *Revue de France* (Apr. 1, 1921), pp. 286–287.

[45] *G.P.*, XXII, nos. 7383, 7385. There is no evidence that Isvolski raised the question during his talks with King Edward at Marienbad, with Schoen at Munich, or with the French statesmen in Paris. He explicitly denied having discussed it with the English (*G.P.*, XXII, no. 7383).

[46] *Ibid.*, XXII, no. 7385; XXV (pt. 1), no. 8506.

[47] *Ibid.*, XXII, no. 7383.

[48] *Ibid.*, XXII, no. 7384; XXVI (pt. 1), 8939.

[49] Franz Conrad [von Hötzendorf], *Aus meiner Dienstzeit* (Vienna, 1921), I, 513, 516, 530.

[50] *G.P.*, XXV (pt. 2), chap. 187 *passim;* Crozier, *Revue de France* (Apr. 1, 1921), p. 299; H. W. Steed, *Through Thirty Years* (New York, 1924), I, 269.

ister, in his address before the delegations, left no doubt of his country's expansive ambitions in the direction of Salonica, and in Russia the announcement of the project had raised a storm of indignation and protest. The tide of national revival had been rising since 1905 and now assumed menacing proportions. There was a loud cry for the resumption of Russia's historic mission in the Near East and for the opening of the Straits. Isvolski sympathized entirely with this demand, but the fervent outburst of the Russian press rendered his plan of an agreement with Austria very difficult. The Sanjak railway project was like a bomb thrown between his legs, as he himself put it.[51]

For the time being there could be no thought of pursuing the confidential negotiations. On the other hand Isvolski's suspicions of Austrian and German policy in the Near East had been greatly strengthened, and it appeared to him more necessary than ever that something should be done. Supported by the Grand Duke Nicholas, the foreign minister decided to resort to heroic measures. In a famous ministerial conference of February 3, 1908, he bitterly indicted his predecessor's policy of passivity and advocated a closer entente with England in order to realize Russia's historic mission in the Near East. He even went so far as to suggest war against the Turks, the pretext to be a frontier dispute between the Sultan and the Persian government. Stolypin, however, was flatly opposed, because of Russia's unpreparedness. He considered it his duty, he said,

> to declare emphatically that at the present time the Minister of Foreign Affairs cannot count upon any support for a determined policy. A fresh mobilization in Russia would add strength to the revolution from which we are only beginning to emerge . . . Any other policy than a strictly defensive one would, at the present moment, be the evil dream of an abnormal government and would spell disaster for the dynasty.[52]

Isvolski was perforce obliged to recur to his former policy. But in his Duma speech of April 17, 1908, he declared that Russia's policy in the Near East must be dictated by a healthy egoism. By this he meant (so

---

[51] *G.P.*, XXV (pt. 2), nos. 8705, 8733, 8739, 8850.

[52] Mikhail Pokrowski, *Drei Konferenzen* (Hamburg, 1920), p. 17; E. A. Adamov, *Konstantinopel i Prolivi* (Moscow, 1925), I, 8–10; *Diaries of General Polivanov* (Moscow, 1924), quoted by Gunther Frantz, "Die Meerengenfrage in der Vorkriegspolitik Russlands," *Deutsche Rundschau* (February 1927), pp. 142–160; *G.P.*, XXV (pt. 2), no. 8725. There were reports that during the crisis the English once more offered the Russians a free hand at Constantinople (*ibid.*, no. 8727). This Benckendorff denied (*ibid.*, no. 8699).

he told the German ambassador) that Russia must not allow herself to be misled by exaggerated emotions and by anxiety for the fate of other Slav peoples to the extent of neglecting her own purely Russian interests.[53]

The problem was still how to square the Austrians. Until this had been accomplished there was no object in going farther, and Isvolski therefore did not mention the matter in his conversations with King Edward and Hardinge at Reval in June 1908.[54] But on July 2 he forwarded to Vienna an aide-mémoire recapitulating the negotiations which had grown out of the Sanjak railway affair and suggesting an entente. The European character of the questions of Bosnia-Herzegovina on the one hand and of Constantinople and the Straits on the other was recognized, but a discussion "in a spirit of friendly reciprocity" was invited.[55] To the German ambassador Isvolski explained that Russia desired only the status quo and the maintenance of the balance of power. She had no wish to see the breakup of the Ottoman Empire or the aggrandizement of any one Balkan state, nor did she aspire to territorial gain or preponderant position for herself. Isvolski's dream was that Russia might secure the free passage of the Straits, not for aggressive purposes, but solely in order to enable her to play a role in the Mediterranean commensurate with her position. The realization of this dream would be quite possible without the possession of Constantinople. All Russia needed were "juridical rights," and in return for these she would be ready to give guarantees for the maintenance of Turkey's integrity and the renunciation of any preponderant political or economic influence in Turkey.[56]

Meanwhile the Young Turk revolution broke out and successfully established itself. For the moment the Near Eastern situation was chaotic, and the Russians once more considered an unprovoked attack upon the Bosphorus.[57] Apparently this was still impracticable, and it

[53] *G.P.*, XXV (pt. 2), no. 8745. Cf. Heinrich Friedjung, *Das Zeitalter des Imperialismus* (Berlin, 1922), II, 219, based in large part on unpublished Austrian documents.

[54] At any rate there is at present no evidence that the subject was discussed, despite the assertion of B. Molden, *Graf Aehrenthal* (Stuttgart, 1917), p. 44.

[55] Text in *G.P.*, XXVI (pt. 1), no. 9055, app.; cf. also Conrad, *Aus meiner Dienstzeit*, I, 104; Friedjung, *Zeitalter des Imperialismus*, II, 220.

[56] *G.P.*, XXV (pt. 2), no. 8852.

[57] *Polivanov Diaries*, quoted by Frantz, *Deutsche Rundschau* (February 1927), pp. 142–160. The matter was discussed in a ministerial conference on August 3, 1908. Cf. also the *Nation* (London), Oct. 24, 1908, on the hostility of the Russians to the Young Turk revolution in its earlier stages.

turned out very soon that the revolution was resulting in a great weakening of the Austro-German position at Constantinople. Fraternization between Slavs and Turks, together with endless demonstrations in favor of England and France, confounded all calculations. Prospects of a Russo-Turkish entente became rosy and Isvolski's hopes began to rise high.[58] In a circular note to the powers on August 7 he announced the suspension of reform projects for Macedonia and declared that

> Russia will follow with the most sympathetic attention every effort of Turkey to secure the proper functioning of the new regime, and that on her side Russia would abstain from all interference that might complicate this task, and would exercise all her influence to forestall and prevent any disturbing action on the part of the Balkan states.[59]

The Austrians, naturally enough, were much worried by these developments. The annexation of Bosnia and Herzegovina appeared more urgent than ever, and Aehrenthal therefore drafted a reply to the Russian memorandum of July 2. It was accepted by the ministry on August 19 and dispatched on August 27. After discussing the possible annexation of the two provinces the note closes by saying that in regard to Constantinople and the Straits, the Austrian government would be disposed to enter upon a confidential and friendly exchange of views if the question arose.[60]

Aehrenthal intended to treat this matter as circumspectly and dilatorily as possible, but it was expected that the question would be raised when the two statesmen met at Buchlau on September 16.[61] Isvolski, says his inspired apologist, was ready for a new plunge into *la haute politique*, "for since his success with Japan and Great Britain he had acquired the taste for the highest kind of statesmanship." [62] Without awaiting the Austrian reply he had drawn up a draft convention with Austria comprising seven articles, one of which stipulated the opening of the Straits to the Russian fleet. Having secured the approval of the Tsar he set out for the west on August 19, his plan being not only to meet Aehrenthal, but to go on to Italy, France, and England to secure

---

[58] *G.P.*, XXV (pt. 2), chap. 191 *passim;* Steed, *Through Thirty Years*, I, 291.

[59] Text in *G.P.*, XXV (pt. 2), no. 8872; *Journal des débats*, Aug. 21, 1908; *Schulthess' Europäischer Geschichtskalendar, 1908* (Munich, 1861–1946), p. 396.

[60] Text in *G.P.*, XXVI (pt. 1), no. 9055, app.; Conrad, *Aus meiner Dienstzeit*, I, 107–109.

[61] *G.P.*, XXVI (pt. 2), no. 8927.

[62] Vox et Praeterea Nihil, "Baron Aehrenthal and M. Izvolsky," *Fortnightly Review* (September 1909), pp. 383–401.

the consent of these powers to the Russo-Austrian agreement and to a European conference to introduce the necessary changes into the Treaty of Berlin.[63]

At Buchlau the two statesmen conferred for fully six hours.[64]

> They laid the Treaty of Berlin on the table [said Isvolski's secretary shortly after], and they read and re-read it, page by page, article by article, the whole length and breadth of it, from one end to the other, not once, but twice, beginning with the beginning and starting over again from the end.[65]

Isvolski, after a rather sharp debate, promised finally to observe a benevolent attitude in the event of the annexation of Bosnia and Herzegovina. His suggestion that territorial compensation be given the Serbs was flatly rejected, and he did not press the matter. It was, however, agreed that Bulgaria might be pacified by a recognition of her independence, and Greece by the cession of Crete.[66] Isvolski was anxious that neither of these states should go to war with the Turks, for they both had good chances of success. The idea of the occupation of the Turkish capital by either was abhorrent to him. He gave the most solemn assurances that Russia herself had no designs on Constantinople. On the contrary Russia's interest demanded the maintenance of Turkey's territorial integrity as long as possible. Even in case of disruption Russia would insist on the continuance of Turkish sovereignty over Constantinople and the Straits. All he asked was the opening of the passage to Russian warships.[67]

Aehrenthal was extremely cautious, but finally agreed to observe a friendly attitude if the question were raised, provided that Rumania and Bulgaria were given equal rights and that Russia gave guarantees for the independence of the Sultan and the safety of Constantinople.

---

[63] I am relying here upon unpublished material, the authenticity of which is beyond question. In view of all this it is hard to put much faith in the assertion made later that Isvolski declared to Aehrenthal that he was travelling merely as a tourist, and that "he possessed no powers whatever to treat with his colleague on any political question" (Vox et Praeterea Nihil and the reply by Vox Alterae Partis, *Fortnightly Review* [September and November 1909]).

[64] Vox Alterae Partis, *Fortnightly Review* (November 1909), pp. 776–789; *Neue Freie Presse*, Sept. 17, 1908.

[65] Crozier, "L'Autriche et l'avant-guerre," *Revue de France* (Apr. 15, 1921), p. 563.

[66] Friedjung, *Zeitalter des Imperialismus*, II, 226–230. This may be taken as the authentic account from the Austrian angle.

[67] *G.P.*, XXVI (pt. 1), nos. 8934, 8935. Cf. also the account written by Isvolski about ten days later and printed in Lee, *King Edward VII*, II, 630–631, note.

Furthermore, he asked that the regulations in force at Suez be applied to the Straits. Only one warship was to pass every twenty-four hours. Both statesmen were agreed that a European conference should be summoned to approve the necessary changes in the existing treaties.[68]

From Buchlau Isvolski went to Berchtesgaden, where he consulted the German foreign minister, von Schoen. He spoke to the German statesman in much the same strain as to Aehrenthal. Schoen listened sympathetically and let it be understood that the German government would not present insuperable obstacles, though its attitude would depend upon the details of the Russian plan.[69] A few days later Isvolski visited Tittoni at Desio, and found full approval for the Austro-Russian programme. The details of the transaction are not clear, but evidently Italy was to be compensated in Albania or Tripoli. The Italo-Russian entente which finally led to the Racconigi agreement was already outlined at this time.[70]

The Russian statesman's progress thus far had been little short of phenomenal. It seemed certain that neither France nor England would be able to resist the Russian plan after the central powers had shown themselves so favorably disposed. Isvolski went on to Paris, and just as he was reaching the outskirts of the French capital he learned from the newspapers of the coming annexation of Bosnia and Herzegovina.[71] There is no evidence that he was particularly surprised. When he arrived on the evening of October 4 he found a letter from Aehrenthal definitely announcing Austria's coming action.[72] He saw Clemenceau and Pichon almost immediately, and the French statesmen, who had

---

[68] Molden, *Graf Aehrenthal*, p. 65; Friedjung, *Zeitalter des Imperialismus*, II, 221; A. F. Přibram, *Austrian Foreign Policy* (London, 1923), p. 26; *G.P.*, XXVI (pt. 1), nos. 8934, 9055. The Austrian obligation was further attested by the letter of Francis Joseph to the Tsar on Jan. 28, 1909 (printed by Zaionchkovski in *Krasnyi Arkhiv*, no. 10, and translated in *Die Kriegsschuldfrage*, IV [April 1926]). Cf. also the letter of Isvolski of Nov. 9, 1911, in Marchand, *Un Livre noir*, I, 160.
[69] *G.P.*, XXVI (pt. 1), no. 8935.
[70] *Ibid.*, no. 9055; Friedjung, *Zeitalter des Imperialismus*, II, 231–232. Tittoni's idea was to bring about an Austro-Russo-Italian agreement in regard to the Balkans (Brandenburg, *Von Bismarck zum Weltkrieg*, p. 272).
[71] There was nothing startling about the declaration of the annexation. Ever since September 20 the newspapers had been full of rumors and discussions, e.g., *Neue Freie Presse*, Sept. 26, 29; Oct. 1, 2, 3. The delivery of the Emperor Francis Joseph's letter to President Fallières by Count Khevenhüller on October 3 was immediately known (*Neue Freie Presse*, Oct. 4, 1908). It must have been this news that Isvolski learned on the train at Meaux (Crozier, *Revue de France* [Apr. 1, 1921], p. 571).
[72] Friedjung, *Zeitalter des Imperialismus*, II, 247.

been forewarned of coming events, very likely reproached him for having kept them in ignorance.[73] Isvolski denied having given his consent to the annexation and apparently succeeded in placating his allies. No doubt he pointed out that a conference had been arranged for. In any case he had no real reason to complain of the Austrian action, and the attitude of the French does not seem to have been so outspoken as to determine him to repudiate his agreement with Aehrenthal and assume a hostile attitude.[74] In the first day or two Isvolski spoke only of the necessity of summoning the conference, and left no doubt that he meant to include the Straits question in the programme, by way of compensation to Russia.[75]

It was apparently not until October 7 that Isvolski turned definitely against Austria. What is the explanation of this change? Historians have generally attributed it to the unfavorable attitude of the French and English in the matter of the Straits; but this is obviously a fallacious line of reasoning, for Isvolski certainly took a hostile stand towards Austria before he left for England, whereas he had been in Paris and had conferred with the French leaders several times before he adopted his new tactics.[76] Very possibly the outspoken declarations in the French

[73] The French statesmen had been continually warned by their ambassador in Vienna. See Crozier, *Revue de France* (Apr. 1, 1921), pp. 562, 564. On the conferences between Isvolski, Pichon, and Clemenceau see *The Times* (London), Oct. 6, 1908; *Neue Freie Presse*, Oct. 6.

[74] On Clemenceau's attitude see Friedjung, *Zeitalter des Imperialismus*, II, 247–248. See Isvolski's denials of his complicity, *G.P.*, XXVI (pt. 1), no. 8987. In any case it is clear that both the French and Isvolski had at least two days before the announcement of the annexation to protest and did nothing. In an interesting letter of April 1909 Sir Charles Hardinge recognizes that Isvolski had hopelessly compromised himself and was at Aehrenthal's mercy (Lee, *King Edward VII*, II, 675).

[75] *G.P.*, XXVI (pt. 1), nos. 8989, 9008, 9010; the raising of the Straits question was already foreshadowed in the *Nation* (London), Oct. 3, 1908: "If Bulgaria were to declare her independence, Austria might, with less risk, annex Bosnia, Greece absorb Crete, and Russia violate the arrangement which confines her navy to the waters of the Black Sea." Similarly *The Times* (London), Oct. 5, 6; *Neue Freie Presse*, Oct. 6. Isvolski told Tardieu on October 7 that, since the Treaty of Berlin had been violated, Russia would demand relief from the clauses that were burdensome to her (interview in *Le Temps*, Oct. 7). Most instructive for Isvolski's attitude in the first days was his talk with the Serbian minister in Paris on October 5, in which he argued for the acceptance of the annexation. See Ger., F.O., *Deutschland Schuldig?* (Berlin, 1919), p. 100.

[76] Not only the older writers like Sosnosky, *Die Balkanpolitik Oesterreich-Ungarns* (Berlin, 1914), II, 168–170, and Friedjung, *Zeitalter des Imperialismus*, II, 248, but more recent scholars like Brandenburg, *Von Bismarck zum Weltkrieg*, p. 273, and F. Stieve, *Deutschland und Europa* (Berlin, 1926), p. 85, who had the use of the German documents, give this erroneous interpretation which can be disproved by a simple constellation of dates.

and English press made him anxious, but he could not have made his decision lightly, for to disavow his agreement with Aehrenthal in a sense involved the abandonment of all hope that Austria and Germany would support him in the Straits question. The truth of the matter seems to be that Isvolski did not voluntarily deny his past, but that his future course of action was marked out for him in a letter from St. Petersburg, which reached him in Paris.

Before leaving for the West, Isvolski had laid his programme before the Tsar and had secured his approval. He had not, however, consulted Stolypin or any other of his colleagues. They had rejected his proposals too often and had no sympathy with an active policy at a time when Russia was completely unprepared. It so happened that the assistant minister of foreign affairs, N. V. Charykov, was a keen rival of his chief and apparently opposed his policy. Immediately after receiving the report of Isvolski's success at Buchlau, Charykov informed Stolypin, Kokovtsev, and General Roediger, the minister of war. Stolypin was beside himself. As a staunch nationalist he refused to admit that Russia could deliberately consent to the annexation of Bosnia and Herzegovina by a German and Roman Catholic state, and insisted that Russia could not barter away her approval for political advantages, however great. Russia must refuse her consent, even though she could not prevent the annexation itself. He threatened to resign if Isvolski's plan were adhered to. The other ministers supported him and the matter was laid before the Tsar, evidently on October 3 or 4. Nicholas II's sympathy seems to have been entirely with his foreign minister, and his desire to score a success in the Straits question was quite as pronounced as his father's yearning for Constantinople. But Stolypin was indispensable, and so it was finally decided that Isvolski's personal feelings must be sacrificed. There must have been prolonged debates, for the new instructions sent to Isvolski did not reach him before he arrived in Paris, in fact, not before October 6 or 7.[77]

[77] I am relying here upon unpublished material. Isvolski sent a draft agreement to St. Petersburg for the Tsar's approval on September 22, 1908; and this Charykov submitted to the Tsar on September 26. But it was not until October 3 or 4 that the other ministers made representations to the ruler (*Neue Freie Presse,* Oct. 6). The delay is explained by the fact that Nicholas was at the time cruising off the Finnish coast and was not easily accessible. Charykov had not got back to St. Petersburg by noon of October 5, so that the new instructions could not have been sent before the evening of that day. Before his return it was erroneously reported from St. Petersburg that he had gone to secure the Tsar's approval of the Russian demand for compensation in the shape of a revision of the Straits treaties (*Neue Freie*

These new instructions explain the Russian minister's sudden change of front and the personal animus which he introduced into the subsequent discussion. To be sure there was nothing in the new instructions that precluded a continuance of the negotiations with regard to the Straits, but in being obliged to protest against the annexation Isvolski was being forced to throw away the approval of Austria and presumably Germany. The new attitude of the Russian government was bound to find an enthusiastic reception in Paris and London, but the applause of France and England would be purchased at a very high cost. Furthermore, Stolypin and his group, who were uncompromisingly opposed to asking any compensation for Russia, saw to it that their views were well reflected in the Russian press.[78] Certain newspapers began to abuse Isvolski for having secretly conspired with Aehrenthal, and on October 8 the *Novoie Vremia,* the leading nationalist organ, published a startling article in which it raised the question whether Isvolski had sold the Slav provinces to Austria.

> Russia [it declared] has in her foreign policy one Holy of Holies, the Slav idea—the supreme embodiment of Russian patriotism. To offend the Slav idea as was done by the Reichstadt Agreement is to offend Russian patriotism.

On the following day it declared that Russia must not sell the Slav heritage for a mess of pottage, and asserted that the opening of the Dardanelles was unnecessary, since Russia was not contemplating war or aggression. Other newspapers joined in the chorus of attack, and the London *Times* correspondent, after consulting various statesmen, reported that "public opinion will be almost unanimously on the side of a disinterested policy," and that the Duma would take the same stand.[79]

As a matter of fact there appears to have been a good deal of sentiment in favor of compensation in the shape of revision of the Straits treaties, but little of this was allowed to become known in London.[80]

Press, Oct. 6). On Stolypin's attitude see also *G.P.,* XXVI (pt. 1), no. 9185 note; Schwertfeger, *Zur europäischen Politik,* III, 147; Otto Hoetzsch, *Russland* (Berlin, 1913), p. 429.

[78] Apparently Stolypin had failed to induce the Tsar to give up the idea of compensation, though he had forced the decision to protest against the annexation.

[79] *The Times* (London), Oct. 9, 10, 14, 1908; *Neue Freie Presse,* Oct. 7, 8, 10; F. Charmes, "Chronique," *Revue des deux mondes* (Oct. 15, 1908).

[80] *G.P.,* XXVI (pt. 1), nos. 8994, 9004, 9185; *Journal des débats,* Oct. 16, 1908: "Le libre passage des détroits pour nos naivres de guerre s'impose donc. C'est une necessité pour nous; c'est un droit naturel." *Ibid.,* Nov. 6: "Les patriotes sincères

The English themselves had taken a strong stand against Austria from the very beginning. Grey's sympathies were all with the Young Turk régime, and in a speech at Wooler on October 7 he had plainly stated:

> Our relations with the government of Turkey have changed from friction and remonstrance to very deep sympathy . . . Hatred, strife, and oppression have been swept away and have been replaced by fair play, peace, and good-will.[81]

He had indeed encouraged Isvolski to hope for a favorable arrangement in regard to the Straits, but that was before the Young Turk revolution. In his apologia he argues that

> the moment was very inopportune. Turkey was hurt and sore at the slight put upon her by Austria and Bulgaria. It was hard enough that she should suffer this at the outset of what we hoped was a new and better era at Constantinople. We could not agree to add to her hardships by forcing upon her at once the embarrassing question of the Straits.[82]

Undoubtedly his attitude was also influenced by the thought that English influence was once more in the ascendant at the Porte and that, with the collapse of the German position, there was no longer an urgent need of strengthening the Russian position. In any case the larger part of the English press took its stand by Grey and avidly devoured all information from St. Petersburg tending to show that Russian opinion was itself averse to bringing up the subject.[83]

---

avouent ici que les détroits, actuellement fermés à tout le monde, doivent être ouverts à tout le monde." Cf. *The Times* (London), Oct. 6, 7. The St. Petersburg correspondent had to admit (*The Times* [London], Oct. 14) that so influential an organ as the *Birzheviia Viedomosti* was for compensation, and added disdainfully that "while enlightened Russia is strongly opposed to a revival at the present stage of the Dardanelles question, provincial opinion remains obscured to some extent." The German attaché, von Hintze, spoke of serious people being opposed to raising the question, while the newspapers and public opinion unthinkingly demanded it (*G.P.*, XXVI ([pt. 1], no. 9075).

[81] *The Times* (London), Oct. 8, 1908.

[82] Grey, *Twenty-five Years*, I, 172.

[83] The whole governmental attitude was foreshadowed in the London *Nation* on October 3, 1908: "The discovery that the Turks can reform themselves and restore their empire may have shaken some of our traditional prejudices, but it threatened none of our interests. On the contrary, it relieved us from the difficult duty of forcing reforms by coercion, allowed us without dishonour to recover our old influence at Constantinople and opened up the attractive vista of a progressive and tolerant Islamic renaissance . . . The duty of Europe, and in particular of Great Britain, is to shield the most promising movement of our generation from foreign complications and to meet with an uncompromising resistance any race or any

Pichon had persuaded Isvolski to postpone his proposal for a conference until after he had spoken to Grey. Nothing definite had been said about the Straits question, though apparently the French minister, relying upon English opposition, had spoken sympathetically and promised to use his influence. *Le Temps,* at that time the mouthpiece of the government, wrote on October 11 that the existing arrangements placed upon Russia and the coastal states of the Black Sea one of the most irksome restraints possible.

> Provided that a legal and correct method of procedure is followed, we confess that for our part we have no tender feeling for treaties which are absolutely contradictory, hypocritical, and ineffectual. A fresh arrangement, more sincere and less vexatious, would seem to us to be the pledge which is to be desired for a better future.[84]

The Russian minister arrived in London on October 9, still determined to have the conference and still hoping to secure a measure of success in the Straits question. Grey, on the other hand, was resolved to have this problem shelved if possible, and, if this course proved to be impracticable, to demand the opening of the passage to the battleships of all nations.[85] On his arrival Isvolski was greeted with an article in *The Times* which read:

> We recognize fully that for Russia to adopt the same self-denying attitude as the two western powers may involve a possible sacrifice of long-cherished desires, but we feel convinced that in the gratitude of a regenerated Turkey she will obtain a far more gratifying and durable reward. Russia has nothing to gain by joining in an undignified scramble, whereby she would alienate Turkey and lose the good will of the Powers with which she is on the best possible terms.[86]

---

power which seeks to endanger its progress." The conservative organs, however, took a different view. The *Saturday Review* was dubious about the Young Turk renaissance from the beginning (Sept. 9 and Oct. 24), and could not see why so much fuss should be made about the action of Bulgaria and Austria (Oct. 10, 1908). The *Spectator* (Oct. 10) could not see why Russia's desires should be opposed.

[84] *G.P.,* XXV (pt. 2), no. 8843; XXVI (pt. 1), nos. 9009, 9031, 9079, 9185 note; *The Times* (London), Oct. 12; Auguste Gauvain, ed., *L'Europe au jour le jour* (Paris, 1917), VIII, 35–36, entry for Oct. 8, 1908.

[85] *G.P.,* XXVI (pt. 1), nos. 9003, 9014; *Spectator,* Oct. 10, 1908. There had been long discussion on the program of the projected conference between Isvolski, Pichon, and Bertie in Paris, but no agreement had been arrived at (*Neue Freie Presse,* Oct. 7, 9, 1908).

[86] *The Times* (London), Oct. 10, 1908. The English were not very enthusiastic at the prospect of a conference of any sort. Cf. the *Nation* (London), Oct. 10: "There is reason to fear that a congress would resolve itself into a highly predatory

The auspices were not exactly favorable, and the Russian minister was soon pressed to the wall. After a two hours' discussion with Grey on October 10 he finally agreed that the Straits problem should not be included in the agenda of the conference, but should first be made the subject of a separate Russo-Turkish agreement. Time and again he assured the English statesman that Russia had no designs on Constantinople and desired only to see it remain in Turkish hands. All Russia wanted was free passage for her own ships of war and those of the coastal states, not more than three ships to go through at one time, and these without anchoring. Grey pointed out the unfavorable impression the Russian plan would make in Turkey, and argued that the proposal was too one-sided. In time of war at least reciprocal rights should be granted, in order to prevent Russian raids on Mediterranean shipping. It would greatly facilitate matters if English public opinion could be convinced that Russia sincerely approved the reform movement in Turkey.[87]

Isvolski's proposals were laid before the cabinet on October 12. Their decision was quite unfavorable, for they agreed with Grey that the moment was "exceedingly inopportune," and that public opinion could not be won over to a one-sided agreement. The Russian minister suggested that in time of war, if Turkey were not involved, the Straits might be opened to all alike. He urged Grey to consider the bad effect which a refusal would have upon the future of Anglo-Russian relations, and finally induced the foreign secretary to resubmit the Russian plan in its revised form to the cabinet.[88]

---

festivity, in which most of the powers would unite to 'compensate' themselves at Turkey's expense for the wrongdoing of Austria and Bulgaria." "Russia's main object is, we suppose, to obtain free passage for her warships through the Dardanelles. We can have no selfish objection to that concession, for it would admit our superior naval force on the same terms to the Black Sea. But unless the Turks should themselves desire to abandon a measure designed for their protection, we can be no party to it." Similarly, the *Saturday Review*, Oct. 10.

[87] Grey, *Twenty-five Years*, I, 172 ff.; G.P., XXVI (pt. 1), nos. 9023, 9024, 9031, 9035, 9039, 9062; *Neue Freie Presse*, Oct. 12, 1908. The whole thing was a compromise: Grey agreed to a conference to discuss compensation not only for Turkey, but for Serbia and Montenegro; Isvolski agreed to the exclusion of the Straits question.

[88] The text of Isvolski's proposals in Marchand, *Un Livre noir*, II, 457; on the cabinet and its decision see Grey, *Twenty-five Years*, I, 174–176. The *Neue Freie Presse*, Oct. 13, 15, 1908, published accurate reports of all the details, drawn from the accounts in the *Petit Parisien* and the *Daily Graphic* (Lucien Wolf). The correspondence between Asquith and the King is very instructive. On October 12 Asquith reported that Isvolski had raised the "delicate and difficult question."

The result was the note of October 14, which, in a sense, amounted to an acceptance of the modified proposals, though it made an agreement conditional on the previous consent of Turkey. Grey promised to use his good offices to secure this consent, but refused to employ pressure of any sort. If obtained at all, it must be obtained "by satisfactory voluntary agreement, and not by pressure or squeeze," as he put it in his memoirs.[89] The same idea was expressed by *The Times* on October 14:

> Great Britain will assuredly be no party to the admission of any demands for "compensation" at Turkey's expense to which Turkey herself objects. She will neither herself put pressure upon Turkey to sanction such demands, nor will she support them, even if the Turk should not reject them, unless she is satisfied that Turkey is acting of her own free will. On the other hand, we are not likely to reject any arrangement of which Turkey may really approve, unless we are convinced that they are incompatible with our own permanent interests.[90]

An authoritative statement was issued on October 16, just as Isvolski left for Paris:

> There is no intention of submitting the question of the Straits to the conference. It is a question in which Russia and Turkey are primarily concerned and there is no desire on the part of the former to settle it in any sense hostile to Turkey or to seek for it as compensation, for Russia enters the conference as one of the disinterested parties.

Isvolski was left to draw what consolation he could from the remark that "the abnegation, the self-restraint, the loyalty, and the candour of which she (Russia) has given us proof have excited our respect and imagination." [91] On his return to Paris the Russian minister once more talked the matter over with the French statesmen. They now subscribed

---

Edward urged the necessity for some concession, lest Isvolski should return to Russia a discredited man who would have to resign. The Anglo-Russian entente would thereby be endangered. On October 13 Asquith reported that he agreed with Grey, Haldane, and McKenna that the existing restrictions on Russia's egress are of no strategic value to Great Britain, but that Morley and Crewe objected to the one-sidedness of Isvolski's proposals (Lee, *King Edward VII*, II, 639–640).

[89] Text of the British note in Marchand, *Un Livre noir*, II, 458; see also Grey, *Twenty-five Years*, I, 172; G.P., XXVI (pt. 1), no. 9056.

[90] *The Times* (London), Oct. 14, 1908; *Neue Freie Presse*, Oct. 16; *Nation* (London), Oct. 24.

[91] *The Times* (London), Oct. 16, 1908. The communiqué is also printed by G. P. Gooch in *Cambridge History of British Foreign Policy* (1923), III, 405.

entirely to Grey's view: the moment was as inopportune as possible. Isvolski was sent away with the assurance that he had French sympathy in his aims and with promises, though not written promises, that France would give general support in realizing them.[92]

So far as this particular problem was concerned everything now depended upon an agreement with the Turks. An arrangement of this sort had been in the mind of Isvolski for some time, though he regarded it originally as the sequel rather than the prelude to his negotiations with the powers. Before leaving for London he had broached the subject in conversation with the Turkish ambassador in Paris, Naoum Pasha. The Straits question, he had remarked, must be settled in a frank and legal manner. The situation as laid down in the treaties was a "crying injustice," as had been shown by the Japanese war. He had then expounded his scheme of opening the passage for the warships of Russia and the coastal states, while maintaining the closure for others. "Russia desires to re-establish the relationship with Turkey as provided for in the Treaty of Unkiar Skelessi." Clearly this would be to the advantage of Turkey, he argued, for it would safeguard the possession of Constantinople against every foreign power.[93]

Meanwhile the question had been raised in St. Petersburg as well. Charykov was an energetic exponent of this policy and had persuaded Nicholas II to allow him to open negotiations. There was every chance of success, he thought, for now Russia could offer the Porte assistance in its protest against the action of Austria. On October 8, therefore, he approached the Turkish ambassador, Turkhan Pasha, saying that Russia asked for the opening of the Straits, but would make use of this privilege only in special cases and in such manner that the Porte would have no occasion for anxiety. In return Russia would be willing to guarantee the European possessions of the Ottoman Empire, to abolish the capitulations, and to support and protect Turkey in all political questions.[94] The Turks had not reacted to this suggestion, evidently thinking it best to bide their time and await developments. But they were at least prepared when, on October 15, Grey sounded the Turkish ambassador in London regarding the attitude of the Porte and the possibility of a

---

[92] Marchand, *Un Livre noir*, I, 145–146, 178; Stieve, *Der diplomatische Schriftwechsel Isvolskis*, I, 140, 184; *G.P.*, XXVI (pt. 1), no. 9079; XXVI (pt. 2), no. 9330.

[93] *G.P.*, XXVI (pt. 1), no. 8999; reported on October 11 by the *Tanin*, the organ of the Committee of Union and Progress (*Neue Freie Presse*, Oct. 12, 1908).

[94] I am making use here of unpublished material. For Charykov's proposals to Turkhan see *G.P.*, XXVI (pt. 1), no. 9001.

Russo-Turkish agreement concerning the Straits. The reply given was that the Porte considered the regulation of the Straits as part of international law, which the Turks proposed to uphold. Changes could be introduced only in agreement with all the contracting parties, and not through negotiations with any one state. Therefore the Porte could not make any concessions to Russia without knowing what consequences the other powers would draw from such an arrangement.[95]

There was, then, no prospect whatsoever of Russia's being able to fulfill the preliminary condition laid down by Grey. The whole plan had failed and there was nothing to do but return home. On his way Isvolski stopped in Berlin. The German government was fully informed not only of what had transpired in London, but also of the steps taken in Constantinople.[96] Since there was no chance of the scheme's materializing, and since the question was not one of primary importance to Germany, there could be no harm in appearing generous. Isvolski was told that Germany would not combat the Russian policy, though she could not support it actively by pressure upon others because of the general international alignments. Isvolski attempted to profit by this benevolent attitude, and on October 26 submitted a very confidential memorandum in which the Germans were asked to promise to receive favorably the agreement which it was hoped might be made with Turkey. To this, however, the Germans were careful not to reply.[97]

On October 28 Isvolski was back in St. Petersburg, a disappointed and disillusioned man. There appear to have been some rather warm discussions between the foreign minister and his colleagues, and the

[95] Grey told the Turks from the start that England would not exert pressure and reserved the right to claim any privileges that might be extended to Russia. On this whole episode see *G.P.*, XXVI (pt. 1), nos. 9047, 9178; *Neue Freie Presse*, Oct. 16, 1908. Even before this the Turks had indicated their unwillingness to entertain proposals. See *G.P.*, XXVI (pt. 1), no. 9004. Cf. also *Neue Freie Presse*, Oct. 9, where a Turkish diplomat says: "Die Oeffnung der Meerengendurchfahrt kann die Hohe Pforte um keinen Preis zugeben." The Turkish stand was also fully expressed by Naoum Pasha, the ambassador in Paris, in *Le Temps*, Oct. 16.

[96] *G.P.*, XXVI (pt. 1), nos. 9031, 9035, 9039, 9056.

[97] *Ibid.*, nos. 9061, 9068 note, 9079; XXVI (pt. 2), nos. 9217, 9220. The text of the Russian memorandum was as follows: "Le Cabinet de St. Pétersbourg est prêt, dans le but de faciliter la solution de la crise actuelle, à exclure la question des détroits du programme de la conférence. Mais si le Gouvernement Russe établit avec la Turquie une entente aux termes de laquelle, le principe de la clôture du Bosphore et des Dardanelles étant maintenu, exception de ce principe serait faite en faveur des bâtiments de guerre des États Riverains de la Mer Noire à des conditions garantissant efficacement la sécurité de la Turquie, le Gouvernement Allemand fera à cet arrangement un accueil favorable soit au cours des travaux de la Conférence soit ultérieurement."

former offered to resign. But the Tsar, who evidently was entirely of Isvolski's mind, insisted on his staying. He did so, but without enthusiasm: "I am no longer a minister of foreign affairs, but merely a *chinovnik* in uniform," he remarked to one of his colleagues.[98]

His failure he attributed entirely to Aehrenthal, because he could not afford to reveal the true circumstances and a campaign of vilification directed against Austria was bound to be popular and aid in rehabilitating himself.[99] It was not until after his return that the tide of nationalist agitation reached the flood stage, and the international crisis assumed dangerous proportions.[100] With the details of the annexation crisis we are not concerned, but a curious little postlude bearing upon the Straits questions deserves mention.

The Kaiser believed that much might be done to conciliate the Russians by frankly offering to support them in the matter of the Straits and thus exploiting the reluctance of England. If the Germans came forward, the English would be compelled either to assume the odium of again refusing concessions or else estrange the Turks and other Mohammedans by accepting the Russian program. Bülow suggested that Russia be asked to enlist French mediation in London, but the Kaiser insisted that Germany and Austria must take the initiative in order to receive the credit. In reply it was pointed out that in all probability England would reject the proposal, and that then Germany would receive the blame for having raised the question.[101] Because of this disagreement nothing specific was done, excepting that the Tsar was informed once more that Germany would not oppose the desires of Russia. The Tsar was agreeably surprised. He admitted that, when the annexation of Bosnia and Herzegovina had been announced, his first idea, and that of Isvolski and of a good many other people had been that, since the treaty of Berlin was being broken, an opportunity had arisen to bring up the Straits question for discussion.

But I want to settle that question legally, by negotiations with the signatories of the Berlin Treaty [he continued. The work of the conference should not be impeded by raising the question]. But in the future, in the near future, I wish this question to be dealt with, and

[98] *G.P.*, XXVI (pt. 1), no. 9185 note, and unpublished material.
[99] Lee, *King Edward VII*, II, 645, Hardinge to the King (Apr. 7, 1909) shows that the English fully appreciated Isvolski's errors. Hardinge speaks of him as "a very unscrupulous and unreliable man."
[100] *The Times* (London), Oct. 29, 1908; *Saturday Review*, Oct. 31, 1908.
[101] *G.P.*, XXVI (pt. 1), nos. 9181, 9182, 9184. This was in December.

then I shall have great pleasure in availing myself of His Majesty's help. I hope to get the consent of all the interested powers, or, at least, of most of them; of course, Turkey is the power mostly con-concerned.[102]

To the Kaiser personally the Tsar wrote to the same effect, pointing out that "now is not the moment for raising that affair, we have got difficulties enough, if I may say so, plenty of diplomatic food to digest for many months to come." [103] And with that the first important stage in the pre-war development of the Straits question came to an end.

Isvolski had failed to attain his object, but there is no denying that progress had been made. The possibility of modifying the existing conventions had been recognized in principle by all the great powers. There was nothing absurd about Isvolski's scheme and it is quite conceivable that an arrangement might have been made. The trouble was not with the idea, but with the execution of the plan. The first fundamental error was made when Isvolski decided to barter consent to the annexation of Bosnia and Herzegovina for concessions in the Straits question. He himself had little interest in the historic mission of Russia to protect the southern Slav states, and he felt that Russia was so deeply committed by previous agreements with Austria that objection to the annexation of the two provinces would be senseless and unprofitable. In all this he showed pathetic lack of appreciation for the growing strength of the nationalist movement in Russia itself. It was a fatal mistake not to consult Stolypin and the other ministers, who had a keener understanding of the national mind. On the other hand, Isvolski no doubt realized that Stolypin and many Russian statesmen had little sympathy with the idea of opening the Straits. The old divergence of opinion on the matter, to which reference has already been made, spelled disaster. Isvolski desired to avoid acrimonious discussion, and hoped that, if he could present his colleagues and the country with a *fait accompli*, he would be irresistible, especially since the Tsar was, at heart, with him. From the moment that Charykov revealed his chief's plans the scheme was already wrecked.

But of hardly less importance was Isvolski's second mistake, which lay in his failure to assess at its true value the change that had come over Europe with the Young Turk revolution. His scheme was sub-

---

[102] *Ibid.*, no. 9185. It was evidently this assurance of the Kaiser that Isvolski referred to later, in 1911 (Marchand, *Un Livre noir*, I, 148, 160).
[103] *G.P.*, XXVI (pt. 1), no. 9185 note.

mitted to Aehrenthal in July. Could he have gone on with it then he might have found but little opposition on the part of the powers. Certainly the view of the English would have been quite different. They would not have raised a finger to protect the Hamidian régime. As it was, however, Isvolski brought forth his suggestions at what, for both France and England, was truly the most inopportune moment. The English hopes of the Young Turk régime were ludicrously exaggerated, but they were sincere. Grey and his countrymen genuinely resented the blows delivered at Turkey by Austria and Bulgaria, and they felt the need of justifying the confidence of the new régime by raising the hue and cry. There was no use in Isvolski's repeated assertions that he had no designs on Constantinople and that he too was benevolently disposed to the New Turkey. Doubts as to his sincerity were only too well justified. He would have fought the Turks or befriended them in order to get what he wanted. But besides this, the obvious answer to his declarations was that, if he really wished the Turks well, he should show his goodwill by abstaining from demands which the Turks could not regard with anything but apprehension. The outcry of the nationalist press in Russia against Isvolski fortified the English in their stand, and the Russian statesman, stabbed in the back, could not hope to wage an uphill battle with any chance of success. The remarkable thing is not that he failed, but rather that his failure was not more complete.

Author's Note.—The unpublished material referred to above (notes 63, 77, 94, and 98) consists of a manuscript written by Monsieur Charykov and shown to the writer by the late Professor A. C. Coolidge in the belief that the author was no longer alive. Since this article went to print the substance of this information has been published by Monsieur Charykov himself in the *Contemporary Review* for October 1928. In the circumstances it has seemed best to leave the references as they stand.

3

The 1908 Prelude to the World War

1929

In the winter of 1908–1909 Europe quivered in fear of a general war. It was barely a year after the Triple Entente had been completed by the agreement between England and Russia, and hardly two months since the Young Turk Revolution had upset the traditional alignment of the powers in the Near East. These two factors—the grouping of the powers and their rival interests in the Near East—supplied the setting for the crisis. The trouble arose from the precipitate action of the Austro-Hungarian government in proclaiming the annexation of Bosnia and Herzegovina, two provinces of the Ottoman Empire which had been occupied by the Dual Monarchy under a mandate from the powers since the Congress of Berlin in 1878. Yet the conflict that threatened was not one between Austria and Turkey, but between Austria and Serbia; for Serbia herself had designs on these two Slav provinces. In other words, the so-called Bosnian annexation crisis of 1908–1909 had obvious points of similarity with the July crisis of 1914. It may, in fact, be aptly described as the prelude to the World War, for it raised issues which were not again to come to rest. In both cases there was the same Austro-Serbian tension, the same threat of intervention on the part of other powers, the same division of Europe into two opposing groups. The question naturally arises why war was avoided in 1909 but not in 1914. An examination of the events of the earlier crisis in the light of the voluminous material that has now been made available will illuminate the more remote origins of the World War and at the same time clarify the course of developments in the crucial months of 1914.

Bismarck had established the ascendancy of Germany in Europe by building up the Triple Alliance and drawing into its orbit almost every

Note: Reprinted from *Foreign Affairs*, VII (July 1929), 635–649, copyright the Council on Foreign Relations, Inc., New York. This article was stimulated by the publication of *British Documents on the Origins of the War, 1898–1914*, vol. V. *The Near East: The Macedonian Problem and the Annexation of Bosnia, 1903–1909*, ed. G. P. Gooch and Harold Temperly (London and New York, 1928).

76

nation of international consequence, including England and excepting only France. The alliance between France and Russia, concluded within a few years of the Iron Chancellor's dismissal, represented a serious breach in this system and once again set up something resembling a balance of power on the continent, as Bismarck's successor frankly recognized. The Franco-Italian agreements of 1900 and 1902, in strengthening the French position, weakened the Triple Alliance correspondingly; while the Anglo-French entente of 1904 marked the definite turn of English policy from the Central Powers. According to the Germans this was the first step in the direction of the encirclement of Germany, a development of the greatest moment. Whatever may be said of the German attitude in the Moroccan crisis of 1905, it can hardly be denied that on the part of Baron von Holstein at least the object in view was to break up the new combination by dragooning France. The Kaiser, by the famous Björkö Treaty with Russia, hoped to attain the same result by gentler means. What actually happened was the very reverse of what the Germans had expected. At the Algeciras conference the Germans were deserted by all the powers excepting Austria. The Anglo-French entente was more firmly established and the unfavorable nature of Germany's position was more marked than ever.

The one bright spot on the horizon, as the Germans saw it, was the exhaustion of the Russians after the disastrous war with Japan and the revolutionary outburst of 1905–1906. But even this bit of consolation disappeared in a very short time. Alexander Isvolski, who became Russian foreign minister in 1906, promptly set to work to iron out what difficulties with Japan had remained after the Peace of Portsmouth, and in August 1907 signed an agreement with England that settled the age-old problems of the two countries in Asia. At the famous Reval meeting between King Edward and the Tsar in June 1908 the question of Macedonian reform was discussed and the new Anglo-Russian entente thereby extended to the Near Eastern terrain.

The statesmen in Berlin were greatly exercised by these events. The relations between Germany and England had become steadily worse since 1901 and threatened to become serious as a result of the German naval program. The Germans refused to yield, and consequently the future of Anglo-German relations looked darker than ever.

Baron Aehrenthal, the Austrian foreign minister, was more concerned with the Near Eastern aspect of the problem. For a full decade the perennial question of the Balkans had been allowed to rest. Russia, engaged in the Far East, had concluded a number of agreements with Austria aimed at the preservation of the status quo and had cooperated with Austria in the program of Macedonian reform. It was expected in Vienna that after their rebuff in the Far East the Russians would devote themselves again to their traditional aspirations in the Near East. Isvolski was distinctly a "westerner" in this respect and did not disappoint expectations. But he did not desire to arouse the hostility of Germany and Austrian and never tired of giving assurances that neither the entente with England nor the Reval meeting was directed against the Central Powers. An exceedingly adroit man, he was ever ready for a plunge in *haute politique*, as his apologist says.[1] According to Sir Vincent Corbett, who knew him well, "he seemed to believe that the rest of the world existed to be outwitted by himself." "He loves academic discussions in which he can review the world from China to Peru, but he does not like the hard give and take of an argumentative conversation," said Sir Arthur Nicolson, the English ambassador to St. Petersburg. Isvolski's idea was evidently to play the two ends against the middle, and to extract concessions from the Central Powers by demonstrating his friendship with the western powers. Already in the autumn of 1907 he had revealed to the Germans and Austrians his desire to see the Straits of the Bosporus and Dardanelles opened to Russian warships. Since her defeat in the Far East, he said, Russia's center of naval development lay in the Black Sea, and she must secure access to the Mediterranean.[2] In Berlin and Vienna no opposition was made to these academic remarks, for it was believed that England, the traditional opponent of concessions to Russia in this question, would wreck the scheme as soon as it assumed concrete form. In this the German and Austrian statesmen were profoundly mistaken.[3] The English had long since given up the idea of maintaining the Turkish Empire at any cost, the more so as the German influence had entirely displaced the English at Constantinople.

General Conrad von Hötzendorf, the Austrian chief of staff, suggested

[1] Vox et Praeterea Nihil, "Baron Aehrenthal and M. Isvolsky," *Fortnightly Review* (September 1909), pp. 383–401.

[2] Johannes Lepsius, Albrecht Mendelssohn-Bartholdy, and Friedrich Thimme, eds., *Die grosse Politik der europäischen Kabinette, 1871–1914* (Berlin, 1922–1926), XXII, nos. 7383, 7385.

[3] See "Russia, the Straits Question, and the European Powers." [Part I, Number 2, of this volume] and especially M[ikhail] de Taube, *La Politique russe d'avant-guerre* (Paris, 1928), p. 186.

to Aehrenthal that, if Russia intended to raise the question of the Straits, Austria should seize the opportunity to bargain and secure in return the consent of Russia to the annexation of the two Turkish provinces of Bosnia and Herzegovina, which had been occupied by the Austrians under a mandate from the powers given at the Congress of Berlin in 1878.[4] The problem of annexation had become an acute one since 1903, when, as a result of the murder of King Alexander and his queen, a new dynasty had ascended the throne in Serbia. The relations between Serbia and Austria had become rapidly worse and there was, undoubtedly, a great deal of agitation and Serb propaganda in the occupied provinces. The famous "pig war," or tariff conflict of 1906–1907, had made matters even worse, and the demand for vigorous action was becoming louder and louder in Vienna. Aehrenthal himself was not a partisan of rigorous measures. According to the British diplomats he did everything he could to remove the bad feeling between the two countries, while Pashitch, the Serb nationalist leader, was determined to free Serbia from Austrian political and economic influence and provoked Austria into taking a more and more aggressive attitude by making offers which, while only too reasonable from the Serbian point of view, were certain to be rejected at Vienna. Nevertheless Aehrenthal continued to hope for a pacific settlement, and desired to postpone the question of annexation of the two provinces until other clauses of the Berlin Treaty came up for discussion. His idea was still to cooperate as closely as possible with Russia.[5]

The change in his attitude came about after the dispute concerning the projected Austrian railway through the Sanjak of Novi-Bazar to connect with the Turkish railroad to Saloniki. Austria had a right to such construction under the terms of the Berlin Treaty, but Isvolski took a stiff attitude and maintained that a "bomb had been thrown between his legs." Unwilling to see Austria score a point, he declared that the Austro-Russian entente had been broken up through the action of the Vienna government. This did not prevent him from soon recovering, and in July 1908 he suggested to the Austrian government an entente and a discussion of the problems of Bosnia and Herzegovina on the one hand and the Straits on the other, "in a spirit of friendly re-

[4] Franz Conrad [von Hötzendorf], *Aus meiner Dienstzeit* (Vienna, 1921), I, 513, 516, 530.
[5] *Ibid.*, I, 519; also Joseph Baernreither, *Fragmente eines politischen Tagebuches*, (Berlin, 1928), p. 77.

ciprocity." Although, in a number of earlier agreements with Austria, the Russians had given their consent to the eventual annexation of the two provinces, Aehrenthal was evidently much impressed by the willingness of Isvolski to abandon the cause of the southern Slavs. Conrad had for some time been urging the desirability of cooperating with Bulgaria against Serbia and the ultimate division of Serbia between the two, Austria to incorporate the territory as far south as Nish. Aehrenthal had looked upon this as the only method of satisfactorily cleaning out "the Serbian revolutionary nest," but apparently it was not until August 1908 that he began to regard the solution as a matter of practical politics. Isvolski's attitude, together with the uncertainty resulting from the Young Turk Revolution of July 23, 1908, evidently led him to believe that some such settlement, followed by the establishment of a southern Slav state within a reorganized "trialistic" Hapsburg Monarchy, might be possible.

Both sides were, even at this time, playing a fast game. Isvolski said nothing of his plans to his ally France, or to his friend England. He did not even consult Stolypin, the vigorous president of the Russian council, whose opposition he had reason to fear. All intent upon the realization of his scheme to open the Straits to Russian warships, he was prepared to resort to any method. In February and again in the first days of August 1908 he had suggested in the council that some pretext be found for an attack upon Turkey, but on both occasions Stolypin had vetoed his proposals on the ground that mobilization in Russia would only add strength to the revolutionary movement and that "any policy other than a strictly defensive one would be the evil dream of an abnormal government and would spell disaster for the dynasty." [6] The little Slav brothers in the Balkans did not concern Isvolski at all. Russia's policy, he had told the Duma in April, must be dictated by a healthy egoism—by which he meant, as he said to the German ambassador, that Russia must not allow herself to be misled by exaggerated emotions and by anxiety for the fate of the other Slav peoples to the detriment of purely Russian interests. He was simply hypnotized by the idea of securing the opening of the Straits for Russian ships, al-

[6] M. Pokrowski, *Drei Konferenzen* (Hamburg, 1920), pp. 17–30; E. A. Adamov, *Konstantinopel i Prolivi* (Moscow, 1925), I, 8–10; Gunther Frantz, "Die Meerengenfrage in der Vorkriegspolitik Russlands," *Deutsche Rundschau* (February 1927), pp. 146–147.

though in Russian government circles there was considerable doubt whether such a concession was desirable or worthwhile.

The negotiations between Russia and Austria in July and August, and the development of the international situation after the Young Turk Revolution, resulted in the decision of the Austrian government to carry through the annexation. The plan was to take the wind out of the sails of the Serbian agitators by granting the two provinces some sort of constitution, and to obviate the danger of a reassertion of sovereignty by the Turks by severing the last tie between the provinces and the Ottoman Empire. A meeting between Isvolski and Aehrenthal was arranged for, though only with considerable difficulty. Aehrenthal was still angry about the attitude taken by the Russians in the Sanjak railway affair, and Isvolski was filled with distrust of the Austrian and of his Balkan schemes. The famous interview took place on September 16, 1908, at Buchlau, where the two statesmen conferred in private for fully six hours. Exactly what was said and what was decided upon will perhaps remain forever a mystery, since there was no witness. We do know, however, that the two statesmen "laid the Treaty of Berlin on the table, read it and reread it, page by page, article by article, the whole length and breadth of it, from one end to the other, not once, but twice, beginning with the beginning and then starting over again from the end." [7] Russian consent to the annexation of the two provinces was promised in return for Austrian approval of Russia's desires in the Straits question, under certain conditions. It seems fairly clear that Aehrenthal indicated that the annexation would take place in the near future, and that he agreed, at least in principle, to the eventual convocation of a European conference to approve the changes made by the Russian-Austrian bargain. But it is equally clear that at Buchlau the two statesmen did not deal frankly and honestly with each other, as one of Aehrenthal's acquaintances remarked.

The annexation was publicly announced by the Austrian government on October 6. Through an indiscretion on the part of the Austrian ambassador to Paris, the French government knew of it on October 3, and it now appears that Aehrenthal had also informed Sir Charles Hardinge, the English under-secretary for foreign affairs, by private letter on the same day. Even then it was no surprise. The newspapers had

[7] Statement made immediately afterwards by Isvolski's secretary and quoted by Philippe Crozier, "L'Autriche et l'avant-guerre," *Revue de France* (Apr. 15, 1921).

been filled with rumors for weeks and the step to be taken by Austria had long since become a "roaring whisper." Isvolski, who had spent the intervening period in visiting Schoen, the German foreign secretary, and Tittoni, the Italian statesman, got the news only as he reached Paris. Undoubtedly he would have preferred to approach the French and English statesmen himself, but he does not appear to have been much exercised by Aehrenthal's action. He had already seen Milovanovic, the Serbian foreign minister, and had left him in despair. In Paris he spoke to Vesnic, the Serb representative, and administered "some cooling medicine." While Vesnic declared the annexation to be a "great national catastrophe" and a menace to peace in the Balkans, Isvolski assured him that he had foreseen the Austrian action and asserted that the excitement of the Serbs was incomprehensible, that the Serbs were in actual fact losing nothing, while they were gaining Russian support.

But before long Isvolski changed his tone, when he learned from St. Petersburg that Stolypin and the government were opposed to recognition of the Austrian action and that the press would not hear of the abandonment of Russia's "Holy of Holies," the Slav idea. The Russian minister was practically forced to deny his past and himself go back on the agreement with Aehrenthal, although obviously this involved the ultimate failure of his plan to open the Straits. He therefore denied that Russia had given her consent to the annexation and insisted on a European conference to discuss the matter and consider what compensation should be granted to other powers. It was his last chance to secure what he wanted. If the friendly arrangement with Austria had fallen flat, perhaps the end could be attained by international pressure.

French statesmen took an attitude of the greatest reserve, deciding to leave the English to settle with Isvolski. The idea of a conference appealed to them, because they had hopes that a preliminary agreement could be reached between Russia, France, England, Italy, and Turkey, and that Austria and her ally, Germany, could once again be isolated and out-voted as at Algeciras. But the English position was unusually difficult. The statesmen in London resented having been left in the dark and they distrusted Isvolski.[8] With the merits of the question they had little concern. "Quite seriously," wrote the *Saturday Review* on October 10, "what has been done is so obviously the right thing,

---

8 John Morley, *Recollections* (New York, 1917), II, 277: "There has been such a quantity of intrigue, secrecy and downright lying that we don't know whether we stand on firm ground or on treacherous bog."

that, except for the breach of diplomatic etiquette and the sentimental offence to the Turkish party of reform, every sensible man should approve it . . . Those who hope to gain by fishing in troubled waters will prefer a conference; those who want a quiet settlement will prefer an exchange of notes." Even the Russian proposals in regard to the Straits did not, in the abstract, upset them, and they had long since indicated their willingness to make concessions on this point. The crux of the matter with them was that Austria by the annexation, and Bulgaria by her declaration of independence, had upset the status quo, that Isvolski's secret parleys with Aehrenthal had revealed the basic weakness of the Anglo-Russian entente, that the Central Powers were about to score a great success, and that, above all, the recent developments threatened to undermine the new influence acquired by England in Turkey after the revolution.

All this was made clear to Isvolski when he came to London. Sir Edward Grey pleaded with him that the moment was very inopportune for the realization of his plans. "Turkey was hurt and sore at the slight put upon her by Austria and Bulgaria. It was hard enough that she should suffer this at the outset of what we hoped was a new and better era at Constantinople. We could not agree to add to her hardships by forcing upon her at once the embarrassing question of the Straits." [9] Isvolski finally agreed to delete the Straits clause from the projected program of the conference, but urged some concession on the part of the English. Twice the matter was before the cabinet. The King, Sir Edward Grey, Asquith, and many other ministers were in favor of acquiescence, but feared the force of public opinion. There was no advantage in the English right of ingress, they were agreed on that. "It is already a settled principle of naval warfare with us that in no case would our fleets enter the Straits unless Turkey were our ally. The condition of reciprocity, however, is a shop-window ware, since the public do not understand these strategical considerations," wrote Hardinge. So Isvolski had to content himself with a compromise. In case of war, if Turkey were not involved, the Straits should be opened to all alike. In any case Russia was to reach an agreement with the Turks and no pressure should be applied at Constantinople. The attitude of the Turks was perfectly clear, so that Isvolski had little to hope for. He left London a disappointed man, with nothing to console him except the compliments of

---

[9] Edward Grey, *Twenty-five Years* (London, 1925), I, 172.

the English press upon his abnegation, self-restraint, and loyalty, and the assurances of Grey that he was not opposed to the Russian desires in principle: "On the contrary, I positively desire to see an arrangement made, which will open the Straits on terms which would be acceptable to Russia and to the riverain states of the Black Sea, while not placing Turkey or outside Powers at an unfair disadvantage."

With that Isvolski's scheme had fallen flat and he was a broken man. Both King Edward and Grey wrote letters to St. Petersburg supporting him in order maintain him in office and avoid the humiliation of his defeat. The game was already up and the rest of the crisis is the story of the play of two rival groups of powers centering on the question of recognition of the Austrian action. On the side of the Entente the policy was positively an insane one, because the two groups were in no sense equally matched. Austria was backed to the limit by Germany and both these powers would have taken recourse to arms if necessary. Not that the Germans were favorably impressed by Aehrenthal's high-handedness. The Kaiser, who learned of the annexation later than the chief of any other state, was bitter in his denunciation of the Austrian action and felt that Germany had been duped in the most outrageous fashion. But with the conclusion of the Triple Entente, Berlin was practically forced to stand by Austria through thick and thin. "For our attitude in Balkan affairs the needs, interests and wishes of Austria are decisive," Bülow had written before the crisis. He now demanded "la loyauté sans phrase," and the Kaiser agreed that it was the only course Germany could follow. Vienna was told that even in the event that difficulties and complications should arise, Germany's ally could count upon her. In a few words, Austria's humiliation would be Germany's humiliation.

As the crisis developed negotiations were opened between the German and Austrian general staffs to determine the conditions of the campaign if war should result. In a letter to Conrad dated January 21, 1909, the German chief of staff, Count Moltke, stated that Germany would support Austria if the latter were attacked by Russia. This was in accord with the terms of the treaty of 1879. But Moltke went on to envisage the possibility of an Austrian invasion of Serbia to put an end to Serbian provocation. "I believe," he said, "that only an Austrian invasion of Serbia would bring about eventual intervention by Russia. In that event the *casus fœderis* would arise for Germany." What it amounts to is this, that Moltke recognized an attack by Russia upon Austria resulting from an Austrian invasion of Serbia as obligating Germany to

84

support Austria. It has been claimed that this represents an extension of the alliance beyond the sense given it by Bismarck, but it should be remembered that Moltke, though his letter was approved by the Kaiser and Bülow, could not in this way bind the German government.[10] Arrangements of this kind were frequently discussed and made by the general staffs of all countries. Furthermore, it should be noted that while Bismarck refused to support Austria if she provoked Russia, the situation in 1887 was fundamentally different, and even Bismarck in his heart of hearts was determined to rescue Austria from defeat in any case, for he regarded the continued existence of the Dual Monarchy as a great power as a primary interest of Germany. The crucial point is that Bismarck, unlike Moltke, scrupulously avoided informing the Austrians of his ultimate intentions. But it cannot be denied that the existence of the Triple Entente had put Germany in a position where she thought she had to support Austria and Austrian policy in the Balkans, almost *sans phrase*. The German statesmen genuinely feared that Austria might go over to Russia with "flying banners."

Both Russia and England knew, in 1908, that Germany was determined to go the limit, for the Germans told Grey and Isvolski on numerous occasions just how they viewed the situation. The English, at least, did not resent this. In fact, Grey told the German ambassador that he understood the German attitude "because it was what we should have done in Germany's place." What the English were concerned with was their position in Turkey and above all the future of the entente with Russia. They knew all about Isvolski, but felt that they had to do their best to support him, such as he was. While greatly desiring a naval agreement with Germany they felt that the Russian friendship was more important: "We have no pending questions with Germany, except that of naval construction, while our whole future in Asia is bound up with the necessity of maintaining the best and most friendly relations with Russia. We cannot afford to sacrifice in any way our entente with Russia—even for the sake of a reduced naval program," wrote Hardinge.

The English, then, were determined to back the Russians, just as the Germans were clear as to the necessity of backing Austria. The great difference was that the English, from the start, had limited their sup-

[10] H. Kanner, *Der Schlüssel zur Kriegsschuldfrage* (Munich, 1926), and the review by S. B. Fay in *American Historical Review*, XXXII (January 1927), 317–319.

port to diplomatic assistance. It was the only thing to do, for the English public would certainly have refused to support the government in any more adventurous policy, and the Russians were so notoriously unable to fight after the disasters of the Japanese war that Isvolski himself had told Aehrenthal at the outset that Russia would not make the annexation a *casus belli*. As for the French, they were never more disinclined to fight for Russia on the Balkan issue. Clemenceau was literally haunted with the fear of European complications, which, in the last count, would compel France to bear the brunt of the German attack. In fact the French seem to have had hopes of eventually weaning Austria from her alliance to Germany much as they had already drawn Italy away from the Triple Alliance.[11]

In international affairs it is not good policy to announce in advance that you cannot or will not fight. This is what the powers of the Triple Entente did, and consequently their defeat diplomatically was a foregone conclusion. The English, from the start, were exposed to a serious setback in supporting Russia, for Isvolski was determined to have his revenge. He fulminated against Aehrenthal to anyone who would listen, and people who came in contact with him in these months found him "suffocating with indignation." Russia no longer had anything to hope for from a conference excepting the humiliation of Austria. But Isvolski saw an opportunity for revenge in pressing the case of the Serbs, who from the beginning had taken the view that they were entitled to compensation, a claim which the Austrians naturally denied. Aehrenthal at first paid comparatively little attention to the Serbs and concentrated on an agreement with the Turks. His theory was that once the Turks had been satisfied the other powers no longer had a leg to stand on. In February 1909 the arrangement with the Turks was complete and the Austrians were able to devote themselves to the Serbian problem.

There was not the slightest indication that the Serbs would yield. Their attitude was throughout a reckless one. Even before the annexation the Serbian foreign minister, Milovanovic, who was an unusually moderate man, had spoken to the English representative in terms of despair, saying that many Serbs felt that an adventure, even with the certainty of defeat, could not make the situation worse: "Even if the

[11] Philippe Crozier, "L'Autriche et l'avant guerre," *Revue de France* (June 1, 1921), pp. 576–617; Raymond Poincaré, *Au Service de la France* (Paris, 1926), I, 245 ff.

Austrian armies swept Serbia and she was annexed to the Dual Monarchy, her patriots would at least have the satisfaction of feeling that they were united with their brethren now under Austrian and Hungarian rule." After the annexation the Serb policy was unequivocal: "Either we shall make Serbia a huge cemetery or we shall make Greater Serbia," said one Belgrade paper.

Neither Germany nor England cared much about the Serbian claims. "Germany had little interest in the fate of Serbia, but she had a great one in the fate of Austria-Hungary. She would stand by her ally and protect her if necessary," said the German ambassador in Vienna. And Grey wrote: "I have not, myself, much sympathy with the clamour of Serbia and Montenegro for territorial compensation. If they are afraid of the Austrian advance, they had better sit still, put their own houses in order, make friends with Turkey and hope that she will get strong under the new régime. But I do not want to cold-shoulder Isvolski on the Serbian question, if the Russians are keen about it." In actual fact the Russians were not keen about Serbian claims as such. Isvolski's attitude has already been discussed. The Tsar's was not far different. To the German naval attaché he said that Serbia and Montenegro were comparatively indifferent to him. The point was that Isvolski saw in Serbia the instrument of his revenge and so Serbia became the focus of the situation. Whereas Isvolski had originally put aside the Serbian pretensions as impossible, he now began to encourage the Serbs to hope for compensation at the expense of Austria. It is true that he warned them about precipitating war, but at the same time he strengthened them in an aspiration which could be realized only by war. When the Serbian Crown Prince and Pashitch came to St. Petersburg they were given advice that could be interpreted in various ways. The Tsar said to the English ambassador: "I told him that because you consider yourself injured that is no reason why you should crack your skull against a stone wall. You can gain nothing by that. You say that there are many Serbians under foreign domination: but do you think that this is a grievance peculiar to your country?" But we know that he also said that the Bosnian question could be settled only by war and that he would not recognize the annexation. The Tsar regarded an eventual conflict between Germanism and Slavdom as inevitable.

The English knew that the Russians had given the Serbs great encouragement, but Grey had promised to support the Russian position and he stuck by his promise. At the same time he backed the Russians in urging upon Serbia a defensive alliance with Bulgaria and Turkey to block the Austrian advance, a matter concerning which a great deal is to be learned from the British documents. The upshot is that the tension between Serbia and Austria became greater and greater, till in February and March 1909 it seemed more than likely that war would result. Conrad urged this course eloquently, but Aehrenthal had given up his idea of settling the Serbian question by dividing the country between Austria and Bulgaria, and was now determined to effect a peaceful settlement if possible. In the end the English used their utmost influence to mediate, and finally found a satisfactory formula for the note which the Serbs were to hand in at Vienna. The solution came in the nick of time, for the Austrians had just decided to mobilize and make war.

By this time the Russian policy had collapsed completely. In order to bring the crisis to an end Aehrenthal threatened to publish certain compromising documents which would have exposed Isvolski and his scheming. The Russians asked the Germans for good offices, but when the Germans presented a note enquiring whether Russia would agree to recognize the annexation by an exchange of notes should Austria request it, Isvolski could not bring himself to make the sacrifice. After some delay the Germans followed their first note by a second, couched in stiff language, and Isvolski gave in. He had not consulted either France or England, who had no objection to the German suggestion, but desired to make recognition of the annexation dependent on a satisfactory settlement of the Austro-Serbian crisis. Recognition in advance would have deprived them of the last leg they had to stand on, for it would have deprived the Serb claim of all justification. But here again they could not be too outspoken in their reproaches of Isvolski, who insisted that the German summons was the equivalent of a "diplomatic ultimatum." The Austro-German alliance, he claimed, had obviously been extended to include the Balkans, and Austria "was browbeating Russia through Germany." A Russian refusal would have led to an immediate attack on Serbia by Austria and perhaps an attack on Russia by Germany. France had left him entirely in the lurch. Her attitude was tantamount to a denunciation of the Franco-Russian Alliance.

The English were not deceived by these jeremiads. They had replied to the German note by making acceptance of the annexation conditional on the Austro-Serbian settlement, and the French had done likewise. "Had he [Isvolski] given a reply such as we gave to Metternich, it would have been impossible for the Germans to base an ultimatum upon it," wrote Hardinge. "In that event," wrote Grey, "there would have been no war—the result would have been just as it is now . . . The result [of the crisis] would not have been so bad, if only Isvolski had withstood German hustling for forty-eight hours." Finding that he had not made a very good impression, Isvolski himself soon changed his mind. "Russia had received nothing more than a temporary diplomatic check and this was preferable to having been launched into war which might have had disastrous consequences," he told Nicolson, and later on he denied everything, describing himself "as the innocent lamb who had been destroyed by the wicked wolf." As for the reputed German ultimatum "he asserted that nothing approaching an ultimatum had been delivered to him; in fact, Germany had acted in a friendly spirit and had merely declared that if war broke out between Austria and Russia it would be very difficult for her not to stand by her ally . . . In fact, Pourtalès came to Isvolski like a cooing dove bearing a message of peace." On this note we may close.

The analogy between the crisis of 1908–1909 and the crisis of July 1914 has often been drawn. In both cases there was acute tension between Austria and Serbia, arising in large measure from the corroding Serbian propaganda against the Monarchy. In 1909 Austria all but declared war; in July 1914 she took the fatal step. On both occasions Germany supported her ally, while attempting to localize the conflict. England, on the other hand, backed Russia, which amounted to the generalization of the crisis.

So much for the points of similarity. They must not be pressed too hard. The situation in 1908–1909 was fundamentally different from that of 1914. King Edward is reputed to have said that England in 1908 had fine friends: the one, Russia, could not fight, while the other, France, would not. From the start Isvolski had announced that Russia would not fight, and it seems more than doubtful whether she could have done so even if Austria had attacked Serbia. The French, while asserting their loyalty to the alliance, made it sufficiently clear that they did not approve of the Russian tactics, and here, too, there is room for grave doubt whether they would actually have gone the limit in supporting Russia.[12] England was consistent throughout, but had de-

[12] In February Isvolski maintained that France had gone over to Austria "bag and baggage." On March 23 he told Nicolson that Russia had "no reason for trusting to the cooperation of France were she disposed to push matters to extremities."

clared at the very beginning that she would not go beyond diplomatic support. In 1914, on the other hand, the Russians were ready to fight and there was no Stolypin to hold them back by reasonable arguments. The French, even if they did not actually encourage the Russians, certainly did little enough to hold them back. The English, too, were prepared to see the thing through, however much they may have desired to avoid the conflict.

The crisis in 1908 was due in very large measure to the scheming and intrigue of Isvolski. Aehrenthal's tactics were not sound and certainly not commendable, but the more we learn about Isvolski the more it appears that he was "a very unscrupulous and unreliable man" to use the words of Sir Charles Hardinge. Mendacious to the last degree, high-strung and emotional, he was constantly engaged on selfish projects which were based upon ruthless lack of consideration for others, friends as well as foes. Under normal conditions his disavowal and dismissal would have been a matter of course. But he had to be held and he had to be supported, because Europe, in 1908 as in 1914, was divided into two hostile camps, each of which dreaded disruption and humiliation and in each of which the members had to be prepared to fight on an issue in which they had no direct interest. In 1908 the new-born entente was not ready for the conflict, but the scene was set. In 1914 the preparations were complete and it took only the least impulse to set the European cart going on the road to perdition.

Somewhat later he asserted that France had made it clear that she would not lend material support. His apologist explains (Vox et Praeterea Nihil, *Fortnightly Review* [September 1909]) that the French press had not been given a "refresher nor a retaining fee."

4

Russia, the Straits Question and the Origins of the Balkan League, 1908–1912

1928

In 1908 Alexander Isvolski, the Russian foreign minister, had, like many of his predecessors, fallen a victim to the intrigue, jealousy, and diversity of views which were so characteristic of the old régime.[1] He had assumed office in 1906 with a clean-cut program of action: to effect the return to Europe after the disastrous Far Eastern adventure, and to reestablish Russian influence in the Near East by securing for his country the free passage of her ships of war through the Bosporus and Dardanelles. His plan was to prepare the way by negotiations with the powers, and the Anglo-Russian agreement of 1907 was merely the first step in a policy which the Russian minister had hoped to crown by his interviews with Aehrenthal at Buchlau, with Schoen at Berchtesgaden and with Tittoni at Desio. The Young Turk Revolution had upset his plans somewhat, and he was told in London that the English government could not and would not support any scheme which failed to meet with the free approval of the Porte and thus put an abrupt end to the newly acquired influence of the English at Constantinople. This part of the program might, in the end, have been satisfactorily arranged, but Isvolski was obliged to shelve the whole Straits policy because of the opposition to his plan which developed in St. Petersburg during his absence.

There was no unity of opinion in Russia in regard to the advisability or desirability of changing the existing Straits convention, and Nelidov, a friend of Isvolski, had seen his own plan brought to grief in 1896 because of the opposition of Witte and Pobiedonostsev. In order to avoid complications and futile discussions, Isvolski had embarked upon his policy without consulting any of his colleagues, though he had, of

---

Note: Reprinted from *Political Science Quarterly*, XLIII (September 1928), 321–363.
[1] See "Russia, the Straits Question and the European Powers 1904–1908." [Part I, Number 2, of this volume.]

course, secured the approval of the Tsar. It was his misfortune that his assistant, Charykov, was also his rival, and seized the earliest opportunity to let the cat out of the bag, so to speak. Stolypin, the prime minister, Kokovtsev, the minister of finance, and General Roediger, the minister of war, were apprised of what was going on, and immediately joined in a vigorous protest to the Tsar. They were flatly opposed to the pursuit of an active policy at a time when Russia was militarily quite unprepared, but what they objected to particularly was the idea of bartering Russia's consent to the annexation of Bosnia and Herzegovina by Austria for concessions in the Straits question. Stolypin may not have been an expert in matters of foreign policy, but he had been brought up in the Slavophil tradition and firmly believed in Russia's historic mission to liberate and protect the little Slav brothers in the Balkans. To allow a Catholic power like Austria to annex two Slavic Orthodox provinces without protesting would amount to treason to the Slavic cause. By threatening to resign Stolypin forced a change in policy and obliged Isvolski to withhold recognition of Austria's action. Though he failed to have a stop put to the negotiations in regard to the Straits he ruined the foreign minister's chances of success by obliging him to go back on his agreement with Aehrenthal and thus knocked out the keystone of the whole structure.

When Isvolski returned to St. Petersburg his colleagues heaped reproaches upon him. They spoke of a "diplomatic Tsushima" for which he was responsible, and nicknamed him the "Prince of the Bosporus." He himself felt like a ruined man, and offered to resign. The Tsar, who sympathized with his aims, induced him to stay, but he considered himself merely as a *chinovnik* in uniform, not as a foreign minister. Indeed, it was said that he was obliged to promise to submit his policy to the approval of the prime minister in the future.[2] Apparently he never learned of Charykov's duplicity and really held Aehrenthal accountable for his discomfiture. At any rate the only possible course for him to pursue was to join in the general outcry against the Austrian action and, if possible, to outdo his fellow countrymen in their indictment of Russia's rival. Personal rancor together with an insurmountable suspicion of Austrian plans became the determining motives in Isvolski's policy after 1908.

[2] Johannes Lepsius, Albrecht Mendelssohn-Bartholdy and Friedrich Thimme, eds., *Die Grosse Politik der europäischen Kabinette, 1871–1914* (Berlin, 1922–1926), XXVI (pt. 1), no. 9185 note.

For the time being, however, he was in entire eclipse, discredited and distrusted. Charykov, who had worked hand in glove with Stolypin, saw a free field for the exercise of his own policy, which he had worked out just as carefully as Isvolski had worked out his own scheme. He had had long experience at Eastern posts and was known to be narrow-mindedly Pan-Slavic, a typical Russian agent in the Orient, strongly tinged with the disease which afflicted most of them, as one of his acquaintances put it.[3] Like Isvolski he was wedded to the idea of opening the Straits for Russian warships, but he was quite out of sympathy with his chief's westernism. Instead of buying the approval of the powers by various concessions he meant to attempt a revival of the Treaty of Unkiar Skelessi of 1833, which had practically established a Russian protectorate over the Ottoman Empire. In order to attain this end he, like Isvolski, was quite ready to sacrifice the interests of the southern Slav states, the difference being that the foreign minister was prepared to sacrifice these interests to the great powers, while his assistant was ready to sacrifice them to the Turks. The one hoped to open the Straits by negotiating with the powers first and then forcing the settlement upon the Porte, the other dreamed of "guillotining the Turks by persuasion" to use a phrase of Gabriel Hanotaux, and ignoring the powers, on the theory that the whole question of the Straits was one which concerned only Russia and the Turkish government. Neither showed any of the simple-minded and thoroughly sincere solicitude for the little Slav brothers which is so characteristic of the Stolypin group.

Immediately after the Austrian annexation of Bosnia had been announced Charykov had begun to exploit the tension between the Austrian and Turkish governments. He approached the Turks with the proposal that they open the Straits to Russian warships and take in return a Russian guarantee of their territory and Russian support in opposition to Austria. The Turks were suspicious and realized only too well that Russian warships in the Bosporus would mean, sooner or later, the domination of the Muscovite over Constantinople and the whole em-

[3] *G.P.*, XXV (pt. 2), nos. 8707, 8725. N. V. Charykov: born 1855; entered the foreign service in 1875 and took part in the war against Turkey; representative at Bokhara, 1883–1890; secretary at Constantinople, 1890; chargé in Egypt, 1891; counsellor at Berlin, 1893; diplomatic agent at Sofia, 1896; minister to the Vatican, 1897; minister to Belgrade, 1900; minister to Holland, 1907; assistant to the foreign minister, 1908–1909; ambassador to Constantinople, 1909–1912. On his character see the estimate of Nekludov in *Carnets de Georges Louis* (Paris, 1926), I, 167; J. von Szilassy, *Der Untergang der Donaumonarchie* (Berlin, 1921), p. 186; H. Friedjung, *Das Zeitalter des Imperialismus* (Berlin, 1922), II, 219.

pire. Discovering that the support of England could be relied upon, they rejected the Russian advances. Obviously the ground had not been adequately prepared, so Charykov adopted a more circuitous course. The Russians would attempt to iron out the difficulties between Bulgaria and Turkey and would attempt to form a huge Balkan bloc to act as a barrier to the Austrian advance. In preparation for the favorable reception of the Russian proposals in regard to the Straits, the press had already been singing the praises of the new régime in Constantinople. Now, on October 14, the *Novoie Vremia*, a leading nationalist organ, came forward with the new policy:

> Russia, having shown repugnance to derive selfish profit at Turkey's expense from the spoliation of the Slav provinces, and being therefore in a position to enjoy the confidence of the Balkan Slavs and Turkey, should encourage the idea of a Balkan Confederation under Turkish hegemony, as the best method of safeguarding Balkan interests and providing the necessary counterpoise to Austria.

On the following day the same newspaper published a direct plea for a close understanding:

> Russia and Turkey have shed more of each other's blood than was necessary. The time has come to understand that sincere friendship on the basis of mutual interests will render more profit to each than futile reminiscences of buried feuds. Muscovites and Osmanlis are really nearer each other than anybody else.

Other newspapers took up the cry and united in declaring that a national policy in the Near East, based on the interests of the Russians and Slavs, could not be other than friendly to a regenerate Turkey.[4]

The program had obvious advantages: it was sufficiently anti-Austrian to appeal to any Russian; its Turcophilism would find favor in England; it promised to prevent the outbreak of hostilities in the Balkans at a time when Russia could not hope to take part; and finally it offered the only prospect of securing what both Isvolski and Charykov desired most; the opening of the Straits. Isvolksi's position demanded that he subscribe to the nationalist view, and so he identified himself with the plan. In his famous Christmas speech in the Duma he openly avowed his adhesion. After emphasizing his friendship for a regenerate Turkey and voicing his hopes for an early agreement between Bulgaria and the Porte, he continued, amid cries of "Bravo!":

[4] Reported in *The Times* (London), Oct. 15, 16, 24, 1908.

We clearly intimated to Bulgaria that our future relations with her will depend, not upon her conduct in the past, but on her conduct in the future, so far as she may remain faithful to the solidarity of the other Slav States in the Balkan Peninsula. Gentlemen, we addressed the same counsels to Serbia and Montenegro. These three states must become imbued with the consciousness of the necessity of moral and political union. Our aim must be to bring them together and combine them with Turkey in a common ideal of defence of their national and economic development . . . With this aim we must show Turkey our good will towards her efforts to renovate her internal organization, and, above all, must make it clear that we do not menace her security. But the above-mentioned object is attainable only on one condition—that events in the Balkan Peninsula are allowed to develop peacefully.[5]

While his audience hailed the new policy with the greatest enthusiasm, the speech was received in Berlin and Vienna with profound scepticism. Isvolski, it was said, was merely trying to frighten his adversaries by conjuring up a bogey.[6] After all, the idea of a Balkan confederation was not new. It ran like a red thread through the history of the Near East in the nineteenth century, from Rhigas and Ypsilanti down. Some plans had called for a purely Slavic union, others for the inclusion of Greece or Rumania. Occasionally even the idea of associating the Turks had been suggested, though this was the most novel part of the Russian program.[7] The important point was that all schemes of

[5] *The Times* (London), Dec. 26, 1908. The substance of the speech was forecast on December 11 by the Berlin *Lokalanzeiger*. Isvolski himself had come to realize the necessity of having Turkey on the right side. See Edward Grey, *Twenty-five Years* (New York, 1925), I, 175; M. Bogitschewitsch, *Kriegsursachen* (Zurich, 1919), p. 159.

[6] *G.P.*, XXVI (pt. 2), nos. 9243, 9295, 9296, 9299, 9302: "Die . . . Kombination eines Balkanbundes inklusive der Türkei mit einer feindlichen Spitze gegen uns möchte ich nicht ernst nehmen" (Aehrenthal); "Nach meiner Ansicht ist der Balkanbund mit oder ohne Türkei eine Utopie" (Marschall); "Einen alle kleineren und grösseren Balkanstaaten umfassenden und unter Führung der Türkei einhermarschierenden Bund kann sich nur eine krankhafte Phantasie als etwas in die Wirklichkeit Umzusetzendes vorstellen" (Bülow).

[7] On the numerous early projects for a Balkan confederation see especially M. R. Ivanovitch, "The Future of the Balkans," *Fortnightly Review* (June 1909), pp. 1040–58; V. Viktorov-Toporov, "Balkanskie soglasheniia i soiuzy," *Russkaia Mysl* (April 1915), pp. 123 ff.; R. Pinon, *L'Europe et la jeune Turquie* (Paris, 1911), pp. 446 ff.; K. Nicolaides, *Griechenlands Anteil an den Balkankriegen* (Vienna, 1914), pp. 16 ff.; J. D. Bourchier in *The Times* (London), June 4, 1913; R. W. Seton-Watson, *The Rise of Nationality in the Balkans* (London, 1917), pp. 144 ff.; E. Jäckh, *Deutschland im Orient nach dem Balkankrieg* (Munich, 1913), pp. 105 ff.; D. Mitrany, "The Possibility of a Balkan Locarno," *International Conciliation*, no. 229 (April 1927), pp. 23 ff. According to Izzet Pascha, *Denkwürdigkeiten*

union even against the Turk had been frustrated by the rivalries and dissensions long existing between the various states. Was the prospect of success any better now? Rumania was known to be in alliance with Austria, and made a point of cultivating the friendship of the Turk in order to maintain a check upon Bulgarian aspirations. The Bulgarians, Serbs, and Greeks all had their eyes riveted on the Turkish province of Macedonia, and had for years been cutting each other's throats in the secluded mountain fastnesses. The Bulgars and Serbs had been bitter enemies since the day of Slivnitza in 1885, and the Bulgars were now on the verge of war with the Turks, while the Serbs were breathing fire and flame at the Austrians. Bulgaria had no quarrel with Vienna, while the Serbs had a real interest in maintaining good relations with the Porte, at least until an outlet had been secured on the Adriatic. As for the Greeks, their quarrel with the Turks on the Cretan question was a long-standing one and continued to color the relations between the two countries. To iron out all these difficulties would require a master mind indeed.

As a matter of fact Isvolski himself had no faith in the program. He was simply blowing Charykov's horn in order to drown out criticism of himself and convince public opinion that he had been misjudged. A huge Balkan confederation directed against Austria was a pious wish at best. Meanwhile more immediate problems were urgently demanding a solution. Russia's defeat would be turned into complete disaster unless some obstacle could be placed in the way of Aehrenthal's victorious advance. Isvolski therefore did all that was humanly possible to frustrate the Austrian attempt to reach a separate agreement with the Porte. But even more important was the Bulgarian question. It was in Sofia that the key to the whole situation lay, for while the Serbs could be counted on by Russia, and the Rumanians were hopelessly enthralled to Austria, Bulgaria had for years been wavering between Austria and Russia. Prince Ferdinand had long since discovered that a policy of having two irons in the fire was most likely to yield results. With great adroitness he had led the Russians on and held them off at the same time. Isvolski was not unaware of the crucial nature of Bulgaria's position, and for some time attempts had been made to negotiate a military convention to replace the outworn pact of 1902. In fact,

---

des Marschalls Izzet Pascha (Leipzig, 1927), p. 89, Abdul Hamid was himself considering a league with the Balkan states just before the revolution.

during the weeks preceding the Bulgarian declaration of independence Ferdinand had been pressed to accept a plan of joint action.[8] But the wily Coburger knew Russia only too well. He preferred to act independently and before making his final decision he visited not St. Petersburg, but Budapest. Isvolski was enraged by this treasonable action. but he could not afford to carry his resentment too far. He quickly became reconciled to the inevitable and remembered that Bulgarian independence had long been a cardinal aim of Russian policy.[9] At any cost Bulgaria must be prevented from going to war with the Turks, for such a conflict might well end with the Bulgarians at Constantinople, all at a time when Russia was militarily helpless. Isvolski therefore exerted himself to the utmost to smooth out the problems at issue between Sofia and Constantinople and to draw both powers to the Russian side in order to prevent their falling into the clutches of Austria.

But the players on the other side were hardly less adroit than Isvolski himself. The Turks were more afraid of the Russian and the Bulgarian designs than of the Austrians. They gently evaded the Serbian offers of an alliance against the Bulgarians, and, through the Young Turk press, cajoled the Russians while they negotiated a settlement with Vienna.[10] Ferdinand, on the other hand, could see no harm in making a *beau geste* to Russia. He had no intention of going to war, and was interested merely in exploiting an enviable situation. In February 1909 he journeyed to St. Petersburg, allowed himself to be recognized as Tsar of the Bulgarians and listened to the seductive proposals made to him. Isvolski, who had just proclaimed to the world his love for the reformed Turk and the need for peaceful cooperation in the

[8] A. L. Popov, ed., "Diplomaticheskaia Podgotovka Balkanskoi Voiny 1912 g.," *Krasnyi Arkhiv*, VIII (1925), 8. Popov published these important documents with an introduction in two installments of *Krasnyi Arkhiv:* VIII (1925), 3–48, and IX (1925), 3–31. A number have been published in German translation in *Die Kriegsschuldfrage*, December 1925.

[9] Bogitschewitsch, *Kriegsursachen*, pp. 153, 157, 163; *G.P.*, XXVI (pt. 1), no. 8977; XXVI (pt. 2), chap. 202 *passim*.

[10] On the Serbian offers of an alliance against Bulgaria see Bourchier in *The Times* (London), June 11, 1913; B. Molden, *Graf Aehrenthal* (Stuttgart, 1917), pp. 78, 94; *G.P.*, XXVI (pt. 1), no. 9026; B. Schwertfeger, ed., *Zur europäischen Politik* (Berlin, 1919), III, 174; L. von Chlumecky, "Politische Uebersicht," *Oesterreichische Rundschau* (Oct. 21–29, 1908); Izzet Pascha, *Denkwürdigkeiten*, p. 107. There was also much talk of an alliance between Greece and Turkey against Bulgaria. See E. Driault and M. Lhéritier, *Histoire diplomatique de la Grèce* (Paris, 1926), V, 8, 13. On the Young Turk press see the interesting quotations in A. Mandelstam, *Le Sort de l'Empire Ottoman* (Paris, 1917), pp. 56–58; also *G.P.*, XXVI (pt. 2), nos. 9243, 9244, 9295; *The Times* (London), Oct. 22, 1908.

Balkans, now showed his real aims. Ferdinand was encouraged to hope for Russian support in realizing Bulgaria's aspirations in Macedonia at the expense of the Turk. In writing to the Russian minister at Sofia, Isvolski revealed his hand completely: "The Constantinople *rayon* and the Straits come into the exclusive sphere of Russian interests," he pointed out. Bulgaria "will have the right to strive for the expansion of her boundaries to the extent of the San Stefano Bulgaria," while Serbia might have "territories that give her access to the coast of the Adriatic Sea."

Ferdinand allowed the Russians to settle the Bulgarian dispute with the Porte at Russian expense, but, while in St. Petersburg this was regarded as a great victory, the wary Balkan ruler had no intention of selling himself to the Muscovites.[11] In vain Isvolski waited for concrete Bulgarian proposals in regard to an alliance. Nothing came of the agreement which had been decided on "in principle." At the same time the Serbs were to meet with disappointment. No doubt instigated by the Russians, they had opened negotiations in Sofia. Whereas in October 1908 they had been willing to aid the Turks against the Bulgarians, they were now prepared to make an agreement with their rivals at the expense of the Turks. Milovanovic, the able Serbian foreign minister, went to Sofia in March and opened *pourparlers* which continued until June. The ultimate object of the Serbs was, of course, to lay mines against the Austrians, but no agreement was possible without a settlement of conflicting claims in Macedonia. They were ready to plan a partition of the province on terms favorable to the Bulgarians, but the latter had no interest in an anti-Austrian policy and besides were unwilling to entertain the idea of abandoning any part of Macedonia. What they desired was autonomy for the whole province, their hope being that, once the stage of self-government had been reached, the road to union with Bulgaria would be a short one. On this rock the

[11] Popov, *Krasnyi Arkhiv*, VIII, 9–10. On Russia's part in effecting a settlement of the Bulgarian-Turkish dispute see *G.P.*, XXVI (pt. 2), nos. 9314 ff.; Mandelstam, *Le Sort de l'Empire Ottoman*, pp. 109 ff.; Friedjung, *Das Zeitalter des Imperialismus*, II, 254; J. Larmeroux, *La Politique extérieure de l'Autriche-Hongrie* (Paris, 1918), II, 107–108. The Russians were at least successful in forestalling an Austrian attempt to bait the Bulgarians by indicating the possibility of eventually acquiring Serbian territory. See *G.P.*, XXVI (pt. 2), no. 9301; Franz Conrad [von Hötzendorf], *Aus meiner Dienstzeit* (Vienna, 1921), I, 204–205; B. von Siebert, *Diplomatische Aktenstücke zur Geschichte der Ententepolitik der Vorkriegsjahre* (Berlin, 1921), p. 524.

negotiations were once more wrecked.[12] The Serbs thereupon promptly reverted to their earlier approaches to the Porte, only to find that the Turks were no more ready to pursue an anti-Austrian policy than were the Bulgarians. Instead, they were attempting to negotiate an agreement with Rumania.[13]

During the first nine months following the annexation of Bosnia no progress had been made by the Russians toward the establishment of a barrier against Austria or toward the reestablishment of Russian influence at Constantinople. Charykov had been rushed off to the Turkish capital as ambassador, but had been unable to accomplish anything.[14] Obviously the time had come for a return to Isvolski's earlier program of negotiation with the great powers. Already in May 1909 a step had been taken in this direction when a draft treaty to be concluded with Germany was submitted to the Tsar. Under its terms Germany was to join the revived Austro-Russian Treaty of 1897 and was to guarantee Austria's obligation to abstain from all military enterprises in the Balkans. Point IV provided that "pending the establishment by the signatory powers of the Treaty of Berlin of formal sanctions indispensable for a change of the treaty, Germany would lend Russia the effective diplomatic support desirable for a definitive solution of the question of the Straits." [15] Nothing is known of the further history of this project, but certainly the famous Racconigi agreement between Russia and

[12] On these negotiations see especially Popov, *Krasnyi Arkhiv*, VIII, 9; Siebert, *Diplomatische Aktenstücke*, pp. 112, 137–139, 141, 293; S. Sazonov, *Fateful Years* (New York, 1927), pp. 52–53. The anti-Austrian point comes out clearly from Schwertfeger, *Zur europäischen Politik*, III, 172–173, 213–214: "Une combinaison de ce genre fortifierait la position de la Serbie vis-à-vis de la Monarchie Habsbourgeoise"; "Ces tendances, qui sont ouvertement dirigés contre la pénétration du Germanisme dans les Balkans . . ." Similarly Milovanovic to Gruic, April 14, 1909: "Eine serbisch-bulgarische Gemeinsamkeit wäre die erste, unumgängliche Bürgschaft, dass wir bewahrt bleiben vor einer Ueberraschung seitens Oesterreich-Ungarns." See Ger., F.O., *Deutschland Schuldig?* (Berlin, 1919), p. 115. Isvolski's fears of Austrian policy appear from *G.P.*, XXVI (pt. 2), nos. 9552, 9568, 9569; cf. also M. Hoschiller, *L'Europe devant Constantinople* (Paris, 1916), p. 63; V. Valentin, *Deutschlands Aussenpolitik* (Berlin, 1921), p. 111.

[13] Schwertfeger, *Zur europäischen Politik*, III, 174–175; Siebert, *Diplomatische Aktenstücke*, pp. 142–143; *G.P.*, XXVII (pt. 1), nos. 9756, 9760, 9762.

[14] On Charykov's mission and aims at this time see Bogitschewitsch, *Kriegsursachen*, pp. 32–33; *G.P.*, XXVII (pt. 1), nos. 9729, 9730; *Carnets de Georges Louis*, I, 36–37; Nikolaides, *Griechenlands Anteil*, p. 24.

[15] E. Laloy, *Les Documents secrets des archives du ministère des affaires étrangères de Russie* (Paris, 1920), pp. 50–51. Charykov seems to have inspired this move, working on the theory that it would serve to check Austrian designs while Russia was unprepared. See *G.P.*, XXVI (pt. 2), no. 9546.

Italy in October 1909 was quite in accordance with the policy long pursued by Isvolski. It was frankly directed against Austria and aimed at maintaining the status quo in the Balkans. In case the existing situation could not be maintained the Habsburg monarchy was to be excluded from any share in the spoils.[16]

Naturally enough this spectacular meeting gave rise to all sorts of rumors and apprehensions in the Balkans. The Turks renewed their overtures to Austria and Rumania, and even the Slav states were in dread lest the arrangement might prove detrimental to their interests.[17] It was probably for this reason that Hartwig, perhaps the greatest Russian expert on matters concerning the Balkans, was sent to Belgrade to give the necessary reassurance.[18]

During the winter of 1909–1910 the situation continued to be extremely uncertain. While Charykov was hard at work attempting to effect a *rapprochement* between the Balkan states and the Porte, Isvolski renewed his efforts to draw the Bulgarians to the Russian side. In December 1909 a projected treaty was worked out in St. Petersburg. It provided that in case of war between Russia on the one hand and Germany, Austria, and Rumania, or Austria and Rumania on the other hand, or in case of war between Russia and Turkey, no matter which power took the initiative, Bulgaria should, on the demand of Russia, mobilize all her forces and begin operations according to plans previously worked out. Operations should continue until all war aims had been attained and should in no case cease without the consent of the Russian government. In case Bulgaria were attacked by Austria as a result of an alliance with another power not provoked by Bulgaria,

[16] Text of the agreement in R. Marchand, ed., *Un Livre noir* (Paris, n.d.), I, 357. The pact had probably been made informally in September 1908. On the agreement and its implications see *G.P.*, XXVII (pt. 1), nos. 9877 ff.; Siebert, *Diplomatische Aktenstücke*, chap. 11 *passim;* G. Giolitti, *Memoirs of My Life* (London, 1923), pp. 202 ff.

[17] Siebert, *Diplomatische Aktenstücke*, pp. 456–457, 120–121; *G.P.*, XXVII (pt. 1), nos. 9734–44, 9774, 9780–85; Popov, *Krasnyi Arkhiv*, VIII, 9; A Diplomatist [George Young], *Nationalism and War in the Near East* (Oxford, 1915), p. 164. It is extremely difficult to evaluate the advances made by Milovanovic to Aehrenthal at this time. See Molden, *Graf Aehrenthal*, pp. 145–146; Joseph Baernreither, "Aehrenthal und Milovanovic," *Deutsche Revue* (January 1922), pp. 84–89; Philippe Crozier, in *Revue de France* (June 1, 1921), pp. 595–596; A. Gauvain, *L'Europe au jour le jour* (Paris, 1917), II, 303 ff., these last two reporting completely contradictory utterances of Milovanovic.

[18] On the Russian assurances see Siebert, *Diplomatische Aktenstücke*, p. 457. Charykov redoubled his efforts to bring the Balkan states together. Schwertfeger, *Zur europäischen Politik*, III, 184–186; *G.P.*, XXVII (pt. 1), nos. 9737, 9738.

Russia would lend active military aid, but in case of an unprovoked attack by Turkey upon Bulgaria, Russia agreed merely to mobilize some of her forces, reserving liberty of further action, unless a third power, unprovoked by Bulgaria, should take part in the war on the side of Turkey. In the event of a successful war against Austria and Rumania, Russia would aid Bulgaria in acquiring the Dobrudja; in the event of a successful war against Turkey, Russia would do her utmost to secure for Bulgaria "localities with Bulgarian population, for example those within the limits fixed in the preliminaries of peace concluded at San Stefano." [19]

In March 1910 Milovanovic paid visits to St. Petersburg, Constantinople, and Sofia, while Ferdinand of Bulgaria and Peter of Serbia followed each other in visits at the Russian and Turkish capitals. On these occasions the whole problem of Balkan politics was gone over in detail, the Russians urging upon both the Bulgarians and the Serbians the necessity for solidarity and the desirability of maintaining friendly relations with the Turks. The chief question, however, was the future of Russian-Bulgarian relations, for no barrier could be erected against Austria unless the Sofia government would agree to become a party. When Ferdinand arrived in St. Petersburg, accompanied by Malinov and Paprikov, Isvolski handed him the draft treaty drawn up some months before. It was, of course, a thoroughly one-sided agreement, all in favor of Russia, and one can hardly blame the Bulgarians for having given it a cool reception. The project was discussed in Sofia in April and May, in conferences arranged by the Russian representative and attended by Malinov and Paprikov, but little progress was made. The Russian minister complained bitterly of the "suspiciousness and stubbornness" of the Bulgarians, but his efforts proved of no avail, and once more the Russian scheme hung fire. [20]

[19] Text of the draft in *Dokumente aus den russischen Geheimarchiven* (Berlin, 1918), pp. 27–31; in abbreviated form in Laloy, *Les Documents secrets*, pp. 52–58; independently printed also by Bogitschewitsch, *Kriegsursachen*, pp. 115–121. Radoslavoff's statement that no agreement was made at this time is true, but in no way disproves the existence of the draft or the fact that it was made the basis of negotiations later. Radoslavoff in *Die Kriegsschuldfrage* (May 1926), pp. 272–273.

[20] Popov, *Krasnyi Arkhiv*, VIII, 10; Viktorov-Toporov, *Russkaia Mysl* (April 1915), pp. 128, 132. Sazonov later said that it was the Bulgarians who had first submitted a draft. See letter of Georges Louis, January 29, 1913, in E. Judet, *Georges Louis* (Paris, 1925), p. 209. On these visits generally see *The Times* (London), Mar. 9, 14, 1910; Bourchier in *The Times* (London), June 11, 1913; Schwertfeger, *Zur europäischen Politik*, III, 194–197; G.P., XXVII (pt. 1), nos. 9747–9751; XXVII (pt. 2), no. 10155; Seton-Watson, *The Rise of Nationality in*

The projected Balkan barrier was still in the realm of ideals, and the gathering of princes for the celebration of Nicolas's jubilee at Cettinje in August 1910 was nothing more than a demonstration. It did, however, frighten the Turks, who once more opened negotiations with Rumania. Apparently the advances, as on previous occasions, proved futile, though Europe was flooded with rumors of a Turkish-Rumanian military convention.[21] The Bulgarians, who felt particularly menaced, never freed themselves entirely of the dread of such a combination and henceforth proved more amenable to the Russian program. The negotiations with Russia took a more favorable turn. Sazonov, the new Russian foreign minister, in December 1910 instructed his representative in Sofia to make concessions in the direction of equalizing the obligations of the two powers under the treaty, adding, however, that Russia would nevertheless regard herself as exempt from fulfilling her promises. It is said that the pourparlers had almost come to a satisfactory close when, in March 1911, Malinov fell from power.[22]

At the same time negotiations had been opened between Bulgaria on the one hand and Serbia and Greece on the other. They were countenanced, if not directly encouraged, by Russia and were of a friendly

---

the Balkans, p. 150; Nikolaides, *Greichenlands Anteil*, p. 25. There was a good deal of talk at the time of including Turkey in the League, and the Russian official communiqué on the occasion of King Peter's visit emphasized the desirability of maintaining good relations with Turkey. Text in *Deutscher Geschichtskalendar, 1910* (Leipzig, 1885–1933), pp. 286–287. In public, however, it was denied that there was any intention of establishing a confederation. Milovanovic in an interview said: "Il ne s'agit pas le moins du monde, comme on l'a dit, de conclure, de concert avec la Bulgarie, une fédération balkanique. Sans doute la fédération reste pour nous une combinaison idéale; c'est elle qui assurerait définitivement notre indépendence. Mais nous connaissons trop les difficultés qui s'opposent à réalisation actuelle et les soupçons que feraient naître des pourparlers préparatoires, pour nous lancer aujourd'hui dans les négotiations scabreuses." Gauvain, *L'Europe au jour le jour*, II, 303 ff., 328.

[21] *G.P.*, XXVII (pt. 1), no. 9790 ff.; Siebert, *Diplomatische Aktenstücke*, p. 145; Schwertfeger, *Zur europäischen Politik*, III, 203–204; Molden, *Graf Aehrenthal*, pp. 148–149. The general uneasiness was increased by the fact that the Turks purchased two German warships at this time. *G.P.*, XXVII (pt. 1), chap. 212, app.; G. Trubetzkoi, *Russland als Grossmacht* (Stuttgart, 1917), pp. 154–158.

[22] Popov, *Krasnyi Arkhiv*, VIII, 10; Viktorov-Toporov, *Russkaia Mysl* (April 1915), pp. 128, 132–133. Apparently everything had been settled excepting the future Bulgarian frontier in Thrace. The Russians offered the San Stefano boundary or the Enos-Midia line. The Bulgarians insisted on the inclusion of Adrianople. See pamphlet by Mishev, quoted by Balkanicus [S. Protic], *The Aspirations of Bulgaria* (London, 1915), pp. 158 ff. It is interesting to note that as late as May 1912 Danev was trying to persuade Sazonov to assign Adrianople to Bulgaria. See Siebert, *Diplomatische Aktenstücke*, pp. 522–525; I. E. Guéchoff, *L'Alliance balkanique* (Paris, 1915), pp. 76–77.

anti-Turk nature.[23] Apparently this change in the Russian attitude was due to Sazonov, the new foreign minister. Not essentially conversant with Balkan affairs, he was content to follow the school of his brother-in-law, Stolypin, and subscribed entirely to the ideas of Hartwig, whose aim was a union of the Slavic states of the Balkans, disregarding Turkey. In Isvolski's policy the Turks had played a distinctly secondary role. Charykov hoped eventually to be able to hug them to death. Hartwig and Sazonov, on the other hand, dreamed of smashing the Ottoman Empire by means of a Balkan league. Not in the near future, to be sure. Nothing could be done so long as the Austrian menace overshadowed everything else. But the beauty of a Balkan league would be that it could be used like a two-edged sword, against the Austrians or the Turks, as the situation demanded.[24] Thus far the chief difficulty had been in making the anti-Turk element (Bulgaria) sufficiently anti-Austrian, and the anti-Austrian element (Serbia) sufficiently anti-Turk.

There was little room for Charykov's plans in the policy of Sazonov, and the Russian ambassador to the Porte felt profoundly disappointed by this new development. Isvolski had at least allowed him to go ahead. Sazonov would almost certainly veto any attempt to realize his scheme.[25] As a matter of fact the idea of a Balkan federation under

---

[23] Bourchier in *The Times* (London), June 5, 1913; Protic, *The Aspirations of Bulgaria*, pp. 158 ff.; A. Nekludoff, *Diplomatic Reminiscences* (London, 1920), p. 2; Siebert, *Diplomatische Aktenstücke*, pp. 146–147; Jäckh, *Deutschland im Orient*, pp. 113–114; Louis de Saint-Victor de Saint-Blanchard, "L'Équilibre balkanique," *Revue des sciences politiques* (Feb. 15, 1914), pp. 12–48.

[24] *G.P.*, XXVII (pt. 1), no. 9871, illustrates Sazonov's suspicions of Austria's plans. Cf. also *G.P.*, XXVII (pt. 2), no. 10155: "Tscharykow, so liess er durchblicken, habe seine Freundschaft für die Türkei bisweilen zu stark affichiert." Miliukov writes in the *Retch*, July 25, 1916: "Sazonoff, receiving in heritage a situation thus complicated, formed a new resource—an alliance of the Balkan States which finally blocked the path of Austria to the South" (quoted in H. N. Brailsford, *A League of Nations* [New York, 1917], p. 64). Trubetzkoi, a close friend of Sazonov, writes: "Ein Bündnis der Türkei mit den Balkanstaaten stellt sich uns als eine Idylle dar, zu der das Bild der Wirklichkeit gar nicht stimmen will." See also *Carnets de Georges Louis*, I, 27, and Popov, *Krasnyi Arkhiv*, VIII, 10. On Hartwig and his views see Nekludoff, *Diplomatic Reminiscences*, p. 50; Friedjung, *Das Zeitalter des Imperialismus*, III, 170; M. Martchenko, *La Catastrophe austro-hongroise* (Paris, 1920), pp. 144 ff.: "Hartwig ne s'entendait pas avec Isvolski . . . A son avis, le dilemme austro-serbe ne pouvait être resolu un jour que par les armes." Similarly Brailsford, *A League of Nations*, p. 64; Young, *Nationalism and War*, pp. 163–164.

[25] *G.P.*, XXVII (pt. 1), no. 9753: "Es versteht sich von selbst, dass meine Ideen betreffs des Balkanproblems, wiewohl ich sie keineswegs zu abandonnieren gewillt bin, dennoch dieser geänderten Orientation akkommodiert werden müssen."

Turkish leadership would certainly have died then and there had it not been for two important changes which took place in March 1911. In the first place Sazonov was taken so seriously ill that he was forced to abandon his post for nine months. His assistant, Neratov, was a henchman of Isvolski and worked hand in glove with him.[26] As a subordinate he lacked the necessary prestige and authority to enforce his own views and so the prospects for Charykov suddenly became more rosy than ever. The second change was due to the fall of the Malinov ministry in Bulgaria. The new Gueshov-Danev cabinet, was, if anything, even more Russophil than its predecessor, but was also very well disposed to the Turks.[27] Furthermore, for some reason or other, perhaps because of jealousy and because of Ferdinand's distrust of the new cabinet, Malinov said nothing about the negotiations with Russia, which were nearing completion. The whole correspondence was transferred from the archives of the foreign office to the police archives, and the Russians themselves seem to have taken no steps to initiate Gueshov.[28]

The first act in the field of foreign politics taken by the new Bulgarian premier was to cut short the anti-Turk negotiations carried on by his predecessor, and to reject new advances made by the Serbs and the Greeks.[29] His first object was to smooth out the difficulties between Sofia and Constantinople, and during the summer of 1911 he discussed

[26] "Neratoff. C'est celui qui travaille le plus avec Isvolski." *Carnets de Georges Louis*, I, 31–32.

[27] Popov, *Krasnyi Arkhiv*, VIII, 10. The Russian chargé at Sofia wrote: "There is still much work ahead, but the conditions for this work are now extremely easy, and the work may be productive in the extreme . . . Bulgaria has now entered the orbit of Russian politics." Cf. M., "The Balkan League: History of Its Foundation," *Fortnightly Review* (March 1913), pp. 430–439, evidently an authoritative article. See also Guéchoff, *L'Alliance balkanique*, especially p. 4. It is hard to see how Larmeroux, *La Politique extérieure*, II, 194, knowing Gueshov's book, could write: "M. Guéchoff comprit que la Bulgarie n'avait rien à gagner à diriger sa diplomatie vers la Turquie." This is characteristic of the whole work.

[28] Viktorov-Toporov, *Russkaia Mysl* (April 1915), pp. 128, 132.

[29] M., *Fortnightly Review* (March 1913), pp. 430–439. According to Popov, *Krasnyi Arkhiv*, VIII, 10, the Serbs proposed that a revolt be started in Macedonia and war be declared on Turkey. See also Bourchier in *The Times* (London), June 5, 6, 1913; H. W. Steed, *Through Thirty Years* (New York, 1924), I, 360–361; Guéchoff, *L'Alliance balkanique*, p. 63; *Report of the International Commission to Inquire into the Causes and Conduct of the Balkan Wars* (Washington, 1914), p. 43 (hereafter cited as *Report*); Seton-Watson, *The Rise of Nationality*, p. 154; Saint-Victor de Saint-Blanchard, *Revue des sciences politiques* (Feb. 15, 1914). Danev appears to have had no Turkophil leanings and to have disapproved of the cavalier manner in which Gueshov rejected all offers. See Siebert, *Diplomatische Aktenstücke*, pp. 150–151; Nekludoff, *Diplomatic Reminiscences*, p. 27.

the matter with Assim Bey, the Turk minister. Progress was slow, but it was quite characteristic of the general situation that both Milovanovic and Venizelos in public speeches proclaimed their adherence to the idea of an entente with the Porte.[30]

Then, suddenly, in the last days of September, came the Italian ultimatum to Turkey and the declaration of war. The outward calm of Balkan politics was rudely disturbed. From the very beginning it was clear that the conflict might lead to complications in the Balkans, especially if operations were carried on in Europe. None of the great powers, not even Italy, desired a disturbance of the status quo, and the Austrian warnings to the Italians not to extend the theater of war to Europe were at this time quite superfluous.[31] But the Russians as well as the Balkan states had for years suspected the Austrians of sinister designs, and they feared that the Vienna government would take advantage of the situation to advance its own interests in the Sanjak or in Serbia. While giving assurances of their pacific intentions the Balkan states decided to close ranks.[32] The Bulgarians had finally made up their minds to seek an alliance with Serbia, partly to be able to present a united front against Austria, but also in order to frustrate any attempt on the part of the Turks to avenge a defeat by the Italians by an attack on their neighbor. The Russians gave the plan their blessing. They had been urging it for years and had been devoting great efforts to it during the preceding months.[33]

But Russian policy was not to be restricted to this purely secondary role. Isvolski, now ambassador to Paris, saw a golden opportunity for realizing grander schemes and old ambitions. France was just securing

[30] Guéchoff, *L'Alliance Balkanique*, p. 8; Nikolaides; *Greichenlands Anteil*, p. 27; Seton-Watson, *The Rise of Nationality*, p. 154; *Documents diplomatiques: Affaires balkaniques* (Paris, n.d.), I, no. 24.

[31] *G.P.*, XXX (pt. 1), nos. 10835, 10842, 10857, 10858, 10861, 10863. The Russians urged upon the Balkan states the necessity for preserving the peace. See Popov, *Krasnyi Arkhiv*, VIII, nos. 3, 6, 8; Molden, *Graf Aehrenthal*, pp. 187–188; Giolitti, *Memoirs of My Life*, pp. 282 ff., 265–267.

[32] The excitement in the Balkan capitals comes out most clearly in the Russian documents. In Belgrade, Milovanovic was bitterly attacked for his passivity. See Popov, *Krasnyi Arkhiv*, VIII, nos. 3, 8. Hartwig believed that the Austrians were "only waiting for an opportunity to come out with at least some sort of justification in defence of the staus quo."

[33] Popov, *Krasnyi Arkhiv*, VIII, nos. 7, 9; Guéchoff, *L'Alliance balkanique*, p. 15; *Affaires balkaniques*, I, no. 24. It appears that the first moves on the part of the Bulgarians were due to Rizov, the minister in Rome, who had conducted the negotiations in the spring of 1911, and to Todorov, the foreign minister. Gueshov himself seems to have been distinctly hesitant and dubious.

control of Morocco after the Agadir crisis, and Italy was proceeding to the conquest of Tripoli. The favorable moment must not be allowed to pass without some gain being made for Russia. France and Italy must be called upon to give renewed assurances of support for Russia's ambitions in the Straits question, and Russia, while doing her utmost to maintain peace in the Balkans, must seize the opportunity to extort an agreement with the embarrassed Turks.[34]

Charykov had the same inspiration. The Balkan states were drawing together and the Turks were in a tight place. This was the ideal moment for bringing them all together, for posing as the protector of the Turks and for seducing them into accepting a new edition of the Treaty of Unkiar Skelessi:

> For us it is extremely desirable that the process of mutual rapprochement and accord between the Balkan governments and nationalities should be hastened and intensified [he wrote home on September 30]. Whenever the Balkan representatives speak to me on this subject I tell them that their interests, which in the present case coincide with the interests of the powers, make it desirable at the present time, in spite of the Italian-Turkish war, to preserve the peace and the status quo. But in view of the impossibility of predicting the effect which the Italian attack may have upon the Turkish Empire, it would be advisable for the Balkan States to come to an agreement concerning their common interests. Not by any means for the purpose of attacking Turkey or in any way departing from their correct attitude towards her, but in order to avoid fighting each other in case of a Turkish catastrophe and in order to be able to act safely, by common friendly efforts, in defense of their interests.[35]

Neratov was carried away by the arguments of the ambassadors and authorized Isvolski to secure from the French a general promise not to oppose the wishes of Russia in regard to the Straits question when Russia should consider it necessary to raise that question.[36] At the same time Neratov, closely following the suggestions of Isvolski, wrote to Charykov asking him to begin negotiations for a revision of the Russian-Turkish railroad agreement of 1900. In case the Turks appeared to

---

[34] Marchand, *Un Livre noir*, I, 136; F. Stieve, ed., *Der diplomatische Schriftwechsel Isvolskis* (Berlin, 1924), I, no. 125; Siebert, *Diplomatische Aktenstücke*, p. 494.

[35] Popov, *Krasnyi Arkhiv*, VIII, no. 2; Marchand, *Un Livre noir*, II, 468, the Bazili Memorandum of September 17, 1912, summarizing the negotiations of these years concerning the Straits.

[36] Marchand, *Un Livre noir*, I, 140; Stieve, *Der diplomatische Schriftwechsel Isvolskis*, I, no. 132.

be well-disposed he was to raise other questions "of more general import," one of which was the Straits question. On this point Neratov was closely sticking by Isvolski's program of 1908, amplified by the ideas of Charykov. Russia was to give the Turks effective support in maintaining the existing régime in the Straits, while extending this to include the adjacent territory. In order to facilitate the execution of this clause the Turks should agree not to oppose the passage of Russian warships through the Straits, on condition that they should not stop without previous arrangement. Russia asked only a general promise from the Turks not to oppose the Russian interests in the matter. Negotiations with the other powers were carefully reserved.[37]

During the following months the Russian diplomats were busily engaged on three different policies. Hartwig at Belgrade and Nekludov at Sofia were attempting to engineer a Balkan league, constructed at the expense of Turkey to block Austria, and perhaps in the distant future to realize Russia's own ambitions in Turkey. Isvolski was negotiating with the powers to secure a free hand in the Straits question, preliminary to extorting a favorable settlement from the Turks. Charykov was energetically at work trying to effect a *rapprochement* between all the Balkan powers under Turkish leadership and Russian protection, hoping eventually to sell the Turks a guarantee of their territory (at the expense of the Balkan states) for extensive concessions to Russia in the Straits. Russian diplomacy was nothing less than transparent.

Nekludov had already hurried off to Davos to consult Sazonov in respect to the projected Serbian-Bulgarian negotiations: "Well, but this is perfect! If only it could come off!" exclaimed the Russian foreign minister. "Bulgaria closely allied to Serbia in the political and economic spheres; five hundred thousand bayonets to guard the Balkans—but this would bar the road forever to German penetration, Austrian invasion." Any aggressive anti-Turk proclivities, he felt sure, could be held in check by Russia. In any case the combination was so important that Sazonov felt that Russia must gamble on it.[38]

[37] Marchand, *Un Livre noir, II*, 458–459. Authorization to begin discussions was given on October 7.

[38] Nekludoff, *Diplomatic Reminiscences,* pp. 45–46. Molden, *Graf Aehrenthal,* p. 210; Young, *Nationalism and War,* pp. 163–164; Brailsford, *A League of Nations,* p. 64, all emphasize the fact that what the Russians wanted was a league to check Austria, not to dismember Turkey. This crucial point is very well developed by Saint-Victor de Saint-Blanchard in *Revue des sciences politiques* (Feb. 15, 1914): "Dans la pensée russe, comme dans la pensée serbe, la crainte du péril

In reality, however, there were still many obstacles to overcome. The Bulgarian readiness to negotiate was largely due to fear of Turk aggression. There were rumors of mobilization on the Bulgarian frontier, and the statesmen at Sofia had temporarily lost their heads. Gueshov alone remained cool, and appealed to the powers to secure for Bulgaria assurances against Turkish attack. He allowed the negotiations with Serbia to be opened, but he was not exactly enthusiastic and evidently would have wished to definitely associate the Russians in order to protect Bulgaria from the wrath of Austria and Rumania.[39] On October 11 he himself, returning from Paris and Vienna, had a long conversation with Milovanovic on the railroad between Belgrade and Liapovo. Recognizing the impossibility of action at the moment and emphasizing the necessity for complete Russian approval, the Serbian minister suggested a general defensive alliance providing against attack by any power and against any state that might attempt to occupy Macedonia, Old Serbia, or northern Albania. The plan was outspokenly anti-Austrian and reflects the Serb fears of Austrian designs in northern Albania. Macedonia and Old Serbia were brought in because it was obviously impossible to effect a settlement without deciding the future disposition of these territories. Milovanovic therefore suggested an offensive clause looking to the liberation of Macedonia and Old Serbia whenever the situation should seem favorable to both parties or whenever it should become necessary to end the anarchy and massacres in the provinces where vital interests of either or both parties were engaged. Tentatively he suggested previous assignment of undisputed regions to each side and Russian arbitration in disposing of the intervening zone. "Ah, yes," he added; "if, at the same time as the liquidation of Turkey the disintegration of Austria-Hungary could take place, the solution would be greatly simplified." [40]

Gueshov did not take very kindly to these suggestions. The Russians had induced the powers to give assurances against Turkish attack and

---

autrichien domine manifestement les ambitions d'expansion." This is more than sufficiently borne out by the Russian documents published by Popov.

[39] Popov, *Krasnyi Arkhiv*, VIII, nos. 9, 10, 11, 15, 18, 20, 22, 23, 24, 25, 26, 28, 37 (Oct. 8–18).

[40] Guéchoff, *L'Alliance balkanique*, pp. 22 ff.; Popov, *Krasnyi Arkhiv*, VIII, nos. 16, 27, 32; Bourchier in *The Times* (London), June 11, 1913; M., *Fortnightly Review* (March 1913), pp. 430–439; Bresnitz von Sydacoff [Philip F. Bresnitz], *Aus den Geheimnissen des Balkankrieges* (Leipzig, n.d.), pp. 14 ff. Saint-Victor de Saint-Blanchard, "L'Europe et la guerre balkanique," *Revue des sciences politiques* (January–February 1913), pp. 24–47.

had themselves brought pressure to bear in Constantinople. This they were obliged to do in their own interest, for a conflagration in the Balkans would have been disastrous for Russia at that time. Nevertheless these assurances went a long way toward calming the excitement in Bulgaria and strengthening Gueshov's hands as against the more belligerent elements. He still felt that it would be better if Bulgaria could arrange things directly with the Turks and thus avoid sacrificing part of Macedonia. His sympathies were with Russia, but he did not want to be a mere cat's-paw to be used against Austria.[41] Assim Bey, the Turk minister in Sofia with whom Gueshov had carried on conversations throughout the summer of 1911, had just assumed the post of foreign minister and had promised faithfully to do his utmost to bring about an entente between Turkey and Bulgaria. His assumption of office had, in fact, greatly contributed to the relaxation of tension in the middle of October.[42]

The Russians, too, looked askance at Milovanovic's proposals. The one thing they were anxious to avoid was trouble in the Balkans which would give Austria a pretext to intervene. They had, therefore, discouraged the idea of a military convention suggested by Venizelos to Gueshov, though the agreement was to have been at least technically defensive. The Russians warned the Sofia government of the danger of becoming involved in the Cretan question and refused to approve any arrangement that was not designed to preserve the status quo. Gueshov was by no means eager and showed no inclination to give the suggestion of the Greeks serious consideration.[43] In regard to the Serbian proposals the Russians made their attitude equally clear. Nekludov suggested to Gueshov a vague and very diluted text to replace the offensive clause of the Serbian draft and furthermore proposed the addition of a provision for the adherence of the other Balkan states, Greece, Montenegro, and Turkey. Neratov himself urged the necessity of carefully

---

[41] Popov, *Krasnyi Arkhiv*, VIII, nos. 27, 28, 31, 37.

[42] Guéchoff, *L'Alliance balkanique*, p. 63; M., *Fortnightly Review* (March 1913), pp. 430–439; Siebert, *Diplomatische Aktenstücke*, pp. 303–304; Popov, *Krasnyi Arkhiv*, VIII, nos. 37, 38. Assim is said to have accepted office only on the condition that an entente with Bulgaria should be sought. Before leaving Sofia he gave Todorov categorical assurances that he would devote his efforts to this end. Already on October 30 Nekludov could report from Sofia that "the most amicable relations again have been established between Sofia and Constantinople."

[43] Guéchoff, *L'Alliance balkanique*, p. 63; M., *Fortnightly Review* (March 1913), pp. 430–439; Popov, *Krasnyi Arkhiv*, VIII, nos. 29, 33, 39, 41.

avoiding anything that might offend the Turks and believed that Russia should stay as much as possible in the background. Under these circumstances the negotiations between Belgrade and Sofia made little progress.[44]

The Russian attitude had to some extent been conditioned by the *pourparlers* in which Charykov was engaging with the Turks. On October 7 he had been instructed to begin conversations, but before doing so he had suggested a number of changes in the Neratov draft. These had to do chiefly with the Straits question. Charykov believed that this part of the program should be taken up immediately. Above all he held that the whole Straits problem should be linked up with the projected Balkan league and that Russia should promise Turkey her mediation in establishing with the Balkan states firm relations based upon the maintenance of the status quo. This seemed to Neratov a rather dangerous procedure, but Charykov had already broached the matter to Bompard, his French colleague, and had opened introductory discussions with Said Pasha, the Turkish prime minister, before Neratov had a chance to raise objections.[45] On October 14 Charykov, unofficially and informally, submitted to Said a written draft, embodying the changes he had suggested to Neratov. This draft provided for the abrogation of the railroad agreement of 1900 and its replacement by new arrangements far more favorable to Turkey. In addition the Russian government expressed its readiness to consider the question of abolishing the capitulations and to receive favorably any economic or financial proposals which the Turks might make. But the main thing was the Straits. Here the draft followed the project sent by Neratov on October 2, but it included a clause embodying Charykov's fundamental idea: Russia would promise to use her good offices to facilitate the establishment of stable neighborly relations on the basis of the status quo between Turkey and the Balkan states. Furthermore, the new régime proposed for the Straits was to be subject to the approval of the powers signatory to the London Convention of 1871.[46]

[44] *Ibid.*, nos. 33, 36.
[45] Marchand, *Un Livre noir*, II, 459–460; I, 143; Stieve, *Der diplomatische Schriftwechsel Isvolskis*, I, no. 137.
[46] The text of Neratov's original instructions and of Charykov's project in Marchand, *Un Livre noir*, II, 462–464. Summaries in Siebert, *Diplomatische Aktenstücke*, pp. 675 ff., and in M. Moukhtar Pacha, *La Turquie, l'Allemagne et l'Europe* (Paris, 1924), p. 210. The important passages dealing with the Straits in Charykov's draft read as follows: "4) Le gouvernement Impérial de Russie s'engage en outre à donner au gouvernement Ottoman son appui efficace pour le maintien du

By this action Charykov had far exceeded his instructions, and he soon managed to raise a storm. Neratov wrote him sharply, reminding him that he had been asked to discuss the railroad agreement and that the government had intended to reserve action on the other matters. This was not quite accurate, for the ambassador had been empowered to raise the question, though he certainly had no authority to put it into so definitive or extensive a form. Neratov expressed decided disapproval of Charykov's wording of the project, insisted on the retention of the original and objected to the provision for the consent of the other powers.[47] Quite rightly he argued that this procedure might create complications. His plan, which was that of Isvolski, had been to get definite assurances from France and Italy and then to sound the other powers before officially opening the question at Constantinople. Negotiations with France and Italy were already under way and Neratov had explicitly stated to the French chargé d'affaires that Russia desired French support at Constantinople when the question was raised. Isvolski himself was much chagrined to learn of Charykov's precipitate action, the news coming to him indirectly from London at a time when the Russian government had not yet breathed a word to its own ambassador to England.[48]

---

régime actuel des Détroits du Bosphore et des Dardanelles, en étendant le dit appui également aux territoires adjacents, dans le cas où ceux-ci seraient menacés par les forces armées étrangères. En vue de faciliter l'exécution de la clause précitée, le gouvernement Impérial Ottoman s'engage, de son côté, à ne pas s'opposer en temps de paix, comme en temps de guerre, au passage des navires de guerre russes par les Détroits, à condition que ces navires ne s'arrêtent point dans les eaux des Détroits, sauf accord. L'application de cette interprétation de la convention conclue à Londres le 1/13 mars 1871, demeure subordonnée au consentement préalable des autres Puissances signataires de la dite convention. 5) Le gouvernement Impérial de Russie s'engage également à employer ses bons offices pour faciliter l'ésablissement entre le gouvernement Impérial Ottoman et les États Balkaniques, des rapports stables de bon voisinage, sur la base du statu quo." (In Moukhtar Pacha's version this last clause reads: "La Russie formerait une alliance des États Balkaniques sous l'hégémonie de la Turquie.")

[47] Marchand, *Un Livre noir*, II, pp. 460–461, Neratov to Charykov, October 22. Already on October 10 he had written objecting in a general way and warning the ambassador against initiating negotiations on too large a scale, even in a private way. Now he wrote that Charykov's letter to Said "ne trouvera point ici d'approbateurs." According to Molden, *Graf Aehrenthal*, p. 197, Neratov and Charykov were confirmed opponents.

[48] Marchand, *Un Livre noir*, I, 142–147; II, 465; Stieve, *Der diplomatische Schriftwechsel Isvolskis*, I, nos. 135, 137, 138, 140, 141; especially Isvolski to Neratov, October 12, 1911: "Apparemment Tcharykof a déjà entrepris quelques pas à Constantinople; je crains qu'avec sa précipitation coutumière il ne se hâte trop et gâte les choses." On October 15 the *Neue Freie Presse* printed a St. Petersburg

Although Charykov had exceeded his instructions, the moment for his action was not ill-chosen. There were rumors afloat that the Italians were planning to extend operations to the Aegean, and this would almost certainly mean trouble in the Balkans.[49] Under the circumstances the Turks were not averse to a guarantee of their European possessions. Assim Bey, in fact, frankly avowed his desire for an understanding with Russia as well as Bulgaria. Gueshov was distinctly well-disposed, and Milovanovic was anything but Turkophobe. What the Turks objected to was not a Balkan league as such, but the idea of a league under Russian direction. The traditional distrust could only be enhanced by the fact that Charykov had linked the idea of a territorial guarantee and a Balkan league with the Straits question. The ulterior motive was too obvious to escape attention.[50]

The Turkish statesmen therefore decided to sound out Russia's friends and, if possible, to remove the objectionable features of the plan by associating England and perhaps France. On October 16 Said Pasha, the Grand Vezir, told the Chamber behind closed doors that the situation was critical. The Turks, he said, had pursued a policy of isolation, much to their own detriment. The Porte must now seek assistance in extricating itself from the existing difficulties. Alliances could be easily concluded, but the Turkish government could not consider an agreement that would put the empire under the tutelage of another power. He then indicated that he had hopes of concluding an entente which would cost some geographical, political, and commercial sacrifices, but these sacrifices would have to be made. In any case the government would apply itself to the task of strengthening the relations

---

dispatch stating that while Russia regarded the existing arrangements as burdensome, there was no intention of raising the Straits question at the moment. According to Moukhtar, *La Turquie*, p. 210, Said immediately communicated the Charykov note to the English ambassador.

[49] *The Times* (London), Oct. 17, 1911; *Neue Freie Presse*, Oct. 17; *G.P.*, XXX (pt. 1), no. 10929.

[50] Siebert, *Diplomatische Aktenstücke*, pp. 303–304; Schwertfeger, *Zur europäischen Politik*, III, nos. 133, 136; *G.P.*, XXX (pt. 1), no. 10911; XXXIII, no. 12044, Marschall to Foreign Office, October 23: Assim says "er strebe nach einer Entente der Türkei mit allen Balkanstaaten einschliesslich Rumäniens auf der Basis der gegenseitigen Zusage, sich einer Aggressivität zu enthalten . . . Auf den von Russland gewünschten Balkanbund dagegen werde er nicht eingehen, weil bei (diesem) die politische und nicht die ökonomische Entwicklung im Vordergrund stehe. Ein solcher Balkanbund werde unter russischer Direktive stehen und Oesterreich-Ungarn zum unversöhnlichen Gegner haben." This is substantially what he told the Belgian minister. See also Moukhtar, *La Turquie*, p. 210.

with all the powers, particularly the Balkan states: "We desire to maintain and strengthen our normal and sincere relations with the Balkan states on the basis of mutual confidence and the reconciliation of our common interests." [51]

More the Grand Vezir refused to say, but from that day on the question of a Balkan confederation was the all-absorbing topic in the Turkish capital. Public opinion, estranged from the Triple Alliance as a result of the Italian aggression, had become outspokenly favorable to the Entente powers and it was generally supposed that Said had hinted at an English alliance which might involve giving England Koweit and concessions in the Bagdad railway question.[52] As a matter of fact the English government was actually approached and proposals for an alliance were submitted. It was suggested that France and Russia might be associated later. The Turks asked, in return for the alliance, that England should give substantial aid in defending the Ottoman sovereignty in Tripoli. In reply Sir Edward Grey expressed his sympathy for an agreement with the Porte, but pointed out that England could not depart from her policy of neutrality in the Tripolitan conflict.[53]

Meanwhile the Turks put off the reply to Charykov's letter from week to week. Everything hung in the balance. The negotiations between Serbia and Bulgaria were tied up pending further developments of the Turkish policy.[54] The Turks were taking soundings before decid-

---

[51] I have pieced this account together from the versions given by Marschall (*G.P.*, XXX [pt. 1], nos. 10897, 10898, 10901) and in *The Times* (London), Oct. 19, 20, 1911; *Neue Freie Presse*, Oct. 19, 20, 21, 22, 25, 26. See also Conrad, *Aus meiner Dienstzeit*, II, 178–179, report of the Austrian military attaché in Constantinople, October 24, 1911.

[52] *G.P.*, XXX (pt. 1), nos. 10897, 10898, 10901. Cf. also *The Times* (London), Oct. 30, 1911 and the *Neue Freie Presse*, Nov. 8, 9, which are astonishingly accurate. See also Schwertfeger, *Zur europäischen Politik*, III, no. 136; E. J. Dillon, "M. Tsharykoff and the Latest Phase of the Straits Question," *Contemporary Review* (January 1912), pp. 122–123; Driault and Lhéritier, *Histoire diplomatique*, V, 60.

[53] *G.P.*, XXX (pt. 1), no. 10912; Siebert, *Diplomatische Aktenstücke*, pp. 304–305; *Neue Freie Presse*, Oct. 21, and the interesting correspondence between Djavid Bey and Winston Churchill in W. Churchill, *The World Crisis* (New York, 1923), I, 523–524. According to Moukhtar, *La Turquie*, p. 211, Said approached the English only after he had in vain sounded the Austrians and Germans. Charykov also believed that there had been negotiations with Germany (Siebert, *Diplomatische Aktenstücke*, p. 679), but there is no evidence of this in the German documents.

[54] On November 4 Neratov wrote definitely that in the view of the Russian government any treaty must leave Turkey the opportunity to join. A draft submitted by Milovanovic on November 3 seemed to Neratov entirely too aggressive and anti-Turk, though it hardly went beyond the outline discussed by Gueshov

ing on a definite course, and at the same time Neratov was continuing his efforts to get from the powers an expression of their attitude in regard to the Straits question. The English government had already learned in an indirect way of Charykov's action and had been approached by the French government for an expression of opinion. Nicolson and Grey took their stand by the promises made in 1908. They once more pointed out that the moment was ill-chosen, but stated that the foreign office recognized the memorandum of October 14, 1908. Any further project would have to be examined in the light of the treaties and submitted to the cabinet. Furthermore Nicolson raised the question as to how Russia could guarantee the integrity of the Turkish territory on the Straits while Turkey was engaged in war.[55]

The French government, meanwhile, was waiting to see what the English would do. As in 1908, they were content to leave the odium to their friends.[56] In order to bring the discussions to an end, Neratov on November 2 instructed the ambassadors in London and Paris to get written declarations from the French and English governments. France was asked to give Russia "entire liberty of action," while Russia would give assurances that there was no intention on her part to involve France in an action in behalf of Russian interests. England was requested to give simply a written expression of opinion on the question of Russia's freedom of navigation and of the projected agreement with Turkey. Russia, it was repeated, was not planning an immediate solution of the problem.[57]

---

and Milovanovic on October 11. Nekludov reported on November 6: "I declared categorically to Spalaikovic [Serb minister to Sofia] that Russia would not hear of any aggressive actions or schemes of partition directed against Turkey and that an alliance between Serbia and Bulgaria must be a purely defensive one designed to maintain the status quo" (Popov, *Krasnyi Arkhiv*, VIII, no. 42; IX, no. 45).

[55] Marchand, *Un Livre noir*, I, 147–149, 151; II, 467; Stieve, *Der diplomatische Schriftwechsel Isvolskis*, I, nos. 141, 148; Siebert, *Diplomatische Aktenstücke*, pp. 674, 675, 679, 680. It is hard to understand how, in 1914, Grey could make the assertion that the Straits had not been discussed by Russia and England during the preceding five years (*British Documents on the Origins of the War, 1898–1914* (London, 1926), XI, no. 5).

[56] Marchand, *Un Livre noir*, I, 150; II, 465; Stieve, *Der diplomatische Schriftwechsel Isvolskis*, I, no. 147. The negotiations with the powers are summarized in E. A. Adamov, *Konstantinopel i Prolivi* (Moscow, 1925), I, 14 ff.

[57] Marchand, *Un Livre noir*, II, 466–467; Siebert, *Diplomatische Aktenstücke*, pp. 681–682.

So far as is known, the English government successfully evaded a written declaration, and evidently the Russians did not press the point in view of the reluctance of the French. Isvolski had taken advantage of the conclusion of the Franco-German treaty regarding Morocco to submit a note to the Quai d'Orsay on November 4. In this he included a clause of his own expressing the Russian conviction that the French government, in return for the benevolent attitude of her ally in the Moroccan question, would be ready to give assurance that it recognized Russia's freedom of action in the Straits regions and would not refuse its assent to measures Russia might take to guarantee her interests and consolidate her position. The French government was still suspicious and, even after assuring itself that the Russian note was more than an independent act on the part of Isvolski, did nothing during November. M. Georges Louis, temporarily director of the Quai d'Orsay, made it clear that he disliked the idea of giving Russia complete liberty of action. In spite of Isvolski's assurance that the Russian note had no connection with the Charykov proposals but was simply a matter of principle, no move was made in Paris to draw up a written reply.[58]

Meanwhile the Russian ambassador in Berlin had been informed. No real opposition was expected from either Germany or Austria. Indeed, on November 16 the German ambassador in St. Petersburg volunteered the information that Germany would probably put no obstacle in Russia's way, provided Germany were allowed to participate in the negotiations. Official soundings were then taken in Berlin and Vienna. The Germans made no difficulties and the Austrians, while holding back, recognized Russia's special interests in the Straits, while empha-

[58] Marchand, *Un Livre noir*, I, 154, 155, 162, 164, 166, 169; Stieve, *Der diplomatische Schriftwechsel Isvolskis*, I, nos. 153, 154, 156, 158, 159, 162, 178. The negotiations with France dragged on and it was only on January 4, 1912, that a written reply was handed to Isvolski. The essential passage read: "D'une manière générale, je suis heureux de confirmer de nouveau à Votre Excellence les déclarations du Gouvernement français, à l'occasion des événements de 1908, relativement aux satisfactions que le Gouvernement russe pourrait être amené à poursuivre dans la question du Détroit du Bosphore et des Dardanelles. Le Gouvernement français reste disposée à échanger des vues à cet égard avec le Gouvernement russe, si les circonstances nouvelles rendaient necessaire un examen de la question des Détroits." See Marchand, *Un Livre noir*, I, 179; Stieve, *Der diplomatische Schriftwechsel Isvolskis*, I, no. 185. For a summary of the negotiations with France see Marchand, *Un Livre noir*, II, 464 ff.; Stieve, *Der diplomatische Schriftwechsel Isvolskis*, II, no. 182; Judet, *Georges Louis*, pp. 95–96, 160 ff.; R. Poincaré, *Au Service de la France* (Paris, 1926), I, 346–347.

sizing the need of finding a formula which would guarantee Austria against an attack by the Russian fleet.[59]

The general result of the Russian soundings in the European capitals was, on the whole, promising. No far-reaching assurances or blanket promises had been given, but it was quite evident that arrangements might be made with the powers if the Turks could be brought to accept the Russian view. The prospects for this were, as we have seen, not entirely black. Charykov was hard at work urging on all sides the necessity for a Balkan confederation. The matter was being discussed in the press and in Constantinople there was a fair amount of favorable sentiment. But the Turkish statesmen, knowing the price asked by Russia, could not bring themselves to a decision.[60]

Meanwhile, towards the middle of November, there were more rumors of the extension of the war to the Aegean and of a coming attack by the Italian fleet on the Dardanelles, Saloniki, Smyrna, or Beyrut. The powers of the Triple Entente were distinctly opposed to any such action, and when the Turks threatened to take measures of defense in the Straits the Russian government proposed to the powers that steps be taken to warn Italy against so dangerous an enterprise. No real representations were made, for the Italian government anticipated action by declaring that no blockade of the Dardanelles or attack upon Turkish ports had been envisaged.[61]

The incident is important, for it gave Charykov another opportunity to play up Russia as the friend and protector of the Turks and to urge once more the necessity for concessions to Russia in the Straits question.

---

[59] Marchand, *Un Livre noir*, I, 160; II, 468–470; Stieve, *Der diplomatische Schriftwechsel Isvolskis*, I, no. 155; *G.P.*, XXX (pt. 1), nos. 10970, 10973–77, 10990, 10992, 11005; von Szilassy, *Der Untergang der Donaumonarchie*, p. 207. The Germans were more favorably disposed than the Austrians. Aehrenthal evidently intended to ask compensation for any gains made by the Russians. From the German documents it appears that neither Germany nor Austria gave more than a promise to consider favorably any proposals the Russians might make. The Russian memorandum in Marchand gives the impression of far more extensive assurances.

[60] Popov, *Krasnyi Arkhiv*, VIII, no. 40; Conrad, *Aus meiner Dienstzeit*, II 189–190; *The Times* (London) and *Neue Freie Presse*, Nov. 10–15. A commission of deputies was actually formed to study the idea, and similar organizations were projected in Sofia and Belgrade. See Schwertfeger, *Zur europäischen Politik*, III, no. 136; *Neue Freie Presse*, Nov. 21, 1911.

[61] Popov, *Krasnyi Arkhiv*, IX, nos. 48, 49; *G.P.*, XXX (pt. 1), nos. 10941, 10942, 10944, 10945, 10948, 10951 ff.; Marchand, *Un Livre noir*, II, 485; Stieve, *Der diplomatische Schriftwechsel Isvolskis*, I, no. 163; *The Times* (London) and *Neue Freie Presse*, Nov. 22–29, 1911.

The Turks feared the Russian action more than they welcomed it, for they suspected that Charykov would not allow the chance to slip by.[62] They were right. Charykov, having never received a reply to his unofficial draft of October 12, now resubmitted the same draft officially, with only one change. According to the first version the Russian-Turkish arrangement was to be subject to the approval of the powers. In the new version it was merely stated that the two governments should notify the powers of the agreement.[63]

There is no evidence that Charykov was in any way authorized to proceed officially in this matter, or that he had even taken the trouble to consult his government. Apparently he regarded the situation as ripe for action and relied upon the original vague instructions which Neratov had sent him. Of course the Turks could know nothing of all this. All they could see was that Russia had officially raised a question of the greatest moment. The whole import of the problem forced itself upon them. The presence of Russian warships in the Bosporus would be synonymous with the end of Turkish independence. They had always relied upon England to prevent such a catastrophe. Now, they argued, Russia must have secured the consent of England, and the fate of the Ottoman Empire had been decided.[64]

In a flash the Anglophil and Entente sympathies so prevalent in Constantinople after the outbreak of the Tripolitan War disappeared. Assim Bey hurried to von Marschall, the German ambassador with the exclamation: "The great blow has just been struck at us," and communicated the full text of the Charykov note. In great excitement he declared that what Russia proposed was nothing less than a protectorate and that if Russia were successful it would mean not only the end of Turkey but the end of Austria's Balkan policy and Germany's Oriental policy as well. Russia, by taking advantage of Turkey's critical situation, showed plainly enough that she was aiming at the disruption of the empire. The

[62] *G.P.*, XXX (pt. 1), no. 10945. The threatened closing of the Dardanelles had caused a temporary paralysis of Russian trade and consequently there was every prospect that the Russian government would capitalize on the situation. See *Neue Freie Presse*, Nov. 23, 27, reporting conditions at Odessa.

[63] The Russian draft was submitted in the form of a letter on November 27. See Marchand, *Un Livre noir*, II, 461. Summaries of the draft in *G.P.*, XXX (pt. 1), nos. 10978, 10985, in part verbatim. Cf. also Dillon, *Contemporary Review* (January 1912).

[64] *G.P.*, XXX (pt. 1), nos. 10978, 10982. Assim suspected that the Russians themselves had raised the spectre of an Italian attack in order to supply a pretext for opening the Straits question. Marschall inclined to the same view, but there is nothing in the Russian documents to bear this out.

suggested Balkan league would be merely a preliminary step to the breakup of Turkey's European possessions.[65]

Marschall was duly impressed and declared frankly for the status quo. Kiderlen, the German foreign minister, was more sceptical, and the ambassador therefore bombarded the foreign office with memoranda setting forth the dangers of the situation. The Russian proposals were almost a word-for-word repetition of the famous treaty of Unkiar Skelessi of 1833. They implied Russian domination of Constantinople and this in turn meant the collapse not only of the Ottoman Empire but of Germany's position in the Near East. There could be no doubt whatsoever, he thought, that the whole thing was being engineered by Russia with the approval of England and Italy. France would not dare oppose.[66]

Marschall was wrong in suspecting an entente conspiracy, as Assim soon found out after sounding the English government. Grey replied that he regarded the Russian *démarche* as out of place at the moment. At any rate the approval of the powers would be necessary.[67] This was enough for Assim. The affair had already leaked out and was everywhere discussed in the newspapers. The *Feni Gazetta* was practically invited to take a strong stand and on December 6 wrote:

> The Russian move is the most important event that has taken place in Turkish history in the last forty years . . . The attitude of the Porte in this affair is clear: we remain immovably attached to our most vital interests. No government, no Turk could for a moment entertain the idea that the Ottoman Empire might fall to the level of a Russian vassal.[68]

[65] *G.P.*, XXX (pt. 1), no. 10978: "Es handle sich um ein russisches Protektorat über das türkische Reich. Russland werde, wenn seine Kriegsschiffe die Meerengen frei passieren, zur ausschlaggebenden Vormacht in Konstantinopel . . . Die ganze oesterreichische Balkanpolitik und auch die deutsche Orientpolitik brechen zusammen, sobald Russland hier der entscheidende Machtfaktor werde."

[66] *G.P.*, XXX (pt. 1), nos. 10980, 10981, 10987, 10988. Marschall went so far as to hand in his resignation, but the Kaiser sided with him against Bethmann and Kiderlen (*G.P.*, XXX [pt. 1], nos. 10993, 10998).

[67] *G.P.*, XXX (pt. 1), no. 10983; *Neue Freie Presse*, Dec. 7, 9, 11, 1911. There appears to have been a general appeal sent out on December 4. Cf. Hoschiller, *L'Europe devant Constantinople*, pp. 64–66.

[68] *G.P.*, XXX (pt. 1), no. 10983; Schwertfeger, *Zur europäischen Politik*, III, no. 137; Hoschiller, *L'Europe devant Constantinople*, pp. 64–65; C. Vellay, *Le Problème méditerranéen* (Paris, 1913), pp. 62–63; *The Times* (London), Dec. 6, 7, 1911; *Neue Freie Presse*, Dec. 3–6, but especially Dec. 7. The Turkish newspapers were all opposed to concessions, and when Hussein Djavid, the editor of the *Tanin*, who was closely connected with the Russian Embassy, suggested the possibility of an arrangement, he was almost expelled from the Committee of Union

When Charykov appeared on the evening of December 6 with a formal written note, Assim confined himself to a few remarks, emphasizing the fact that the Porte regarded the Straits question as of far greater importance than the railroad agreement. He would submit the whole matter to the cabinet.[69] Three days later he was not yet in a position to give a reply. Charykov wrote home for permission to initiate the French and British ambassadors. This permission was never given.[70] Neratov had not approved of Charykov's independent action and already on December 6 the *Novoie Vremia* published a semi-official communiqué stating that the Russian government was not negotiating officially with the Turkish government about the Straits and that it had no knowledge of private conversations between Charykov and Assim Bey on this question.[71]

At this very moment Sazonov arrived in Paris on a tour preliminary to the resumption of his ministerial duties. There he conferred not only with the French statesmen, but with Isvolski and Benckendorff, who had come from London to be present. No doubt he learned in detail what the attitude of the French and English governments was, and we may imagine that Isvolski gave a not too favorable review of Charykov's high-handed action.[72] Besides this, he must have been put *au courant* of the negotiations between Serbia and Bulgaria, for Milovanovic had conferred in Paris with Stanciov and Rizov on November 18–19. The French had been more or less initiated into the project from the beginning and had given it their blessing. Milovanovic had spoken eloquently

---

and Progress. See Mandelstam (who was first dragoman of the Russian embassy), *Le Sort de l'Empire Ottoman*, p. 66; *Neue Freie Presse*, Dec. 11, 1911.

[69] Marchand, *Un livre noir*, I, 173; II, 461; Stieve, *Der diplomatische Schriftwechsel Isvolskis*, I, no. 171.

[70] Marchand, *Un livre noir*, II, 461. Neratov merely suggested at Paris that the French ambassador be informed (*ibid.*, I, 173; Stieve, *Der diplomatische Schriftwechsel*, I, no. 171).

[71] Marchand, *Un livre noir*, I, 173; II, 461; Stieve, *Der diplomatische Schriftwechsel*, I, no. 171. Especially Neratov to Isvolski, December 9, where he speaks of the "six points malheureusement déjà transmis officiellement par Tcharykof à Hassim Bey, dont le texte complet, et par son essence et par sa rédaction, provoque de notre part les observations que Tcharykof connaît déjà." Cf. also Dillon, *Contemporary Review* (January 1912), who says he can vouch for the disapproval of Neratov and Sazonov. The Russian *démenti* of December 6 in the *Neue Freie Presse*, Dec. 6, 7; Hoschiller, *L'Europe devant Constantinople*, p. 65; Vellay, *Le Problème méditerranéen*, p. 63.

[72] *The Times* (London), Dec. 7, 8, 9, 1911; *Neue Freie Presse*, Dec. 8. According to K. Helfferich, *Der Weltkrieg* (Berlin, 1919), I, 93–94, Benckendorff begged Sazonov on his knees to have the scheme dropped.

of the Austrian designs in northern Albania and the French statesmen had declared themselves prepared to further the solution of Serbia's national problems in every respect. They were distinctly sceptical about a Balkan confederation, while they sympathized entirely with the idea of a Serbian-Bulgarian treaty which would create an "effective barrier against German-Austrian pressure."[73]

This was quite in accordance with Sazonov's own views and therefore it was not likely that he would recognize Charykov's action, especially as it did not promise success. On December 8 he declared to Stephen Lauzanne of the *Matin* that there was no "Dardanelles Question" properly speaking, and that Russia had not engaged in negotiations or attempted any *démarche*. There had merely been discussions designed to keep the Straits open to commerce. On the following day he wired home that Charykov was to be instructed to establish clearly the absolutely private character of his exchange of views.[74]

With that the game was really up. On December 14 Charykov asked Assim to regard his action in the Straits question as *"non avenu"* and explained that Sazonov had been inadequately informed on the matter. Neratov, he insisted, had given his approval.[75] On the very same day the Austrian ambassador declared to the Turkish foreign minister that Austria would stand by the existing arrangements until a solution could be found that would safeguard the interests not only of Russia and of

[73] Guéchoff, *L'Alliance balkanique*, pp. 40 ff.; Popov, *Krasnyi Arkhiv*, IX, no. 51. As early as October 1909, Milovanovic had discussed with Pichon the idea of a closer union between the Balkan states and had requested the French to bring pressure upon the Bulgarians. Pichon had expressed complete sympathy with the idea (*ibid.*, p. 9). The French view on a Balkan confederation to include Turkey is well brought out in Gauvain, *L'Europe au jour le jour*, II, 313, 328, but especially in the report of Panafieu, the chargé at St. Petersburg, December 22, 1911: "Comment les populations chrétiennes des Balkans pourraient-elles accepter un lien politique quelconque qui les mettrait sous la dépendance de la Turquie et les forcerait à l'inaction, alors que toutes ont des appétits à satisfaire soit sur la Turquie elle-même, soit sur quelqu'un de leurs voisins? Leur rivalité est trop ancienne et trop aiguë; les sentiments que les Grecs, Bulgares, Roumains, Serbes manifestent à l'égard les uns des autres sont trop peu bienveillants, malgré la communauté de religion et un régime identique, et à plus forte raison à l'égard de leurs anciens maîtres les Turcs, pour qu'il soit permis d'escompter la formation d'une confédération, même sous la direction d'une grande puissance quelconque" (Driault and Lhéritier, *Histoire diplomatique*, V, 61).

[74] *Matin*, Dec. 9; *Temps*, Dec. 9; *The Times* (London), Dec. 9; *Neue Freie Presse*, Dec. 9; Marchand, *Un Livre noir*, II, 462; Gauvain, *L'Europe au jour le jour*, III, 230; *Journal des débats*, Dec. 15, 1911.

[75] *G.P.*, XXX (pt. 1), no. 10999; *Neue Freie Presse*, Dec. 14, 1911.

Turkey, but also those of the other signatory powers. The German ambassador followed with an analogous statement on the next day.[76]

Charykov evidently thought that the final word had not yet been said. He told his Rumanian colleague that the question would be raised again in the near future, and continued to urge upon the Turk statesmen the desirability of an understanding on this matter. In fact he went so far as to tell the Porte that a reply to his note was still expected. On December 21 Assim therefore handed him the following declaration:

> The Imperial government, in conformance with the treaties concluded prior to 1878 and ratified at the Congress of Berlin, cannot authorize the exclusive passage of the Russian fleet through the Straits in time of peace or in time of war and declares that all rights to the Straits belong exclusively to the Ottoman nation and its sovereignty, for the safeguarding of the integrity of its territory.[77]

This is the last that we hear of the incident. It seems likely that Sazonov, on his return to St. Petersburg, looked into the matter more closely and sent even more categorical instructions to the ambassador. To the Serbian minister he spoke in almost scathing terms of the whole incident:

> M. Charykov [reported Popovic], whom many regard as a somewhat muddle-headed politician, knows that this question is one of great importance for Russia, and that the statesman who succeeds in solving it will cover himself with glory. Since M. Neratov directed the foreign office until a few days ago, M. Charykov made use of the weakness of the interregnum to pluck a few laurels for himself, by raising the question at Constantinople on his own responsibility. With Sazonov's return the matter immediately took on a different aspect.[78]

---

[76] *G.P.*, XXX (pt. 1), no. 10997; *The Times* (London), Dec. 18, 1911; *Neue Freie Presse*, Dec. 17; Hoschiller, *L'Europe devant Constantinople*, p. 66.

[77] *G.P.*, XXX (pt. 1), nos. 11000, 11002, 11003; text of the reply in *Schulthess' Europäischer Geschichtskalender, 1911*, p. 521; Hoschiller, *L'Europe devant Constantinople*, p. 66; Adamov, *Konstantinopel*, p. 16. The date generally given, December 8, is obviously old style, though the Turkish cabinet seems to have reached its decision on December 7 or 8 new style (*Neue Freie Presse*, Dec. 9, 1911).

[78] Bogitschewitsch, *Kriegsursachen*, p. 167; similarly *G.P.*, XXX (pt. 1), no. 11004; *Neue Freie Presse*, Dec. 15, 1911. Also a letter of Georges Louis, December 30: "M. Tcharykoff, emporté-par son ardeur habituelle et convaincu qu'en allant de l'avant il serait approuvé par l'Empereur, a pressé le Gouvernement turc plus que ne le souhaitait M. Neratoff, beaucoup plus en tout que ne le voulait M. Sazonoff, qui a compris tout de suite qu'il fallait arrêter net des démarches qui découvraient si inopportunément le gouvernement russe" (Judet, *Georges Louis*, p. 166).

Had Sazonov had his way Charykov would have been recalled immediately. As it was he was allowed to stay until mid-March 1912, almost till the very moment that the Serbo-Bulgarian treaty was signed.[79] Negotiations for this important pact had taken a more energetic course since the reappearance of Sazonov. Hartwig, who was in entire sympathy with the foreign minister's views, had long been chafing at Charykov's schemes. The confederation which the latter advocated he regarded as a Utopia. Serbia and Bulgaria, he reported on November 5, would agree to it if the Russian government insisted, but neither was enthusiastic and the whole negotiations might be jeopardized if the point were pressed. Besides, the confederation could never be a stable institution. At best it would be merely a temporary expedient designed to gain time not only for the Balkan states, but for Russia, whose ultimate aim, after all, must be the realization of an age-old mission: to set foot upon the shores of the Bosporus, the entrance to the "Russian Sea." [80] As a matter of fact the Bulgarians had no desire to see the Russians gain control of the Straits and they were profoundly dismayed by the news of Charykov's *démarche*. On December 6, the very day on which the Russian government had issued a denial that negotiations were being conducted at Constantinople, Neratov wrote to the Russian minister in Sofia:

> You may inform Gueshov confidentially that an exchange of opinions is taking place between the Turks and ourselves in regard to questions interesting us in particular. In this we are treating with especial care the questions which may affect the interests of the Balkan countries. In particular, as regards the Bulgarian interests, we contemplate no deals affecting those matters which formed the subject of our confidential proposals to Bulgaria in 1910 . . .[81]

[79] On December 29 the *Neue Freie Presse* reported that Charykov would be recalled on January 14, that is, the Russian New Year. Similarly *G.P.*, XXX (pt. 1), no. 11046. When finally recalled, Charykov was practically disgraced. The exact reasons for this are not clear, but it was generally agreed that his disappearance meant the end of the Russian pro-Turk policy (*Neue Freie Presse*, Mar. 14, 1912; *The Times* (London), Mar. 13, 1912; Schwertfeger, *Zur europäischen Politik*, IV, no. 7; Gauvain, *L'Europe au jour le jour*, IV, 13; *Affaires balkaniques*, I, no. 25). Moukhtar, *La Turquie*, p. 211, thinks Charykov was recalled at the instigation of the English and the French.

[80] Hartwig to Neratov, November 5. See further Popov, *Krasnyi Arkhiv*, VIII, no. 44.

[81] Guéchoff, *L'Alliance balkanique*, p. 59; Popov, *Krasnyi Arkhiv*, IX, no. 56. On the Bulgarian view in respect to the Straits see the numerous quotations in Protic, *The Aspirations of Bulgaria, passim.*

One could hardly imagine a more deceptive statement. In any case, the Charykov incident showed the need of hurrying the negotiations between the Balkan states. The Austrians were making efforts to engineer a league between Bulgaria and Rumania with which Turkey would in all likelihood be associated.[82] The Turks themselves were suggesting to Bulgaria an entente providing that neither party should interfere in the domestic affairs of the other, that each should so regulate its home affairs that its neighbors should have no reason to complain, and that each should promise not to undertake to enlarge its frontiers for a period of perhaps ten years. This was the Turk reply to the suggestions which Gueshov had made two months before. He was justified in suspecting their sincerity, therefore, and looking upon the whole move as an attempt to sound out the position of Bulgaria.[83]

In any case it was too late for such combinations. Returning from a visit to Vienna, Ferdinand appears to have become convinced that the Entente powers were in the ascendant and that little was to be hoped from Austria. He was more disposed than he had ever been to accept the alliance with Serbia, especially as the Russians were now urgently pressing the point. Neratov suggested that the agreement should be based on the principle of mutual support in case of the violation of the status quo and the delimitation of spheres of cultural influence. This would protect both parties from attack and would obviate the necessity of deciding in advance the problems of the future. All efforts of the Russian representatives were now concentrated on this problem, and by the end of December almost all the difficulties had been removed.[84] There remained only the drawing of the line of partition in Macedonia, upon which both sides insisted. By the end of February even this point

---

[82] Popov, *Krasnyi Arkhiv*, IX, nos. 54, 57, 59, 60. The Austrians appear to have offered the Bulgarians a free hand in Macedonia.

[83] *Ibid.*, no. 58. Guéchoff, *L'Alliance balkanique*, pp. 8–10, gives the text of Assim's note, but says it was never submitted to the Bulgarian government. The Russian documents show that this is a plain misstatement.

[84] Popov, *Krasnyi Arkhiv*, IX, nos. 57, 59, 62, 65; Guéchoff, *L'Alliance balkanique*, p. 58; Siebert, *Diplomatische Aktenstücke*, p. 153. Already on December 11 Milovanovic had jubilantly declared in the Skupchtina that the Balkan States were drawing together and that this gave him greater confidence in the future. See *Neue Freie Presse*, Dec. 12, 16. New fears of Austrian aggression had made the Serbs more pliable. See Popov, *Krasnyi Arkhiv*, IX, no. 52; *Affaires balkaniques*, I, nos. 1, 2. Ferdinand evidently felt uneasy about the anti-Austrian implications of the treaty until the very end. See Nekludoff, *Diplomatic Reminiscences*, p. 63.

had been settled. There was no more serious talk of including Turkey or even of Russian-Turkish friendship. In fact Sazonov began the new year with vigorous attempts to mediate between the Italian government and the Porte, taking a distinctly friendly attitude towards Italy throughout. It may well be that the Italian government was not entirely a stranger to the Serbian-Bulgarian negotiations.[85] At any rate, with the conclusion of the Balkan alliance the Charykov incident passed into history and a new chapter in Russian foreign policy was begun.

"It is difficult, even after the event, to get any clear idea of the purpose and proceedings of Russian diplomacy, further than that it has been going to and fro in the earth and walking up and down in it; for even when it plays Providence, it moves in a mysterious way," says "A Diplomatist" in his interesting book on *Nationalism and War in the Near East* (p. 162). The purpose of this paper has been to elucidate one of the most obscure chapters in the history of Russian pre-war diplomacy. The aim has been to show how the Russian policy was dominated by two fundamental considerations, which were closely connected. The first was to gain control of the Straits and the second to block the *Drang nach Osten* of the central powers. In ultimate aims there was perhaps little difference between the Russian statesmen, but in regard to methods there was no unity whatsoever. Each thought that he had the key to the situation, and none of them hesitated to double-cross the other in the attainment of the goal. The critical moment came with the outbreak of the Tripolitan War. Germany and Austria, as allies of Italy, were temporarily discredited at Constantinople. Isvolski believed that the moment when Italy was realizing on the Racconigi agreement and France was establishing her position in Morocco presented a golden opportunity for Russia to demand freedom of action in the Straits. There is no indication that he favored definite action at Constantinople just then. As in 1908 he thought it more important to square the great powers first. On the other hand Charykov believed the time had come for a real step in advance. Turkey's embarrassment could be exploited in Russia's interest. The Balkan states were drawing together. Turkey

---

[85] The statement of Italian complicity has often been advanced. Cf., for example, Saint-Victor de Saint-Blanchard in *Revue des sciences politiques* (January–February 1913), pp. 24–47: "L'historien futur devra rechercher les origines du bloc balkanique dans la coopération de l'Italie et de la Russie depuis les accords de Racconigi jusqu'aux menées de M. Isvolsky et de M. Tittoni." The Turkish government certainly believed in Italian intrigues. See also Popov, *Krasnyi Arkhiv*, IX, no. 55.

could be sold membership in the league and a guarantee of the territory adjacent to the Straits for the price of concessions to Russia in the shape of free passage for her warships in time of war as well as peace.

Neratov, temporarily in charge of the foreign office, was apparently a man of no authority. He was a tool of Isvolski, but was unable to force through the one ambassador's program as against the other's. His instructions to Charykov betray uncertainty and indecision. They were ill-defined and left too much to the ambassador's discretion. Charykov, an incurable optimist (he was nick-named *"à la bonne heure"* by his colleagues), plunged into the work of realizing his favorite idea, drew up unwarranted proposals on his own initiative, and gave the whole procedure a much more formal character than had been intended.[86] The scheme was bound to fail. Russian public opinion and Russian official circles were interested in the Straits and regarded the idea of a Balkan confederation as at best a means to the end.[87] In Constantinople, on the other hand, there was considerable interest in the confederation, but the old suspicions of Russian policy persisted and were only enhanced by the reopening of the Straits question. The Turks desired a confederation solely in order to forestall aggressive tendencies on the part of the Balkan states. They feared the hand of Russia and in any case were unwilling to purchase protection at the Russian price.

The net result of Charykov's action was that he estranged the great powers and made the realization of Isvolski's plan once more impossible; he also estranged the Turks and drove them back into the arms of the central powers; and finally he contributed indirectly to the conclusion of a Balkan alliance which not only left out the Turks but actually established the principle of success at the expense of the Turks. In the end the Balkan league, which the Russians had always intended should be primarily a barrier against the Austrian advance, became an instrument of aggression in the opposite direction. The whole idea had become distorted and the results were disastrous for European peace. For it should be particularly emphasized that the Russians at this time

[86] On Charykov's character see Nekludov's estimate (March 1911): "Il est très allant et dépasse souvent ses instructions. Son imagination l'entraîne, son optimisme aussi, et il ne voit jamais qu'il se trompe. Il est tellement saisi par son idée du moment qu'il croit n'en avoir jamais eu d'autre. See *Carnets de Georges Louis*, I, 167; similarly von Szilassy, *Der Untergang der Donaumonarchie*, p. 186.

[87] On Russian opinion see Hoschiller, *L'Europe devant Constantinople*, p. 75; Mandelstam, *Le Sort de l'Empire Ottoman*, p. 66; Conrad, *Aus meiner Dienstzeit*, II, 213 ff.; but especially *Neue Freie Presse*, Nov. 22, and *The Times* (London), Nov. 13, 1911.

had no aggressive plans. They were quite unprepared for war and everybody knew it. In encouraging the Balkan league they were merely trying to prevent the exploitation of their weakness by their rivals. Isvolski, Charykov, Sazonov, all alike desired nothing more fervently than the maintenance of the status quo. But Isvolski and Charykov hoped to secure it by acquiring control of the key to the Near East, the Straits. Sazonov, on the other hand, like Hartwig, believed that the far-flung schemes of the two ambassadors were not realizable. At best one could hope to bring the Balkan states into the same anti-Austrian fold. If this could be done only by giving the combination an anti-Turkish turn as well, the chance must be taken. After all, they argued, Russia, which had stood sponsor to the whole plan, would be able to control the actions of these small states. The evidence on this point is overwhelming. Until the end of the summer of 1912 Sazonov brought pressure to bear upon the Balkan states to prevent the outbreak of hostilities.[88] He failed

---

[88] The Confederation, Russia fondly believed, "would prove a docile instrument in her hands and serve the double purpose of maintaining peace in the Balkans and of barring an Austrian advance to the Aegean" (George Buchanan, *My Mission to Russia* [London, 1923], I, 121). The correctness of this view is borne out by Sazonov's own letter to Isvolski and Benckendorff on March 31, 1912, notifying them of the conclusion of the Serbo-Bulgarian pact: "Since there is a special clause which obliges both sides to consult Russia before taking active measures, we believe that this gives us the means of bringing pressure on both parties and that at the same time we have taken protective measures to oppose the expansion of the influence of a larger power in the Balkans" (Siebert, *Diplomatische Aktenstücke*, p. 154). See also Sazonov, *Fateful Years*, p. 54; Kiderlen's letter to King Carol, April 15, 1912, in E. Jäckh, *Kiderlen-Waechter* (Berlin, 1924), II, 186. When Danev, on a mission to Livadia in May 1912, hinted at the possibility of war against Turkey, Sazonov was horrified. Russia, he said, sympathized with an alliance for defense, but not with one which envisaged offense. Russian opinion would not countenance such action on the part of the Balkan States. See Siebert, *Diplomatische Aktenstücke*, pp. 522–525; Nekludoff, *Diplomatic Reminiscences*, pp. 82–83; Guéchoff, *L'Alliance balkanique*, p. 73 ff.; Velchev's pamphlet, *The Full Truth about Bulgaria's Collapse* (1913) quoted in *Schulthess' Europäischer Geschichtskalendar*, *1913*, pp. 759–760. When Poincaré came to St. Petersburg in August 1912 and was shown a copy of the treaty, he pointed out its implications in dismay, but Sazonov reassured him with these words: "We warned Bulgaria and Serbia of Russia's intention not to recognize the alliance concluded by them excepting as a defensive measure aiming to guarantee the independence and liberty of these countries against the designs of Austria-Hungary and that we did not wish in any way to collaborate in projects of aggression on their part" (Marchand, *Un Livre noir*, II, 342; *Affaires balkaniques*, I, no. 57). As late as September, Sazonov told the Bulgarian minister in London to avoid war, because war would bring Russia into conflict with the Triple Alliance or Turkey: "We do not want to be exposed to this danger. We have not yet liquidated one war, do you want to force us into another one? No, we shall leave you to your fate and your own statesmen shall bear the responsibility for the catastrophic results. Our idea of an agreement among the Balkan states was intended to protect the peninsula against foreign

entirely to foresee that the Balkan bloc, prepared by Russia to obstruct the road of the Austrian advance, would automatically turn against Turkey. With the rest of Europe he was taken unawares by the outbreak of the war.[89]

Of the Balkan states themselves little need be said. In the years from 1908 to 1912 each and all of them were torn by conflicting motives. They all felt the need of protection, either against Austria or against Turkey. At the same time they were unwilling to give up their grand ideas. In order to guard themselves against the enemy and further their designs they were ready to stoop to any means, even to an agreement with the enemy if necessary. There is nothing edifying in the picture here presented either of Russian policy or of the policy of the various Balkan states. But, like their patron, the small states in 1911 were still thinking primarily in terms of defense. The military leaders were all impressed with the strength of the Turkish army; and the Serbs, at least, intended that the alliance, if it ever functioned at all, should function against Austria.[90] It was Danev and other Bulgarian leaders of the same stamp who finally precipitated the crisis and gave the whole league its outspokenly anti-Turkish character. The Serbs were unable to stem the tide. Like Sazonov they had not reckoned on being outwitted, though all were playing a game the object of which was to exploit one's friends in one's own interest.

---

conquest. We had no thought whatsoever of an alliance with aggressive purposes" (Velchev, quoted in *Schulthess' Europäischer Geschichtskalender, 1913,* pp. 759–760).

[89] Miliukov in the *Retch,* July 25, 1916, quoted by Brailsford, *A League of Nations,* p. 64. Similarly the Bulgarian newspaper *Volia:* "The Balkan War broke out against the wish of Russia, which had created the Balkan Alliance in the hope of directing it against Austria, when the moment for a declaration of war on Germany should arrive" (quoted by Protic, *The Aspirations of Bulgaria,* p. 154).

[90] Bourchier in *The Times* (London), June 13, 1913, says that in February 1912 he found Milovanovic still worried at the idea of a rupture with the Porte. Cf. also M., *Fortnightly Review* (March 1913): "When the question of an alliance was first mentioned the possibility of a war did not seriously enter into the calculations of the contracting parties." This is amply proved by the story of the negotiations, as outlined above. In March 1912 Milovanovic described as the chief object of the treaty "protection against Austria" (Bogitschewitsch, *Kriegsursachen,* p. 35). Herbert Adams Gibbons, *The New Map of Europe* (New York, 1914), p. 267, rightly emphasizes the fact that until the actual outbreak of the war the military leaders were greatly impressed with the Ottoman strength in the Balkans. It is well known that throughout Europe it was feared that the Balkan states would be defeated.

5

Bismarck as a Dramatist

1961

In the political memoir literature there is probably no passage comparable in vividness and dramatic force to Bismarck's account of the outbreak of war with France in 1870 as it appears in his *Gedanken und
Erinnerungen*. We are told by the editors of his collected works that
these memoirs, though not published until 1898, were dictated soon
after the chancellor's dismissal in 1890. Furthermore, that the twenty-
second chapter, dealing with the crisis of July 1870, was the one he
worked on last and the only chapter he left substantially in its original
form. It is interesting to note that Bismarck entitled this chapter "The
Ems Despatch," thus giving particular prominence to what was undoubtedly his favorite story: how, during dinner with Moltke and Roon
on the evening of July 13, 1870, they were saved from utter despair by
the arrival of a telegram from Ems which, after appropriate editing by
Bismarck, saved the situation by provoking the French government to
declare war. The episode was so colorful that the iron chancellor—as
great a raconteur as a statesman—related it on countless occasions. A
dozen or more instances have been recorded by those who were associated with him, thus providing the historian with a most unusual opportunity for critical comparison. In view of the fact that there are still
many obscurities in the story of the origins of the Franco-Prussian
War, it should be well worth while reviewing the evidence in its chronological sequence and evaluating it in the light of materials which have
in recent years been added to the record.[1]

It should be emphasized at the outset that this essay does not deal
with the larger issue of responsibility for the outbreak of the war, nor,

Note: Reprinted from *Studies in Diplomatic History and Historiography in
Honor of G. P. Gooch*, ed. by A. O. Sarkissian (London, 1961).

[1] Robert Pahncke, *Die Parallel-Erzählungen Bismarcks zu seinen Gedanken und
Erinnerungen* (Halle, 1914), attempted to do just this, but in the matter of the
Ems dispatch his inspiration failed him, and he was unable to advance beyond a
pedestrian catalogue of similarities and differences among the various accounts.

in a narrower sense, with Bismarck's role in the Hohenzollern candidacy for the Spanish throne, nor even with the transactions between King William and the French ambassador, Count Benedetti, at Ems on July 13. The purpose of the paper is a restricted one: to examine the various accounts given by Bismarck of the dinner party with Moltke and Roon and, through analysis, to attempt to establish the facts which, I believe, have been seriously distorted in the chancellor's telling and retelling. The crucial passage in Bismarck's memoirs has been appended to the text (pp. 144–146), in English translation, for the convenience of the reader.

It will suffice here to recall that, according to Bismarck, he had decided to resign his offices and was engaged in argument with his two guests when a telegram arrived from Heinrich Abeken, counsellor of the Prussian foreign office, in attendance upon the King during the latter's cure at Ems. The chancellor read this telegram aloud to Moltke and Roon, who thereupon became so dejected that they lost their appetite. Bismarck, however, noted the authorization given him to publish the fact that Benedetti, the French ambassador, had asked the King to promise not to approve any future revival of the candidacy, and the further fact that the King had refused. Having received assurances from Moltke that the Prussian army was ready and that the sooner war broke out, the better, he edited the Abeken telegram by greatly reducing its length and by giving it a tone of brusqueness and finality. On hearing the new version Moltke, ordinarily so taciturn, broke out with the enthusiastic exclamation: "Now it has a different ring; it sounded before like a *schamade* [i.e. a parley]; now it is like a *fanfare* in answer to a challenge." Bismarck proceeded to explain that if he sent this report at once to the newspapers and telegraphed it to the Prussian missions in South Germany and abroad, it would soon be known in Paris and would act like a red rag on the Gallic bull. This explanation brought the two generals to a surprisingly joyous mood. They recovered their pleasure in food and drink. Roon thanked God for not letting them perish in disgrace, while Moltke "glancing up joyously towards the ceiling and abandoning his usual punctiliousness of speech, smote his hand upon his breast and said: 'If I live to lead our armies in such a war, then the devil may come directly afterward and fetch away the old carcass.' " [2]

[2] Otto von Bismarck, *Gedanken und Erinnerungen* (Berlin, 1951 ed.), pp. 231–232.

In order to appreciate this story at all, it is essential to go back a few days, not only to recall the circumstances of Bismarck's coming to Berlin on July 12 and the impact of Prince Anthony's renunciation of the Hohenzollern candidacy in behalf of his son, but also to consider the role of Moltke and Roon. The generals were agreed that the Prussian army was superior to the French, whatever the French might think. They also believed firmly, as did Bismarck, that German unity could never be achieved without a prior reckoning with France. And finally, they were convinced that the moment was favorable, since in the future France might not only strengthen its forces but might actually secure the alliance of Austria and Italy. Already in the council of March 15, 1870, Moltke had been completely reassuring as to the military situation. In early July, when the situation became suddenly acute through the provocative statement of the French foreign minister in the *Corps législatif*, Moltke was living quietly on his estates in Silesia, as Bismarck was at Varzin in Pomerania. But on the afternoon of July 11 the Prussian ministers who were still in Berlin conferred at length on the situation. Those present were Hermann von Thile, the undersecretary of the foreign office, Count Eulenburg, the minister of the interior (a man who enjoyed Bismarck's full confidence), the ministers of justice and of commerce, and, on the military side, General von Roon, the minister of war, General von Podbielski (Roon's deputy) and Colonel von Stiehle, Moltke's deputy and a man in whom the chief-of-staff put the greatest trust. It is difficult to believe that such a council would have met without Bismarck's approval. The chancellor had already decided to leave Varzin and go to Ems, but was unable to reach Berlin until the following day, July 12.

The council of July 11 discussed what military measures should be taken in view of the likelihood that France would make the Hohenzollern candidacy an occasion for war. The decision was to advise the King against taking special or partial measures: if and when he regarded war as inevitable, the only proper course would be to order total mobilization.[3] The council further considered sending Roon or Eulenburg to the King at Ems, and furthermore dispatched, through Stiehle,

[3] Robert H. Lord, *Origins of the War of 1870* (Cambridge, Mass., 1924), pp. 59–60, first called attention to the importance of this meeting. On the confidence of Stiehle and the military men, see also the telegram of the Crown Prince to Bismarck, July 11, in George Bonnin, *Bismarck and the Hohenzollern Candidature for the Spanish Throne* (London, 1957), p. 247, and Holstein's note in Norman Rich and M. H. Fisher, *The Holstein Papers* (Cambridge, 1955), I, 41.

a telegram recalling Moltke to Berlin. This message was brought to the chief-of-staff as he was out driving, and he must have received it in time to enable him to take the train at about 7 P.M., bringing him to Berlin before 6 A.M. on July 12.[4] On that same day Bismarck travelled from Varzin to Berlin, where he expected to spend only the evening, before going on to Ems by the night train. The chancellor had been much surprised by the strong language of Gramont's declaration of July 6, which seemed to him a clear indication of the French intention to make war. He was even more disturbed by the news that the French ambassador, Count Benedetti, had arrived at Ems and had, on July 9, begun discussions with the King.[5]

Since Bismarck's position throughout was that the Hohenzollern candidacy was a matter of the Hohenzollern princes with which the Prussian government had no concern, he at once warned his master not to become involved in transactions with the ambassador and in fact offered to come to Ems himself. By the afternoon of July 11 he had the King's instructions to come, and on July 12 he went on to Berlin, where he arrived about 6 P.M. He had arranged beforehand to have Roon and Eulenburg dine with him. Moltke, having already arrived, also joined in the conferences that took place.[6] It is important to note, then, that there

---

[4] There has been the greatest confusion about the date of Moltke's return to Berlin, the more so as his presence was evidently kept secret and was not announced until July 15. See the discussion in Pahncke, *Die Parallel-Erzählungen Bismarcks*, based on the earlier inquiries of Richard Fester, *Briefe, Aktenstücke und Regesten zur Geschichte der Hohenzollernschen Thronkandidatur in Spanien* (Berlin, 1913), II, 428. The records of the office of the chief-of-staff revealed that Moltke had arrived in Berlin on July 12, which is further supported by the now incontrovertible fact that he dined with Bismarck that evening (see below). Eberhard Kessel, *Moltke* (Stuttgart, 1957), p. 542, states that it was on July 12 that the general received the summons, which simply must be wrong.

[5] According to Bismarck's remarks to Moritz von Blankenburg, which date from late July 1870 and were transmitted through Roman Andrae (see Pahncke, *Die Parallel-Erzählungen Bismarcks*, pp. 159–160), his first reaction to Gramont's speech, which he read on July 8 was to wire the King urging immediate mobilization and attack before the French were prepared. His uneasiness about the appearance of Benedetti at Ems is recorded by Robert von Keudell, *Fürst und Fürstin Bismarck* (Berlin, 1901), p. 441.

[6] For Bismarck's invitation to Roon and Eulenburg, see his note on a telegram from Eulenburg, July 11, and his telegram to Thile, same date, in Bonnin, *Bismarck*, pp. 243, 245. The *Provinzial-Korrespondenz* on July 13 reported Bismarck's consultation with Roon and Eulenburg, but did not mention Moltke (see Horst Kohl, *Bismarck-Regesten* [Leipzig, 1891], I, 396), but Bismarck on July 13 told Prince Gorchakov that he had conferred on the previous evening with Moltke as well as Roon. See Chester W. Clark, "Bismarck, Russia and the War of 1870," in *Journal of Modern History*, XIV (1942), pp. 195–208. He later repeated the statement in his memoirs.

were actually two dinner parties on successive evenings, with the same two guests. It would be natural for anyone in looking back after the crowded events that followed, to confuse what was said or done on the one occasion with what occurred on the other. I consider the evidence quite conclusive that this was what happened in Bismarck's case. What we read in his many accounts of the dinner party of July 13 (especially that in his memoirs) applies in large part to the gathering of the previous evening, which in turn puts an entirely new complexion on the accepted story of the Ems dispatch.

It is impossible, with the data presently available, to reconstruct the exact sequence of events on the evening of July 12. What we know is that the chancellor, on his arrival in Berlin about 6 P.M., found a number of telegrams. Most important of these was the one reporting the renunciation of the Hohenzollern candidacy by Prince Anthony on behalf of his son. The information from Ems left little doubt that King William, who had always disliked the project, had been using his influence to bring about the withdrawal. There was certainly a real possibility that the King, in the hope of preserving the peace, might lend his name to the renunciation and perhaps even give it official approval. Evidently Bismarck conferred with Roon and Eulenburg immediately after his arrival. In their behalf as well as his own he telegraphed His Majesty and Abeken urging that no explanation of any kind be given to Benedetti. In view of French threats any concession on the part of the King would make a bad impression on German public opinion. His Majesty had already gone a long way in receiving Benedetti after the threatening language of Gramont. A few minutes after dispatching these messages, Bismarck wired Ems that because of exhaustion he felt unable to go to Ems that night, but that Eulenburg would arrive in the morning in his stead.

Bismarck tells us in his memoirs that the news of Leopold's withdrawal came to him as a staggering blow, since it followed upon the bellicose utterances of Gramont and the vituperation of the French press. Under these conditions it constituted a humiliation even worse than that of Olmütz in 1850 and one for which he could not assume responsibility. His first inclination, therefore, was to resign. The stain on Prussia's honor could be wiped out only through war. Since the French would presumably accept the renunciation as a great victory for themselves, it would be impossible to bring about a conflict without seeming to provoke it deliberately.

This argumentation seems altogether reasonable under the circumstances and it is, in fact, borne out by the available evidence. It was more than suggested in the telegram wired to Abeken, and was clearly reflected in the chancellor's remarks to Prince Gorchakov somewhat later on the same evening. In succeeding years the chancellor referred to his reaction and his intended resignation a number of times in quite explicit terms.[7] There is, to be sure, no documentary evidence that he did in fact proffer his resignation, but it is altogether likely that Eulenburg was sent not merely to forestall further conferences between the King and Benedetti, but also to suggest Bismarck's intention to resign if further concessions were made.

Moltke appears to have arrived at Bismarck's home only in time for dinner that evening. We may assume that he, like Roon, reproached the chancellor for his talk of resignation. In any event it is noteworthy that in his earlier accounts of these stirring days, Bismarck liked to stress the fact that Moltke became dejected and irritable as he realized that the favorable moment for war was likely to slip away. He always looked ten years younger or older as the prospect for war became better or worse. And so it was when he heard of the renunciation and the continued compliance of the King.[8] To Moritz Busch he remarked on October 4, 1870: "I rememer that, when the Spanish business became hot, Moltke at once looked ten years younger. Then, when I told him that the Hohenzollern prince had reneged, he at once became quite aged and weary." [9]

[7] So to the Russian diplomat Stremoukhov in April 1873 (*Krasnyi Arkhiv*, I [1922], pp. 10 ff.); to Lucius in September 1876 (R. S. Lucius von Ballhausen, *Bismarck-Erinnerungen* [Stuttgart, 1921], pp. 91–92); to Busch in October 1877 (Moritz Busch, *Tagebuchblätter* [Leipzig, 1899], II, 481 ff.); to Horst Kohl in November 1891 (see Otto von Bismarck, *Die gesammelte Werke* [Berlin, 1923–35], IX, 175). See also Keudell, *Fürst und Fürstin Bismarck*, p. 442, and Herman Hofmann, *Fürst Bismarck* (Stuttgart, 1914), I, 174.

[8] Bismarck's remarks to Bamberger, August 2, 1870, in *Die geheimen Tagebücher Ludwig Bambergers* (Frankfurt, 1932), p. 141.

[9] Busch, *Tagebuchblätter*, I, 258 ff. See also Bismarck's talk with Stremoukhov in 1873, note 7 above, and his remarks to Hohenlohe on May 6, 1874, on the reaction of Moltke and Roon to the news of the renunciation. See Chlodwig zu Hohenlohe-Schillingsfürst, *Denkwürdigkeiten* (Stuttgart, 1907), II, 119 ff. The undated remarks of Bismarck to Kardorff in Siegfried von Kardorff, *Wilhelm von Kardorff* (Berlin, 1936), p. 188, probably belong to this same period. They give a vivid picture of Moltke's senescence and rejuvenation as Bismarck observed it at a conference with Moltke and Roon. Moltke seemed very worn and hardly fit for another campaign: "He sat there quite distracted and lost in thought. Suddenly he realized that we were on the verge of war, and in a moment he was transformed; the old man had changed into a youth, and I said to Roon: 'Look at that. Would you have credited our friend Moltke with such blood-thirstiness?' "

Bismarck told Gorchakov on the following day that both Moltke and Roon were in favor of immediate war, arguing that the advantage would be all on the side of Prussia if it acted at once. He himself, he went on, opposed such a decision, since neither reason nor religion permitted the precipitation of war. Anything, he added, might happen. Meanwhile the least that could be done would be to recall Baron von Werther, the Prussian ambassador in Paris, on indefinite leave "in order to show the country that the government had not been insensible to the arrogant language of France." [10]

This concluding remark indicates that before the evening was over, Bismarck was already plotting ways and means for resuming the course he had embarked upon before the news of the renunciation had upset his calculations. His inspiration came, no doubt, from the telegrams from Paris which awaited him on his arrival in Berlin. Dated July 10 and 11, they reported statements of Gramont to various foreign diplomats indicating that unless the Hohenzollern candidacy were withdrawn, France would make war on Prussia. Particularly ominous was an article in the *Moniteur Universel* which was known to be the mouthpiece of the French premier, M. Ollivier, and which, according to information which reached the Prussian *chargé d'affaires* from a reliable source, had been read to the council of ministers before being published. This article spoke of the need for guarantees, mentioning the full implementation of the treaty of Prague, the garrison at Mainz and the military agreements between the North German Confederation and the South German states.[11] Obviously talk of this sort played directly into the chancellor's hands. At 9:45 P.M. (July 12) he sent a telegram to Ems substantially in the terms of his conversation with Gorchakov: the German public expects at least a satisfactory explanation of the Gramont speeches. In order to meet this situation he proposed that His Majesty suggest to Werther that he take indefinite leave. It might be well for the ambassador not to conceal the reason for his departure.[12]

It should be obvious, even from this brief recapitulation of the

---

[10] Clark, *Journal of Modern History*, XIV, 200–202, prints Gorchakov's reports of July 12 and 13.

[11] Solms to Bismarck, July 10 (in Lord, *Origins*, no. 907). For Gramont's remarks to foreign diplomats see also *ibid.*, no. 96. The article in the *Moniteur* was regarded as so important that it was communicated at once to the Crown Prince (Kaiser Friedrich III, *Das Kriegstagebuch von 1870/71* [Berlin, 1926], pp. 2–3).

[12] Lord, *Origins*, no. 147.

course of events on the evening of July 12, that they fit remarkably well the narrative given by Bismarck of the dinner party of July 13. There was the shock of the Hohenzollern withdrawal, the feeling of almost irreparable humiliation, the resolution to resign, the reproaches of Roon and probably somewhat later of Moltke, the grief of the military men as they saw the golden opportunity escaping them, the reconsideration of the telegrams that had come in, the dawning of a new idea for reviving the crisis, the recovery of good spirits on the part of the generals, and finally the initiation of the new course of action. I submit that much of Bismarck's account of what happened at the dinner party on July 13 really refers to the dinner on the previous evening. Objective study of the developments of July 13 will, I believe, reveal the untenability of Bismarck's account.

The chancellor devoted most of his effort, on that eventful day, to the furtherance of the counteroffensive so admirably analyzed by the late Robert H. Lord, to whose book the reader may turn for a wealth of detail. In the present context the essentials are these: during the morning, news came from Ems that Benedetti has asked for an audience in order to request of the King a declaration or communication which the French government could lay before the legislature. Bismarck's reaction was to wire Werther at once that unless within the next few days the Prussian government were to receive from the French government completely reassuring statements about France's intentions, he would propose to His Majesty that the *Reichstag* be summoned for the beginning of the following week, for consultation regarding the course to be taken.[13]

It must have been some time in the mid-afternoon that Bismarck received a second visit from Prince Gorchakov, whom he informed of Benedetti's design. According to Gorchakov's report to the Tsar: "Bismarck has telegraphed to Werther: The Hohenzollern incident being settled, he is to demand of Gramont guarantees on the present intentions of France and to tell him that if the replies are not satisfactory, the Reichsrat [*sic*] would be convoked a week hence to vote the funds necessary for the mobilization of the entire army." This, the chancellor admitted, would mean war, but "in the uncertainty in which France has kept us, we would have no other recourse."[14] The Russian chancellor did not quarrel with this statement, for he was himself convinced

---

[13] Sent at 2:25 P.M. See *ibid.*, nos. 159, 162.
[14] Clark, *Journal of Modern History*, XIV, 201.

that the French were bent on war and that the Prussian King had done his utmost to avoid it. Indeed, he presently made available to Bismarck a telegram from Okunev, the Russian chargé d'affaires in Paris, reporting that Gramont had told Werther that Leopold's renunciation did not settle the affair, for there remained the *mauvais procédé*. This, if true, was news of the utmost importance. Bismarck at once (4:10 P.M.) telegraphed Werther inquiring as to the facts and somewhat later (5:10) repeated his inquiry with added urgency. Suspecting that Werther's messages were being interfered with, he cabled London at 6:50 P.M. requesting that the British ambassador in Paris be instructed to find out from Werther when the latter had sent his most recent message.[15]

It is perfectly clear that Bismarck was eager for confirmation of further French demands, oblique references to which began to come in from other capitals. Banking upon them, he now proceeded to push his own offensive. In conversation with Lord Loftus, the British ambassador, who had come to congratulate him on the termination of the crisis, he dilated on the provocative attitude of the French, the indignation aroused thereby in the German people and the reports that Paris was not satisfied even with the renunciation. There were, he said, indications of French military preparations which, if persisted in, would oblige the Prussian government to demand explanations. "After what has occurred, we must require . . . some guarantee that we shall not be subjected to a sudden attack; we must know that, this Spanish difficulty once removed, there are no other lurking dangers which may burst upon us like a thunderstorm." Among other things the French would have to explain or withdraw Gramont's declaration of July 6.[16]

Bismarck certainly counted on his remarks to both Gorchakov and Loftus being relayed to the French, as they were. In short, he was now about to challenge the French government. By the late afternoon of July 13 he knew from incoming reports that the important European governments thoroughly disapproved of further French demands. He knew also that it was most unlikely that Austria-Hungary would support the French militarily and that the South German states, even Württemberg, were disgusted with the French attitude and would sup-

[15] Lord, *Origins*, nos. 166, 172, 175.
[16] Great Britain, House of Commons, *Sessional Papers*, 1870, LXX, no. 53; Augustus Loftus, *Diplomatic Reminiscences*, 2d ser. (London, 1894), I, 274 ff.

port the North German Confederation in a war. He had, of course, known for some time that the military men believed that the French were overestimating their power, that the Prussian army was definitely superior and that, even without the support of South Germany, victory was almost certain.[17]

It is against this background that the account of the dinner party with Moltke and Roon, as given in Bismarck's memoirs, must be scrutinized. It is hard indeed to see why, at this time, the chancellor should have been talking of resignation, the more so as he knew that the King would not receive Benedetti again prior to Eulenburg's arrival, that he would refuse Benedetti's request for a statement, and that he proposed to tell the ambassador that, since Paris and Madrid had learned of the renunciation before he (the King) had heard of it, he had nothing further to tell him.[18] It is equally difficult to understand why the three men should have been low in spirit, for it was by this time reasonably certain that the French were going to advance further demands and that these could be made the occasion for war. The chancellor, as we know from his conversations with Gorchakov and Loftus, had decided to demand guarantees of the French. It was entirely in keeping with his determination to turn the tables on the French that he wrote out longhand a telegram which was sent to the King at 8:10 P.M.: In view of the growing exasperation of public opinion (said the message) he, Bismarck, considered it necessary that a summons (at first he wrote *ultimatum*) be addressed to France to explain her intentions with respect to Germany. In order to draft such a document, Moltke and Roon joined him in urging His Majesty to return at once to Berlin.[19]

It was at this point that Bismarck was handed the text of Abeken's most recent telegram from Ems (sent at 3:10 P.M.; arrived at 6:09 P.M.; certainly deciphered before 8 P.M.). He read it to his two guests who,

[17] On the confidence of Moltke's deputy, Colonel von Stiehle, see Lord, *Origins*, no. 93, and Kaiser Friedrich III, *Kriegstagebuch*, p. 2.

[18] According to Lord, *Origins*, no. 159, it was sent from Ems at 10:15 A.M., evidently before Abeken knew of the King's famous interview with the ambassador on the promenade. The telegram was received in Berlin at 12:25 P.M.

[19] *Ibid.*, no. 181. Lord points out that in view of the time necessary to encipher such a message, Bismarck must have written it at about 7 P.M. Since there is in it no trace of recent news from Ems, it must have been sent off to be enciphered before Abeken's famous Ems dispatch had been deciphered. Bismarck was told of the arrival of Abeken's telegram, and it is strange that he should have sent off so important a message as that cited above without awaiting the deciphering of the incoming telegram.

according to Bismarck's oft-repeated story, were completely floored by it, becoming so dejected that they lost all appetite and laid down their knives and forks.[20]

Historians have long been at a loss to explain the general gloom in which this historic dinner was from the outset shrouded. For a long time it was supposed that news of Gramont's proposal to Werther that King William write Napoleon a letter of explanation and regret was at the bottom of it. But this thesis became untenable when the publication of the documents by Lord showed that nothing was known of this in Berlin until just before midnight. Lord was probably right in conjecturing that the temper and the talk at dinner was quite different from what Bismarck would have us believe: "It seems much more likely that the conversation turned upon the tantalizing vagueness of the news from Paris, upon the plans for a diplomatic offensive which Bismarck had outlined to Loftus, and upon the impatience of all three men for immediate action." [21]

As for the staggering effect of the Abeken telegram from Ems, this is, by any standard, quite incomprehensible. Actually the telegram contained what for all three should at that time have been good news. Benedetti had accosted the King on the public promenade and had requested him urgently to promise never again to give his approval to a Hohenzollern candidacy for the Spanish throne. The King had flatly refused. Having, however, promised Benedetti on an earlier occasion that he would let him know when he received confirmation of the withdrawal, he later sent an adjutant to say that he now had such confirmation and that he had nothing further to say to the ambassador. Eulenburg had arrived at Ems about noon and had dissuaded the King from receiving the ambassador personally to communicate this news. How, under these circumstances, Bismarck could speak of the Abeken telegram as a second Olmütz and complain that the King was continuing

[20] Bismarck's conversation with Busch, December 19, 1870, and October 20, 1877 (Busch, *Tagebuchblätter,* I, 545 ff.; II, 481 ff.); with Lucius, September 26, 1876 (Lucius von Ballhausen, *Bismarck-Erinnerungen,* pp. 91–92); with Mittnacht, February 23, 1889 (Hermann Mittnacht, *Erinnerungen an Bismarck* [Stuttgart, 1905], pp. 65–66), and several conversations following the dictation of the memoirs in 1890.

[21] Lord, *Origins,* no. 98. More recently Jochen Dittrich, "Bismarck, Frankreich und die Hohenzollernkandidatur," *Die Welt als Geschichte,* XIII (1953), 42–57, has pointed out, in my opinion quite rightly, that the evening of July 12, not that of July 13, might have been the gloomy one.

to yield all along the line passes the ordinary understanding.[22] The telegram, which for the first time provided reliable information about further French demands, should by all odds have brought elation rather than dejection. In view of what is now known of the general situation it is hard to escape the conclusion that Bismarck's account of the impact of the telegram from Ems is entirely fictitious.[23]

In Bismarck's memoirs one then arrives at the most dramatic passage: while his guests were lost in gloom, a light dawned on the chancellor as he reread the Abeken telegram. The King had authorized him to publish Benedetti's new demand and its rejection, and this he proceeded to do, but only after inquiring of Moltke how soon military preparations could be completed. On learning that the sooner war broke out, the better, he "edited" the Abeken telegram leaving, as he once put it, only the head and tail and, instead of merely reporting the rejection of the demand, concluded his release with the statement: "His Majesty the King thereupon decided not to receive the French ambassador again and sent an aide-de-camp on duty to tell him that His Majesty had nothing further to communicate." [24]

Bismarck would have us believe that the mere reading of the terse, revised text was enough to rouse Moltke from his listlessness and to induce him to exclaim: "Now it has a different ring. Before it sounded like a *schamade* [parley]; now it is like a *fanfare* [flourish] in reply to a challenge." On Bismarck's further explanation that if the announcement were released at once to the newspapers and sent to the Prussian missions abroad, it would be known in Paris by midnight and, not only for its contents but because of the method of its distribution, would have the effect of a red rag on the Gallic bull, his guests fully recovered their spirits and rejoiced at the renewed prospect of almost certain war. Their appetite returned and while Roon thanked the Almighty for not

[22] The limit was certainly reached in Bismarck's talk with Lucius (September 26, 1876) when he insisted that the King had even agreed to the demand for a guarantee against renewal of the candidacy.

[23] In roughly half of the known versions of this event, it is the renunciation which is spoken of as a second Olmütz, and so it is in the memoirs. In the other half it is the Abeken report that is so characterized, in my opinion quite erroneously.

[24] The editing of the Ems telegram or dispatch has been subjected to a great deal of critical analysis, which need not be repeated for purposes of the present paper. In general, recent writers are much less severe on Bismarck's procedure than they were a generation ago.

139

letting them die in disgrace, Moltke smote his breast and cried: "If I live to lead our armies in such a war, then the devil may come directly afterwards and fetch away the old carcass."

Unfortunately even this colorful passage will not withstand critical scrutiny. In the three versions of the episode that date from 1870 the emphasis, as noted above, was on the fact that Moltke seemed older or younger as war seemed more remote or more close. Only in 1876 does there appear any reference to Moltke's and Roon's loss of appetite (conversation with Lucius), and this motif does not recur prior to the dictation of the memoirs in 1890. After that it was repeated several times, showing how pleased the chancellor was with it. But least authentic is probably the story of the enthusiastic exclamations of Moltke and Roon. There is no suggestion of these in the earlier accounts. In December 1870 Bismarck told Busch that on reading his edited version, the two generals said: "Yes, that will do." Years later, in 1877, Bismarck recalled the famous supper party in the very presence of Moltke and Roon and made no mention whatever of their reaction to his editing.[25] In his remarks to Busch in October 1877, he reported the two generals as saying: "that would do." Not until much later was a more dramatic note introduced. Narrating the episode to a group of deputies, probably some time in the 1880s, the chancellor had Moltke and Roon react to his reading of the edited text with the cry: "Splendid, that will surely work!" And finally, in his account to Freiherr von Mittnacht in 1889, he had Moltke declare that it sounded "like a challenge with trumpets." [26] From there it was but a short step to the vivid account in the memoirs, which were dictated in the following year. In this definitive form it suited Bismarck so well that in the accounts postdating the composition of the memoirs he repeated many of the phrases, invariably including the picturesque words *schamade* and *fanfare*.[27]

One more item calls for consideration: Bismarck's contention that the revised Ems dispatch and its communication to foreign govern-

[25] Lucius, *Bismarck-Erinnerungen,* pp. 97 ff.

[26] Mittnacht, *Erinnerungen an Bismarck,* pp. 65–66. The account to the deputies, undated and anonymously reported, appeared in the *Neue Freie Presse,* Nov. 21, 1892, and was reprinted in Heinrich von Poschinger, *Bismarck und die Parlamentarier* (Breslau, 1894–96), II, 128–130.

[27] As a piquant detail it may be remarked that in the only known non-Bismarckian account, that of Roon's son (in *Kreuzzeitung,* May 14, 1891), there is no suggestion of enthusiasm on the part of the generals: "He [Bismarck] read the abbreviated version to his two guests and received their approval."

ments did in fact enrage the French to the point of declaring war. The subject is too large and too complicated to be given adequate treatment here, but Bismarck's thesis has long since been questioned and a strong case can in fact be made for the proposition that the dispatch played only a subsidiary role. In Paris a hot and unequal contest had been going on for days between those demanding the humiliation of Prussia even at the cost of war, and those still striving to preserve peace. Recent studies suggest that the prevailing mood of the public was bellicose and the thirst for revenge for Sadowa great.[28] On the other hand, Gramont was at all times in advance of public opinion in his determination to win a victory, either diplomatic or military. The Ems dispatch did not appear in the Paris newspapers until July 14, and then in a curiously garbled version. For to the Havas report from Berlin, giving the text as published in the semiofficial *Norddeutsche Allgemeine Zeitung* at 10:00 P.M. on July 13, was added another statement, of uncertain origin, saying that King William had approved the renunciation of the candidacy (which indeed he had, though Bismarck did not know this at the time he edited the Ems telegram). Thus the Paris press was uncertain whether France had obtained satisfaction or not. It was only at 7:30 P.M. that the Paris *Soir* appeared with the story that a public affront had been offered the French ambassador, and it was only in the late evening that the council of ministers at St. Cloud made the decision for war. It may well be that this decision was influenced by news that the Ems dispatch had been officially communicated to other governments and that in at least some cases there had been added to it the statement that Benedetti, in order to present his demand for a guarantee, had accosted the King on the promenade in a provocative manner and against His Majesty's will.[29]

From this supplementary statement one can only conclude that Bismarck did not regard the text of the revised Ems dispatch, which allegedly enraptured his guests, as strong enough to achieve his purpose. The original Abeken telegram made clear that Benedetti had in fact been unpleasantly persistent. This was enough to provide Bismarck

[28] See especially Lynn M. Case, *French Opinion on War and Diplomacy During the Second Empire* (Philadelphia, 1954), pp. 243 ff., and Jean Stengers, "Aux Origines de la guerre de 1870: Gouvernement et opinion publique," *Revue belge de philologie et d'histoire*, XXXIV (1956), 701–747, supplementing the earlier study of E. Malcolm Carroll, "French Public Opinion on War with Prussia in 1870," *American Historical Review*, XXXI (July 1926), 679–700.

[29] Texts in Lord, *Origins*, no. 187.

with the basis for a story that Benedetti had been disrespectful if not positively insolent. Already on the evening of July 13 the Spanish ambassador, after seeing Bismarck, reported home that Benedetti had approached the King in a narrow passage and, when His Majesty refused to stop or speak to him, followed him in order to present his demand for a guarantee. The King thereupon turned, looked down on him with an air of contempt, and went his way. Later, when Benedetti requested an audience, the King sent an adjutant to say that he did not wish to receive him or to hear anything more from him.[30] On the morning of July 14 the chancellor spoke to the Russian ambassador in similar terms: Benedetti had tried to extort from the King, in an improper way and on the promenade, a promise, and so forth.[31] Furthermore, the *Norddeutsche Allgemeine Zeitung* on the morning of July 14 published an additional note to this effect: "Benedetti so far ignored the rules of diplomatic intercourse that he did not hesitate to disturb the King in his cure, to interpellate him on the promenade, and to attempt to extract assurances from him."

The evidence would suggest, then, that Bismarck from the very outset regarded some embellishment of the Ems dispatch as essential if it was to have its intended provocatory effect. The Ems legend very quickly came to overshadow the Ems dispatch. On July 14 the Berlin correspondent of the London *Times* began to speculate whether such disrespectful behavior on the part of a seasoned diplomat like Benedetti was not intentional. Presently it was said that the ambassador had received instructions from his government to be brusque with the King (*brusquez le Roi*) and that, after the King had turned his back upon him on the public promenade, within sight of many bystanders, Benedetti followed him to his quarters, where the King had to order an adjutant to show him the door. It need hardly be said that this spectacular, though imaginary, episode provided inspiration to many an eager artist.[32]

[30] Rascon to Sagasta, July 13, 1870, in Conde de Romanones, *Amadeo de Saboya* (Madrid, 1935), pp. 200–201. This long report does not appear among Lord's documents from the Spanish archives, where there is, however, a short telegram (Lord, *Origins*, no. 249) sent by Rascon at 10:40 P.M., July 13, in which Bismarck is reported to have said that the King, on hearing of the new French demand, treated Benedetti "with great scorn."

[31] Clark, *Journal of Modern History*, XIV, 203.

[32] Karl Abel (*Times* correspondent), *Letters on International Relations Before and During the War of 1870* (London, 1871), II, 128. See also Georg Hirth,

Reviewing the situation in July 1870, as it now appears, one might say that Gramont, like a large segment of French opinion, was eager to make the most of the Hohenzollern candidacy and, with complete confidence in France's military superiority, decided to force the Prussian government to back down or accept war. Bismarck, for his part, seems to have been prepared to make war from the very moment (July 8) when he read Gramont's declaration of July 6. He and perhaps Roon planned to go to Ems to convert the reluctant King and induce him to order mobilization. The news of the renunciation of the candidacy was undoubtedly a severe blow and, if the French had been content with it, might well have made it appear that Prussia had suffered a humiliating setback in the face of French threats. But Bismarck, as a resourceful statesman, was not slow in meeting the situation. His plan was to turn the tables by himself demanding explanations and guarantees. It is now quite possible to trace the development of his counteroffensive step by step. But he himself, looking back on the crowded and hectic events of July 12 and 13, tended to telescope them and, with his strong tendency to condense and dramatize, ended by seriously distorting them. The German people no doubt believed that they went to war not only because of the unreasonable French demands, but because their revered monarch had been insolently treated by the French ambassador. To that extent they were the victims of the Ems legend, to which Bismarck himself succumbed. With the passage of years he became more and more convinced that the crucial link in the chain of events was his editing of the telegram from Ems, which to present-day historians appears far less horrendous than the chancellor would have the world believe. Having reached this conviction, Bismarck allowed all else to crystallize around this one episode. The feeling aroused by the renunciation of the candidacy came to be focused on the Abeken telegram, and the revival of hope in the two generals, probably due to Bismarck's plan for a counteroffensive, became attributed to the rewording of the message from Ems. The rest of the story consists largely of embroidery.

Tagebuch des deutsch-französischen Krieges (Berlin, 1871), pp. 102 ff., for extensive quotations from the German press on July 14 reporting Benedetti's "boundless insolence." I have consulted many contemporary German and English books, all of which carry much the same story and several of which, like Hermann Fechner, *Der deutsch-französische Krieg* (Berlin, 1871) have illustrations of Benedetti's being shown the door.

So we are left with the conclusion that Bismarck's favorite story and his most successful dramatic effort is, in terms of historical evidence, of highly questionable value.

Bismarck's Memoirs on the Dinner Party of July 13, 1870

"Having decided to resign, in spite of the remonstrances Roon made against it, I invited him and Moltke to dine with me alone on the 13th, and communicated to them at table my views and projects for doing so. Both were greatly impressed, and reproached me indirectly with selfishly availing myself of my greater facility for withdrawing from service. I maintained the position that I could not offer up my sense of honor to politics, that both of them, being professional soldiers and consequently without freedom of choice, need not take the same point of view as a responsible foreign minister. During our conversation I was informed that a telegram from Ems, in cipher, if I recollect rightly of about 200 'groups,' was being deciphered. When the copy was handed to me it showed that Abeken had drawn up and signed the telegram at His Majesty's command, and I read it out to my guests, whose dejection was so great that they turned away from food and drink. On a repeated examination of the document I lingered upon the authorization of His Majesty, which included a command immediately to communicate Benedetti's fresh demand and its rejection both to our ambassadors and to the press. I put a few questions to Moltke as to the extent of his confidence in the state of our preparations, especially as to the time they would still require in order to meet this sudden risk of war. He answered that if there was to be war, he expected no advantage to us by deferring its outbreak; and even if we should not be strong enough at first to protect all the territories on the left bank of the Rhine against French invasion, our preparations would nevertheless soon overtake those of the French, while at a later period this advantage would be diminished. He regarded a rapid outbreak as, on the whole, more favorable to us than delay."

[There follows a rather lengthy passage in which Bismarck explains why he himself regarded war as inevitable if Germany was to be unified.]

"With this conviction I made use of the royal authorization communicated to me through Abeken, to publish the contents of the telegram; and in the presence of my two guests I reduced the telegram by striking out words, but without adding or altering, to the following form:

Ems, July 13, 1870.
After the news of the renunciation of the hereditary Prince of Hohenzollern had been officially communicated to the Imperial French Government by the Royal Spanish Government, the French ambassador further demanded of His Majesty the King at Ems, that he would authorize him to telegraph to Paris that His Majesty the King bound himself for all time never again to give his consent, should the Hohenzollerns renew their candidature. His Majesty the King thereupon decided not to receive the French ambassador again and sent the aide-de-camp on duty to tell him that His Majesty had nothing further to communicate."

[The difference in the effect of the abbreviated text of the Ems telegram as compared with that of the original was not the result of stronger words, but of the form, which made this announcement appear decisive, while Abeken's version would only have been regarded as a fragment of a negotiation still pending, and to be continued at Berlin.]

"After I had read out the concentrated edition to my two guests, Moltke remarked: 'Now it has a different ring; it sounded before like a *schamade* [parley]; now it is like a *fanfare* [flourish] in reply to a challenge.' I went on to explain: If in execution of His Majesty's order I at once communicate this text, which contains no alteration in or addition to the telegram, not only to the newspapers, but also by telegraph to all our embassies, it will be known in Paris before midnight, and not only on account of its contents, but also on account of the manner of its distribution, will have the effect of a red rag upon the Gallic bull. Fight we must, if we do not want to act the part of the vanquished without a battle. Success, however, essentially depends upon the impression which the origination of the war makes upon us and others; it is important that we should be the party attacked, and this Gallic overweening and touchiness will make us, if we announce in the face of Europe, so far as we can without the speaking tube of the Reichstag, that we fearlessly meet the public threats of France.

"This explanation brought about in the two generals a revulsion to a more joyous mood, the liveliness of which surprised me. They had suddenly recovered their pleasure in eating and drinking and spoke in a more cheerful vein. Roon said: 'Our God of old lives still and will

145

not let us perish in disgrace.' Moltke so far relinquished his passive equanimity that, glancing up joyously towards the ceiling and abandoning his usual punctiliousness of speech, he smote his hand upon his breast and said: 'If I may live to lead our armies in such a war, then the devil may come directly afterwards and fetch away the old carcass.' "

6

Red Rag and Gallic Bull:
The French Decision for War, 1870

c. 1961

Bismarck, in a highly dramatic chapter of his memoirs, tells the story of his rewording of the famous telegram from Ems reporting King William's discussions with the French ambassador and then quotes himself as having said to his dinner guests: "If I not only publish this text . . . at once in the newspapers, but also transmit it by telegram to our embassies, it will be known in Paris before midnight and, not only because of its contents but because of its mode of publication, will have the effect of a red rag on the Gallic bull." [1]

Various items of the chancellor's vivid account of his dinner party with Moltke and Roon on the evening of July 13, 1870, are open to question and there may be some reason to query also the role actually played by the so-called Ems telegram in deciding the French government to declare war.[2] A definitive answer may be forever impossible, for the record is extraordinarily scant, consisting primarily of the extended apologia of the prime minister, M. Ollivier, the short and often confused account of the foreign minister, the Duc de Gramont, and scraps of information provided by the papers of other participants and made available by Pierre de La Gorce in his *Histoire du Second Empire*. Furthermore, it is obvious that the crucial day, July 14, marked only the culmination of a crisis that had been developing since July 3 and which, in a very real sense, was determined by the evolution of Franco-Prussian relations ever since Prussia's victory over Austria at Sadowa in 1866.

Recent biographers of Ollivier and Gramont, like those statesmen themselves, make much of the influence of public opinion in the deter-

Note: Reprinted from *Europa und Ubersee: Festschrift für Egmont Zechlin* (Hamburg, n.d.), pp. 135–154.

[1] Otto von Bismarck, *Gedanken und Erinnerungen* (Stuttgart, 1898), II, 91.
[2] I have examined some aspects of the Bismarckian account in "Bismarck as a Dramatist" [Part I, Number 5, of this volume].

mination of French policy in those hectic days.[3] It was therefore entirely logical that historians should analyze in great detail this aspect of the problem. Their conclusions are by no means unanimous, but on certain fundamentals there appears to be substantial agreement. The country at large no doubt desired peace. It had, on the other hand, become deeply imbued with the idea that since 1866 the balance of power had been shifting in favor of Prussia and that France could not afford to countenance further aggrandizement on Prussia's part. The more chauvinistic elements, especially in Paris, went further and considered "revenge for Sadowa" as the only real salve for French pride. In general, then, the government could count on public support throughout the land for a firm policy, that is, for insistence on the renunciation of the Hohenzollern candidacy for the Spanish throne and for satisfaction from the Prussian government in the shape of official disavowal of any intention to offend French susceptibilities. The uncompromising statement of Gramont before the *Corps législatif* on July 6 therefore met with widespread approval, though it clearly involved for Prussia a humiliating retreat or the acceptance of war.

Students of French public opinion concur in thinking that Gramont's declaration, which was approved by the entire cabinet, anticipated the populace and indeed contributed to the general excitement. In the same way Gramont, in formulating the demands for guarantees on July 12, went beyond popular clamor, for the news of the withdrawal of the candidacy by Prince Leopold's father was too recent to have evoked much popular response. However, there is no doubt that there was little satisfaction to be derived from the renunciation so long as the Prussian government refused to acknowledge its responsibility for the candidacy and to give its official imprimatur to its withdrawal. By and large it may be said, therefore, that even though Gramont on two occasions hurried ahead of public opinion, and may even have stimulated it, there is a great likelihood that the foreign minister and at least some of his colleagues correctly assessed the probable popular reaction. Like the Empress Eugenie they were convinced that the newly established lib-

[3] E.g., Pierre Saint Marc, *Emile Ollivier* (Paris, 1950), and Constantin de Grunwald, *Le Duc de Gramont* (Paris, 1950). The emphasis on this aspect of the problem was no doubt encouraged from the outset by Fernand Giraudeau, *La Verité sur la campagne de 1870* (Marseilles, 1871). Giraudeau was, in July 1870, chief of the press division of the French ministry of the interior. Convinced of the heavy responsibilities of the newspaper press, he provided innumerable excerpts to prove his point.

eral regime and indeed the dynasty itself could not successfully weather a further diplomatic reverse. The Paris press in particular was, for the most part, rabidly patriotic, while the public at large, fully confident of France's military superiority, was all too ready to face war rather than accept anything less than full satisfaction.[4]

The point to be made in the present context is that the so-called Ems telegram, published by the *Norddeutsche Allgemeine Zeitung* in Berlin in the late evening of July 13, had little if any discernible effect on French public opinion and therefore no significant bearing on the deliberations of the government on July 14. The telegram was not known in Paris before midnight of July 13, as Bismarck anticipated, but only on the morning of July 14, and then for the most part in garbled form. The *Correspondance du Nord-Est* brought a summary of the telegram as it appeared in the Berlin paper, but the more authoritative Havas agency made it appear that the telegram, while dated from Berlin, was a report from a correspondent at Ems. More seriously, it added a paragraph (from an unknown source) stating that King William had officially approved the renunciation of the candidacy and considered all cause for conflict eliminated. The two paragraphs were obviously contradictory and left the newspaper editors wondering whether or not French demands for satisfaction had been met. Not until the evening of July 14 did five of the Paris papers print the Havas report. Only after 7:30 P.M. did the extremist paper *Soir* appear with the sensational statement that the French ambassador had been affronted by King William. Even then it was difficult to know what to believe. The uncertainty about the treatment of Ambassador Benedetti continued until midday of July 15, when the legislature went into session.[5]

It is clear, then, that the Ems telegram had no important impact upon French public opinion, which, to be sure, was deeply stirred and highly excitable by July 14 and more than ever insistent on guarantees of future good behavior on Prussia's part. There is certainly no reason to disbelieve Ollivier and Gramont when they assert that pressure of

---

[4] The basic studies of French opinion are those of E. Malcolm Carroll, "French Public Opinion on War with Prussia in 1870," *American Historical Review*, XXXI (1926), and *French Public Opinion and Foreign Affairs, 1870–1914* (New York, 1931), pp. 31 ff.; Lynn M. Case, *French Opinion on War and Diplomacy During the Second Empire* (Philadelphia, 1954), pp. 243 ff.; and the exhaustive analysis of Jean Stengers, "Aux Origines de la guerre de 1870: Gouvernement et opinion publique," *Revue belge de philologie et d'histoire*, XXXIV (1956), 701–747.

[5] The fullest account of this curious and mystifying episode is that contained in Carroll's article, to which the Stengers' article is a useful supplement.

public opinion made itself felt acutely not only by members of the cabinet, but by the Emperor himself. In an oft-quoted report of the British ambassador, Lord Lyons, evidently despatched in the afternoon of July 14, it was stated quite unequivocally:

> Although the . . . article in the *North German Gazette* had not become generally known, the public excitement was so great and so much irritation existed in the army, that it became doubtful whether the government could withstand the cry for war, even if it were able to announce a decided diplomatic success. It was felt when the Prussian article appeared in the Paris evening papers, it would be very difficult to restrain the anger of the people, and . . . that the government would feel bound to appease the public impatience by formally declaring its intention to resent the conduct of Prussia.[6]

In short, members of the council deliberated on July 14 in a setting of noisy, patriotic demonstrations and decidedly under popular pressure to declare war.

Nonetheless, Ollivier and several members of his cabinet undoubtedly favored a moderate course and opposed any measure that would aggravate the situation or further inflame the public. This had become evident on the morning of July 13, when the council met in the presence of the Emperor at St. Cloud and learned for the first time of the French demand that King William promise never to permit the renewal of Leopold's candidacy. This requirement of guarantees for the future had been formulated by Gramont in consultation with the Emperor and had greatly troubled Ollivier when he was informed of it belatedly. It certainly shocked several of the ministers—Segris, Louvet, Parieu, Plichon, Chevandier—who at once recognized the implications of a refusal on the King's part. Gramont was taken to task for embarking on so ominous a policy without consultation with his colleagues. Furthermore, the minister of war, Marshal Le Boeuf, was outspokenly critical. As early as July 11, before the renunciation of the candidacy had become known, there had been serious talk of mobilization. This fateful step had been eschewed when the crisis seemed to lift. Now it appeared to Le Boeuf that further tension was being generated. He therefore insisted that the reserves be called up immediately, arguing that every day lost involved further jeopardizing of the country's future. But Ollivier and the other ministers knew only too well that recall of the reserves was tantamount to a declaration of war. The prime min-

[6] Gr. Br., *Parliamentary Papers* (Commons), vol. 70 (1870), Cd. 167 (no. 60), p. 35.

ister argued that the government should content itself with the withdrawal of the candidacy and, in the event of a rejection of the demand for guarantees, should abstain from making an issue of the King's refusal. In the end Napoleon yielded and Gramont followed suit: by a vote of eight to four it was decided to accept the King's approval of the renunciation as adequate satisfaction of French claims.[7]

In these days of crisis the Emperor, suffering as he did in the summer of 1866 from an acute attack of bladder trouble, was certainly torn in mind. Desirous of peace yet quite unable to withstand the pressure of the war party, he avoided a decision as long as possible and evidently staked his hopes on intervention by friendly powers. Gramont, on the other hand, was firm in his conviction that France must take a strong line and accept war rather than suffer a further diplomatic reverse. From the middle of the afternoon of July 13 onward, telegrams arrived from Benedetti at Ems, reporting that King William, while approving unreservedly the withdrawal of the Hohenzollern candidacy, absolutely refused to give assurances as to the future.[8]

According to the decision of the council that very morning, the foreign minister should have contented himself with the King's approval of the renunciation. Instead, he wired Benedetti at 7:00 P.M. instructing him to make a last effort to secure a promise that Leopold would never be permitted to renew his candidacy. In conversation with the British ambassador and with the Russian chargé d'affaires that same evening Gramont reiterated this French demand and stated that in the event of refusal there would be no other alternative to war.[9] The King's approval of the renunciation seemed to him but a small matter, as he wrote in a note to Ollivier before leaving for St. Cloud to inform the Emperor of recent developments. The prime minister quite naturally protested, but it is unlikely that Gramont received his note before leaving Paris. Reporting his conference with the Emperor and his entourage he wrote Ollivier late in the evening: "Great indecision. First, for war. Then doubts, on account of the King's approval. The despatch from Spain

---

[7] Emile Ollivier, *L'Empire libéral* (Paris, 1897–1918), XIV, 284 ff.; Pierre de la Gorce, *Histoire du Second Empire* (Paris, 1904–1906), VI, 272 ff.; Pierre Muret, "Emile Ollivier et le Duc de Gramont les 12 et 13 juillet, 1870," *Revue d'histoire moderne et contemporaine*, XIII (1910), 305–328; XIV, 178–213, 201 ff.

[8] Fr., Ministère des Affaires Etrangères, *Les Origines diplomatiques de la guerre de 1870–1871*, XXVIII (Paris, 1910–1932), nos. 8458, 8469, 8470.

[9] Gr. Br., *Parliamentary Papers* (Commons), vol. 70 (1870), no. 41, p. 48; Robert H. Lord, *The Origins of the War of 1870*, no. 182, p. 229.

(accepting the renunciation) might tip the scales for peace (*pourra peut-être faire pencher vers la paix*).[10]

By the morning of July 14 Gramont's situation was somewhat as follows: his determination to obtain satisfaction from Prussia had led to the formulation of the demand for guarantees. It was known that not only great powers like Britain and Russia, but even some of the South German states regarded such demands as excessive and began to suspect France of seeking a pretext for war. Furthermore, it had become clear that King William would not under any circumstances proffer assurances as to the future. In the meanwhile reports from Berlin described the rapidly mounting excitement in the Prussian capital. The French military attaché replied to Le Boeuf's request for information that Prussian generals and other officers were returning to the capital. The Prussians could have 100,000 men in the Saar within eighteen or twenty days and, so the attaché warned his chief, the French should not for a moment forget that their enemies were in the highest degree audacious, enterprising and unscrupulous.[11]

Since Gramont was clearly determined to disregard the decision of the council, he was obliged to find some justification for his continued recalcitrance. The Ems telegram seems to have arrived most providentially to fill his need. The article from the *Norddeutsche Allgemeine Zeitung* had been sent by the French chargé d'affaires in Berlin during the night and had reached Paris at 3:45 A.M. It reported not only the King's rejection of Benedetti's demand but also His Majesty's refusal further to receive the ambassador. As a communiqué it was offensively terse and was, of course, intended by Bismarck to be so. It is easy to believe that a man of Gramont's temperament should at once have felt its sting. Ollivier tells us that, as he was drafting a pacifying message for the legislature, the foreign minister burst in on him with the telegram from Berlin and exclaimed: "My dear fellow, you see before you a man who has just been given a slap in the face." On reading the document Ollivier had to admit "We must not indulge in further illusions; they want to force us into war." [12] He therefore called in several of his colleagues (which ones is not known), who requested that the Emperor call a full meeting of the council at the Tuileries for that very

---

[10] Ollivier, *L'Empire libéral*, XIV, 349 ff.

[11] *Les Origines diplomatiques*, XXVIII, no. 8491, sent from Berlin at 1:00 A.M. July 14 and arrived in Paris at 4:00 A.M.

[12] Ollivier, *L'Empire libéral*, XIV, 354 ff.

afternoon. Gramont suggests that at least some of the ministers (he actually says "le gouvernement") were unwilling to admit that a foreign newspaper article, no matter what the context, should distract them from their objective: "We were uneasy, but resolved not to commit ourselves until we had full information."

The point has been made by some French historians that Gramont, instead of nursing his wounded pride, might well have wired Benedetti for specific details regarding his relations with King William.[13] The explanation may well be that the foreign minister was all too ready to make the most of the Prussian affront, for when the council met at 12:30 P.M. he at once struck a bellicose note. Throwing his briefcase on the table he declared: "After what has happened, a foreign minister unwilling to decide for war would be unworthy to keep his portfolio." The minister of war was equally positive, reporting on alleged Prussian preparations and demanding the immediate calling up of the French reserves. The atmosphere was definitely warlike, the more so as angry, exigent crowds were surging about the ministry and the chamber.

But on this, as on previous occasions, the moderate faction in the council insisted on holding back. There was no overlooking the fact that the King had officially and unreservedly approved the withdrawal of the candidacy and that, as a matter of fact, Benedetti's telegrams and despatches contained no suggestion of discourtesy on the monarch's part. In view of the King's unwillingness to entertain the French demands, his refusal to see the ambassador for further discussion was entirely natural: "He had done so in courteous terms; no one had been insulting and no one had been insulted." [14] On the other hand, it was difficult to regard the Ems telegram as an ordinary newspaper report. It was clearly a government communiqué and constituted an intentional affront to France, which could only be taken as intolerable. Yet the hazards of war were great. Several of the ministers pleaded for delay, pending further information regarding the King's refusal of an audience. There was some discussion of the state of France's alliances, and even more of France's military position. Le Boeuf was positive in his assurances: France would have a two week's headstart and would lose this advantage if the decision for war were further delayed. There were already numerous reports of Prussian war measures. It was evidently

[13] See especially Henri Welschinger, *La Guerre de 1870, causes et responsabilités* (Paris, 2nd ed., 1910), I, 137.
[14] Ollivier, *L'Empire libéral*, XIV, 360.

Le Boeuf's complete confidence in French military superiority and his insistence on immediate action that turned the tables. At about 4 P.M. the council voted "almost unanimously" to call up the reserves, knowing full well that this was practically the equivalent to a decision for war.[15]

Although Le Boeuf left the council to prepare the necessary orders, argument continued among the remaining ministers. A new telegram arrived from Benedetti which, while it reported King William's readiness to receive the ambassador at the railway station prior to his (the King's) departure for Coblenz on the afternoon of July 14, more particularly underlined the hopelessness of further negotiations on guarantees and suggested that the so-called Ems telegram must have originated in the King's cabinet.[16]

It is hard to accept Ollivier's contention that this message made the King's language to Benedetti seem "less harsh," and so provoked further discussion of a possible peaceful solution. It was in this connection that Gramont is alleged to have suggested a European congress at which, to meet the French need for assurances as to the future, the powers might reaffirm the principle that no prince belonging to the reigning family of a great power should mount a foreign throne without previous agreement. Of those present both Ollivier and Louvet maintained that the foreign minister initiated this proposal. Gramont in his book (published in 1872) not only does not refute the statement but pictures the government as determined, on July 14, to bank on the good offices of the European powers. Yet basically the idea of appealing to others to obtain satisfaction for France was so out of keeping with Gramont's character and so difficult to reconcile with his known aims and policies during the crisis that his initiative in the matter is hardly credible. It is not impossible, however, that he may have thrown out the suggestion either in the thought that thereby Prussia might be isolated and called to account, or that the very suggestion of a congress would demonstrate to his colleagues the inadequacy of such a course. The entire congress proposal is so baffling that heretofore historians have glossed it over, preferring to leave it in obscurity rather than trying to grapple with the scanty and often contradictory evidence.

[15] Neither Ollivier nor Gramont has much to say about the military angle. La Gorce, *Histoire du Second Empire*, VI, 289 ff., provides the most convincing record, based in part on unpublished papers of one of the ministers, M. Louvet.
[16] *Les Origines diplomatiques*, XXVIII, no. 8496.

So much, however, is clear: that Napoleon snatched up the idea with enthusiasm, indeed with tears in his eyes. He seems to have taken little part in the prolonged discussion of the afternoon and may well have shared the reluctance of some ministers to make the Ems telegram a pretext for war. Throughout his reign he had repeatedly proposed a European congress as the best remedy for international ills. It was altogether natural, then, that he should have seized on the suggestion and quickly taken the lead in promoting it. The ministers "without exception," according to Ollivier, adopted it. Efforts were made at drafting a declaration to be made to the Chambers when, at about 5 P.M., the Emperor recessed the council briefly while he retired to speak with Prince Metternich, the Austrian ambassador and a close friend of the imperial family. It must be assumed that Metternich had been called to the Tuileries, probably to try out on him the proposal for a European congress. Since he had that very afternoon been reporting to Vienna the rising popular pressure and the imminence of war unless King William yielded to French importunities, the ambassador must have been surprised when the Emperor showed or read him a rough draft of the proposed declaration, substantially in these terms: "Despite Prussia's rejection of our legitimate demand, we do not consider the conflict imminent. However, we feel obliged to call up the forces. We are prepared to accept a congress at which all the questions at issue (*en litige*) would be definitively solved in the interest of a durable peace." [17]

On his return to the council the Emperor read his suggested text, but this was, understandably, regarded as only a sketch and therefore inadequate. Finally Ollivier struck on a happy phrasing which Napoleon, with tears in his eyes, urged him to write down in the privacy of the imperial study, and which with a few changes was then adopted. The Emperor had hoped that it could be read to the Chambers that very evening, but they had already adjourned and the weary ministers were glad to postpone further action until the next morning. But before leaving the Tuileries for St. Cloud, Napoleon wrote a note to Le Boeuf suggesting that perhaps the recall of the reserves was not as urgent as had been supposed. Clearly at 6 P.M. the Emperor and the council were in substantial agreement on the congress proposal. They regarded the Ems telegram as an intentional affront, but they had obviously abandoned

[17] Metternich's telegram to Beust, sent at 7:50 P.M. on July 14, in Hermann Oncken, *Die Rheinpolitik Kaiser Napoleons III* (Berlin, 1926), III, no. 888.

the idea that it was intolerable for France. Their demand for guarantees for the future had been rejected, but they hoped to save face by inducing the European powers to adopt formally a principle which would have given France the assurances they deemed necessary.[18]

Within a matter of hours, however, the tables were turned and the decision for war was made irrevocably by the Emperor and the council. The circumstances were, briefly, as follows: Ollivier, who claims to have been at best but lukewarm about the congress proposal, soon came to recognize it for what it was: an illusory act of cowardice (*une chimérique défaillance de courage*). On reaching home he found his family astonished and reproachful when informed of the project. The Emperor, on returning to St. Cloud, met with an even more outspoken reception from the Empress Eugénie who, from the outset of the crisis, had championed war as the only solution for the imperial regime. To add to Napoleon's difficulties, Marshal Le Boeuf arrived at St. Cloud shortly after dinner. He had received the Emperor's note suggesting delay in calling up the reserves and was, quite naturally, disturbed by this new development. Orders had apparently already been given and were about to be sent out to the military commands.[19] He is pictured in Ollivier's memoirs as having been quite ready to accept the Emperor's decision as to the congress, despite the reproaches of the Empress, and to have pressed only for a final answer with respect to military preparations. He did, however, induce the Emperor to reconvene the council for further discussion. At 8:00 P.M. Napoleon telegraphed Ollivier to convoke the ministers for an urgent meeting at St. Cloud.[20]

Ollivier was the first to arrive, probably shortly after 9 P.M. He says in his memoirs that he found the Emperor alone and now somewhat dissatisfied with the proposed declaration in favor of a congress. This gave the prime minister a desired opening: "I feel the same way, Sire; if we take this proposal to the Chamber, people will hurl mud at our carriages and hoot us." The road was clearly open for reconsideration

---

[18] The accounts of Antoine Gramont, *La France et la Prusse avant la guerre* (Paris, 1872), pp. 211 ff. and Ollivier, *L'Empire libéral*, XIV, 364 ff. should be supplemented by that of La Gorce, *Histoire du Second Empire*, VI, 292, and by Metternich's letter to Beust, July 31, 1870, recounting his talk with Gramont on July 15, 1870 (Oncken, *Die Rheinpolitik*, III, no. 934).

[19] They actually went out at 8:40 P.M. Le Boeuf must have arrived at St. Cloud not later than 7:30 P.M., in short, in ample time to countermand the instructions if necessary.

[20] The only detailed account of these developments is that provided by Ollivier, *L'Empire libéral*, XIV, 369 ff.

of the afternoon's decision. The Empress and Le Boeuf had, so it seems, made their influence felt.

By ten o'clock the ministers had gradually assembled and the discussions could begin. Although three members, all of whom belonged to the peace party, were absent,[21] the sentiment at first seems to have been in favor of adhering to the congress idea and therefore suspending military measures. But at this point Gramont intervened. Just before coming to St. Cloud he had had a conference with the Prussian ambassador, Count Werther, to whom it had been suggested a couple of days before that King William write a letter to the Emperor Napoleon assuring him that no offense had been intended by the Hohenzollern candidacy. Werther had been severely reproved both by King William and Bismarck for even entertaining such a suggestion, and had been instructed to inform the French government that he was about to go on extended leave. In conversation with Gramont, the ambassador left no doubt of the reason for his departure. The episode constituted another demonstration, if such were needed, of the King's and Bismarck's flat rejection of French proposals and demands.[22]

More important for the deliberations of the council were the telegrams most recently received by the foreign office, which Gramont had brought along to St. Cloud. Among these was a report from Le Sourd at Berlin, sent on the evening of July 13 and stressing Prussian discontent with the renunciation of the candidacy and recounting a rather gloomy conversation with Lord Loftus, the British ambassador in Berlin. There was also a telegram from Benedetti reporting his leave-taking of the King and the latter's suggestion that any further negotiations should be conducted through Prussian government channels. There may also have been included a telegram for Le Boeuf from a Captain Samuel, in Ems on secret mission. This read: "Serious preparations are beginning." Five companies of artillery and one of pioneers were being

---

[21] M. Segris had not been informed in time; M. Louvet had been forgotten; M. Plichon, who had been away from home, received the summons so late that he arrived only as the council was breaking up. See La Gorce, *Histoire du Second Empire*, VI, 297.

[22] Ollivier, *L'Empire libéral*, XIV, 354 ff. and Gramont, *La France et la Prusse*, p. 208, state that Werther saw Gramont about noon on July 14 and announced his forthcoming leave. But Werther's telegram, sent to Berlin at 9:35 P.M. on July 14, leaves no doubt that he had not seen the foreign minister until just prior to that hour (see Lord, *Origins of the War of 1870*, p. 245). It is difficult to understand how such an error could have crept into the record, but it now seems rather unimportant, since the impact of the Werther episode on developments both in Ems and in Paris has been overrated.

sent from Coblenz to Saarlouis and several batteries had left for Trier: "Considerable movements of troops." [23] And finally, there was a telegram from Berne, sent at 4:30 P.M. and received in Paris at 7:00 P.M., reporting that the Prussian minister had communicated to the President of the Federal Council a telegram from Bismarck announcing the King's refusal to give assurances as to the nonrenewal of the Hohenzollern candidacy and his refusal also to receive the French ambassador again.[24]

Hardly had the foreign minister finished reading this telegram, says Ollivier, when another one (from the Duc de Cadore at Munich, sent at 6:30 P.M. and arrived at Paris at 8:15 P.M.) was brought him by courier. This was of the same tenor, but with this important addition: "M. de Bismarck goes so far (in his telegram to the Bavarian government) as to accuse M. Benedetti of having been discourteous in approaching the King during his promenade; and, in the effort to give the incident importance, he qualifies it as wounding to the pride of a German sovereign, and believes that on this account it will arouse lively resentment in Bavaria." [25]

These telegrams left no shadow of doubt that Bismarck was treating the so-called Ems telegram in an official manner—that he was communicating to foreign governments the fact of the French demand for guarantees and its rejection, and the King's refusal further to receive the French ambassador. The supplement to Cadore's report enhanced the offensiveness of the matter, charging the French ambassador with downright discourtesy. Ollivier, who claims that there had been no hesitation on the part of the ministers from the very outset, argues simply that these telegrams clinched the decision to accept the Prussian challenge by confirming the orders for mobilization. He rather vehemently contests Gramont's assertion that, over and above the provocation involved in Bismarck's procedure, the crucial item was fear of Prussian mobilization: "Everything was being done on the other side of the Rhine as though war had been declared." The French were left no choice. "It was no longer a question of negotiation; we had to defend

---

[23] This telegram was sent from Ems at 2:30 P.M. and arrived in Paris at 7:15 P.M., July 14. Since it was sent in embassy code, it could easily have come to Gramont's attention. The text is in *Les Origines diplomatiques*, XXVIII, 341.

[24] *Ibid.*, p. 343.

[25] *Ibid.*, p. 345. Later on the same evening Cadore was able to transmit the actual text of the Prussian telegram to Munich, *ibid.*, p. 353.

ourselves." [26] To this Ollivier replies that it would have been impossible to conceal the mobilization of a great army and that there was no report of Prussian mobilization on the evening of July 14. But this amounts to little more than a play upon words. Le Boeuf had made it clear from the beginning that the alleged French advantage would be lost if the enemy were allowed a headstart in the matter of military preparations. For some days the French general staff had been receiving reports of Prussian military measures, most of which proved unfounded. But the message referred to above, received in Paris at 7:15 P.M. on July 14, could easily have been available to the council at St. Cloud and was certainly of such a character as to provide Le Boeuf with telling arguments.[27]

This is not to maintain that the Ems telegram and its utilization by Bismarck were not of major importance in influencing French decisions of policy. It is merely to suggest that Ollivier ex post facto tended to emphasize the point of honor to the exclusion of everything else. He is probably misleading in his assertions that there was only informal discussion on the evening of July 14 and that from the very beginning of the meeting the sentiment was against the congress idea and in favor of military action. Gramont may be more accurate in stressing the military factor and in this he is supported to some extent by Le Boeuf, who in later testimony insisted that initially sentiment was for suspending mobilization and that "a certain telegram" brought the reversal. La Gorce, evidently using another source of evidence, also states that one of the telegrams (which one is not known) produced a profound impression and led to the intervention of the Empress Eugénie, who for the first time since the establishment of the parliamentary regime was attending the council. Eugénie in turn was supported by Le Boeuf and the other ministers gradually fell into line, so that by 11 P.M. it was generally agreed that the decision for war should be announced to the Chambers on the following day.[28]

In this context a few other bits of evidence are of considerable interest. Gramont knew from Benedetti's messages that the ambassador had not really been insulted and that, since the King was unwilling to dis-

[26] Gramont, *La France et la Prusse,* pp. 215 ff., 232 ff., 245, 256.

[27] On the whole question of incoming reports of Prussian preparations see Pierre Lehautcourt, *Histoire de la guerre de 1870–1871* (Paris, 1901), I, 180 ff.

[28] See Ollivier's controversy with Le Boeuf and Gramont in his *L'Empire libéral,* XIV, 618 ff.; La Gorce, *Histoire du Second Empire,* VI, 297.

cuss the French demands further, there was nothing remarkable about his refusal to receive the ambassador again. He appreciated also that the Ems telegram was much sharper in tone than the facts warranted. What counted, however, was not the wording of a newspaper communiqué, but the fact that the Prussian government had officially notified foreign governments of the affront to France through its ambassador.[29] Yet there is at least a suggestion in the sources that all the ministers were not prepared to make an issue of the Ems telegram episode. Gramont on July 15 told both Prince Metternich and the special Austrian emissary, Count Vitzthum, that he had had difficulty in persuading the Emperor to drop the congress idea—that, in fact, he had to threaten to resign in order to win his point. In discussing the incident, the foreign minister worked himself into such a fury that he could hardly continue the conversation. Obviously his behavior reflected a previous stormy argument, as did also his actual remarks to Vitzthum: "Yesterday, when the Emperor spoke of a congress to the council, I told him that I would hurl my portfolio at his feet if he continued to talk of the subject. A congress indeed! We called up the reserves, after Marshal Le Boeuf assured us that we were more than ready (*archiprêts*)." [30]

Gramont's irritation at the mere mention of the congress proposal may have been due to the fact that Napoleon, despite his alleged remarks to Ollivier on the latter's arrival at St. Cloud, seems to have persisted in the idea even after the adjournment of the council on the evening of July 14. At 10 A.M. the following morning he received in audience Count Vitzthum, the Austrian diplomat who had been sent on special mission to Paris by his government. Napoleon blamed Ollivier for the situation in which France found itself, remarking that though the prime minister had very good qualities, he was inexperienced in the conduct of international affairs. It was now too late, he continued, for France to retreat, but he was genuinely delighted when his visitor broached the subject of a European congress. Indeed, he hoped that the Emperor Francis Joseph could be induced to propose such a congress. But, he concluded, "this must not keep us from fighting," by which he could only have meant that, in view of the reported Prussian

---

[29] See his remarks to Baron von Werther on the evening of July 14 (Lord, *Origins of the War of 1870*, p. 251), and to Lord Lyons on July 15 (unpublished report of Lyons now printed by Stengers, *Revue belge*, XXXIV.

[30] Metternich's letter to Beust, July 31, 1870; Vitzthum's letter to Andrassy, January 16, 1873; excerpts from Vitzthum's unpublished memoirs, all in Oncken, *Die Rheinpolitik*, III, nos. 890, 891.

military moves, France could not afford to countermand orders for mobilization.[31]

Ollivier was certainly arguing speciously when he maintained that no decision for war was taken on the evening of July 14. Though because of the absence of several ministers no formal vote may have been taken, those present were agreed that the orders calling up the reserves should stand, and these orders were admittedly tantamount to the initiation of war. The point is in any event of little importance, for at 9 A.M. the next morning the full council met at St. Cloud and approved a declaration worked out by Ollivier and Gramont. This statement reviewed briefly the course of the crisis and stressed the fact that France had not broken off negotiations even when King William refused to give the required assurances against the eventual renewal of the Hohenzollern candidacy. The decision for war was attributed rather to the King's refusal to receive Benedetti and to the communication of this refusal to the European governments. The orders to Werther to go on leave and reports of Prussian military preparations provided further arguments.[32]

The wording of the government statement was actually very guarded, and much less instructive than the explanations given by Ollivier in his memoirs: "We did not invoke as the decisive reason either the refusal to give us even by a word a guarantee for the future, nor the refusal to clothe in official form the purely personal approval (of the renunciation), nor even the refusal to receive and listen to our ambassador. We were revolted by this refusal of an audience simply because it had been made a palpable outrage through the publication of the telegram in street posters, and in messages to legations and to the newspapers. In other words, our declaration was nothing but a reply to the slap in the face (*soufflet*) of the Ems despatch, a reply which Germany itself seemed to suggest to us by awaiting it as inevitable." [33]

The prime minister's presentation of the government statement to the *Corps législatif* at noon on July 15 precipitated a long and at times acrimonious debate. Thiers, Favre and Gambetta criticized the government's refusal to content itself with the withdrawal of the candidacy

---

[31] Telegram from Metternich to Beust, sent at 3:30 P.M. on July 15; Vitzthum's letter to Andrassy, January 16, 1873, and Vitzthum's memoirs, *ibid.*
[32] The text is given in full in Ollivier, *L'Empire libéral*, XIV, 397 ff.
[33] *Ibid.*, p. 392.

and demanded proof that France had been insulted. In reply Ollivier was obliged to argue that the government's decision was based not on the offensive terms of the Ems telegram, but on its intentional publication and its communication to foreign powers. There was much debate on whether the government should be required to submit the key documents. Some of them were, in fact, read at least in summary to a committee appointed to hear evidence in support of the government request for credits. These lengthy proceedings have been analyzed in detail by several French historians and need not be examined here. The point of interest in the present context is that Gramont did not himself have the actual text of the objectionable Prussian telegram to foreign governments, on which so much of the government's case rested.[34] He and Ollivier were eventually driven to contend that documents were relatively unimportant—the fact was that the Emperor and France as well had been insulted by the Prussian government's notification to other governments of King William's refusal to receive the French ambassador and continue with him the discussion of the question at issue.

The intervention of Thiers and other critics of the government's policy was dramatic and illuminating, but politically unimportant. The Chamber as a whole had for some days been rabid for war and created the greatest possible din in order to drown out the opposition. Late on the evening of July 15 the war credits were voted 245 to 10. Thereafter the declaration of war was a mere formality.

In reviewing the French decision of July 14–15 one is bound to be impressed with the scantiness of the evidence and the unusual amount of contradiction in the testimony of the participants. In part this is due, no doubt, to the peculiar conditions existing at the French court in the closing months of the Second Empire. Despite the introduction of the parliamentary regime, Napoleon continued to pursue his own policies and to engage in discussions and even negotiations behind the backs of his ministers. During the most critical days he was suffering much physical pain, which prevented him from taking more than spasmodic part in the debates. In addition he was subjected to great pressure by

---

[34] Gramont, *La France et la Prusse*, p. 232. The text had been sent from Munich at 11:00 P.M. on July 14 and had arrived at Paris at 2:00 A.M. on July 15. So Gramont might well have known of it and one can only assume that in the confusion of these critical hours it was not brought to his attention. How great the confusion was is suggested by the fact that Ollivier kept talking of the Ems telegram as though it were a confidential document, apparently not realizing that it had appeared in all the Paris papers.

the Empress and by the court circle, which was in general in favor of drastic measures. It is reasonably clear, too, that the Emperor relied heavily on Gramont, yielding to his arguments even more readily than to those of the Empress. Ollivier, though officially head of the government, was unsure of himself in foreign affairs, tended to follow Gramont's lead, and in general showed himself emotional, wordy, and rather pompous. The Emperor obviously disliked him, if only because he represented the new parliamentary regime. Why he should have made Ollivier rather than Gramont responsible for the dilemma in which the government found itself is not immediately evident. It does seem, however, that Gramont, as a professional diplomat and a member of the highest French aristocracy, managed to set himself up as the arbiter of French interest and honor, and succeeded through his self-confidence and quick temper in having his way.

In retrospect it appears that the accepted notion of the Ems telegram as the red rag that provoked the Gallic bull to charge requires some qualification. Basic to Gramont's policy was the demand for official satisfaction from the Prussian government. This demand was criticized even by friendly governments, like the British and Austrian, was in a sense belatedly disavowed by the French council, and was eventually flatly rejected by King William. In short, Gramont's policy was, by the morning of July 14, completely bankrupt. Since he had, from the outset, been determined to inflict a diplomatic defeat on Prussia or else resort to war, he was in a serious quandary when the arrival of the Ems telegram provided him with a new grievance, the affront to national honor. Even then, the discussions of the afternoon of July 14 suggest that not only the Emperor but a number of the ministers were only half persuaded by Gramont's argumentation. On the one hand they were convinced by Le Boeuf that France had a distinct military advantage provided it acted promptly, on the other hand the Ems telegram seemed a rather flimsy pretext for a test of strength with all its hazards. Hence the decision to call up the reserves, followed almost at once by ready acceptance of the idea of a European congress. It may well be, as Ollivier asseverates, that he and others quickly came to feel that the congress idea was a pusillanimous one, unworthy of them and of France. It is also reasonable to suppose that the mounting popular excitement and the growing clamor for war may have shaken the ministers. But the conclusion is inescapable that on the evening of July 14 two new considerations emerged and in the end tipped the scales for war. One of these was certainly the news that the Ems tele-gram had been communicated by the Prussian government to other European governments, along with an addendum that charged the French ambassador with discourtesy. The other was the accumulating intelligence of Prussian military moves which gave the council good reason to suppose that on the side of the enemy operations were al-ready in full swing.

Since the argument based on military moves was of necessity an uncertain and shaky one, the government perhaps wisely decided not to stress it.[35] The argument based on national honor was clearly the more impressive and, in view of the inflamed state of public opinion, the more effective. One is almost tempted to wonder, however, whether Bismarck, having read the long debates in the French cham-ber on July 15, with their emphasis on the Ems telegram and its com-munication to foreign governments, was not himself somewhat misled: that is, whether he may not have come to attach to the telegram and the use made of it a greater significance than he intended or could have foreseen.

[35] Actually it soon turned out that reports of Prussian military activities were mistaken.

PART II

Imperialism Old and New

7

A Critique of Imperialism

1935

It is now roughly fifty years since the beginning of that great outburst of expansive activity on the part of the great powers of Europe which we have come to call "imperialism." And it is about a generation since J. A. Hobson published his *Imperialism: A Study,* a book which has served as the starting point for most later discussions and which has proved a perennial inspiration for writers of the most diverse schools. A reappraisal of it is therefore decidedly in order. The wonder is that it has not been undertaken sooner.

Since before the outbreak of the World War the theoretical writing on imperialism has been very largely monopolized by the so-called neo-Marxians, that is, by those who, following in the footsteps of the master, have carried on his historical analysis from the critique of capitalism to the study of this further phase, imperialism, the significance of which Marx himself did not appreciate and the very existence of which he barely adumbrated. The neo-Marxians, beginning with Rudolf Hilferding and Rosa Luxemburg, have by this time elaborated a complete theory, which has recently been expounded in several ponderous German works. The theory hinges upon the idea of the accumulation of capital, its adherents holding that imperialism is nothing more nor less than the last stage in the development of capitalism —the stage in which the surplus capital resulting from the system of production is obliged by ever diminishing returns at home to seek new fields for investment abroad. When this surplus capital has transformed the whole world and remade even the most backward areas in the image of capitalism, the whole economic-social system will inevitably die of congestion.

That the classical writers of the socialistic school derived this basic

Note: Reprinted from *Foreign Affairs,* XIV (October 1935), 102–119, copyright the Council on Foreign Relations, Inc., New York. It is a reappraisal of J. A. Hobson, *Imperialism: A Study* (London, 1902).

idea from Hobson's book there can be no doubt.[1] Lenin himself admitted, in his *Imperialism, the Highest Stage of Capitalism*, that Hobson gave "a very good and accurate description of the fundamental economic and political traits of imperialism," and that Hobson and Hilferding had said the essentials on the subject. This, then, has been the most fruitful contribution of Hobson's essay. When we examine his ideas on this subject we refer indirectly to the larger part of the writing on imperialism since his day.

As a matter of pure economic theory it is most difficult to break down the logic of the accumulation theory. It is a fact that since the middle of the last century certain countries—first England, then France, Germany, and the United States—have exported large amounts of capital, and that the financial returns from these investments in many instances came to overshadow completely the income derived by the lending countries from foreign trade. It is also indisputable that industry embarked upon the road to concentration and monopoly, that increased efficiency in production led to larger profits and to the amassing of ever greater surpluses of capital. We must recognize further that, as a general rule, the return from investments abroad was distinctly above the return on reinvestment in home industry. In other words, the postulates of the socialist theory undoubtedly existed. There is no mentionable reason why the development of the capitalist system should not have had the results attributed to it.

But, as it happens, the actual course of history refutes the thesis. The course of British investment abroad shows that there was a very considerable export of capital before 1875, that is, during the climax of anti-imperialism in England. Between 1875 and 1895, while the tide of imperialism was coming to the full, there was a marked falling off of foreign investment. Capital export was then resumed on a large scale in the years before the war, though England was, in this period, already somewhat disillusioned by the outcome of the South African adventure and rather inclined to be skeptical about imperialism. Similar observations hold true of the United States. If the promulgation of the Monroe Doctrine was an act of imperialism, where was the export of capital which ought to have been its condition? Let us concede that the war with Spain was an imperialist episode. At that time

[1] I strongly suspect that Hobson, in turn, took over the idea from the very bourgeois American financial expert, Charles A. Conant, whose remarkable article, "The Economic Basis of Imperialism," *North American Review* (September 1898), pp. 326–340, is now forgotten, but deserves recognition.

the United States was still a debtor nation, importing rather than exporting capital. In Russia, too, the heyday of imperialism coincided with a period of heavy borrowing rather than of lending.

There is this further objection to be raised against the view of Hobson and his neo-Marxian followers, that the export of capital seems to have little direct connection with territorial expansion. France, before the war, had plenty of capital to export, and some of her earliest and most vigorous imperialists, like Jules Ferry, declared that she required colonies in order to have adequate fields for the placement of this capital. But when France had secured colonies, she did not send her capital to them. By far the larger part of her exported funds went to Russia, Rumania, Spain, Portugal, Egypt, and the Ottoman Empire. In 1902 only two or two and a half billion francs out of a total foreign investment of some 30,000,000,000 or 35,000,000,000 francs was placed in the colonies. In 1913 Britain had more money invested in the United States than in any colony or other foreign country. Less than half of her total export of capital had been to other parts of the empire. The United States put more capital into the development of Canada than did England; and when, after the war, the United States became a great creditor nation, 43 percent of her investment was in Latin America, 27 percent in Canada and Newfoundland, and 22 percent in European countries. What she sent to her colonies was insignificant. Or let us take Germany, which in 1914 had about 25,000,000,000 marks placed abroad. Of this total only 3 percent was invested in Asia and Africa, and of that 3 percent only a small part in her colonies. Prewar Russia was a great imperialist power, but Russia had to borrow from France the money invested in her Far Eastern projects. In our own day two of the most outspokenly imperialist powers, Japan and Italy, are both nations poor in capital. Whatever the urge that drives them to expansion, it cannot be the need for the export of capital.

At the height of the imperialist tide, let us say from 1885 to 1914, there was much less talk among the advocates of expansion about the need for foreign investment fields than about the need for new markets and for the safeguarding of markets from the tariff restrictions of competitors. It is certain that in the opinion of contemporaries that was the mainspring of the whole movement. But this economic explanation, like the other, has not been borne out by the actual developments. Very few colonies have done even half of their trading with the mother country and many have done less. Taken in the large it can be proved statistically that the colonial trade has always played a relatively unimportant part in the total foreign commerce of the great industrial nations. These nations have always been each other's best customers, and no amount of rivalry and competition has prevented their trade from following, not the flag, but the price list. The position of Canada within the British Empire did not prevent her from levying tariffs against British goods, nor from developing exceedingly close economic relations with the United States. In the prewar period German commerce with the British possessions was expanding at a relatively higher rate than was Britain's.

If one must have an economic interpretation of imperialism, one will probably find its historical evolution to have been something like this: In the days of England's industrial preeminence she was, by the very nature of the case, interested in free trade. In the palmiest days of Cobdenism she exported manufactured goods to the four corners of the earth, but she exported also machinery and other producers' goods, thereby preparing the way for the industrialization of the continental nations and latterly of other regions of the world. In order to protect their infant industries from British competition, these new industrial powers threw over the teachings of the Manchester school and began to set up tariffs. The result was that the national markets were set aside, to a large extent, for home industry. British trade was driven to seek new markets, where the process was repeated. But the introduction of protective tariffs had this further effect, that it made possible the organization of cartels and trusts, that is, the concentration of industry, the increase of production and the lowering of costs. Surplus goods and low prices caused the other industrial powers likewise to look abroad for additional markets, and, while this development was taking place, technological improvements were making transportation and communication safer and more expeditious. The exploration of Africa at that time was probably a pure coincidence, but it contributed to the movement toward trade and expansion and the growth of a world market. Fear that the newly opened areas of the world might be taken over by others and then enclosed in tariff walls led directly to the scramble for territory in Asia and Africa.

The socialist writers would have us believe that concentration in industry made for monopoly and that the banks, undergoing the same process of evolution, were, through their connnection with industry, enabled to take over control of the whole capitalist system. They were the repositories of the surplus capital accumulated by a monopolistic system and they were therefore the prime movers in the drive for imperial expansion, their problem being to find fields for the investment of capital. This is an argument which does violence to the facts as they appear historically. The socialist writers almost to a man argue chiefly from the example of Germany, where cartellization came early and where the concentration of banking and the control of industry by the banks went further than in most countries. But even in Germany the movement towards overseas expansion came before the growth of monopoly and the amalgamation of the banks. In England, the imperialist country par excellence, there was no obvious connection between the two phenomena. The trust movement came late and never went as far as in Germany. The same was true of the consolidation of the banking system. One of the perennial complaints in England was the lack of proper coordination between the banks and industry. To a certain extent the English exported capital because the machinery for foreign investment was better than the organization for home investment. In the United States, to be sure, there was already a pronounced concentration of industry when the great outburst of imperialism came in the last years of the past century, but in general the trust movement ran parallel to the movement for territorial expansion. In any event, it would be hard to disprove the contention that the growth of world trade and the world market brought on the tendency toward better organization and concentration in industry, rather than the reverse. It is obvious not only that one large unit can manufacture more cheaply than many small ones, but that it can act more efficiently in competition with others in the world market.

But this much is clear—that territorial control of extra-European territory solved neither the trade problem nor the question of surplus capital. The white colonies, which were the best customers, followed their own economic interests, and not even tariff restrictions could prevent them from doing so. In the backward, colored, tropical colonies, which could be more easily controlled and exploited, it proved difficult to develop a market, because of the low purchasing power of the natives. The question of raw materials, of which so much has always been made, also remained open. The great industrial countries got but a fraction of their raw materials from the colonies, and the colonies themselves continued to show a tendency to sell their products in the best market. As for the export of capital, that continued to flow in an ever broader stream, not because the opportunities for investment at home were exhausted, but because the return from foreign investment was apt to be better and because, in many cases, foreign investment was the easier course. Capital flowed from the great industrial countries of Europe, but it did not flow to their colonies. The United States and Canada, Latin America (especially the Argentine), and even old countries like Austria-Hungary and Russia got the bulk of it. The export of capital necessarily took the form of the extension of credit, which in turn implied the transfer of goods. Not infrequently the granting of loans was made conditional on trade concessions by the borrowing country. So we come back to the question of trade and tariffs. In a sense the export of capital was nothing but a device to stimulate trade and to circumvent tariff barriers, which brings us back to the coincidence of the movement for protection and the movement toward imperialism.

This may seem like an oversimplified explanation, and it probably is. Some may argue that imperialism is more than a movement toward territorial expansion and that financial imperialism in particular lays the iron hand of control on many countries supposedly independent. But if you try to divorce imperialism from territorial control you will get nowhere. Practically all writers on the subject have been driven to the conclusion that the problem cannot be handled at all unless you restrict it in this way. When Hobson wrote on imperialism, he had reference to the great spectacle of a few powers taking over tremendous areas in Africa and Asia. Imperialism is, in a sense, synonymous with the appropriation by the western nations of the largest part of the rest of the world. If you take it to be anything else, you will soon be lost in nebulous concepts and bloodless abstractions. If imperialism is to mean any vague interference of traders and bankers in the affairs of other countries, you may as well extend it to cover any form of influence. You will have to admit cultural imperialism, religious imperialism, and what not. Personally I prefer to stick by a measurable, manageable concept.

But even though Hobson's idea, that imperialism "is the endeavor of the great controllers of industry to broaden the channel for the flow of their surplus wealth by seeking foreign markets and foreign investments to take off the goods and capital they cannot sell or use at home," proved to be the most stimulating and fertile of his arguments, he had the very correct idea that imperialism was also a "medley of aims and feelings." He had many other contributory explanations of the phenomenon. For example, he was keenly aware of the relationship between democracy and imperialism. The enfranchisement of the working classes and the introduction of free education had brought the rank and file of the population into the political arena. One result of this epoch-making change was the rise of the so-called yellow press, which catered to the common man's love of excitement and sensationalism. Northcliffe was one of the first to sense the value of imperialism as a "talking point." Colonial adventure and faraway conflict satisfied the craving for excitement of the industrial and white-collar classes which had to find some outlet for their "spectatorial lust." The upper crust of the working class, as Lenin admitted, was easily converted to the teaching of imperialism and took pride in the extension of empire.

No doubt this aspect of the problem is important. The mechanization of humanity in an industrial society is a phenomenon with which we have become all too familiar, and every thoughtful person now recognizes the tremendous dangers inherent in the powers which the demagogue can exercise through the press, the motion picture, and the radio. In Hobson's day propaganda was still carried on primarily through the press, but later developments were already foreshadowed in the activities of a Northcliffe or a Hearst. Hobson himself was able to show how, during the war in South Africa, the English press took its information from the South African press, which had been brought very largely under the control of Rhodes and his associates. Even at that time Hobson and others were pointing out how imperialistic capital was influencing not only the press, but the pulpit and the universities. Indeed, Hobson went so far as to claim that the great inert mass of the population, who saw the tangled maze of world movements through dim and bewildered eyes, were the inevitable dupes of able, organized interests who could lure or scare or drive them into any convenient course.

Recognizing as we do that control of the public mind involves the most urgent political problems of the day, it is nevertheless important to point out that there is nothing inexorable about the connection of propaganda and imperialism. Even if you admit that a generation ago moneyed interests believed that imperialism was to their advantage, that these interests exercised a far-reaching control over public opinion, and that they used this control to dupe the common man into support of imperial ventures, it is obvious that at some other time these same interests might have different ideas with regard to their own welfare, just as it is evident that public opinion may be controlled by some other agency—the modern dictator, for example.

But the same thing is not true of another influence upon which Hobson laid great stress, namely the biological conception of politics and international relations. During the last years of the nineteenth century the ideas of "social Darwinism," as it was called, carried everything before them. Darwin's catchwords—the struggle for existence and the survival of the fittest—which he himself always refused to apply to the social organism, were snapped up by others who were less scrupulous, and soon became an integral part of popular and even official thought on foreign affairs. It not only served to justify the ruthless treatment of the "backward" races and the carving up *in spe* of the Portuguese, Spanish, Ottoman, and Chinese empires and of other "dying nations," as Lord Salisbury called them, but it put the necessary imprimatur on the ideas of conflict between the great imperialistic powers themselves, and supplied a divine sanction for expansion. It was currently believed, in the days of exuberant imperialism, that the world would soon be the preserve of the great states—the British, the American, and the Russian—and it was deduced from this belief that survival in the struggle for existence was in itself adequate evidence of superiority and supernatural appointment. The British therefore looked upon their empire as a work of the divine will, while the Americans and Russians were filled with the idea of a manifest destiny. It will be at once apparent that glorification of war and joy in the conflict was intimately connected with the evolutionary mentality. Hobson, the most determined of anti-imperialists, was finally driven to define the whole movement as "a depraved choice of national life, imposed by self-seeking interests which appeal to the lusts of quantitative acquisitiveness and of forceful domination surviving in a nation from early centuries of animal struggle for existence."

The last phrases of this quotation will serve to lead us to the consideration of what has proved to be another fruitful thought of Hobson. He speaks, in one place, of imperialism as a sociological atavism, a remnant of the roving instinct, just as hunting and sport are leftovers of the physical struggle for existence. This idea of the roving instinct has made but little appeal to later writers, but the basic interpretation of imperialism as an atavism underlies the ingenious and highly intelligent essay of Joseph Schumpeter, *Zur Soziologie der Imperialismen,*[2] the only work from the bourgeois side which has had anything like the influence exerted by the writers of the socialist school. Schumpeter, who is an eminent economist, worked out a most convincing argument to prove that imperialism has nothing to do with capitalism, and that it is certainly not a development of capitalism. Capitalism, he holds, is by nature opposed to expansion, war, armaments, and professional militarism, and imperialism is nothing but an atavism, one of those elements of the social structure which cannot be explained from existing conditions, but only from the conditions of the past. It is, in other words, a hangover from a preceding economic order. Imperialism antedates capitalism, going back at least to the time of the Assyrians and Egyptians. It is, according to Schumpeter, the disposition of a state to forceful expansion without any special object and without a definable limit. Conquests are desired not so much because of their advantages, which are often questionable, but merely for the sake of conquest, success, and activity.

Schumpeter's theory is in some ways extravagant, but it has served as the starting point for some very interesting speculation, especially among German scholars of the liberal persuasion. It is now fairly clear, I think, that the neo-Marxian critics have paid far too little attention to the imponderable, psychological ingredients of imperialism. The movement may, without much exaggeration, be interpreted not only as an atavism, as a remnant of the days of absolute monarchy and mercantilism, when it was to the interest of the prince to increase his territory and the number of his subjects, but also as an aberration, to be classed with the extravagances of nationalism. Just as nationalism can drive individuals to the point of sacrificing their very lives for the purposes of the state, so imperialism has driven them to the utmost exertions and the extreme sacrifice, even though the stake might be only some little known and at bottom valueless part of Africa or Asia. In the days when communication and economic interdependence have made the world one in so many ways, men still interpret international relations in terms of the old cabinet policies, they are still swayed by outmoded, feudalistic ideas of honor and prestige.

In a sense, then, you can say that there is, in every people, a certain

---

[2] Josef Schumpeter, *Zur Soziologie der Imperialismen* (Tübingen, 1919).

indefinable national energy, which may find expression in a variety of ways.

As a general rule great domestic crises and outbursts of expansion follow each other in the history of the world. In many of the continental countries of Europe, and for that matter in our own country, great internal problems were fought out in the period before 1870. The energies which, in Germany and Italy, went into the victory of the national cause, soon began to project themselves beyond the frontiers. While the continental nations were settling great issues between them, England sat "like a bloated Quaker, rubbing his hands at the roaring trade" he was carrying on. In those days the British cared very little for their empire. Many of them would have felt relieved if the colonies had broken away without a fuss. But, says Egerton, the best-known historian of British colonial policy, when the Germans and the French began to show an interest in colonial expansion, then the British began to think that there must be some value as yet undiscovered in the colonies. They not only started a movement to bind the colonies and the mother country more closely together, but they stretched out their hands for more. In the end they, who had the largest empire to begin with, got easily the lion's share of the yet unappropriated parts of the world. Some thought they were engaged in the fulfilment of a divine mission to abolish slavery, to spread the gospel, to clothe and educate the heathen. Others thought they were protecting the new markets from dangerous competitors, securing their supply of raw materials, or finding new fields for investment. But underlying the whole imperial outlook there was certainly more than a little misapprehension of economics, much self-delusion and self-righteousness, much misapplication of evolutionary teaching, and above all much of the hoary tradition of honor, prestige, power, and even plain combativeness. Imperialism always carries with it the connotation of the *Imperator* and of the tradition of rule. It is bound up with conscious or subconscious ideas of force, of brutality, of ruthlessness. It was these traits and tendencies that were so vividly expressed in the poetry and stories of Kipling, and it was his almost uncanny ability to sense the emotions of his time and people that made him the greatest apostle of imperialism.

We shall not go far wrong, then, if we stress the psychological and political factors in imperialism as well as its economic and intellectual elements. It was, of course, connected closely with the great changes in the social structure of the western world, but it was also a projection of nationalism beyond the boundaries of Europe, a projection on a world scale of the time-honored struggle for power and for a balance of power as it had existed on the continent for centuries. The most casual perusal of the literature of imperialism will reveal the continued potency of these atavistic motives. In a recent number of this very journal a leading Italian diplomat, explaining the policy of the *Duce,* recurred again and again to the failure of the other countries to appreciate the fact that Italy is a young and active country "animated by new spiritual values." [3] By the much-decried Corfu episode of 1923, Mussolini, to give a concrete example, "called Europe's attention to the respect due to the new Italy and to the reawakened energies of the Italian people." In the present Ethiopian crisis there is not very much suggestion of economic or civilizing motives on the part of the Italians; rather the *Duce* holds before his followers the prospect of revenge for the defeat at Adua (reminiscent of Britian's thirst to avenge Gordon) and promises them a glorious future. Not long ago he spoke to a group of veterans among the ruins of ancient Rome and told them that every stone surrounding them should remind them that Rome once dominated the world by the wisdom of her rule and the might of her arms and that "nothing forbids us to believe that what was our destiny yesterday may again become our destiny tomorrow." [4] In much the same spirit an eminent Japanese statesman expressed himself recently in *Foreign Affairs:* "As soon as the Meiji restoration lifted the ban on foreign intercourse, the long-pent-up energy of our race was released, and with fresh outlook and enthusiasm the nation has made swift progress. When you know this historical background and understand this overflowing vitality of our race, you will see the impossibility of compelling us to stay still within the confines of our little island home. We are destined to grow and expand overseas." [5] It is the same emphasis given by the Italian diplomat to the need for an outlet for surplus energies.

It is, of course, true that both Italy and Japan have a serious population problem and that Japan, at any rate, has an economic argument to back her imperialistic enterprises in Manchuria and China. But it

[3] Dino Grandi, "The Foreign Policy of the Duce," *Foreign Affairs,* XII (July 1934), 551–566.

[4] *New York Times,* June 17, 1935.

[5] Baron Reijiro Wakatsuki, "The Aims of Japan," *Foreign Affairs,* XIII (July 1935), 583–594.

has been shown long ago that the acquisition of new territory has no direct bearing on the population problem and that emigrants go where their interest calls them, not where their governments would like to have them go. As for Japan's economic needs, it may at least be questioned whether she would not be better off if she avoided political and military commitments in China. Her cheap goods have made very extensive inroads in all the markets of the world, and her eventual conquest of the whole Chinese market is perhaps inevitable. Far from having gained much from her recent policy, she has had to face boycotts and other forms of hostility. In this case, certainly, one might debate whether the game is worth the candle.

Baron Wakatsuki, whose statement is quoted above, was careful to avoid mention of a factor in Japanese imperialism which, as every well-informed person knows, is probably the real explanation of Japanese policy. After the Meiji restoration it was more the exuberance and bellicosity of the military caste in Japan than the enthusiasm of the country at large which determined the policy of the government. If one reads modern Japanese history aright one will find that from 1870 onward the military classes were constantly pressing upon the government for action in Korea. Only with the greatest difficulty did the civil authorities stave off this pressure. In 1894 the Tokyo government more or less rushed into the war with China in order to avoid a dangerous domestic crisis. In other words, the ideas of honor and patriotism were appealed to in order to divert attention from the parliamentary conflict which was then raging. After the Japanese victory it was the military men who, against the better judgment of men like Count Ito and Baron Mutsu, insisted on the cession of the Liaotung Peninsula, which netted Japan nothing but the intervention of Russia, Germany, and France. We need not pursue this subject in all its minute details. The point I want to make is that in the case of Japan, as in the case of many other countries, it is easier to show that the military and official classes are a driving force behind the movement for expansion than to show that a clique of nefarious bankers or industrialists is the determining factor. Business interests may have an interest in the acquisition of territory, or they may not. But military and official classes almost always have. War is, for the soldiers, a profession, and it is no mere chance that war and imperialism are so commonly lumped together. For officials, expansion means new territories to govern and new jobs to be filled.

Hobson, with his pronouncedly economic approach to the problem, held that "the struggle for markets, the greater eagerness of producers to sell than of consumers to buy, is the crowning proof of a false economy of distribution," of which imperialism is the fruit. The remedy, he thought, lay in "social reform." "There is no necessity to open up new foreign markets," he maintained; "the home markets are capable of indefinite expansion." These contentions sound familiar enough in this day of world depression. Whether the home markets are capable of indefinite expansion is a question on which the economic internationalists and the advocates of autarchy hold different opinions. The interesting thing for us to consider, however, is the fact that movements towards autarchy should have developed at all and that so much stress should now be laid upon the problems of redistribution of wealth, of building up purchasing power, and, in general, of domestic social reform. The current of activity has shifted distinctly from expansion to revolution, peaceful or violent. Perhaps it may be argued from this that the socialist thesis regarding imperialism is now being proved; that capitalism has already transformed the backward areas to such an extent that the markets are ruined, and that the capitalist system is rapidly choking. This view might be acceptable if it were not for the fact that the colonies and backward areas are still very far from developed and if it were not for the futher fact that before the depression the colonial trade with the older countries was steadily increasing. In the last five years, to be sure, international commerce has sunk to an unbelievably low point, but the difficulty has been chiefly with the trade between the great industrial powers themselves. It is quite conceivable that the crisis is primarily due to the special situation arising from the World War and that the root of the trouble lies in the impossibility of fitting tremendous international payments into the existing framework of trade relations. The fantastic tariff barriers which have been set up on all sides have simply aggravated a situation which has been developing since the teachings of Cobdenism first began to fall into disrepute.

But whatever the true explanation of our present difficulties, very few voices are raised in favor of a solution by the methods of imperialism. Indeed, the movement toward autarchy is in a way a negation of imperialism. Economically we have been disillusioned about imperialism. We have learned that colonies do not pay. Britain's expenditure for the defense of the empire alone is enormous, yet she has never yet devised a method by which anything like a commensurate return could be secured. The French military outlay on the colonies in 1913 was more than five hundred million francs, at a time when the entire trade of France with her colonies came to hardly three times that figure. Similar statistics could be quoted for Germany, and it is a well-known fact that the colonies of both Spain and Portugal were much more of a liability than an asset.

In the same way it has turned out that foreign investments of capital are not all that they were expected to be. The higher returns from colonial investments have often been counterbalanced by the greater insecurity that went with them. European countries had more than one opportunity to learn the lesson even before the war. We need only recall the Argentine fiasco of 1890 and the wildcat Kaffir boom in South African securities in 1895 as classical examples of what might happen. But of course all these instances are completely dwarfed by the experiences of the postwar—or perhaps better, the predepression decade. Foreign investments have caused acute international tensions and have resulted in phenomena like American dollar diplomacy in Latin America. The expenditure has been immense, and what has been salvaged has been unimpressive enough. The nations of the world are still on the lookout for markets, as they have been for centuries, but the peoples of the world have become more or less convinced that the markets, if they can be got at all, can be got only by the offering of better and cheaper goods and not by occupation, political control, or forceful exploitation. As for foreign investments, no one has any stomach for them and most of those fortunate enough to have money to invest would be glad to learn of a safe investment at home. The assurance of needed sources for raw materials is as much if not more of a problem today than it was a generation ago, but there is little sense in taking over the expensive administration of tropical or other territory to guarantee a source of raw materials, because somehow or other it usually turns out that the other fellow has the materials that you want, and it has long since become obvious that the idea of controlling sources of all the materials you may need is a snare and a delusion.

In 1919, at the Paris Peace Conference, the struggle among the victors for the colonial spoils of the vanquished reached the proportions of the epic and the heroic. It seems like a long time ago, because so much has happened since and because we have come to see that in large measure it was a case of much ado about nothing. To meet the demands for some sort of ethics in imperialism, the German colonies and large parts of the Ottoman Empire were set up as mandates under the League, the principle being wholly in consonance with the demand already put forward by Hobson that there be an "international council" which should "accredit a civilized nation with the duty of educating a lower race." But no one will deny that the mandate-seeking nations had other than purely altruistic motives. Though they should have known better, they still proceeded on the principle that some good was to be gotten out of colonies. But the sequel has shown that, just as the more backward regions imported producers' as well as consumers' goods from Europe and thereby laid the foundation for an independent economy by no means favorable to European industrialism, so they imported from Europe the ideas of self-determination and nationalism. Since the disaster suffered by the Italians at Adua in 1896 Europe has had ample evidence of what may happen when these ideas are taken up by native populations and defended with European implements of war. The story of the last generation has been not only the story of the westernization of the world, but also the story of the revolt of Asia and Africa against the western nations. True to Hobson's prediction, the attacks of imperialism on the liberties and existence of weaker races have stimulated in them a corresponding excess of national self-consciousness. We have had much of this in India and China, and we have lived to witness the rise of Mustapha Kemal and Ibn Saud, to whom, for all we know, may be added the name of Haile Selassie. France has had her battles in Morocco, and the United States has at last come to appreciate the depth of resentment and ill-feeling against her in Latin America.

That these are not matters to be trifled with has by this time penetrated not only the minds of the governing classes and of the industrial and financial magnates, but also the mind of the man in the street. Who is there in England, for example, who puts much store by the mandates? Since the war England has allowed Ireland to cut loose, and she is trying, as best she can, to put India on her own. Egypt has been given her independence, and the mandate over Iraq has been abandoned. It would probably not be overshooting the mark to say that the British would be glad to get out of the Palestine hornet's nest if they could, and it is whispered that they would not be averse to turning back to Germany some of the African colonies. But it is not at all clear that Hitler really wants the colonies back. There obviously are other things that he wants more and the return of the colonies is more a question of vindication and prestige than anything else. In like fashion the United States has reversed the rambunctious policy of interference and disguised control in Mexico, the Caribbean, and Latin America. We are about to withdraw from the Philippines with greater haste than the Filipinos desire or than many Americans think wise or decent. Neither Britain nor America has shown much real appetite for interfering against Japan in the Far East. Public opinion would not tolerate it, and even among those who have interests at stake there seems to be a growing opinion that if the Japanese wish to make the expenditure in blood and money necessary to restore order and security in China, they ought to be given a universal blessing.

France, to be sure, has shown no inclination to give up any of her vast colonial possessions, while Italy and Japan are both on the warpath. But the case of France is a very special one. Being less industrialized than England, Germany, or the United States, she never felt to the same extent as those countries the urge for markets and sources of raw material. The imperialist movement was in France always something of an artificial and fictitious thing, fanned by a small group of enthusiasts. It takes a great and splendid colonial exposition to arouse much popular interest in the greater France. It might be supposed, therefore, that France would be among the first nations to beat the retreat. But there is a purely military consideration that holds her back. Like England, she can draw troops from her colonies in time of crisis. In the British case this is always something of a gambling proposition. England has no choice but to defend the empire so long as it exists, but whether the dominions and colonies will support England is a question which they decide in each case as they choose. They elected to support the mother country in the Boer War and in the World War, but they did not choose to support her in the Near East when Mustapha Kemal drove the Greeks from Anatolia and appeared at the Straits in 1922.

With France the situation is different. In 1896 an eminent French statesman told Tsar Nicholas II, in reply to an inquiry, that France needed her colonies if only because they could supply her with manpower. The exploitation of that manpower reached large dimensions during the World War, and it is now an important and generally recognized factor in France's military establishment. So far, so good, but the French must realize, and no doubt they do realize, that this may not go on forever. Who can say how long the "Senegalese" will be willing to pour out their blood in defense of French interests? Who can say when they will make use of the training and equipment that has been given them and turn upon their own masters? The spectacle of black troops holding down the population in the Rhineland was one which roused misgivings in the minds of many who think of Western civilization in terms other than those of might and political exigency.

As for Japan and Italy, perhaps the less said the better. Japan is motivated by ideas which were current in Europe a generation ago and which are now being discarded. She has serious economic problems which have come with industrialism, and she is trying to solve them by means of territorial expansion and political control. But the peculiar thing is that, with all her progress, little headway has been made in the direction of breaking the power of the former feudal, military caste. Ideas of conquest, power, and prestige are still dominant, and they explain, more perhaps than economic considerations, the rampant imperialism of the present day.

The Italians, on the other hand, have involved themselves deeply in the Ethiopian affair for reasons which are hardly at all economic. If they were to conquer Abyssinia, what good would it really do them? The country is populated by some 6,000,000 to 8,000,000 warlike natives and it would cost a fortune in blood and treasure, poured out over a long term of years, to hold them in subjection. Can anyone seriously maintain that such an area would prove a suitable one for the settlement of very considerable numbers of Italian colonists, or that emigrants from Italy would choose Ethiopia so long as the door in Latin America is even the least bit open? It may be that there are oil reserves or gold in the country, but talk on this point is to a large extent speculation. The story of Ethiopia's wealth will, in all probability, be exploded as was the myth of Yunnan's treasure in the nineties. Taken in the large, it has been proved on many an occasion that "pegging out claims for the future" is in the long run a poor proposition. But Dino Grandi has said in so many words, in the article quoted above, that Italy's claims to empire were ignored and neglected at Paris in 1919 and that Italy must now teach the world to respect her. If that is indeed the object, Mussolini has failed to note the trend of world opinion since the war. The greatness of a nation is no longer necessarily measured by the extent of the national color on the maps of the world, and on many sides empire has come to be regarded indeed as the "white man's burden." In other words, *Il Duce* is behind the times. I think much of the disapproval of the Italian policy in the world at large is due to the fact that other nations have grown out of the mentality that has produced the Ethiopian crisis.

Imperialism as it existed in the last two generations will never again be possible, for the world has been definitely divided up and there are but very few unclaimed areas still to be appropriated. There may be exchanges of territory between the imperial powers, and there will undoubtedly be aggression by one against another, but, in the large, territory has, in this age of rabid nationalism, become so sacred that its permanent transference has become more and more difficult and in many places almost impossible. The tightness of the territorial settlement in Europe long since became such that changes were possible only as the result of a great cataclysm, and the same petrifaction of the territorial status quo now tends to hold good of the general world settlement. If we are to give up empire, it will probably be to the natives to whom the territory originally belonged. If the tide of native resistance continues to rise, as it is likely to do, that course will become inevitable. We shall have more and more nations and more and more margin for conflict between them unless the mentality of nationalism undergoes a modification and there is some divorce of the ideas of nationalism and territory. In the interval the hope of the world would seem to be in the gradual evolution of voluntary federative combinations between groups of nations, regional pacts. The British Commonwealth, the Soviet Federation, and the Pan-American bloc may point the way to a transition to some form of super-national organization for which the present League of Nations will have served as a model and a guide. But all this may be merely wishful thinking.

8

The Struggle for the Nile

1936

In the course of the present African crisis Great Britain has consistently taken its stand with the angels. It has done more than any other major power to make the League an effective instrument of action against an aggressor state, and through leading members of its government it has announced on more than one occasion its determination not to accept a settlement of the dispute repugnant to the League. To be sure, in the London press reference has been made here and there to the fact that the British, whatever their interest in peace and in the strengthening of the League, have other interests of a purely national character which are endangered by the Italian policy and which must therefore be defended. But this aspect of the problem has generally been glossed over. The English, as a people, have been well satisfied with themselves in an altruistic role. In the words of one of their leading political writers, they have long enjoyed freedom of speech because they can be trusted to leave unsaid the things that would be discreditable or embarrassing.

At the root of the present difficulties there lies, no doubt, the general apprehension, shared alike by Britain and France, of the new wave of nationalism and colonialism which has been sweeping Italy since the advent of the Fascist régime. Anyone who has followed at all closely the last decade's flood of expansionist propaganda and the story of Fascist organization and activity in the countries of the Mediterranean basin will hardly have escaped the conclusion that the aspirations of the new Italy have created an entirely new situation—a situation fraught with latent danger to the two powers which, hitherto, have shared between them the control of northern Africa. It has been suggested on some sides that M. Laval's visit to Rome last January was actuated as much by fear of Italian designs on Tunis as by alarm at Hitler's plans for Austria, and that the French premier sold out the

Note: Reprinted from *Foreign Affairs*, XIV (January 1936), 259–273, copyright the Council on Foreign Relations, Inc., New York.

well-established French interests in Ethiopia in order to avoid trouble nearer home. This may or may not have been so, but it is beyond question that Fascist propaganda in all the region from Algiers on the west to Egypt and Syria on the east has caused genuine uneasiness and has obliged the governments of both Paris and London to reconsider the Mediterranean problem.

So far as England is concerned, the new colonialism of the Italians touches most directly the time-honored problem of Egypt; and for England the Egyptian question has always been indissolubly linked to the Suez Canal and to the general safeguarding of the route through the Red Sea to the Far East. This is certainly not the place to review the British policy either in Egypt or in the Suez area, but it may be worth recalling that the London government has always been sensitive about the establishment of any strong power on the coasts of the Red Sea. Long before the Suez Canal was built, the English occupied Aden as a reply to the activities of Mehemet Ali in Arabia. Much later in the nineteenth century they put every conceivable obstacle in the way of Turkish efforts to establish effective control along the same coast. They intervened only a few years ago to save the Imam of Yemen from the consequences of his defeat by Ibn Saud, and are clearly anxious to keep the conquests of the great Arab within bounds so far as the coastline is concerned.

On the other side of the Red Sea the story has been the same. The English were filled with misgivings about the expansion of Egypt to the south in the days of the Khedive Ismail. They insisted, at great cost, on holding Suakin and the coast line of the Sudan against the onslaughts of the Mahdi's followers, and they themselves occupied British Somaliland as a reply to the establishment of the French at Obock and Jibuti. It is true that they encouraged the Italians to take over Massaua, but the Italians were then their friends and clients, and it certainly does not follow that because they once desired Italian help against the dervishes they are now prepared to see the erection of a large Italian empire on the Red Sea. On the contrary, it is an obvious British interest to frustrate Italian aspirations of such a magnitude.

While acknowledging, then, the very real interests of Britain in the Mediterranean and Red Seas, let us turn to an examination of the motives of British policy more specifically in Ethiopia. The newspapers often mention Lake Tana and its importance for the Sudan and Egypt. But the present significance of Lake Tana is not sufficiently realized, nor has the fact that British policy in Ethiopia has for almost fifty years centered on the protection of this lake been properly underlined.

Appreciation of the facts came rather late to the English, it must be confessed. When the decision was made, in 1884, to abandon the Sudan, even General Gordon wrote: "The Sudan is a useless possession, ever was so, and ever will be so . . . I think Her Majesty's Government are fully justified in recommending the evacuation." And as late as 1889 Lord Cromer could report home: "I have pointed out over and over again during the last five years that the true interests of Egypt are not to reconquer, but to trade with the Soudan." All of which indicates that to the English mind the Sudan had meant nothing to Egypt but a paradise for slave traders and ivory hunters, a paradise for officials bent on ruthless extortion.

But among the Egyptians themselves the situation was viewed from a different angle. Ever since the Middle Ages there had been current a legend that the Emperor of Ethiopia could shut off the water of the Nile as one would shut off a faucet. Even within the last few months a high Egyptian official has explained Egyptian sympathy for the Ethiopians as a form of gratitude for the fact that the highlanders never tampered with the Egyptian water supply. More than likely one of the motives behind the Egyptian conquest of the Sudan in the nineteenth century was the desire to secure control over the entire Nile system. The growth of the Egyptian population and the extension of the system of perennial irrigation was rapidly making the increase of the Egyptian water supply the most vital problem of the government, and it was being widely recognized that Egypt could not feel safe until the whole course of the great river was in her hands. That is why, in 1884, the Egyptian government protested so vigorously against the abandonment of the Sudan, and why Riaz Pasha wrote in 1888: "No one will deny, so clear and evident a proposition is it, that the Nile is the life of Egypt. Now the Nile means the Soudan, and nobody will doubt that the bonds and connections which unite Egypt to the Soudan are as inseparable as those which unite the soul to the body . . . I mean by the Soudan the banks of the Nile and the island of Senaar, and the districts of the Eastern Soudan, terminating at Suakin . . . No European power would occupy Suakin without wishing necessarily to extend its power into the interior, with a view to reaching richer districts. But if it attained its object, and took possession of the banks of the Nile, it would be all over with Egypt."

This was the danger to which so eminent an authority as Sir Samuel Baker had called attention. In his famous book "The Nile Tributaries of Abyssinia," published in 1868, he had already put forward the proposal that a series of dams be constructed from Aswan to Khartum, in order to increase the Egyptian water supply and to irrigate the Sudan for the culture of cotton. In 1884 he pointed out what the loss of Khartum would mean: "If a civilised, or even semicivilised, enemy be in possession of that point, the water of the Rahad, Dinder, Blue Nile, and Atbara Rivers could be diverted from their course and dispersed throughout the deserts, to the utter ruin and complete destruction of Egypt proper."

Among British statesmen, Lord Salisbury was undoubtedly one of the first to appreciate the danger. After the very low Nile flood of 1888 he seems to have been convinced by the warning letters written to *The Times* by Sir Samuel Baker; and his daughter has told us, in her biography of her father, that the reconquest of the Sudan became one of the fixed points in his policy. England was not willing to finance that reconquest, and so the actual operation had to be postponed for some years, but in the interval the new orientation of British colonial policy was beginning to show itself in connection with the relations of Great Britain with other European states. The Germans were bought off from Uganda in 1890; and after some years of uncertainty the English took over that crucial area at the source of the White Nile from the British East Africa Company. The Italians were, at the same time, putting forward their pretensions to a protectorate over all Ethiopia, which led Lord Dufferin, at that time ambassador at Rome, to express the fear that they might "attempt to tap the Upper Nile and Sudan." Salisbury agreed, and in the negotiations with Italy, which were then opened, thought that England should insist "on the command of all affluents of the Nile, so far as Egypt formerly possessed them." After much difficulty the agreements of 1891 were made, one clause of which bound Italy "not to construct on the Atbara, in view of irrigation, any work which might sensibly modify its flow into the Nile."

In the meanwhile the water requirements of Egypt had reached the point where some further storage provisions were becoming indispensable. For years the engineers in the Egyptian service discussed various possibilities, finally deciding upon the Aswan Dam, which was built between 1899 and 1902. In the midst of the debates, however, an eminent French engineer put forward the suggestion that dams be built at the outlets of Lakes Victoria and Albert, and at the confluence of the Sobat and the White Nile. Indulging in dangerous speculation, he pointed out that these reservoirs, if built, would control the fate of Egypt, for if they were kept closed Egypt would be deprived of the needed supply, while if they were opened in flood time they could be used to wash out the entire Egyptian civilization. The point is important, because it can be shown that the French, anxious as they were to force the British evacuation of Egypt, formulated their policy in the Congo and in Ethiopia on this idea of getting control of the Nile water. By supporting the Emperor Menelik against the Italians, they secured a preponderant influence at Addis Ababa, encouraged the Emperor in his claims to a frontier on the Nile, and obtained a concession for a railway from Jibuti to Addis Ababa and beyond, to the White Nile. Marchand was sent out from the west to advance to the Nile at Fashoda, while another French expedition, starting from Ethiopia, was to meet him and thus establish a French-Ethiopian belt right through the Sudan. It would then have been easy to force the British out of Egypt by threatening to cut off the water supply. In a recent book, I have followed the development of this crisis in some detail.[1] There is neither need nor space for the repetition of it here, but I should point out that in the Fashoda crisis of 1898 the British were prepared to go to war with France for reasons which, at bottom, were not so very different from those which have driven London to take so uncompromising a stand at the present time.

The French plans were completely frustrated in 1898 and the victorious English, once they had finished with the South African War, were able to devote themselves to the Ethiopian angle. Nothing much is known of the negotiations carried on by the English minister, Colonel Harrington, but he did succeed in having Menelik sign the agreement of May 1902, by which the Ethiopian ruler not only accepted a frontier removed by a considerable distance from the main course of the Nile, but also gave invaluable assurances with regard to Lake Tana. By Article III he engaged "not to construct, or allow to be constructed, any work across the Blue Nile, Lake Tana, or the Sobat which would arrest the flow of their waters into the Nile, except in agreement with His Britannic Majesty's Government and the Government of the Soudan."

[1] William L. Langer, *The Diplomacy of Imperialism* (2 vols., New York, 1935).

The engagement was, to be sure, a purely negative one, but neverthe-less it marked a great advance over the danger and uncertainty of the previous period.

The provisions of the treaty with Menelik already reflected the im-proved knowledge of the régime of the Nile which resulted from the investigations of Sir William Garstin and his associates, investigations which were undertaken at once after Kitchener's reconquest of the Sudan and the ejection of Marchand from Fashoda. I shall not go into the highly complicated details of a hydrological nature connected with the Nile Basin, but something must be said on this score if the im-portance of Lake Tana and the general British stake in Ethiopia are to be understood. Before 1900 knowledge of the peculiarities of the Nile discharges was very scant indeed, but since that time a tremendous amount of study has been devoted to the subject and the main facts, at least, are no longer the subject of dispute.

Although the Nile originates in Lakes Victoria, Albert, and Edward, the true reservoir is Lake Albert, into which both systems flow, and from which the Bahr-el-Jebel issues. A very substantial amount of water, the result of the winter rains in the lake region, emerges from Lake Albert, but almost half of this supply is lost by evaporation in the great swamp area, about four hundred miles long, through which the Bahr-el-Jebel passes between Mongalla and the mouth of the Sobat River. The Sobat itself, the first important confluent on the right bank, brings down the water from the southern part of the Abyssinian high-lands, and, rising in April, just about doubles the amount of water of the White Nile. But the rush of water from the Sobat serves to hold back most of the water from the Bahr-el-Jebel. In similar fashion the Blue Nile, which alone contributes more than half of the entire dis-charge of the Nile, holds back the water of the White Nile in August and September. As the great flood of the Blue Nile begins to subside, this great body of water above Khartum is released, thus continuing for several more months the flood that reaches Egypt. Two-thirds of the total discharge of the Nile passes the frontier of Egypt in August, September, and October, and of this flood two-thirds comes from the Blue Nile, the rest being divided about evenly between the Atbara and the White Nile. But when this great flood has passed and the im-pounded waters of the White Nile take the place of the Blue Nile water, the White Nile supplies about 85 percent of what reaches Egypt.

In other words, the heavy silt-laden water which has made possible the cultivation of Egypt for thousands of years is almost exclusively the contribution of the Blue Nile, which collects it from countless streams in the Ethiopian mountains. It has been estimated that five-sixths of all the water of the Blue Nile enters that river between its outlet at Lake Tana and its crossing of the frontier into the Sudan. In that region the river flows through a tremendous canyon which has never yet been explored by white men, but which is known to drain a very large mountain area. Engineers agree that nothing man can do could in any way check this torrential flow. Egypt's supply of autumn water and fertilizing silt is, in all human probability, completely safe.

The modern problem of Egyptian water, however, arose with the introduction of perennial cultivation in the time of Mehemet Ali. The second crop, which is mainly cotton, requires water during the spring months, when the discharge of the Nile is slight. Cotton has now become the crop on which Egypt depends for her existence. Between 1882 and 1900 the population increased from somewhat less than 7,000,000 to about 10,000,000, and by 1900 most of the land in the delta was under perennial cultivation, though in Upper Egypt there were still almost 2,000,000 acres under annual or basin irrigation. The Aswan Dam, storing about 1,000,000,000 cubic meters of water, permitted the conversion to perennial cultivation of about 400,000 acres in Upper Egypt and tripled the yield of cotton. Between 1908 and 1912 the Aswan Dam was heightened and its capacity more than doubled, thus making possible further conversion of lands under basin irrigation to the perennial system. But the population rose from about 10,000,000 in 1900 to more than 14,000,000 in 1927 and is increasing at the rate of about 300,000 annually. The conversion of all available land has therefore become more and more imperative, but even so the situation is rather desperate, for only about 12,000 square miles of Egypt's 350,000 are at all cultivable. It is estimated that by 1955 all suitable land will have been converted and that then Egypt will be supporting between 18,000,000 and 20,000,000 people.

Ever since the investigations of Sir William Garstin and his associate, Mr. Dupuis, it has been taken for granted that ultimately a dam would have to be built on the Upper Blue Nile, preferably at its outlet from Lake Tana, to supplement the summer water supply of Egypt. The introduction of irrigated cotton culture in the Gezira of the Sudan in 1904 has made this desirable also from the Sudanese standpoint. However, the scheme has been held up by the political difficulty of getting the Ethiopian government to agree. For that reason the project was more or less shelved for years, though surveys were made, with the permission of Addis Ababa, in 1915 and again in 1920–1924. In the interval the Sennar Dam on the Blue Nile was begun in 1913 and finally finished in 1925. This has made possible the extension of the cotton area in the Gezira from 30,000 feddans (a feddan is 1.04 acres) to a possible 300,000, without any detriment to Egypt. At the same time much attention had been given to the possibility of constructing a dam just above Khartum. The Aswan Dam was raised for a second time in 1930, thus doubling the capacity once more, and finally, after much dispute, the Egyptian government proceeded in 1933 to the construction of the great Jebel Aulia Dam, south of Khartum on the White Nile. This dam will be finished in 1937 and will serve to reduce the flood danger as well as to store summer water for Egypt.

The situation as it presents itself now is briefly this. Between March 1 and August 1 of each year Egypt requires about 14,500,000,000 cubic meters of water for the cotton, sugar, rice, and other summer crops. The average flow for the years 1912–1927 was 10,500,000,000. The Aswan Dam, after the second raising, will hold about 5,000,000,000 and the new Jebel Aulia Dam another 3,000,000,000 to 4,000,000,000. Egypt will therefore have more than she needs when the Jebel Aulia Dam is finished, but if she is to develop the land to the limit, as she must, she will need about 26,000,000,000 cubic meters of summer water, and this will have to come from further projects, namely from an Upper Blue Nile Dam and from a dam at the outlet of Lake Albert. The Lake Albert reservoir, if the level were raised by only 1 meter, would store 5,000,000,000 cubic meters, but it would do little good unless the course of the Bahr-el-Jebel were cut deeper and regulated, so that the stream could no longer lose itself in the swamps. This will eventually have to be done, but it will be an extremely costly enterprise.

The Tana Dam, on the other hand, would not be expensive, and would have the added advantage of serving the Sudan as well as Egypt. It is thought that fully 3,000,000 acres could be put under cultivation in the Sudan, if only there were water; in any event cotton now constitutes 60 percent of the exports of the Sudan and is a factor of considerable interest to Lancashire. England's unwillingness to abandon the Sudan to Egypt has been one of the prime reasons for the failure to reach an Anglo-Egyptian agreement, and it demonstrates more clearly than anything else the high value which England assigns to the Sudan. As for the projected Tana Dam, it is unnecessary to say much. The lake, which is about 6000 feet above sea level, is about 40 to 50 miles square and reaches depths in the neighborhood of 200 feet. About 3,500,000,000 cubic meters of water are discharged by the lake annually. The water as it issues from the lake contains no silt; and since the flow takes place at the time of the great Blue Nile flood, it is of almost no account to Egypt at present. About 6,000,000,000 cubic meters could be stored ready for use when needed, by blasting a deeper outlet and erecting a dam. Of this amount about 3,500,000,000 would be released from January to April for use in the Sudan and Egypt, and the rest would be kept in reserve for years of poor flood. By cutting out the cataract, a reservoir could be built without raising the level of the lake, a fact which is important because the Ethiopians have been much exercised by the thought of having the churches on islands in the lake in any way damaged.

Since for more than thirty years the Tana Dam has been an integral part in the projected development of the summer water supply of Egypt and the Sudan, we need not wonder that it should have become the key to British policy in Ethiopia. As aforesaid, the fact is reflected in the agreement made with Menelik in 1902. A second stage was reached in the famous Tripartite Agreement of December 1906 between England, France, and Italy. Of the negotiation of this pact we have only the most fragmentary evidence. However, its general lines seem to have been something as follows.

Towards the end of 1902 the Italians, much alarmed by the progress of British influence at Addis Ababa, and disturbed by the illness of Menelik and the danger of intertribal war at his death, approached the British with a suggestion that the two powers agree on a successor who might if necessary be imposed on the Ethiopians. The English, evidently eager to get Italian support for their efforts to internationalize the French-owned railway concession, entered upon discussion and came to an agreement with the Italians. But in the interval the *entente cordiale* with France had been consummated, and it was deemed necessary to initiate the Paris government. In the course of the negotiations, which dragged out over a period of years, M. Delcassé raised the question of marking out spheres of influence. He was willing to recognize British interests in the Tana region and was willing to abandon the idea of extending the French railway from Addis Ababa westward. But in return he wished to have included in the French sphere not only

Harar, but also Shoa, with the capital. This demand conflicted with the Italian desire for a sphere connecting Eritrea and Italian Somaliland, which presumably would have run just west of Harar. Being the weaker party, the Italians were obliged to give in, if only in order to prevent an Anglo-French agreement to which they were not parties. Their sphere was therefore moved to the west of Addis Ababa, and was apparently to pass to the east of Lake Tana, though this was not made clear. The Italians were dissatisfied with the whole pact, but had to console themselves with the idea that it was better than nothing. The British, on their part, were at last freed from the danger of having French influence extend to the west of Addis Ababa, though, as we realize now, they were letting in the more restless and ambitious Italians.

In 1914, soon after the raising of the Aswan Dam, Lord Kitchener took steps to further the Tana project and in 1915 a joint Egyptian-Sudanese-Ethiopian commission visited the lake. The World War and the internal disorders in Ethiopia no doubt had much to do with the fact that no progress was made. But there is every indication that the British expected to push on with the project as soon as convenient. When in November 1919 the Italian government tried to link up the Ethiopian question with its claims for compensation under the Treaty of London, it had no success whatever. The Italians proposed to support Britain "in order that she may obtain from Ethiopia the concession to carry out works of barrage in the lake itself, within the Italian sphere of influence, pending the delimitation of the extent of the territorial zone to be recognized as pertaining to Great Britain in respect of the latter's predominant hydraulic interests . . ." Italy was also to support an application from Britain to build a motor road from the Sudan to Lake Tana. In return England was to support the Italians in order that they might obtain a concession for a railway from Eritrea to Somaliland west of Addis Ababa. Rome asked further for recognition by Britain of "an exclusive economic influence in the west of Ethiopia and in the whole of the territory to be crossed by the above-mentioned railway."

This proposal is interesting inasmuch as it represents an effort to expand the agreement of 1906. Lake Tana is here described as within the Italian sphere, only a zone of which was to be allowed England. In fact, all of western Ethiopia was to be part of the Italian economic sphere. It is not surprising that the London cabinet rejected the offer, "owing to the strong objection felt to the idea of allowing a foreign Power to establish any sort of control over the headwaters of rivers so vital to the prosperity and even the existence of Egypt and the Sudan." It must be remembered that at the time the English were still expecting to secure the concession from the Ethiopian government. Of the discussions carried on in the years 1920 to 1924 we know nothing specific. An authoritative Italian writer has declared, very recently, that in 1922 the English offered the Ethiopian government the port of Zeila in British Somaliland in return for the concession.[2] Others have maintained that in 1923, presumably at the height of Anglo-Italian tension during the Corfu affair, Lord Curzon threatened to denounce the Tripartite Agreement of 1906. But these are simply a few among the many obscure points in the whole historical background of the present crisis. All we know is that when Ras Tafari (the present emperor) came to London in 1924, the whole matter was gone over with him by Ramsay MacDonald and that negotiations continued even after that. Nothing came of the discussions; apparently the Ethiopian regent made it pretty clear that when the dam was to be built, Ethiopia would undertake the work itself.

Profoundly disappointed by this turn of events, and evidently suspecting that Italian influence had something to do with the Ethiopian's obstinacy, the London government now returned to the Italian offers of 1919, in order, as Sir Austen Chamberlain said later, "to secure that exterior opposition should not intervene to prevent a friendly arrangement." The result was the famous exchange of notes of December 14/20, 1925, which amounted practically to acceptance of the Italian terms of 1919. In return for Italian support in securing the concession for the dam and the road, the English were to support the Italians in getting the concession for the railroad from Eritrea to Somaliland and to recognize "an exclusive Italian economic influence in the west of Abyssinia and in the whole of the territory to be crossed by the above-mentioned railway." "But such recognition and undertaking are subject to the proviso that the Italian Government, on their side, recognizing the prior hydraulic rights of Egypt and the Sudan, will engage not to construct on the headwaters of the Blue or the White Niles or their tributaries or affluents any work which might sensibly modify their flow into the main river." It would appear, from the futher assurance

[2] Maurizio Rava, "L'Inghilterra e l'Etiopia," *Nuova Antologia* (Sept. 1, 1935), pp. 74–90.

of the British government that it would construct and operate the dam so far as possible with locally recruited labor, and from the expression of confidence that the project would increase the prosperity and economic progress of the local inhabitants, that "exclusive Italian economic influence" must have meant more than is usually understood by this admittedly vague phrase.

The further history of this episode need not detain us. When Ras Tafari learned of it in June 1926, he took it to be a plan to bring pressure upon him, appealed to the League, and succeeded in securing reassuring statements from both England and Italy. But the incident left its mark. In his note to the British minister, the Regent pointed out that negotiations between England and Ethiopia had been in progress, adding bitterly, "We should never have suspected that the British Government would come to an agreement with another Government regarding our Lake." In any event, negotiations were taken up again. Of their content we know nothing, but Sir Austen Chamberlain referred later to a British note of May 1927 to which the Ethiopian government replied in September. Very soon after that, on November 3, the *New York Times* reported that negotiations had been practically completed between Dr. Warneth Martin, agent of Ras Tafari, and the J. G. White Engineering Corporation of New York for the construction of the dam, which was estimated to cost $20,000,000. In view of the stir caused by this announcement both in England and in Egypt, Sir Austen Chamberlain declared almost at once that a concession granted without previous consultation with the British government would be contrary to the agreement of 1902. As a matter of fact, Dr. Martin stopped at London on his return journey, gave assurances that no definite contract had been signed, and reaffirmed the respect of the Ethiopian government for the agreement of 1902.

Nothing seems to have happened for more than a year, but in November 1929, Mr. Lardner, the vice-president of the J. G. White Corporation, went to Addis Ababa, and, on the invitation of the Ethiopian government, the Sudan government in January 1930 sent one of its experts, Mr. R. M. MacGregor, to join in a conference. Egypt too had a representative. After two months of discussion it was decided that in addition to the dam a road should be built to the lake from Addis Ababa, not from the Sudan. Engineers of the Company were to make further surveys for the project. Evidently complete agreement was reached with regard to the American contract. The English regretted that their own engineers were not to build the dam, but they argued with some force that the main thing was to have the dam at all. It could be of little use to Ethiopia; consequently, if once built, it would of necessity serve the needs of Egypt and the Sudan.

The surveys, carried out by Major L. B. Roberts, were completed by May 1931, but either because of the world economic conditions or because of unknown reasons, nothing came of the project until in January 1933 another conference was summoned to meet at Addis Ababa. The Egyptian government, which had just decided to build the Jebel Aulia Dam, was not enthusiastic, partly for financial reasons, partly because of the violent opposition of nationalist elements to the construction of works even in the Sudan, to say nothing of Ethiopia. So determined was this opposition that for a time Cairo could find no one willing to act as delegate at Addis Ababa, and when finally a victim was found, he was sent to the conference without power to make an agreement. His mission was simply to find out what the Ethiopian government proposed to do. At the conference itself, in February and March 1933, it was decided that, in the hope of reducing estimates, further surveys should be made by the American engineers both for the road and for the dam. It was proposed that Egypt should vote 50,000 Egyptian pounds for this purpose and that the whole matter should be gone into again in 1935. In July 1933 the Egyptian Chamber actually voted the 50,000 pounds, its purpose being primarily to keep a finger in the pie.

The present Ethiopian crisis, as it developed in the spring of 1935, apparently served to hasten the reopening of the subject. On May 10 the Emperor invited the British, Egyptian, and Sudan governments to send delegates to a new conference at Addis Ababa, but the London cabinet, anxious not to aggravate the dispute with Italy, replied that it favored postponement. Nevertheless the Egyptian government on May 22 adopted a five-year plan of irrigation work at an outlay of £E21,000,000, of which 3,000,000 were set aside for the Tana Dam. At the same time negotiations between the Egyptian and Sudan governments were opened with a view to settling the details of costs and partition of waters, so that all might be clear for the final arrangements with the Ethiopian Emperor as soon as the international situation permitted. On September 4, 1935, the Egyptian cabinet approved an arrangement with the Sudan by which the dam was to be constructed at the expense of Egypt, but the Sudan was to pay for water at a certain rate. The Sudan was to be permitted to take 10 percent of the water at first, but might later increase its quota to as much as 50 percent. It was reported that the Egyptian government would now proceed to make an agreement with the Ethiopian government giving Egypt the right to construct the dam irrespective of future developments in Ethiopia.

The relationship of Italy to these negotiations is not at once apparent. In the earlier days of the crisis the Italian press, and presumably the government, made much of its claims under the 1906 treaty and under the Anglo-Italian exchange of notes of December 1925. It was evidently on the basis of these obligations that Mr. Eden tried to negotiate in Rome in June 1935. But as a matter of fact London can easily evade these earlier arrangements. They are incompatible with the League Covenant in so far as Italy may try to stretch them till they affect the independence and integrity of Ethiopia. Furthermore, as things now stand, England is not securing the concession for the Tana Dam, and therefore is under no obligation to assist Italy to realize her share of the bargain. The dam is going to be built, but officially it is to be constructed for the Ethiopian government by an American engineering firm, even though the Egyptian government will supply Addis Ababa with the necessary funds. The Sudan government may, to all intents and purposes, be under the control of Britain; but the Sudan government will merely buy water when the dam is completed.

With respect to Italy there is another aspect to be considered, that the basis of French policy has been changed. In 1906 it was the French objections that made the Italians accept a sphere in western Ethiopia. What they really wanted was a broad belt in eastern Ethiopia, running behind French and British Somaliland. They have themselves sneered at the fantastic idea of a railway through the mountains in a great circle passing west of Addis Ababa. Now the present situation has all the appearance of resting on French approval. The Italians are pushing forward toward Harar both from the north and from the south, yet one hears no protests from France and no suggestion that the Italian advance will interfere either with the railway or with the French zone. From this one can only conclude that M. Laval sold out completely in making the agreement of January 1935 and that the Italians, if no one stops them, will get the sphere they originally wanted, and of course as much more as they can. This would also explain the oft-reiterated statements from Italy that Britain need not fear for her interests or for

198

Lake Tana, and that Italy is fully prepared to guarantee those interests. It makes it by no means impossible that before the crisis is over, Britain, guided by France, will strike a bargain with Mussolini. If it is at all within reason, this can be forced down the throat of Haile Selassie and presented to the League as an agreement satisfying to all parties concerned. If England does eventually yield to temptation and allow her imperialism to get the better of her internationalism, we may be sure at least of this, that the Lake Tana region will remain outside the Italian sphere and that it will be either under the control of a rump Ethiopia or within the sphere of the Sudan and of England.

9

Alliance System and League

1936

In the good old days war was a much more casual thing than it has come to be in our harassed time. Even in the period of the great Napoleon, months of inactivity often followed a declaration of war, and during the lag the opposing states devoted themselves to the building up of coalitions. As late as the middle of the last century the Crimean War took an unconscionable time to get itself declared, and alliance negotiations continued throughout the period of the conflict. But since that time the acceleration of life which followed in the train of the industrial revolution has made itself felt in international affairs as in other aspects of human activity. Warfare has become more and more mechanized and speed has become a crucial matter. Governments could no longer afford to leave the alignment of other powers to chance. Just as the army staffs have had to provide plans for all possible contingencies, so foreign offices have had to prepare in advance for the aid of others, that is, for allies. And so Bismarck, much against his will at first, became the architect of the first great peacetime coalition, the Triple Alliance, which in turn provoked the formation of the Franco-Russian Alliance and ultimately the Triple Entente.

These combinations were decidedly defensive groupings, but from the very nature of the case the division of Europe into two armed camps led to increased tension. Indeed, this division of the nations into competing coalitions has not without justice been assigned a leading place among the causes that produced the World War, and the League of Nations was in large measure designed to obviate the necessity for peacetime alliances. The primary purpose of the League was to provide security through collective action, and security, it must be remembered, has become the chief and all-absorbing objective of all foreign policy.

Those who realize to the full not only the horror of modern war, but also its terrifying threat to our civilization have watched with uneasi-

Note: Reprinted from *Polity* (February 1936, pp. 10–11).

ness and apprehension the development of the League. They have bemoaned its initial weakness and have seen with distress its inability to function as a political organ in cases where the interests of first-class powers were concerned. The present Ethiopian crisis derives its world importance largely from the fact that it has developed into a great and crucial test of League action. All thoughtful people are at one in the recognition that this is a question of make or break, and that if the League fails in this matter its doom is sealed. We shall be back to the prewar situation—every nation for itself and infinitely more hatred, infinitely more antagonisms making for a cataclysm.

This present crisis has served not only to bring into the spotlight the problem of collective security, but it has also illuminated the duality that has existed in international affairs since the last great conflict. For, to tell the truth, no European power has been willing to stake its future on the effectiveness of the League. Since 1920 Europe has seen the emergence of peacetime coalitions, just as it did after 1871. The situation up to 1924 or 1925 was rather chaotic, but after that the division into revisionist and anti-revisionist groupings became increasingly obvious, and since the advent of Hitler, a profound change of alignment has been taking place. In order to understand this process of coalescence it is necessary to have clearly in mind the basic aims of the various powers and to consider the various factors that have made for union or antagonism.

In the beginning there was France. Her preponderance on the continent in 1920 was beyond question. Germany was defeated and rendered entirely helpless by the unbelievably harsh Treaty of Versailles; the Austro-Hungarian monarchy had dissolved, and its place had been taken by a number of second-rate powers; Italy was submerged in domestic difficulties and could be treated as Cinderella with impunity; and Russia was just coming out of a long period of civil war and was so engrossed in the problem of social revolution that the danger of a Bolshevik crusade was only a passing phenomenon. For the moment France had complete security, but, naturally enough, the Quai d'Orsay was not blind to the fact that the policy of Versailles might result in a German policy of revenge and the future might bring dangers much greater than those of the past. So the French devoted themselves to the cultivation of the League and to the maintenance of the alliance with England. But at the same time the French foreign office concluded an alliance with Poland and gave its blessing to the attempts at coalition which were being made in central Europe under the leadership of Benes. The Little Entente between Czechoslovakia, Rumania, and Yugoslavia was evolved in 1920–1921 with the object of presenting a united front to any efforts made to restore the Hapsburgs in Austria or Hungary, and this combination, together with Poland, flourished under the aegis of France, which staked much money upon it. With Polish help the Paris foreign office hoped to hold Germany in check in any eventuality; with the aid of the Little Entente France could hope to frustrate any attempt to disturb the status quo along the Danube and to prevent the realization of restless Italy's aspirations in the Adriatic at the expense of Yugoslavia; and both Poland and the Little Entente could be relied upon for aid if the Bolshevik menace should materialize, for the antagonism between Russia and Poland was almost axiomatic, and Czechoslovakia had forgotten, temporarily at least, the idea of Pan-Slavism, while Rumania was at daggers drawn with Russia on account of the Bessarabian difficulty.

The position of France would have been entirely secure, had it not been for the fact that all these states were still in their infancy, beset by endless domestic difficulties, and for the most part quite unstable. Nevertheless, they represented, even at their worst, a useful second string to the French bow. If the system of collective security through the League should fail, if England, like the United States, should reject any responsibility for continental affairs, there were still France's allies to fall back upon, and these states, it should be remembered, commanded not inconsiderable manpower.

The advent of Mussolini in Italy first besmirched this idyllic picture. Bismarck, who made an alliance with the Italians, had never respected them. He described them as a first-class power only by courtesy and jested that their appetite had come before their teeth. The Italians, in fact, themselves suffered before the war from a feeling of inferiority, which the great conflict and the peace settlement did little to allay. In French eyes the military accomplishment of the Italian armies was not nearly as great as present-day Fascist writers would have the world believe, and for that reason little was done to satisfy the cravings of the Italians when they came to Paris in 1919. They remained discontented and disillusiond, and the prevalence of these feelings had not a little to do with the rise of Fascism and the victory of Mussolini. Hardly was he firmly in the saddle when the Duce demonstrated to the world his intention of changing things. The bombardment of Corfu in 1923 was meant to serve notice that Italy was resuming her claims in the Adriatic and in the Balkans. Nothing was accomplished, due to the strong attitude taken by both England and France, acting through the League. But from that time on Mussolini devoted himself to the construction of an anti-French alliance system in the Balkans. We cannot stop to examine this policy in all its details, but it is important to note that it has been by no means entirely unsuccessful. Since 1926–1927 Albania has been largely under the thumb of Italy; there has been a marriage alliance with Bulgaria and a concerted effort at even closer relationship; above all, both Austria and Hungary have been drawn into the orbit of Rome. The Hungarians, deprived of a great deal of territory by the peace treaties, some of it with right but much of it quite unjustly, have been consumed with the desire for treaty revision and were brought into Mussolini's revisionist camp without much difficulty. In Austria Dollfuss was persuaded that the independence of the little country was both desirable and feasible. He became the advance guard of the Italian dictator, and even his successors have been unwilling or unable to throw off the connection. So that the Italians have, for years, been able to count upon three or four clients in central and eastern Europe. The members of the Italian group were, to be sure, less powerful and less important than the members of the Little Entente, but they could serve at least as a spear-head and helped to give weight to the revisionist policy of the Duce.

But the picture of Italian policy would not be complete unless some reference were made to Mussolini's attempts to draw Greece and Turkey into his grouping. Greece was a more or less unaccountable factor, but for a time the Italian influence at Athens was fairly pronounced. But Mustapha Kemal (the new name "Kemal Atatürk" seems so strange) proved obdurate. He had no use for either England or France after their support of the Sultanate and of the Greeks in the stormy years from 1919 to 1922, but neither had he any faith in the Italians, who, through the possession of the Dodecanese, were a standing menace to the Turkish coast and whose efforts to establish themselves in Adalia were not forgotten. Mustapha Kemal had driven on to victory with the support of Russia, and with Russia he continued to stand. For years he devoted himself to a policy of retrenchment and reconstruction, concentrating his attention in foreign affairs on the improvement of Turkish relations with his neighbors to the east. For the rest, the Ankara government showed a commendable desire to establish friendly relations with the

Balkan states and to take an active part in the building up of a coalition which would liberate the Balkan nations from their dangerous dependence on the western powers. In the unofficial or semi-official Balkan conferences which took place annually after 1930, the Turks played a prominent part. There emerged gradually the astounding alliance between Greece and Turkey, as a result of which the two traditional enemies buried the hatchet and established the closest cooperation in all foreign affairs. There can be little doubt, I think, that, when in 1933 this alliance was joined by Yugoslavia and Rumania to form a new Balkan Entente, Italian policy suffered a major setback. By blocking all prospect of Italian expansion in the Balkans or in the eastern Mediterranean, the Balkan Entente drove Mussolini into the resumption of activity in Africa.

For the French there was nothing but good to be expected from this new alignment, which came at a most crucial moment. Hitler came into power in January 1933, and his advent was bound to accentuate all the French fears of German revenge. For a moment there seemed to be an acute danger that Hitler and Mussolini might join forces in a campaign for revision, peaceful if possible, but warlike if necessary. Fortunately for the Quai d'Orsay the meeting of the two dictators led to nothing. Apparently they could not see eye to eye and before long they were at daggers drawn over the Austrian question, where Mussolini, ironically enough, was playing the game of France's friends of the Little Entente. Still, the German demand for equality of armaments, Germany's withdrawal from the League, the Saar plebiscite, and the scrapping of the disarmament clauses of the Versailles Treaty have kept the French and all Europe at fever heat. Hitler's readiness to shelve the great dispute with Poland over the corridor to the Baltic and his success in concluding a ten-year pact with his eastern neighbor set all Europe by the ears. France felt constrained to undertake a complete overhauling of her relationships in Europe. This was the great objective of the late M. Barthou, who, if he was unable to keep the Poles in line, nevertheless reaffirmed the bonds which held the Little Entente to France, laid the basis for the pending alliance between democratic France and communist Russia, and paved the way for the most revolutionary turn of French policy, the agreement with Italy. In the face of the German menace nothing else counted for the French. The Russians, greatly exercised by the avowed German aim to expand towards the east and seriously threatened by the Japanese policy in the Far East, entered the

204

League and joined hands with the French. The Italians, on the other hand, had to be bought off. There can be no reasonable doubt that M. Laval a year ago sold out to the Italians in Ethiopia, in order to assure himself of Italy's presence in a united front as paraded before Hitler at the Stresa conference. The settlement of the Russian-Rumanian difficulty, in the meantime, has obviated all antagonism between the Soviets and the Little Entente. If the German threat to France is greater than it was, France has a stronger and more united alignment to present to it.

But M. Barthou and M. Laval failed to give due weight to some very important factors. In the first place they seem to have underestimated Mussolini's determination to get something and to proceed at once to the eating of the Ethiopian pie. In the second place, they failed to appreciate the latent popular interest in the League and the world-wide hope in the system of collective action and security through the League. Hardly was the ink dry on the Franco-Italian agreement of last January than Mussolini embarked on his great adventure and began to ship large numbers of troops to Africa. The Italian case against Ethiopia was weak in itself, but the presentation of that case by the Italians was even weaker. It was, in fact, the most pathetic presentation in the whole history of modern diplomacy. The result was that it outraged public opinion throughout the world and at once focused all eyes on Geneva. No matter from what angle the problem was regarded, there was no way of reconciling the Italian action either with the letter or with the spirit of the covenant. M. Laval was, from the outset, in a most serious dilemma, for the support of Italy against Germany implied a carte blanche for anything Mussolini might see fit to do in Ethiopia, but the carte blanche to Italy estranged France's anti-Italian allies and outraged all those who looked for security beyond the revived system of alliances to the new system of collective action.

The situation was endlessly complicated by the attitude of Britain. Throughout the entire postwar period the world interests of the British Empire have tended to make Downing Street turn its back on continental affairs. The French have for years bewailed the halfhearted cooperation of England in the furtherance of collective action, and the Conservatives in England have, in very truth, shown a pronounced tendency to devote themselves to their own affairs and to rely upon their own armed power for the protection of their interests. But with the rise of the Hitler danger there has come, in England, a revival of interest in the League, which found its most eloquent expression in the astounding peace poll of the spring of 1935, an experiment which may well, in the long run, prove to have been nothing less than epoch-making. The most recent events have shown beyond cavil that the peace poll was meant to be taken seriously and that no English government, conservative or otherwise, can possibly act contrary to the popular will expressed therein. The British have very real interests in the Mediterranean, in Suez, in the Red Sea, and in Ethiopia itself. Possibly the Baldwin government, before as after the recent elections, may have been willing and ready to make a dicker with the Italians to protect those interests, but all moves in that direction have been wrecked by public opposition.

The London government has, then, been driven into action through the League and lo and behold, it has found that action good. Italy has been proclaimed the aggressor and sanctions, which have long been regarded as little more than ornamentation of the covenant, have been imposed upon her. Whatever the outcome of the present crisis, these are world-moving developments, which will stand in the textbooks long after the details of the crisis have been forgotten. Their effect has been electric. In France itself faith in the League has been revived and strengthened. The Quai d'Orsay has, indeed, been reminded that not only France but France's allies prefer the League system to any other, and that the alliances are really only a second string. For that reason France, despite her obligations to Italy, has been more or less forced to follow the lead of England at Geneva, and France's allies, the nations of both the Little and Balkan Ententes, have taken their place by the side of England, promising support in the event of an Italian attack in reply to sanctions and other League action. Not only Turkey, but Greece, the two states most directly involved, have come out against Italy. Mussolini's efforts to secure the friendship of Greece through Marshal Kondylis and through the restored King George appear to have fallen flat in every way.

What we have, then, is the astonishing situation in which both the revived alliance systems of olden days and the League system of postwar origin are working together in the interest of peace and security. The combination, if it continues to operate in this fashion, is absolutely irresistible. It may well be that the Ethiopians will defeat the Italians without outside aid. But if they do not, and if the mere sight of Europe united against them does not induce the Italians to draw back, it is almost certain that they can be forced to yield by the application of oil or other sanctions and that no general European war would result from such a course. Mussolini began by declaring that nothing less than the whole of Ethiopia would satisfy him; he has since been ready to take much less. Time was when he threatened to leave the League if it took a hostile stand, but he has thought better of that. Last summer he declared roundly that sanctions meant war, but they did not. Then he proclaimed that the oil sanction would be regarded as a hostile act, but now the newspapers report him less uncompromising on this point. If the League will only persist, its success seems almost unquestionable.

But with all this favorable development in international affairs, it should not be out of place to close on a word of warning. The League has without doubt been in the past too much a combination of the victors against the vanquished and the postwar alliance systems have been too exclusively designed for the preservation of the status quo. When the covenant was drawn, it was the intention of President Wilson that the League should act as an organ for the revision of treaties, for he, like all thinking persons, recognized that the world is not static and that all efforts to preserve a given situation are bound to lead to serious explosions later. Take Austria, for example. There is the most alarming danger spot in Europe. The country is hardly viable, and the overwhelming desire among the people is for union with Germany, even with Nazi Germany. Both Italy and France believe that the independence of Austria from Germany is a major interest of theirs, for reasons that are not entirely convincing. The Little Entente takes the same attitude, for more obvious reasons. Yet it is fairly clear that the *Anschluss* must come, and that if it cannot be managed by peaceful means, the ultimate resort will be to force. Other urgent problems could be easily enumerated and they all point to the fact that it is not enough to maintain peace by collective action. It is necessary to go further and provide for a just peace. I have no ready-made solution for this problem, but I am reasonably certain in my own mind that far too little thought has been given to it in the past and that this aspect of international relations is bound to be the great issue of the future.

10

The Revival of Imperialism

1937

Now that Mussolini has conquered Ethiopia he is touting through Europe for financial aid to help him develop the country. The story is, by this time, an old one: "backward" regions, which are a "disgrace" to European civilization, are rescued from barbarism. In the old days the process was accomplished by Maxim guns, which have by now given way to more advanced weapons like the aerial bomb and the gas projector. But in any event the white man continues to assume the burden in the hope that charity, which ought to begin at home, may be made to pay abroad. As in the past, it turns out that the business requires a considerable initial investment, not only in men, but in money. In all likelihood the experience of Fascist Italy will not differ materially from that of the expansive great powers of the past generation. The mother country will be drained for funds to be poured into Ethiopia and in the end the colony will prove to be more of a liability than an asset, and there will be little satisfaction beyond what can be derived from seeing a large blotch of the national color on the face of the globe.

And yet this African adventure bids fair to mark a turning point in European and perhaps world politics, for it has done more than deliver the coup de grâce to the system of collective international action as represented by the League of Nations. It has called to life all the latent energy, blind discontent, and animal bellicosity of a congested and restless Europe. It may be argued that this whole development reaches back of Mussolini's defiant outbreak and that the action of Japan in Manchuria had already set the pace. It would, indeed, be naive to overlook the significance of the Far Eastern crisis of six years ago. It undoubtedly weakened the international structure and demonstrated anew that God is on the side of the strong battalions. But from the standpoint of Europe there is an immense difference between what

Note: Reprinted from *Harvard Guardian* (March 1937), pp. 3–7.

Japan does in China and what a power such as Italy does anywhere. The Chinese situation for years has been like a great boiling pot. No one expects a real solution or anything more than reasonable stability within the next generation or more. As for Japan, she is clearly suffering from growing pains, from the aches and pressures that go with the transformation of an essentially medieval economy into a modern industrialism. Japan has about reached the stage of economic development attained by the western European nations and the United States a generation ago. Just as they felt the need to expand, so did Japan. So long as the matter went no further it might be hoped that Japan too would ultimately come to recognize the futility of trying to solve domestic social and economic problems by the diversion of national energy and national wealth to foreign adventure and expansion.

With Italy the situation was quite different. She is a member of the European family (if one can speak of such a thing); she cannot move without sending a tremor through the house; if she misbehaves and escapes punishment the whole family becomes demoralized. Now the Ethiopian adventure was initiated with the laying down of the usual smoke screen. There was the usual talk about the violation of treaties and frontiers by the villainous Ethiopians, and a formidable dossier was presented to the League to prove that these monsters were unworthy of even ordinary consideration. But this part of the Italian offensive made little impression and was soon abandoned. The aggressors themselves seemed to dislike having their tongues in their cheeks. Before long they were proclaiming *urbi et orbi* that they were out for gain, sordid gain, plain and simple. Italy was overpopulated (Mussolini having done his best to make it more so) and undersupplied with raw materials and markets. The Ethiopians had been chosen (a chosen people in a new sense) to solve Italy's problems. As usual, they were not consulted in the matter. They have been saved despite themselves.

It was almost inevitable that the Italian success should have aroused the hopes and cupidity of others. For the most part the intellectual classes in Europe had become disillusioned about imperialism, the more so since it has been shown over and over again and proved to the hilt with statistics that colonies are not a paying proposition. But in these last years Europe, like all the world, has been suffering real want. With the exchange situation chaotic and international trade reduced to hardly more than a trickle, people at large have been ready to pounce upon any theory that promised relief. While here people were worshipping at the shrines of social justice and the Townsend plan, in Europe the cult of expansion was being taken up again. Even the British, who had long ceased to expect much from their empire ("commonwealth" is really a much more appropriate term), began to think that if others wanted territory perhaps it might have some hidden value. As the imperialist clamor has become more strident, the Conservative party at least has become more plainspoken in its opposition to the abandonment of any possession whatever.

The crux of the situation, however, is the attitude of Germany. The rearmament of the *Reich* has set all Europe by the ears. While Mussolini was despatching the League system, Hitler was upsetting the whole structure of military alliances so carefully elaborated by French statesmen in the previous fifteen years. The satiated nations, as Bismarck called them, are much annoyed by their restless neighbor. The family is upset by the unruly, fast-growing boy. Threats and rebukes have been used aplenty, but it is generally understood that the offender is too strong for an old-fashioned caning. Within broad limits he has been given his own way, and there has even been some suggestion that it might be wise to reason with him and try to solve his problem by understanding cooperation. As the German battalions grow, we may look for increasingly sympathetic treatment.

By this time the Germans have erased most of the clauses of the unfortunate peace treaties. But one very important one remains; that which deprived Germany of her colonies on the plea that she was not fit to have them. This argument has long since been discarded by all those who know anything of the history of colonial administration. The Germans were as able and as acceptable colonial masters as were any other European people. As a matter of fact they never did what the French have done on a large scale, namely draft the natives into the army to fight in Europe. During the Great War they proposed that military operations in the colonies be renounced. The suggestion was rejected by the Allies, and the war was carried into Africa and the Pacific. The Germans put up a heroic, not to say epic struggle, notably in East Africa and at Tsing-tao. They lost the colonies because they were defeated in Europe. They want them back, partly as a matter of prestige and partly for the usual economic reasons. Being realists they eschew all moralizing. Dr. Schacht, the minister of finance, who is the leading proponent of the colonial program and who has converted the somewhat reluctant *Führer*, put the case very frankly in a recent number of *Foreign Affairs*. Germany, he says, must have colonies whence she may draw raw materials. She cares little about technical questions of sovereignty, army, police, the churches, or international collaboration; all she insists on is that the colonies be part of the German monetary system, so that raw materials may be purchased there with German currency. Germany, he promises, will subject these colonies, if she gets them, to a high-pressure system of exploitation unthought of before the war. There will be no peace in Europe, he concludes, until this problem is solved.

In the speech he delivered to the *Reichstag* on January 30, Hitler made it clear that he subscribes to Schacht's arguments. Germany, he declared, asks for no colonies from powers who did not take a share of hers, which puts the matter up squarely to those that did: the British Commonwealth, France, Japan, and Belgium. There is no further evading the issue. Something must be done, and the only possible thing is to return to Germany the colonies of which she was deprived in 1919. It is most improbable that this would do much to relieve the German economic problem; in fact almost all past experience speaks against it. It is equally unlikely that such a move would usher in a millenium of peace. The tension and restlessness of the modern world goes back to deeply rooted social problems, and the mere removal of a few symptoms will not do much to cure the disease. But the retrocession of the colonies will not constitute a very great sacrifice to Britain, France, and the others, while it will give the German people a sense of vindication and satisfaction. In a world system where territory is valued for its own sake, where those who have not are accustomed to taking if they are able, it is inconceivable that a people like the Germans, able, energetic, and filled with an almost messianic enthusiasm, will long continue to be without. They have not and will not have the sea power necessary to take back their colonies, but that has little bearing on the situation. The great colonial questions have always of necessity been settled by the relations of power in Europe. If the Germans are thwarted in Africa, their discontent will vent itself in much more dangerous places.

Under the circumstances it is most fortunate that the former German territories, instead of being annexed outright by the victors, were placed under the newly invented mandate system. That means that they can be given up without serious loss of prestige by those who now hold them. The thing would have to be done through the League of Nations, but there is no reason to suppose that a program of retrocession would meet with insurmountable opposition. A settlement is urgently necessary and it will, in all probability, be made in the not too distant future. Whether thereafter the surge of imperialism will subside or whether we are on the eve of a new epidemic of *Milomania*[1] no one can say. In an epoch of political emotionalism the voice of reason is hardly discernible above the din.

[1] This term, meaning a thirst for more territory (a "mania for miles"), was common in the anti-imperialist literature of the late nineteenth century.—Ed.

11

Tribulations of Empire: The Mediterranean Problem

1937

Two years ago the British and the Italians were on the very verge of conflict in the Mediterranean, and in the course of the past twelve-month the situation in that sea has been thrown into utter confusion by the Spanish civil war. Anyone who tried to make predictions for the future would obviously be rash indeed. But much may be learned about the present position from an analysis of the various stages which have led up to it and by an examination of the basic factors involved.

Ever since the opening of the Suez Canal in 1869 and the occupation of Egypt by British forces in 1882 the interest of Britain in this shortest route to her Asiatic possessions has been axiomatic. It requires no further elaboration here. But some consideration may profitably be given to the policy that was formulated to protect this route. In the decade following the opening of the canal the British were fascinated by the danger that seemed to threaten from Russia. Disraeli's whole thought was to block the advance of the Muscovite colossus either in the Balkans or in the Caucasus. When the crisis of 1878 had at last blown over, Britain was discovered in occupation of Cyprus, which was thought of as a *place d' armes* and a point of departure for meeting Russian encroachment either by sea or by land through Anatolia. The fact that Lord Salisbury offered the French a free hand in Tunis in return for support of the British policy shows more clearly than anything else how little thought was then given to the possibility of Anglo-French antagonism. The conflict of interests came only later. When the French cashed their check on Tunis in 1881 the government of Mr. Gladstone was profoundly displeased, but there was no idea of active opposition. In fact, the French themselves were acting mainly from motives of prestige and certainly had no conception of the strategic value of Tunis.

Note: Reprinted from *Foreign Affairs*, XV (July 1937), 646–660, copyright the Council on Foreign Relations, Inc., New York.

It was only after the occupation of Egypt that the Mediterranean rivalry between England and France developed. During the eighties, however, the British still felt justified in regarding the threat from France with equanimity. For in the time of Crispi the danger of a clash between France and Italy overshadowed everything else. The Italians, despite their formidable naval power, were in constant dread of a French attack upon their exposed coastal cities and therefore clutched the apron strings of Britannia for all they were worth. The situation as it was at that time was best reflected in the famous Mediterranean Agreements of 1887, concluded under Bismarck's auspices between England and Italy and adhered to by Austria-Hungary and Spain. Leaving out of account the Near Eastern aspects of these pacts, it is important to note that they provided for the preservation of the status quo in the Mediterranean and that they were directed against the further expansion of French power in North Africa. It is perfectly clear that any forward movement on the part of France would have been met, at that time, by united action by England and Italy.

The famous Franco-Russian Alliance of 1891–1893 was at least in large measure a reply to the Mediterranean Agreements and the association of Britain with the powers of the Triple Alliance. When a Russian squadron visited Toulon in October 1893 the English were under no illusions regarding the possible consequences. They had a powerful squadron in the Mediterranean, based upon Malta, but the French Toulon squadron was hardly inferior in number and probably superior in quality, and France was completing the great fortifications at Bizerta which gave them a second *point d' appui* and bade well to assure them control of the western basin. France's Russian friends had a half dozen new warships in the Black Sea which could have come out into the eastern Mediterranean without fear of serious opposition from the Turks. In that event the British fleet would have been caught in the center, with only the Italian squadrons to rely on for aid. The upshot of it all was that in the winter of 1893–1894 the British experienced an acute naval panic. Among the experts the whole Mediterranean problem was gone over in minute detail, while in Parliament no less a person than Joseph Chamberlain expressed the opinion that in the event of war "the British Navy in the Mediterranean would have to cut and run—if it could run." Men like Dilke and Brassey had already despaired of England's ability to protect her commerce against French cruisers and destroyers and were recommending that in case of conflict the entire merchant marine should be transferred to foreign registry. Food, it was hoped, would not be declared contraband.

The immediate results of the crisis were the impressive "Spencer building plan," supplementing the famous Naval Defense Act of 1889, and the desperate though abortive efforts of Lord Rosebery to revitalize the Mediterranean Agreements and to enlist the support of Germany. Fortunately for the British, the attention of the Russians was very soon diverted to the Far East, and when the storm broke between England and France in the great Fashoda crisis of 1898, France, deserted by her ally and deeply immersed in the Dreyfus scandal, was too unprepared to face the prospect of a naval conflict with Britain. Delcassé climbed down and Britannia's rule of the waves was once again undisputed.

During his unprecedented tenure of office, Delcassé worked systematically for an entente with England, which he hoped would lead ultimately to an Anglo-Russian entente and the weakening of the Triple Alliance. Camille Barrère, the eminent French ambassador at Rome, succeeded in weaning the Italians from their German connections by exchanging a free hand in Tripoli for a free hand in Morocco. In the same way the Spaniards were baited with the prospect of a share in the Moroccan spoils. After the Spanish-American War, the Madrid government was unutterably weak and in constant dread of losing the Canaries or the Balearics to some great power like Germany, which was supposed to have far-reaching designs in both the Atlantic and the Mediterranean. The pressure from Paris was great, but the Spaniards did not dare conclude an arrangement without the approval of Britain. Delcassé had to square the London government before he could hope for much success in Madrid; and this he did in the famous entente of April 8, 1904, the basis of which was the abandonment of French claims in Egypt for the withdrawal of British opposition to French policy in Morocco.

The negotiations for the entente led quite naturally to a consideration of the Mediterranean scene. England's traditional policy in Morocco had always been "that any attack on the Mediterranean coast of Morocco, and especially on Tangier, should be resisted by force." Delcassé, hounded by the fear of German ambitions, was ready to give full assurances and in fact proposed an arrangement to preserve the status quo within a radius of five hundred miles from the Straits of Gibraltar to nip in the bud any German hopes of acquiring the Balearics. This seemed to the British to be going too far, but in the final agreement it was provided that no fortifications should be erected on the Moroccan coast between Mellila and the Atlantic and that Tangier should be given a special, neutral position. When, in November 1904, Spain made her Moroccan agreement with France, she was obliged to accept these arrangements, though northern Morocco was part of the Spanish zone. England had already secured from Spain a promise not to fortify Algeciras, whence the new long-range guns might threaten Gibraltar, and so the British concern for the freedom of the Straits seemed well taken care of.

The crushing naval strength of England and France in the Mediterranean practically forced the weaker powers, Italy and Spain, into close relations with the entente. Italy managed to keep at least one foot in the other camp, but Spain became little more than a subsidiary of the main combination, just as Portugal was hardly more than a British protectorate. After the acute Morocco crisis of 1905 both England and France were much exercised by the threat of German expansion. From every successive Portuguese foreign minister the English extracted a promise not to grant the Germans a coaling or naval station in the Madeiras or Azores, and on May 16, 1907, the Madrid government, despite the resentment felt at French action in Morocco, was induced to exchange notes with Paris as well as London (the Pact of Cartagena) providing for the maintenance of the status quo in the Mediterranean and that part of the Atlantic which washes the shores of Europe and Africa. Each of the three powers declared that in pursuance of this policy it was firmly resolved to preserve intact its rights over its insular and maritime possessions in those regions. Thus were the Balearics and Canaries safeguarded from a grasping Germany.

From 1907 until 1912 the situation remained substantially unchanged, despite the fact that the Agadir crisis of 1911 raised once again the specter of German designs in Morocco and at the same time evoked a good deal of friction between France and Spain. This was not resolved until conflicting claims were settled by the agreement of November 1912. It was the war of Italy against Turkey, which broke out in September 1911, that brought about a basic transformation in the Mediterranean. The annexation of Tripoli secured for the Italians a footing on the African shore and gave them a splendid potential base at Tobruk. But even more serious was the occupation of the Dodecanese Islands in May 1912, which brought them to the very coast of Anatolia and established them athwart the routes from Malta and Constantinople to the Suez Canal. This move created something like consternation both in Paris and in London. The French feared, and rightly, that the Italians were preparing to challenge the French cultural and economic position in the Near East, and the British were profoundly disturbed by the naval aspects of the problem. An admiralty report of June 1912 declared that the naval authorities had always proceeded on the proposition that no possible opponent at sea should be permitted to have a base less than one thousand miles from Suez, in other words east of Malta. The strategic potentialities of the Dodecanese were great, and might in future be greater yet: "None can foresee the developments of material in warfare, and the occupation of the apparently most useless island should be resisted equally with the occupation of the best."

For Britain and France the situation was much aggravated by other considerations. The growing sea power of Germany made it necessary for England to withdraw her battle fleet from the Mediterranean in the summer of 1912 in order to reinforce the North Sea fleet, while the French were obliged to concentrate all their battleships in the south in view of the steady growth of the Italian navy and the emergence of Austria-Hungary as a factor to be reckoned with. For the moment the French squadrons were slightly superior to the combined Austro-Italian forces, though the latter included some recent dreadnoughts and had an advantage in the heaviest guns. It was chiefly because of the uncertainty of the French position that Delcassé introduced the great naval building program of 1912, while England kept four battle cruisers and some lighter cruisers in the Mediterranean and planned to send some dreadnoughts as soon as they were available. There was constant fear in both Paris and London that the Italians might make over to the Germans a naval base in Tripoli or in the Dodecanese, or that the Central Powers, inspired by Italy's success, might take steps of their own to establish themselves in the east. "There would be a regular scramble," said Sir Edward Grey, "and the whole applecart would be upset." In no uncertain terms the British Ambassador at Madrid declared: "Once Italy is in possession of a naval base in the eastern Mediterranean, the Triple Alliance will be mistress of those shores."

The question was how to meet this new threat. Paul Cambon recommended from London that the Bosporus and Dardanelles be opened to Russian ships so that the Black Sea squadron might be used to redress the balance in the Mediterranean, but this idea met with little favor. Instead, the Entente powers began to consider the conclusion of a pact with Italy to guarantee the status quo, which would spare them further surprises and forestall Italy's falling entirely under German-Austrian control. Both Cambon and Barrère, French ambassadors respectively in London and Rome, urged the expediency of this policy, and Grey supported it. After the conclusion of peace between Italy and Turkey in October 1912 the matter was taken up with the Rome government, but nothing came of the negotiations because the Italians asked as a price that they be allowed to keep at least one or two of the islands, while the British and French insisted on their evacuation. Discussions continued, on and off, until the very eve of the Great War.

In the treaty with Turkey the Italians had promised to evacuate the Dodecanese as soon as the Turks had withdrawn their troops from Tripoli. On one score or another they delayed action, despite the strong, not to say threatening, language of the British and the French, and the constant efforts of these to have the islands turned over to the Greeks and given a neutral status. The Italians gave abundant assurances but did nothing. In the spring of 1914 relations were so strained that Grey complained to the Italian ambassador: "During the last year or two the Italian government had encroached more upon British interests than any other two European Powers put together."

The chief result of this quarrel was that it drove Italy back into the arms of Austria and Germany. In November 1912 Germany for the first time established a Mediterranean division, consisting of the new battle cruiser *Goeben* (launched 1911, 24,000 tons, speed 30 knots) and seven smaller cruisers. There seemed every reason to suppose that the Triple Alliance (renewed in December 1912) was extending the sphere of its activity to the eastern Mediterranean. With the balance of power already precarious, the Entente governments were only too glad to receive offers of Spanish support. The recently published French documents have revealed the eagerness of King Alfonso to have Spain join the Triple Entente. In 1912–1913 he made concerted efforts in this direction, paid a visit to Paris (May 1913), and entertained Poincaré at Madrid and Cartagena, where there was an imposing naval demonstration attended by a British battle cruiser (October 1913). The King gave the French repeated assurances that in the event of war they need pay no attention to the Pyrenees frontier, and pointed out further to Poincaré that if Spain were allied to France, the French might make use of the ports of the peninsula and of the Balearics, that they might transport their African forces by rail across Spain, and so forth. Poincaré, so it seems, avoided too extensive commitments, being unwilling to assume responsibility for all Spain's possessions and evidently fearing trouble with Germany with regard to Spanish Guinea. Nevertheless, Spain could be counted on to be friendly and in the last analysis the Spanish naval forces, greatly strengthened since 1908, might have been of some account.

When the great crisis of July 1914 culminated in the first declarations of war, not only Spain but Italy proclaimed neutrality. Spain maintained this policy throughout, though there was considerable sentiment for joining the Allies and some talk of securing Gibraltar in exchange for Ceuta as a reward. The Italian neutrality was probably, in the first instance, the reflection of public dislike of Austria; but unpreparedness certainly played a part. The abstention of the Italians was of the utmost importance for France, for it ruined the plan laid down in the naval convention of the Triple Alliance (November 1913) for an attack upon the French troop transports from Algeria. What might have happened may be guessed from the achievement of the *Goeben* and the *Breslau*. By bombarding Philippeville and Bône these two ships drove the French admiral to violate his instructions and use his ships to convoy transports individually, thereby delaying troop movements considerably. If the Italians had joined in it is not unlikely that the famous French XIX Corps would never have reached Europe in time, for the combined squadrons of the Triple Alliance had a distinct advantage over the French and British in battleships. By May 1915 this advantage was, if anything, somewhat greater, if the naval forces concentrated at the Dardanelles are left out of account. It is easy to understand, then, why the Allies were so eager to bring Italy into the war on their side, and nothing demonstrates more clearly their anxiety than the fact that the Treaty of London assigned the Dodecanese to Italy in full sovereignty. Only just before the war, M. Doumergue had heard from Grey's own lips (April 1914): "The Italians must return the islands. They must not keep them; we shall never agree to that."

Once the Italians had joined the Entente powers there was no further problem. The German and Austrian submarines wrought havoc with shipping in the Mediterranean and drove much of the usual commerce to take the route around the Cape of Good Hope; but actually the command of the sea was secure in Allied hands. In the course of the war British troops were moved to and from the various theaters of war, and the French were able to bring several hundred thousand men from their African colonies to the European battlefields. The effect of the critical years 1912–1918 was to throw into high relief the various aspects of the naval problem and to indicate the relative importance of the elements that made the balance. Spain's role throughout was a secondary one, while Italy's was decisive. In the last count the powerful combination of Britain and France attracted the others to the Entente, though the price for Italian support was a high one.

In the period immediately following the war the situation was much less acute, though the underlying antagonisms remained. The disappearance of Austria-Hungary removed one of the prewar threats, but on the other hand it gave Italy complete control of the Adriatic and permitted her to devote her whole attention to the Mediterranean proper. All the efforts made between 1919 and 1922 to induce the Italians to give up the Dodecanese broke down and the Treaty of Lausanne once again recognized their sovereignty. In the interval Mussolini had come into power and almost from the dawn of Fascist rule he made it clear that he meant to follow the Mediterranean aspirations which were so ardently expressed by the men of the *Risorgimento* and by the Nationalists of the prewar years. *Mare nostro* became more than a dream, it became a policy.

So long as Fascist Italy stood alone there was no immediate danger to British and French positions. Mussolini, having suffered a setback in the Corfu episode, could do little more than cultivate the friendship of Spain. Primo de Rivera, who was particularly sensitive about Gibraltar, gave ear to the siren-calls from Rome. In 1923 King Alfonso visited Italy and in the following year Victor Emmanuel journeyed to Madrid. A treaty of friendship was concluded in August 1926 and the two powers worked together to undermine the preponderant position of France in Tangier. Whether there ever existed, as some have claimed, a naval convention giving the Italians the right to use the Balearics in time of war it is hard to say; but the Spanish plan to tunnel under the Straits of Gibraltar caused no little uneasiness in France, and we may assume that the fall of the Spanish dictator was not deeply regretted north of the Pyrenees. Until recently France kept nearly her whole naval power in the Mediterranean and the rivalry of Italy was one of her chief preoccupations.

The Ethiopian crisis of 1935–1936 revealed in a flash a number of profound changes that had been taking place in the Mediterranean situation in the postwar years. The interests of both Britain and France had grown enormously. Both having extensive possessions in the Far East, they are equally interested in the Mediterranean as a commercial and strategic route. Of all imports brought by this route, oil has become for both the most important. Britain gets almost three-quarters of her supply from the East Indies, Iran, Iraq, and Rumania, while France takes half of hers from Iraq. These supplies come normally through the Mediterranean, the Iraq oil arriving by the Anglo-French pipelines ending at Haifa and Tripoli-in-Syria. Both powers hold important positions in the Near East (Syria, Palestine, Egypt, Transjordania, Iraq) involving distinct obligations of defense. England has made the eastern Mediterranean the junction of her imperial airways to the Far East and Africa, and France is steadily developing similar communications. In addition France has become ever more dependent on her African colonies for troops. Fully a third of the French standing army is stationed in Africa and the problem of transporting them to Europe is a matter of life and death for her. Further details need not be given. It is perfectly obvious that politically, strategically, and commercially the Mediterranean is far more important for England and France now than it was twenty years ago.

The conditions of defense have undergone an even more drastic change. We do not need to give too much attention to the submarine, which was fairly well under control at the end of the war. It is the development of the airplane, particularly in the last three or four years, that has upset all traditional calculations. Fighting planes and bombers, flying at 200 to 250 miles an hour, have made the Mediterranean a very narrow passage and have given riparian states like Italy and Spain an advantage they have never enjoyed before. At the same time they have greatly reduced the strength of positions like Gibraltar and Malta, which were chosen purely for their naval importance.

It is common knowledge that in September 1935 the British, having assembled an immense armada from the four corners of the globe, were obliged to withdraw their naval forces from Malta and concentrate them at Alexandria and Haifa, where the larger part remained until a year later. The British were caught frankly unprepared. Their fleet had been neglected, their bases were not up to par, their air power in the Mediterranean wholly inadequate. They made the best they could of a very nasty situation. Several hundred airplanes were rushed to Egypt and Palestine, and agreements were made with France, Yugoslavia, Greece, and Turkey providing for cooperation in the event of war resulting from any action take under League auspices. Even under the circumstances, Mussolini took a long chance; but his daring brought its reward in the shape of the Ethiopian prize.

In view of the collapse of the League system and the surprising strength of Italy in the Mediterranean, the British were not at all certain that they could maintain themselves in that sea in time of war. In the spring of 1936 there were many who advocated the abandonment of the route and a policy of sealing it at either end. In that case the commerce from the Middle and Far East would be transferred to the Cape route. As this is 80 percent longer, the carrying capacity of the merchant marine would be reduced proportionately. For more than a generation the British have been accustomed to the thought of having to fall back on the Cape route, but this solution presents serious difficulties at the present time. Since 1914 British shipping tonnage has declined by nine percent, the number of ships dropping from 9,240 to 7,246. Sir Archibald Hurd, the outstanding authority, thinks Britain would need at least 700 more ships to maintain her food supply in wartime. If the efficiency of British shipping were further reduced by being forced to take a much longer route, the problem would be aggravated. Nevertheless, there is no illusion about the importance of the Cape route, and the naval bases at Simonstown and Sierra Leone are being taken in hand in preparation for a possible evil day.

But the British Government is determined to use the shorter route if it is humanly possible to do so. It has embarked upon an elaborate program of naval and air rearmament which will give Britain 25 capital ships and the corresponding number of cruisers, destroyers, and submarines by 1942 and which will bring the air force up to about 5,000 planes by 1940. Though the Italians have also decided to develop their fleet to the limit of their financial capacity, there is no likelihood that they will continue to be a major threat to England on the sea. The chief British problem is that of bases. After a visit of inspection to the Mediterranean in August and September 1936, Sir Samuel Hoare announced publicly that "far from there being any question of our abdicating our position in the Mediterranean or scuttling from Malta, we intend to face these new and difficult problems, to make our future position secure." Malta is being completely refortified and a third airfield is being built. Ultimately it will probably be able to withstand attack from Sicily (only twenty minutes distant by air) and possibly an air fleet stationed there will be able to take the offensive. It also will be made into an important submarine base. But there seems little likelihood that it can be used by the fleet in wartime, for if the experts are right, a hostile air force could, if it broke through the anti-aircraft defense, register something like 50 percent of hits on a dockyard or on a fleet at anchor. The Italian situation is in this respect, then, very favorable. The British naval forces will have to be concentrated to the east. As neither Alexandria or Haifa is adequate and as neither is located in British territory, the great hope of the future is Cyprus, regarded until recently as utterly useless but now spoken of as the solar plexus of the empire. The harbor of Famagusta can be developed to accommodate at least some battleships. But Cyprus is most promising as an air base, to counterbalance the Italian position at Leros in the Dodecanese. The central plain will provide any number of airfields and Lake Akrotiri can be used for seaplanes. Imperial Airways has recently decided to make Cyprus the junction of its Asian and African lines and is already constructing subterranean hangars. Strategically the island will serve to cover Suez and the Haifa pipeline and to support the ships based on those points. In the Red Sea the British are working on Akaba (taken in 1925) and on Aden. Rumor has it that they are out to get other positions in the Farsan Islands or at Sheikh Said. The Iraq Petroleum Company recently obtained from Ibn Saud a concession to exploit the resources of the whole Arabian coast of the Red Sea for a distance of 100 kilometers inland.

Diplomatically the English have been just as active. In October of last year British squadrons visited all the key ports of Greece and in November a Turkish force paid a visit to Malta, stopping at the Piræus on the return voyage. It is essential for England to keep Greece on her side, for the Greek harbors would be invaluable in time of war. But Turkey is even more important, and the British are happy to think that their relations with Kemal Atatürk are better than they have ever been since the war. A regional pact between Turkey, Iraq, Iran, and Afghanistan is under discussion, and within the last eighteen months an important alliance has been concluded between Iraq and Saudi Arabia. Egypt has signed a treaty with Arabia, and it seems only a matter of time before the Yemen is brought into the bloc. These combinations are all more or less under British auspices, and their general effect is to create a solid Turkish-Arabian front to any attempt of Mussolini to encroach on the Near East.

223

In many discussions of the Mediterranean problem there has been a tendency to underestimate the potential strength of the British position. If they keep enough airplanes, cruisers, destroyers, and submarines in the Mediterranean, they may be able to pass at least part of their normal commerce over this route by the convoy system. Italy's defensive position is more precarious, for her whole empire lies along this route and fully 80 percent of Italy's imports come to her by sea. If the British confined their efforts to closing the sea at either end, the result would be disastrous for Italy. In reply to British moves, Mussolini has decreed the fortification of Pantellaria (an admirable base between Sicily and Tunis) and of Assab at the southern end of the Red Sea. Even so, the Italians will remain at a distinct disadvantage.

In the Anglo-Italian accord of January 2, 1937, both parties recognized "that the freedom of entry to, exit from and transit through the Mediterranean is a vital interest both to the different parts of the British Empire and to Italy and that these interests are in no way inconsistent with each other." The two powers expressed their desire to contribute to the cause of peace and security and to "the betterment of relations between them and all Mediterranean Powers." But, even at the time, the statement seemed somewhat unreal in view of the Italian policy in Spain. And since then the Anglo-Italian relationship has been further clouded by the proclamation of Italian friendship for the Moslems made in the course of Mussolini's demonstrative visit to Libya.

The Spanish civil war added the problem of the western Mediterranean to that of the eastern and presented both France and England with a fresh set of dangers. The possibility of a Fascist victory there at once raised the specter of Italian or German establishments in the Balearics, Morocco, Ifni, Rio de Oro, or the Canaries. The prompt aid given to Franco by Mussolini and Hitler brought all these questions at once to the acute phase. The British recognize that in these days Gibraltar, exposed to long-range guns from the mainland and without an adequate airfield, exists more or less on sufferance; hence they are keenly interested in having the Balearics, Ceuta, and Tangier in friendly neutral hands. The French, despite their grand base at Bizerta and the new works at Mers-el-Kebir (near Oran), have no confidence in their ability to bring oil from Syria or to transport their troops from Algeria. They are providing for huge oil stores in France and plan if need be to take their African troops to the Atlantic coast of Morocco and send them from Casablanca and Rabat to Bordeaux, even though this would mean the loss of several days in the critical first period of a conflict. But there are even worse contingencies to consider. The Italians entrenched in the Balearics[1] would be able to command both the east-west and south-north routes of the western part of the sea; but the Germans established on the Canaries or in Rio de Oro would be a serious menace to British or French shipping not only on the Cape route, but also on the South American route.

In the early months of the struggle, Franco, Mussolini, and Hitler all gave assurances that there was no intention of changing the status quo and that there would be no territorial cessions. Anyone acquainted with the ideology of the Spanish nationalists must realize that Franco would hardly feel able to give up Spanish territory. But the question of territorial sovereignty is really beside the point. The World War showed how friendly ports could be used by submarines. In the same way friendly airfields will be used in the future. Even if Franco were to cede the Balearics to Italy, these islands could probably not be held against the combined power of England and France. In the same way the Germans would be unable to maintain themselves in Morocco, in West Africa, or in the Canaries. But both the Balearics and the Canaries are marvellous submarine and air bases and permission to make use of them would be invaluable in time of war.

The French, on their side, have been losing sleep for years over German activities in Morocco and on the African west coast. On the Portuguese Bissagos Islands (halfway between Konakry and Dakar) the former *Kamerun Eisenbahn Gesellschaft* has been operating since 1923 as the *Companhia Agricola e Fabril da Guiné*, ostensibly manufacturing vegetable oils for export, but, according to the French, actually storing oil for submarines and airplanes. Rio de Oro and Ifni, they say, are nothing but German headquarters for anti-French propaganda. The Moroccan scare of January 1937 showed how alert the French are to note any German encroachment further north. They have built the battleships *Strasbourg* and *Dunkerque* to offset the German pocket battleships of the *Deutschland* type and the new Italian *Littorio* and *Vittorio Veneto*, and they have evidently used strong language to check the flow of Italian and German volunteers to Spain.

---

[1] The island of Minorca, regarded by Admiral Mahan as the strongest position in the Mediterranean, is still in the hands of the Spanish government. See "The Balearic Islands in Mediterranean Strategy," *Foreign Affairs*, XV (January 1937), 384–385.

There seems little that can be said in definite terms about the future of the Mediterranean problem until after the Spanish conflict has been decided. And how can it be decided so long as England and France refuse to allow the Fascist powers to send sufficient help to assure a Fascist victory in Spain and so long as Italy and Germany refuse to entertain the notion of a radical government there? Plainly the Mediterranean problem is to be with us for a long time yet as a major focal point of international relations and international dispute.

12

When German Dreams Come True

1938

Now that the "miracle" of the *Anschluss* has been performed, the world turns again to Adolf Hitler's *Mein Kampf* for some indication of the miracles that are still in store. But is that book really a safe or adequate guide? Much of it is biographical, and by far the largest part has nothing whatever to do with foreign policies. Where Hitler does discuss international affairs, the marks of the stress under which the book was written are everywhere apparent. He indulges in a fairly extensive criticism of German prewar policy, but there the points he makes are in no sense novel. Then he proceeds to an analysis of Germany's postwar situation, demanding the nullification of the peace treaties and the restoration of German self-respect, prestige, and power. None of this differs in any essential respect from what any patriotic or nationalist German might have written in 1924 or 1925. The speculation on Russia's early collapse and, above all, the violent Francophobia of the book reflect, in the first place, the confused state of Russia after the introduction of the New Economic Policy and the death of Lenin, and, in the second place, the tension and excitement following the French invasion of the Ruhr.

A good deal of what Hitler has said and done since 1933 is not in consonance with the policy he laid down in *Mein Kampf;* his repeated and unqualified assurances to France, for example, have an entirely different ring. We have no way of knowing whether the book or the much later statements give the real clue to his policy. And, as a matter of fact, the *Führer* has at no time revealed very fully his ultimate objectives. We read on page one of *Mein Kampf* that Austria must return again to the Greater German Fatherland, even though *Anschluss* might mean economic loss to Germany, for "the same blood belongs to the same empire." Beyond this, there is nothing more than general reflection. He derides the colonial and commercial policy of William II, which netted Germany nothing but the hostility of England. He is bound to

Note: Reprinted from *Yale Review*, XXVII (Summer 1938), 678–698.

eschew it and to angle for the support of England and Italy, in order that Germany's deadly enemy, France, may be isolated. After the reckoning with France, Germany would have a free hand to pursue the only correct policy, namely, expansion in the east—expansion which, so Hitler asserts, could, in the first place, be realized only at the expense of Russia and the Russian border states.

If *Mein Kampf* were to be taken at face value we should have to expect that Hitler, now that the Treaty of Versailles has been demolished, and Austria annexed, would follow up the agreement with Italy by a similar agreement with Britain (purchased at no matter what cost), after which he should settle the score with France and then embark on a crusade against Lithuania, Latvia, Estonia, and ultimately Russia. The oft-discussed designs on the Ukraine are not mentioned in his book, but the author speaks explicitly of resuming the march of the Teutonic Knights, whose exploits were confined to East Prussia, Poland, and the Baltic states. Of course, we may wake up some morning to read of a German advance in that direction, but for the moment it is the fate of Czechoslovakia that holds the breathless attention of the world. On German policy in this problem, little or nothing is to be learned from *Mein Kampf*, but some enlightenment may be derived from a reconsideration of the traditional German *Drang nach Osten*, the drive towards the east, the pertinent doctrines of Pan-Germanism, and the relation of Hitler to that school of thought.

At bottom, there is very little originality in any of the teachings of National Socialism. They are really little more than a projection and adaptation of the ideas of German nationalism and Pan-Germanism as they have been advanced for a hundred years. Already in the time of the great national uprising against Napoleonic rule, the poet Arndt, answering his own question "What is the German's Fatherland?" could write:

> Where'er is heard the German tongue,
> And German hymns to God are sung,
> There take thy stand
> And call that land thy Fatherland.

Throughout the literature of the German romantic school, kindred ideas crop up, shrouded in an almost mystical devotion to the German *Volk* and marked by an insuperable yearning for national unity. To all of which was soon added the economic factor. Friedrich List, preoccupied with the problems of German agriculture, industry, and population increase, was convinced of the need for expansion and settlement in the lower Danube region and declared, in 1842, that "the banks of the Danube on the right and on the left from Pressburg as far as the mouth, the northern provinces of Turkey, and the western shores of the Black Sea offer German emigrants an abundance of unoccupied and naturally fertile land."

When, in 1848, the liberal-nationalist movement came to a head in Germany and in the Hapsburg dominions, many of the most prominent leaders were hardly less intent on the formation of a great economic bloc in Central Europe than on the establishment of a German empire. The project of a Greater Germany, to include at least the German lands of the Austrian monarchy, broke down under the weight of Hapsburg opposition to the dismemberment of the empire, while the schemes for a huge middle European economic union of sixty million inhabitants were actively fostered by the Austrian statesmen Schwarzenberg and Bruck, only to be wrecked on the resistance of Prussia. But it is worth recording that in the subsequent years, before Bismarck's advent to power, Austrian diplomacy attempted to exploit the Crimean War to secure control of what is now Rumania, and that even then voices were raised in favor of an independent Ukrainian state, which might act as a bulwark against the encroachment of Russia in Central Europe.

Bismarck established the German Empire in 1866–1870 by excluding Austria from the new state and by defeating France. His was the "Little German" solution, but after long years of hope and frustration, even this dénouement was enough to secure him the enthusiastic support of his former enemies, the Liberals. The great majority was blinded by success, albeit the success was but partial. Yet the "Great German" idea was not dead, as may be seen from the *Deutsche Schriften* of Paul de Lagarde, the eminent Orientalist, who was the father of Pan-Germanism and National Socialism, if any one man can be credited with the paternity. In Lagarde's teaching may be found, at least in embryo, almost every essential tenet of the National Socialist faith: the belief in mystic powers in history, working through selected individuals (has not Hitler recently confessed to a divine mission?); the dislike of liberalism as a foreign importation; the distrust of parliamentarism; the anti-Semitism; the demand for a new national religion to overcome the traditional conflict of Catholicism and Protestantism among the Germans; the preoccupation with the maintenance and development of pure Germanism; the aversion to industrialism and the divorce of the people from the soil; the project of schools, to be organized on the monastic model and established in the open country, for the building of character and the education of an aristocratic leading caste. Lagarde was convinced that, great as was Bismarck's achievement, the "Little German" empire would have to give way to the "Great German." He advocated the closest relations between Germany and Austria and believed that, under the leadership of the Hohenzollerns and Hapsburgs, the Austro-Hungarian monarchy should be thrown open to colonization by Germans and that similar settlement should be carried out in the Polish provinces. As an ultimate goal he envisaged all of Central Europe as a preserve of the Germans. "It is necessary," he wrote, "to create a Central European power which will guarantee the peace of all the continent from the time when the Russians and southern Slavs are cleared from the Black Sea and when we shall have conquered for German colonization large territories to the east of our present frontiers. We cannot abruptly enter into the war which must bring this Central Europe into existence. All we can do is familiarize our people with the idea that this war will eventually occur."

Bismarck was far too much a realist to be touched by such theories. Indeed, in this day and age we can look upon him only as the very embodiment of moderation and common sense. For him, after 1870, it was enough to protect what he had won. Austria-Hungary was, in his view, an effective barrier to the Russian colossus, and if he had had his way the alliance with the Hapsburg monarchy in 1879 would have been put on a constitutional rather than a mere contractual basis. For colonies he had but little use, preferring to concentrate on continental problems. Repeatedly he spoke of Germany as a "satiated nation." Yet below the glamour of German success in the prewar period ran a strong current of unrest and discontent which found expression, soon after Bismarck's fall in 1890, in the foundation of the Pan-German League. This organization, though its leaders always hoped to make it a broad, popular movement, could never boast a very large membership and at bottom remained the organ of certain academic groups and of middle class business interests. But to minimize its influence would be a great mistake. It issued a large body of literature, and through its association with some fifty or sixty other organizations it colored the thought of the whole country.

The Pan-German League, while paying tribute to Bismarck as a great German, was unwilling to accept his dictum about "satiation."

Much of its inspiration was drawn from Friedrich List and Paul de Lagarde, though it adopted also the teachings of racial superiority of the Germans as worked out by Count Gobineau and somewhat later by Houston Stewart Chamberlain. During the period of the World War, the Pan-German writings served admirably for purposes of Allied propaganda, and thereby much misapprehension was spread as to their real aims. Writers of the group at times put forward perfectly fantastic claims and spoke even of a great Teutonic union to include Scandinavia, the Low Countries, German Switzerland, the German parts of Austria-Hungary (which invariably meant Bohemia and Moravia as well), the Baltic provinces of Russia, and so on. Others were more interested in the economic aspects of the problem, advocating a Central European customs union, into which the Low Countries, Switzerland, and possibly Rumania would be drawn. Still others were fascinated by the famous Berlin-Baghdad railway scheme and advanced extensive claims to Anatolia in the event of Turkey's disruption. Lastly, the Pan-Germans were fairly well united in support of an active colonial policy and all that this implied. In short, they called for everything to which the Germans, on national or economic grounds, could lay claim with any show of reason. They did not advocate war to attain their objectives, though they encouraged the cultivation of the military virtues and undoubtedly looked forward to a great conflict as the means to realize their aspirations.

It is important to remember, however, that the most immediate interest and the most concrete aims of the Pan-Germans had to do with the fate of the German communities in the states bordering Germany in the east, and this brings us back to the unsolved problem of the Germans in the Hapsburg monarchy. There a great conflict of nationalities had broken out in 1879, when the Prime Minister, Count Taaffe, undertook to govern with a coalition of Poles, Czechs, and German clericals. The German Liberals, fearing the loss of German control in the monarchy, founded the Vienna School League to keep alive the feeling of German nationality and to carry on the fight against the Slav elements. The leader of the movement was Georg von Schönerer, an able and somewhat fanatical agitator, who indirectly supplied a goodly part of Hitler's political education. In the view of Schönerer, the Hapsburg dynasty was committing treason against the German *Volk* and was preparing, with the aid of the Roman Catholic Church, to turn over the empire to the Slavic populations. He therefore organized the *Los von Rom*

(Away from Rome) movement, through which several thousand conversions to Protestantism were effected each year. The objective of this movement, however, was not religious but political. It was designed to weaken the clerical hold on the German population and to prepare the way for Protestant Germany. "One People, one Emperor, one Faith" was the original version of the present-day slogan "One People, one Reich, one Leader." The German Nationalists in 1897 fought tooth and nail the famous Badeni language ordinances (which made concessions as to the use of the Czech language in Bohemia), exhibiting a ruffianism and brutality in their tactics which remind us of these later days. At the height of the crisis, in 1898–1900, the Nationalists went so far as to cheer the German Emperor in the Austrian parliament. In a public speech Schönerer expressed the hope that he might see the day when the German armies would march into Austria and "deliver" the German people.

Now, this great conflict of nationalities in the Hapsburg monarchy had important international aspects. Czech leaders, like Karel Kramář, were in close touch with the Russian Pan-Slavs and with prominent French publicists, like André Chéradame and René Henry, who believed that the British had given the Germans a free hand and that, through the Pan-Germans, the disruption of the monarchy was being prepared. As a matter of fact, the German government was not unmoved by the threat to German dominance in Austria. "The Austrian state idea," reported the German ambassador at Vienna, "has taken refuge in clericalism, and in clericalism the dynasty sees its most powerful support, while at the same time it looks upon Slavdom as an indispensable bulwark against Pan-Germanism." The German authorities, to be sure, did not encourage the movement for dismemberment of the monarchy and annexation of the German provinces to Germany, for in Berlin Bismarck's view that Austria-Hungary must be maintained as a barrier against Russia was still upheld. But the evidence would indicate that in 1899–1900 the German government brought pressure on Vienna to prevent further concessions to the Slavic groups and to bring about the downfall of the objectionable Premier, Count Thun. To that extent, the Berlin government demonstrated its determination to support the German interest, and from that time until the outbreak of the World War the situation was never again so critical.

But even though the German government pursued a circumspect policy, the Pan-German League, together with innumerable associations connected with it, took an active part in the struggle. The League, like the present National Socialist Party, was organized in local and district groups (*Gaue* and *Ortsgruppen*). It maintained the closest contact with the Nationalists in Austria, received their delegates at its meetings and, in turn, sent representatives and secret agents into all the Austrian storm centres. It supported the German proposal for the division of Bohemia into German and Czech districts and, in general, did everything possible to assure the protection of German interests and the maintenance of Germanism. The prospect of Austria's disruption did not frighten the Pan-Germans, but they were determined, in that event, that not only the areas that could be classed as German but also Slovenia, with Trieste ("the gateway to the Mediterranean"), should be annexed to the German Empire. It was in the course of this struggle that much of the technique and many of the methods of German nationalist propaganda appear to have been worked out.

In the decade before the World War, the Austrian situation was somewhat easier, but the Pan-Germans found ample scope for activity in the furtherance of the colonial movement and in redoubled agitation for economic expansion in the Danube basin. There is no need here to repeat what has already been said, but it is important to realize how widespread was the idea of this German mission. Sir Harry Johnston, writing in *The Fortnightly Review* in 1905, was convinced that, with Britain, the United States, France, and Russia controlling huge territories, the Germans were entitled to the Balkans and Near East as their sphere of expansion. "The German Empire of the future," he maintained, "will be, or should be, a congeries of big and little States, semi-independent in many respects, bound together by allegiance to a supreme Emperor, by a common Customs Union, an Army and Navy for defence of their mutual interests. This Empire will include the present German kingdoms, duchies, principalities, and republics, and, in addition, a Kingdom of Bohemia, under a Hapsburg or a Hohenzollern, a Kingdom of Hungary, Kingdoms of Rumania, Servia, Bulgaria, Principalities of Croatia, Montenegro, Macedonia, a Republic of Byzantium, a Sultanate of Anatolia, a Republic of Trebizond, an Emirate of Mosul, a Dependency of Mesopotamia; the whole of this mosaic bound together by bands and seams of German cement." Sir Harry indicated, characteristically, that England should offer no opposition to the realization of this huge program, provided Germany renounced all idea of incorporating Holland, Belgium, and Luxembourg, returned

North Schleswig to Denmark, and restored Metz and French Lorraine to France. Austria should give up the Trentino to Italy.

On the outbreak of the World War, the Pan-German League was almost the first organization to bring forward definite war aims. These culminated in the demand for "a Greater Germany, which would afford the new generation possibilities of settlement and work for a long time to come, with frontiers which promise security against another attack." More specifically, it called for land in Poland, Lithuania, and the Baltic provinces.

In more than one way the great conflict was bound to stimulate ideas of Central European union. Germany, Austria, Bulgaria, and Turkey were united for military purposes, and the German leadership became ever more pronounced. It was this circumstance that induced Friedrich Naumann to publish his book *Mitteleuropa* (1915), persuasively written and sold in hundreds of thousands of copies, easily the most influential document on the subject. Naumann's line of thought in some ways reminds one of Hitler's. For years he had been working to organize a National Social League, which should reconcile social democracy with bourgeois nationalism and expansionism. He foresaw in the organization of a great Central Europe a spread of German technique and system—"Thus there grows up from all sides a State or national socialism, there grows up the 'systematized national economy.'" But, for all his devotion to ideas of what we call autarchy, his approach was by no means a purely economic one. On the contrary, he saw all the obstacles to economic cooperation. His main thought was that the war had shown that Germany alone could not stand and that in the future small states could not exist. The emphasis, then, was on the integral association of Germany and Austria-Hungary, leaving the Balkan states and Turkey to be brought in later, if possible.

It was largely under the pressure of opinion created by Naumann's book that the German and Austrian governments in November 1915 began negotiations for a customs union. The scheme was delayed by the necessity for renewing the economic arrangements between Austria and Hungary, and by countless technical difficulties. Actually no agreement was come to until October 11, 1918, on the very eve of the collapse. We need not, therefore, enlarge upon the project here. But it is important to recall that the success of the German campaigns in Poland, the Baltic provinces, and the Balkans—more particularly the conquest of Rumania and the breakdown of Russia—opened the prospect for the Central Powers of realizing an idea which had become deeply rooted, but which men like Naumann had thought it would take a generation to accomplish. Even the most moderate and sensible historians and economists were under the spell of grand visions. Hermann Oncken, in his widely discussed book, *The Old and the New Middle Europe* (1917), argued that with Germany, Austria, Bulgaria, and Turkey united, Serbia and Rumania would be forced into association with this bloc. Professor Spiethoff, writing a semi-official analysis of the Austro-German economic problem, declared: "The establishment of a sphere of economic influence from the North Sea to the Persian Gulf has been for nearly two decades the silent, unspoken aim of German foreign policy . . . It is indeed in this region, and in this region alone, that Germany can break out of her isolation in the centre of Europe into the fresh air beyond, and win a compact sphere of economic activity which will remain open to her independently of the favor and the jealousy of the great powers." In a collaborative study of peace aims, "Germany and the Peace," the historian Walter Goetz maintained that the Baltic states, Rumania, Bulgaria, and Serbia would be bound to gravitate into the orbit of the Central European combination. "The Ukraine and Russia, Turkey and the hinterland of the Black Sea," he wrote, "are the natural prolongation of this Middle European economic domain." Another writer in the same scholarly work declared that "on the basis of the peace treaty with Russia (of Brest-Litovsk), the Black Sea opens to view not only Georgia, recently liberated, but, beyond Turkey, Persia and Afghanistan, the independence of which are explicitly provided for in the treaty with Russia." Germany, asserted yet another contributor, required an independent Ukraine not only because it would weaken Russia economically, but because it would serve as a barrier for the protection of Middle Europe.

The defeat of Germany blasted these dreams of expansion for the time being, the more so as the Hapsburg monarchy fell to pieces. The succession states, it was hoped in Paris, would serve as effective obstacles to the resumption of the German advance, and we know from the Czech memoranda submitted to the peace conference that Masaryk and Beneš founded their territorial claims not only on ethnographic, strategic, and economic considerations, but on the need of a substantial state to dam up Pan-Germanism. Yet discerning writers even then recognized that the disappearance of Austria-Hungary involved the breakdown of the most effective obstacle to the Greater Germany. Alfred

Dumaine, for years French ambassador at Vienna, warned his countrymen that the defeat of Germany did not mean the end of Pan-Germanism. "In place of the old Pan-German leagues," he wrote in 1919, "others will arise under new names—democratic, popular, national—only the label will be changed. Like ants, who do not lose a moment in rebuilding their hills if they are destroyed, the Pan-Germans will resume their interrupted work." Jean Darcy, who urged the French to do their utmost in support of all particularist movements in Germany, already envisaged a new Caesar, who would realize the German national aspirations.

As a matter of fact, the peace treaties created more German minorities than had ever before existed and so provided new grounds for agitation. The Pan-German League at once called for national regeneration, a new army, *Anschluss* with Austria, repeated demands for Alsace and Lorraine and for Polish territory, resettlement of the proletarians on the land, anti-Semitism, and so on. Similar programs were put forward by other nationalist groups, and the first point in the twenty-five point National Socialist platform of 1920 was: "We demand the union of all Germans, on the basis of the right of self-determination of peoples, to form a Great Germany."

Which brings us to Adolf Hitler, the inheritor of a hundred years of theorizing, whose advent to power in January 1933 meant the adoption of the Pan-German doctrine for the first time by the government. Hitler's views need startle no one who has considered his career or really studied his book. He was born and brought up in the old Austria, filled with the conflict of German and Slav and with the fanatical Pan-German agitation of Schönerer and the German Nationalists. His family belonged to that very *petite bourgeoisie* from which the extremists drew their greatest strength. What wonder, then, that Hitler's book reveals on almost every page a deep-seated hatred of the Hapsburgs, traitors to Germanism and traffickers with the Slavs. It must have been a profound satisfaction to the *Führer* when, recently, he was able to snatch Austria from under the nose of young Otto and his supporters. As for Schönerer, Hitler pays him a profound tribute in *Mein Kampf,* but with great discernment points out the crucial weakness in the Austrian leader and his movement. Schönerer, he says, never succeeded in reaching the masses and was too much content with middle class support. For the rest, he had a sound appreciation of the importance of race, which in Hitler's thinking, of course, overshadows all else.

Hitler's book and his speeches leave no doubt that he has absorbed most of the ideas advanced by men like Friedrich List and Paul de Lagarde, as they have come down through the literature of nationalism and Pan-Germanism. For him the great mistake of prewar policy (and in this respect he diverges from the Pan-Germans) was to embark upon an overseas colonial and trade policy which was bound to antagonize England and drive her into the arms of France and Russia. The real task, the neglected task, was to unite the Germans in one empire, and, what was no less important, to acquire additional territory to support a growing German population. Of the frontiers of 1914 he speaks with scorn, since they were neither logical nor adequate. The only solution for the German problem is expansion towards the east, resumption of the millennial German crusade against the Slavs. There is nothing sacred about frontiers. They are made and unmade by men, usually by the use of force. Paper protests about German minorities are not only ludicrous, but dangerous, for they serve only to hold together the hostile coalition of the war period. Two things are essential: the building up of national power and the reformation of the European alliance system. The great opponents of the German aspirations are, first and foremost, the Slavs led by Russia and, secondly, the French, who, according to Hitler, cannot tolerate Germany as a great continental power on any account. Hence his repeated admonition of an alliance with England and Italy that would isolate France, and hence his violent antagonism to the Franco-Russian alliance.

"We start anew where we terminated six centuries ago," reads an oft-quoted passage in *Mein Kampf*. "We halt the eternal German move to the south and west of Europe and turn our eyes on the lands to the east. We bring to a close the colonial and trade policies of the prewar period and pass to the land policy (*Bodenpolitik*) of the future." As has been already said, the author leaves no doubt that the aim can be accomplished only at the expense of Russia and the border states of Russia. The details are left open, and the reader is bound to wonder how the redemption of German minorities is to be reconciled with expansion in that region. There are but few Germans in Lithuania (except for Memel), not more than a few hundred thousand in Latvia, almost none in Estonia. Those in Russia proper are scattered, except for the colonies on the lower Volga. And the plain fact of the matter is that Hitler's gaze has of late been turned more and more to the southeast and the Balkans rather than to Russia. The reason for this may be that his appraisal of the Russian situation has changed since he wrote his book. There he harps on the idea that the Russian state was not the achievement of the Slavs, but of the German element in Russia; that this element had been well-nigh destroyed by the war; and that Russia had fallen into the hands of the Jewish Bolsheviks, all of which, in his opinion, could presage nothing but decomposition. "The gigantic empire in the east," he asserted, "is ripe for collapse." And the breakdown, he appears to have hoped, would open the road to German expansion. How differently he expressed himself in his talks with Lord Londonderry a year or two ago, when he dilated on the growth of Russian power since 1924 and declared: "A German attack on Russia would be practically impossible, as a strip of land seven hundred kilometers broad, thank Heaven, divides us from Russia!"

Let us assume, then, that the annexation of Austria and the precipitation of the Czechoslovak problem indicate the diversion of Nazi interest to the southeast. The German economic penetration of the Balkan area has already made great strides. Ever since France was obliged to discontinue the huge loans made to the Little Entente states for a dozen years after the war, Dr. Schacht, with his elaborate devices of barter, blocked marks, and so on, has been able to pose as the economic savior of the Balkans, relieving these undeveloped countries of their agricultural surpluses and paying in manufactured goods, preferably armaments. The statistics indicate that already in 1935 Germany took 41 percent of Bulgarian exports, 58 percent of the Greek, 61 percent of the Yugoslav, 80 percent of the Rumanian, and 93 percent of the Turkish. World conditions being what they are, the economic middle Europe has become a reality already, and it is hard to see what could be done to check the trend, for it lies in the very nature of things. German economic influence and penetration in the Balkans are, in a sense, merely the counterpart of Britain's position in the British Commonwealth or of our own position in the Caribbean and Central America.

But what the world is primarily interested in, at least for the moment, is not so much the commercial as the political side of German policy. Does Hitler envisage a huge political bloc, based upon the economic, and if so, what would it include, how far would it extend? Does he accept the old German slogans, "Berlin-to-Baghdad," or even "Hamburg-to-Herat," and does he follow the Pan-Germans in their insistence upon Trieste as an outlet to the Mediterranean? On the theory of "One

People, one Reich" and following the principle of self-determination, why should he not reunite the Germans in Czechoslovakia with the empire? But why, again, should he stop there, and forget the large German minorities in the South Tyrol, Hungary, and Rumania? And what, in that case, would become of the non-German populations of the Balkan states? How could they be fitted into an empire in which racial purity has become a veritable fetish?

Perhaps some of these difficult questions can be answered by further reference to past doctrine. In the first place, it must be recalled that the Pan-Germans were primarily concerned with the fate of the Hapsburg monarchy. They insisted that all the territory of the old Germanic confederation should be included in the German empire. This involved the annexation not only of the purely German provinces, but also of Bohemia and Moravia and, in the south, Slovenia with Trieste; in other words, territories in which there was a large non-German population. The solution put forward by Paul de Lagarde was that these non-German peoples should be given special rights and should be restricted to specific areas or reserves, while the rest of these provinces should be systematically colonized by Germans, beginning with solid German settlements along the frontiers. The same idea was expounded by later writers, some of whom even went so far as to propose that the non-Germans be moved out and settled elsewhere. Richard Tannenberg, in his *Grossdeutschland* (1911) blandly asked why, if England had managed to force the emigration of some four million Irish, Germany should not hope to achieve something similar. In 1914 the Pan-German League advocated specifically that non-Germans should be moved out of the territories to be acquired.

Now the important thing is that this suggestion, first made by Lagarde, is found reproduced and recommended by Hitler in his book. The colonization of new territory, he says, must not be left to chance, but must be conducted according to special principles. Racial commissions should be set up to test the fitness of each colonist, and fitness would depend, of course, on racial purity. "Thus border colonies could be gradually formed, the inhabitants of which would be the embodiment of the highest racial purity and therefore of the highest racial promise."

Following this train of thought, we can understand readily enough why the Czechoslovak problem should have followed so rapidly upon the annexation of Austria and why, Rome-Berlin axis or no, the questions of Trieste and the South Tyrol are just around the corner, await-ing the favorable moment for solution. We may assume, I think, that despite all asseverations to the contrary, the ultimate objective is the annexation of all Bohemia and Moravia, Teschen to go to the Poles and Slovakia perhaps to the Hungarians. The Czechs can look forward only to the possession of special districts, in which they would be given special national rights, while strong semi-military colonies of pure Germans would be organized along the frontiers. From these areas the Czechs would unquestionably be removed, probably by the process outlined by Goering for dealing with the Jews in Germany: make their sojourn so uncomfortable that they will be glad to leave, even without their property. So the exchange of populations would be applied in Central Europe, as it has been in Eastern Europe, a pro-cedure unbelievably hard on the victims, but undoubtedly effective in establishing the "clear frontiers" for which many Pan-Germans clam-ored.

As for the other Central European and Balkan states, some clue to their future as the Germans see it may be found in the favorite Pan-Germanic doctrine of federalism, which envisaged German and non-German nationalities bound together by a loose connection under German leadership. The principle was expounded in detail by Con-stantin Frantz, one of the earliest and one of the most influential of the Pan-German writers, who was followed by Lagarde and many others. Naumann, for instance, declared frankly: "We wish to detach the west-ern Slavs from Russia and in company with them form the soul of *Mitteleuropa*," but at the same time he insisted that within the great league the non-Germans should be given the utmost national freedom. Oncken, again, flatly denied that the Germans aimed at domination and held that the objective should be simply "a free political-economic-cultural community of interest between large and small peoples which, by combining, seek a counterweight to the oppression of the predatory powers." So strong was this federalist current that in 1917 a League for a Middle European Federal State was organized in Germany.

It is no secret that German agents and German money have by this time established effective Nazi influence over all the German minorities scattered through the Balkans and that, in all of those countries, strong native fascist movements have got under way. Several of the Balkan states already have dictatorships well disposed towards Germany. We need not assume that any of them, passionately nationalistic as they are, would voluntarily abandon their independence and allow themselves to be merged in a huge Central European federation such as the Germans dream of. On the other hand, there is at least the likelihood or possibility that, under economic or military pressure, they might be brought into some federal system and that a new Danubian empire might emerge to replace the defunct Hapsburg monarchy. The new bloc would, undoubtedly, be more inclusive than the old, and the German hegemony would be far more effective.

The great question, of course, is whether Hitler and the Germans will be free to carry out their schemes. Bismarck, if he cherished any Pan-German aspirations, felt obliged to suppress them because he suffered from the nightmare of coalitions. In his day the shadow of the Russian colossus fell right across Central Europe, and there was the constant dread of a Russian-French combination that would threaten Germany on two fronts. Under William II this coalition became a reality and the government was obliged, if anything, to be more circumspect. When the Hapsburgs undertook, on their own hook, to advance their position in the Balkans, the German government in no sense approved, despite its growing economic interests in Turkey. And, in the last analysis, the Austrian policy brought on the World War, and France backed Russia in her resistance to the "German" policy.

As we look back on the results of the World War, it is hard to escape the conclusion that, for political as well as economic reasons, the disappearance of the Hapsburg monarchy has only simplified the realization of the Pan-German dream. The existence of large German minorities has stimulated German national ardor, and the principle of self-determination has supplied an unanswerable argument. The Czechoslovak state was intended by the Allies to serve as a barrier to the German advance, and the Little Entente, heavily financed by France, was thought of as an added precaution. Hitler himself believed, when he wrote his book, that France would have to be defeated before any progress could be made in Eastern Europe. But the French have played the Nazi game well. In the first place, they frustrated the projected German-Austrian customs union in 1931, which might have paved the way for *Anschluss* with the German republic, and might have so strengthened the liberal régime in Germany as to make the victory of Hitler impossible. Then, when the economic crisis made the continuance of French loans to the Balkan states impracticable, Barthou set out to construct an anti-German front by making agreements with Russia and Italy. But this policy proved utterly disastrous, for the agreement with Russia, while it gave Czechoslovakia ostensible support, estranged Rumania and Yugoslavia, as well as Poland, so that now the Little Entente is but a feeble reed. In like manner, the deal with Italy, far from establishing a solid Franco-British-Italian front, proved to be merely the prelude to the Ethiopian adventure, which, in turn, brought about the collapse of the League system and the emergence of British-Italian antagonism. Considerations of Mediterranean security almost certainly lay behind Mussolini's adventure in Spain and this, again, brought the Rome-Berlin axis into being. Hitler has annexed Austria without creating more than a ripple, and now that he is established on the Brenner Pass and can look down on Trieste, he has Mussolini more firmly than ever in his grasp.

There was every reason why Hitler should move next towards his Czechoslovak objective. The first steps may be taken before we have got used to the annexation of Austria. In the long run, effective opposition is unlikely. Russia, preoccupied with domestic affairs and with the Far Eastern situation, is all but out of the picture, French policy, under the threat of the Hitler-Mussolini combination, is subject to British approval, and the British themselves show no disposition to fight for Czechoslovakia. It is in their interest to leave Hitler a free hand in Central Europe in order to avoid a recurrence of conflict in the colonial sphere. We may, therefore, look for the "commonwealth of nations in middle Europe," to the realization of which, according to Franz von Papen, the annexation of Austria was but the first step. Hitler appears, then, as the consummator of an age-old urge and an age-old dream. The German *Drang nach Osten,* in one form or another, goes back a thousand years. It may be compared to Russia's steady advance in Central Europe. Call it Germany's manifest destiny if you will. While many of Germany's best minds have been fascinated by it in the course of the past century, it remained for Hitler to give it the mass appeal and to muster the power in Germany to take advantage of an international situation that promised success.

But there is this one point to bear in mind. Even the Pan-Germans came to recognize that Central Europe alone would not suffice for Germany's economic needs. An essentially agrarian region, it can supply but few of the raw materials needed for modern industry. Hitler himself, despite the scathing denunciation of colonial policy in his book, has come to see that ultimately autarchy can be attained only by securing sources of raw materials abroad. And so the resumption of colonial policy awaits only the solution of the Central European problem. When that day comes the British may find that they have been living in a fool's paradise, for the new Greater Germany promises to be infinitely stronger than the antagonist of 1914.

13

Farewell to Empire

1962

Now that the liquidation of Europe's overseas empires is all but complete, the world is in travail, beset by problems of readjustment and groping for new relationships that may make possible the peaceful and prosperous coexistence of more than a hundred states of widely differing characters and needs. The age-old expansion of Europe in terms of military power, settlement, trade, proselytism, territorial rule and, finally, social dominance has come to an abrupt end. Thoughtful people, particularly in the Western world, are bound to reflect on this epochal upheaval, and to realize that one of the very great revolutions in human affairs has taken place. They must be impressed, not to say awed, by the thought that the political and social structure of our planet has undergone such fundamental alterations at the very time when science and technology are opening to view the vast possibilities as well as the dangers of the space age.

Historians and political scientists have for some time been grappling with the problems of expansion without, however, having come to anything like generally accepted conclusions. Political controversy has seriously beclouded the meaning of the terms *imperialism* and *colonialism,* while scholarly analysis has revealed ever more clearly how loose and unmanageable these words and concepts really are. I take it that, in its broadest sense, imperialism means domination or control of one nation or people over another, recognizing that there may be many forms and degrees of control. But there is probably no hope of ever constructing a generalized theory of imperialism. Indeed, the most violent differences of opinion persist with regard to the causes and character even of modern European expansion, with little if any prospect of reconciling the Communist doctrine, so positively formulated by Lenin, with the manifold theories advanced by Western "bourgeois" writers.

However, among the non-Communist critics and students substantial

Note: Reprinted from *Foreign Affairs,* XLI (October 1962), 115–130, copyright the Council on Foreign Relations, Inc., New York.

progress is being made in the evaluation of European imperialism. The initial phase of expansion, consequent to the great discoveries of the fifteenth and sixteenth centuries, involved large-scale settlement of Europeans in sparsely populated areas of the world. This in turn led to the gradual conquest of vast territories, along with complete subjection and at least partial extermination of the natives. But this earlier stage of imperialism, while it certainly remade much of the globe in the European image, had relatively little bearing on recent and contemporary problems of expansion. For in the late eighteenth and early nineteenth centuries most of the American colonies of Britain, Spain, and Portugal attained their complete independence of European rule. In the sequel Canada, Australia, New Zealand, and eventually South Africa became British dominions, independent of the mother country in all but name. Meawhile Siberia, which was overrun and partially settled by the Russians in the seventeenth century, became an integral part of the contiguous Tsarist state.

This process of settlement and territorial expansion occasionally brought in its train the destruction of highly developed cultures like those of the Inca, Maya, and Javanese. But in general it touched only primitive, thinly populated regions, which previously had been outside the main stream of history. Such was the case also with the trading posts and military establishments acquired in the East by the Portuguese, Dutch, British, and French in the seventeenth and eighteenth centuries. Only with the military victories of the British over local potentates and the repeated extension of their territorial domination in India did modern imperialism, in the sense of the rule or control of one state or nation over an alien people or culture, become a reality. Even so, India remained a rather special case, an almost unique instance of a private company over a long period of time ruling a huge area of highly developed cultures and constantly expanding its territorial control even at times when the home government was opposed to any extension of its responsibilities. For the European powers had, by the early nineteenth century, become highly skeptical about overseas commitments. It is true that both the British and the French made substantial territorial acquisitions in these years, but they resulted largely from the efforts of local officials to safeguard existing establishments and further trade. Only in Russia, where the government engaged in systematic encroachment and eventually in the conquest of the Transcaucasian principalities, was there anything like purposeful expansionism, though on this side of the

Atlantic the war against Mexico was certainly a comparable demonstration of imperial acquisitiveness.

Imperialism revived only in the period after 1870 when, however, it developed to such a degree that most of Africa was quickly partitioned among a few European powers and some form of domination or control was established over many Asian peoples. Concurrently Russia, operating against adjoining countries, imposed its rule upon most of Central Asia and, having earlier acquired the Maritime Province on the Pacific, inaugurated a policy of peaceful penetration of Manchuria and Korea.

To account for this phenomenal spread of European authority is certainly a fascinating and challenging assignment for the historian. Innumerable theories, both general and special, have been advanced in the search for an adequate explanation. They run the gamut from the hard-hitting, straightforward propaganda of Lenin's *Imperialism, the Highest Stage of Capitalism* to the highly sophisticated and daringly original speculation of Schumpeter's *Sociology of Imperialism*. But the one conclusion to be safely drawn from all this ratiocination is that modern imperialism constituted a most complicated episode of recent history, that it was the expression of many and varied forces and motives, and that the economic explanation, so cogently argued by Hobson in his *Imperialism: A Study* (1902), and so fondly cherished by Lenin, is as inadequate as it is popular. Humanitarian, religious, and psychological factors were clearly important, to say nothing of considerations of national power and pride. It should never be forgotten that the present condemnation and rejection of imperialism by the Western world is a very recent development. Prior to 1920, if not even later, European rule of overseas colonies was considered honorable and altruistic—definitely in the best interest of the "backward" peoples. It has been pointed out with complete justice that the campaign against the slave trade and the effort to propagate Christianity were among the prime motive forces behind modern expansion, and that the imperial powers as well as their agents were moved, with some exceptions, by a desire to play a beneficent role in the world, to fulfill a noble, national mission.

Recent monographic studies of various aspects of modern imperialism suggest also that certain elusive, not to say irrational, forces contributed to the dynamism of expansion. Schumpeter, and indeed both Kautsky and Hobson before him, gave emphasis to the atavistic feature of imperialism. That is to say, they saw it as a survival in modern society of an outworn, feudal-militaristic mentality, devoted to conquest for its own sake, without specific objective or limit. One might underline also the importance of basic human traits such as aggressiveness and acquisitiveness, along with the urge to dominate, as fundamental to any analysis of imperialism. To do so would leave open, however, many instances in which powerful states with dynamic populations showed no inclination to express these drives in terms of expansion and domination. The American people's rejection of imperialism almost as soon as it was tried, in the wake of the war with Spain, would be a case in point.

Yet it does seem that there was something feudal or at least aristocratic about imperialism, even in its modern phase. It was, in fact, frequently criticized on this score. Colonies, it was said, were desired by the ruling classes in order to provide for their "clamorous and needy dependents." They were, according to James Mill, "a vast system of outdoor relief for the upper classes," and, in the words of Richard Cobden, a "costly appendage of an aristocratic government." [1] And much later, in 1903, Henry Labouchere referred to imperialists as magpies: "They steal for the love of stealing." Certainly the men who made the decisions for expansion were, in England, peers and great landowners, and on the continent aristocrats, notables, and soldiers. Bismarck, than whom no statesman of modern times had a keener sense of the requirements of power politics, reckoned at all times with the dynamism of the traditional military castes. He encouraged Russian expansion in Central Asia on the theory that it was better to have the military engaged there than on the European front. In the same spirit he attempted to divert the attention of the French from the blue line of the Vosges by supporting their activities in North Africa. And a particularly clear demonstration of the operation of feudal-military forces is provided by the history of modern Japan. The Genyosha Society, which was the driving power behind Japan's expansion, represented primarily the samurai elements which had been eclipsed by the Restoration.[2]

It may be argued that the above theory is at least in part invalidated by the fact that imperialism enjoyed great popular acclaim. But actually this proves very little, for it was more true of England than of other countries, and in England, it will be conceded, the lower classes were

[1] Klaus Knorr, *British Colonial Theories, 1570–1850* (Toronto, 1944), pp. 356 ff.
[2] E. H. Norman, "The Genyosha: A Study in the Origins of Japanese Imperialism," *Pacific Affairs,* XVII (1944), 261–284.

traditionally interested in the doings of the aristocracy and readily applauded its achievements. Actually the common man, in England as elsewhere, knew little of the issues and policies involved in imperialism. Colonial affairs, like foreign affairs, remained the preserve of the ruling class. As for continental countries, it is perfectly clear that popular interest in and support for colonial enterprise were never widespread or sustained. Explorers, missionaries, publicists, professors, and certain business interests were the prime movers in the cause of overseas undertakings.

With further reference to the economic interpretation of imperialism, I would say that recent studies of specific cases reinforce the proposition that business interests were much less important than considerations of national power and prestige, to say nothing of national security. A new analysis of the partition of Africa contends convincingly that Britain, concerned by the disturbance of the European balance of power by the German victories of 1870–1871, was driven primarily by concern for its communications with India to assume control of Egypt, and that this move in turn had such repercussions on international relations as to precipitate the "scramble for Africa." [3] It certainly becomes increasingly clear that much of modern imperialism reflected problems of power in Europe itself during a period when the alliance systems had produced a temporary deadlock.

The competition for markets and for sources of raw materials as well as the search for new fields for capital investment were much talked of in the heyday of imperialism and underlay the argumentation of a host of writers on economic imperialism. But it is well known now that in actual fact the colonies played a distinctly subordinate role in the foreign economic activities of the major imperial powers. These powers at all times remained each others' best customers. At the height of the colonial age, in the early twentieth century, less than a third of Britain's exports went to the dominions and colonies, and less than one-half of British foreign investment was in the Empire. The major European investments in this period were in the United States, Russia, the Ottoman Empire, and Latin America, where there could hardly be any question of true imperial domination.

If in fact the European governments in the 1880s and 1890s plunged headlong into the scramble for colonies, they were evidently acting in

[3] Ronald Robinson and John Gallagher, *Africa and the Victorians* (New York, 1961).

panic. Confronted with the entirely novel problems arising from progressive industrialization, and alarmed by the depression that set in in 1873, as well as by the strong tendency on the continent to abandon free trade in favor of protection, they sought to safeguard their overseas economic interests by acquiring actual control of as much territory as possible. They hoped thereby to ensure themselves against unknown eventualities. Failure to act seemed improvident and dangerous. I would call this "preclusive imperialism," and would describe it as obviously a concomitant of the onrushing industrial revolution. A misguided effort, this reaction to hypothetical dangers, as we can now recognize; but in the late nineteenth century it evidently was so compelling that most statesmen, even the skeptical Bismarck, were carried away by it.

The final accounting suggests that the colonies brought their masters but indifferent returns. It has been frequently argued that even though the European governments may have spent more on their overseas possessions—especially in terms of defense, police, administration, and public health—than they ever received in return, private interests made huge profits through the ruthless exploitation of native labor and natural resources. Bookkeeping in these matters is extremely difficult, because it is impossible to isolate and allocate specific items of expense. The best recent studies indicate that the governments, and so the home countries, did in fact make large and continuing outlays, in many ways anticipating more recent policies of aid to underdeveloped nations. An admirable analysis of the finances of the Congo arrives at the conclusion that that colony, unusually rich in raw materials such as ivory, rubber, and copper, was indeed a source of considerable enrichment for Belgium as a country, but that between 1908 (when the Belgian government took over the colony from King Leopold II) and 1950 the Brussels government spent 260,000,000 gold francs on the Congo in return for only 25,000,000 francs in taxes and other income.[4] In like manner an eminent French authority has estimated that even in the period prior to 1914 the Paris government spent 2,000,000,000 gold francs on the French colonial empire.[5]

In the large, the profits taken by private interests seem to have been anything but exorbitant—indeed, little above the average returns of

[4] Jean Stengers, *Combien le Congo a-t-il coûté à la Belgique?* (Brussels, 1957).
[5] Henri Brunschwig, *Mythes et réalités de l'impérialisme colonial français* (Paris, 1960).

home investments. Of course there were instances of huge profits made through forced labor and other forms of ruthless exploitation, as in the Congo of King Leopold, in German Southwest Africa, and in British South Africa. No one would excuse or condone such practices, but again it is important to retain a proper sense of proportion. The mercantilist idea that colonies existed solely for the purpose of enriching the mother country persisted for a long time. Leopold II of Belgium, for example, was an ardent admirer of the Dutch "culture system" as enforced in the East Indies, and was interested in the Congo exclusively for the revenue it might bring. As for the treatment of the natives, it may be doubted whether it was any worse than that meted out to Russian serfs and American Negro slaves until past the middle of the nineteenth century. Sad though it may be, the fact is that the human race became sensitive only at a very late date. When one considers the heartless attitude taken toward the miseries of the early factory workers or even toward the Irish peasantry in the days before the great famine, one is bound to marvel at the callousness of human nature, obviously not restricted to the brutalities of Hitler's Nazi régime.

Students of the problem have of late devoted much attention to the advantages which accrued to the colonies from European rule. They included defense and public order, suppression of tribal warfare and restriction of patriarchal tyranny, the establishment of adequate administration and justice, the furtherance of public health, and, in many cases, substantial contributions to the development of communications.

No doubt the price paid by the colonies was a high one: the subversion of traditional institutions and social forms, not necessarily intentional, but none the less effective. To some Europeans as well as to many natives this has been a matter of real regret. But if in fact European expansion was the ineluctable expression of a dynamism generated by the economic and social revolution of the nineteenth century, then it follows that the progressive destruction of static, traditional societies was inevitable under the impact of outside forces. Thinkers and statesmen of the Ottoman Empire, of Japan, and of China recognized this feature of the situation at an early date. They saw that the only hope of survival lay in the adoption of Western technology and institutions, however distasteful they might be. The remaking of the world in the Western image began long before the tide of imperialism came to the flood.

The South African War (1899–1902) not only drained imperialism of much of its emotional content but also induced the British and other imperial governments to reconsider their relations to the colonies. Far more thought was given to the welfare of the colonial peoples, and far more effort was made in the direction of development and improvement. The more liberal régimes encouraged the education of the natives and their participation at the lower levels of the administration. Thereby they fostered the growth of the native élite, members of which presently began to apply the lessons learned from the West to the task of getting rid of Western control. The imperial powers, having themselves inculcated the ideas of equality, self-determination, independence, and nationalism, thereby prepared the way for the destruction of their own dominion. For it would hardly seem possible, in historical retrospect, that Western rule could have long withstood the weight of the arguments drawn from its own intellectual armory. Imperialism was bound to lose its moral basis as soon as the principle of equality was recognized and the notions of responsibility and trusteeship were generally accepted. The reaction of British liberals, radicals, and socialists to the war in South Africa was in itself irrefutable proof of the incompatibility of democracy and imperialism. Without doubt the anti-colonialist movement that developed in Europe and in the United States following the war with Spain contributed heavily to the growth of nationalism in various colonies during the early twentieth century. So also did the defeat of the Russians by Japan in 1904–1905, for that defeat broke the spell of European superiority and invincibility.

The First World War then set the stage for the actual breakdown of imperialism. The fratricidal conflict within the European master race deflated whatever prestige the ruling nations may still have had, while the employment of hundreds of thousands of colonial troops and laborers in the great war opened the eyes of multitudes of natives to conditions in the more advanced countries of the world. It is generally recognized that in 1919, while the victorious powers were busily applying the principle of self-determination to European peoples and as consistently ignoring it as regards the colonial peoples, imperialism had already received the mortal blow. The subsequent inter-war period then witnessed the rapid development of nationalist movements in many additional areas, despite the drastic measures of repression employed by some of the imperial governments. It took only the Second World War, fought as it was in many of the most remote places of the world, to

251

loose the impounded floodwaters of colonial nationalism. The European nations were now so weakened and discredited that they could no longer offer effective resistance. Those which, like France, attempted to hold their possessions found themselves involved in long and costly wars, ending invariably in colonial triumph. In less than twenty years, millions of subject peoples attained their independence and more than fifty new states appeared on the international scene.

Ever since its advent to power in Russia, the Soviet government has proclaimed the right of self-determination and has given all possible encouragement and support to the national movements aimed at liberation of the European overseas colonies from imperial rule. Soviet propaganda has to a large extent succeeded in restricting the definition of "imperialism" and "colonialism" to these overseas territories and in fostering the idea that Russia, having no such colonies, has had no part in imperial domination. Actually, it is impossible to draw a valid distinction between the expansion of Russia and that of other European states. The conquest of Central Asia was basically equivalent to the extension of British power in India. It began with trade interests, followed by conquest and annexation for reasons of security and prestige. And at the end of the nineteenth century Russian penetration of Manchuria and Korea was an integral part of the European effort to "partition" the Celestial Empire. Eminent Russian hisorians like Kliuchevski and Miliukov were just as bitterly critical of Russian expansion as were the anti-colonialists of the West with reference to the overseas empires.

The Russo-Japanese War put an early end to Tsarist aspirations in China, while the First World War, by precipitating the revolution in Russia, brought on a premature struggle for independence or autonomy on the part of almost all the subject peoples of the old empire. In this extremity Lenin and Stalin proclaimed the most conciliatory policy, even going so far as to recognize the right of any people to cast off all ties to Russia. It soon turned out, however, that these moves were purely tactical. Self-determination was to be restricted to the "workers" of the subject nations, which were warned by Stalin that if they seceded, they would surely fall victim to world imperialism. It was inconceivable, he added, that these peoples should abandon the Soviet Union, which was so dependent on them for food and raw materials. They clearly had an important contribution to make to the victory of socialism. In order to forestall "treason" on their part, the Soviet government proceeded to suppress liberation movements, by force if necessary, carrying on a protracted war against even the avowedly Communist leaders of the various Turkic peoples.

For geographical reasons it is much easier for Soviet Russia to hold adjacent peoples in subjection than it was for countries like Britain and France to maintain their hold on distant overseas possessions. For a time following Hitler's attack in 1941, Soviet rule was, nevertheless, again seriously jeopardized. In revenge, the Kremlin in its hour of victory meted out the most ferocious treatment to the disaffected peoples and furthermore set up on its western borders a system of satellites reminiscent of the client system through which the great Napoleon controlled so much of the continent. Whether for ideological or for security reasons, the Soviet government now exercises effective control over adjoining states all the way from Finland in the north to Bulgaria in the south. To safeguard that control it will, if necessary, resort to military force, as was demonstrated so clearly in the case of Hungary.

In short, the Soviet government has taken advantage of its contiguity to hold in subjection not only the ancient states of Eastern Europe, but also Armenians, Georgians, and other Caucasian peoples, as well as some millions of Turkic peoples in Central Asia. Under the old régime, spasmodic attempts were made at Russification and at forced conversion to orthodoxy. In Central Asia much of the best land was appropriated by the conquerors, while the natives were subjected to heavy taxation. On the other hand, the nomadic tribes were left largely to themselves and the well-developed khanates of Khiva and Bokhara enjoyed a large measure of autonomy. The Soviet government, especially in Stalin's time, was much more repressive. The status of the subject nationalities as federated republics was altogether misleading, for all important political and economic posts were held by Russians or by carefully selected native Communists. Besides, the economic life of these puppet republics was regulated entirely by the needs of the Kremlin. For a time the Soviet government carried on propaganda directed even at the language, religion, and culture of the subject peoples.

In some respects this policy is still in effect. In any event, the subject nationalities have been deprived of all hope of freedom. Their leaders disappear before they can become dangerous. Unobstrusively, Russians are being settled among the native populations, so that by now some six or seven million Europeans are established in Central Asia. In Kazakhstan it has been reported that fully half of the population is now

European. Furthermore, the Russian language is an obligatory subject in all schools and a Cyrillic-type alphabet has been introduced for the Turkic languages. While there is no concerted attack on non-Russian cultures, it has been made abundantly clear that the chances of success in life depend largely on identification with Russianism as well as with Communism.

In view of the realities of Russian imperialism, it is surprising that the Soviets have been so successful in their efforts at concealment and have managed so well to exploit the issue of "colonialism" to the detriment of the West. It is likely, however, that the effectiveness of their propaganda has already passed its peak. After all, the world cannot ignore the fact that the overseas empires have now been largely liquidated. Besides, the experience of some of the new states with Soviet guidance and aid has been disillusioning and disquieting. Already at the Bandung Conference (1955) there were round denunciations of Soviet imperialism, accompanied by pointed warnings against Communist designs on the freedom of colonial peoples.

It is unrealistic to suppose that either the European satellites or the subject nationalities of the Soviet Union can obtain their independence so long as the Soviet government remains what it is and its objectives are unaltered. How long that may be is certainly a debatable question. The Soviet régime, having itself become outspokenly nationalistic and having systematically supported nationalist movements in the overseas colonies, can no longer condemn nationalism among its own subjects as a reactionary deviation. Furthermore, Soviet society is steadily evolving along lines familiar to us from Western history. It is at least not inconceivable that its transformation under the impact of industrialization may become accelerated and that, with the growth of representative institutions and the development of a more democratic mentality, there will come a change of attitude toward the imperialism that is now so basic to Russian policy. At the same time the economic evolution of the satellites and subject nationalities is speeding their Westernization and strengthening forces which in the long run the Kremlin may find it difficult to hold in check.

The Soviet government, with its prodigious military and economic power, can for the present certainly hold in subjection the adjacent nationalities of Europe and Asia. It may, indeed, succeed in exploiting the nationalist theme to the point of luring some of the newly liberated peoples into the Communist camp and thereby bending the anti-colonialist sentiment of the entire world to the purposes of the world revolution. But the subjection of weaker peoples by the stronger runs counter to the democratic sentiments characteristic of modern industrial societies. There may be serious lapses, such as the Nazi interlude in Germany. But the example of Western nations suggests that industrial populations are basically peace-loving and definitely averse to the subjugation and exploitation of other peoples. In the later nineteenth century the imperial aspirations of the French government met their strongest obstacle in the opposition of democratic and socialist elements. It is most unlikely, therefore, that the Soviet Union, simply by denying its imperialism, will be able, in the long term, to shield itself from the forces inherent in modern society.

In this context, some reference to the forces of Chinese Communist expansion and indeed to the entire problem of world Communist domination is perhaps unavoidable. Communist China's imperialist aspirations permit of no doubt. They appear, however, to derive from traditional notions of universal or at least Asian empire as well as from more immediate considerations of national security or ideological zeal. The Chinese thus interpret their efforts to establish control over Korea, Taiwan, and the countries of southeastern Asia as a gathering-in of the *membra disjecta* of the millenary Celestial Empire, less as the conquest of new than the recovery of ancient domains.

As for the world revolution and the new world of Communism, it would seem that whatever validity this program might have would depend on its ideological content. If neither Napoleon nor Hitler could dominate Europe, it can hardly be supposed that Soviet leaders—on the whole a sober and realistic lot—imagine it possible for the U.S.S.R. to control the entire world. The developments of recent years must suggest to them the difficulties of managing even the present Communist domain. No doubt the Soviet Union would feel more secure in an all-Communist world, just as the United States would in a world made safe for democracy. But as the Soviet Union grows in strength this consideration is bound to lose some of its importance. It is quite possible, in fact, that Marxism, already so largely overtaken by events, may in time lose not only its revolutionary fervor but also its incentive to world domination.

The end of European political domination in Africa and Asia does not alter the fact that the stamp of European ideas and institutions has now been put upon the whole world. Even the Soviet and Chinese Communists rely for their power upon Western technology and to a considerable extent upon the imitation of Western institutions. As for the newly liberated peoples, they have set themselves the same course. No doubt there are in all of them conservative and even reactionary elements which would like, if possible, to return to their traditional society. But in most countries the ruling group consists of men educated in Western schools and convinced that the future lies with the adoption of Western techniques. They have no intention whatever of reverting to pre-imperialist days. On the contrary, they want more and more of what imperialism brought them: greater productivity and a higher standard of living through industrialization, social improvements of every kind, and especially more and better education as a basis for democracy.

Their problems are many, and by no means exclusively economic. The transformation of assorted tribes into modern nations is in itself a stupendous undertaking. Besides, these new states are for the most part too weak militarily as well as economically to stand on their own feet. Their political independence therefore does not by any means imply complete independence. Because of their almost unlimited need for economic and technical assistance they are certainly in some danger of falling again under the influence if not the control of powerful advanced nations, be they Western or Communist.

They can find some insurance against such threats in the antagonism between the free world and Communism, which enables their leaders to play off one side against the other. They are bound to derive some protection also from the strong anti-imperialism that has come to pervade the entire free world and will probably become ever more deeply enrooted. Indeed, the new underdeveloped states will be fortunate if Western disillusionment with empire does not reach the point where it will obstruct seriously the aid programs without which many of the former colonies cannot hope to survive. Happily some progress is being made in the coordination of the economic efforts of the free world through the Organization for Economic Cooperation and Development. The Western world has such a great potential for aid that it should be possible, with even a modicum of statesmanship, to maintain the connection of Europe and the United States with the erstwhile colonial world.

It is truly noteworthy that, for all the heat and rancor generated by anti-colonialism, so many liberated colonies have chosen to remain members of the British Commonwealth or the French Community. The enthusiastic reception accorded to Queen Elizabeth in India and Ghana provided occasions for the expression, on the part of their governments, of appreciation for the important contribution made by imperial rule. No doubt considerations of security have a significant bearing on the attitude of the former colonies, but it would seem that in the world at large the old—shall we say atavistic, aristocratic?—notion of domination and exploitation has given way to the concept of association and collaboration. Even in the Communist world it has become fashionable to speak of the "Socialist Commonwealth."

In bidding farewell to empire we cannot and must not suppose that human nature has undergone a sudden, radical change—that basic aggressive urges will disappear completely and that sweetness and light will soon prevail. The argument of this essay has been that fundamental drives lay behind imperial expansion; that European dynamism, combined with technological superiority, enabled the European nations to settle the largely unoccupied continents and to found European communities all over the globe. It permitted them also, in the sequel, to impose their rule over many peoples of old and highly developed, as well as of primitive, cultures. So marked was Europe's material power and so alluring its political and economic institutions that within a comparatively short span of time the stamp of European civilization was put upon the whole earth.

Europe's political domination is gone. Its cultural influence remains, and there is no likelihood that it will be supplanted in the forseeable future. The new states, while still vociferously denouncing "colonialism," may genuinely fear that cultural influence will eventually change to economic control and so to some new form of political domination. The Soviet government is already accusing the Common Market of being a new device by which the Western powers will attempt to keep the colonial world in an economically subordinate and undeveloped state. In this connection the importance of the erstwhile colonial areas as sources of raw materials for the industrialized nations remains a prominent consideration. But imperialism provided no real solution for this problem, while for the future more, it would seem, is to be hoped from cooperation than from domination and exploitation.

It is highly unlikely that the modern world will revert to the imperialism of the past. History has shown that the nameless fears which in the late nineteenth century led to the most violent outburst of expansionism were largely unwarranted. The Scandinavian states and Germany since Versailles have demonstrated that economic prosperity and social well-being are not dependent on the exploitation of other peoples, while better distribution of wealth in the advanced countries has reduced if not obviated whatever need there may have been to seek abroad a safety-valve for the pressures building up at home. Even in the field of defense, the old need for overseas bases or for the control of adjacent territories is rapidly being outrun.

It is often said that human nature does not change, but it is none the less true that it does undergo changes of attitude. With reference to imperialism it is certainly true that there has been over the past century a marked alteration of mood, reflecting greater sensitivity to human suffering and a greater readiness to assume responsibility for the weak and helpless. In our day, anti-imperialism runs as strong in the West as did imperialism a couple of generations ago. Domination and exploitation of weaker peoples by the stronger, which seemed altogether natural in the past, is now felt to be incompatible with the principles of freedom, equality, and self-determination so generally accepted in modern societies. Imperialism has been on its way out since the beginning of the century and particularly since the First World War. Writing on imperialism in this very journal in the days when Mussolini was embarking on the conquest of Ethiopia, I ventured to disparage his undertaking and to describe him as being behind the times.[6] The world, I opined, had outgrown the mentality of imperialism. I could not, of course, foresee that the edifice of colonialism would collapse so suddenly and so completely after the Second World War, but I suggested that if the tide of native resistance continued to rise, the abandonment of the colonies would soon become inevitable. To make this forecast did not require any particular prescience, but only recognition of the forces at work in modern society. At the present day the Soviet Union may still pose as the doughty opponent of a system that is already done for, but by maintaining its own imperial sway it is appearing more and more in the role of champion of an outworn and discredited system.

Imperialism's one great achievement was to open up all parts of the world and to set all humanity on the high road to eventual association and collaboration. In the process much has been lost of cultural value, but much also has been gained in the suppression of abuses, in the alle-

---

[6] See "A Critique of Imperialism," Part II, Number 7, of this volume.—Ed.

viation of suffering, and above all in the raising of the standard of living. The seamy sides of industrial society are familiar to us all, but it should never be overlooked that the machine age for the first time in history provided the common man with more than the requirements of the barest subsistence. This in itself has given human life a new dimension. It was perhaps the greatest of Europe's contributions to the world. Without the imperialist interlude it is difficult to see how the static, secluded, backward peoples of the globe could possibly have come to share in it. So much at least seems certain: without the period of European rule none of these peoples or states, not even India, would today be embarked on the course leading to a better and richer life.

PART III

The United States as a World Power

14

The Faith of Woodrow Wilson

1941

The dedication of Woodrow Wilson's birthplace as a national memorial, coming as it does in the midst of a great international crisis, should serve not only to recall the memory of a truly great American but to remind us of his message to his country and to mankind. Confronted with a highly organized, unbelievably efficient, and utterly ruthless dictatorship, the few democracies remaining in the world today see before them the fate of Europe. On many sides may be heard the question whether democracy can be saved and whether it is worth saving.

Wilson's reply in the crisis of the World War was unequivocal: he spoke for democracy and was unshakable in his conviction of its superiority over any other system of government or life; he had boundless faith in the ultimate victory of democracy over autocracy, imperialism, and militarism; he believed that men have the right to govern themselves, that small nations are entitled to respect along with the large, and that the world must be organized to prevent the ruthless exploitation or complete extermination of the weak by the strong.

What is going on in Europe today is the complete negation of everything that Wilson stood for: tyranny is the order of the day, and the terrible power of Nazism, scoffing at ideas of liberty, equality, and international cooperation, rolls like a juggernaut over one free nation after another, reducing millions to a state of servitude. Now, indeed, is the time to recall the teaching of Wilson and to draw fresh inspiration from his message.

We know how Wilson viewed the great conflict of his time. We recall the circumstances under which we associated ourselves with the opponents of Germany; we appreciate the part played by this country in bringing about the final victory and drafting the terms of the peace settlements. It may be very instructive, however, to review and recon-

Note: From the *New York Times Magazine* (May 4, 1941), p. 5. © 1941 by The New York Times Company. Reprinted by permission.

sider the policies and objectives of our World War president, and to raise the question of their applicability to the present crisis.

One ought to begin, I think, by stressing Wilson's intense and unswerving faith in democracy, his profound conviction that the democratic way of life and the democratic system had proved themselves in this country and that from the experience of the American colonies something useful might be derived for the world at large.

Woodrow Wilson had no use for "governments clothed with the strange trappings and the primitive authority of an age that is altogether alien and hostile to our own." Already in the autumn of 1914 he saw that if Germany won, "it would change the course of our civilization and make the United States a military nation," whence it followed that "England is fighting our fight" and that we should put no obstacles in her way.

To be sure, it was almost three years after the beginning of the war before Wilson took this country into the fray. But this was not because the President was an isolationist. Quite the contrary; like many other prominent Americans he realized that the conditions of the modern world make isolation an illusion.

Addressing the League to Enforce Peace in May 1916, he declared: "We are participants, whether we would or not, in the life of the world. The interests of all nations are our own also. We are partners with the rest." And similarly in a speech at Long Branch in September 1916: "We can no longer indulge our traditional provincialism. We are to play a leading part in the world drama whether we like it or not." And finally, in his address at Shadow Lawn in November 1916: "It does not suffice to look, as some gentlemen are looking, back over their shoulders, to suggest that we do again what we did when we were provincial and isolated and unconnected with the great forces of the world, for now we are in the great drift of humanity which is to determine the politics of every country in the world."

Despite the Lusitania and other provocations, Wilson kept us out of war because he believed that we had a mission to fulfill toward mankind at large. As a great power standing aside, we could at the crucial moment step in as disinterested mediators, perhaps influence the terms of peace in the direction of moderation and justice, and certainly see to it that provision should be made for some type of international organization and action that would prevent the recurrence of such a catastrophe.

In the end this policy proved impossible; the German submarine campaign landed us in the war. But Wilson was more intent than ever on the organization of collective security after victory had been attained. He envisaged a league of democratic states: "A steadfast concert for peace can never be maintained except by a partnership of democratic nations. No autocratic government should be trusted to keep faith with it or observe its covenants."

He wanted self-determination for nations, and insisted that the rights of small states should be respected as are those of the great powers: "Shall there be a common standard of right and privilege for all peoples and nations, or shall the strong do as they will and the weak suffer without redress?" The new world order, he held, must guarantee the political independence and territorial integrity of all states and must make provision for common action against aggressors.

Nor did he shun the eventual application of military force to attain this end: "If you say, 'We shall not have any war' you have got to have the force to make that 'shall' bite"; "If the peace presently made is to endure, it must be a peace made secure by the organized major force of mankind"; "If the moral force of the world will not suffice, the physical force of the world shall."

There is no need to analyze here the way in which these ideas were translated into the Covenant of the League of Nations, nor even to recall Wilson's insistence that the Covenant be made an integral and inextricable part of the peace settlements. The Covenant was essentially the expression of Anglo-American views and was a great disappointment to the French, who had thought in terms of a league of victors to hold down the vanquished and had advocated an international army which would have ignored accepted ideas of national sovereignty.

As a matter of fact, the Covenant as it stood proved to be too much for the American digestion. Plain ignorance on the part of many, slavish adherence to outworn slogans on the part of others, the letup in crusading fervor on the part of most, and the exploitation of the situation by Wilson's political enemies resulted in rejection of the treaty and the Covenant.

Whether the American people in 1919–20 were really opposed to the League is still a moot question. Whether Wilson was maladroit in his handling of the situation can be debated *ad nauseam*. The fact of the matter is that the United States did not join the League. The

President, who had suspected and distrusted the greed and wrong-headedness of the Europeans, was let down by his own people, in whom he had had boundless confidence and of whom he could never have dreamed that they would fling his Covenant into the gutter to rot, as Lloyd George puts it.

Of the League but little is heard in these hectic days. That it turned out a failure is a widely held opinion, and there are not a few Americans who have thanked Providence that we did not allow ourselves to be implicated. But a few points perhaps require consideration.

In the first place it is clear that the League with the United States as a member would have been a very different thing from what it became as a result of our defection. Our relative disinterestedness, our power, our prestige would have made all the difference in the world. Instead of the dynamic, creative force which Wilson had envisaged, it tended to become a mere method of preserving the status quo.

We who thought once more to wash our hands of responsibility and to stand aloof from the European mess may well in these cataclysmic days return to Woodrow Wilson. He had a vision and he had a message. Within the League, we might have helped to forestall disaster. We refused to play the role which Wilson regarded not only as desirable in the cause of humanity, but necessary in the interest of our own country.

Of course international collaboration means sacrifices, involves contributions. Wilson knew that too, but he was convinced that the game was well worth the candle, that for the good of the world and for our own good we would have to shoulder the burden. "The League is dead; long live the League." Wilson can still guide us, for it becomes more and more obvious that if the future of mankind is once more in jeopardy, the trouble has lain not with too much international organization and activity, but with too little.

15

The American Attitude Towards Europe: An Historical Approach

1948

I. FAREWELL TO EUROPE

The subject of my lectures is the historical evolution of the American attitude towards Europe. The heart of the matter is to examine the factors that led us, as a nation, to adopt a policy of isolation, and to trace the influences which brought us later to active and indeed leading participation in European and world affairs. I fully expect from you, as Englishmen, a substantial measure of understanding for the problem, for after all Britain, ensconced in her island, was for long devoted to a policy of isolation, tempered only by regard for the requirements of the continental balance of power. Europe and the world grew beyond the predilections of the British. More recently we Americans have in turn seen the force of circumstances narrow the Atlantic to the span of a channel and sweep aside many time-honored preferences and prejudices.

Within the lifetime of many of us here present, the United States has intervened, actively and perhaps decisively, in two great wars—wars which, though world-wide in scope, were essentially European in origin and crucial for the future of European civilization. In each case, it should be noted, the conflict raged for more than two years before the United States entered the lists, that is, before the country could convince itself that its own interests were at least indirectly at stake. European governments and peoples have, I am sure, found it hard to understand these delays and have, on occasion, resented them. Today, as the world crisis moves into yet another phase, they quite naturally fear that in a future emergency there will be the same hesitation and indecision and that, given the tremendous acceleration of tempo in all human affairs, American intervention may next time come too late. We all know that in the present parlous state of the world, policies and plans

Note: A series of three hitherto unpublished addresses delivered at the University of London (Spring 1948).

267

have to be drawn long in advance and that no nation, however powerful, will be given years or months or even weeks for debate and decision. The future of our civilization will depend in large measure on what the United States will do, and particularly on how quickly it will do it. For Europe, then, as for the whole world, it is a matter of prime importance to know what attitude the United States is likely to take in any foreseeable crisis.

It is hardly necessary to remind an English audience that in my country, as in yours, the ultimate course of policy and action is determined by the popular will as expressed through innumerable organs of opinion and above all through the machinery of democratic election. The key to our problem would therefore seem to lie in the attitude of the American people. I am sure that, as an historian, I will be pardoned if I take the view that in order to understand the present climate of opinion one must re-examine past development, attempting to establish what factors and considerations went into the original formulation of the popular view and what has been the evolution of sentiment under the impact of successive events. I do not propose in these lectures to discuss the history of American diplomacy nor even to analyze the relations of the United States with any particular European country. These, you will realize, are large and complicated subjects, to which nothing approaching justice could be done in a few hours. My concern must necessarily be restricted to a review of the American position towards Europe and towards European questions in general and my effort must be concentrated upon sketching the main features of a broad orientation.

I need hardly say that I am fully aware of the difficulties inherent in the analysis of public opinion, even in these days of joyous questioning and exuberant polling. I realize only too well that it would be extremely hard if not impossible to determine with any degree of scientific accuracy the public reaction to any specific issue of a century ago. But for my purposes I am convinced that technical considerations need not be a deterrent. The broad currents of feeling that I am dealing with are usually not difficult to establish. For the most part they find open and free expression, though it stands to reason that there are always subtle shadings and qualifications. These we shall have to ignore here, but it will be wise to bear them in mind for this as for any other effort at broad analysis.

At the root of our historical problem lies the fact that the nucleus of what is now the United States was a territory settled by Europeans, in fact by Englishmen for the most part, and that the settlers in the New World left the old country for what they considered good and sufficient reasons. We have always chosen to underline the issue of religious freedom and no doubt it was prominent in the minds of the early colonists. As we see it now, of course, their conception of religious liberty was a rather narrow one, which certainly did not include much of the idea of toleration. Indeed, there is interesting evidence that the original European immigrants were as much intent as their successors on finding better economic opportunities. For example, in the years from 1640 to 1660, within a decade of the Massachusetts Bay settlement, almost more people returned to England than arrived in the colony. The Great Rebellion offered promising opportunities at a time when conditions were anything but rosy in the New World. It seems that fully a third of the graduates of Harvard College in the first score of years of its existence returned to England, where most of them found attractive positions in the church, in the universities, and even in the army.[1]

Be that as it may, there can be no question that for the discontented of England and of other countries the New World beckoned. They came in large numbers and the overwhelming majority of them were well-content to have come. Despite all hardships the New World seemed infinitely better than the old. In 1677 Increase Mather could exclaim in pious enthusiasm:

> There never was a generation that did so perfectly shake off the dust of Babylon both as to ecclesiastical and civil constitution as the first generation of Christians that came into this land for the Gospel's sake.

Other Colonial leaders, like William Bradford and Edward Winslow, echoed the sentiment, while one of the leaders of the Pennsylvania Germans wrote home full of relief at having left "the old, unhappy system of Europe." More than that, the idea soon became current that Providence, in the words of Jonathan Edwards, had singled out America as "the glorious renovator of the world"; that the colonists, like the Israelites in the past, were a chosen people designed to build a new and more godly society.[2]

[1] William L. Sachse, "The Migration of New Englanders to England, 1640–1660," *American Historical Review*, LIII (1948), 251–278.

[2] Max Savelle, "Colonial Origins of American Diplomatic Principles," *Pacific Historical Review*, III (1934), 334–350; J. Fred Rippy and Angie Debo, *The*

Unfortunately for the colonies, whatever their opinion of Europe or their high estimate of their own worth and future, they had no choice but to be involved in the great conflicts of Europe. From 1688 until the Revolution, the Second Hundred Years' War between England and France was fought out in the New World as in the old. Considering what the English colonies suffered from the depredations of France's Indian allies, it is no wonder that there grew up an intense hatred of France as a government and a people, and beyond that an ever greater resentment of the European system that produced unending antagonism and war. "The French," wrote one colonial author, "are the common Nusance and Disturbers of Europe, and will in a short time become the same in America, if not mutilated at Home." Other writers pictured them as immoral, wily, and godless, "busy frizzing their hair and painting their faces, without faith or morals." [3]

There can be no doubt, I think, that the so-called French and Indian Wars served at best to maintain in the English colonies a sense of patriotism and even of reliance on the home country for protection against a common foe. But after the great victory which in 1763 produced the Peace of Paris and the British acquisition of Canada, sentiment rapidly underwent a change. Among the colonists many felt that the victory was really their achievement and even more of them realized that, once the great external danger had been exorcised, there was no further reason for dependence. I do not mean at all to imply that there was popular or even widespread sentiment for casting off the connection with England. As a matter of fact the patriot leaders were most reluctant even in 1776 to go the whole way to independence. For the most part they still thought in terms of compromise and dreamed to the last of attaining something like modern dominion status within the British Empire. But it was characteristic of the colonials to think in large and far-ranging terms. It is interesting to note that John Adams, one of the deepest and most original thinkers of the Revolutionary period, should have been speculating in the following way as far back as 1755 when the most deadly war between England and France was only beginning:

Historical Background of the American Policy of Isolation, Smith College Studies in History, IX (1924), 71 ff.; Merle Curti, *The Roots of American Loyalty* (New York, 1946), pp. 6, 67.

[3] Howard M. Jones, *America and French Culture, 1750–1848* (Chapel Hill, 1927), chap. 1; Dixon R. Fox, *Ideas in Motion* (New York, 1935), pp. 50 ff.; Max Savelle, "The Appearance of an American Attitude Towards External Affairs, 1750–1775," *American Historical Review*, LII (1947), 655–666.

If we can remove the turbulent Gallicks, our people, according to the exactest computations, will in another century become more numerous than England itself. Should this be the case, since we have, I may say, all the naval stores of the nation in our hands, it will be easy to obtain the mastery of the seas; and then the united force of all Europe will not be able to subdue us.[4]

It is no part of my purpose to examine here the involved train of events that led to the Revolution and the American War of Independence. An American authority has expressed some wonder that involvement in European wars was not advanced as an argument for independence from the very start. It was not, however, mentioned in the Declaration of Independence, from which one must conclude that the leaders "looked upon such involvement as a matter of course, an ineluctable turn of fate, like tide and time and death." It appears to have been Tom Paine (*Common Sense*, 1776) who first argued for independence on the grounds that "it is the true interest of America to steer clear of European contentions, which she can never do while, by her dependence on Britain, she is made the makeweight in the scale of British politics." This idea seems to have opened the eyes of the patriots. At any rate, following Paine, the argument was repeated *ad nauseam* in political debate from that time on.[5]

Unhappily for the colonies, however, it was highly doubtful whether they would be able to withstand the power of England. Knowing the burning desire of the French for revenge, many minds turned to the idea of enlisting French aid, which would be tantamount to exploiting European rivalries for colonial ends. The idea was tempting, but full of danger. John Adams, who favored negotiation for aid, was nevertheless rabidly intent on keeping out of European involvements. Addressing the Continental Congress in 1776, he formulated the policy of non-entanglement which was to become traditional in the United States:

We ought to lay it down, as a first principle and a maxim never to be forgotten, to maintain an entire neutrality in all future European wars . . . Foreign powers would find means to corrupt our people, to influence our councils and, in fine, we should be little better than puppets, danced on the wires of the cabinets of Europe. We should be the sport of European intrigues and politics.[6]

[4] J. Fred Rippy, *America and the Strife of Europe* (Chicago, 1938), p. 58.
[5] Samuel Bemis, *The Diplomacy of the American Revolution* (New York, 1935), p. 12.
[6] Rippy and Debo, *Historical Background*, pp. 75–76.

271

In the end, the Continental Congress decided to negotiate for a commercial treaty with France. This was in no way intended to lead to an alliance. Indeed, the decision was due in part at least to fear lest Britain and France might come to an agreement and divide the American colonial empire between them. France furnished supplies surreptitiously, but it was not until 1778 that the treaty of alliance was concluded. The terms were not exactly what the patriot leaders had envisaged, but they had to accept the French conditions and console themselves with the thought that the treaty, while recognizing American independence, involved no obligation on the part of the United States to participate in European affairs.

It is common knowledge that the French contribution to the American cause in men and ships was substantial and perhaps even decisive. Nor can there be any doubt that French aid was deeply appreciated, just as the splendid conduct of the French officers and men brought about a genuine revision of earlier conceptions of the French character. And yet the American leaders were not without distrust, were never quite free of suspicion that the French government was not doing as much as it might and that in the end it might make a deal with England at America's expense. The peace negotiations which followed the surrender of Cornwallis were marked throughout by lack of faith, more or less on both sides. When the war was at last over the American leaders were deeply relieved and firmly determined in the future to keep out of the European cockpit. To quote again from John Adams, who was one of the most experienced and articulate of the American statesmen:

> America has been long enough involved in the wars of Europe. She has been a football between contending nations from the beginning and it is easy to foresee that France and England will endeavor to involve us in their future wars. It is our interest and duty to avoid them as much as possible, and to be completely independent, and to have nothing to do with either of them, but in commerce.[7]

When, in 1783, the United States emerged as an independent nation, the uppermost thought in the minds of the leaders was to hold aloof from future involvement in European affairs at all costs. Their attitude was in large measure due to the tribulations of a century of conflict, culminating in the experiences of the Revolution—the disheartening

[7] *Ibid.*, pp. 113 ff.

negotiations with London and the constant dangers inherent in the great struggle between England, France, and Spain. They saw no possible advantage in ever again being drawn into the maelstrom, and they were eagerly intent on organizing the new republican government free of all interference from abroad. More than ever they felt their system to be different from that of the Old World—as it was—and better. They sensed the hostility of the old order and wanted freedom to work out their own system by themselves. Furthermore, there was a continent to settle and develop. After all, no less a person than Adam Smith had painted a brilliant picture of the American future once the colonies were independent. So it is not to be wondered at that imaginative Americans should already have dreamed of taking over the whole continent even to the Pacific. The fathers of the country, if somewhat more modest in their aspirations, were nevertheless expansionists almost to a man. They wanted free navigation of the Mississippi, which was natural, but beyond that they kept in constant sight Louisiana, the Floridas, and Canada, if only because they had the uncomfortable feeling that these colonies would of necessity always be pawns in the European political struggle. As such they might at any time draw the new country into conflicts in which it had no interest. Very quickly there developed the idea that not only should we abstain from European affairs but that Europe likewise should leave us a free hand on this side of the Atlantic.[8]

And so, in 1783, the Congress voted to abstain from association with the League of Armed Neutrality on the plea that "the true interest of these states requires that they should be as little as possible entangled in the politics and controversies of European nations." Indeed, the Congress went so far as to consider recalling our ministers from European courts and sending embassies only on special occasions. Adams in particular was anxious to avoid having his country become "the sport of transatlantic politicians of all denominations, who hate liberty in every shape and every man who loves it, and every country that enjoys it." Thomas Jefferson went even further and thought it might be well, in order to escape entanglement, to scrap our commerce with Europe. "I should wish the United States to practice neither commerce, nor navigation, but to stand, with respect to Europe, precisely on the footing of China," he wrote in 1785.

[8] Gilbert Chinard, *Thomas Jefferson, Apostle of Americanism* (2nd ed., Boston, 1939), introduction.

Jefferson, like many of his colleagues, was deeply disturbed by the continued hostility of England:

> In spite of treaties, England is still our enemy. Her hatred is deep-rooted and cordial, and nothing is wanting with her but the power to wipe us, and the land which we live on, out of existence.

Four years of residence in France (1785–1789) made him if anything more aware of the shortcomings of the European system. Europe to him was a place

> where the dignity of man is lost in arbitrary distinctions, where the human species is classed into several stages of degradation, where the many are crushed under the weight of the few, and where the order established can present to the contemplation of a thinking being no other picture than that of God Almighty and His angels tramping under foot the hosts of the damned.

This applied to France as well as England, though in the last analysis he thought the French still to be preferred to the "rich, proud, hectoring, swearing, squibbling, carnivorous animals who live on the other side of the Channel." [9]

The more Jefferson saw of Europe, the more convinced he became that the United States should be "a standing monument and example for the aim and imitation of the people of other countries." His later rival, Alexander Hamilton, echoed the same idea in the *Federalist* (1787):

> Let the thirteen states, bound together in a strict and indissoluble union, concur in erecting one great American system, superior to the control of all trans-atlantic force or influence, and able to dictate the terms of the connection between the old and the new world.

To which George Washington, in his inaugural address (1789) added:

> The preservation of the sacred fire of liberty and the destiny of the republican model of government are justly considered perhaps as deeply, as finally staked on the experiment intrusted to the hands of the American people.

The presidency of George Washington marked the inauguration of the federal constitution, the adoption of which finally welded the thirteen states into one nation. Although it is patently impossible to enlarge

[9] *Ibid.*, pp. 208, 212, 217; Rippy and Debo, *Historical Background*, pp. 120 ff., 130 ff.

upon this fundamental departure here, it is necessary to point out that among other factors which induced the sovereign states to surrender part of their sovereignty was the constant fear that foreign powers would exploit disunion and would intrigue with one state against another. The proposal that the Congress should elect the President was rejected for fear that outside powers would intrigue for votes, as in the Polish elections. The same apprehension led to the requirement that treaties with other powers should be approved by a two-thirds vote of the Senate. There were some who questioned seriously the wisdom or need for having a secretary for foreign affairs. Indeed, his functions were finally included in a Department of State which originally dealt with all domestic affairs excepting finance and the army. And finally, as a reflection of profound suspicion, the Constitution forbade all officials to accept "any present, emolument, office or title of any kind whatsoever, from any King, Prince or foreign state." [10]

Taken by and large, then, there can be no question that the leaders of the new republic were united in their dislike and suspicion of the entire European system; that they were determined, so far as possible, to stand aloof from it, though they were by no means averse to profiting from the rivalries of European states to extend the territory of their own country. Convinced that the republican regime was far superior to that of Europe and that indeed it was the hope of the world, they were easily persuaded that continental expansion was a positive duty, to say nothing of the practical consideration that by taking over the remaining European colonies they would be eliminating the danger of future involvement in foreign conflict.

But just as the new republic came into being, the great revolution broke out in France. American opinion was tremendously exercised, the more so as the popular movement in France was generally attributed to American influence. As on later occasions, there was an outcry for support of the revolutionaries, the champions of liberty.[11]

Leaders like Washington, Adams, and Hamilton, to be sure, feared the possible excesses of the revolutionaries and were from the outset determined not to allow the American republic to be drawn into the French imbroglio. "I trust we shall never go so far," wrote Washington to Gouverneur Morris in 1791, "as to lose sight of our own interest and

---

[10] Rippy and Debo, *Historical Background*, pp. 136 ff.
[11] Charles D. Hazen, *Contemporary American Opinion of the French Revolution* (Baltimore, 1897).

happiness as to become, unnecessarily, a party in their political disputes." The issue in any case did not become an acute one until war broke out in 1793 between republican France and other European powers, thus raising the question of American obligations under the treaty of alliance of 1778. Since our leaders were one and all determined not to become involved, it was argued by Hamilton and others that the treaty was concluded with the government of Louis XVI, which no longer existed, and that, furthermore, France's war could not properly be defined as a defensive one. The French government, for reasons of its own, did not raise the issue, and Washington therefore issued a proclamation of neutrality, which was the logical expression of the American policy of abstention from European affairs.

Unhappily the new republic was not entirely a free agent. Apart from the continued pressure for intervention from the pro-French party, the government was constantly confronted by arbitrary attacks on American trade, by unrestrained agitation and intrigue on the part of French agents, and by the danger of seeing European antagonisms settled on the basis of American territorial exchanges. The highly complicated details must be omitted here, but it should be pointed out that the total effect was to heighten the aversion to any involvement. In 1795 Alexander Hamilton, the close collaborator of Washington, could write:

> If you consult your true interest, your motto cannot fail to be: Peace and trade with all nations; beyond our present engagements, political connection with None. You ought to spurn from you as the box of Pandora, the fatal heresy of a close alliance . . . with France. This would at once make you a mere satellite of France, entangle you in all the contests, broils and wars of Europe. 'Tis evident that the controversies of Europe must often grow out of causes and interests foreign to this country. Why, then, should we, by a close political connection with any power of Europe, expose our peace and interest, as a matter of course, to all the shocks with which their mad rivalship and wicked ambition so frequently convulse the earth? 'Twere insanity to embrace such a system.[12]

The same ideas were expressed in Washington's Farewell Address (September 17, 1796), much of which was drafted by Hamilton. Since to many Americans, even today, this famous address is a basic statement of principles, the salient passages at least must be quoted in full. The retiring President began by stating:

[12] Samuel F. Bemis, "Washington's Farewell Address," *American Historical Review*, XXXIX (January 1934), 250–268.

The great rule of conduct for us in regard to foreign nations is, in extending our commercial relations, to have with them as little political connection as possible . . .

The reasons were the familiar ones:

Europe has a set of primary interests which to us have none or a very remote relation. Hence she must be engaged in frequent controversies, the causes of which are essentially foreign to our concerns. Hence, therefore, it must be unwise in us to implicate ourselves by artificialities in the ordinary vicissitudes of her politics or the ordinary combinations and collisions of her friendships or enmities . . . Our detached and distant situation invites and enables us to pursue a different course . . . Why forego the advantages of so peculiar a situation? Why, by interweaving our destiny with that of any part of Europe, entangle our peace and prosperity in the toils of European ambition, rivalship, interest, humor or caprice?

It was left for Jefferson, in his first inaugural address (March 4, 1801) to sum it all up in the classic phrase, "Peace, commerce and honest friendship with all, entangling alliances with none."

Many writers have pointed out that it was Jefferson, not Washington, as popularly supposed, who used the words "entangling alliances." This is a minor point. Of greater importance is the fact that Jefferson, supposedly the friend of France and often suspected of having wanted us to intervene in France's behalf, should have expressed himself so definitely in the same sense as his rival, Hamilton. M. Adet, the French minister to the United States in 1796, showed better judgment in this respect than many later American authors:

Although Jefferson is a friend of liberty and science, although he is an admirer of the efforts we have made to cast off our shackles and to clear away the cloud of ignorance which weighs down the human race, Jefferson, I say, is an American, and as such, he cannot sincerely be our friend. An American is the born enemy of all the peoples of Europe.[13]

Other commentators have noted the fact that Washington, in his address, did not advocate out and out isolation. In another part of his message he drew a distinction between permanent and temporary alliances, thus:

'Tis our true policy to steer clear of permanent alliances with any portion of the foreign world . . . Taking care always to keep our-

[13] *Ibid.*, p. 267.

selves, by suitable establishments, on a respectable defensive posture, we may safely trust to temporary alliances for extraordinary emergencies.

This passage is certainly interesting, the more so as it leaves no doubt that Washington recognized the possibilities of unforeseen situations arising that might, in our own interest, necessitate foreign involvement. The fact of the matter is that the Father of His Country was almost certainly not wedded to the idea of complete isolation, but thought rather in terms of neutrality and independence whenever possible. Like the hardheaded, experienced men that the founders of the republic were, he thought primarily in terms of the state's interests and security and was prepared, if the occasion demanded, to take any steps, even to the conclusion of alliances, which seemed expedient. This was true even of Jefferson, the friend of France and the author of the phrase about "entangling alliances." Faced, in 1802, with the cession of Louisiana by Spain to France, he wrote to the American minister in Paris:

> The day that France takes possession of New Orleans . . . seals the union of two nations who, in conjunction, can maintain exclusive possession of the ocean. From that moment, we must marry ourselves to the British fleet and nation. We must turn all our attention to a maritime force, for which our resources place us on very high ground; and having formed and connected together a power which may render reinforcement of her settlements here impossible to France, make the first cannon which shall be fired in Europe the signal for the tearing up of any settlement she may have made, and for holding the two continents of America in sequestration for the common purposes of the United British and American nations.

Later, in 1810, Jefferson realized full well that it would not be in the interest of the United States to allow Napoleon to dominate Europe. At that time he warned that we might be obliged to send an army overseas if such a contingency seemed likely to materialize.[14]

It is quite clear, then, that our early statesmen took a realistic view of the national requirements. But in the sequel this fact was ignored. Washington's reference to the possible desirability of temporary alliances was soon forgotten and in actual fact the United States never again concluded an alliance, properly speaking, either temporary or permanent. Washington's political testament has weighed heavily with

[14] This whole matter is well discussed by Walter Lippmann, *United States Foreign Policy* (Boston, 1943), pp. 63 ff.

the American people—the more so, no doubt, as it was an accurate re-flection of the popular viewpoint and temper, to say nothing of the fact that for the next hundred years our position was well protected by the British command of the seas.

A few words must suffice to close out the development of our theme during the early years of our national existence. One of our most prom-inent contemporary historians, Professor Carlton J. H. Hayes of Colum-bia University, remarked recently in his presidential address to the American Historical Association that our success in keeping out of the European wars in this period was due less to our policy of aloofness than to the knowledge and experience of our statesmen with respect to Europe.[15]

There is certainly more than a grain of truth in this interpretation. The United States, in its infancy, was blessed beyond any reasonable expectation in having a veritable galaxy of brilliant leaders—men of great intellectual power, of wide knowledge, and of unusual experience in the conduct of affairs.

Indeed, it is hard to overlook the fact that during the stormy years of the French Revolution and the Napoleonic Empire, although we did become involved in an undeclared naval war with France, we managed to exploit the rivalries of the European states and the shifting balance of power to such an extent that our future was well assured. From Spain we secured the freedom of trade on the Mississippi and from Napoleon we managed to purchase the entire Louisiana territory, which opened up the continent to American settlement as far as the moun-tains. These were tremendous gains, which would be unthinkable ex-cept in the context of European strife. Furthermore, it was no mean achievement to have avoided embroilment in war until 1812. Merely to recall the precariousness of our position during the great Anglo-French duel and the ruthless, indiscriminate attacks on our trade by both an-tagonists is sufficient to make us realize that. Jefferson's embargo of 1807 has been harshly dealt with by historians, and there are many who regard the War of 1812 with Britain as altogether unwise, if not gra-tuitous. The situation, looking backward, was not unlike that of the First World War. In either case we ultimately felt ourselves impelled to go to war with that nation which most ruthlessly violated our neutral-ity and attacked our commerce. Added to that, however, was the burn-

[15] Carlton J. H. Hayes, "The American Frontier: Frontier of What?" *American Historical Review*, LI (January 1946), 199–216.

ing expansionism, which had already marked Canada and the Floridas as the next additions to the republic of virtue. As it turned out, our "patriots" overreached themselves. On land, at least, we took a severe drubbing; without the adroit exercise of diplomacy we might not have been able to extricate ourselves from our headstrong adventure before Britain had settled the continental score and turned her full force against us. If the War of 1812 was any lesson to us, it tended to confirm the basic national feeling and vindicate the teachings of the fathers.

As the young republic emerged, then, from the long period of international conflict that extended from 1756 to 1815, it was fully convinced of the rightness of certain basic propositions: that as colonies we had been exploited in the interests of European nations whose concerns were not ours; that the French alliance, though necessary, had endangered us almost as much as it helped us; that the new republican system was infinitely superior to the old regime in Europe; that we had an obligation to cherish it for the good of humanity; that we must protect it as a thing apart; that the best way of doing this was to hold aloof from foreign quarrels and concentrate the national energy on the elimination of foreign colonies on the American continent; and finally that, even though our sympathies might lie with European peoples struggling for liberty, we could not afford to aid them for fear of involving our own security.

Of course the United States was never either isolated or insulated from Europe excepting in the strictly political and military sense. The economic bond was always there. It meant a good deal to the European nations and it was highly important to the infant republic. In moments of extreme abhorrence a man like Jefferson would pronounce himself against any development of industrialism because it might mean further trade involvement. On the other hand, even Jefferson in his calmer moods recognized the need for a certain amount of commerce and was forever trying to reconcile his yearning for isolation with the obvious requirements of international economics. Hamilton on his side was strongly in favor of industrialization on the plea that only so could we become really and fully independent of Europe. And so the argument went, while the actual fact of close commercial intercourse existed and indeed was the primary and dominant cause of our troubles with Europe.

Isolation, then, was only a partial thing—more of an ideal than a reality. But for our present purposes it is important to remember that it was the ideal, that we not only longed for it but longed for more of it. To Americans this continent was full of promise and we wanted to work at its development without being constantly diverted or obstructed. "We specially ought to pray," wrote Jefferson in 1812, "that the powers of Europe may be so poised and counterpoised among themselves, that their own safety may require the presence of all their forces at home, leaving the other quarters of the globe in undisturbed tranquility." [16] All of which leads us to the obverse of the basic program of American foreign relations: while determined to keep out of Europe's affairs we came around more and more to the related proposition that Europe should abstain from all interference on this side of the Atlantic. Once we had Louisiana and the Floridas, this additional ideal was at least within the scope of attainment. It will be analyzed in the next lecture.

II. THE HEYDAY OF ISOLATIONISM

When the great wars of the Napoleonic era came to a close in 1815 the American people heaved sighs of relief, hoping ardently that at last the danger of entanglement was over. Though they had gone to war against England in 1812, suspicion and hatred of Napoleon and his France had run strong and deep, especially in Federalist circles. In the words of Henry Clay, we had called the Emperor "every vile and opprobrious epithet in our language . . . he has been compared to every hideous monster and beast, from that mentioned in the Revelations down to the most insignificant quadruped." [17]

And now the subverter of European republics had fallen. Great was the rejoicing, warm was the reception for the restored Bourbons, wild was the enthusiasm for Alexander the Liberator. This exultation, centered particularly in New England, was, however, short-lived. As the Bourbon Restoration showed itself in its true colors and the European powers began to band together in the Holy Alliance and the Quadruple Alliance, Americans could only conclude that the Old World was incorrigible. Europe, wrote John Quincy Adams in 1816, "has burst asunder the adamantine chains of Bonaparte, to be pinioned by the rags and tatters of monkery and popery. She cast up the code of Napoleon and re-

[16] Chinard, *Thomas Jefferson*, p. 480.
[17] Quoted by Elizabeth B. White, *American Opinion of France* (New York, 1927), p. 16.

turned to her own vomit of Jesuits, inquisitions and legitimacy as Divine Right." [18]

Added to this was the intense dislike and suspicion of the British and their policies, which led men like Jefferson to fear that the United States might be even more exposed to European machinations now that the Anglo-French antagonism had come to an end.[19] When, in 1820, the European Alliance began to take steps to suppress the revolutionary movements in Italy, the indignation on this side of the Atlantic mounted rapidly, and the average American became more and more deeply persuaded that there could be no reconciliation between the reactionary system of Europe and the free republicanism of the New World. Replying in 1820 to the well-intentioned efforts of Tsar Alexander to associate the United States with the Holy Alliance, John Quincy Adams, who had many years of experience in European chancellories behind him, wrote:

> To stand in firm and cautious independence of all entanglement in the European system has been a cardinal point in their (i.e., United States') policy under every administration of their government from the peace of 1783 to this day . . . [F]or the repose of Europe as well as of America, the European and American political systems should be kept as separate and distinct from each other as possible.[20]

Such was the American temper in the early 1820's, against which must be viewed the promulgation of the famous Monroe Doctrine on December 2, 1823. This doctrine, incomparably the most important of all foreign policy formulations in American history, has been examined in minute detail by a host of American historians and has by now been competently analyzed in all its many aspects.[21] It would be impossible to review the problem here, even in its brief outlines, and after all, that is not my purpose. I am not concerned here with the specific questions, such as the Russian pretensions on the Pacific coast or the status of Spain's revolted colonies in Latin America, nor with the highly compli-

[18] Quoted by Edward H. Tatum, Jr., *The United States and Europe, 1815–1823* (Berkeley, 1936), p. 218; see also White, *American Opinion,* chap. 2.

[19] Tatum, *The United States and Europe,* pp. 190 ff.

[20] Quoted by Samuel E. Morison, "The Origins of the Monroe Doctrine, 1775–1823," *Economica,* no. 10 (February 1924), pp. 36–37.

[21] To mention only a few of the more recent and illuminating treatments: Morison, *Economica,* no. 10 (February 1924), 27–51; Dexter Perkins, *The Monroe Doctrine, 1823–1826* (Cambridge, Mass., 1927), which is the most important single study; Tatum, *The United States and Europe;* Arthur P. Whitaker, *The United States and the Independence of Latin America* (New York, 1941).

cated negotiations and discussions that preceded President Monroe's pronouncement. In other words I am, in the context of these lectures, less interested in the particular issues and their treatment than I am in the general attitude reflected in American policy and in the implications of that policy for the future.

Enough has already been said to prove beyond a shadow of a doubt that the ideas behind the doctrine had their origins as far back as colonial times, that they were well-established and almost universally accepted. We were convinced that European quarrels were none of our concern, and we wanted no part in them. By way of corollary we thought we were justified in demanding that Europe keep out of American affairs. So far as we were able, we had followed this line with truly remarkable fidelity. In other words, one might say that the Monroe Doctrine existed in practice before it was so solemnly proclaimed as a principle in 1823.

But in the years from 1820 to 1823 there was real danger, as there was in 1789–1790, that we might be diverted from the chosen path by our intense interest in the cause of liberty wherever men were fighting for it. Even George Washington, who was the soul of circumspection in such matters, had declared in one of his last speeches: "My anxious recollections, my sympathetic feelings, and my best wishes are irresistibly excited whensoever, in any country, I see an oppressed nation unfurl the banners of freedom."

Most of our early leaders shared these sentiments, which had flared up in the days of the French Revolution and which glowed with even greater ardor after 1820, when the Italians, Spaniards, and Greeks rose against their governments. The aged Jefferson, when he heard of the Spanish insurrection, hoped that it would "end in an universal insurrection of continental Europe and in the establishment of representative government in every country of it." [22] Others, like Henry Clay and Daniel Webster, and even President Monroe, were deeply stirred and possibly at times tempted to translate their feelings into action. As the tide of philhellenism rose in the United States, President Monroe in his message to Congress one year before the proclamation of the Monroe Doctrine declared that Greece "fills the (American) mind with the most exalted sentiments and arouses in our bosoms the best feelings of which our nature is susceptible." He expressed a strong hope that the Greeks

[22] White, *American Opinion*, chap. 30.

would recover their independence. And a year later, in drafting the message embodying the famous doctrine, he actually wrote in a statement that would have been tantamount to a recognition of Greek independence.[23]

But the Secretary of State, John Quincy Adams, had from the outset seen the contradiction between our traditional standpoint and a program of crusading for liberty. In his Independence Day Address (July 4, 1821) he had expressed himself most definitely on this point:

> Wherever the standard of freedom and independence has been or shall be unfurled, there will her (i.e., United States') heart, her benedictions, and her prayers be. But she goes not abroad in search of monsters to destroy. She is the well-wisher to the freedom and independence of all. She is the champion and vindicator only of her own ... She well knows that by once enlisting under other banners than her own, were they even the banners of foreign independence, she would involve herself beyond the power of extrication, in all the wars of interest and intrigue, of individual avarice, envy and ambition, which assume the colors and usurp the standard of freedom.[24]

This, I believe, expressed the general sense of the American public and certainly of Congress. On this and later occasions we found an emotional outlet in meetings and resolutions, but at no time did we seriously or intentionally plan intervention in behalf of other peoples' freedom. By 1823 the European powers had suppressed the revolutions, with the exception of the Greek, which was in a class by itself. The issues that presented themselves to us were the Russian claims in the Pacific Northwest and more particularly the fate of Spain's revolted colonies in the New World.

The first item is of importance here chiefly because it enabled Adams to work out the principle of noncolonization in the future by European powers in America. As for the rest, it is common knowledge that the British foreign secretary, George Canning, had, through his conversations with the American minister, Richard Rush, given the impetus to the formulation of the Monroe Doctrine. In the summer of 1823 there appeared to be real danger that France, supported by the other continental great powers, might attempt to reconquer the American colonies of Spain. The United States government, acting on its own, had,

[23] Myrtle A. Cline, *The American Attitude Toward the Greek War of Independence* (Atlanta, 1930).
[24] Quoted by Tatum, *The United States and Europe*, p. 244.

albeit reluctantly, recognized the independence of the new Latin American states in 1822. Both Britain and the United States had a common interest—commercial as well as political—in preventing European intervention. A joint pronouncement, then, would have made perfectly good sense.

The matter was considered and discussed at great length in American government circles in the autumn of 1823. The differences of opinion need not delay us. The Sage of Monticello, when consulted by President Monroe, was certainly torn in his feelings, and fell back on the argument that temporary alliances for special purposes might be useful. In his reply he argued in this fashion:

> Our first and fundamental maxim should be, never to entangle ourselves in the broils of Europe; our second, never to suffer Europe to intermeddle with cisatlantic affairs. America, north and south, have a set of interests distinct from those of Europe and peculiarly our own. She should therefore have a system of her own, separate and apart from that of Europe; while the last is laboring to become the domicile of despotism, our endeavor should surely be to make our hemisphere that of freedom.

But here was a special case, where American interests might be served by cooperation. Jefferson continued,

> Great Britain is the nation which can do us the most harm of any one, or all on earth; and with her on our side we need not fear the whole world. With her, then, we should the most sedulously cherish a cordial friendship; and nothing would tend more to knit our affections than to be fighting once more side by side, in the same cause. Not that I would purchase her amity at the price of taking part in her wars. But the war in which the present proposition might engage us, should that be its consequence, is not her war, but ours. Its object is to introduce and establish the American system, of keeping out of our land all foreign powers, of never permitting those of Europe to interfere with the affairs of our nations. It is to maintain our principle, not to depart from it.

This sounded eminently reasonable, but it did not appeal to the administration. Most members of Monroe's cabinet were suspicious of British designs and were not at all sure that Canning's suggestion was not aimed at a self-denying ordinance on our own part. Since the British consistently refused to recognize the independence of the Spanish colonies, there seemed to be even more grounds for circumspection. And

Adams argued that it would be more dignified to act on our own and not appear as a cockboat in the wake of the British man-of-war.

The end result was that in December, after Canning had convinced himself that there was no immediate danger, and after he had all but forgotten his original advances to Rush, President Monroe made his famous utterance, only the salient passages of which can be quoted here:

> In the wars of the European powers, in matters relating to themselves, we have never taken any part, nor does it comport with our policy so to do. It is only when our rights are invaded or seriously menaced that we resent injuries or make preparation for our defense. With the movements in this hemisphere we are, of necessity, more immediately connected, and by causes which must be obvious to all enlightened and impartial observers. The political system of the allied powers is essentially different in this respect from that of America . . . We owe it, therefore, to candor, and to the amicable relations existing between the United States and those powers, to declare that we should consider any attempt on their part to extend their system to any portion of this hemisphere as dangerous to our peace and safety. With the existing colonies or dependencies of any European power we have not interfered and shall not interfere. But with the Governments who have declared their independence and maintained it, and whose independence we have, on great consideration and on just principles, acknowledged, we could not view any interposition for the purpose of oppressing them, or controlling in any other manner their destiny, by an European power, in any other light than as a manifestation of an unfriendly disposition toward the United States . . .
>
> Our policy in regard to Europe, which was adopted at an early stage of the wars which have so long agitated that quarter of the globe, nevertheless remains the same, which is not to interfere in the internal concerns of any of its powers.

Here, then, is the barest outline of the steps that led to the classic formulation of American policy: no interference in Europe's affairs, but in return abstention by European nations from intervention in the Americas. Of course the Monroe Doctrine was not always observed. On our own side it at times fell into almost complete oblivion. At other times it was abused, reinterpreted, and extended. But for our present purpose the important thing is that the American people hailed it at the time and that ever since it has been regarded with almost religious reverence. The reason for this is obvious: the Monroe Doctrine expressed what Americans felt most deeply; namely, the profound cleavage between the European system and the American, the sharp distinction between European interests and those of the New World.

Limitations of time forbid my reviewing, even in the most casual way, the diplomatic relations between the United States and European countries during the nineteenth century. Disputes there were with all of them, excepting Russia, and at times, as during the Civil War, relations were strained to the breaking point. But these matters, however important and interesting, are of secondary significance to our theme. Needless to say, none of them served to increase our love for Europe. British and French interests and activities in the Caribbean region, the heated dispute over the Oregon boundary, the threat of intervention during the Civil War, and the French attempt to establish an empire in Mexico—all these things were irritating and they were deeply resented. To the European, no doubt, the American claims under the doctrine of "Manifest Destiny" seemed extravagant and outrageous, but on this side of the ocean they appeared altogether reasonable and even necessary. Actually we invariably had our way, primarily because European tensions frustrated the opposition. Jefferson's hope that the European nations might be always poised and counterpoised so as to require their keeping their forces at home was, in the main, realized. Without European interference, we were able to expand over the continent and to settle a world of our own.

What, then, remains to be said of the American attitude toward Europe in the course of the last century? Two aspects, I think, deserve our consideration. The first of these touches the nonpolitical angles and requires some consideration of cultural relationships. The second hinges on the great changes wrought by large-scale immigration and the impact of the vast influx of European settlers on our general attitude towards "the old country."

With respect to the first item, it cannot be said too frequently or too forcefully that for all our political farewells to Europe, we remained culturally a dependency, particularly of England. Let us remember that prior to 1800 the American states were inhabited very largely by Englishmen. During the entire colonial period the contacts with England were close. We derived our learning, our ideas, to a certain extent our social system, from England. Colonists of the upper classes went abroad not only for trade, but for education and enjoyment. Most of our early statesmen, like our writers, had lived abroad, and many of them had wide experience of European conditions. They thought in European terms and had an understanding of European problems which unfortunately became rare later on.

But with the Revolution came the first exhortations to cultural independence. One of our fiery revolutionary poets, Philip Freneau, cried in exasperation, with reference to the Mother Country:

> Can we never be thought to have learning or grace,
> Unless it be brought from that damnable place?

Somewhat later Noah Webster, exuberant and argumentative schoolmaster and eventually our first great lexicographer, called for a national language as well as a national government. For him it was a matter of honor that we have a system of our own, based on a simpler, republican-democratic orthodoxy and style.[25]

Joel Barlow, one of the most vigorous protagonists of the French Revolution, in turn composed a formidable if hopelessly pompous American epic, the *Columbiad,* as a first step towards a national literature.

For the time being these were feeble voices crying in the wilderness. Though Jefferson deplored the migration of American students to Europe and feared for the corruption of their republican virtue, they continued to go, if anything extending their travels to continental countries. It was only after the War of 1812, which left very sore feelings on both sides, that a concerted demand developed for a purely national literature. A number of prominent British journals seemed to take a peculiar delight in taunting the uncouth Americans with their barbarism and vulgarity and with their failure to produce anything noteworthy or original in literature or art. In the so-called War of the Reviews, the newly-founded American magazines replied in kind, pouring ridicule on the antiquated British social system and the servility of the average Briton. Puffed up by their spectacular naval victories in the recent war, American critics began to call for a national literature dealing exclusively with American themes in an appropriately American way.[26]

---

[25] H. L. Mencken, *The American Language* (4th ed., New York, 1943), p. 10; Harry R. Warfel, *Noah Webster, Schoolmaster to America* (New York, 1946), pp. 124 ff.

[26] Robert E. Spiller, *The American in England* (New York, 1926), chaps. 2 and 3; Tatum, *The United States and Europe,* pp. 66 ff; John C. McCloskey, "The Campaign of Periodicals after the War of 1812," *Publications of the Modern Language Association,* L (March 1935), 262–273; George Stuart Gordon, *Anglo-*

This agitation, fanned by a number of American academicians, culminated in Ralph Waldo Emerson's vibrant address, *The American Scholar* (1837):

> Perhaps the time is already come . . . when the sluggard intellect of this continent will look from under its iron lids and fill the postponed expectation of the world with something better than the exertions of mechanical skill. Our day of independence, our long apprenticeship to the learning of other lands, draws to a close. The millions that around us are rushing into life, cannot always be fed on the sere remains of foreign harvests. Events, actions arise, that must be sung —that will sing themselves . . . We have listened too long to the courtly muses of Europe.

For years Emerson, and after him Melville and Whitman, to mention only a few, harped on the same theme, calling for treatment of homely American subjects—"our banks and tariffs, our Methodism and Unitarianism, our logrolling and stumps and politics, our Negroes, Indians, Northern trade and Southern planting, Western clearings, Oregon and Texas" (Emerson), in short, for a literature based on American democracy, free of feudalism, designed not for the noble but for the farmer in the kitchen.[27]

Such was the program, but the realization of it was little short of pathetic. To be sure, after the Revolution we severed our religious connections with the Old World and gradually worked out our own legal system. In 1828 Noah Webster was able to publish his cherished *American Dictionary of the English Language*. A group of American artists emerged as the Hudson River School, and George Bancroft began publishing his ardently democratic and nationalistic *History of the United States* (1834–1866). But in the main, things remained as they were in the literary field. Of all books published in the United States in 1820, only 30 per cent were written by Americans. No doubt the lack of a protective copyright law had something to do with it. American publishers found it more profitable to pirate outstanding English works than to introduce new American writers. But beyond this remains the

---

American Literary Relations (Oxford, 1942), pp. 35 ff.; William Charvat, *The Origins of American Critical Thought, 1810–1835* (Philadelphia, 1936), pp. 28 ff.

[27] Benjamin T. Spencer, "A National Literature, 1837–1855," *American Literature*, VIII (1936), 125–159; Harry H. Clark, "Nationalism in American Literature," *University of Toronto Quarterly*, II (1933), 492–519; A. M. Schlesinger, "History and Literary History," in Norman Foerster, *Reinterpretation of American Literature* (New York, 1928), pp. 160–180; Karl H. Pfeffer, *England im Urteil der amerikanischen Literatur vor dem Bürgerkrieg* (Leipzig, 1931).

fact that the demand was for established European authors. American critical thought was derived from Scottish philosophers. The great British reviews, like the *Edinburgh* and the *Quarterly*, were regularly published in American editions. Many of the writers of our classical period, for example Cooper, Longfellow, and Lowell, were skeptical of the possibility of a truly national literature, much though they may have resented British criticism of American efforts. In general, the development of American literature followed the European modes, and almost all of our leading authors paid devotional visits to the historical and literary shrines of the English world. "My native country was full of youthful promise," wrote Irving, "but Europe was rich in the accumulated treasures of ages." The same feeling was echoed by Hawthorne, who remarked:

> While an American willingly accepts growth and change as the law of his own national and private existence, he has a singular tenderness for the stone-incrusted institutions of the mother country.

Or again:

> After all these bloody wars and vindictive animosities, we have still an unspeakable yearning towards England. When our forefathers left the old home, they pulled up many of their roots, but trailed along with them others, which were never snapt asunder by the tug of such a lengthening distance, nor have been torn out of the original soil by the violence of subsequent struggles, nor severed by the edge of the sword.[28]

But I must resist the temptation to pursue this fascinating theme in greater detail. The point I want to leave with you is the same made by Margaret Fuller when she wrote from Italy in 1847:

> Although we have an independent political existence, our position toward Europe as to literature and the arts is still that of a colony, and one feels the same joy here that is experienced by the colonist in returning to the parent home.[29]

"Your literature suits its each whisper and motion/To what will be thought of it over the ocean," wrote Lowell in his *Fable for Critics*

---

[28] Quoted by Philip Rahv, *Discovery of Europe* (Boston, 1947), pp. 184, 202. On American critical thought see Charvat, *The Origins of American Critical Thought*, pp. 28 ff.; the copyright issue is illuminatingly discussed in Gordon, *Anglo-American Literary Relations*, pp. 82 ff.

[29] Quoted by Rahv, *Discovery of Europe*, p. 166.

(1848). In a word, our great literary lights wrote English, and they wrote it as Englishmen, or tried to. The public devoured English books and welcomed a long procession of English lecturers, even though the visitors often spoke with perhaps unnecessary brutality of our shortcomings. All through the century our students hurried overseas, bringing back the knowledge and techniques on which our higher learning is based. And all this time what the Mid-Westerners called the "real" America was but little heard from. It was too busy conquering a new world, and literary America, which meant primarily New England and New York, was but little touched by it, at least until after the Civil War. In Emerson's words: "Europe extends to the Alleghenies; America lies beyond." Ultimately the "real" America would make itself heard, but for the nineteenth century at least the Anglo-American element remained dominant.[30]

Our close cultural ties with Europe, reinforced by the deep-seated American interest in the progress of liberty and republicanism, made it inevitable that we should follow the revolutionary movements beyond the Atlantic with the utmost attention. In a sense, Americans were always waiting to see the oppressed and benighted Europeans come to their senses. Hence the ardor of our philhellenism in the 1820's and our enthusiastic reception of the July Revolution of 1830 in France, led for the moment by our own beloved Lafayette. In like manner we hailed the English Reform Bill of 1832 with sympathetic approval as a first move on the road to democracy. But our greatest enthusiasm and our highest hopes were reserved for the great revolutionary movement of exactly a century ago, which swept the continent from France to what is now Rumania. France itself proved a disappointment, for the movement there sank rapidly into what was regarded in America as dangerous radicalism, only to emerge as the dictatorship of Louis Napoleon. To most good Americans it was clear that France was unprepared for liberty and only too prone to fall in line behind a despicable charlatan.[31]

But the German Revolution was different, for it aimed not only at

[30] See Gordon, *Anglo-American Literary Relations,* pp. 62 ff., on the British visitors; for the rest, see the highly stimulating essays in Foerster, *Reinterpretation of American Literature,* and Howard M. Jones, *Ideas in America* (Cambridge, Mass., 1944), especially chap. 11.

[31] White, *American Opinion,* chaps. 4 and 5; E. N. Curtis, "American Opinion of the French 19th Century Revolutions," *American Historical Review,* XXIX (January 1924), 249–270.

liberty, but at federal organization, which was most flattering to the American soul. Our minister at Berlin was instructed to indicate our desire to see a constitution drawn up for all Germany "which will render that nation great and powerful, and will secure to every German citizen the blessings of liberty and order." At one time Daniel Webster thought of going himself to Germany in order to help establish a federal system. But here too we were to be disillusioned. The famous Frankfurt Parliament turned out to be composed of "moon-struck professors" instead of practical men. Before long it became aggressively nationalistic and toadied to Austria and Prussia. Finally all that was left of the revolutionary movements was the doughty resistance of the Hungarians to the Hapsburgs and their Russian mentors.

The Hungarians, strange though it may seem, were clearly "the Americans of Europe" and Kossuth was their Washington. Excitement ran high and even the government came uncomfortably close to recognizing Hungarian independence and breaking relations with Austria.

After the defeat of the Hungarians, Kossuth, having fled to Turkey, was brought to the United States under American auspices. He was welcomed with frantic enthusiasm, and managed to raise almost $100,-000 for his cause. The hero on his part made no secret of his hope of provoking American intervention in Europe, and for a time there was some sentiment for such action. Senator Cass of Michigan declared that the United States must cease being a "political cipher" and that the world must be taught that there are "twenty-five millions of people looking across the ocean at Europe, strong in power, acquainted with their rights, and determined to enforce them." Webster went far beyond the bounds of propriety in dealing with the situation, and the so-called "Young America" group in the Democratic Party proclaimed as its principle: "no more neutrality; active alliance with European republicanism throughout the world."

And yet, looking backward, we can see that much of this was spread-eagleism designed for popular consumption. For all the truculent bluster, the government never seriously considered actual intervention. When the agitation had served its political purposes it soon died down. To be sure, as late as 1854 Mr. Buchanan, then our minister to England and later president, sat at table in London with the leaders of the European Revolution—Kossuth, Mazzini, Garibaldi, Ledru-Rollin,

Orsini, Ruge, and Herzen—but this was hardly more than a piquant detail, devoid of all larger significance.[32]

As before, then, the United States continued to be the "well-wisher to the freedom and independence of all," but the "champion and vindicator only of her own." It is interesting to note, in this connection, that the enthusiasm for action in the Kossuth period was centered primarily in the West, that important region which was emerging into political prominence. This leads me to say a few words, in concluding this lecture, of the influence of the frontier and the influx of immigrants upon our attitude towards Europe.

One of our greatest historians, Frederick Jackson Turner, pointed out more than fifty years ago that

> at the frontier the environment is at first too strong for the man . . . Little by little he transforms the wilderness, but the outcome is not the old Europe, not simply the development of Germanic germs . . . The fact is, that here is a new product that is American . . . Thus the advance of the frontier has meant a steady movement away from the influence of Europe, a steady growth of independence on American lines.[33]

Some aspects of Turner's theory have been much debated from that time to this, but no one has seriously questioned the thesis that the settlers of the West grew away from the European traditions and ideals that still held sway east of the mountains. In the West there was not only disdain but positive dislike of Europe, and the Middle West has remained to this day the stronghold of isolationist sentiment. After the Civil War the South, which had been one of the strongholds of British influence, lay in ruins and the preponderance of New England in national affairs was soon ended by the weight of the West. Once the issues of slavery and separatism had been settled in war, the energies of the country went more than ever into the development of its enormous western domain. The war left us sore and distrustful of both

---

[32] The literature on all this is extensive. See Evarts B. Greene, *American Interest in Popular Government Abroad* (Washington, 1917); Merle Curti, *Austria and the United States, 1848–1852*, Smith College Studies in History, XI (1926); John G. Gazley, *American Opinion of German Unification* (New York, 1926), chap. 2; Arthur J. May, *Contemporary Opinion of the Mid-Century Revolutions in Central Europe* (Philadelphia, 1927), *passim;* Eugene Pivany, *Hungarian-American Historical Connections* (Budapest, 1927). Merle Curti, "Young America," *American Historical Review*, XXXII (October 1926), pp. 34–35.

[33] F. J. Turner, *The Frontier in American History* (New York, 1958), p. 4.

British and French policy. Less than ever did we want to deal with Europe. We had reached the limits of our continental expansion and we wanted above all to apply ourselves to the consolidation of our holdings.

It might be supposed that the enormous influx of immigrants might have counteracted this attitude of indifference, the more so as so many of the newcomers settled in the Mid-West. But such was not the case. Although no less than 9,500,000 immigrants entered the country between 1840 and 1880, they played at best a subordinate part in American public life. Prior to 1848 the immigration was largely Irish and German and predominantly Catholic. As such the newcomers were unpopular, and their coming provoked the formation of the anti-Catholic Native American and Know Nothing parties, with the slogan "Our country, our whole country and nothing but our country."

The revolutions of 1848–49 brought to America a good many educated political refugees, many of whom played prominent roles in the Civil War period. But the great influx of Europeans came in search of economic betterment. Almost half of them were Germans or Scandinavians, who, despite many hardships, for the most part found opportunity and even prosperity in the great farmlands of the West. Many of them retained a romantic attachment to the old countries and scrupulously cultivated their native languages in church and society. But even in the cultural sense the American melting pot reduced them in a remarkably short time. How it was done it is hard to say, but there can be little doubt that the public school system played a large role. Our textbooks were probably not much better nor much worse than those of other countries. They instilled patriotism, of course, but they also aimed at conveying the idea, which was strongly fortified by public opinion, that the American system was unique and far superior to that of the rest of the world—that the United States was the land of opportunity and that all were blessed who were privileged to live therein. It has often been remarked that immigrant children sang almost more lustily than the native-born: "Land where our fathers died, land of the Pilgrim's pride." Lord Bryce, among many others, noted the deep attachment of Americans to their institutions which, he added, "are believed to disclose and display the type of institutions toward which, as by a law of fate, the rest of civilized mankind are forced to move, some with swifter, others with slower, but all with unresting feet."

294

The millions of immigrants, he concluded, "vie with the natives in their exultant pride in being citizens of the United States." [34]

It is perfectly true, of course, that the character of the immigration changed fundamentally after 1890. From that time on the Teutonic influx diminished, and the majority of the newcomers were Slavs (Czechs, Poles, Slovaks), Hungarians, Italians, Greeks, Jews, and Levantines. These later immigrants were, on the whole, on a lower cultural level than their predecessors. Few of them settled on the land, the great majority being absorbed by the great industrial centers. Many of them came without their families. They sent their earnings back home and dreamed of returning to the home country themselves. They were admittedly more difficult to assimilate and for that reason restrictive legislation was later adopted. But in any case there is no reason to suppose that their presence in any way affected the basic attitude of Americans towards Europe. Many of the later immigrants were politically under the thumbs of Irish politicians and were notoriously anti-British and on the whole isolationist.

As the century closed, then, the United States had enjoyed more than a century of independence. Culturally, we were still very much a part of the western European world, part of the Atlantic community. Economically, too, we were deeply in Europe's debt and completely enmeshed in the world trade system. But politically speaking, it was the heyday of isolationism. The center of gravity had already shifted to the Middle West, and the Middle West was genuinely American in its ignorance of Europe and its preoccupation with its own affairs. Men like William T. Stead, Cecil Rhodes, and Andrew Carnegie might dream, at the turn of the century, of an ultimate reunion of the "Anglo-Saxon race," but nothing was further removed from the average American's thought. Nothing illustrates the point better than the fact that as a rule we were quite content at that time to send abroad as ambassadors or ministers local politicians and placemen whose ignorance of Europe was often abysmal. In the words of an eminent American his-

---

[34] James Bryce, *The American Commonwealth* (London, 1888). On the whole question of the effects of immigration see George M. Stephenson, *A History of American Immigration* (Boston, 1926), especially chap. 15; E. A. Benians, *Race and Nation in the United States* (Cambridge, 1946); the masterly study of Marcus L. Hansen, *The Atlantic Migration* (Cambridge, 1945); and Ray A. Billington, "The Origins of Middle Western Isolationism," *Political Science Quarterly*, LX (1945), 46–64.

torian, our general attitude was one of "good natured indifference, not to say superiority." [35]

III. THE UNITED STATES AS A WORLD POWER

In the preceding lecture I emphasized the fundamental ambivalence in the American attitude towards Europe during the last century. While in political matters we Americans turned our backs on Europe, we were in economic matters more and more bound up with the transatlantic world. Culturally, too, we remained dependent on European leadership and wedded to European traditions. Of course there is a great danger of oversimplifying trends and forces of this magnitude, and I realize fully the desirability of making reservations and recognizing nuances. This will be my particular task in this lecture as I attempt to trace—again only in broad lines—the change that came over the American attitude in the first half of the twentieth century.

To begin with I ought to call attention to an interesting facet of the problem: the emergence of what is often called "internationalism" in contradistinction to isolationism or "continentalism." The roots of internationalism go far back in American history. Like the British, the Americans have long been interested in religious and humanitarian causes. They have always been crusaders, eager to share with others the blessings they enjoyed, and quite prepared to make real sacrifices for a high purpose. At times, no doubt, crusading carried us beyond the strict limits of nonintervention in European affairs. Our missionaries, especially in the Near East, were frequently propagandists of liberty, equality, and democracy, and even our government went so far as to protest against the persecution of Jews in Rumania and Russia. These were extreme examples, but in general we took an active part in the suppression of the slave trade, in the relief of famine, in the furtherance of international law, and in the agitation for international peace. After the turn of the century the impetus given by the Hague Peace Conference resulted in widespread popular interest and active participation by the government in the work for peace. The great vogue of arbitration treaties is eloquent evidence of devotion to peace and "internationalism." It has been estimated that during the generation

[35] Archibald C. Coolidge, *America as a World Power* (New York, 1908), p. 85. See also the discerning remarks by Hayes, *American Historical Review*, LI (January 1946), 199–216.

preceding the First World War the United States government took part in no less than twenty-eight official international conferences, the decisions of which were for the most part approved by the United States Senate.[36]

These conferences, to be sure, dealt almost entirely with so-called "nonpolitical" matters. Nonetheless they illustrate a growing tendency toward international action, brought about quite naturally and inevitably by the development of better communications and the ever greater interdependence among the nations in the economic sphere. As a matter of fact it was probably economic pressure as much as anything that provoked the extraordinary outburst of "colonialism" or "imperialism" that marked the last quarter of the nineteenth century. Almost every major country of Europe took part in this frantic effort to secure new markets and fields for investment and, as we all know, the end result was the appropriation by Europe of just about all of the so-called "unclaimed" regions of Africa and Asia. The United States did not remain free of the imperialist fever. American economists were among the earliest and most persuasive proponents of expansion, and the writings of Admiral Alfred T. Mahan had a universal influence on the movement. Under the circumstances it was not too remarkable that the United States should have embarked on overseas adventure along with other nations. We had pushed our frontier of settlement to the Pacific and had built up extensive trade interests in the Far East. Our war with Spain in 1898 effected not only the liberation of Cuba, but also established us in the Philippines as an imperial power.

What were the repercussions of our imperial ventures on our general attitude toward Europe? The significant thing was the fact that our Far Eastern involvement of necessity brought us into political contact with Europe and threatened to entangle us in the rivalries of European powers. So far as possible we continued to stand aloof. When we had to act we avoided "common" action with European governments but took "parallel" action. But as a practical matter circumstances generally tended to bring us to the British side and to estrange us from the German. This development is noteworthy and of course important. It was not the result of any planned policy but, as I say, was the result

[36] George H. Blakeslee, *The Recent Foreign Policy of the United States* (New York, 1925), p. 20. On the peace movement see Merle Curti, *Peace or War, 1636–1936* (New York, 1936).

of circumstances inherent in the situation. After the unpleasant Venezuela episode and the conclusion of the Hay-Pauncefote Treaty regarding the Panama Canal, there were no major issues outstanding between Britain and ourselves. Such as they were, they were dealt with by Britain in a spirit of accommodation. The same was true of France, which became linked with Britain by the *entente cordiale* of 1904. On the other hand we became steadily more estranged from Germany, partly because of the latter's pretensions in the South Pacific (Samoa and the Manila incident of 1898) and partly because of the ill-concealed hostility of the Berlin government towards the Monroe Doctrine. Added to this was a mounting sense of rivalry in sea power and trade matters and the general dislike of Americans for Prussian militarism and imperial arrogance. For the time being, however, all this amounted to little more than a dull and ill-defined feeling of little, though increasing, importance.

President Theodore Roosevelt and some of his imperialist supporters were not at all averse to active participation in world affairs. It will be remembered that the President intervened energetically to mediate peace between Russia and Japan in 1905 and, what is even more striking, that he interfered in a more strictly European crisis—the clash over Morocco in 1905. Constantly prodded by the German Emperor, but at bottom somewhat concerned about the aims and methods of German policy, the President induced France to agree to the Algeciras Conference, arranged to have the United States officially represented, and used his influence to effect a peaceful settlement. The United States Senate ratified the Act of Algeciras, but cautiously added a reservation reaffirming our traditional policy, "which forbids participation by the United States in the settlement of political questions which are entirely European in their scope." [37]

This characteristic move revealed the caution of Congress and its reluctance to leave the beaten path even in an era of imperialism. Indeed, Theodore Roosevelt's adventurous moves in world affairs can hardly be rated as more than symptomatic. The President took a lively interest in high policy and fancied himself as the chief of a powerful state. But he was no thinker, and I doubt if he ever attempted to ana-

[37] See, as the most recent contribution, L. J. Hall, "A Partnership in Peacemaking: Theodore Roosevelt and Wilhelm II," *Pacific Historical Review*, XIII (1944), 390–411.

lyze systematically the existing or future relationship of his country to Europe. For the most part he operated, in his joyous way, in the less complicated and less dangerous arenas of the Far East and Latin America, where the Big Stick pointed the way for Dollar Diplomacy. As for Europe, there was no thought in his or in the popular mind of any real or effective participation. One of our eminent American historians, the late Archibald Cary Coolidge, who himself recognized the nature of the problems that were opening before us, felt bound to admit, when he wrote *The United States as a World Power* in 1906, that there was little popular knowledge of European affairs and that the American attitude was still one of detachment and indifference.

Had it not been so, it is unthinkable that President Wilson should have been able, in 1914, to call on the country to remain neutral in thought as well as in act. Wilson himself was entirely engrossed in problems of domestic reform and unquestionably resented the troubles in Europe that threatened to interfere with his program. Like most Americans, he was shocked by the callous German violation of Belgian neutrality, but neither he nor his fellow citizens were prepared to draw any conclusions from the imperial assault. Sympathy for the Allies was strong in the East and South, but in the influential Middle West the German-American elements were strongly organized and exceedingly vocal in noting the transgressions of the British. What it all came to was a generally prevalent attitude, only too familiar from the past, that there was not much to choose between the antagonists, that the war was simply one more chapter in the disgusting chronicle of European ambition and conflict, and that the only sensible policy for America was to stay out of it at all costs. In this instance, however, the traditional reaction to European strife was reinforced by fear lest involvement lead to racial strife within the Union. This possibility was constantly in the President's mind, and was succinctly stated some fifteen years later by the most influential isolationist leader, the late Senator William E. Borah:

This country has within her boundary people from almost every land under the sun, still conscious under certain conditions of the "mystic chords of memory." Every civilization has made its contribution to the American civilization. How easy to transfer the racial antipathies and political views and controversies of the Old World into our very midst. Once abandon our policy of aloofness from European controversies and we bring these European controversies into the American home and into our national life.[38]

Of course the President could not overlook entirely the fact that the United States, as a great and powerful nation, was bound to be affected by the outcome of the struggle in Europe. "The interests of all nations are our own also," he said in a speech of May 27, 1916. "We are partners with the rest. What affects mankind is inevitably our affair as well as the affair of the nations of Europe and Asia."

Nevertheless, he fought and won the electoral campaign of November 1916 on the issue of keeping the country out of war. Despite all the tribulations of neutrality, he surely had no intention of intervening on one side or the other. He had gradually become convinced that "we can no longer indulge our traditional provincialism. We are to play a leading part in the world drama whether we wish it or not" (September 2, 1916), but for him this part was to be that of mediator, as midwife to bring about the birth of a new and better world. More than any other American statesman, President Wilson was imbued with the idea of the national mission. As far back as September 27, 1915, he had remarked, "I hope we shall never forget that we created this nation not to serve ourselves, but to serve mankind," and on April 17, 1916, "The only excuse that America can ever have for the assertion of her physical force is that she asserts it in behalf of the interest of humanity."

Wilson's great objective, then, was not to determine and safeguard specific, concrete national interests, but to choose the crucial moment to more or less impose upon Europe a system based on American conceptions of liberty and justice. In his great address of January 22, 1917 —that is, before America's entry into the war—he proposed that all the nations with one accord should adopt the Monroe Doctrine as the doctrine of the world:

> That no nation should seek to extend its polity over any other nation or people, but that every people should be left free to determine its own polity, its own way of development, unhindered, unthreatened, unafraid, the little along with the great and powerful.

> I am proposing that all nations henceforth avoid entangling alliance which would draw them into competitions of power, catch them in a

38 William E. Borah, "American Foreign Policy in a Nationalistic World," *Foreign Affairs*, XII, supplement (January 1934), iii–xii.

net of intrigue and selfish rivalry, and disturb their own affairs with influences intruded from without. There is no entangling alliance in a concert of power.

These principles, declared the President, were American principles, but they were also the principles of forward-looking and enlightened people everywhere: "These are the principles of mankind and must prevail."

Here, then, you have a program not of intervention on one side of a European conflict, but a program of utilizing that conflict to remake the world by the application of American influence and power. Within a matter of weeks we made the fateful decision, and the President was able to proclaim (April 2, 1917) that "the world must be made safe for democracy. Its peace must be planted upon the trusted foundations of political liberty."

I do not propose to discuss here the controversial question of why the United States intervened in the war. My opinion, shared I believe by most serious students, is that the country was not maneuvered into war either by British propaganda or by the machinations of bankers and munitions-makers anxious to save their huge investments. The decisive factor, I am persuaded, was the unrestricted German submarine warfare which, though it involved less material loss than the British interference with our trade, did result in loss of American lives and did constitute an outrageous affront to American rights and honor. As a demonstration of ruthlessness and disdain for legality, the German policy underlined the methods of militarism and brought home to countless Americans a realization that a victory of imperial Germany would mean the end of democracy in Europe and thereby a direct threat to the United States itself. It was recognition of this threat that enabled the President to cut across the lines of conflicting sympathies and unite all elements in the country behind the war effort.

But the United States never took its place, properly speaking, in the ranks of a European coalition. We were never allied with Britain and France. We were only associated with them. Our entrance into the fray came at just the crucial moment when Russia was dropping out and when the future for Britain and France was all but hopeless. Looked at in realistic terms one might argue that we could not afford to let a power like imperial Germany win control of the European Continent. So responsible a writer as Walter Lippmann, who as a young man was associated with Colonel House, has stated very explicitly that these thoughts were prominent in the minds of the President's advisers. It is Lippmann's conviction that "if the Germans had not broken into the Atlantic and threatened the whole structure of our Atlantic defenses, private citizens would still have made faces at the Kaiser, but the nation would not have made war upon him." [39]

But it is not at all clear that the President himself was much moved by such considerations. Indeed, Lippmann takes him severely to task for phrasing the issue in strictly idealistic and moralistic terms. The President and the whole American people felt that they were embarking upon a great crusade, proud to announce that they had no selfish motives, that they were battling against an abominable system in behalf of self-determination, democracy, and a new world order.

The President's ringing wartime addresses were full of religious fervor, to say nothing of almost offensive self-righteousness. When he came to England after the victory, he was at pains to spare the people of Manchester any illusion. In his speech of December 30, 1919 he stated his position uncompromisingly:

> You know that the United States has always felt from the beginning of her history that she must keep herself separated from any kind of connection with European politics, and I want to say very frankly to you that she is not now interested in European politics. But she is interested in the partnership of right between America and Europe. If the future had nothing for us but a new attempt to keep the world at a right poise by balance of power, the United States would take no interest, because she will join in no combination of power which is not the combination of all of us. She is not interested merely in the peace of Europe, but in the peace of the world.

We need not rehearse here the sad experiences of the President at the Paris Peace Conference, where he found more attention for concrete questions of territory and security than interest in the larger schemes for world organization to which he had dedicated himself. Concessions he had to make, but at least he secured agreement on a League of Nations, and to him that was the essential thing. On his return home he was unrepentant and confident. He declared in an address of September 5, 1919,

> America is made up of the peoples of the world. All the best bloods of the world flow in her veins, all the old affections, all the old and

[39] Lippmann, *United States Foreign Policy*, pp. 33 ff.

sacred traditions of peoples of every sort throughout the wide world circulate in her veins, and she has said to mankind at her birth: "We have come to redeem the world by giving it liberty and justice."

There can be little doubt that the American people, and for that matter the European peoples as well, had followed the leadership of Wilson with enthusiasm. Everything points to the fact that in 1919–20 the American public was prepared to accept the responsibility that the war and the peace had imposed. It was conveniently discovered that even Washington had not envisaged isolation as an eternal necessity but had, on the contrary, foreseen the time "when, our institutions being firmly consolidated and working with complete success, we might safely and perhaps beneficially take part in the consultations held by foreign states for the advantage of the nations."

The idea of the League was popular and enjoyed wide support from both political parties. All the influence engendered by the peace and arbitration movements was behind it, and to the federally-minded Americans it made excellent sense. And yet the Senate, after an unprecedently acrimonious debate, rejected both the Treaty of Versailles and the League of Nations.

How are we to explain this extraordinary contradiction? It is, I think, quite generally agreed that the reasons for Wilson's failure were largely personal. Though the majority of Congress was Republican, he had excluded that party from any significant part in the negotiations. Added to this, he had made a fateful concession when, in order to make the League palatable to the French, he had signed a treaty of guarantee which smacked strongly of the old-fashioned diplomacy which he himself had denounced. But above all, the President, though already ill and unable to exercise his influence with the country to the full, showed himself unbelievably headstrong. He flatly refused to accept amendments which might have served as a sop to isolationist sentiment and in general dealt with the Senate in so uncompromising a way that the larger issue became submerged under a flood of personal antagonism. But this is probably not the whole story. It is altogether likely that the President, having put the whole issue on an altruistic basis, failed to demonstrate a vital American interest that would be served by undertaking onerous obligations. In the words of Walter Lippmann, "the longer the Senate debated the Treaty of Versailles with its covenant, the more the people felt that there was no compelling connection between their vital interests and the program which President Wilson offered them." [40]

In any event it is clear that the effect of the great League debate was to drive the American people back into what President Wilson himself described as their "sullen and selfish isolation." Suspicion and dislike characterized our attitude toward Europe once more.

Revelations of the sordid dickering at the Peace Conference, reports of the rampant nationalism of the new European states, the spectacle of new alliance systems of the old type emerging in Europe—all these things played their part in reinforcing popular disgust and reviving the time-honored aversion to all commitments. Worst of all was the dispute about war debts and the flood of criticism of Uncle Shylock from abroad. This seemed like poor recompense for our contribution, and it undoubtedly raised American hostility to the boiling point. The end result was a violent nationalistic reaction. These were the days of the Ku Klux Klan, the days when we imposed rigorous limitations on further immigration, the days when we assiduously purged our textbooks of "Unamericanisms" and applied ourselves in earnest to the task of systematically "Americanizing" the foreign-born. In the economic sphere we were now creditors rather than debtors, and we hastily set up those high tariff walls which were to protect us from the efforts of Europe to pay its debts. Even in the cultural sphere we finally made the great break. "Our cultural humility before the civilizations of Europe is the chief obstacle which prevents us from producing any true indigenous culture of our own," wrote one critic, who concluded that our "cultural chauvinism . . . can hardly be too intense, or too exaggerated." [41]

This sounds a bit brutal, but the fact remains that it led to a remarkable flowering—to what some people regard as the first glorious outburst of truly American literature. At long last we began to have writers of non-English extraction and writers who no longer viewed their country from an Anglo-Saxon standpoint or shunned the problems of the immigrant elements. In the course of a couple of decades American society was subjected to close critical scrutiny in a style that was distinctly a departure from the orthodox. Cheap deflation there was in plenty, but it is decidedly worth noting that the general tone was

[40] *Ibid.*, p. 38.
[41] Randolph Bourne, quoted by Clark, *University of Toronto Quarterly*, II (1933), 503.

affirmative even when critical, and that the tendency was distinctly toward rejection of the Old World in favor of the New. It was a splendid achievement—one which, I might say, has been perhaps more appreciatively recognized abroad than at home.[42]

Yet for all this nationalism it would be a grave error to underrate the strength of sentiment in behalf of continued international cooperation. In nonpolitical matters our government collaborated with the League and at most international conferences we were represented at least by "unofficial observers." In the struggle for disarmament and peace we took a prominent part. The Kellogg-Briand Pact, after all, was as much an American as a European achievement. So also in the economic sphere we could not hold aloof. The Dawes and Young Plans for dealing with the German reparations problem are alone sufficient evidence of this. Indeed, I think it is safe to say that between the two wars American business men were as a group pre-eminent in their appreciation of the world's economic interdependence, just as the intellectuals as a class stood out in favor of international organization. Even in the days of rampant nationalism and isolationism there were always many voices recalling to us our duties and our responsibilities.[43]

This brings us to the decade of the great world depression and the concomitant rise of the aggressive dictatorships. Obviously we cannot here recount all the episodes on the road that led again to cataclysm. On the American side it ought to be said, however, that statesmen like President Franklin D. Roosevelt, Secretary Henry L. Stimson, and Secretary Cordell Hull recognized the eventual dangers at an early date. From the time of the Manchurian crisis of 1931 onward, Washington showed a marked disposition to work with the League in the effort to check aggression. Unhappily some of the leading members of the international organization, for reasons we cannot stop to analyze, were unwilling to face the ultimate consequences. In retrospect we see the sad spectacle of the breakdown and disintegration of the League system just as the United States was coming to the point of assuming its share of the responsibilities. Perhaps I should state the proposition in reverse, but the conclusion would be the same. Rightly or wrongly the American people blamed the European powers for their failure to check aggression. The worse things became, the less we wanted to have to do with them.

[42] Jones, *Ideas in America*, chaps. 1 and 11.
[43] See, e.g., Frank H. Simonds, *Can America Stay at Home?* (New York, 1932).

In the years between the Ethiopian crisis and the downfall of France, American isolationism reached its apogee. In our neutrality legislation of August 24, 1935, it found its most extreme expression. It seems clear that the agitation for rigid neutrality was due in large measure to the report of a Congressional Investigating Committee which had come to the conclusion that munitions and other related interests were the nefarious engineers of our participation in the First World War. It therefore seemed wise to prevent a repetition of the earlier situation. Congress therefore legislated the arms traffic out of existence and, forgetting our traditional assertion of neutral rights, abandoned principles of freedom of the seas in the hope that by staying religiously at home we could avoid getting into trouble.

It stands to reason that this drastic treatment of the situation aroused substantial opposition. Critics maintained that it was immoral, in so far as it failed to discriminate between an aggressor nation and its victim. We might, it was pointed out, actually find ourselves in the position of aiding the aggressor. Furthermore, the policy of neutrality was tantamount to repudiation of our responsibility for peace, and completely ignored the fact that our own interest demanded that we intervene energetically to prevent aggression.[44]

But for the time being, the isolationists or, as they preferred to be known, the "continentalists," were decidedly in the ascendant. The Middle West was almost solidly so, not because of pro-Nazi sympathies, of course, but because of its devotion to pure and unadulterated "Americanism." The whole country, indeed, was flooded with writings highly critical of the European system, most of which concluded with warnings against entanglement. None were more vigorous than the Americans in their denunciation of the British appeasement policy, and there were not a few who came to the uncomfortable conviction that there was little to choose between any of the European powers. They were all defaulters on their debts, all politically inept, and all incorrigible intriguers for power. As for the British and French, they were forever trying to enlist the innocent Americans to fight in behalf of their rotten systems and their outworn empires. Why should the United States sacrifice men and treasure in the interest of others? Let the European nations clean their house in their own way. We fought one war to make the

---

44 An admirable presentation of this side of the argument is given by Allen W. Dulles and Hamilton Fish Armstrong, *Can We Be Neutral?* (New York, 1936).

world safe for democracy, and all we had reaped for our efforts was a crop of dictatorships and a harvest of aggressions. America, surely, had learned its lesson. The greatest contribution we could make would be to stay at home, mind our own business and make sure that democracy retained one safe haven in a world at war.[45]

As aforesaid, President Roosevelt and Secretary Hull did their utmost to convince the American people that even though we had no concern with purely European problems, we had a genuine and direct interest at least in cooperating with other nations to maintain peace. Mr. Hull said on February 16, 1935,

> We have no direct concern with the political and economic controversies of the European states. We have time and again expressly disassociated ourselves from these disputes. Nevertheless, we are deeply interested in the peace and stability of Europe as a whole and have therefore taken part in a number of multilateral efforts to achieve this purpose.[46]

So much at least was unobjectionable. But the President sounded a new and more ominous note in his famous Quarantine Speech of October 5, 1937. In this he called for common action against aggressors, arguing that

> there is a solidarity and interdependence about the modern world, both technically and morally, which makes it impossible for any nation completely to isolate itself from economic and political upheavals in the rest of the world, especially when such upheavals appear to be spreading and not declining.

But this suggestion at once produced an outburst of opposition and protestation. It was clear that the country would have none of such a program and the President himself realized that in future he must be more circumspect. Secretary Hull on March 17, 1938, said:

> We may seek to withdraw from participation in world affairs, but we cannot thereby withdraw from the world itself. Isolation is not a means to security; it is a fruitful source of insecurity.

[45] Among a deluge of writings see Arthur H. Vandenberg, *The Trail of a Tradition* (New York, 1926), and particularly Charles A. Beard, *A Foreign Policy for America* (New York, 1940).

[46] Similarly President Roosevelt's comment on the Neutrality Law, August 31, 1935.

Here and there writers like Lippmann tried to get beyond generalities and down to concrete national interests:

> A fatal blow struck at the heart of the British power would not merely destroy the international unity of the Empire; it would mean the destruction of all international order as we have known it . . . In the final test, no matter what we wish now or now believe, though collaboration with Britain and her allies is difficult and often irritating, we shall protect that connection because in no other way can we fulfill our destiny.[47]

But even in 1939 these admonitions were unwelcome. I do not mean to say that the country had no interest or sympathy one way or the other. Public sentiment was overwhelmingly on the side of the democracies, and there was almost no trace of the racial split that had been so prominent in 1914. But neither Congress nor the country would listen to any policy that might involve us in a second crusade abroad. According to the simon-pure isolationists it was really none of our business. Thus Senator Gerald P. Nye, in a speech of August 24, 1939, assured the country:

> In the present European controversy, the cause of Democracy is no more involved than is the cause of American women's suffrage or liquor prohibition. The cause there is that old, old one of power politics. It is a cause that we cannot meddle in unless we are ready and anxious to jeopardize the life of the one remaining great democracy, our own.

European wars, added Senator Borah, are "wars brought on through the manipulation and unconscionable schemes of remorseless rulers."

As against these self-assured pronunciamentos, Colonel Henry L. Stimson warned (October 5, 1939) "that Britain and France are now fighting a battle which, in the event of their losing, will, whether we wish it or not, become our battle," and President Roosevelt, in his New Year's address of 1940, denounced

> those who wishfully insist, in innocence or ignorance, or both, that the United States of America, as a self-contained unit, can live happily and prosperously, its future secure, inside a high wall of isolation,

---

[47] Walter Lippmann, "Rough-hew Them How We Will," *Foreign Affairs,* XV (July 1937), 587–594; similarly Raymond L. Buell, "Is an Anglo-American Understanding Possible?" *International Affairs,* XVI (January 1937), 45–69.

while outside the rest of civilization and the commerce and culture of mankind are shattered.

But until the Phony War, with its easy assurance of ultimate victory over Hitler by application of blockade, came to an abrupt end, the country was essentially unmoved. As the final testament of isolationism, Senator Arthur H. Vandenberg, at that time a confirmed "nationalist," produced an appeal to reality (February 10, 1940):

> We must ever take counsel of reality. Reality says we cannot hope to control the destiny of power politics in the Old World. We tried it twenty years ago and failed . . . Reality tells us that our own stupendous obligation to democracy is to keep its torch alight in this New World. Reality warns us that if we enter this appalling conflict we shall come from it in bankruptcy and with our liberties in chains.

The great awakening came when Hitler's armies overran the Low Countries, drove the British from the Continent, and turned their deadly power on the staggering French forces. Gone then overnight was the old isolationism. In the President's words (June 10, 1940):

> Some indeed still hold to the now obvious delusion that we of the United States can safely permit the United States to become a lone island, a lone island in a world dominated by the philosophy of force. Such an island may be the dream of those who still talk and vote as isolationists. Such an island represents to me and to the overwhelming majority of Americans today a helpless nightmare, the helpless nightmare of a people lodged in prison, handcuffed, hungry and fed through the bars from day to day by the contemptuous, unpitying masters of other continents.

With anxiety we followed the fate of the French fleet, and with dire apprehension we watched the German air attack on Britain. At one awful stroke most Americans came to the realization that if Britain went under and the British fleet fell into Hitler's hands, we, with our fleets concentrated in the Pacific, would be fully exposed in the Atlantic—exposed to a powerful Germany controlling the resources of a continent.

Gone was the time for hair-splitting arguments or for reverent adoration of tradition. A few die-hard isolationists, like Lindbergh, might tell us that no one had designs upon our territory or wealth and that in any case we could still defend ourselves behind our ocean barrier. Few believed them. Even the isolationists in Congress joined in the mad scramble to vote defense bills as fast as the administration could throw them together. The Atlantic had suddenly become very narrow and Europe very close. Even isolationists hastened to rally to a policy of supporting Britain to the utmost of our then limited ability.

Looking back we can see now that in the summer of 1940 American opinion was seized with panic. There was still strong and almost universal opposition to sending our boys abroad, but many people were coming to see that eventually it might become necessary—necessary in our own interest. As it became clear in the winter of 1940–41 that Britain might hold, there was a final upsurge of isolationism as represented by the American First Committee, but even this was not enough to block passage of the Lend-Lease legislation. We held off intervention as long as we could—indeed until the Japanese solved the problem for us and Hitler and Mussolini obliged us by taking further decisions out of our hands. The details are still fresh in all minds, and I will not labor them. The main idea which I should like to convey is that the summer of 1940 marked for the American people a revolution of attitude towards Europe—a revolution which I for one believe will prove permanent.[48] This opinion I base on the thought that the events of June 1940 revealed to Americans what no amount of argument or suasion had induced them to see, namely, that for us, as for Britons before us, it is intolerable that any one power should control the manpower and resources of the European continent and that therefore any nations that resist such domination must be supported, even to the point of our own military intervention. The ideological considerations are important, and we clearly have an interest in preserving democracy wherever possible. But the crucial thing is, and remains, the relationship or balance of power. There was a time when the British were Little Englanders and felt safe behind a Channel guarded by the world's most powerful fleet. Those days passed and fortunately the British people recognized their passing. The Americans, in the meanwhile, have gone through somewhat the same evolution, underlined by the phenomenal shrinkage of the Atlantic.

To me it is inconceivable that the American people should ever again backslide into isolationism or continentalism. They were halcyon days for us when that was possible. But they are gone beyond recall

---

[48] See in this connection the interesting lecture by W. W. Rostow, *The American Diplomatic Revolution* (Oxford, 1946).

and the conditions which made non-entanglement practicable are not apt ever to return. All of us realize, of course, what the coming of atomic warfare may mean for our own country as well as for the world at large. We know that our fate is closely tied to that of the whole world and that, in fact, the future of the world hinges largely on our leadership. To say that the situation in Europe and the world is today a grave one is to utter the worst of platitudes. No one can say how it will be solved, and we can only express hope that it will not again be necessary to resort to war.

Americans argue incessantly about this great issue, as indeed they should. But the arguments all revolve around such questions as to how the United Nations can be made more effective, how a check can be put upon the inexorable march of the Soviet dictatorship? Excepting for a few diehard isolationists and followers of Henry Wallace there are few who suggest that we wash our hands of Europe and the world or that we enclose ourselves in our own continent or hemisphere. Our armies stand deep in Europe, and we are proposing to support the independence of countries like Greece and Turkey with all our might, not excluding the military. At the same time we are undertaking to apply our every effort to the rehabilitation of western Europe and to its strengthening against possible aggression. Slowly we are coming to see that the system of western Europe is no longer exactly our system of free enterprise. We regret it but we try to understand it.

Meanwhile we shall not falter and I am sure that if, unhappily, western Europe is again obliged to defend its independence and existence, we shall be found in its ranks. In all this, sentiment of course plays its part. We are more conscious than ever that we are all part of the Atlantic community, that in the last analysis there is no greater difference between ourselves and the Europeans than among various European peoples themselves. But beyond sentiment there is that most important factor in all international relations, which is national interest. We saw it dimly in 1917–18 but we looked away. Today it is vivid in the mind of every American. It no longer requires argument or pleading, and for that reason I am convinced the old distinction between the Old and the New Worlds is bound to sink into oblivion.

In bringing this all too hasty survey to a close, I can hardly do better than to recall and mentally expand to all Europe the words of your own great statesman, pronounced at the time of the Destroyers-for-Bases Deal in 1940:

> Undoubtedly this process means that these two great organizations of the English-speaking democracies, the British Empire and the United States, will have to be somewhat mixed up together in some of their affairs for mutual and general advantage. For my own part, looking out upon the future, I do not view the process with any misgivings. I could not stop it if I wished; no one can stop it. Like the Mississippi, it just keeps rolling along. Let it roll. Let it roll on full flood, inexorable, irresistible, benignant, to broader lands and better days.

16

Political Problems of a Coalition

1947

Defeat in war invariably brings in its wake an avalanche of apologetic writing by the losers. The leaders of the vanquished nation are intent on exonerating themselves; men of action, military and political, who made history without much thought of how it would be written, suddenly become concerned about the opinions of posterity. A debate, for the most part quite unedifying, begins at once and is apt to continue far beyond the point where it is of interest to any but historians.

The victors, on the other hand, are less given to post mortems. Having been convinced from the outset of the justice of their cause and the rightness of their policy, they take success as a matter of course. The seamy side of the conflict is soon forgotten, and the uncertainties, the long chances, the wretched blunders are conveniently glossed over if not ignored. Books and articles on this last war there are in plenty, but for the most part they are in the nature of thrilling narrative, panegyrical biography, or personal reminiscence. And yet it is perhaps even more necessary for the victors to take counsel with themselves and essay an honest appraisal of the record. Victory is a heady draught, all too apt to breed overconfidence and self-delusion. History is punctuated by disasters which followed on the heels of success, springing from exaggerated notions of past achievement or extravagant conceptions of national prowess.

Since war is indeed but a continuation of policy by other means, it follows inexorably that once hostilities have broken out political decisions must be subordinated to the requirements of strategy. In such circumstances traditional policies may have to be abandoned, natural sympathies may have to be sacrificed. The problem is further complicated by the fact that most modern wars are fought by coalitions of states that are frequently, nay almost proverbially, strange bedfellows. One overriding interest—that of defeating a common enemy—may

Note: Reprinted from *Foreign Affairs*, XXIV (October 1947), 73–89, copyright the Council on Foreign Relations, Inc., New York.

bring them together, but a dozen other interests may drive them apart. Diplomatic revolutions are the stuff of which the drama of history is made. They are the nightmare of statesmen, whose incessant task during a war is to obviate friction between allies and to reconcile as best may be the diverging aims of the associated powers, at least until the victory is won.

So far as the United States is concerned, the recent world conflict divides naturally into the periods of our nonbelligerency and of our active participation. During the first phase the important decisions were of necessity political, while during the second they were pre-eminently military, though, of course, political considerations remained of moment all the way through and again became predominant as the war drew toward its close.

Under our constitutional system the executive power is concentrated in the President, who is much more the effective head of the government than in most other democratic states. In the field of foreign policy his authority is almost unrestricted. In the words of a Supreme Court decision: "in this vast external realm, with its important, complicated, delicate and manifold problems, the President alone has the power to speak or listen as a representative of the nation." He is, therefore, the very fountainhead of policy, limited in his decision only by his own judgment of what the Congress and the people will approve and support. At the same time, however, he is the commander-in-chief of the armed forces and therefore has the final word in all matters of strategy and operations. Through the union of civil and military authority in one man we are spared the all-too-common and sometimes disastrous conflict between politicians and soldiers, and we avoid serious divergence between policy and strategy. When wisely exercised, the presidential authority makes for singleness of purpose and unity of action. Thus far in our history the system has worked successfully. Whether by divine dispensation or by pure luck, in all major crises we have had presidents who were equal to the occasion.

Franklin D. Roosevelt's role as the maker and director of American foreign policy is likely to be a matter of violent dispute for a long time to come, perhaps even beyond the time when his papers are made available for scholarly study. During the last few years of his life, Harry Hopkins probably knew his mind pretty intimately, but in the first eight or nine years of his administration the President does not appear to have confided much in any one man. His relations with Mr. Hull were based on complete loyalty and tremendous mutual respect, but the two men were so different in temperament that there could be no real intimacy. The President, of course, conferred and discussed with other men too. He relied heavily on Mr. Sumner Welles and for some years was influenced by the views of Mr. Bullitt. But no one person got the whole picture, no one person was permitted the inwardness of the President's thoughts or the vision of his ultimate objectives. Under the circumstances it is hard to speak authoritatively, and in some cases one can do little more than conjecture.

The President was unusually well equipped by education and experience to deal with international affairs, yet during the early years of his administration he appears to have been so engrossed by domestic issues as to have given little attention to foreign problems, either political or economic. He was apparently quite disillusioned about international organization and collective security and quite insensible to the importance of the crisis in international trade. His one compelling foreign interest in the early period was the development of the Good Neighbor Policy and the furtherance of hemispheric solidarity. This, to be sure, was a notable exception and was to prove itself one of the most successful of his policies. It need not be discussed in any detail here, though we may note that, viewed in the context of the early years of the Roosevelt Administration, even the Good Neighbor Policy was only an expression of a modified isolationism. The President, whose thoughts were centered on national reform and national welfare, expanded his conception to the whole hemisphere. Yet basically the idea was the same, reflecting a hope for self-sufficiency.

It was only during the second term, when crisis began to follow crisis both in Europe and the Far East, that the President's attention began to focus on the international scene and his basic foreign policies began to take form. The famous "quarantine" speech at Chicago in October 1937, though still shrouded in considerable mystery, at least revealed an acute sense of the world danger and a keen realization of the possible repercussions of the foreign situation on our own national interests. With a suddenness that shocked the country, the President not only expounded his views but proceeded to outline a policy. The change was too abrupt and the proposal too vague and ominous for popular sentiment. The President drew back, and for more than a year did not again express himself so flatly and forcefully.

Nonetheless, it is beyond doubt that long before the outbreak of the war in Europe Mr. Roosevelt's ideas had taken definite form and had begun to crystallize into policy. He detested the dictatorships and all that they stood for, and he regarded their aggressiveness as at least an ultimate threat to this hemisphere and this country. Although public opinion generally shared his aversion, it was for the most part skeptical about the implications of what was loosely called Fascism. There was a good deal of applause for the President's repeated and sometimes unmeasured castigation of Hitler and his ilk, yet there was almost universal opposition to any specific action by this government, however mild. The President's advocacy of "methods short of war" received a cold reception, and his urgent requests for repeal of the arms embargo were turned down despite his insistence that repeal would strengthen his influence for peace. For all its reprobation of Fascist aggression, the American public in 1939 was disgusted with the rest of the world and was determined not to jeopardize its domestic policies or its peace.

Through the American Foreign Service, the Washington government was probably more fully and accurately informed about the world situation on the eve of the crisis than was any other government in the world. The President and his advisers were under no illusions about the ultimate objectives of Germany, Italy, and Japan, nor did they have exaggerated notions about the ability of Britain and France to resist successfully. Envisaging, as they did, the possibility of a Nazi victory in Europe and an effective combination of the German and Japanese efforts, they appreciated to the full the ultimate danger to Latin America and the United States. Their policy, therefore, was to give all possible support to the democracies, within the limitations of the law and the bounds of public opinion. And so was born the first and most fundamental of American policies connected with the war— the identification of our long-term interests with those of Britain and France and the extension of all possible aid to those countries.

This policy was initiated in a very modest way by facilitating the purchase and manufacture of airplanes in this country. Yet when such aid was accidentally revealed in February 1939, it created such a furor in Congress and in the press that it probably deterred the President from too great insistence on repeal of the arms embargo. Only after the agreement between Hitler and Stalin, and Germany's conquest of Poland, was repeal of the embargo carried through Congress by handsome majorities. Although little public reference was made to the full significance of the repeal, it was well understood that the prime objective of the President was to make munitions and supplies available to the democracies. We may therefore conclude that Congress, in repealing the embargo, reflected a growing willingness on the part of the public to follow the President's lead.

It is common knowledge that during the first winter of war the Allies did not take full advantage of the chance to purchase American supplies. They were costly, and the need of them was not fully appreciated. The period of the "phony war" was brought to an abrupt end by the German invasion of Scandinavia, which sent shivers of apprehension through this country as well as through Britain and France. Then came the spectacular collapse of France. In a matter of weeks the prospects of victory had been completely reversed, and Britain herself appeared to be on the verge of invasion and conquest. Along with many others, the President waited from day to day—one might say literally from hour to hour—for news that the German attack on the British Isles had begun. He realized more clearly than most Americans that if Britain went under, our bulwark in the Atlantic would be gone and that before long we might be faced with a war on two ocean fronts.

But even though Mr. Roosevelt expected the invasion of Britain, he stuck at all times to the hope that the British would be able to resist successfully. Faith in British determination enabled him to make the fateful decision to send abroad all available matériel without delay, though it should be added that American opinion was not slow in grasping the magnitude of the danger and in tacitly approving whatever action the President deemed necessary. The famous destroyers-for-bases deal, put over in the dark days of September 1940, evoked remarkably little criticism, partly no doubt because the whole transaction was a masterstroke, as important for our own security as it was for the maintenance of Britain's supply lines.

Looking back, we can now see clearly enough that the summer and early autumn of 1940 were the most critical phase of the whole war and that Hitler came nearer victory then than at any later period. That being so, it can be said with considerable assurance that the decision to give all possible support to Britain in her most dangerous hour was the most important and courageous decision made by the United States government during the entire war period. Europe was in Hitler's hands, and when we decided to support Britain we knew that we might be putting our money on the wrong horse. But the consequences of Britain's defeat were so ominous that we had to take the chance. No matter how desperate the situation, it was still better for us to throw our weight into the struggle than to abandon the last outpost and await the Nazi advance on this side of the Atlantic. We took a chance on Britain, and we won.

The concluding chapter of the program of aiding the anti-Axis forces was written in the Lend-Lease Act of March 1941, which was precipitated by the inability of the British to continue to pay cash for munitions and supplies. As an operational device the Lend-Lease Act made possible for the first time the extension of unlimited aid not only to Britain but to any government engaged in fighting an aggressor. It was literally the key to victory, opening wide the doors to the American arsenal.

No positive decision comparable to these decisions in our European policy was ever taken with relation to the Far Eastern situation. If reckoned from the Japanese invasion of Manchuria, the crisis in Asia antedated the Roosevelt administration as well as the beginning of aggression by Italy and Germany. In one sense our consistent support of nationalist China against Japan was the prototype of our program of aid to France and Britain. But our policy in Asia, which promised in the first instance to be the touchstone of our entire attitude toward the growing world crisis, never came into clear focus. Originally, Secretary Stimson had proposed a bold move to check aggression, and it is quite conceivable that if his proposal had been accepted not only Japan, but Italy and Germany might have been deterred by collective action. Actually, however, nothing was done to block the realization of the Japanese program, and when the rape of Manchuria was followed by the advance into North China in 1937, the tension in Europe was already so great that it was hardly more feasible for the United States government to take a strong line than for the British to do so. The President and his advisers from that time on adopted an inconclusive position, reflected in the policy of nonrecognition and buttressed by a program of active though modest support for the government of Chiang Kai-shek. We had, of course, much more effective weapons in our armory; and, in general, American opinion was more disposed to use them in the Far East than in Europe. But the President and Secretary Hull felt, no doubt correctly, that the United States could not afford to become seriously involved with Japan without thereby encouraging aggression in Europe. Our decision with regard to the Far East, then, was essentially a negative one. We muddled along, objecting and protesting and trying to deter Japan by shrouding our policy in uncertainty until the Japanese themselves cut the Gordian knot at Pearl Harbor.

It has often been argued that if we had proceeded firmly with a policy of economic sanctions for Japan, we might have discredited the Japanese militarists and strengthened the liberal, civilian elements with which some sort of acceptable compromise might have been worked out. But actually there is little if any evidence that the Japanese warlords could have been deterred in their plans, which they regarded as vital to the national interest. The chances are, rather, that a positive policy on our part would have provoked hostilities when we were unprepared for them, and when lack of American support might have meant defeat for Britain in Europe. Viewed in this light, the decision not to join issue in the Far East was perhaps as important as any positive decision we could have come to. The Japanese militarists were left to assume the odium of aggression, while the astonishingly prompt declaration of war by Hitler and Mussolini relieved the government and the country of a decision which, though it was by that time recognized as inevitable, would nonetheless have been a hard one to arrive at. Had we had our choice, we should probably have elected to stay out of the war for another six months at least. But Pearl Harbor, bad as it was, would have been a greater naval disaster had it come a year or six months earlier; and there were inestimable political advantages to this country in having the ultimate decision to go to war in Asia and in Europe imposed upon it.

Decisions which turn on questions of ideology, are, of course, "political," but they are much less amenable to dispassionate analysis and less susceptible of proof one way or the other than are specific diplomatic problems. We sometimes set them apart by calling them "moral problems." Their effects are usually vague and intangible, yet their importance is great. They were given full weight from the very beginning by so consummate a politician as President Roosevelt. Long before the outbreak of war in Europe the President had hoped to arouse world opinion against the aggressors and had directed his efforts toward building up sentiment against the dictators even in their own countries.

Hitler's position was too strong to enable the President to make much headway in that direction, but he did succeed in unifying and galvanizing opinion in the democracies—in reinforcing the conviction that in the end free men would win. The fact that the Nazi leaders were always apprehensive of his influence is perhaps the best evidence of the importance of his leadership.

In keeping with his belief in the significance of the imponderables, the President began to concern himself from the beginning of the conflict with plans for a peace settlement that would end the era of international conflict. He was convinced that men fought best when they knew what they were fighting for, when they had some vision of a better world to follow the tribulations of war. He recognized that even in the aggressor countries there was an overpowering desire for security and greater economic opportunity. His mind turned rather to these larger issues than to specific questions like territorial disputes. When, in February 1940, Under Secretary Welles was sent on a special mission to Europe to canvass the possibilities of peace, he took with him a memorandum outlining such a program. At the same time the President dispatched a personal representative to the Vatican to enlist the support of the Pope in the cause of an equitable settlement of world problems. Unfortunately most of this activity was unavailing. Instead of ending in a negotiated peace, the war broke into its most violent phase.

No serious political issue was presented by conquered Poland, Denmark, Norway, Belgium or the Netherlands, all of which had set up governments-in-exile which we could and did recognize. But two-fifths of France remained unoccupied under its own government, a government which indeed had concluded an armistice with the Germans and was of necessity more or less under the domination of Hitler, but which nevertheless pretended to some authority in France and to effective control of the French Empire. The question, difficult in itself, was further complicated by the fact that the Vichy government, under Pétain, was decidedly authoritarian in character and made no secret of its hostility to the democratic system.

In this instance, as in later cases, the President refused to subordinate what he believed to be the national interest to purely ideological considerations. He and his advisers had considerable respect for Marshal Pétain, but no sympathy whatever for subordinates like Laval and Darlan. The United States government, like the country, despised the Vichy system and detested the Vichy policy of collaboration with the

Nazis, but the national interest seemed to be best served by maintaining contact with the French and using such influence as we had to prevent the full victory of the collaborationist elements. Of course this meant turning a cold shoulder to de Gaulle and the Free French Committee in London (though we recognized and assisted the Free French in those parts of the empire where they exercised effective control), and it probably threw some shadows over our role as a leader of democracy against Fascism. The fact remains, however, that in cases like this one cannot have one's cake and eat it.[1]

This same problem of compromise with nondemocratic forces was to dog the American government all through the war and beyond the term of hostilities. The main job throughout was to defeat the Nazi and Fascist dictators and the Japanese militarists. In order to do this we had to cooperate with those who held the same purpose. Britain was one of the few democratic régimes on either side of the conflict. No real objection was raised to our support of Chiang Kai-shek, though his régime could be described as a democratic one only by courtesy. But of course the greatest problem was offered by Soviet Russia, where the issue was not compromise with reaction but association with Communism.

The relations between the United States and Russia had not improved after the recognition of the Soviet government in 1933. If anything, they had grown worse as a result of the failure of the U.S.S.R. to live up to its obligations. By 1940 they were about as bad as they could be, and the distrust in government circles was exceeded only by the intense aversion to the U.S.S.R. of the American public. The Communist system, detested as a threat to the social order and a ruthless dictatorship, was at that time in even worse repute as the partner of Nazism.

When Hitler launched his assault on the Soviet Union, the President and the country were confronted with the question whether to support the Communist régime in its struggle against the invader. The choice of government and of the American people was in the affirmative: we would send all possible assistance. In actual fact the United States supplied about 10 percent of the Russian requirements in equipment and munitions, representing crucial items without which the Soviet resistance might have proved futile. Though the decision has certainly pro-

---

[1] William L. Langer, *Our Vichy Gamble* (New York, 1947).

voked much searching of soul in the months since victory was assured, it met with remarkably little criticism at the time. The reason seems to me to be a fairly simple one. At the time the situation of Britain was becoming ever more desperate. The primary question was how the war could be won; and about the only hope of victory seemed to lie in bleeding the Germans white on the plains of Russia. The alternative to aiding Russia was to accept Hitler's oft-renewed peace offers, on the basis of recognizing most of his conquests and giving him a free hand against the U.S.S.R., with the extreme likelihood that he would triumph. And that meant a real and terrible danger of Nazi world conquest. In an explanatory letter to the Pope, President Roosevelt expressed himself quite categorically:

> In my opinion, the fact is that Russia is governed by a dictatorship, as rigid in its manner of being as is the dictatorship in Germany. I believe, however, that this Russian dictatorship is less dangerous to the safety of other nations than is the German form of dictatorship. The only weapon which the Russian dictatorship uses outside of its own borders is Communist propaganda which I, of course, recognize has in the past been utilized for the purpose of breaking down the form of government in other countries, religious belief, et cetera. Germany, however, not only has utilized, but is utilizing, this kind of propaganda as well and has also undertaken the employment of every form of military aggression outside of its borders for the purpose of world conquest by force of arms and by force of propaganda. I believe that the survival of Russia is less dangerous to religion, to the church as such, and to humanity in general than would be the survival of the German form of dictatorship.[2]

In short, the President regarded the Communist dictatorship as the lesser of two evils. But beyond that, as we learn from Mr. Welles' recent book, he at once recognized that understanding and cooperation between Moscow and Washington was one of the indispensable foundations for American foreign policy, and was convinced that a firm agreement with the Soviet government was essential for future peace. He saw no need to fear Communism if an international organization existed, and believed that if Russia could be given security through such an organization, the Communist régime would gradually accommodate itself to the general society of nations. While the Russian and the American systems would probably never meet, they would ap-

[2] *Wartime Correspondence Between President Roosevelt and Pope Pius XII* (New York, 1947), pp. 61–62.

proximate to the point where there would no longer be a serious problem of living together.[3] The President shared an idea common at the time that the cult of world revolution was already receding in the minds of the Soviet leaders and that they were becoming more and more engrossed in purely national problems. And, after all, argued the President, Stalin and his associates could not live forever. It might well be that his successors might adopt a more agreeable line. To all these considerations should probably be added the fact that Russia's strength was underestimated and that there seemed to be reason to suppose that the Soviet régime, even if victorious, would be so seriously weakened as to be dependent on the allied powers and therefore well-disposed to any program of international organization and action.

To what extent this line of reasoning was sound can be determined only after the lapse of years. For the short run, however, it soon proved to be mistaken. During the first six months, when the Germans just barely failed to reach Moscow, the Soviets were cooperative in every way and did their best to play to the western gallery by demonstrations of religious concessions and so forth. But as soon as the tide began to turn, and particularly after the victory at Stalingrad, they began to change their tune. From that time on the British and Americans were in a perpetual quandary, and it would hardly be going too far to say that all the political decisions of the later period of the war hinged more or less directly on consideration of the Russian problem.

In August 1941, the President and Mr. Churchill met in the waters off Argentia, Newfoundland, for the famous conference which produced the Atlantic Charter, a document comparable to the Fourteen Points of President Wilson, but far less specific in its provisions and more general in its appeal. No doubt the primary purpose of the charter was to afford a common program for all anti-Axis forces and to mark out the lines of a peace settlement for which men everywhere would be willing to fight. But aside from its propaganda value in the democratic countries, we may, I think, assume that it was drafted with an eye to Russia. If the Soviet government could be brought to subscribe to the provisions of the charter against territorial aggrandizement and in favor of self-determination of peoples, in favor of equal access to raw materials and freedom of trade, and in favor of a permanent system

[3] Sumner Welles, *Where Are We Heading?* (New York, 1946), pp. 36, 37, 102, 377.

of security and disarmament, clearly the Allied governments could look to the future with a greater measure of assurance. The Soviet leaders made no objection: along with the other anti-Axis governments, they signed the Atlantic Charter and joined the ranks of the United Nations.

But before long the Kremlin began to take a stronger line. There arose the insistent demand for a second front, in addition to the ever-growing requirements for supplies. For a long time a second front in Europe was militarily impossible and had to be evaded or refused. As a result, however, the Allied governments were more and more haunted by the possibility that the Soviet government might find it more advantageous to make a deal with Hitler, an idea which it was obviously in the Soviet interest to circulate. To me it seems that these fears were at all times groundless, for it is difficult to see how any Russian-German pact could have been more than a truce, or how Hitler could possibly have offered Stalin anything to compare to the gains he would make by an Allied victory over Germany. The war gave Russia the chance of centuries to dispose of a chronic menace, and as long as there was even a fair chance of success, the Soviets would have been stupid to accept anything less.

The fact of the matter seems to have been that the Soviet leaders were quite as suspicious of their allies as we were of them. Whether sincerely or otherwise, they took the line that refusal to open a second front was an indication of unwillingness to crush the Nazi power or permit Communist Russia an unqualified victory. It was this mutual suspicion and constant recrimination more than anything else that lay behind the demand for unconditional surrender as formulated by the Casablanca Conference of January 1943 which, incidentally, Stalin refused to attend.

The primary objective of the President and Mr. Churchill at that conference was to reassure the Bolshevik leaders that there would be no compromise with Hitler and that the Allies would fight on to total victory. Whether or not the unconditional surrender formula had the desired effect in the Kremlin we cannot know, but in any event it was a fateful decision; for even if it served to keep the Russians in line, it undoubtedly made the struggle against Nazi Germany more difficult and more prolonged. Far from scaring the Germans into early surrender, it gave the Nazi propagandists their best argument for a last-ditch resistance. On balance it seems that the demand for unconditional surrender was an unfortunate and costly move, and that it was too high a price to pay for Stalin's peace of mind.

The President, influenced no doubt by the widespread criticism of the Paris peacemakers of 1919, seems to have made up his mind at an early date that after the conclusion of hostilities there should be a "cooling-off period" before the negotiation of the final settlement. Like President Wilson before him, he appears to have thought that international organization should come first and that, through collective action, many problems could be disposed of in a spirit of cooperation. Closely related to these ideas was the decision, arrived at with Mr. Churchill, to subordinate everything to the winning of the war and to avoid all political and territorial issues that might provoke dissension among the anti-Axis forces. Sound though this approach might have been, it necessarily presupposed that all parties would postpone final territorial settlements. Actually, the Soviet government never showed the slightest intention of doing so, and serious difficulties arose almost at once. Hardly had the German armies been stopped before Moscow than Stalin began to press General Sikorski for a discussion of the eastern frontier of Poland. It was no secret that the Soviets, while fighting on the side of the western powers, were fully determined to retain all that they had acquired through their partnership with Hitler. Sikorski, and after him Mickolajczyk, firmly refused to sacrifice eastern Poland, insisting that they had no constitutional power to barter with the national heritage. At first both the British and American governments encouraged their stand, though neither Washington nor London was prepared to make an issue of the matter. But by 1943 the British had already weakened considerably, and by 1944 even the President appears to have reconciled himself to Poland's loss of her eastern territories in return for acquisitions at Germany's expense.

By the beginning of 1945 the Soviet armies were already engulfing the Balkan area. Militarily the Allies could do nothing to influence Soviet policy toward countries like Poland, Rumania, Bulgaria, Yugoslavia, Hungary, and even Austria. The remaining possibility was to temper the impending storm by discussion and agreement. The Yalta Conference represented the last, almost desperate effort of the President and Mr. Churchill to hold Stalin to the principles of the Atlantic Charter and to save eastern Europe from Bolshevik domination.

The Yalta Conference, like the preceding meeting at Teheran, concerned itself largely with military matters, in this case with the planning for the final assault on Germany. In reality, of course, the outcome of the war was already assured. The defeat of Germany was merely a matter of time and cost. Neither the western powers nor the Soviets any longer needed each other to clinch the victory. But the President and his advisers, civilian as well as military, still felt that they needed Russian aid to wind up the Far Eastern conflict. It may be, as General Deane says, that no one seriously doubted that the Soviets would eventually enter the war against Japan, for Russian interests in the Far East were too extensive and important to permit of Moscow's exclusion from the final settlement. But it was obviously in Russia's interest to postpone action in the Far East till the latest possible moment, which would mean that the United States forces would bear the entire burden of Japan's defeat. For many months efforts had been made to get Stalin to commit himself, but the timing of Russian intervention was still not fully decided when the Yalta conferees assembled.

Rightly or wrongly the President was prepared to pay a substantial price for a definite agreement by Stalin to participate in the Far Eastern war. The great fear of the Americans at the time was that the Japanese, even after their home islands had been conquered, might attempt to continue the struggle with the large armies they still had in Manchuria and China. Although it seems unlikely that the Japanese could have continued effective operations on the Asiatic mainland, the only guarantee against such an eventuality was active intervention by the Soviet Far Eastern armies. In short, the President felt that the United States still needed Russian support and thereby was put at a disadvantage in discussion with Stalin. He felt obliged to pay a price for Russian intervention, only to discover later that the Soviet contribution in the Far East was little more than a victory parade. Our own atomic bomb served our purposes a hundred times better than did the Soviet armies.

The price paid for this concession in the military sphere was the recognition of Russia's unilateral settlement of the Polish frontier problem, attenuated only by Soviet acceptance of the vague and ill-defined principle that representative, democratic governments should be established in Poland and other liberated countries. And that was not all. With respect to the all-important German settlement, the President agreed to the compensation of Poland by the cession of German territory, accepted the Russian program for reparations in a general way, and consented to the zonal occupation of Germany along lines exceedingly favorable to the Russians. As everyone knows, these arrangements touching Germany were the prelude to the current struggle for power in Europe. It would be interesting and instructive to follow them in all their ramifications, but that would lead us beyond the scope of this essay. Before leaving the decisions of the Yalta Conference, however, something must be said of the agreements bearing on the plans for world organization.

These plans, proclaimed in the Atlantic Charter, were dear to the heart of the President and enjoyed almost universal support in the United States, where there was general agreement that our failure to join the League of Nations was a fatal blunder. Secretary Hull, through his arduous journey to the Moscow Conference in October 1943, had succeeded in aligning the Soviet government with the scheme, and the Dumbarton Oaks Conference of August–October 1944 had produced a preliminary draft for the future United Nations organization. But the Russians had at that time insisted on an all-inclusive veto power for each of the five great powers sitting on the Council and this question had to be left for decision at the highest level. At Yalta the President induced Stalin to retreat somewhat from his initial position, but the real victory remained with the Soviet leader, for the veto power was retained for all but the less important areas of Council procedure. At the San Francisco Conference the Russians refused to be moved from this position, despite all influence that could be brought to bear and despite the vigorous objections of the minor powers. The history of the United Nations organization since its inauguration is still so fresh that no detailed consideration of this decision of the Yalta Conference is required.

At the time of the Yalta meeting the President was already a very sick man. It is more than likely that his failing health had much to do with his decisions on that occasion. But with that aspect we need not concern ourselves here. The long and the short of it is that the consequences of Yalta were unfortunate on almost every count and that the conference represented a rather sad closing chapter to a war which, on the whole, was wisely directed and gallantly fought.

One is drawn to the conclusion that the brilliant phase of American policy was the initial one, which was followed by a middle phase of expediency and compromise, and a closing phase during which we tried in vain to adjust to the Russian problem. Though this problem has emerged as the key issue of international relations, it is too cheap and easy now to say that the President and the country were misled in the decision which threw in our lot with the Soviets in the summer of 1941. We can see clearly now that it was a mistake to believe that the Bolsheviks had given up the idea of world revolution. Maybe they persist in the revolutionary struggle as a matter of faith and principle. More likely they regard it as the most effective instrument for eliminating their rivals and possible enemies, for the creation of a world fashioned in the Russian image, a world which the Soviet Union can dominate and in which it can therefore feel safe. Be this as it may, Europe and the world have been freed of the Nazi menace only to be confronted with the specter of Communist control.

The prospect of such an eventuality confronted the British and American governments six years ago. They elected to support the Soviets because the Nazi danger was immediate and frightful, and it was truly perceived also that past treatment of the Soviet régime was at least partially responsible for the isolation and distrust so characteristic of Moscow. It was reasonable to suppose that after a great common effort the Soviets could be drawn into permanent association with other powers, that mutual confidence and a feeling of security could be developed. After all, the Russian government and people had a great internal problem of social betterment. They had a vast territory and immeasurable resources. They had no need to expand at the expense of neighbors and they had no ideas of racial superiority to drive them on. Looked at in these terms the crucial decision of 1941 still seems sound.

The really debatable part of our wartime conduct of foreign relations does not hinge on the original decision to aid Russia, but on the subsequent development of policy toward the Soviet government. It is impossible to focus this criticism on any one problem or single decision. It was a gradual cumulation of questions, characterized perhaps by two chief errors. First, the President unquestionably overestimated his ability to influence Stalin (though here the "might-have-been" result is forever shrouded in uncertainty by his death), and put excessive hope on the possibility of solving the Russian issue through international organization. Second, both Mr. Roosevelt and Mr. Churchill exaggerated the danger that Russia might quit and make a new deal with Hitler. I find it impossible to believe that at any time, as long as there was even a fair chance of victory, it could have been in Stalin's interest to reverse himself. Actually the Soviets were fully as dependent on allied aid, direct and indirect, as we were on theirs. The idea that during 1942 and 1943 they were carrying the major share of the burden was essentially a mistaken one. Under the circumstances there was no real need for "appeasing" Russia, and certainly no real excuse for acquiescing in Stalin's unilateral action in cases like that of Poland. The idea of side-stepping territorial and other difficult issues may perhaps have been initially sound, but it should not have been adhered to after it had become clear that the Kremlin was exerting its full power to get the settlements it wanted. The United States government should then have taken a much stronger line. In the case of a showdown, we could have planned much earlier and in a much more constructive way for our own security in western and central Europe.

17

Scholarship and the Intelligence Problem

1948

In the long-drawn discussions over the recent "merger" of the armed services little attention was given to one item which seems to me to be of great—not to say vital—importance. This item, which was incorporated in the final legislation, involved the reorganization of the intelligence services of the government. Previously existing agency services have now been subordinated to a new Central Intelligence Agency, which in turn is placed under the new Council for National Defense. Henceforth, in theory at least, all foreign intelligence activity which has a bearing on the national security will be directed and coordinated by the new agency, serving not only the highest echelons of the government, but the President himself.

I do not propose on this occasion to analyze the organization or functioning of this new service. Suffice it to say that it reflects appreciation of a need that was keenly felt during the recent war and that has now been recognized as essential for the formulation and implementation of American foreign and military policy. Things being what they are in the world today, it would be simply laboring the obvious to stress the constant and urgent need for reliable, up-to-date information on foreign powers, with particular reference to their capabilities and intentions. My purpose is merely to examine one aspect of the subject—one which I think should be of interest to members of this society.

The general problem of intelligence involves two quite distinct activities. One is the gathering of materials and information abroad. To many people this suggests at once the glamorous if somewhat dishonorable and un-American work of secret intelligence and espionage, which is indeed part of the job and one that has become particularly important in this age of secret weapons and intense scientific competition, to say nothing of the foreign police systems that have closed huge areas to

Note: Reprinted from the *Proceedings of the American Philosophical Society,* XCII (March 1948), 43–45.

ordinary observation and study. Nonetheless, the popular notion is quite mistaken. Most of the information required concerning other nations can still be obtained by very ordinary, unspectacular methods. Trained collectors under proper guidance and with adequate funds can procure probably 85 to 90 per cent of the needed materials and data.

Far less dramatic but in my opinion much more important is the other aspect of the intelligence problem, namely, the analysis of information and its processing into meaningful reports. The idea has certainly been prevalent, at least in government circles, that anyone with a modicum of common sense could put two and two together and come up with the correct answer. Even though in 1939 our intelligence collecting system was very inadequate, it was infinitely superior to our arrangements for analysis. In certain restricted fields, such as fiscal matters and problems of foreign trade, excellent research was being done in the Treasury, Federal Reserve Board, and Department of Commerce. These agencies had highly trained staffs and were fully aware of the fact that such technical matters as international finance or taxation required specialized study. But in the political field little was done. From time to time some academically-minded official in the Department of State might essay an historical survey or a systematic analysis, but such cases were exceptional. For the most part the department operated on the strength of personal knowledge and accumulated experience. Basic study and long-range planning were all but unknown.

The Army and Navy were almost as casual in their treatment of the problem. They had intelligence branches, but these were staffed by officers mostly without special qualifications, often by men regarded as unsuitable for field or sea command, who, by the mere issuance of orders, supposedly could be transformed over night into "experts." Under the circumstances it would have been little short of a miracle if high-grade intelligence reports had emerged. Actually the estimates and conclusions of the service intelligence staffs were notoriously inadequate and sometimes mistaken to a dangerous degree.

During the war a real effort was made to correct this sad situation. When General William J. Donovan in August 1941 organized what later became the Office of Strategic Services, his chief aim was to bring into government service scholars who, in addition to their specialized knowledge of foreign countries, were trained in particular disciplines and thoroughly grounded in the methods of assembling, selecting, evaluating, and presenting evidence. Later the OSS expanded its activities

331

into other fields and many of you, no doubt, have read thrilling accounts of the adventures and exploits of its secret agents and operatives in even the most remote parts of the world. But throughout the whole war period the original idea was unobtrusively developed. By 1945 the Research and Analysis Branch comprised a staff of some five hundred professional people working in Washington, to say nothing of a couple of hundred others working at various stations abroad and scattered all the way from London to Chungking.

This unpublicized research staff consisted of scholars drawn from all the social science fields—economists, political scientists, historians, geographers, psychologists, archaeologists, and even philologists. The great objective was to get these specialists to work together, to pool their knowledge of the materials and literature and to focus their various techniques on specific problems in the hope of coming up with the best-informed, most comprehensive, and most critical estimates of particular situations.

The idea was excellent, but the operation was difficult. We ran into obstacles internally and externally. Not only did we discover how little competence this country could furnish in certain fields, but we were shocked—some of us at least—to find how narrow much of our specialization had become and how difficult it was to get people from the various disciplines to work together. For example, it turned out not only that we had very few people competent in the Russian, Far Eastern, and Near Eastern fields, but also that few if any of our American economists or psychologists had concerned themselves with foreign problems. In like manner there was, especially at the outset, much suspicion of the procedures and conclusions arrived at by unfamiliar techniques. To mention only one instance, in the Russian field the economists were sure that they alone could deal adequately with economic problems, while the Russian specialists pointed out, with considerable cogency and much persistence, that the economists not only knew nothing of the Russian materials, but were abysmally ignorant of the peculiar Russian conditions.

I will not dwell at length on these difficulties. Gradually they were overcome and in the end I believe we went a long way towards our original objective. Many excellent reports were produced in greatly diverse fields and I am certainly not overstating the case when I say that new standards and indeed new techniques were established for many types of work.

332

Externally the arrival of the professors was greeted in characteristic Washington fashion, with some derision and more suspicion, not to say outright and avowed hostility. I recall that at first we were solemnly warned never to use the word "strategy," so as not to evoke too violent antagonism from the services. This did not prevent our emergence, after a year, as the Office of Strategic Services. Then we were told to avoid scrupulously any reference to "policy," so as not to arouse the suscepti- bilities of the State Department. Yet at the end of the war the entire research branch was transferred to the State Department on the plea that it was essential for the study and formulation of policy.

In a word, the strain and stress of war hastened the process of edu- cation. Originally we had to grope our way and apply ourselves to those things that seemed important and within our competence. Often we did not learn until too late of real needs, and often we labored hard only to find that our effort was simply duplication. Many of our most solid and valuable reports, I am sure, never reached those people who could have profited most from them. But all this is part of the general Washington experience and I will not dwell on it. What seems to me to be of perma- nent importance is that the OSS staff demonstrated the value and need of specialized research. Towards the end of the war recognition of our work was so general that we were hopelessly pressed. Even in purely operational fields such as bomb targets and determination of enemy losses our help was regarded as indispensable. But, above all, in the study of the capabilities and intentions of foreign powers I think we went far beyond anything previously known in Washington or previ- ously attempted anywhere else, even in Germany. On these problems we could bring our full competence to bear, analyzing all possible as- pects of the problem and integrating the results into a comprehensive report.

The most convincing proof that we had made our mark was the de- cision made to maintain the research branch when the rest of the OSS was disbanded in 1945. At that time there was much heated debate re- garding the allocation of the organization and this, in my opinion, is a really very difficult organizational problem, which I will not attempt to discuss here. The essential thing is that, under the State Department, the activity has continued uninterruptedly, and that there is little like- lihood that in the future it will be seriously curtailed or jeopardized.

What we have, then, in the government is something like a huge social science research institute devoted to the exploration of certain types of problems bearing directly on the national security. Whether it remains in the State Department or is ultimately transferred to the new Central Intelligence Agency is no doubt important, but not decisive. The principle has been established and the need recognized. I cannot conceive of the government ever being willing to dispense with it, and I am confident that, for the future, the work of the organization will serve as an incentive to closer coordination in the social sciences. Already the regional studies programs in many institutions reflect its influence on the universities.

But this new departure, like most others, has its shady side. The question of personnel is and undoubtedly will remain for a long time the controlling factor in determining success or failure. During wartime the staff was built up by draining the universities, but that could never be anything more than an emergency procedure. It stands to reason that, with the end of the conflict, many members of the staff and more particularly the senior, directing members, should have returned to their habitual callings—after all, the needs of the universities after demobilization were just about as great and as urgent as those of the government during hostilities. The result has been that the intelligence research staff has been decapitated and generally depleted, with only faint prospect of improvement in the immediate future. The plain fact of the matter is that we have far from enough trained people in these fields to staff both the universities and the government.

This is obviously a question that should be considered in connection with the government program for training and research. In the social science fields the results are of course less concrete and spectacular than in the fields of science and invention. Furthermore, the exact preparation is difficult to define and organize. But it is, I am convinced, very necessary that encouragement be given and that concerted efforts be made to enable promising students to get training in the less familiar fields, as well as to study and live abroad. The regional programs in the universities represent hopeful beginnings, but the load is heavy and the road is long. My hope is that, as appreciation of the problem spreads, something larger and more systematic will be undertaken and that, ultimately, it will be realized that the country has a real stake in the type of study that is clearly essential for any nation which, whether it likes it or not, is called upon to play a major part in world affairs.

18

American Objectives

1952

The United States government has been frequently charged, particularly of late, with failure to determine, proclaim, and pursue consistently its basic objectives. Eminent critics like George F. Kennan have denounced our inveterate habit of following what he calls the legalistic-moralistic line, that is, the habit of attaching ourselves to abstract moral principles, such as freedom and justice, and looking to the orderly processes of international law to protect our interests, and assure our security. Personally I agree that this approach to international problems, however laudable in itself, is apt to lead to misconceptions and result in disappointments. The time has passed when we could afford to delude ourselves with pious hopes, high-sounding shibboleths and sanctimonious protests. Faced by a major crisis it is urgently necessary that we get down to brass tacks, decide what it is that we should strive for, determine what our capabilities are for attaining our objectives, and lay concrete plans for their implementation. Without clear definition of objectives it is impossible to plan sound strategy, impossible to make and hold friends, impossible to impress potential enemies.

Parenthetically is may be remarked that our mechanisms for planning policy are still woefully inadequate. While, through the Central Intelligence Agency, provision has now been made for the effective coordination of all foreign intelligence and for the production of national intelligence estimates, there is as yet no analogous staff organization under the National Security Council for the long-range study of national objectives and policies. Neither is there adequate provision for consultation and coordinated action between the executive and legislative branches. If there were, it is inconceivable that such dickering as we have recently seen over the Mutual Aid appropriations should take place. This reckless cutting and slicing, to the tune of hundreds of millions of dollars, to me reflects a disregard for careful factual study, and

Note: A lecture delivered at the Naval War College, June 10, 1952. Reprinted from the *Naval War College Review,* V (September 1952), 14–30.

a lack of understanding of national aims that can only confuse the country and shake the confidence of the world at large.

Let it be said at once, however, that the definition of positive national objectives is no easy matter. In an age of increasing tempo, of shrinking space, and of terrifying complexity it becomes, indeed, exceedingly difficult.

Reduced to the simplest terms, the basic objectives of any nation must be the preservation of its society and its territory against disintegration from within and against assault from without. These objectives, in turn, presuppose adequate resources and a sound social and political structure on the one hand and adequate military power for defense in any emergency on the other.

It is unlikely that any nation will ever have the means to assure itself of absolute security. However, for a brief spell in the later nineteenth century, our own country approximated that happy state. Having severed the ties that bound it to Europe, and having overcome a domestic crisis of the most serious character, the United States was left undisturbed to develop its social and political system, to open up and exploit the vast resources of a continent, and in general to build up wealth and power far beyond that attained by any other nation in history. Secure behind the barrier of the oceans on the east and west, flanked by thinly populated and generally undeveloped countries on the north and south, the United States could afford isolation and could hold itself aloof from the problems that plagued most other peoples of the globe.

Seen in the larger historical perspective this period was, however, but a brief interlude. In the context of the present world crisis it is worth recalling that in the beginning of our history the fathers of the then weak and infant republic were also confronted with an ideological menace. They were all too painfully aware of the strength of the feudalistic, monarchical, undemocratic system of Europe. Because they feared reconquest by the old order against which they had rebelled, they made themselves experts in international politics and diplomacy. They bent their every effort toward playing off one power against another. In view of British seapower they did not regard even the broad Atlantic as an adequate protective barrier. What, after all, was the purpose of the Monroe Doctrine if not to extend the defense lines of the nation by thousands of miles and in principle at least to seal off the entire hemisphere against the renewed intrusion of a social and political system that was regarded as unalterably hostile to the ideals and objectives of the New World?

The threat that confronts us today is not dissimilar, though it is more immediate, because the number of genuinely great powers has been reduced to two and because the distances between them have been greatly narrowed by the improvements in communication. True, the threat now comes from the left rather than from the right; it is revolutionary and subversive rather than conservative and reactionary. But this appears to have made the antagonism all the more bitter and irreconcilable. It would indeed be difficult to exaggerate the depth of the gulf dividing American democracy and Soviet Communism, or to overplay the menace of Communism to American institutions and national security. Soviet leaders have been taught by Marx and Lenin to speculate on the collapse of the system of free enterprise, but in the interval to do everything possible to undermine and weaken it. Through the brutality of their dictatorship they have been able to harness the power of a vast territory and a huge and rapidly growing population for the realization of their purpose, which is avowedly to make the whole world safe for Communism. Finally, through the ruthless exploitation of want and discontent throughout the world they have already subverted many neighboring governments and have expanded the circle of their power over European satellites and over the vast territory and population of China.

Returning to the question of American objectives it is clear that first and foremost this country must look to its defenses. We do not have and should not have any aspirations towards territorial expansion. The imperialist aberration of the late nineteenth and early twentieth century was never really popular among us and soon proved disappointing. The empires of the European powers have disintegrated and are in the process of liquidation. The idea of empire is dead, and no one in this country, so far as I know, believes that the security of the United States can be strengthened by direct control of foreign peoples. The posture of the United States is, therefore, a defensive one. Directly threatened by a powerful state and a hostile ideology, it must rededicate itself to democracy and apply itself with renewed vigor to the solution of social, economic, racial, religious, and kindred problems that tend to weaken and divide it, that create the climate for Communist agitation and subversion. To pursue this phase of the problem through all its ramifications would distract us from the issues with which this group is chiefly concerned. Besides, these are issues with which every thoughtful American is painfully familiar. It is sufficient, therefore, to remind this audience that historically speaking social and political systems that fail to provide a reasonably satisfactory mode and standard of living for the population are bound to be supplanted by other systems. The much vaunted "new order" may in our day be of the Fascist or the Communist variety. We as democrats may be convinced that, in terms of freedom and respect for individual rights, both varieties are the negation of freedom and progress. Nonetheless, they hold the promise of novelty, always a potent appeal to desperate men.

In terms of military power it is inconceivable that for the foreseeable future the United States can escape the burden of conscription and of heavy expenditure for defense. Obligatory military service, in addition to its cost in terms of labor power, is by its very nature distasteful to a free and individualistic people. The appropriation of a substantial part of the national income to unproductive and quickly outmoded military equipment is equally objectionable. No doubt the late President Roosevelt was right in holding that sane international relations are possible only if based on drastic disarmament all around. But there is, at the present, no even remote possibility of reaching agreement with the Soviet Union on such a program. The Kremlin retained a huge military establishment when, in 1946, the West hastily liquidated the great armies that might have served as a deterrent to Soviet expansion.

The facts are familiar to all: for a period of five years all western Europe lay defenseless before Soviet power. If in fact the Kremlin did not press its gains beyond Czechoslovakia it was certainly not for lack of divisions, planes, and other equipment. It may have been from fear of taking over so large and so recalcitrant an area. More likely it was from fear of atomic retaliation on the part of the United States. Reluctant though I am to accept a simple explanation, I find it increasingly difficult to reject Mr. Churchill's view that the atomic bomb was in fact the decisive deterrent. But America's atomic superiority is no longer unchallenged. The race for atomic power is already on. The Communists undoubtedly have a bomb, and there is at least a strong probability that they have already built up a stockpile sufficiently large to enable them to wreak havoc on American cities and seriously, if not critically, impair the war making potential of the United States. It is impossible to speak with any assurance on these matters, but the very depth of our uncertainty dictates a supreme effort on our part. Since the Soviet Union has steadfastly refused to accept such control of atomic production as we regard necessary, we have no choice but to live with the threat and counter it to the best of our ability.

This country is as yet far from a state of preparedness even for self defense. The value of the atomic bomb as a deterrent has been reduced by the Soviet's presumed capability for retaliation. Under present circumstances it is all but impossible to foresee any alternative to large-scale rearmament and to redoubled efforts to devise ever more effective and consequently more terrible weapons. This is a dismal conclusion to arrive at, for it would seem that other methods than those of the jungle could be discovered for settling issues among nations. Yet given the apparently irreconcilable conflict between West and East no one, to my knowledge, has been able to produce any other solution. With two antagonists acting on incompatible principles and not even speaking the same language of international relations, I see no alternative to armament and more armament, at all cost short of national ruin.

Even among those who fully recognize the threat of Communist power to the security of the United States there have long been two schools of thought. Some hold that, with resources which are after all limited, the United States would do best to concentrate on strictly national or at least on hemisphere defense. There is no prospect, they argue, that determined Soviet aggression in Europe or Asia can be contained. We are therefore in danger of having our capabilities drained by futile efforts to strengthen others or by hopeless attempts to check our opponent in far-off places where no decision is possible.

The other school, of course, insists that if eventually one has to fight, it is better to engage the enemy as far away as possible from one's own frontiers. This is the principle on which the system of hemisphere solidarity is based. It is the system which proved itself in both recent wars. For my own part, I believe it the only sound strategy. Indeed, when I hear people debating whether we should devote so and so much money and equipment to the defense of others, I am always tempted to say that the real issue is not whether we should support others, but whether we can, at whatever price, induce others to stand by us. For it cannot be a matter of indifference to us whether the Soviet Union overruns, subverts, or in any way establishes control over all Eurasia. Perhaps other nations of the West do not like us. Perhaps they are apathetic and listless. Perhaps they would put up a miserable fight against Soviet aggression. Nonetheless, we need them. Actually we cannot expect them to fight for love of us, but only in their own cause, in their own interest. In any case, the essential issue for the United States is that they should provide us facilities, support our position, and resist as long as possible.

Quite aside from any positive contribution which Western Europe might make in an armed conflict with the Soviet Union, we have the greatest interest in denying that area to the enemy. The loss of China to the Communists has been a calamity. How much more so would be the loss of Western Europe! For the resulting accretions to the Kremlin in terms of manpower, skills, resources, facilities and equipment would be such as to make it impossible for the United States to check Communist inundation of the Middle East and Africa, and probably even to protect the Western hemisphere from subversion and conquest. The military strength of the South American nations is so limited that that continent could hardly be defended against a major hostile power in control of West Africa. In the light of these facts it appears that our agreements with the other American republics involve grave liabilities unless supplemented by provisions for the utmost possible defense of Western Europe.

The foregoing considerations suggest that it is incumbent upon us to rally as many of the free nations as possible to our side and to give them all available support, economic and military, to strengthen their powers of resistance. In the most generalized terms this policy dictates adherence to and support of the United Nations' contribution not only to the peaceful solution of international differences but also to the frustration of aggression. The high cost in men and treasure of the Korean intervention and the disheartening deadlock that has ensued must not be permitted to blind us to the epoch-making importance of prompt international action in this instance. Failure to act would undoubtedly have entailed the complete collapse of international organization and a total loss of confidence in the purposes of the United States and other leading nations of the free world. Whatever the solution of the current stalemate, the fact remains that the Communist assault on South Korea was frustrated and that its immediate effect has been to dispel whatever doubts may have remained as to Communist aims and tactics. As a result of Korea, the United States and the West generally are today in a state of military preparedness far beyond what would otherwise have been possible, and it is not unreasonable to suppose that further aggressions, as on Taiwan or Indo-China in the east, or in Iran or Yugoslavia, have been forestalled. The Korean action has certainly involved us in a remote and difficult theater. It holds the danger of too great commitment in what is strategically a secondary area. But our opponents can hardly be expected to act in accordance with our interests. On the contrary, we can probably count on them always to strike where it is most difficult for us to react effectively.

With respect to Europe, the United States is now fully obligated, by the terms of the North Atlantic Treaty and by the commitments inherent in the recent contractual agreement with the West German Republic and the European Defense Community, to support the free nations of the Old World in the event of attack.

The numerous agreements concluded between West European powers in recent years, supplemented by the creation of the Council of Europe and the mechanism of the Schuman Plan and the European Defense Community, have brought these nations more closely together than they have been since the decay of the Holy Roman Empire. Indeed, federation is now frankly envisaged as the ultimate solution of Europe's economic and military weakness. It is quite conceivable that eventually the United States might find a united Europe a formidable economic competitor and politically a somewhat obstreperous colleague. Nonetheless, I believe it important if not essential to build up this additional power center, to consolidate the European powers as at least a partial counterweight to the Soviet Union. Individually none of these countries can offer effective resistance to Communism. United they can certainly do much to redress the balance.

With American aid, advice, and leadership something of a miracle has already been achieved in the line of economic reconstruction through the Marshall Plan, and it would be a mistake to underrate the progress that has been made in the direction of building military strength. Possibly the original schedules for rearmament, hastily drawn, were too sanguine. The effort to even approximate them has led to grave financial difficulties, discouragement and even unrest. On the other hand, there is good reason to suppose that as the defensive posture of Western Europe becomes stronger, the hopelessness and despair that has characterized the popular attitude in some countries and has facilitated the spread of Communism, will give way to a new confidence. The great danger, as I see it, is that we ourselves may become impatient and disillusioned. The recent Congressional debates on the Mutual Security appropriations seem to highlight this danger. As aforesaid, I take this attitude of impatient criticism to rest on the mistaken notion that American aid is a matter of generosity, if not charity, and that Europe alone is on the receiving end. Actually the vital issue is to hold Western Europe in line, in our own as well as in the interest of others. This is no easy matter, for Western Europe will for several years at least remain relatively indefensible unless the development of new weapons upsets present military calculations. Europeans know this and many of them are still prone to despair. While being no expert on national economics, I would judge that this country could afford up to ten billion dollars a year in foreign aid. In terms of the cost of our own defense preparations, and even more in terms of the cost of a great war the investment of such a sum to reinforce our own overseas defense lines would not appear unreasonable or exorbitant.

The question of European defense has raised such subsidiary questions as the rearmament of Western Germany, the extension of aid to Franco Spain in return for base facilities in that country, and the provision of economic and military support to Communist Yugoslavia. Considering the nature of the emergency under which we live, all these policies can be defended as a matter of expediency. The case of Germany is in itself relatively simple, for it involves no ideological conflict and requires only the establishment of adequate safeguards against the abuse of renascent German military power. By contrast the idea of cooperation with Fascist Spain and Communist Yugoslavia is abhorrent to many Americans, for such collaboration seems a betrayal of the democratic cause. This argument is difficult to answer convincingly, but it is worth recalling that the records of history, even of recent history, are full of examples of such relationships, entered upon when national interests seemed to require them. In the present case it should be remembered that prior to the time of Woodrow Wilson our relations with other states were determined without reference to their internal régimes. We have happily outgrown the rather naive idea that the democratic system is the only desirable and suitable one, whatever the conditions and the circumstances. If we are to be purists and deny our friendship and support to all nations following a course other than our own, we shall soon find ourselves in self-imposed isolation, since almost all foreign régimes are to varying degrees socialistic or undemocratic. Actually there is reason to suppose that extremist régimes like those of Spain and Yugoslavia may see the errors of their ways more readily in cooperation with freer systems than while in a state of ostracism. Meanwhile both Spain and Yugoslavia are strategically of such importance to the defense of Western Europe and are of themselves so little a threat, actually or potentially, to American interests, that we can ill afford to renounce the aid they may provide.

However deficient may be the power of Western Europe, that area is a pillar of strength compared to North Africa, the Middle East, and South Asia, the soft underbelly of Eurasia. The countries comprising that huge belt are almost without exception in a state of ferment. The opening up of these areas by European imperialism has brought in its train the introduction of European ideas, such as nationalism and self-determination, which have made the continuance of the imperial relationship impossible. European influence and the impact of great wars have made these colonial peoples conscious and resentful of want and oppression which their forefathers suffered for generations as a matter of course. Almost everywhere in these regions the social system is antiquated and the old agrarian structure is being shaken by the impact of modern industrialism. In many instances the traditional ruling classes are maintaining their privileged position despite the facade of democracy which has been erected. Invariably they exploit national feeling to throw off the shackles of European control or, where they have already achieved that objective, to divert popular attention from social problems.

Bad enough in itself, this situation provides an ideal setting for Communist activity, for the Kremlin has long shown itself expert in directing and exploiting the forces of discontent. Supposedly internationalist, according to the gospel of Marx, Soviet leaders have found no difficulty in championing the cause of nationalism where it serves their purposes. Their promises of a popular democratic régime, of expropriation of the upper classes, or of economic equality are so familiar as to require no elaboration. I do not say that the disorders in Morocco and Tunisia, the crisis in Anglo-Egyptian relations, the chaos in Iran, or the unrest seizing all of South Asia are the achievements solely of Soviet propaganda and subversion. I do say that they threaten the loss of parts or all of this important area to the West. No one can deny that relationships of these countries with the West have already seriously deteriorated.

What, in this context, should be the United States objective? Obviously to hold this area if possible, if only to deny it to the enemy. But how? If we support the dominant groups in these countries against their

European masters, for example France, we definitely run the risk of estranging countries vital to the defense of Europe. Furthermore, if we countenance the existing régimes in their often benighted domestic policies, we will sooner or later find ourselves in opposition to emerging popular forces. The problem in each case is a complex and difficult one, for which a general solution is not apt to be found. It would appear, however, that little is to be gained simply by adroit maneuvering. We have already made clear to the European powers that we consider imperial rule done for and that we welcome the liquidation of overseas empires. Beyond that we must look to fundamentals and do what we can to remove or alleviate the basic ills from which this part of the world is suffering and which tend to accentuate the unbalance in the world's forces. No doubt the Point IV program is an important initial step in this direction. Over the years it may prove crucial and turn out to have been the most worthwhile investment of all. It certainly is a potential demonstration of democracy in action. By reducing misery it opens the prospect of effectively countering Communism, of paving the way for reform and modernization of the social and political systems of undeveloped areas. In short it promises a vast return on a relatively modest investment, as witness the results of agricultural instruction, in India for example, by a mere handful of experts.

Furthermore, the work of education, health and technical aid introduces a positive element into American policy. The objectives of the United States cannot be purely defensive or static. As John Foster Dulles has rightly said, if we merely hold our own in Asia our position in a few years will be hopeless. Communism being dynamic and aggressive, fired with the conviction of eventual triumph, it can only be fought successfully by a positive and constructive program. Publicity and information are important as weapons of refutation and instruments of truth. But they must be supplemented with the promise of improved living conditions and increased freedom. The unbalance in the world today, in terms of standards of living, population pressures, essential resources and industrial capabilities, are such that unless we can manage to raise the level of the lowly we are sure to be forced to reduce our own.

There is at present no prospect that the burdens entailed by the objectives of the United States can soon be lightened—that is, that the threat confronting our security and culture can soon be surmounted.

On the other hand, progress has undeniably been made, and it is not impossible, indeed it is likely, that growing strength will check the progressive implementation of the Soviet program. Since the seizure of Czechoslovakia in 1948 there has been no further aggression in Europe. On the contrary, Yugoslavia has been lost to the Kremlin. In the Middle East the Soviets have thus far failed to make capital of the unrest and tension, even in Iran. India seems to be veering steadily towards the West and in Southeast Asia the Communist cause has made no significant progress. With the Communist victory in China the Kremlin appears to have had relatively little to do, and one may assume that the emergence of the new régime in China has its dark as well as its bright sides for the Soviets. The Korean adventure has at least been frustrated, while the peace treaty with Japan has been put through despite Soviet opposition and protest. It may be taken for granted that even in the European satellites the Kremlin still has many problems to solve. In the Soviet homeland itself, there may be more latent dissatisfaction and hostility to the régime than we realize. Believing as we do, in the dignity of the individual and the virtues of democracy grounded in law, we cannot accept the idea that the brutality and oppression of totalitarian régimes can last forever. Mr. Kennan, who knows infinitely more about these matters than I, has noted that there are limits beyond which peoples cannot be driven. He believes in the possibility, indeed in the strong possibility, that Soviet power, like the capitalist world of its conception, bears within it the seeds of its own decay and that the sprouting of these seeds is already well advanced. Certainly the increasingly severe controls in Communist states would seem to reflect a growing need for such controls.

Consequently there is nothing implausible in the idea that Stalin and his confreres will try to avoid major armed conflict in the future as they have in the past, if only to safeguard their own dictatorship. There is nothing in their doctrine to suggest a time table for achievement of their objectives. In the past they have shown themselves patient and flexible. They will, unquestionably, exploit, as it arises, any situation that promises success. Indeed, much of their effort is devoted to creation of such situations. We must expect them to move here, there and anywhere—to keep us on the run. But we may also expect them to avoid the ultimate test, at least so long as we retain certain elements of strength and can rally the support of the free world. The men of the

Kremlin, unlike Hitler, have not shown themselves to be gamblers. There is reason to suppose that they hope and expect to attain their objectives without involving the Soviet Union in major armed conflict and that they would retreat rather than embark on a war in which the chances of success were uncertain. There remains a constant and grave danger that through miscalculation or through a tragic mistake on either side, a general war may develop. But barring such a contingency we may expect peace—a peace, however, that will long remain precarious, an armed peace maintained under pressure and in the midst of unbroken tension.

There are those who argue that in this situation, the United States might be well advised to strike while it still has the presumed superiority in atomic weapons, that is, that it should loose a preventive war. The argument is so logical as to be disturbing. Remember, however, that historically preventive wars have rarely served their purposes, and remember, above all, that modern wars are so destructive that they harm the victor almost as much as the vanquished. The ruin and misery attending a war with the Soviet Union might well prepare the ground for the spread of the very social revolution we are intent on combatting.

Certainly it would be reckless to launch a preventive war and thereby lose the moral support of the free world so long as there is a reasonable chance of attaining our objectives by other means. On the theory that the Communist system cannot last forever, that power to resist will check its further spread, and that gradual improvement of conditions throughout the world will sap its appeal, it would seem to be the part of wisdom to learn patience and perseverance. Quite conceivably the situation may develop to the point where certain issues can be adjusted by agreement, even if but partially and temporarily. Such opportunities we should always seize and exploit, for even though they may not strike at the root of the matter, they may provide further time, and time has frequently proved the most effective solvent of apparently irreconcilable differences.

In any event, the main thought I should like to leave with you is that in this great crisis, in this great clash of ideas and cultures, American objectives cannot and should not be selfish, narrow, or purely defensive. As human society is constructed today, we cannot hope to attain security for ourselves alone. Our fate is bound up with that of the entire free world. Consequently our interests, our objectives and our obligations strike across meridians of longitude and parallels of latitude. They extend as far as our influence can reach. As the greatest world power in the annals of history, tremendous responsibilities and burdens have been thrust upon us. Our objectives must be to discharge the obligations assigned to us by circumstances and events. Anything less holds promise only of disaster and defeat. On the other hand we have every reason to suppose that clarity of purpose, unity and resolution in action, and faith in the rightness of our cause will eventually lead us, even without war, to triumph over the dangers that presently beset us.

19

Woodrow Wilson: His Education in World Affairs

1956

Few statesmen of modern times were in their own day raised so high in the public esteem as Woodrow Wilson, or cast down so deeply into disrepute. Less than two score years ago, during the American participation in the First World War, he was hailed as the leader in the crusade for democracy—the man to whom millions in the enemy countries as in the allied nations looked as the champion of a just peace and the harbinger of a new and better international order. Yet when he died five years later Wilson was a broken man, whose passing aroused a measure of public sympathy but little more. America's crusading days were forgotten and the country was delighted to return to normalcy, which was equated with isolation and material prosperity. Peace and the new world order were relegated to the realm of dreams, while Wilson's attempted world leadership was widely regarded as an ill-advised, not to say dangerous, aberration.

Within yet another decade compassion had turned into active hostility. As the world sank into the great depression, as totalitarianism made gigantic strides in Europe, as collective action for peace became enfeebled and the threat of Fascist-Nazi aggression became immediate, Wilson appeared to more and more of his countrymen as the man who had foolishly abandoned blessed isolation and had purposely involved his people in all the tribulations of world politics. Some went so far as to stamp him a hypocrite who, having secured re-election in November 1916 on a platform of continued neutrality, straightway took the country into war against the Central Powers. Many welcomed the supposed "findings" of the Nye Committee, which pictured Wilson as a simple-minded professor, easily misled by British propaganda and unwittingly victimized by powerful banking and munitions interests intent on driving the country into war so as to safeguard their huge investment in the Allied

Note: Address delivered at the Harvard commemoration of the birth of Woodrow Wilson, March 7, 1956. Reprinted from *Confluence*, V (Autumn 1956), 183–194.

cause. Even the more charitable could see in Wilson little more than a starry-eyed idealist who, overlooking or ignoring the real interests of the United States, staked all on an impossible program for peace, only to be completely outmaneuvered by slick European politicians. All he got for his pains, it was said, was a paper scheme for a League of Nations; and even this he could not prevail upon the Senate to ratify without reservations on which, again, he was too inept or too obstinate to accept a reasonable compromise.

The years that have elapsed since the outbreak of the Second World War have taught the American people many painful lessons, and with their learning there has come a revival of interest in and appreciation of Wilson's aims and policies. It is now easy to see how desperate was the need for collective action in the 1930's to forestall totalitarian aggression and how ineffectual League action was bound to be in the absence of the full participation or support of the United States. The experience of 1939–1941, in turn, revealed the weakness if not the hopelessness of traditional neutrality, to say nothing of isolation. The American people, albeit haltingly and reluctantly, were driven by events to recognize their immense stake in the security of the Atlantic sea-lanes and consequently in the continued independence and integrity of the United Kingdom. The genuine and whole-hearted participation of the United States in the establishment of the United Nations and the strong American initiative in the Korean crisis of June 1950 are eloquent proofs of the now general acceptance of Wilson's doctrine. The main features of his foreign policy are no longer controversial, and it would therefore hardly be worth the time and effort necessary to refute the preposterous charges brought against him twenty years ago. Most of his principles and policies have, indeed, become integral parts of American thinking on world problems. If the world of today, instead of living in peace and harmony, is racked by cold war and plagued by the nightmare of atomic annihilation, the explanation is clearly not to be sought in too much, but rather in too little Wilsonism.

Wilson, like many great men, was patently in advance of his time. In one of his early addresses he remarked of Edmund Burke, whom he admired greatly, that he had been not only wise too soon, but wise too much, for "he went on from the wisdom of today to the wisdom of tomorrow, to the wisdom which is for all time," and it was impossible for ordinary mortals to follow him so far. The same might be said with equal justice of Wilson, the grandeur of whose principles, the strength of whose convictions, and the depth of whose faith tended to blind him to the meanness of human nature and the realities of political life. But this having been said, it should be realized that Wilson did not arrive at his program solely by way of inspiration, but also by way of harsh experience.

When he assumed the office of president, he was still living in a cloud of misapprehension about international affairs. Only under the pressure of events did he gradually fight free of illusion and face up to the most unpleasant aspects of reality. The lessons he learned were those that the American people were ultimately also to learn. But Wilson was forced by circumstances and by the requirements of his own personality to apprehend in three years what it took most Americans thirty years to grasp. To review some of these lessons will not only clarify his statesmanship but will also illuminate some of the basic issues which have determined and still do determine the action of the United States on the world stage.

Long before the onset of the First World War, Wilson, like a small minority of American statesmen and writers, had come to the conclusion that isolation, however desirable, was rapidly becoming impossible for the United States. The passing of the frontier, the ever-developing domestic pressures, the constant multiplication and acceleration of communications and many other factors were making it imperative that the country assume its fair share of responsibility in world affairs just as it was demanding its fair share of opportunity. But Wilson had not pursued this idea to anything like the point eventually reached by men such as Admiral Alfred Thayer Mahan or even President Theodore Roosevelt. For him participation in world affairs continued to mean little more than the use of American influence and power in behalf of arbitration, mediation and, in general, organization and action for international peace. He was interested primarily in domestic politics and he went abroad merely for short pleasure tours in Britain or possibly France. There is no evidence that he ever studied the details of any foreign issue, and it is hard to escape the harsh conclusion that the breaking of the storm in Europe in 1914 found the President of the United States woefully ignorant of and still utterly indifferent to the origins and issues of the cataclysm. As late as 1916 he could refer to the European war as "a drunken brawl in a public house," and could expose himself to obloquy by stating publicly that Americans had no concern with the causes and objects of the conflict.

The fact of the matter was that the President regarded the war as merely the latest manifestation of the ruthless ambition and political amorality of the European states, the details of which were as unimportant as they were unedifying. In these circumstances it was the sole mission of the United States to use its influence and power to put an end to hostilities and to see that peace, when concluded, was so reasonable and just as to make future conflict unlikely. This mission he attempted to fulfill when the war was only a few days old. In the following months he was to renew his efforts repeatedly, each time with greater insistence. He found, however, that the belligerents had no desire for American intervention; that, on the contrary, they were determined to avoid it at all costs.

Nothing is more instructive, in this connection, than the story of the second mission of Colonel House to Europe in the early months of 1916. The purpose of his mission was to arrange for a conference of the belligerents under American auspices in the hope of putting an end to the hostilities and in this way forestalling the growing danger of American involvement. Knowing from past experience that the British and French were, if anything, even more opposed to American interference than the Germans, the President was willing to make substantial concessions to secure the concurrence of the London government. Through House he offered to leave the date for the convocation of the conference to the British, which meant that the latter could fight on until their cause appeared hopeless, at which time they could count on American intervention. Furthermore, Mr. Wilson was prepared to promise that at the prospective conference he would use his best efforts to ensure that the peace terms were "not unfavorable" to the Allied side. In the event of German refusal to attend the conference, the President stated through House, the United States would probably enter the war on the Allied side.

This extraordinary proposal was accepted by the British Foreign Secretary, Sir Edward Grey, but the British government made no move to take advantage of what was tantamount to an American offer to intervene in the conflict unless the Germans agreed to come to the conference table and accept terms "not unfavorable" to the Allies. Mr. Wilson and Colonel House were surprised and deeply disappointed that nothing came of their plan. Henceforth they became more and more intolerant of the highhanded British treatment of neutral trade, and even more suspicious of the war aims of the Entente powers.

The point is that the experience of the years of American neutrality taught the President not only that continued neutrality was impossible if one of the belligerents chose to violate it, but also that once locked in mortal combat great nations will fight on until their vital interests are fully assured. They will not, if they possibly can help it, accept foreign mediation, which means decision by an outside power with respect to their basic interests. The British desired American participation in the war against Germany, certainly; but not if it involved acceptance of American direction in the making of peace. Even so liberal and well-disposed a person as Sir Edward Grey would have none of American mediation if it could in any way be avoided. The lesson which Mr. Wilson had drummed into his mind in these years was that the European powers were fighting not out of mere cussedness, but out of the deep conviction that their independence, security, and prosperity depended upon victory. They would accept outside interference only if forced on them by overwhelming military and economic power. In short, he was brought to realize that the nation that desires to play a leading role in international affairs must have the knowledge to act intelligently and understandingly; it must have the power to reinforce its policies and decisions; and it must be willing to assume an appropriate share of responsibility for the consequences of its acts.

The President's abortive attempt to engineer peace on American terms soon dispelled whatever illusions he may have had about the ultimate aims of the belligerents. "The fight," said Mr. Lloyd George in the autumn of 1916, "must be to the finish—to a knock-out." To this Sir Edward Grey, in a secret memorandum to the Cabinet at the same time, added: "As long as the naval and military authorities believe that Germany can be defeated and satisfactory terms of peace can eventually be dictated to her, peace is premature, and to contemplate it is to betray the interests of this country and of the Allies." In a word, not even the monstrous losses of human life suffered by both sides would bring them to yield. All the belligerents were set on a total victory that would permit them to impose their terms on their enemies. They were equally decided that those terms should not only ensure substantial territorial and economic gains, but should also leave the vanquished helpless to wage another major war in the foreseeable future.

Mr. Wilson was quick to see that under these conditions the outlook for durable peace was dim indeed. His espousal of the program for a League of Nations (May 1916) no doubt reflected his realization that nations could be dissuaded from imposing Draconian terms on their vanquished enemy only if their security could be guaranteed through an international organization providing for collective action against aggression. At any rate when, on the very eve of American involvement in the conflict, the President addressed the Senate on January 22, 1917, his thought had taken full form, and he unflinchingly presented a program of "peace without victory." Though this program was anathema to the activists, the experiences of the next generation were to be such as to make it well worthy of further reflection. "Victory would mean peace forced upon the loser, a victor's terms imposed upon the vanquished," Mr. Wilson warned. "It would be accepted in humiliation, under duress, at an intolerable sacrifice, and would have a sting, a resentment, a bitter memory upon which terms of peace would rest, not permanently, but only as upon quicksand." A durable peace could not be based on a victor's terms, but could be only a peace without victory: "Only a peace between equals can last. Only a peace the very principle of which is equality and a common participation in a common benefit. The right state of mind, the right feeling between nations, is as necessary for a lasting peace as is the just settlement of vexed questions of territory or of racial and national allegiance."

When, after the entry of the United States into the war, the President learned of the secret treaties between the Allied governments, he must have felt that his worst apprehensions had proved well-founded. During the summer of 1917 he had Colonel House organize a group of scholars to study the various issues to come before the future peace conference and above all to make policy recommendations with respect to them. The publication of the secret treaties by the Bolsheviks in November 1917 obliged the Western powers to pronounce themselves publicly on their peace aims. It was this situation that produced the Fourteen Points (January 8, 1918) which at once became basic to the American position. It may be remembered that the President's programmatic address to Congress was anticipated by the British Prime Minister's speech to the British Trade Union Congress on January 5. A comparison of the Wilson and Lloyd George programs leaves no room for doubt

353

that by this time the two statesmen were openly competing for control of the prospective peace negotiations.

Fate decreed that the Germans should put greater trust in the President than in the Prime Minister. When the time came for the Imperial government to sue for an armistice, it turned to Mr. Wilson with the request that he arrange peace negotiations on the basis of the Fourteen Points. For three weeks the President discussed the details of this matter with the Germans without even consulting the Allied governments. Only after he had secured German acceptance of his conditions did he lay his proposal before the Allies to either take or leave. Colonel House, sent to Europe to secure official acceptance of the Fourteen Points, met with such resistance that he found it necessary to suggest the possibility of a separate peace between the United States and Germany if the Allies refused to conclude an armistice and negotiate a settlement based on the principles and terms already accepted by the Germans.

To the President the distinction between a victor's peace and a just peace was crucial. He had learned from his dealings with European governments what a punitive, dictated peace might involve, and he knew that only a just peace, resting on an international organization to provide security, could endure. In a speech on the eve of his negotiations with the Germans he had stressed that "the impartial justice meted out must involve no discrimination between those to whom we wish to be just and those to whom we do not wish to be just. It must be a justice that plays no favorites and knows no standard but the equal rights of the several peoples concerned." The record leaves no doubt that he was determined to prevent Germany's being ground under foot or even condemned without a hearing. It was his full intent that the vanquished should have a chance to state their case and that the peace should be a negotiated, not a dictated one. Furthermore, the Germans were to be members of the League of Nations from the outset and free to appeal to the League for the revision of any injustices that might appear in the settlement. Unfortunately developments took a very different turn. The peace that was imposed at Versailles was far harsher than that envisaged by the Fourteen Points. Had the President's principles and plans prevailed, the world would undoubtedly have been spared much future woe.

Opinion has always been much divided with respect to the President's decision to attend the peace conference in person. Obviously his doing so had many disadvantages, especially with respect to the domestic political situation. But it is hard to see how he could have done otherwise if one bears in mind the situation as he saw it. Expecting serious conflict with Allied statesmen over peace terms, he considered it indispensable to be on the scene himself at least while the League of Nations was being organized. And in this connection, too, Mr. Wilson learned fundamental lessons. Originally he had thought of the League as a very loose organization, hardly more than a covenant between states committing them to peace and to collective action against peace-breakers. To the very eve of the peace negotiations he had resisted commitment to any of the quite numerous detailed schemes for international organization, and had stuck by his conviction that nothing more than an ambassadorial conference was needed to serve as supreme tribunal and executive organ. But once the issue came under debate, he soon realized that without much detailed organization effective action would be difficult if not impossible; that the rights and responsibilities of member states would have to be scrupulously defined; and that the preservation of peace involved so many factors as to make fairly elaborate administrative machinery imperative.

With respect to the actual terms of the Treaty of Versailles, the idea has become well-established that Mr. Wilson was so wrapped up in the drafting of the League Covenant and so intent on securing its approval by his European colleagues that he unwittingly permitted Lloyd George, Clemenceau, and other statesmen to work out a highly punitive settlement fundamentally at variance with the Fourteen Points. This is certainly an oversimplification, for it can be shown that the harshness of the Versailles Treaty was due to many factors, most of them complex. Among other things the President's lack of information on and understanding of concrete questions had much to do with some of the objectionable decisions. President Emeritus Seymour of Yale has recorded the fact that Mr. Wilson was surprised to learn that millions of Germans lived in the territory assigned to the new Czechoslovakia. "Why," he exclaimed, "Masaryk did not tell me that." His hasty recognition of the Italian claim to the Brenner frontier was clearly another instance of action taken in ignorance of basic facts. His staff experts were, to be sure, well-equipped with statistical and other factual data. On technical matters, such as reparations, their judgment was remarkably sound. On the other hand, they lacked political experience and judgment to sense the errors inherent in many decisions. Had this not been so, it would be hard to explain the readiness of both the experts and the President to assume what soon proved to be fantastically heavy and even dangerous commitments in the Middle East. Surely the American experience at Paris demonstrated to the hilt the need for deep knowledge as a prerequisite of effective leadership in international affairs.

The President must furthermore have learned that too much reliance must not be placed upon public opinion, for it would seem that he made his greatest error in this connection. It is generally agreed that during the war Mr. Wilson had proved himself a master propagandist and that, through his speeches and diplomatic notes, he had succeeded in undermining the morale of the enemy peoples as much as in firing the imagination and war spirit of the Allied populations. The ovations with which he was received in Europe in December 1918 were so enthusiastic as to warrant his thinking that his program had the support of the peoples of the world and that therefore he would, in any crisis, be able to prevail against the old-fashioned politicians. This proved very definitely not to be the case. Europeans were undoubtedly sincere in hailing Wilson for his and his country's contribution to the victory, but the elections held in both Britain and France that same December left not a shadow of doubt that there was strong and wide-spread sentiment for a "tough" peace. The spring of 1919 demonstrated with equal clarity that people everywhere were intent on providing for their future security and attaining their national aspirations. Wilson's attempt to appeal to the Italians over the heads of their leaders was a pathetic failure. Other examples could be cited to prove how strong was the popular pressure for a "realistic" settlement. It is well known that the French were profoundly disappointed by the failure of their statesmen to secure the detachment of the Rhineland from Germany. And it should be remembered that the allegedly "idealistic" American people were no less implacable. For the most part they were opposed to an armistice in November 1918 and shared Pershing's desire to annihilate the German armies and dictate peace in Berlin. And little objection was raised in the United States to the harsh Versailles Treaty itself. On the contrary, opposition was directed almost entirely at the well-intentioned Covenant of the League of Nations, which had been made an integral part of the treaty.

Experience, then, proved that Mr. Wilson was wrong in attempting to draw a distinction between governments and peoples and in thinking that the common man would support his program in preference to the search for security in traditional terms. Speaking of the Senatorial opposition to the League, the President once remarked that his adversaries did not know what the people were thinking: "They are as far from the people, the great mass of the people, as I am from Mars." On another occasion he declared that he was not obeying the mandate of party or politics, but the mandate of mankind, "the great compulsion of the Common Conscience." When his breakdown came in September 1919 he was stumping the country because he would not believe that the people, if they knew the full facts, would not insist on ratification of the Covenant of the League. It is by no means certain that Mr. Wilson was ever prepared to admit his mistake in relying too simply on public opinion. But his speaking tour in the West shows that at least belatedly he saw the need for much greater information for and instruction of the public mind. The common man may by instinct favor what is good and noble, but one can hardly escape the conviction that modern, total war involves such an effort and requires such aggressive impulses and hostile sentiments that, in the hour of victory, it is hardly possible to gear down and create a climate in which a just and reasonable settlement would find popular support. If indeed Mr. Wilson could never bring himself to acknowledge this lesson, it is none the less essential that mankind understand that modern war, from its very nature, precludes any improvement in international relationships. On the contrary, its legacy promises always to be the heightening of old and the creation of new antagonisms.

PART IV

Explorations in New Terrain

20

The Rise of the Ottoman Turks and Its Historical Background[1]

1932

Who were the Ottoman Turks, and how is their phenomenal rise to power and empire to be explained? The question has baffled and mystified historians ever since the house of Osman came to play a prominent part in European history. It was in 1551 that Hieronymus Beck von Leopoldsdorf first brought to Vienna a chronicle written in the Turkish language. Forty years later Johannes Leunclavius (Loewenklau) published his great collections of sources for Turkish history, which, as we now know, included in one form or another nearly everything in the way of Turkish chronicles that had any bearing on the early period of Ottoman history.[2] During the seventeenth and eighteenth centuries Turkish studies made rapid progress in Europe. Ignace Mouradja d'Ohsson's *Tableau Général de l'Empire Ottoman* (Paris, 1788–1824) is but the most striking evidence of the erudition and careful systematic work that was devoted to the subject.[3]

Note: Reprinted from the *American Historical Review*, XXXVII (April 1932), 468–505. Robert P. Blake was co-author.

[1] The authors are deeply indebted to Mr. Walter L. Wright, Jr., and Mr. George C. Miles, both of Princeton University, for a critical reading of the manuscript and for a number of valuable suggestions.

[2] Johannes Leunclavius, *Annales Othmanidarum a Turcis sua Lingua scripti*, etc. (Frankfurt, 1588); German translation of Leunclavius with the addition of the Pandects (Frankfurt, 1590); and the *Historiae Musulmanae Turcorum de Monumentis ipsorum exscriptae*, etc. (Frankfurt, 1591).

[3] The development of Turkish studies is well surveyed by Franz Babinger, "Die türkischen Studien in Europa bis zum Auftreten Josef von Hammer-Purgstalls," *Die Welt des Islam*, VII (1919), 103–129, with additions and corrections by Carl Ausserer, "Zur Frühgeschichte der osmanischen Studien," *Der Islam*, XII (1922), 226 ff. The history of Turkish studies at Vienna is treated in the introduction of vol. I of the *Mitteilungen zur osmanischen Geschichte* (Vienna, 1921). See also Franz Babinger, *Stambuler Buchwesen im 18. Jahrhundert* (Leipzig, 1919), and the introduction to his *Die Geschichtsschreiber der Osmanen und ihre Werke* (Leipzig, 1927); J. H. Kramers, *Over de Geschiedschrijving bij de osmaansche Turken* (Leiden, 1922). The recent work of Turkish historians is well reviewed by Ettore Rossi, "Gli Studi di storia Ottomana in Europa ed in Turchia nell'ultimo venticinquennio, 1900–1925," *L'Oriente moderno*, VI (1926), 443–460.

In 1827 there appeared at Budapest the first volume of Josef von Hammer's *Geschichte des osmanischen Reiches.* The author stated in the preface that he had spent thirty years in preliminary studies and in the collection of materials. Of the fifty sources which he listed for his first volume only five had been previously used by European historians. There is relatively little in the way of Turkish chronicles that Hammer did not know and make use of. He was the greatest authority of his time, perhaps of all time. His history and his special studies are still veritable mines of information. It is not to be wondered at that his successors were content to draw on him for facts and that little progress was made in the study of Turkish history for almost a hundred years after the appearance of his monumental work. Neither Zinkeisen, in his history of the Ottoman Empire in Europe, nor Nicholas Iorga, in his general history of the Ottoman Empire, nor Herbert Adams Gibbons, in his special study of the foundations of the Ottoman Empire, was able to make use of Turkish sources except as they had been translated into western tongues. For the most part they were forced to rely upon the information contained in Hammer.[4]

Yet Hammer, for all the loving care with which he assembled manuscript material, did not approach Ottoman history in the spirit of modern critical scholarship. He was quite content to give a coherent narrative, based upon the chronicles, and frequently, when dealing with the obscure question of the rise of the dynasty, preferred the more elegant and finished works of later Turkish historians to the confused accounts of the early writers. Until the last decade even the most elementary work of comparing and collating, to say nothing of editing and publishing the basic chronicles, remained undone. Much of it still remains undone, though several German scholars have devoted themselves to the task and have done pioneer work in clearing away part of the debris. In 1922 Friedrich Giese examined a considerable number of anonymous *Tewārīḫ-i āl-i ʿOsmān,* or early chronicles which, as he noticed, bore much similarity to each other and probably had a common origin.[5]

[4] J. W. Zinkeisen, *Geschichte des osmanischen Reiches in Europa* (7 vols., Hamburg, 1840–1863). N. Iorga, *Geschichte des osmanischen Reiches nach den Quellen dargestellt* (5 vols., Gotha, 1908–1913). H. A. Gibbons, *The Foundation of the Ottoman Empire* (Oxford, 1916).

[5] F. Giese, *Die altosmanischen anonymen Chroniken,* Teil I, *Text und Variantenverzeichnis* (Breslau, 1922); Teil II, *Uebersetzung* (*Abhandlungen für die Kunde des Morgenlandes* [Leipzig, 1925], XVII, no. 1). See also F. Giese, "Einleitung zu meiner Textausgabe der altosmanischen anonymen Chroniken," *Mit-*

From these researches it appears that these chronicles, or their prototype, were written between 1490 and 1512, that is, in the reign of Bayezid II. Furthermore, they formed part of Leunclavius's collection, published toward the end of the sixteenth century. The original writer was evidently a mere compiler, who drew from the same source as two of the oldest identified Turkish historians, ʿAšiḳpašazāde and Nešrī. Efforts have been made, especially by Paul Wittek, to determine the relationship between these earliest writers. Nešrī was used by Hammer in the version published by Leunclavius and known as the *Codex Hanivaldanus.* ʿAšiḳpašazāde he was, to his great sorrow, unable to buy, though he made use of the beautiful manuscript acquired by Queen Christina of Sweden and now in the Vatican Library (*Codex Vaticanus*). Wittek was able to prove the close relationship of these two writers, and concluded that Nešrī, who wrote a world history of which only the sixth part, dealing with the Ottoman Turks, has come down to us, was a compiler who wrote not earlier than 1512. ʿAšiḳpašazāde, who was born in 1400, but who wrote his history only in his ripe old age, about 1485, has evidently survived only in later versions, which contain continuations by other writers. Wittek believed that both the writer of the ʿAšiḳpašazāde supplement and Nešrī drew on the original version of ʿAšiḳpašazāde, who, in turn, relied upon a yet earlier chronicler, Yaḫšī Kaḳīh, for his account of events prior to 1389 or 1403. No manuscript of Yaḫšī Faḳīh, whom ʿAšiḳpašazāde himself mentions as his source, has yet been discovered. But in recent years a number of manuscripts in European libraries have been identified as copies of ʿAšiḳpašazāde. Giese, who has published a critical edition of the text, lists twelve of them, and another has been found in Cairo. At least three of these newly identified manuscripts are better than the *Codex Vaticanus,* but they fail to settle the problems connected with this important source. The supplementary chapters vary considerably in the different versions. All we can be reasonably certain of is that ʿAšiḳpašazāde himself ended his account with the year 1485 or 1486, and that the later chapters were probably written around the year 1510.[6]

teilungen zur osmanischen Geschichte, I (1922), 49–75; L. Bonelli, "Di una Cronaca Turca del 1500," *Rendiconti della R. Accademia dei Lincei,* Classe di scienze morale (1900), pp. 423 ff.

[6] Paul Wittek, "Zum Quellenproblem der aeltesten osmanischen Chroniken," *Mitteilungen zur osmanischen Geschichte,* I (1922), 77–150, and the lengthy discussion of this article by J. H. Mordtmann, *Der Islam,* XIII (1923), 152–169;

The work of classifying the early chronicles has led to the careful scrutiny of many manuscripts in European and Turkish libraries, and to the discovery and identification of works hitherto unknown. In 1922 the eminent Turkish historian, Fuad Köprülü, pointed out the importance of Šükrüllāh, who in 1457 wrote a concise world history in Persian, and thus antedates all known Ottoman chroniclers. This important account has now been translated into German by Theodor Seif.[7] Soon afterward Babinger discovered in the Bodleian Library a manuscript containing the chronicle of Uruj 'ibn 'Ādil, written in the time of Meḥmed the Conqueror, and next to Šükrüllāh the oldest known Ottoman prose history. Several other manuscripts have, since then, been identified as copies of Uruj, and a critical edition of this work has been published.[8]

At about the same time J. H. Mordtmann identified a number of anonymous chronicles of the late fifteenth century as the work of Rūḥī Edrenewī, while the Turkish historian Mükrimin Halil Yinanç made an even more important discovery of a chronicle dating from the time of Meḥmed the Conqueror. Babinger has identified this as the work of Qaramānī Meḥmed Paša, grand vizier from 1478 to 1481. Parts of this chronicle have now been published in the *Historical Review* of the Ottoman Historical Institute (*Tā'rīkḫ-i Türk Enjümeni Mejmū'asī*, vol. XIV., 1924), but it has not yet been made available in any Western language.[9]

further, Paul Wittek, "Neues zu 'Ašikpašazāde," *Mitteilungen zur osmanischen Geschichte*, II (1923–1925), 147–164; Franz Babinger, "Chronologische Miszellen," *Mitteilungen zur osmanischen Geschichte*, II (1923–1925), 311–319; Hüsejn Nāmik, "Jahšy Faḳih," *Mitteilungen zur osmanischen Geschichte*, II (1923–1925), 319–321; F. Giese, "Zum literarischen Problem der frühosmanischen Chroniken," *Orientalistische Literaturzeitung*, XXIX (1926), 850–854, and Giese's introduction to his critical edition, *Die altosmanische Chronik des 'Ašikpašazāde* (Leipzig, 1929). The beginnings of Nešri's chronicle were translated by Theodor Nöldeke and published in the *Zeitschrift der Deutschen Morgenländischen Gesellschaft*, XIII (1859), 176 ff.

[7] Köprülüzāde Meḥmed Fu'ād [Fuad Köprülü], "Bemerkungen zur religionsgeschichte Kleinasiens," *Mitteilungen zur osmanischen Geschichte*, I (1922), 203–222; Theodor Seif, "Der Abschnitt über die Osmanen in Šükrüllāh's persischer Universalgeschichte," *Mitteilungen zur osmanischen Geschichte*, II (1923–1925), 63–128.

[8] Franz Babinger, *Die frühosmanischen Jahrbücher des Urudsch* (Hanover, 1925); *Berichtigungen und Verbesserungen* (Hanover, 1926); and the review by G. Bergsträsser in *Orientalistische Literaturzeitung*, XXIX (1926), 433–438.

[9] J. H. Mordtmann, "Rūḥī Edrenewī," *Mitteilungen zur osmanischen Geschichte*, II (1923–1925), 129–136; Franz Babinger, "Die Chronik des Qaramānī Meḥmed Paša, *Mitteilungen zur osmanischen Geschichte*, II (1923–1925), 242–247. Franz Babinger, in his *Die Geschichtsschreiber der Osmanen und ihre Werke*, catalogues the various historians in chronological order, states what is known of their lives,

The investigations of these German scholars have demonstrated more clearly than ever before that we have no Turkish sources antedating the middle of the fifteenth century. The chronicles are, therefore, of doubtful value to the student of the origins of the empire. They unquestionably contain a certain amount of useful tradition, but they must be used with the utmost caution. They are crude and naïve and generally confine themselves to a legendary account of the beginnings of the empire. A conventional genealogical table tracing the descent of Osman from Japhet and Noah relieves the writers of their embarrassment when they discuss the origins of the dynasty. They are, moreover, full of confusion and contradictions so serious that, as Babinger says, even the most unbridled imagination cannot reconcile them. The truth is that, from the Turkish chronicles alone, no date in Ottoman history prior to 1421 can be fixed with any degree of certainty. No wonder that Hammer frequently relied upon the later historians and ignored the earlier sources.[10]

It might be thought that, failing Turkish sources, the Byzantine historians would be of service in clearing up the obscure story of early Ottoman history. Hammer, Iorga, and Gibbons all relied heavily upon them. Yet very little information is to be derived from the contemporary Greek writers. The Ottoman Turks were evidently too unimportant in the time of Osman to invite special attention, and the Byzantines were too much taken up with the spectacular dynastic struggles of the Paleologi to devote attention to events in Asia. Besides, the tendency toward classicism rampant among Byzantine historians after the twelfth century helped to veil the information about the irksome intruders behind a decorous rubric on the Persians, the Medes, and so forth. Consequently, only three contemporary Byzantine historians are worth mentioning at all. They are Nicephoras Gregoras, whose history covers the years 1204–1359; Pachymeres, dealing with the years 1261–1307; and John Cantacuzene, whose history treats the stormy period 1320–1356. Later historians, who, like Phrantzes and Chalcocandyles, are often

lists the known manuscripts of their works and the published editions, and gives references to discussions of their writings. This list, though necessarily provisional, is of immense value.

[10] The variations in the genealogical tables have been studied by Paul Wittek, "Der Stammbaum der Osmanen," *Der Islam*, XIV (1925), 94–100; for further discussion see Babinger, *Mitteilungen zur osmanischen Geschichte*, II (1923–1925), 311–319, and the same author's "Byzantinisch-osmanische Grenzstudien," *Festgabe für August Heisenberg, Byzantinische Zeitschrift*, XXVII/XXVIII (1929–1930), 411–415.

quoted, wrote in the middle of the fifteenth century, that is, long after the events here under discussion. They are not without value, for, like the first Turkish chroniclers, they evidently drew upon earlier sources which are now lost. But, like the Turkish chroniclers, they can be accepted only with distinct reservations. Their story is much like that of their Turkish contemporaries, and anyone who has taken the trouble to read it will come away with the conviction that the critical historian can derive from them very little reliable data regarding the beginnings of the Ottoman Empire.[11]

There remain the Arab writers, of whom three must be considered. First and foremost the great traveler, Ibn Baṭūṭāh, who traversed Asia Minor in the 1330's and visited Nicaea soon after its conquest by the Turks. His description of the country and of prevalent conditions is of great interest, but he says nothing whatever of the history of the Ottomans.[12] The second writer is Shihāb ad-Dīn al-ʿUmarī, the learned scribe of Damascus and Cairo, who in the 1340's wrote a huge historical and geographical work covering most of the Mediterranean world. Al-ʿUmarī, too, gives a detailed account of conditions in Asia Minor, but is silent in regard to the beginnings of the Ottoman state.[13]

Neither of these two writers, so far as we can see, was made use of by Iorga, though Gibbons drew heavily upon them for his account of Asia Minor at the beginning of the fourteenth century. Since his time, notice has been drawn to an interesting passage in the famous world history of Ibn Khaldūn. It deals directly with the origins of the Ottoman power, and, since it was written prior to 1402, is the oldest known account. Unfortunately it is very brief and adds little to our knowledge.

[11] R. Guilland, *Essai sur Nicéphore Gregoras* (Paris, 1926); J. Draeseke, "Zu Johannes Kantakuzenos," *Byzantinische Zeitschrift*, IX (1900), 72–84; William Miller, "The Historians Doukas and Phrantzes," *Journal of Hellenic Studies*, XLVI (1926), 63–71; and the same author's "The Last Athenian Historian, Laonikos Chakokondyles," *Journal of Hellenic Studies*, XLII (1922), 36–49. The traditional story of Turkish origins, as found in Turkish and Byzantine sources, has been republished by two competent scholars: J. Draeseke, "Der Uebergang der Osmanen nach Europa im XIV. Jahrhundert," *Neue Jahrbücher für das klassische Altertum*, XXXI (1913), 476–504, and F. von Kraelitz, "Das osmanische Herrscherhaus und die Gründung des osmanischen Reiches," *Oesterreichische Montasschrift für den Orient*, XL (1914), 38–40.

[12] C. Defrémery and B. R. Sanguinetti, *Voyages d'Ibn Batoutah* (Paris, 1877), II, 317 ff.

[13] French translation by M. Quatremère, "Notice de l'ouvrage qui a pour titre Mesalek Alabsar fi Memalek Alamsar," *Notices et extraits des manuscrits*, XIII (1838), 151–384. There is now a critical edition of the part of Al-ʿUmarī's work dealing with Asia Minor, by Franz Taeschner, *Al-ʿUmarīs Bericht über Anatolien in seinem Werke Masālik al-absār fī Mamālik al-amsār* (Leipzig, 1929).

Attention was first called to it by the late Clément Huart, the eminent French scholar, who published a translation of it. Some years later it was noted by Richard Hartmann, who published a summary, evidently without knowing of Huart's translation.[14]

In the absence of literary records, the historian is frequently able to derive valuable information from the study of coins or monuments. Here again the prospect for Turkish studies is disheartening. Osman coined no money, but very interesting coins, struck in the first year of the reign of Orkhan, have recently been published by a Turkish scholar.[15] As for inscriptions, the earliest yet discovered is on the castle at Brusa, and dates from the reign of Orkhan, probably from the year 1337 or 1338. There is another dating from the reign of Murad I (*c.* 1378) on the Yeshil Jami at Ismid, but the splendid long inscription in Turkish at Kutahia, dating from the year 1411, belongs to the last Kermian ruler, and not to the Ottomans. Such buildings as were erected by the early sultans at Nicaea and were still standing in our day were mostly destroyed by the retreating Greek armies in 1921–1922, so that there is little chance for valuable results from archaeological investigation.[16]

It is obvious that, for lack of the source material usually at the disposal of the historian, the whole question of the origins of the Ottoman Empire cannot be approached directly. The problem must be attacked from the rear, so to speak. We must find out not only who the Turks were, but also what was the background of their rise to power. Recent historians have recognized the necessity for this procedure. Iorga, for example, devotes one hundred and fifty pages of his five volume work to a discussion of the Seljuq Turks, whereas Hammer disposed of this matter in forty pages, though his history took ten volumes to reach the time of the treaty of Küchük Kainarji. Gibbons, in his *Foundation of the Ottoman Empire,* made an even more valiant effort to throw light upon the conditions in Asia Minor. Relying on Ibn Baṭūṭāh and Al-

---

[14] Clément Huart, in his review of Gibbons's book (*Journal asiatique,* 2nd ser., IX [1917], 345–350); the translation in Huart, "Les Origines de l'Empire Ottoman," *Journal des savants,* n.s., XV (April 1917), 157–166; see also Richard Hartmann, "Das 'älteste' uns erhaltene 'Osmanische Geschichte enthaltende Werk,'" *Mitteilungen zur osmanischen Geschichte,* II (1923–1925), 306–308.

[15] 'Ali, "Osmanlı Imparatorluğunun ilk sikkesi ve ilk akçesi," *Tarih-i Osmanı Encümeni Mecmuası,* VIII (1917), 48.

[16] Franz Taeschner, "Anatolische Forschungen," *Zeitschrift der Deutschen Morgenländischen Gesellschaft,* LXXXII (1928), 83–118; Franz Taeschner and Paul Wittek, "Die Vezirfamilie der Gandarlyzäde und ihre Denkmäler," *Der Islam,* XVIII (1929), 60–115.

'Umarī, he studied the disruption of the Seljuq state, while from the Byzantine historians he drew the material for his account of the weakness of the Greek Empire. His stress upon the utter impotence of the Byzantine state and his emphasis upon the essentially European character of early Ottoman expansion is without question the most important contribution made by his monograph. Yet neither Iorga nor Gibbons had much to go by on the Oriental side: for the early history of the Turks, the books of writers like Vambéry and Cahun, excellent perhaps in their day but now superseded; on the history of the Seljuqs, not a single scholarly monograph. The fact is that the history of the Seljuq sultanate of Rum has not been adequately treated even in our own day, at least not in any Western language. Most of the Seljuq sources that have been published by Houtsma, Melioranski, and others, deal with the earlier period of Seljuq domination, and refer primarily to the eastern parts of the Seljuq empire. Turkish historians have, in recent years, published a certain amount of inscriptional material from former Seljuq centers in Anatolia, and have written some good monographic studies on the history of the succession states of the sultanate of Rum. But the history of that sultanate, say from 1100 to 1300, still requires systematic treatment.[17] Of geographical or descriptive material there is nothing on the Turkish side. During the sixteenth century the Turks translated some of the Arab writers, but it was only at the very end of the sixteenth and the beginning of the seventeenth century that serious works like those of Meḥmed al-'Āsiq and Ḥājjī Khalīfa made their appearance.[18] As for the Arab geographers, Ibn Baṭūṭāh and Al-'Umarī, valuable as their observations are, they do not strike at fundamentals. Their descriptions of the Ottoman territories are brief and anecdotal. Ibn Baṭūṭāh was more interested in the hot baths and sanatorium built by Sultan Orkhan

[17] M. T. Houtsma, *Recueil de textes relatifs à l'histoire des Seldjoucides* (Leiden, 1886–1902); some portions of the Seljuq-namé have been translated and paraphrased by P. Melioranski, "Sel'dzukname, kak Istočnik dlya Istorii Vizantii v XII i XIII Vekakh," *Vizantiiskii Vremennik*, I (1894), 613 ff. The best account, though not definitive, is to be found in the first volume of Fuad Köprülü's *History of the Turks* (*Türkiye Tarihi*, Constantinople, 1923). The article on the Seljuqs by H. M. J. Loewe, in the *Cambridge Medieval History* (vol. IV, chap. 10 [B]) is hardly more than the usual catalogue of battles, rulers, and dynasties. In English, the best treatment is still that of E. G. Browne, *A Literary History of Persia* (London, 1906), II, 165 ff., 297 ff., but see also M. T. Houtsma, "Some Remarks on the History of the Saljuks," *Acta Orientalia*, III (1924–1925), 136 ff. Most of the monographic studies in Turkish are listed by Babinger in the introduction of his *Die Geschichtsschreiber der Osmanen und ihre Werke*.

[18] Franz Taeschner, "Die geographische Literatur der Osmanen," *Zeitschrift der Deutschen Morgenländischen Gesellschaft*, LXXVII (1923), 31–80.

at Brusa than in the problems which concern us. Al-'Umarī was himself never on the ground, and relied upon what he could learn from other travelers whom he met at Cairo.

In order to understand the rise of the Ottoman Turks one must have clearly in mind various factors inherent in the geography and history of Asia Minor, as well as certain fundamental developments in the conditions of Anatolia in the period just preceding the appearance of Ertoghrul, Osman, and their followers. The Anatolian plateau forms a geologic unit. It is a relatively barren plain with a salt sink in the center, and is surrounded on all sides by rather lofty mountain ranges. Its surface is so diversified that it is hard to maintain communication between the different parts. The salt sink in the center, to the west of the Halys River, impedes direct longitudinal traffic; the wooded areas on the coast have little in common and no connection with the barren plains of the uplands; and the deep river valleys are effectually sundered from each other by the mountains. While the mountain ranges do not cut up the terrain to the same extent as in the Balkans, the general relief is distinctly broken. These individual and sharply marked geographical units form the districts and cantons which play a large part in the life of Asia Minor. They are the warp and woof of which the changing web of Anatolian history has been woven. If they play but little part in the written records, the reason is that the Byzantine sources contain little information about the provinces of the empire, while the Armenian historians were for the most part locally minded.

At any rate, the canton was a characteristic phenomenon of the Anatolian plateau. The unending list of principalities ruled by the Hittite monarchs, by Mithridates Eupator, Tigranes, and other potentates, must have been of this type.[19] They were organized on a clan basis and even when small and weak were remarkably tenacious of life. Especially in eastern Anatolia they continually emerged unscathed from the wreck of larger kingdoms. Thus geography made for disruption, and explains the strong tendency in Anatolian history toward the formation of small social and political entities.[20]

[19] See the *Cambridge Ancient History*, II, chaps. 1 and 5; L. A. Meyer and J. Garstang, "Index of Hittite Names, Geographical with Notes," British School of Archaeology, *Supplemental Papers* (1923), and the same authors essay, "Kizzuwadna and Other Hittite States," *Journal of Egyptian Archaeology*, II (1925), 23–35.

[20] Cantonal structure in Armenia and Georgia is well discussed by I. Džavakhov, *Gosudarstvennyï Stroï drevneï Gruzii i drevneï Armenii* (St. Petersburg, 1905); and N. G. Adonts, *Armeniya v Epokhu Iustiniana* (St. Petersburg, 1909). J. Lau-

The counterpart of the cantonal structure was the confused linguistic map of the region. The diversity of tongues spoken in Asia Minor was very great and went back to the dawn of recorded history. The Hittite kings used prayers in seven distinct tongues in the state liturgies.[21] Speaking of the Caucasus region Strabo says: "At any rate seventy tribes come together in it (Dioscurias), though others, who care nothing for the facts, actually say three hundred. All speak different languages because of the fact that, by reason of their obstinacy and ferocity, they live in scattered groups and without intercourse with one another."[22] Neither the Hellenization attempted by the Seleucids and the Pergamene kings, nor the partial Latin or Greek urbanization which took place under the Roman Empire effactually extirpated the native dialects and patois. Isaurian and kindred Asianic dialects remained in current use at least until the seventh century. Knowledge of Greek was apparently rather superficial and probably sporadic in the villages, a thin gloss over the underlying barbarism of customs and speech.[23]

The confused racial and linguistic conditions in Anatolia were accentuated by religious factors. With the appearance of Christianity and the adoption of the Zoroastrian cult by the Sasanid rulers of Persia (226 A.D.), missionary activity and persecution began to take place.[24] Then came the first Islamic deluge, in the seventh century. This, to be sure, left but few traces in western and central Asia Minor, and even in the East, where the new frontier of the Byzantine and Arab empires ran through Armenia, there was little contact between the Moslem towns and the Christian countryside. A good many Armenian and Georgian families emigrated southward and westward, but those that remained under Moslem rule appear to have gotten along very well with the conquerors. In the tenth century we actually find members

rents, *L'Arménie entre Byzance et l'Islam depuis la conquête arabe jusqu'en 886* (Paris, 1919), is wholly useless except as a collection of material.

21 See E. Forrer, "Die Inschriften und Sprachen des Hatti-Reiches," *Zeitschrift der Deutschen Morgenländischen Gesellschaft*, LXXVI (1922), 174–269.

22 Strabo, *Geography*, bk. 11, pt. 2, sec. 16 (trans. H. L. ones, Loeb Library edition, V, 208 ff.).

23 See K. Holl, "Das Fortleben der Volkssprachen in Kleinasien in nachchristlicher Zeit," *Hermes*, XLIII (1908), 240–254; W. M. Ramsay, *The Cities and Bishoprics of Phrygia* (Oxford, 1895–1897), I, 9 ff.; Richard Leonhard, *Paphlagonia* (Berlin, 1915), chaps. 7, 9, 10. The interesting and instructive linguistic evolution of a Caucasian district is given by N. Marr, *Georgii Merčul, Zitie sv. Grigoriya Khandzt' üskago* (St. Petersburg, 1911).

24 J. Labourt, *Le Christianisme dans l'empire perse sous la dynastie sassanide* (2nd ed., Paris, 1904).

of the Armenian and Georgian nobility, who were Christians, adopting Moslem names.[25]

Of much greater importance was the appearance of the Turks. First into Persia and Mesopotamia, then into Armenia and Anatolia proper, came successive infiltrations, impelled by the same pressure from the rear that their kindred and congeners, the Pečenegs and Kumans, were sensing in the northern steppes. Great advances have been made in recent years in the study of the racial affinities, the ethnological position and the religious status of these Turks. For the purposes of this paper it is unnecessary to discuss the interesting researches of Thomsen, Marquart, Pelliot, Barthold, and others who, by the use of Chinese sources and the discovery of early Turkish inscriptions, have succeeded in tracing back the existence of Turkish tribes to the beginning of the Christian era, or even further.[26]

When the first waves of Arab invasion reached the banks of the Oxus, Turkestan was in the hands of Turkish tribes. For the space of a generation, in fact from 560 to 585, a mighty Turkish khanate existed whose confines stretched from the Sea of Azov to the Altaï, and relations with it formed the central point of the diplomatic endeavors of both the Roman emperors and the Sasanid Shahan-shahs. This overweighty structure collapsed almost as soon as it was erected, and the congeries of tribes, Turkish and others, resolved itself into an eastern and a western branch. These groups have left traces behind them in the monuments, carved and written. To them are attributable the Orkhon inscriptions belonging to the eastern kingdom, the fragments of literature in the Uighur dialect, written in a script derived from the Syriac, as well as documents written not only in Uighur characters, but also in Nestorian Syriac, Manichaean, Brahmi, and other alphabets, and other monuments which have been found in the sands and caves of Turkestan. The culture of the Turkish races was largely external, and was based

---

[25] M. Ghazarian, *Armenien unter der arabischen Herrschaft biz zur Entstehung des Bagratidenreiches* (Marburg, 1903); J. Laurents, *L'Arménie*; K. Kostaneanc, "Vimikan Taregir," *Bibliotheca Armeno-Georgica* (Petropolis, 1913), II; H. Hübschmann, *Grammatik der armenischen Sprache* (Leipzig, 1807), II, pt. 2, 285 ff., 320–321.

[26] See especially the late W. W. Barthold's address to the First Turcological Congress at Baku in 1926, now published in German translation by Paul Wittek under the title, "Der heutige Stand und die nächsten Aufgaben der geschichtlichen Erforschung der Türkvölker," *Zeitschrift der Deutschen Morgenländischen Gesellschaft*, LXXXIII (1929), 121–142; the bibliography in Marie A. Czaplicka, *Turks of Central Asia in History and at the Present Day* (Oxford, 1918); and W. W. Barthold, "Turks, History," *Encyclopaedia of Islam*, IV (1931).

upon the syncretistic civilization, partly Christian, partly Manichaean, partly Buddhist, which we find in the forgotten states of Chinese Turkestan. Chinese influences were also operative. After long struggles the Turkestan area was subdued by the Arabs in 758–759, and the Turkish tribes of the region, who belonged to the family of the Ghuzz (Oguz) gradually adopted Islam during the ninth and tenth centuries. The eastern branch maintained itself with ups and downs only until 745, when it was overthrown by the Uighurs.[27]

In the tenth century the conquests of the Chitai, a Mongolian race, seem to have started the Turks moving westward into Islamic regions. But long before this, at least as early as the middle of the eighth century, Turkish slaves were kept at Baghdad and had become the most influential element in the armies of the caliph. There must have been thousands of them in Mesopotamia and eastern Asia Minor before the Ghuzz tribes arrived in the tenth and eleventh centuries. But it was the newcomers who set up the Seljuq dynasty and in a short time reunited the scattered states of Islam, thus consolidating the Mohammedan power just in time to meet the onslaughts of the Crusaders. From the start the Seljuqs proved themselves valiant champions of religion. It is hardly too much to say that they saved Islam and laid the basis for the Turkification of Asia Minor.[28]

The history of the Seljuqs yet remains to be written, but certain outstanding factors in the Turk invasion are fairly clear. The Seljuqs, like most of the Turk tribes of Central Asia, were nomadic in their habits and forms of organization. But the social structure of the newcomers was in no sense a hindrance to their settlement in large numbers in Asia Minor. From time immemorial the agricultural, village-dwelling populations of the Anatolian plateau had been the neighbors of nomadic stocks. The villages, for the most part, were located along the slopes of the foothills or in the more fertile and well watered river valleys.

[27] W. Radloff, *Die alttürkischen Inschriften der Mongolei* (St. Petersburg, 1895; N.F., 1897); Barthold, "Turks, History," *Encyclopaedia of Islam.* There are now German and English translations of the Orkhon inscriptions, based upon the Danish translations of Wilhelm Thomsen, by H. H. Schaeder, *Zeitschrift der Deutschen Morgenländischen Gesellschaft,* LXXVIII (1924), 121–175, and E. D. Ross, *Bulletin of the School of Oriental Studies,* V, pt. 4 (1930), 861–876.

[28] Barthold, "Turks, History," *Encyclopaedia of Islam;* Wittek, *Zeitschrift der Deutschen Morgenländischen Gesellschaft,* LXXXIII (1929). By far the best studies of this period are Fuad Köprülü's *Türkiye Tarihi* (Constantinople, 1923), I, and W. W. Barthold's *Turkestan down to the Mongol Invasion,* Gibb Memorial Series, V (London, 1928). A good brief introduction is Eugen Oberhummer's *Die Türken und das osmanische Reich* (Berlin, 1917).

They did not extend to the upland pastures which are thickly blanketed with snow during the winter, nor out into the barren, grass covered, and fairly arid steppe beyond the foothill belt. These areas had long been the habitat of what we might term the synoecious nomad, a social phenomenon much more familiar to us from the history of Iran than from the history of Asia Minor.[29] On the Iranian plateau the symbiosis of nomad and cultivator has continued unbroken to the present day. The adjustment between the two elements is easily made and a *modus vivendi* is not hard to establish. It is less commonly known that the very same phenomenon is characteristic of Asia Minor at the present day, and the same is true, though to a lesser extent, of the Balkans.[30] The last, westernmost representatives of this movement are probably the gypsies. So far as Asia Minor is concerned these peoples evidently go back to very remote times. It appears from the Hittite tablets that in the thirteenth and fourteenth centuries before Christ a tribe of nomads who lived in the center of Asia Minor and were primarily engaged in horse breeding spoke a language closely akin to pure Sanskrit, and differing decidedly from the *Ursprache* of the dominant folk, Indo-Europeans though they were.[31] Our material does not suffice to show whether during the Byzantine period these nomad elements were racially of a different stock than the populations around them, nor can we show this for Armenia, except perhaps in the case of the Kurds. There seems to have been some diversity of race between the various unsettled or nomadic elements.

At any rate, the peculiar populational conditions in Asia Minor made it possible for large numbers of Turks, arriving over a period of many decades, to slip through the normal channels of life without causing much disturbance. They brought with them the nomad's ferocity and energy, but also the nomad's willingness to submit to discipline. Gradually they settled down to an agricultural life, living in villages side by side with the original non-Turkish settlements. The local population, accustomed to living with an intrusive nomad element, cared but little to what stock the intruders belonged. To be sure, some individuals and even families moved out, especially those belonging to the upper classes.

[29] The Bakhtiyars are a good modern example, but the Parthians retained certain nomadic characteristics down to the fall of their state.

[30] F. W. Hasluck, *Christianity and Islam under the Sultans* (Oxford, 1929), I, 5 ff. See an interesting passage in the life of St. George the Athonite in P. Peeters, *Histoires monastiques géorgiennes* (Brussels, 1923), pp. 102 ff.

[31] P. Giles, "The People of Asia Minor," *Cambridge Ancient History*, II, 13.

For the most part they moved into Byzantine territory, migrating southward along the Taurus.[32] But the large mass of the population, not only in the country, but also in the towns, gradually became submerged by Islam or apostasized.[33] The result was the striking disappearance of the Greek language and culture from the interior of Asia Minor, an important development which deserves far more study than it has received.

This process can be understood only if one remembers that the Greek population in many parts of Asia Minor could never have been very dense, and that Greek culture was hardly more than a veneer so far as the mass of the people was concerned. Along the frontiers the population tended to be heretical in a large measure—Armenians, Paulicians, Mardaites, Nestorians, who were not Greek by origin and were distinctly unsympathetic to the Greeks in a religious way.[34] In a number of instances we find serious disturbances arising because of the persecution of these heretics by the orthodox authorities. After the Seljuq conquest a distinctly nationalistic and chauvinistic trend made its appearance in the Orthodox Church itself, so that there was less chance than ever for the Greeks to carry on successful propaganda outside Byzantine territory.[35]

The accuracy of this view may be established by a study of the areas of Asia Minor where the Greek language survived up to modern times.[36] We must exclude later colonies of islanders who established themselves upon the seacoast, and we must except also the trading elements present in every Turkish town. This having been done we find that Greek is (or was) spoken in the interior of Asia Minor in but two areas: Pontus, in the valleys leading back from the seacoast from Rizé to Kerasund,

[32] The importance of this movement is emphasized in the otherwise useless book of the late F. W. Bussell, *The Roman Empire: Essays on the Constitutional History from the Accession of Domitian, 81 A.D., to the Retirement of Nicephorus III, 1081 A.D.* (London, New York, 1910). The effects of the nomad infiltrations are well discussed by Ramsay, *The Cities*, II, 302.

[33] H. Gelzer, "Abriss der Kaisergeschichte," in Karl Krumbacher, *Geschichte der byzantinischen Literatur* (2nd ed., Munich, 1896), p. 1012, is almost certainly wrong in assuming that there was a sudden and wholesale apostasy. See R. Oberhummer and H. Zimmerer, *Durch Syrien und Kleinasien* (Berlin, 1899), chap. 16.

[34] See A. Vogt, *Basile Ier* (Paris, 1908), pp. 295 ff., and A. A. Vasiliev, *Vizantiya i Araby za Vremya Makedonskoi Dinastii* (St. Petersburg, 1905), *passim*.

[35] This is exemplified in the affair of Johannes Italos (1085). See F. Chalandon, *Essai sur le règne d'Alexis I. Comnène* (Paris, 1900), pp. 310 ff., and especially N. Marr, "Ioann Petritsi, Gruzinskii Neoplatonik XII-go Veka," *Zapiski Vostočnago Otdeleniya Imp. Rossïiskago Arkheologičeskago Obščestva*, XIX (1909), 53–114.

[36] See the excellent study of R. M. Dawkins, *Modern Greek in Asia Minor* (Cambridge, 1916).

some inland colonies between Pontus and Cappadocia near Shabin-Kara-Hissar, and some twenty-six villages in Cappadocia in the neighborhood of Tyana and Nazianos. To these we can add Silli near Konia, Livisi in Lycia, and Gyolde in Lydia. The dialects spoken in these places show that the Greek population goes back to Byzantine times and further. All other colonies date definitely from the Turkish period.

One or two interesting deductions can be made from this distribution. First, the Greek character of the Pontic area was obviously due to the continued existence of the empire of Trebizond. Second, Greek disappeared wholly from western Asia Minor. Third, the Cappadocian centers were probably stimulated by the presence of the Pontic ones. Clearly, the hold which Hellenism had on the Anatolian plateau was relatively slight.

Even if it is true, and there is evidence to substantiate the view, that the Turks, whether Seljuq or Ottoman, pursued destructive tactics in making their conquests, it seems to be equally true that, once an area was subjugated, conditions rapidly became settled. Sir William M. Ramsay, most eminent of modern students of Anatolian history, has drawn a vivid picture of the course of events in the Byzantine-Seljuq frontier area in Phrygia during the period from the end of the eleventh to the end of the twelfth century. The evidence indicates, he says, that much of the territory was voluntarily abandoned to the Turks by the warring claimants to the Byzantine throne, who were not scrupulous in choosing their friends. The Seljuq conquest was at first merely nominal, and involved little more than the payment of tribute. To be sure, there was more or less campaigning in this area throughout the whole period, and the warfare was ferocious and destructive. But it was spasmodic and inconclusive. Apart from the raids and the campaigns, the country was quiet and the rule of the Turks lenient and tolerant. "Even the prejudiced Byzantine historians," says Sir William, "let drop a few hints that the Christians in many cases preferred the rule of the sultans to that of the emperors." So far as one can detect, the inhabitants submitted without offering resistance. There is no mention of defense. "Each city stood until the Turks gathered power to overthrow it." Furthermore, there is no trace of religious persecution by the Seljuqs. Most of the Christians evidently became Mohammedan, and Ramsay thinks that the Oriental substratum in the population asserted itself and took naturally to an Oriental religion. However that may be, a study that has been made of the evolution of the Christian archdioceses in

Asia Minor after the beginning of the Seljuq conquest indicates that there was a very rapid decrease in the number of Christians and a very rapid impoverishment of the congregations. Since it is fairly clear that the conquerors spared the inhabitants and granted them religious freedom, it must be assumed that the population went over voluntarily to the new faith, either in order to retain its property or else to avoid being at a disadvantage in other ways. Apostasy was evidently a practical measure for many people, and one which did not occasion much searching of hearts.[37]

It seems to us that the important process of Islamization in Asia Minor can be made yet more easily understandable if the peculiar color of Turkish Islam is borne in mind. It will be remembered that, almost from the beginning, there was a pronounced mystical trend in the teaching of Islam. The literature on the subject is immense, yet the problem still presents innumerable difficulties and still leads to sharp differences of opinion among competent authorities. Here it need only be said that in Islam, where there was no organized church government or single authority, there was more room for variant interpretations and divergent viewpoints. The ascetic, mystical strain in Islam was traced back by the mystics themselves to the earlier part of the Prophet's own career, as set forth in the Koran. Some scholars have tried to connect this attitude with the strong movement of opposition which developed against the Omayyads and eventually led to the establishment of the 'Abbāsid caliphate. But the forces which finally overthrew the Omayyads came from the confines of the empire, from Khurāsān, a region which was one of the strongholds of Messianism. This Messianic movement, while it was in a sense mystical, appears to have been quite distinct from Islamic mysticism (Ṣūfiism) properly speaking, as it developed in the time of the 'Abbāsids. In any event, the theory and practice of mysticism was worked out more especially in Iraq, Syria, and Egypt. How much of Christian influence, of Neo-Platonism, of Manichaeanism, of Buddhism, and of other Persian and Indian elements went into its makeup we need not stop to inquire. The subject is one on which even the most distinguished authorities seem unable to agree. In fact it is almost impossible to determine even the relation of this movement to unorthodox Islam (Shī'ah), if, indeed, there was a connection. All we can say is that both involved a belief in an esoteric

[37] Ramsay, *The Cities*, I, 15 ff., 26 ff., 300–301; II, 695 ff.; A. H. Wächter, *Der Verfall des Griechentums in Kleinasien im XIV. Jahrhundert* (Leipzig, 1903).

doctrine which had supposedly come down from the Prophet through his son-in-law, the fourth caliph, 'Alī.[38]

Central Asia, that great trade emporium of the early Middle Ages, lay at the junction of many Eastern religious currents. Fuad Köprülü, the eminent Turkish historian, has made a detailed study of the religious evolution of the Turks while they were still in that region, and has, with the aid of many unpublished documents, done more than anyone to throw light on the utterly obscure religious history of Asia Minor in the times of the Seljuq and early Ottoman rulers.[39] He stresses the fact that the Turks, even after their conversion to Islam, retained many elements of their earlier pagan religion. They disliked the rigorous tenets of orthodox Islam, because these tenets conflicted with their own traditions. For that reason they, like most nomad peoples, leaned strongly in the direction of mysticism, and favored the holy men, monks, and dervishes. The Central Asian cloisters and orders became more and more powerful, and had a larger popular following at times than the rulers themselves.[40]

The greatest figure in the history of Turkish mysticism was Aḥmed Yasawī, who lived in Central Asia in the eleventh century and founded the first dervish order using the Turkish language. It was he who translated the ideas of Ṣūfiism into Turkish. His following was immense and his influence on the later development of other orders was of prime

---

[38] Of recent discussions we mention, as among the best, the various works of R. A. Nicholson; D. B. Macdonald, *The Religious Attitude and Life in Islam* (Chicago, 1909); Ignaz Goldziher, *Vorlesungen über den Islam* (2nd ed., Heidelberg, 1925); French translation: *Le Dogme et la loi de l'Islam* (Paris, 1920); H. Lammens, *L'Islam: Croyances et institutions* (Beirut, 1926); Louis Massignon, *La Passion d'Ali-Hallâj* (Paris, 1914–1921), with exhaustive bibliography; Theodor Nöldeke, "Zur Ausbreitung des Schiitismus," *Der Islam*, XIII (1923), 70–81; Richard Hartmann, "Zur Frage nach der Herkunft und den Anfängen des Sufitums," *Der Islam*, VI (1916), 31–70; H. H. Schaeder, "Manichäer und Muslime," *Zeitschrift der Deutschen Morgenländischen Gesellschaft*, LXXXII (1928), lxxvi–lxxxi.

[39] Köprülüzäde Mehmed Fu'äd [Fuad Köprülü], *Türk Edibiyatinda ilk Mutasavviflar* (Constantinople, 1919); "Les Origines du Bektachisme," *Actes du congrès international d'histoire des religions* (Paris, 1925), II, 391–411. There is an excellent analysis of the former work by Theodor Menzel, entitled, "Köprülüzäde Mehmed Fu'äds Werk über die ersten Mystiker in der Türkischen Literatur," *Körösi Czoma-Archiv* (*Zeitschrift für türkische Philologie und verwandte Gebiete*), II (1927), 28–310. Menzel's article, "Die aeltesten türkischen Mystiker," *Zeitschrift der Deutschen Morgenländischen Gesellschaft*, LXXIX (1925), 269–289, is hardly more than a summary of the same work. See also the review of Köprülü by Clément Huart, "Les Anciens Derviches tores," *Journal des savants*, XX (1922), 5–18, and "Turks, Literature," by Köprülü, *Encyclopaedia of Islam*, IV (1931).

[40] Barthold, *Turkestan*, pp. 310 ff.

importance. With their conquest of Asia Minor the Seljuqs transplanted all these orders into their new possessions. The princes themselves were strictly orthodox (Sunnite) and Islamic mysticism, which reached its highest development in the time of the Seljuqs in the persons of Ibnu'l-'Arabi and Jalāl ed-Dîn i-Rumî, was officially in complete consonance with the demands of strict observance. The great Mevlevi order, founded by Jalāl ed-Dîn, was always orthodox. But among the common people all sorts of heterodoxy flourished, mixed with primitive religious practices. The popular dervishes propounded theories which, as Köprülü says, were a conglomerate of esoteric Moslem elements, indigenous beliefs of Asia Minor and Iran, and an admixture of various schismatic forms of Christianity, together with philosophic Ṣūfic ideas. Evidently it was not far from these primitive religious tenets to the popular religion prevalent in Asia Minor in the form of heterodox Christianity. At the present day Asia Minor is still full of seminomadic tribes whose religion is a mixture of Shīʿah Mohammedanism and Christianity, with a strong substratum of pagan animistic elements.[41]

Now it is a general phenomenon throughout the Near East that, inasmuch as religious faith was closely connected with linguistic and cultural influences, a change of religion tended to bring about a change of culture as well. A striking instance of this is perhaps the fate of the Chalcedonite Armenians, who were ultimately absorbed by the Georgians. The apostates tended naturally to lose their national peculiarities and ultimately also their native language.[42] The upshot of the Seljuq invasion and conquest of Asia Minor was, then, the disappearance of Christianity and Greek influence in the larger part of Asia Minor, and the effective Turkification and Islamization of this region. Idrīsī, describing the country in 1117, still used the old names, while Ibn Baṭūṭāh, traversing the region in the 1330's, used purely Turkish names. This is a striking illustration of the transformation that had taken place. It will

41 Köprülü, *Türk Edebiyatinda*; Franz Babinger, "Der Islam in Kleinasien," *Zeitschrift der Deutschen Morgenländischen Gesellschaft*, LXXVI (1922), 126–152, and the vigorous reply by Theodor Nöldeke, *Der Islam*, XIII (1923), 70–81. See furthermore, the illuminating discussion in Hasluck, *Christianity*, I, 128, 139 ff., and chap. 13; "Shīʿa," by R. Strothmann, in *Encyclopaedia of Islam*, IV, (1931), 350–358.

42 N. Marr, "Kreščenie Armyan, Gruzin, Abkhazov, Alanov sv. Grigoriem: Arabskaya Versiya," *Zapiski Vostočnago Otdeleniya Imp. Rossïiskago Arkheologičeskago Obščestva*, XV (1904–1905), 63 ff.; also his "Arkaun, Mongol'skoe Nazvanie Khristian v svyazi s Voprosom ob Armyanakh Khalkedonitakh," *Vizantïiskïi Vremennik*, XII (1906), 1–68.

readily be seen how important a preparation this was for the later establishment of Ottoman rule.[43]

The thirteenth century was a memorable period in the history of the Near East, and especially of Asia Minor. It witnessed the establishment and disappearance of the ephemeral Latin Empire and the temporary transfer of the Greek Empire to Nicaea, as well as the decline and disintegration of the Seljuq sultanate of Rum (Konia) and the first great Mongol conquest. For the moment we must confine our attention to these latter developments.

The Mongols, having conquered Armenia, defeated the sultan of Rum in 1243 and temporarily occupied the capital of the Seljuq state. From that time on the Seljuq ruler was a tributary of the Mongol Great Khan or his lieutenants. Just what did this mean? We do not know exactly, for we lack information as to how the Mongols governed territories of this type. Suffice it to say, however, that the Mongols never really occupied Asia Minor. Their headquarters were in Armenia. Military authorities were established at Konia and other key places, and they certainly interfered in the domestic affairs of the vassal states. Occasionally the vassal rulers were obliged to furnish contingents for new Mongol expeditions. In fact, it is said that the sultan of Rum was defeated largely by Armenian and Georgian contingents fighting in an army only the nucleus of which was Mongol. The Mongols appear never to have been very numerous.[44] But the chief duty of the Mongol agents was to see to the collection and payment of the tribute in the territories not actually occupied by their armies. Thus we are told that the sultan of Rum had to deliver annually 1,200,000 hyperpers, 500 pieces of silk, 500 camels, and other things, and that he had to supply the Mongols, whenever they were in his territory, with horses, provisions, and other necessities.[45]

We do not believe, therefore, that the Mongol conquest made any very profound changes in Anatolia. It served to drive many more Turks from Central Asia into the peninsula, but it caused little permanent social or cultural change, despite the ravages and devastations of the armies. Once a country was conquered, a lenient régime was instituted

[43] Leonhard, *Paphlagonia,* chap. 10. This important transformation is well discussed by T. Kowalski, "Turkish Dialects," *Encyclopaedia of Islam,* IV (1931).

[44] Georg Altunian, *Die Mongolen und ihre Eroberungen in kaukasischen und kleinasiatischen Ländern im XIII. Jahrhundert* (Berlin, 1911), p. 80.

[45] C. d'Ohsson, *Histoire des Mongols* (Paris, 1834), III, 83.

and the greatest toleration shown the Christians. Thus the most magnificent Armenian manuscript now extant was written at Erznga (Erzinjan) between the years 1269 and 1271, that is, during the Mongol rule. It is a complete manuscript of the Old and New Testaments, with what is unquestionably the finest series of Biblical illuminations now in existence, extraordinary in technique and flawless in execution.[46] That the Mongol rule in no way affected the greatness of Persian literature is a well-known fact.[47]

The decline of the Seljuq power had already begun when the Mongols appeared upon the scene. The reasons for this phenomenon were evidently deep-seated. Apart from the peculiar conditions in Asia Minor, all empires set up by nomadic peoples like the Turks showed a strong tendency toward disintegration, because they were built up on units like the family and tribe, which could only be held together for a short time by some dominant personality. Furthermore, there was no tradition of strong autocracy among the Turks. The dominions of the ruler would often be divided among his sons, with the result that partitions frequently ended in dissolution, especially if defeat at the hands of a rival power intervened. The Mongols defeated the Seljuqs in 1243. In 1260 they were themselves defeated by the Mamelukes of Egypt. From that time on till the end of the century both the Mongol and the Seljuq powers were wracked with dynastic struggles and antagonisms, in which Egypt played a very prominent part. Under the circumstances it is difficult to see how the Mongol conquest can be made to explain the conditions in the sultanate of Rum.[48]

The most potent cause for the breakup of the Seljuq state was probably the habit of the rulers of granting territory in fief to their followers. The nature of these grants is, however, very obscure and our information on the later twelfth and thirteenth centuries so scant that it is almost impossible to make a definite pronouncement. The older theory, advanced by Hammer, that this practice, like most of the Seljuq culture, was taken over from the Persians, is no longer accepted by students

[46] MS 2555 of the library of the Armenian convent of St. James in Jerusalem. Some of the miniatures have been reproduced, rather badly, by A. Tchobanian, *La Roseraie d'Arménie* (Paris, 1918), vol. I., and by F. Murat, *Yaytnut'iun Yovhannu: Hin Hay T'argmanutiun* (Jerusalem, 1905–1911).

[47] E. G. Browne, *A Literary History of Persia*, II, 443; *idem, A History of Persian Literature under Tartar Dominion* (Cambridge, Eng., 1920), p. 17.

[48] The peculiar nature of the Turk state formations is discussed by Barthold, in *Turkestan*, pp. 305 ff. See also the anonymous article on the Seljuqs in the *Encyclopaedia of Islam*, IV, 208–213; and Hasluck, *Christianity*, I, 135.

of the problem. It is true that the Arab caliphs, borrowing the custom from the Persians, assigned large properties and even provinces, or the right to farm the taxes in certain areas, to the great leaders of the state or to soldiers. But it was not until the period of Turkish influence at Baghdad, not until the ninth or tenth century, that this system became closely bound up with the idea of a return in the form of military service rather than in money payments. In 1087 the great vizier of the Seljuqs, Nizāmu'l-Mulk, regularized the practice and established a system of military fiefs. For the first time the grants became hereditary. It stands to reason that this system, the dangers of which Nizāmu'l-Mulk himself recognized as clearly as anyone, was bound to lead to the formation of semi-independent or wholly independent states, especially at times when the ruler was weak or the throne in dispute.[49]

There are at least two instances of considerable grants of this type made by the sultans of Rum in the thirteenth century. About the middle of the century the sultan granted his powerful minister Mu'in ud-Dīn the territory about Sinope, with the right to pass it on to his son. This was done. There was a direct line of four rulers, who added to their dominions by further conquests, until, about 1300, this area was acquired by the rulers of Kastamuni, who had received that region in the same manner from the Mongol Ilkhan. Even more interesting is the history of the state of Karamania, which played a great part in Anatolian history until its acquisition by the Ottomans in the fifteenth century. Apparently, about the year 1223, a grant of territory was made on the frontier of Rum and Little Armenia, which the Seljuq ruler had conquered from the Armenians. The grantee was given "some Turkman tribes to establish there and guard the frontier." [50] In the last years of the thirteenth and the first years of the fourteenth century it seems that many similar grants were made by the sultans, for these principalities

[49] Joseph von Hammer, *Des osmanischen Reichs Staatsverfassung und Staatsverwaltung* (Vienna, 1815), I, 338 ff.; corrected by the writings of Alphonse Belin, "Du Régime des fiefs militaires dans l'Islamisme," *Journal asiatique*, ser. 6, XV (1870), 187–301. Paul Andreas von Tischendorf, *Das Lehnswesen in den moslemischen Staaten* (Leipzig, 1872) adds but little to Belin. The best recent studies are those of C. H. Becker, "Steuerpacht und Lehnswesen," *Der Islam*, V (1914), 81–92; Barthold, *Turkestan*, pp. 305 ff.; M. Sobernheim, "Iktā'," *Encyclopaedia of Islam*, II (1927), 461–463; Charles Schefer, *Siasset Nameh: Traité de gouvernement composé pour le Sultan Melik-Châh par le Vozir Nizam oul-Moulk*, Persian text (Paris, 1891), French trans. (Paris, 1893); and Köprülü, *Türkiye Tarihi*, I, 181–184 (bibliography).

[50] D'Ohsson, *Histoire des Mongols*, III, 489 ff., 500; J. H. Kramers, "Karamanoghlu," *Encyclopaedia of Islam*, II, 748–750.

cropped up like mushrooms. When Ibn Baṭūṭāh passed through this region about 1340 he noted some twenty-five of them.[51]

The earliest Ottoman chronicles are unanimous in saying that Ertoghrul received territory as a fief from the sultan of Rum for having helped him in his wars with the Mongols. The idea has been rejected with some vehemence by H. A. Gibbons, who stresses the fact that the authority of the Seljuq ruler was, at the time, of the most shadowy character, and who insists that the first Ottomans were "self-made men." There is no evidence to support this contention. On the contrary, there is every reason to suppose that the tradition as we find it in the chronicles is substantially correct. Like the forebear of the Karamanian dynasty, Ertoghrul was sent to the frontier with a certain number of Turkman tribesmen, to settle there and do guard duty.

Who, more exactly, were Ertoghrul, Osman, and their followers? So far as one can make out, the stories told in the chronicles are true in all essentials. They were evidently part of the Qayi tribe of the Ghuzz branch of the Turks, the same racial group from which the Seljuqs came and with which the Qun, ancestors of the Cumans of southern Russia, were connected.[52] If Professor Marquart's theory is correct, they came from the east side of the Caspian Sea, from the region now known as the Krasnovodsk Peninsula. The name Balkan Mountains was evidently transferred to Europe from the Balkan Mountains of that Asiatic area. Marquart accepts the story told by the early chroniclers, that the ancestors of the Ottomans came into Armenia under the leadership of a certain Soleiman, who belonged to the army of the Khwārezm-shāh Jelāl ud-Dīn Mankobirtī. The latter took the town of Achlat in 1229, and, as we know from his contemporary biographer, distributed fiefs in the vicinity. Soon afterward he was defeated and driven out by the Mongols; Soleiman, say the chroniclers, decided to return to Khurāsān, but was drowned on the way as he tried to ford the Euphrates.[53]

51 These are listed in H. A. Gibbons, *The Foundation of the Ottoman Empire,* app. A, on the basis of the information in Ibn Baṭūṭāh and Al-'Umarī.

52 M. T. Houtsma, "Die Ghuzenstämme," *Vienna Oriental Journal* [*Wiener Zeitschrift für die Kunde des Morgenlandes*], II (1885), 219–233.

53 Mohammed en-Nesawi, *Histoire du Sultan Djelal ed-din Mankobirti,* trans. O. Houdas (Paris, 1895), pp. 337 ff. On this matter see Josef Marquart, "Ueber das Volkstum der Komanen," in *Abhandlungen der königlichen Gesellschaft der Wissenschaften zu Göttingen,* Phil. Hist. Klasse, N.F., XIII (1914), 25–240. Paul Pelliot, in his detailed review supplementary to Marquart ("A propos des Comans," *Journal asiatique,* ser. II, XV [1920], 125–185), does not touch upon this aspect of the problem.

The chronicles go on to say that Ertoghrul, Soleiman's son, turning westward, came to the aid of the sultan of Rum and was given territory about Süğüd in return for his assistance. H. A. Gibbons throws out the whole story, on the plea that the reputed fifty thousand followers of Soleiman are not even mentioned by the biographer of Jelāl ud-Dīn Mankobirtī. It stands to reason that this figure must not be taken literally. Ertoghrul is said to have settled about Süğüd with four hundred families, which is quite likely near the truth. He was in all probability the leader of one of the numerous small Turkish tribes that entered Anatolia at this time, very possibly driven westward by the pressure of the Mongol advance. Even at the present day there are nomadic or seminomadic tribes in Anatolia with names evidently taken from Central Asian villages. These Anatolian names go back to this period.[54] As for Ertoghrul, he was almost certainly assigned the territory about Süğüd by the sultan of Rum, for it is inconceivable that he should have taken, of his own free choice, one of the most crucial and necessarily most closely watched spots, the frontier of the Greek Empire, for the settlement of a nomadic or seminomadic population.

Ertoghrul himself plays no important part in Ottoman history. So far as we can make out he conquered no territory worth mentioning. Presumably he simply held the front, as he was supposed to do. It was Osman who is reputed to have declared his independence in 1299 and to have set out on a career of conquest. This does not mean that he made a formal pronunciamento of any kind. The fact was that the Seljuq state went to pieces in the last years of the thirteenth century and that Osman, like many of his fellow vassals, set up on his own, from necessity as much as from choice. The question then arises, how were Osman and Orkhan able, in a short period, to make such important conquests as those of the cities of Brusa (Bursa), Nicaea (Iznik), and Nikomedia (Ismid)?

H. A. Gibbons makes a special point of stressing the weakness of the Byzantine Empire as one of the important factors facilitating the expansion of the Ottoman Turks. He contrasts the relatively strong position of the Anatolian emirates and khanates with the debility of the Greeks, and repeatedly emphasizes the fact that these considerations explain why the Ottoman conquests first extended into Europe, rather

[54] Hasluck, *Christianity*, I, 128; Leonhard, *Paphlagonia*, chap. 10. It is worth noting that there is little difference between the old Ottoman language and the Seljuq Turkish. See Kowalski, *Encyclopaedia of Islam* (1931).

than toward the south and east. This is a view to which we heartily subscribe. Yet it must be confessed that Gibbons does not go very deeply into the fundamentals. He contents himself with a discussion of the dynastic and religious struggles of the first half of the fourteenth century, and dilates on the dangerous policy of the emperors in calling in men like Roger de Flor and his Catalan followers to meet the raids of the Turks. All this is certainly important, but it is by no means the whole story. Neither does it help much to explain the very first Ottoman conquests in Asia Minor. Everyone knows that the empire of the Paleologi was merely "a slender, dislocated, miserable body upon which rested an enormous head, Constantinople," and that the last two centuries of its existence were a period of "slow and lamentable agony, not worth spending much time upon." They were the last pathetic years of an "ageing organism," years not only of decay, but of veritable wasting away.[55]

But these generalities are not very enlightening. What is needed is a series of detailed studies on the administrative, military, and social history of the empire after 1261. The recent monographs on the Nicaean period and on Michael Paleologus add nothing on this side.[56] Dölger has illustrated a number of points in the governmental and financial problems of the later period, and Tafrali has published an excellent monograph on the social struggle in Thessalonica in the fourteenth century. This is the type of investigation that is needed for the understanding of conditions in Bithynia.[57] Taken by and large the best general account of the various aspects of the decline and fall of the Greek Empire is that in the recent volume by Charles Diehl.[58]

Our object must be to recreate, as well as may be, a picture of conditions on the Asiatic front in the late thirteenth century. The Greek

[55] Charles Diehl, "L'Empire byzantin sous les Paléologues," in his *Études byzantines* (Paris, 1905), pp. 220, 223; A. A. Vasiliev, *History of the Byzantine Empire* (Madison, 1929), II, 265–266; Ernst Stein, "Untersuchungen zur spätbyzantinischen Verfassungs- und Wirtschaftgeschichte," *Mitteilungen zur osmanischen Geschichte*, II (1923–1925), 1–62.

[56] Alice Gardner, *The Lascarids of Nicaea* (London, 1912); Conrad Chapman, *Michel Paléologue, restaurateur de l'empire byzantin, 1261–82* (Paris, 1926).

[57] F. Dölger, "Beiträge zur Geschichte der byzantinischen Finanzverwaltung besonders des 10. and 11. Jahrhunderts," *Byzantinisches Archiv*, Heft 10 (Leipzig, 1927); O. Tafrali, *Thessalonique au quatorzième siècle* (Paris, 1912). Still of great value are the researches of V. G. Vasil'ievskii, "Materialy dlya Vnutrenneï Istorii Vizantiiskago Gosudarstva," *Zurnal Ministerstva Narodnago Prosveščeniya*, CCII (1879), pt. 2, 160–232, 386–438; CCX (1880), pt. 2, 98–170, 355–404.

[58] Charles Diehl, *Byzance, grandeur et décadence* (Paris, 1919).

domination at Constantinople had been reestablished only a short time before, and the imperial possessions in Anatolia were still essentially what they had been in the time of the Nicaean emperors. That is to say, the frontier ran somewhere on the plateau just north of Eskišehir (Dorylaeum), leaving to the Greeks the three important cities of Nicaea, Nikomedia, and Brusa. From the beginning of the restoration period the Paleologi were unable to pay much attention to this area. Controlling only a few fragments of the territories once held by their predecessors, challenged in their position by the ejected Latins, confronted by the demands of the Genoese, Venetians, and other Italians for extensive trading privileges, deprived of anything like an adequate income, and sorely in need of an army and navy, the restored emperors were hardly able to maintain themselves in the face of ecclesiastical and social struggles at home and the standing menace of invasion from abroad.

The Byzantine historian Pachymeres says that Michael VIII, on a visit to his Asiatic possessions sometime after 1261, found this region in the most appalling condition. The cities were ruined and deserted, trees and vegetation were destroyed, and the countryside in many places could not be traversed. The immediate cause for this destruction was undoubtedly the constant raiding of roving Turkish tribes. But other factors were unquestionably of great contributory importance. It must be remembered that for centuries the Anatolian provinces had been the scene of the growing power of what we may call feudalism. Large estates had been emerging, and not even the energetic rulers of the tenth century had been able to put a stop to the process. The Anatolian aristocrats, together with the powerful abbots and ecclesiastical dignitaries were, perhaps, the most virile, active, and able men produced by the later empire, but this does not alter the fact that they became a menace not only to the imperial power, but to the health of the social structure. The investigations of Vasil'ievskii, referred to above, showed that in the period we are considering there were still free peasants in the areas about the Sea of Marmora. This social class had not entirely disappeared, but it is probably true that the large mass of the agricultural population held land under a variety of forms either from a feudal lord or from a monastery. Of the misery of the peasantry there can be little doubt. Weighed down by payments due to their lords, they were more and more exposed to the exactions of the tax collectors sent out by a government which became increasingly indigent. From the time of the first Turkish invasions the agricultural regions tended to become depopulated. Evidently the peasants were glad rather than sorry to change masters. Others, when they could, escaped to the towns, though it may be questioned whether they found a better lot there. One thing, at any rate, may be taken as certain, that the population of the Byzantine Empire in Asia was not in a very prosperous or happy state of mind. The great Zealot and Hesychast controversies of the fourteenth century, which centered in Thessalonica, were social as much as religious movements. They throw a lurid light on the almost unbearable wretchedness of the common people.[59]

Militarily speaking, the emperors were not able to offer serious resistance to an invader. Ever since the first Arab incursions in the seventh century, a long line of fortified posts had been established to protect the frontier. These were located in or about the mountain passes, and were manned with frontier troops (*akritai*). These forces were quite distinct from the provincial army corps (*tagmata*), and operated only from their strongholds. Rarely were they drawn off on campaigns in other areas. In the earlier period they were composed of rough and ready military men, of great daring and energy. The emperors placed implicit trust in them and rewarded them with large grants of land or military fiefs. When the frontier was thrown back into northwestern Asia Minor as a result of the Seljuq invasions, less adequate fortifications appear to have been erected, so the frontiersmen were of greater importance than ever. The Nicaean emperors treated them with great consideration, endowing them with lands, relieving them of taxation, and looking indulgently upon their great wealth. It seems that a worse element established itself in this line of work. In the famous tenth century epic of Digenis Akritas, the frontier guards appear as the valiant defenders of the empire and Christianity against the infidel—splendid men, great in valor and great in love. But by the end of the thirteenth century, traits of cruelty and violence had become more prominent.

Evidently the *akritai* had become more of a bane than a blessing. After the reconquest of Constantinople in 1261, Michael VIII proceeded

[59] Stein, *Mitteilungen zur osmanischen Geschichte*, II, 1–62; Vasiliev, *Byzantine Empire*, II, 147 ff., 386 ff.; Charles Diehl, "Byzantine Civilization," *Cambridge Medieval History*, IV, chap. 24, and especially his *Byzance*, bk. III, chaps. 2, 3, 6.

against them. He had a census taken and in 1265 confiscated all their landed property, giving the owners a compensation of only forty pieces of gold. It turned out, however, that the soldiers were stronger than the emperor. They rose in revolt in the usual fashion, and the decrees could not be put into effect. After this the defense system seems to have become completely demoralized. The emperors at best could muster an army of only ten or twelve thousand men and when, in 1329, Andronicus II and John Cantacuzene proceeded against the Ottoman Turks they took only some two thousand trained troops with them. All the rest of the army was mere rabble, intent on saving its own hide and plundering the country as it went. The burden of the battle was borne by some three hundred knights, and they made a poor enough showing. Under the circumstances it is easy to understand how the first Ottoman rulers, even with their small following, were able to accomplish what they did.[60]

Our understanding of the course of the earliest Ottoman conquests will be considerably facilitated if we bear in mind the peculiar topographical conditions of the region in which Ertoghrul and his men had been established. They were on a high and rather barren tableland north of Eskišehir. In all probability they had come along the great trunk road from Armenia, the course of which has been so well studied by Taeschner.[61] The winter pastures of these tribes appear to have been north of Süğüd, while the summer pasturage was farther to the west, on the Dumanij Dagh. In their first conquests the Ottomans simply pushed along the road, that is, northward down the valley of the Kara Su, along which, in the opposite direction, went the Crusaders and along which runs the modern railway. This brought them, along the old roads retraced by Taeschner, to Bilejik and then to the lower country in which lie the cities of Brusa, Yenišehir, Nicaea, and Āq-Hiṣṣār. Such is the

[60] Chapman, *Michel Paléologue*, chap. 11; Vasiliev, *Byzantine Empire*, II, 292 ff.; Diehl, *Byzance*, bk. III, chap. 7. The best study of the military organization in this period is by P. Mutafčiev, "Voiniski Zemi i Voinitsi v Vizantiya prez XIII–XIV Veka," *Spisanie na Bolgarskata Akademiya na Naukite*, Kn. XXVII, Klon Istorio-Philologicen i Philosofsko Obščestven, XV (1923), 1–113. See also the detailed review of this article by F. Dölger, in *Byzantinische Zeitschrift*, XXVI (1926), 102–113.

[61] Franz Taeschner, "Das anatolische Wegenetz nach osmanischen Quellen," *Türkische Bibliothek*, nos. 22, 23 (Leipzig, 1924, 1926); Franz Taeschner, "Die Verkehrslage und das Wegenetz Anatoliens im Wandel der Zeiten," *Petermanns Mitteilungen*, LXXII nos. 9–10 (1926).

account of the earliest known chroniclers, Šükrüllāh and Uruj, and we have no reason to question it. The movement from the dry, barren uplands to the thicker vegetation of the river valleys and the better grazing areas on the north side of Olympus and ultimately to the richer, busier lowlands about Brusa and Yenišehir was the most natural thing in the world.[62]

Whatever may have been the exact state of cities like Brusa and Nicaea at the beginning of the fourteenth century, we know that they were strongly walled towns, probably surrounded by many smaller forts and outworks. Nicaea must have been a town of some thirty to forty thousand inhabitants. It had enjoyed a period of splendor during the thirteenth century, when it was the capital of the Greek Empire.[63] So far as one can make out, it was still quite a busy place about 1300.

According to the early chronicles, the Ottomans besieged these places for many years, building forts opposite the Greek outworks and gradually cutting off these cities until they surrendered. We do not question the accuracy of this account of Turkish tactics, but the question arises why nomadic or seminomadic tribes should have wanted to go to all this trouble. H. A. Gibbons gives a peculiar reply to this query. After rejecting most of the traditional account and making fun of the ridiculous stories concerning the origins of the Ottomans which were circulated by Western writers in the sixteenth century, he seizes upon the story told by the Turkish chroniclers of a dream attributed to Ertoghrul or Osman and upon the Arabic name of Osman in order to build up the theory that Osman and his followers first became converted to Islam at this time and embarked upon their conquests from religious motives. Now the story of the dream is utterly unconvincing. It appears in the chronicles in the most divergent forms. One can not even decide whether it was Ertoghrul or Osman who saw the vision of empire.

[62] Taeschner, *Zeitschrift der Deutschen Morgenländischen Gesellschaft,* LXXXII (1928), 83–118. Wilhelm Tomaschek, "Zur historischen Topographie von Kleinasien im Mittelalter," *Sitzungsberichte der kaiserlichen Akademie der Wissenschaften,* CXXIV, Abh. 8 (Vienna, 1891) deals chiefly with the coastal areas and the routes of the Crusades, but see Colmar Freiherr von der Goltz, *Anatolische Ausflüge* (Berlin, 1896) and the detailed geological and geographical study of Alfred Philippson, "Reisen und Forschungen im westlichen Kleinasien," Heft III, *Petermanns Mitteilungen,* Ergänzungsheft no. 177 (1913). Richard Hartmann's *Im Neuen Anatolien* (Leipzig, 1928) is predominantly archaeological and artistic.

[63] See especially Johannes Soelch, "Historisch-geographische Studien über bithynische Siedlungen: Nikomedia, Nikäa Prusa," *Byzantinisch-neugriechische Jahrbücher,* I (1920), 263–337.

Besides, the prototype of the story can be found as far back as the history of Herodotus. It is not a very firm foundation for a key argument.[64] Neither is Osman's name of any consequence.[65]

It is almost a certainty that the Ottoman Turks, like almost all Turks, were Moslems even before they left Central Asia. In fact, it is very likely that the Mongols, who were pagans but who were much more favorably disposed toward the Christians than toward the Moslems,

---

[64] See especially J. H. Mordtmann's observations, *Der Islam*, XIII (1923), 152–169.

[65] This question has caused so much trouble for so long a time (see Theodor Nöldeke, in *Zeitschrift der Deutschen Morgenländischen Gesellschaft*, XIII [1859], 185, n. 5) that a few words of explanation may be in order. In Anatolia, proper names are so frequently and so completely corrupted that philological derivations are of little use. Al-'Umarī calls Osman *Taman*, and Pachymeres and Nicephoras Gregoras call him *Atman*, so that the suggestion has been made that his name may really have been Turkish—*Azman* or something like it (see F. Giese, "Das Problem der Entstehung des Osmanischen Reiches," *Zeitschrift für Semitistik*, II [1923], 246–271). On the other hand, Ibn Baṭūṭāh calls him Osman, and so he appears on the first coins, struck in the reign of Orkhan ('Ali, *Tarih-i Osmanî Encümeni Mecmuası*, VIII [1917], 48). Of course, this in itself does not prove that his name was originally Osman, or that he was always a Moslem. It should be recalled that after the Turkish invasions many Armenian and Georgian Christians adopted Islamic names, and that Ertoghrul's father bore the common Arabic name, Soleiman. A clue may be found in Ibn Baṭūṭāh's statement that Osman's name had a suffix, -*jiq* or -*juq*. He says this signified Osman the Little, to distinguish him from Osman the third caliph. Giese thought that it might have been a term of endearment, and Huart, (*Journal asiatique*, 2nd ser., IX [1917], 345–350) has suggested that it might have been connected with the town of Osmanjiq (or zich), just south of Sinope on the Qizil Irmaq. This idea has been developed by J. H. Kramers, "Wer war Osman?" *Acta Orientalia*, VI (1927), 242–254, who has pointed out that the town had the name in the early thirteenth century and that the practice of naming persons from the locality of their birth was by no means unusual. From the confusion of the early chronicles regarding the names of Ertoghrul's sons, Kramers tried further to establish the theory that Osman was not a real son, but a man who joined Ertoghrul as he and his followers passed through Osmanjiq. It may be, however, that Osmanjiq was a perfectly good Turkish name. Mahmūd of Ghazna, the great Turkish conqueror of Persia and India, had, according to a contemporary writer (Al-'Utbī in the early eleventh century) an uncle named Bughrājuq and a general named Tughānjuq (see Muhammad Nāzim, *The Life and Times of Sulṭān Mahmūd of Ghazna* (Cambridge, 1931), pp. 32, 37, 39, 46, 48, 67), and a later Turkish writer tells of a Turkish general of the eleventh century named Osmanjiq Beg. Ḥājjī Khalīfa, the great Turkish traveler, says the town of Osmanjiq got its name because it was conquered by a general named Osman in the tenth century! (See A. D. Mordtmann, "Die Dynastie der Danischmende," *Zeitschrift der Deutschen Morgenländischen Gesellschaft*, XXX [1870], 467–486.) As a piquant detail it may be mentioned that Donado da Lezze, one of the earliest Italian historians of the Ottomans, says explicitly that the first member of the dynasty was Zich, who was the father of Ottoman (Donado da Lezze, *Historia Turchesa, 1300–1514*, ed. Ursu [Bucharest, 1910], I, 4). We do not know what this suffix -*jiq* or -*juq* signified and the original form of Osman's name evidently cannot be determined.

forced the emigration of the Turk tribes from Central Asia by their religious persecution, of which the Arab and Persian sources make bitter complaint. After all, racially the Mongols and the Turks were very closely related.

Though we think that Gibbons's theory of the conversion of Osman to Islam will hold no water whatever, we do believe that religion played some part, perhaps an important part, in the story of Ottoman expansion.

We have already pointed out the mystical trend and the dervish influence in Turkish Mohammedanism, as well as the part played by these factors in the Turkification and Moslemization of Asia Minor in the time of the Seljuqs. Now the Mongol conquests sent another flood of dervishes and holy men into Asia Minor from Transoxania, Persia, Iraq, and Syria. In all probability they moved along in the company of the migrating Turkish tribes. It is interesting to note that the ancestor of the Karaman dynasty was a Ṣūfi sheikh and that the Sarukhan dynasty in the fourteenth century was closely connected with the Mevlevi order of dervishes.[66] We have every reason to suppose that the early Ottoman rulers were under similar religious influence. It is said that the earliest document bearing on religious grants in the Constantinople archives goes back to 1294–1295, and it is a fact that among the earliest Ottoman buildings in Brusa were mosques and medresses.[67] It has been claimed, in fact, that the Janissary corps was established through the efforts of Ḥājjī Bektash, the founder and patron of the famous Bektashi order and the reputed friend and adviser of Osman or Orkhan. If true, the story would go far toward explaining the *élan* of the early Ottoman conquerors.

The story is found in many of the early chronicles, though it is warmly disputed by one of the oldest, ʿAšiḳpašazāde. A classic version of it is contained in a recently published dervish manual attributed to Bektash himself. The book dates from the early fourteenth century, and is therefore older than any known Turkish account of the origins of the Ottoman Empire. Erich Gross, the editor, was disposed to attribute to it considerable value as an historical source, though the nature of the

[66] J. H. Kramers, "Karamanoghlu," *Encyclopaedia of Islam*, II, 748–752; Franz Babinger, "Sarukhan," *Encyclopaedia of Islam*, IV, 177–178.
[67] J. Deny, in *Histoire et historiens depuis cinquante ans* (Paris, 1927), I, 453; Taeschner, *Zeitschrift der Deutschen Morgenländischen Gesellschaft*, LXXXII (1928), 83–118; Taeschner and Wittek, *Der Islam*, XVIII (1929), 60–115.

book is against its acceptance as serious historical material.[68] As a matter of fact, there appears to be nothing substantial in this legendary account. The researches of other scholars, like Browne, Jacob, Köprülü, and Hasluck, have shown convincingly that Bektash himself lived in the early part of the thirteenth century and that he was a popular, none too orthodox dervish leader. He had nothing to do with the founding of the order that bears his name, nor, in fact, with the establishment of the Janissaries. His disciples, about 1400, fell under the influence of a Persian mystic and agitator named Faḍlu'llah, the founder of the Ḥurūfi sect. With this sect the followers of Bektash became merged. They may have had some connection with the serious religious and social upheaval under Sheikh Bedr-ed-din in 1415–1416, and they were certainly involved in the uprising of the first quarter of the sixteenth century. It was only after this period that their connection with the Janissaries began. The association was recognized in the late sixteenth century, and from that time on the Bektashi dervishes lived in the barracks of the Janissaries and accompanied them on their campaigns. The point is important, for the Bektashi were as much a sect as an order, and were far removed from good Sunnite orthodoxy. They were careless of matters like circumcision, veiling of women, regular prayer, abstention from drink, and so forth, and were closely related to Shī'ah Mohammedanism and even Christianity. These traits are still very pronounced among the Kizilbash tribes of Anatolia, who are visited each year by a Bektash dervish, known by them as a rabbi, who administers to them the sacrament![69] It cannot be that this association of Janissaries and heterodox dervishes was welcome to the Ottoman government. Evi-

---

[68] Erich Gross, "Das Vilajet-name des Haǧǧi Bektasch," *Türkische Bibliothek,* no. 25 (Leipzig, 1927), especially pp. 199 ff. See the severe criticism of the editor's conclusions by H. H. Schaeder, "Zur Stifungslegende der Bektaschis," *Orientalistische Literaturzeitung,* XXXI (1928), 1038–57. The story is given in the traditional form in Theodor Menzel, "Das Korps der Janitscharen," *Beiträge zur Kenntnis des Orients,* I (1902–1903), 45–95.

[69] E. G. Browne, "Further Notes on the Literature of the Hurufis and Their Connection with the Bektashi Order of Dervishes," *Journal of the Royal Asiatic Society* (July 1907), 533–581; Georg Jacob, "Beiträge zur Kenntnis des Derwish-Ordens der Bektaschis," *Türkische Bibliothek,* no. 9 (Leipzig, 1908); Georg Jacob, "Die Bektaschijje in ihrem Verhältnis zu verwandten Erscheinungen," *Abhandlungen der philosophisch-philologischen Klasse der königlich-bayerischen Akademie der Wissenschaften,* XXIV (1909), pt. 3; Fuad Köprülü, "Les Origines du bektachisme," *Actes du congrès international d'histoire des religions* (Paris, 1925), II, 391–411; Hasluck, *Christianity,* I, 159 ff.; II, chap. 40; Leonhard, *Paphlagonia,* chap. 11.

---

dently the weak sultans who followed Soleiman the Magnificent were unable to do anything about it, but it is significant that Maḥmud II, in 1826, attempted to abolish the Bektashi order together with the Janissaries. On the other hand, he showed great favor to the orthodox and perfectly loyal Mevlevi order.

Though the Bektashi, as such, evidently had no connection with the first Ottoman rulers, other dervishes did. Taken by and large, the dervishes aimed at the reconciliation of Christianity and Islam. They put little store by doctrinal differences and ceremonial practices. Some were downright missionary in their aims, like the Isḥāqī, who are reputed to have converted to Islam thousands of fire worshipers and Jews in Persia, India, and China before they appeared in Anatolia.[70] There were not a few shrines in Anatolia that were frequented indiscriminately by Christians and Moslems alike. In fact, it is difficult to draw any fundamental distinction between the Turkish dervishes on the one hand and on the other the numerous zealots, mendicant monks, pilgrims, wanderers, and madmen who swarmed through Byzantine territory in the time of the first Paleologi. H. A. Gibbons is probably right in assuming that there was widespread apostasy on the part of the Greeks, who found the change of religion a not very considerable one and discovered that it was a useful expedient. Many accepted Islam outwardly, while still remaining Christian in faith and feeling. There is a most curious letter, written in 1338 by the patriarch at Constantinople to the Greeks at Nicaea, in which he offers to take them back into the Church, even if they made no public renunciation of Islam. There was a Christian monastery in Nicaean territory as late as 1395, as there were many Christian monasteries at all times in lands ruled by Moslems. Dawkins quotes a document of the year 1437, which shows clearly what took place:

> Notandum est, quod in multis partibus Turcie reperiuntur clerici, episcopi et arci-episcopi, qui portant vestimenta infidelium et locuntur linguam ipsorum et nihil aliud sciant in greco proferre nisi missam cantare et evangelium et epistolas. Alias autem orationes dicunt in lingua Turcorum.[71]

[70] Fuad Köprülü, "Abū Isḥāq Kazerūni und die Isḥāqī Derwische in Anatolien," *Der Islam*, XIX (1930), 18–26.

[71] Dawkins, p. 1, n. 1, cited from *Neos Hellēnomnēmōn*, VII (1910), 366. On the Anatolian shrines, see Hasluck, *Christianity*, II, chap. 26. The letter of the Greek patriarch in Wächter, *Der Verfall des Griechentums in Kleinasien im XIV. Jahrhundert*, pp. 56–57. The conditions in the Greek Church and the activities of popular agitators are discussed by Vasiliev, *Byzantine Empire*, II, 366 ff., and by Diehl, *Byzance*, bk. III, chap. 4.

We have still to consider the military side of the activities of the first sultans, and here we come into a most difficult subject, on which the final word cannot be said yet. Ibn Baṭūṭāh, recounting his experiences in Anatolia in the period just after the conquest of Brusa and Nicaea, tells of associations of men which he found in all the towns, and which did much to make his stay pleasant. They were called *Akhi,* and were composed of unmarried men of the same profession who selected a chief and established a community. A house was built and furnished. The members of the association worked all day and brought to the chief the money which they earned. With this the necessary supplies were bought. The whole thing was on a communal basis, but beyond providing for the exigencies of everyday life the Akhi made a special point of housing and entertaining strangers. The great Arab traveler was immensely impressed with this organization and its hospitality. He says specifically that at Brusa he stayed at one of their hospices.[72]

Exactly what were these associations, which, incidentally, had a certain religious basis? Hammer believed that the religious orders of the Islamic world were the prototypes of the orders of chivalry in the Western world. There are some recent writers who still insist that not only the medieval orders like the Templars but later Christian organizations like the Society of Jesus drew their inspiration from this source.[73] Whatever the truth in this matter may be, considerable progress has been made of late in the study of the Akhi organizations. These recent investigations have been based, in very large part, upon the Futūvvetnāmé, or Book of Chivalry, written, so it seems, in the fourteenth century by a certain Yaḥyā ben Khalīl. Chivalry is perhaps a misleading term, for the Futūvva included all the ideas which we associate with chivalry, together with the moral ideas of Moslem religious brotherhood and the ideas of professional solidarity. The word Akhi does not come from the Arab word for brother, as Ibn Baṭūṭāh thought, but is a purely Turkish word meaning knightly or noble. It is likely, therefore, that the Akhi were Turkish organizations fitting into the general framework of Moslem chivalry or Futūvva. They go back at least to the time of the

[72] Defrémery and Sanguinetti, *Voyages d'Ibn Batoutah,* II, 260 ff.
[73] Joseph von Hammer, "Sur les passages relatifs à la chevalerie dans les historiens arabes," *Journal asiatique,* 5th ser., VI, 282–290; D. B. Macdonald, *Religious Attitude and Life in Islam* (Chicago, 1909), p. 219; G. Bonet-Maury, "Les Confréries religieuses dans l'islamisme et les ordres militaires dans le catholicisme," *Transactions of the Third International Congress for the History of Religions* (Oxford, 1908), II, 339–345.

Caliph Nasir (1180–1225) for the Arab sources tell of his reformation of the organization and his protectorate over it.[74]

Following suggestions made by Huart and Babinger, Giese first worked out the connection between these Akhi organizations and the early Ottomans. He was able to mention by name a number of Akhi associated with the first sultans, and recalled that the chronicles tell us that Osman surrounded himself with "fast young men" who evidently belonged to these groups. Kramers, in the article already referred to, went so far as to suggest that Osman may himself have been a leader of the Akhi, who joined Ertoghrul as he passed through Osmanjiq, a town which seems to have been a veritable center of dervish organizations.[75] But these investigators tended to lay too much emphasis on the religious aspects of the Akhi organizations, and to identify them with the dervish orders. Taeschner was able to show that in Angora, for example, they played a prominent part in governing the city during the fourteenth century, and German scholars who have interested themselves in the problem are now inclined to put more stress on the mundane side of their activity.[76]

So far as one can determine, the Akhi were the more prominent men in the community, joined in professional groups and living according to certain religious precepts. Their rise and spread in the thirteenth and fourteenth centuries may well have had some connection with the expansion of trade and the revival of towns under Seljuq rule. In Anatolia the town or municipality had not played a prominent role before this period. Individual cities may have reached a considerable degree of

[74] Hermann Thorning, "Beiträge zur Kenntnis des islamischen Vereinswesens," *Türkische Bibliothek,* no. 16 (Berlin, 1913); the articles of Vladimir Gordlevski in *Zapiski Kollegii Vostokovedov,* II (1926–1927), 235–248, and *Izvestia Akademii Nauk SSSR* (1927), pp. 1171–94; Köprülü, *Türk Edebiyatinda, passim;* and especially Franz Taeschner, "Beiträge zur Geschichte der Achis in Anatolien," *Islamica,* IV (1929), 1–47. On the Futuvva, see M. Deny, "Fütüwwet-name et romans de chevalerie turcs," *Journal asiatique,* ser. 2, XVI (1920), 182–183; H. Ritter, "Zur Futuwwa," *Der Islam,* X (1920), 244–250; Franz Taeschner, "Das Futuvvetnāme des Jahjā b. Halil," *Orientalistische Literaturzeitung,* XXI (1928), 1065–66, and his more recent article, "Die türkischen Futuvvetnames und ihre religions-geschichtliche Stellung," *Zeitschrift der deutschen morgenländischen Gesellschaft,* LXXXIV (1930), 87–88.

[75] F. Giese, . . . *Zeitschrift für Semitistik,* II (1923), 246–271; Kramers, *Acta Orientalia,* VI (1927), 242–254.

[76] See especially Taeschner's review of Rudolf Tschudi's *Vom alten Osmanischen Reich* (Tübingen, 1930), in *Deutsche Literaturzeitung,* ser. 3, I (1930), 1665–67, and the discussion in Taeschner, *Zeitschrift der Deutschen Morgenländischen Gesellschaft,* LXXXIV (1930), 87–88.

prosperity and of population through political or economic causes, but so far as we can see the rulers of the surrounding territory always kept a firm and solid grip upon these urban centers. The Seljuq and Mongol conquests appear to have wrought a decided change in the situation. In Armenia the Mongols built new roads and cleared the old ones of bandits and robbers. During the thirteenth century many of the towns along the chief trading routes displayed unusual prosperity and the population took an active part in seeing that this prosperity was maintained. One of the most striking ruins in the capital of the Armenian dynasty of the Bagratids at Ani is the tremendous caravanserai of the city, which recent investigations have shown was built by the merchant guilds during the thirteenth and fourteenth centuries, when the very existence of the town was not noted in the historical annals. Similar great structures in this area and in other districts of Asia Minor were constructed, enlarged, or rebuilt at this time. The private organizations which did the work exhibited an energy and enjoyed a control of resources that is truly quite startling.[77]

The immensity of the Mongol conquests made extensive trade much simpler than it had been. It was the time of the journeys of Marco Polo, Plan de Carpini, and other famous European travelers. The towns on the main routes began to boom. But it seems that the arrangements for the escort of travelers, as well as for their reception and housing, were managed by the merchant guilds rather than by the Mongol authorities. The influence of the merchants certainly grew rapidly at this time. When disturbances closed the trade routes, these people tended to emigrate *en masse* to more fertile centers of enterprise, such as the Crimea, Constantinople, and the various harbor towns of the Levant.

Were the Akhi guilds pure and simple? It depends on what is meant by the term. They bear little resemblance to the guilds which were widespread in the Greek world from Hellenistic times onward, or to the Byzantine guilds, of which we know relatively little. These organizations were more strictly economic. The Byzantine guilds were under close government supervision and resembled the medieval guilds of

---

[77] The best general sketch is still that of W. Heyd, *Histoire du commerce du Levant au moyen âge*, trans. Furcy Raynaud (Leipzig, 1883), II, 3 ff., 73 ff. See also the itineraries through Asia Minor in F. Pegolotti, *Pratica della Mercatura*, ed. Pagnini (Lisbon, Lucca, 1766), pp. 7–13. On Ani, see the detailed archaeological study of N. Marr, in *Revue des études arméniennes*, no. 4 (1921), 395–410.

western Europe more than the associations of the Islamic world.[78] W.
M. Ramsay, who was struck by Ibn Baṭūṭāh's account of the Akhi, tried
to establish a connection between them and the Xenoi Tekmoreioi, or
Bearers of the Sign, who were organized along similar lines, had distinct religious connections, kept a communal treasury, and made hospitality one of their chief duties. He pointed out that Ibn Baṭūṭāh found
the Akhi chiefly in towns of Anatolia where there was a large non-Greek
and presumably pre-Greek population. One thing is certain. The Akhi
were economic organizations.[79] Ibn Baṭūṭāh says that at Adalia the
society consisted of two hundred silk merchants. But they also pursued
political, perhaps even military, activities. The old Turkish chronicler,
'Ašikpašazāde, says that there were parallel organizations of dervishes
and soldiers, and even a women's association. Of these we know nothing definite. We are not even able to speak with great assurance of the
Akhi. But if Osman was an Akhi leader, if he had these people in his
entourage, the fact is of great importance. It helps to explain not only
the Ottoman push to the cities of the Bithynian lowlands, but also the
remarkable ability shown by the Ottomans from the very beginning in
matters of state organization. For a people purely nomadic or even
seminomadic this was truly astonishing.

The "fast young men" in Osman's following, whether they were Akhi
or members of some kindred organization, may well have been the fore-
runners of the Janissaries. The origin of this famous body is still a
mystery, though it can be said with assurance that H. A. Gibbons's
theory that the rapid Islamization of Christian territory was due in
large measure to the tribute in Christian children exacted by the sultans
is devoid of foundation. Neither Ibn Baṭūṭāh nor Schiltberger (late
fourteenth and early fifteenth centuries), nor La Broquière (mid-fifteenth century) speaks of such a tribute in connection with the organization of the Ottoman forces. Their silence can not, of course, be taken
as conclusive, but the system as we know it from a later period is the
more remarkable in that it was contrary to the essential principles of

---

[78] See Franz Poland, *Geschichte des griechischen Vereinswesens* (Leipzig,
1909), and the article, "Berufsvereine," in Pauly-Wissowa, *Real-Encyclopedie der
classischen Altertumswissenschaft,* Supplementband IV (1924), 155–211; Hans
Gehrig, "Das Zunftwesen Konstantinopels im 10. *Jahrhundert,*" *Jahrbücher für
Nationalökonomie und Statistik,* ser. 3, XXXVIII (1909), 577–596; Albert Stöckle,
"Spätrömische und Byzantinische Zünfte," *Klio,* Beiheft 9 (Leipzig, 1911); G.
Zoras, *Le Corporazioni Bizantine* (Rome, 1931).

[79] Ramsay, *The Cities,* I, 97

Islam, which prescribed that all non-Moslems outside the Arabian Peninsula should be free to practice their religion on condition that they paid a capitation tax. Nothing like this levy of children can be found in the history of any other Moslem state.[80] The Janissaries evidently grew out of an earlier body of troops known as the Yayā, which, in turn, may have been a derivation from some sort of military, semi-religious organization. There was much in the organization of the Janissaries analogous to the Christian orders of knighthood.[81] In any case, the Yayā were a sort of enlisted infantry, established to supplement the irregular cavalry known by the name of *Akinji*. They are interesting because they antedated the first standing armies of France and even the companies of archers in England. If Huart is right, the Janissary corps were modeled on the legions of the Byzantine Empire, which, in turn, were derived from the Roman legions. Throughout the fourteenth century they were probably recruited as they were in the fifteenth, not from the Christian tribute children, but from war prisoners. There was nothing novel in this system. The Turkish Mameluk sultans of Egypt built up their power by means of a slave army, recruited almost exclusively from Christian territory. Impressment and the levy of Christian children were only gradually and irregularly resorted to in Turkey in order to keep the ranks of the regiments filled. The numbers of the Janissaries were very small, even in the time of Soleiman. But their peculiar weapons and their admirable training and discipline seem to have been wonderfully effective in all their engagements with Christian forces.[82]

The Ottoman state, then, rose from among a fairly large number of small principalities that succeeded to the heritage of the sultanate of Rum. Its position was peculiarly favorable, because it made possible considerable conquests at the expense of the moribund Byzantine Empire. But the first sultans had more than a mere horde of nomads to rely

[80] Hasluck, *Christianity*, II, chap. 40; J. H. Mordtmann, "Dewshirme," *Encyclopaedia of Islam*, I, 952–953; Clément Huart, "Janissaries," *Encyclopaedia of Islam*, II, 572–574; Menzel, "Das Korps der Janitscharen," *Beiträge zur Kenntnis des Orients*, I (1902–1903), 51–52.

[81] Heinrich Schurtz, "Die Janitscharen," *Preussische Jahrbücher*, CXII (1903), 450–479.

[82] Huart's review of Gibbons's book in *Journal asiatique*, ser. 2, IX (1917), 345–350; Huart, "Les Origines de l'empire ottoman," *Journal des savants*, XV (1917), 157–166; Giese, *Zeitschrift für Semitistik*, II (1923), 246–271; Taeschner and Wittek, *Der Islam*, XVIII (1929), 60–115; Menzel, *Beiträge zur Kenntnis des Orients*, I, 50–52.

upon. There was an efficient military organization which was evidently based upon something resembling merchant guilds and religious orders. These organizations supplied the impetus to the conquest of the Greek cities in Bithynia, they enabled the sultans to establish a governmental system, and they facilitated the conversion of a large part of the Christian population to Islam, thus giving the new state a firm popular basis. Much undoubtedly remains to be learned about them and about the whole early history of the Ottomans. But enough is already known to make possible a thorough revision of ideas that have been current all too long.

21

The Historian and the Present

1952

The impressive attendance here today may be taken, I suppose, as evidence of the widespread and lively interest in modern history and its problems. In this respect there has been a marked change over the past twenty-five years, for I remember that when some of us here present undertook to organize a modern history group and launch the *Journal of Modern History,* we had but a modest following and were on occasion warned that there would be but few subscribers to the new journal and that scholarly contributions would be hard to come by in sufficient number to fill its pages. Time has belied these dire forebodings. No doubt the University of Chicago Press would be delighted to have a larger subscription list and the editors still yearn, as editors do at all times and in all places, for more significant and better-written articles. But the fact remains that the *Journal* has survived depression and inflation, that, due in large measure to the hard and devoted work of its successive editors, it has been and still is an interesting and valuable organ for those working in the modern field, and that the Modern History Group has grown to its present imposing size.

No one any longer disputes the validity of the study and teaching of modern history, but there has developed of late much argument for and against what is called contemporary history. By this, I take it, no one means actually current history, which is patently a contradiction in terms. The debate really centers on the study of the recent past, say the period of the last generation or two. Nor has the issue been raised in this country only. The French have long had a *Review of Contemporary History* and the Germans have just established one. The British, traditionally conservative in such matters, have also engaged in the discussion and have, in fact, produced some noteworthy protagonists of the cause.

Note: Address delivered before the Modern History Group of the American Historical Association, Washington, D. C., Dec. 29, 1952. Reprinted from *Vital Speeches of the Day,* XIX (Mar. 1, 1953), 312–314.

I gather from the proceedings of the last meeting of the Association (which I was unable to attend) that there was on that occasion much adverse criticism of what many regard as the prevalent overemphasis on recent history. Professor C. E. Nowell's remarks, reprinted in the current number of the *Journal of Modern History,* rightly called attention to the growing neglect of the study and teaching of earlier periods and even went so far as to raise the question whether the past is to continue to have a place in history.

I do not propose to reopen this debate or to re-examine the validity of contemporary history or even the methodological problems which it presents. These matters were cogently discussed by Sir Llewelyn Woodward at last year's meeting of the Association and have since been clearly and succinctly restated by Professor Hans Rothfels in the introductory essay of the new *Vierteljahrshefte für Zeitgeschichte.* From my own efforts in the writing of contemporary history you may take it that I believe in the desirability and feasibility of useful work in this field.

For the rest I need only remind you that we already have numerous textbooks on contemporary history, that the subject is widely taught in our schools, and that many volumes of studies of the recent past are constantly pouring from the presses. Whether we like it or not, contemporary history is an established discipline and, considering the tempo of the modern world—the rapidity with which the present becomes the past—I think there is but a slight likelihood that the subject can or will be argued out of existence.

Despite contentions to the contrary, I should say that the popularity of contemporary history is decidely a reflection of the need felt by the public as well as by students for some analysis and explanation of the world we live in. This need, it seems to me, is world wide. In many areas where Communism has taken root and is spreading there appears to be a general feeling that Marxism-Leninism-Stalinism provides a complete philosophy of history, a convincing analysis of modern society, and a persuasive program for the future. The free world, on the other hand, is unable to provide a statement, comprehensive yet succinct, of the philosophy and program of liberal democracy and free enterprise.

It is most unlikely, as I think you will all agree, that such an analysis or prospectus can or will be made. From the very nature and principles of the free world it becomes impossible to reduce it to anything like the singleness of view and objective that is basic to authoritarian systems. While dictators like Lenin, Hitler, or Stalin not only can but in a sense

400

must denounce "bourgeois anarchist individualism" (the phrase is Lenin's) and ruthlessly suppress originality and all forms of modernism even in the arts, we take it for granted that there should be wide divergencies in thought and expression. Western civilization has never been without its heresies, its protestors, and its critics. We hold differences of view to be not only permissible but desirable and believe that in general good comes from the development of new ideas and the constant clash of conflicting opinions.

Nonetheless, I think we are touching here upon a serious problem, significant for our own culture as well as for the fate of the non-European world. We are all keenly aware of the fact that during the past half-century our society has been passing through a major crisis—a crisis so profound and severe that some believe it unprecedented in human annals. The tremendous technological changes of recent times have altered completely the conditions of life and have been accompanied by an intellectual revolution so extensive and far-reaching as to have called in question just about all the previously accepted values of our civilization. Two stupendous world conflicts have rocked society to its foundations, have taken an enormous toll of life and property, have left a legacy of widespread human misery, and have set the stage for the translation of revolutionary doctrine into revolutionary action.

If out of all this turmoil there were emerging a new philosophy, a new religion, a new political or social doctrine, or a new style, we might at least be able to get our bearings and catch a glimpse of the light at the end of the tunnel. But the trends and movements that we see and sense about us all suggest disruption if not total destruction of our society. Even if I had the knowledge, I would not have the temerity to attack this vast problem in any detail in the few minutes available to me here.

In any case it is hardly necessary, among a group of historians, to do more than recall the devastating attacks on modern culture going back to Dostoevski and Nietzsche, if not to Wagner and Kierkegaard as well as to Marx; the loss of faith in religion and in the ethical teaching of Christianity, particularly since the emergence of the doctrine of evolution; the rapid disintegration of nineteenth century philosophy, the ensuing triumph of irrationalism, and the rise of many new competing schools extending all the way from materialism and realism through pragmatism and vitalism to the presently popular existentialism; the severe impact of Freudian teaching, with its emphasis on the dark

401

forces of the subconscious; the profound revolution in the conceptions of science since the early writings of Planck and Einstein; and finally, the loss of faith in freedom and democracy, leading to the rapid spread of activist movements and the establishment of authoritarian, totalitarian systems of government.

Professor Huizinga (*The Shadow of Tomorrow*) has noted that the prevalence of anti-intellectualism is something truly novel in the history of human culture. Along with the general attack on individualism and equality it has vindicated Nietzsche's prediction of a period of atomistic chaos, well reflected by the breakdown of style in the arts and the rapid succession of movements and schools. Prominent artists like Picasso and Stravinsky have undergone in their own work an amazing number of changes, while artists in general have exhibited a most disquieting indifference, not to say hostility to the values of Western society. To quote Arnold Hauser (*Social History of Art*) modern art has renounced all illusions of reality and "destroys pictorial values in painting, carefully and consistently executed images in poetry, and melody and tonality in music." Hugo Leichtentritt (*Music, History and Ideas*) sees only "much agitation, much speculation and clever experiment, a passionate striving after a new basis, but no clearness about the really efficient measures to be taken, no real style, no well-defined course." Maurice Stern ("Cezanne Today," in *The American Scholar*, Winter 1952) reports nothing but disorientation and "desultory efforts in every direction."

All along the line, then, our age reflects uncertainty, confusion and blind groping for security. Since not even the educated can find their way out of what many of them have described as the current chaos, it is hardly to be wondered at that the proverbial man in the street is unable to find a footing. The prevalent mood is one of impending gloom, of resignation and of pessimism, so characteristic of artists like Picasso, James Joyce, Kafka, and innumerable others and even more so of the common man, in so far as he thinks of these matters at all. The achievements of science are wonderful and suggest that nothing is impossible to man. On the other hand, Eddington has warned that "something unknown is doing we don't know what," and there is no good reason to suppose that the worst as well as the best is not possible. Freud, in one of his later works (*Das Unbehagen in der Kultur*) underlined the sense of insecurity and anxiety arising from the feeling of being surrounded by unknown, unfathomable, and indefinable dangers. In brief, Western society has lost its moorings to such an extent that the schemers of the Kremlin are already speculating on the next economic crisis to give the Western world the coup de grâce.

In this welter of confusion and apprehension it seems to me that the historian has a function to perform. We may, I suppose, take it for granted that the public supports historical work in the hope that knowledge of the past will provide some understanding of the present, if not some clue to the future. In the past historians have recognized and tackled this task with the result that they frequently formed or at least influenced the thought and aspirations of their time. But of late they have tended to abdicate this function and leave it to the newspaper and radio commentators to whom, as Professor Nowell has pointed out, the public now looks for explanation and guidance.

My own feeling, then, is that we need more contemporary history and, above all, a broader conception and profounder treatment of the subject. I am not unmindful of the excellent work that has been done in intellectual history, political thought, and social theory. We are coming to have a better understanding of the inter-relations of various trends of thought and of the ways in which they were translated into programs of action and systems of political-social organization. But despite a number of recent studies of the origins of Nazism and of the evolution of totalitarianism generally, I suspect that there is still much to be done along this line, more particularly in uncovering the contribution of Western revolutionary thought and techniques to the doctrine and methods of Lenin. The influence of Nietzsche has been pretty carefully scrutinized, and I would say that the impact of men like Bergson is fairly well understood, but I doubt if the larger role of men like Maurras and Sorel has been sufficiently clarified.

Furthermore, it strikes me that perhaps there is a tendency to over-emphasize the movement of thought at the expense of systematic analysis of the conditions which provoked the new ideas and provided the basis for their implementation. No doubt this takes us on to more slippery ground and confronts us with problems that are far less tangible and may in many instances prove insoluble. But we do recognize that behind some of the great movements of recent date there were forces which we must take into account. Alfred Weber (*Farewell to European History*) suggests that "an indefinable objective *something* broke loose that swept away values taken for granted and held to be unshakable, in a universal psychic wave. A collective, supra-personal force, chained and hidden till then, burst from captivity." It would obviously be of the utmost importance to analyze and determine the nature of this force, the more so as we cannot delude ourselves that Nazism, though defeated, has become definitely a thing of the past.

More concretely, however, I should say that we still have much to learn about such forces as imperialism, to say nothing of the effects of its recession in western Europe and the new impetus that has been given it in the Soviet Union. Possibly even more important would be studies of various aspects of the population problem. The enormous increase of the European population must certainly have been a primary factor conditioning recent historical development. Yet so far as I know we still lack adequate analyses of the effect on Europe of the huge drain of population by emigration. Neither has sufficient attention been given to the implication of the vast expansion of the base of the political-social structure. In many if not most European countries universal suffrage and general education are recent introductions and one can hardly believe that the advent of the so-called "masses" has not been a development of immense importance, coloring the complexion of all European culture.

Ortega y Gasset has pointed out that the increase of human beings has been so great and so rapid that it was quite impossible to saturate the new masses with the traditional cultural values. The result has been an ever widening gap between the cultured minority and the untutored elements of the population, endowed with ever greater political and social power. Nietzsche and many others sensed the dangers inherent in this development, denounced the barbarism of the herd and saw no salvation save through the self-assertion and aloofness of the elite. Nietzsche warned that "intellectual enlightenment is an unfailing means to make people more uncertain, weaker-willed, more desirous of union and support." Similarly Gustave Le Bon in 1895 foretold the behavior of mass man as revealed later in the surge toward collectivism and authoritarianism. Pareto held that the nineteenth century had carried individual liberty, experiment, and novelty to a point where society could no longer hold together and where a reaction toward authority, collectivism, and order had become inevitable. More recently Erich Fromm (*Escape from Freedom*) has argued that the masses are incapable of enjoying freedom and tend to escape it by seeking security and relief from responsibility in uncritical activism and in submission to authoritarian systems.

Clearly this problem calls for careful analysis. We can all see the

404

dangers involved in the impact of modern thought on the mind of the common man. He is fed vast doses of miscellaneous knowledge through radio, television, comics and all the other methods of mass communication, and he is in a position, in the free world, to translate his half-baked ideas into action. True, opinions differ as to the actual influence of modern ideas on the average person. My colleague, Professor Brinton, by nature an optimist, holds that the average man is not much touched by irrationalism and that essentially he still thinks in good eighteenth century terms. He may talk in alarming ways, but he acts in accordance with accepted precepts. Yet according to Professor Hans Morgenthau this is exactly the root of our trouble, that man still thinks too much in terms of reason, science, and progress and has lost the sense of history and tragedy in human life.

We certainly cannot resolve this question here and now. It seems to me impossible, however, to overlook the fact, noted by Mussolini, that "modern man's disposition to believe is unbelievable" and to ignore the social threat involved if the larger part of the population fails to acquire and support the values of culture and drifts thoughtlessly in the direction of collectivist despotism. If in fact there is nothing to be done with the masses, the situation in terms of democracy and freedom would appear to be veritably hopeless.

It remains a very great question, however, whether education and improved social conditions and facilities will not bring, if they have not already brought, some change for the better. There are certainly some indications that the center of the great storm of our time has passed. The contrast between the iconoclastic and exuberantly revolutionary decade following the First World War and the apathy and discouragement of the last half dozen years could hardly be more striking. The great conflagration of ideas seems to have burned itself out, and there have of late been no major revolutionary doctrines or significant new movements at all comparable to those of the first decades of the century. In all fields one senses a tendency to return to old values and traditional forms. Extravagant hopes and daring programs have been exploded. In literature, art, and music some of the great innovators are still active, but the years just past have brought forth no striking personalities or novel ideas among the younger generation. On the contrary, there appears to be a trend towards something like neoclassicism, as there is a trend towards revival of traditional religion. We may be on the verge of a period of relative acceptance and consolidation, reflecting not only the deflation of past hopes and delusions, but also progressive adjustment to the conditions of the new age.

But I must not allow myself to become involved in discussion of specific issues, however fundamental, and I would like, in closing, merely to conjure up the vision of a yet broader synthesis, one that would draw together all the many different strands of recent cultural development. Admittedly this is a tall order, calling for something like the type of encyclopedic man who has become impossible in a world so specialized—so unavoidably specialized—as the one we live in. How can anyone be expected to encompass all aspects of modern thought and activity when within a single discipline it has become impossible for anyone to command more than a segment? Obviously it cannot be done by anyone working from the ground up, that is, working from the original sources. But if we could stop disparaging the scholar who attempts to synthesize the results of countless specialized studies and instead commend those heroic souls who try to make use of detailed findings which have significance only in a larger connection, I think it not inconceivable that headway could be made. There have already been some interesting and profitable efforts to link up developments in different fields. For instance, we recognize the influence of Bergson on Debussy and on the evolution of religious modernism, and the impact of Freudian teaching on writers like Lawrence and Joyce and on the Surrealists is fairly obvious.

More could certainly be done in this direction and the need for it is demonstrated by the efforts of scientists to philosophize and by the attempts of men like Arnold Hauser (*Social History of Art*) and R. H. Wilenski (*Modern French Painters*) to tie up the movement of art with other social forces. I confess that most of these efforts have been rather unsuccessful and I think they are bound to be so when undertaken by people, however competent in their particular fields, who lack historical training. After all, it is the historian who, by education and temperament, should be peculiarly fitted to view human development in all its aspects and with a dispassionate yet sympathetic eye. Historians, too, are about the only ones of the scholarly guild who mercifully have thus far eschewed the unintelligible jargons which perforce close the books of modern learning to the rank and file of mankind. As aforesaid, historians have, however, tended to evade this high function and have abandoned it to sociologists and to far less learned popularizers.

Perhaps this is due to the fact that historians realize more clearly than others the magnitude and difficulty of the task, which no one will deny. On the other hand I still insist that the historian could and should assume a larger share of the burden. With all respect for original research, he should combat his aversion against the secondary treatment which is, after all, what his own original work becomes the moment anyone else attempts to extract from it whatever good it may contain.

I appreciate the fact that, in raising these large issues I run the risk of being put down as a visionary, but a gathering like this seems to me the appropriate occasion to voice even somewhat extravagant hopes and aspirations. It is only because I have so high an opinion of the breadth of mind, the analytic power, and the sympathetic understanding of the trained historian that I am so loath to see him abdicate a high social function and abandon to the journalist or commentator the grave and inspiring task of providing his fellow men with bearings in the present as well as with an anchorage in the past.

22

The Next Assignment

1958

Anyone who, like myself, has the honor to serve as president of this association and to address it on the occasion of its annual meeting may be presumed to have devoted many years to the historical profession, to have taught many successive college generations, to have trained numerous young scholars, and to have written at least some books and articles. The chances are equally great that he has reached those exalted levels of the academic life which involve so many administrative and advisory duties, as well as such expenditure of time and energy in seeing people, in writing recommendations, and in reading the writings of others that he is most unlikely ever again to have much time to pursue his own researches. Nonetheless, his long and varied experience and his ever broadening contacts with scholars working in many diverse fields have probably sharpened his understanding of the problems of his own profession and enhanced his awareness of the many lacunae in our knowledge of the world and of mankind, both in the past and in the present. It would seem altogether fitting, therefore, that I, for one, should make use of this occasion not so much for reflection on the past achievements of the profession (which is what might be expected of a historian), as for speculation about its needs and its future—that is, about the directions which historical study might profitably take in the years to come.

I am sure to sense, at this juncture, a certain uneasiness in my audience, for historians, having dedicated their lives to the exploration and understanding of the past, are apt to be suspicious of novelty and ill-disposed toward crystal-gazing. In the words of my distinguished predecessor, they lack the "speculative audacity" of the natural scientists, those artisans of brave hypotheses. The tendency of many historians

Note: Presidential address delivered to the American Historical Association, New York City, Dec. 29, 1957. It first appeared in the *American Historical Review*, LXIII (January 1958). A later version was published with minor changes in *American Imago*, XV (Fall 1958), 235–266, and is reprinted here.

to become buried in their own conservatism strikes me as truly regrettable. What basically may be a virtue tends to become a vice, locking our intellectual faculties in the molds of the past and preventing us from opening new horizons as our cousins in the natural sciences are constantly doing. If progress is to be made, we must certainly have new ideas, new points of view, and new techniques. We must be ready, from time to time, to take flyers into the unknown, even though some of them may prove wide of the mark. Like the scientists, we can learn a lot from our own mistakes, and the chances are that, if we persist, each successive attempt may take us closer to the target. I should therefore like to ask myself this evening what direction is apt to lead to further progress in historical study; what direction, if I were a younger man, would claim my interest and attention; in short, what might be the historian's "next assignment."

We are all keenly aware of the fact that during the past half century the scope of historical study has been vastly extended. The traditional political-military history has become more comprehensive and more analytical and has been reinforced by researches into the social, economic, intellectual, scientific, and other aspects of the past, some of them truly remote from what used to be considered history. So far has this development gone that I find it difficult to envisage much further horizontal expansion of the area of investigation.

There is, however, still ample scope for penetration in depth and I, personally, have no doubt that the "newest history" will be intensive rather than extensive. I refer more specifically to the urgently needed deepening of our historical understanding through the exploitation of the concepts and findings of modern psychology. And by this, may I add, I do not refer to classical or academic psychology which, so far as I can detect, has little bearing on historical problems, but rather to psychoanalysis and its later developments and variations as included in the terms "dynamic" or "depth psychology."

In the course of my reading over the years I have been much impressed by the prodigious impact of psychoanalytic doctrine on many, not to say most, fields of human study and expression. Of Freud himself it has been said that "he has in large part created the intellectual climate of our time." [1] "Almost alone," remarks a recent writer in the *Times Literary Supplement*, "he revealed the deepest sources of human endeavor and

---

[1] "Freud and the Arts," *Times Literary Supplement* (London), May 4, 1956.

remorselessly pursued their implications for the individual and society." [2] Once the initial resistance to the recognition of unconscious, irrational forces in human nature was overcome, psychoanalysis quickly became a dominant influence in psychiatry, in abnormal psychology, and in personality study. The field of medicine is feeling its impact not only in the area of psychosomatic illness, but in the understanding of the doctor-patient relationship. Our whole educational system and the methods of child-training have been modified in the light of its findings. For anthropology it has opened new and wider vistas by providing for the first time "a theory of raw human nature" and by suggesting an explanation of otherwise incomprehensible cultural traits and practices. It has done much also to revise established notions about religion and has given a great impetus to pastoral care and social work. The problems of mythology and sociology have been illuminated by its insights, and more recently its influence has been strongly felt in penology, in political science, and even in economics, while in the arts almost every major figure of the past generation has been in some measure affected by it.[3]

Despite this general and often profound intellectual and artistic reorientation since Freud published his first epoch-making works sixty years ago, historians have, as a group, maintained an almost completely negative attitude toward the teachings of psychoanalysis. Their

[2] *Ibid.* See also Abram Kardiner, *The Psychological Frontiers of Society* (New York, 1945), p. 11; Goodwin Watson, "Clio and Psyche: Some Interrelations of Psychology and History," in *The Cultural Approach to History*, ed. Caroline Ware (New York, 1940), pp. 34–47; Hans W. Gruhle, *Geschichtsschreibung und Psychologie* (Bonn, 1953), p. 7; *The Social Sciences in Historical Study*, ed. Hugh Aitken, Social Science Research Council Bull. No. 64 (New York, 1954), pp. 61 ff.

[3] See the article by Henry W. Brosin, "A Review of the Influence of Psychoanalysis on Current Thought," in *Dynamic Psychiatry*, ed. Franz Alexander and Helen Ross (Chicago, 1952), pp. 508–553; Ernest Jones, *What Is Psychoanalysis?* (new ed., New York, 1948), pp. 80 ff.; Iago Galdston, ed., *Freud and Contemporary Culture* (New York, 1957). See also J. A. Gengerelli, "Psychoanalysis: Dogma or Discipline?" *Saturday Review* (Mar. 23, 1957), pp. 9–11, 40; Gardner Murphy, "The Current Impact of Freud upon Psychology," *American Psychologist*, XI (1956), 663–672; A. Irving Hallowell, "Culture, Personality and Society," in *Anthropology Today*, ed. A. L. Kroeber (Chicago, 1953), pp. 597–620; Clyde Kluckhohn, "The Influence of Psychiatry on Anthropology in America During the Past One Hundred Years," in *One Hundred Years of American Psychiatry*, ed. J. K. Hall (New York, 1944), pp. 589–618, and "Politics, History and Psychology," *World Politics*, VIII (1955), 112–123; Harold D. Lasswell, "Impact of Psychoanalytic Thinking on the Social Sciences," in *The State of the Social Sciences*, ed. Leonard D. White (Chicago, 1956), pp. 84–115; R. Money-Kyrle, *Superstition and Society* (London, 1939); Walter A. Weisskopf, *The Psychology of Economics* (Chicago, 1955); Erich Fromm, *Psychoanalysis and Religion* (New Haven, 1950); F. J. Hoffman, *Freudianism and the Literary Mind* (Baton Rouge, 1945); Louis Schneider, *The Psychoanalyst and the Artist* (New York, 1950).

lack of response has been due, I should think, less to constitutional obscurantism than to the fact that historians, as disciples of Thucydides, have habitually thought of themselves as psychologists in their own right. They have indulged freely in psychological interpretation, and have no doubt shared the fear that the humanistic appreciation of personality, as in poetry or drama, might be irretrievably lost through the application of a coldly penetrating calculus.[4] Many have considered psychoanalytic doctrine too biological and too deterministic, as well as too conjectural, and they have, furthermore, been reluctant to recognize and deal with unconscious motives and irrational forces. Psychoanalysis, on the other hand, was a young science and therefore lacked the prestige to make historians acquire a guilt-complex about not being more fully initiated into its mysteries.[5] Almost without exception, then, historians have stuck to the approach and methods of historicism, restricting themselves to recorded fact and to strictly rational motivation.[6] So impervious has the profession as a whole been to the new teaching that an inquiry into the influence of psychoanalysis on modern thought, written a few years ago, made no mention whatever of history.[7]

This is as remarkable as it is lamentable, for, on the very face of it, psychoanalysis would seem to have much to contribute to the solution of historical problems. Many years of clinical work by hundreds of trained analysts have by now fortified and refined Freud's original theory of human drives, the conflicts to which they give rise, and the methods by which they are repressed or diverted. Psychoanalysis has long since ceased being merely a therapy and has been generally recognized as a theory basic to the study of the human personality. How can it be that the historian, who must be as much or more concerned with human beings and their motivation as with impersonal forces and causation, has failed to make use of these findings? Viewed

[4] Raymond B. Cattel, *An Introduction to Personality Study* (London, 1950), pp. 13–14. Harold D. Lasswell, *Psychopathology and Politics* (Chicago, 1930), p. 11, refers to "the obscurantist revulsion against submitting the sacred mystery of personality to the coarse indignity of exact investigation." Keats is said to have feared that spectrum analysis would ruin his enjoyment of the rainbow. See Jones, *What is Psychoanalysis?* pp. 12 ff.

[5] Sidney Ratner, "The Historian's Approach to Psychology," *Journal of the History of Ideas,* II (1941), 95–109.

[6] Edward N. Saveth, "The Historian and the Freudian Approach to History," *New York Times Book Review* (Jan. 1, 1956); Gruhle, *Geschichtsschreibung und Psychologie,* pp. 116 ff.; Richard L. Schoenwald, "Historians and the Challenge of Freud," *Western Humanities Review,* X (1956), 99–108.

[7] Brosin, *Dynamic Psychiatry,* pp. 508–553.

in the light of modern depth psychology, the homespun, common-sense psychological interpretations of past historians, even some of the greatest, seem woefully inadequate, not to say naive.[8] Clearly the time has come for us to reckon with a doctrine that strikes so close to the heart of our own discipline.[9]

Since psychoanalysis is concerned primarily with the emotional life of the individual, its most immediate application is in the field of biography. Freud himself here showed the way, first in his essay on Leonardo da Vinci (1910) and later in his analytical study of Dostoevsky (1928). He was initially impressed by the similarity between some of the material produced by a patient in analysis and the only recorded childhood recollection of the great Italian artist. With this fragmentary memory as a starting point, Freud studied the writings and artistic productions of Leonardo and demonstrated how much light could be shed on his creative and scientific life through the methods of analysis. No doubt he erred with respect to certain points of art history. Quite possibly some of his deductions were unnecessarily involved or farfetched. Nonetheless, recent critics have testified that he was able, "thanks to his theory and method, and perhaps even more to his deep sympathy for the tragic and the problematic in Leonardo, to pose altogether new and important questions about his personality, questions which were unsuspected by earlier writers and to which no better answer than Freud's has yet been given." [10]

The striking novelty and the startling conclusions of Freud's essay on Leonardo had much to do with precipitating the flood of psychoanalytic or, better, pseudo-psychoanalytic biographical writing during the 1920's, almost all of which was of such a low order—ill-informed,

---

[8] Gruhle, *Geschichtsschreibung und Psychologie*, pp. 127 ff., cites a number of instances from the writings of eminent German historians; and Max Horkheimer, "Geschichte und Psychologie," *Zeitscrift für Sozialforschung*, I (1932), 125–144, argues the complete inadequacy of the psychological concepts of the classical economists. Alfred M. Tozzer, "Biography and Biology," in *Personality in Nature, Society, and Culture*, ed. Clyde Kluckhohn and H. A. Murray (2nd ed., New York, 1953), pp. 226–239, plays havoc with the simple-minded biological twist in much biographical writing.

[9] This thought is more or less explicitly expressed by Louis Gottschalk, "The Historian and the Historical Document," in *The Use of Personal Documents in History, Anthropology and Sociology*, Social Science Research Council Bull. No. 53 (New York, 1945), and in *The Social Sciences in Historical Study*. See also Lewis Namier, "Human Nature in Politics," in his *Personalities and Powers* (London, 1955); Schoenwald, *Western Humanities Review*, X (1956), 99–108.

[10] Meyer Shapiro, "Leonardo and Freud: An Art-Historical Study," *Jour. Hist. Ideas*, XVII (1956), 147–178, and other critics there cited.

sensational, scandalizing—that it brought the entire Freudian approach into disrepute. I have no doubt that this, in turn, discouraged serious scholars—the historians among them—from really examining the possibilities of the new teachings. Only within the last generation has the situation begun to change. The basic concepts of psychoanalysis, such as the processes of repression, identification, projection, reaction formation, substitution, displacement, and sublimation, have by now become more firmly established through clinical work and have at the same time increasingly become part of our thinking. Meanwhile, concerted efforts have been made to build up systematic personality and character study on a psychoanalytic basis and the so-called neo-Freudians, advancing beyond the narrowly environmental factors, have done much to develop the significance of constitutional and cultural influences.[11]

While recognized scholars in related fields, notably in political science, have begun to apply psychoanalytic principles to the study of personality types and their social role, historians have for the most part maintained an iron curtain between their own profession and that of the dynamic psychologists. It is, indeed, still professionally dangerous to admit any addiction to such unorthodox doctrine.[12] Even those who are in general intrigued by the potentialities of psychoanalysis are inclined to argue against its application to historical problems. They point out that detailed evidence on the crucial early years of an individual's life is rarely available and that, unlike the practicing analyst, the historian cannot turn to his subject and help him revive memories of specific events and relationships. To this it may be answered that the historian, on whatever basis he is operating, is always suffering from lack of data. Actually there is often considerable information about the family background of prominent historical personalities and the sum

[11] Erich Fromm, "Die psychoanalytische Charakterologie und ihre Bedeutung für die Sozialpsychologie," *Zeitschrift für Sozialforschung,* I (1932), 253–277, and *Psychology and Religion,* pp. 10 ff.; Karen Horney, *The Neurotic Personality of Our Time* (New York, 1937), chap. 1; Franz Alexander, *Fundamentals of Psychoanalysis* (New York, 1948), chap. 6; Ralph Linton, *The Cultural Development of Personality* (New York, 1945); Kardiner, *Psychological Frontiers of Society,* especially chap. 14; Gerald S. Blum, *Psychoanalytic Theories of Personality* (New York, 1953); Gordon W. Allport, *Becoming: Basic Considerations for a Psychology of Personality* (New Haven, 1955); Georges Friedmann, "Psychoanalysis and Sociology," *Diogenes,* no. 14 (1956), 17–35.

[12] Bernard Brodie, in his review of the excellent study of *Woodrow Wilson and Colonel House* (New York, 1957) by Alexander and Juliette George, notes that the authors, while using very effectively the concepts of psychoanalysis, are scrupulous not to mention the fact. "A Psychoanalytic Interpretation of Woodrow Wilson," *World Politics,* IX (1957), 413–422.

total of evidence about their careers is in some cases enormous. Furthermore, the experiences of earliest childhood are no longer rated as important for later development as was once the case, and the historian, if he cannot deal with his subject as man to man, at least has the advantage of surveying his whole career and being able to observe the functioning of significant forces.[13] In any event we historians must, if we are to retain our self-respect, believe that we can do better with the available evidence than the untrained popular biographer to whom we have so largely abandoned the field.

The historian is, of course, less interested in the individual as such than in the impact of certain individuals upon the society of their time and, beyond that, in the behavior of men as members of the group, society, or culture. This leads us into the domain of social or collective psychology, a subject on which much has been written during the past twenty-five years, especially in this country, but in which progress continues to be slight because of the difficulty of distinguishing satisfactorily between large groups and small groups, between organized and unorganized aggregations, between such vague collectivities as the crowd, the mob, and the mass.[14] Much certainly remains to be done in this area, especially in the elaboration of a theory to bridge the gap between individual and collective psychology.

Freud himself became convinced, at an early date, that his theories might have a certain applicability to historical and cultural problems.[15] He accepted the conclusions of Gustave Le Bon's well-known study of the psychology of crowds (1895) and recognized that a group may develop "a sort of collective mind." [16] As the years went by, his clinical work led him to the conclusion that there were close parallels between the development of the individual and of the race. Thus, the individual's unconscious mind was, in a sense, the repository of the past experiences of his society, if not of mankind.[17] In his most daring and provocative

[13] Gruhle, *Geschichtsschreibung und Psychologie*, pp. 127 ff.
[14] Gustave Le Bon, *La Psychologie des foules* (Paris), was published in 1895. The earliest texts, those of William McDougall, *An Introduction to Social Psychology* (London), and of Edward A. Ross, *Social Psychology* (New York), were first published in 1908. See M. Brewster Smith, "Some Recent Texts in Social Psychology," *Psychological Bulletin*, L (1953), 150–159.
[15] Freud's letter to C. G. Jung, July 5, 1910, quoted in Ernest Jones, *The Life and Work of Sigmund Freud* (New York, 1955), II, 448–449.
[16] Sigmund Freud, *Group Psychology and the Analysis of the Ego* (New York, 1921).
[17] Jones, *What is Psychoanalysis?*, pp. 20 ff.

works, *Totem and Taboo* (1913) and his last book, *Moses and Monotheism* (1939), Freud tried to determine the effect of group experience on the formation of a collective group mind.

Anthropologists, like historians, will probably continue to reject Freud's historical ventures as too extravagantly speculative, but the fact remains that anthropological and sociological researches suggest ever more definitely that certain basic drives and impulses, as identified by Freud, appear in all cultures and that the differences between cultures derive largely from varying methods of dealing with these drives.[18] Furthermore, social psychologists are increasingly aware of the similarity in the operation of irrational forces in the individual and in society.[19] Everett D. Martin, an early but unusually discerning student of the subject, noted in 1920 that the crowd, like our dream life, provides an outlet for repressed emotions: "It is as if all at once an unspoken agreement were entered into whereby each member might let himself go, on condition that he approved the same thing in all the rest." A crowd, according to Martin, "is a device for indulging ourselves in a kind of temporary insanity by all going crazy together." [20] Similarly, Freud's erstwhile disciple, C. G. Jung, has characterized recent political mass movements as "psychic epidemics, i.e. mass psychoses," and others have noted that the fears and rages of mass movements are clearly the residue of childish emotions.[21]

All this, as aforesaid, still requires much further exploration. It does seem, however, that we shall have to learn to reckon with the concept of "collective mentality," even on the unconscious level, and that the traits of that mentality—normally submerged and operative only in association with others or in specific settings—can best be studied as a part of, or extension of, individual psychology. That is to say that progress in social psychology probably depends on ever more highly refined analysis of the individual—his basic motivations, his attitudes, beliefs, hopes, fears, and aspirations.[22]

[18] Geza Roheim, *Psychoanalysis and Anthropology* (New York, 1950).

[19] Clyde Kluckhohn, "The Impact of Freud on Anthropology," in *Freud and Contemporary Culture*, pp. 66–72.

[20] Everett D. Martin, *The Behavior of Crowds* (New York, 1920), pp. 35–36. Martin was well versed in the psychoanalytical literature of his time.

[21] Jung, quoted by Ira Progoff, *Jung's Psychology and Its Social Meaning* (New York, 1953), p. ix; Erik H. Erikson, "The First Psychoanalyst," *Yale Review*, XLVI (1956), 40–62; Melitta Schmideberg, "Zum Verständnis massenpsychologischer Erscheinungen," *Imago*, XXI (1935), 445–457.

[22] See especially Erich Fromm, "Über Methode und Aufgabe einer analytischen Sozialpsychologie," *Zeitschrift für Sozialforschung*, I (1932), 28–54.

In this connection it is worth recalling our venerable French colleague, Georges Lefebvre's, long-standing interest and concern with the character and role of mobs and crowds in the French Revolution, and especially his impressive study of the mass hysteria of 1789 known as "The Great Fear." Although Lefebvre thought Le Bon superficial and confused, he was convinced by his own researches that there was such a thing as a "collective mentality." Indeed, he considered it the true causal link between the origins and the effects of major crises.[23] Without specific reference to psychoanalytic concepts, Lefebvre arrived at conclusions altogether consonant with those of modern psychology. His truly impressive studies have in a sense prefaced the more recent analyses of totalitarian movements which, in my estimation, have clearly demonstrated the vast possibilities opened to social scientists by the findings of dynamic psychology.[24]

As historians we must be particularly concerned with the problem whether major changes in the psychology of a society or culture can be traced, even in part, to some severe trauma suffered in common, that is, with the question whether whole communities, like individuals, can be profoundly affected by some shattering experience. If it is indeed true that every society or culture has a "unique psychological fabric," deriving at least in part from past common experiences and attitudes, it seems reasonable to suppose that any great crisis, such as famine, pestilence, natural disaster, or war, should leave its mark on the group, the intensity and duration of the impact depending, of course, on the nature and magnitude of the crisis. I hasten to say in advance that I do not imagine the psychological impact of such crises to be uniform for all members of the population, for if modern psychology has demonstrated anything it is the proposition that in any

[23] Lucien Lefebvre, "Foules révolutionnaires," in his *Étude sur la Révolution Française* (Paris, 1954), pp. 271–287, and *La Grande Peur de 1789* (Paris, 1932). Philip Rieff, "The Origins of Freud's Political Psychology," *Jour. Hist. Ideas*, XVII (1956), 233–249, is equally hard on Le Bon.

[24] To mention a few titles: Nathan Leites, *A Study of Bolshevism* (Glencoe, Ill., 1953); Gabriel A. Almond, *et al.*, *The Appeals of Communism* (Princeton, 1954); Hannah Arendt, *The Origins of Totalitarianism* (New York, 1951); Henry Pachter, "National-Socialist and Fascist Propaganda for the Conquest of Power," in *The Third Reich*, ed. M. Baumont, J. H. E. Fried, and E. Vermeil (New York, 1955), pp. 710–741, and the discussion of it by Carl E. Schorske, "A New Look at the Nazi Movement," *World Politics*, IX (1956), 88–97. See also Hadley Cantril, *The Psychology of Social Movements* (New York, 1941), for a discussion of various modern mass movements, and Raymond A. Bauer, "The Psycho-Cultural Approach to Soviet Studies," *World Politics*, VII (1954), 119–132, for a critical review of several analyses of Soviet society.

given situation individuals will react in widely diverse ways, depending on their constitution, their family background, their early experiences, and other factors. But these varying responses are apt to be reflected chiefly in the immediate effects of the catastrophe. Over the long term (which is of greater interest to the historian) it seems likely that the group would react in a manner most nearly corresponding to the underlying requirements of the majority of its members, in other words, that despite great variations as between individuals there would be a dominant attitudinal pattern.

I admit that all this is hypothetical and that we are here moving into unexplored territory, but allow me to examine a specific problem which, though remote from the area of my special competence, is nevertheless one to which I have devoted much study and thought. Freud once stressed the fact that present-day man, living in a scientific age in which epidemic disease is understood and to a large extent controlled, is apt to lose appreciation of the enormous, uncomprehended losses of life in past generations, to say nothing of the prolonged and widespread emotional strain occasioned by such disasters.[25] This is not entirely true, however, of historians of the ancient world who, since the days of Niebuhr, have concerned themselves with the possible effects of widespread disease and high mortality on the fate of Mediterranean civilizations. A strong case has been made for the proposition that malaria, which seems to have first appeared in Greece and Italy in the fourth or fifth centuries B.C., and soon became endemic, led on the one hand to serious debilitation, sloth, and unwillingness to work, and on the other to excitability, brutality, and general degradation. Recent researches suggest that malaria may have been one of the main causes of the collapse of the Etruscan civilization and may have accounted, at least in part, for the change in Greek character after the fourth century, especially for the growing lack of initiative. With reference to the Roman Empire, Professor Arthur Boak has recently reexamined the striking loss of population in the third and fourth centuries A.D. and has attributed it largely to the great epidemics of A.D. 165–180 and 250–280, thus reaffirming the view of Niebuhr and others that the Empire never really recovered from these tragic visitations.[26]

[25] Sigmund Freud, "Thoughts for the Times on War and Death" (1915), in *Collected Papers* (London, 1924–1934), IV, no. 17.

[26] W. H. S. Jones, *Dea Febris: A Study of Malaria in Ancient Italy* (n.p., n.d.) and *Malaria and Greek History* (Manchester, 1909); W. H. S. Jones, Major R. Ross, and G. G. Ellet, *Malaria, a Neglected Factor in the History of Greece and*

The literature on these and subsequent epidemics is, however, devoted largely to their medical and sanitational aspects, or at most to their economic and social effects. My primary interest, as I have said, is with the possible long-range psychological repercussions. To study these I think we may well pass over the great plague of Athens in 430 B.C., so vividly reported by Thucydides, and the so-called plague of Justinian of the sixth century A.D., not because they were unimportant but because there is much more voluminous and instructive information about the Black Death of 1348–1349 and the ensuing period of devastating disease.

Western Europe seems to have been relatively free of major epidemics in the period from the sixth to the fourteenth century. It may well be that the revival of trade and the growth of towns, with their congestion and lack of sanitation, facilitated the spread and establishment of the great mortal diseases like plague, typhus, syphilis, and influenza.[27] At any rate, the Black Death was worse than anything experienced prior to that time and was, in all probability, the greatest single disaster ever to have befallen European mankind. In most localities a third or even a half of the population was lost within the space of a few months, yet the great visitation of 1348–1349 marked only the beginning of a long period of pandemic disease with a continuing frightful drain of population. It is hardly an exaggeration to say that for three hundred years Europe was ravaged by one disease or another, or more usually by several simultaneously, the serious outbreaks coming generally at intervals of five to ten years.[28] Professor Lynn Thorndike,

---

Rome (Cambridge, Eng., 1907); Nello Toscanelli, *La malaria nell'antichità e la fine degli Etruschi* (Milan, 1927), especially pp. 237 ff.; A. E. R. Boak, *Manpower Shortage and the Fall of the Roman Empire in the West* (Ann Arbor, Mich., 1955).

[27] Bernard M. Lersch, *Geschichte der Volksseuchen* (Berlin, 1896), pp. 52 ff.; L. Fabian Hirst, *The Conquest of Plague* (Oxford, 1953), p. 10. It is highly likely that the arrival of rats in Europe in the twelfth century had an important bearing on the spread of bubonic plague. See Hans Zinsser, *Rats, Lice and History* (Boston, 1935), pp. 195 ff.; Major Greenwood, *Epidemics and Crowd-Diseases* (New York, 1937), pp. 289 ff.

[28] August Hirsch, *Handbook of Geographical and Historical Pathology*, trans. Charles Creighton (London, 1883–1885), I, chap. 10; Georg Sticker, *Die Pest*, Abhandlungen aus der Seuchengeschichte und Seuchenlehre, I (Giessen, 1908), pp. 74 ff.; Hirst, *Conquest of Plague*, p. 13; Josiah C. Russell, *British Medieval Population* (Albuquerque, N. Mex., 1948), pp. 2, 14 ff.; Lynn Thorndike, "The Blight of Pestilence on Early Modern Civilization," *American Historical Review*, XXXII (1927), 455–474; C. W. Previté-Orton, *Cambridge Medieval History* (Cambridge, Eng., 1932), intro.; David A. Stewart, "Disease and History," *Annals of Medical History*, n.s., VII (1935), 351–371; Herman B. Allyn, "The Black Death,

who thirty years ago wrote in the *American Historical Review* of the blight of pestilence on early modern civilization, pointed out that the period of greatest affliction was that of the Renaissance and Reformation, and especially the years from about 1480 until 1540, during which period frequent severe outbreaks of bubonic plague were reinforced by attacks of typhus fever and by the onset of the great epidemic of syphilis, to say nothing of the English Sweat (probably influenza) which repeatedly devastated England before invading the Continent in 1529. The bubonic plague began to die out in Western Europe only in the late seventeenth century, to disappear almost completely after the violent outbreak at Marseilles in 1720. But the Balkans and Middle East continued to suffer from it until well into the nineteenth century and the pandemic that broke out in India in the 1890's was evidently comparable to the Black Death in terms of mortality and duration.[29]

The extensive records of the Black Death have long been studied, not only with reference to their medical aspects, but also in connection with the economic and social effects of so sudden and substantial a loss of population. The English population is estimated to have fallen from 3,700,000 in 1348 to 2,100,000 in 1400, the mortality rates of the period 1348–1375 far exceeding those of modern India. While the figures for continental countries are less complete, the available data suggest that the losses were comparable.[30] Cities and towns suffered

---

Its Social and Economic Results," *Ann. Medical Hist.*, VII (1925), 226–236; the excellent, succinct review by Yves Renouard, "Conséquences et intérêt démographique de la peste noire de 1348," *Population* [Paris], III (1948), 459–466, and "La peste noire de 1348–1350," *Revue de Paris* (March 1950), 107–119. According to Charles Mullett, *The Bubonic Plague and England* (Lexington, Ky., 1956), p. 18, there were no less than twenty attacks in England in the course of the fifteenth century.

[29] Hirsch, *Handbook*, I, chaps. 3, 10, 11; II, chap. 2; Justus F. K. Hecker, *The Epidemics of the Middle Ages*, trans. B. G. Babington (London, 1844), pp. 188 ff.; Charles Creighton, *A History of Epidemics in Britain* (Cambridge, Eng., 1891), I, chap. 8; Herman Meyer, "Zur Geschichte der Pest im 15. und 16. Jahrhundert," *Schauinsland*, XXVIII (1901), 13–32; Hirst, *Conquest of Plague*, p. 16. It is likely that the replacement of the black rat by the brown rat in Europe in the early eighteenth century had an important bearing on the decline of the plague, since the black rat was much more domesticated than the brown (see Zinsser, *Rats, Lice and History*, pp. 195 ff.), and it may well be that the growing severity of the European climate, beginning with the late sixteenth century, may have reduced the reproduction rate of the rat flea which is the carrier of the plague bacillus. See Gustaf Utterström, "Climate Fluctuations and Population Problems in Early Modern History," *Scandinavian Economic History Review*, III (1955), 3–47.

[30] Julius Beloch, "Bevölkerungsgeschichte Europas im Mittelalter," *Zeitschrift für Socialwissenschaft*, III (1900), 405–423; Russell, *British Medieval Population*, pp. 263 ff., 375, and "Medieval Population," *Social Forces*, XV (1937), 503–511;

particularly, but in some areas as many as 40 per cent of the villages and hamlets were abandoned, the survivors joining with those of other settlements or moving to the depopulated towns where opportunity beckoned.[31] Although a generation ago there was a tendency, especially among English historians, to minimize the social effects of the Black Death, more recent writers like G. G. Coulton acknowledge that the great epidemic, if it did not evoke entirely new forces, did vastly accelerate those already operative.[32] The economic progress of Europe, which had been phenomenal in the thirteenth century, came to a halt and was soon followed by a prolonged depression lasting until the mid-fifteenth century and in a sense even into the seventeenth.[33]

Renouard, *Population,* III (1948), 459–466; Maxim Kowalewsky, *Die ökonomische Entwicklung Europas* (Berlin, 1911), V, 227 ff., 321 ff., 362 ff., 400 ff.

[31] On the desertion of villages and the depopulation of the countryside see Francis A. Gasquet, *The Great Pestilence* (London, 1893), pp. 28 ff., 54, 68, and chaps. 9, 10, *passim;* Creighton, *History of Epidemics,* I, 122, 177, 191; Maurice Beresford, *The Lost Villages of England* (London, 1954) who, however, attributes the abandonment of villages to increasing enclosures for grazing, at least in the first instance. By far the best treatments are those of Friedrich Lütge, *Deutsche Sozial- und Wirtschaftsgeschichte* (Berlin, 1952), pp. 144 ff., and Wilhelm Abel, *Die Wüstungen des ausgehenden Mittelalters* (2nd ed., Stuttgart, 1955).

[32] So far as Germany is concerned the reaction to exaggerated claims was first expressed by Robert Hoeniger, *Der Schwarze Tod in Deutschland* (Berlin, 1882), pp. 77 ff. In England the reversal of opinion was brought about largely through the researches of A. Elizabeth Levett, "The Black Death on the Estates of the See of Winchester," *Oxford Studies in Social and Legal History,* V (1916), 1–120, and was strongly reflected in such writings as Helen Robbins, "A Comparison of the Effect of the Black Death on the Economic Organization of France and England," *Journal of Political Economy,* XXXVI (1928), 447–479. For the best-informed recent evaluations, see G. G. Coulton, *The Black Death* (London, 1929), chap. 5; also the very judicious review by Eileen E. Power, "The Effects of the Black Death on Rural Organization in England," *History,* n.s., III (1918), 109–116; the basic study for Spain by Charles Verlinden, "La Grande Peste en Espagne: Contribution à l'étude de ses conséquences économiques et sociales," *Revue belge de philologie et d'histoire,* XVII (1938), 101–146; and the admirable summaries of Renouard, cited above, n. 28.

[33] So eminent an authority as Wilhelm Abel, "Wachstumsschwankungen mitteleuropäischer Völker seit dem Mittelalter," *Jahrbuch für Nationalökonomie und Statistik,* CXLII (1935), 670–692, holds that pestilence, famine, and war were not enough to account for the enormous decline in population and that psychological forces, as yet unanalyzed, led to a reluctance to marry and raise a family. E. J. Hobsbawm, "The General Crisis of the European Economy in the 17th Century," *Past and Present* (1954), no. 5, 33–53 and no. 6, 44–65, notes that the economic crisis, which had been in process since about 1300, came to an end at just about the time the plague died out. On the general economic depression see especially M. Postan, "Revisions in Economic History: The Fifteenth Century," *Economic History Review,* IX (1930), 160–167; John Saltmarsh, "Plague and Economic Decline in England in the Later Middle Ages," *Cambridge Historical Journal,* VII (1941), 23–41; Édouard Perroy, "Les crises du xiv⁰ siècle," *Annales,* IV (1949), 167–182, who stresses the fact that the Black Death created a demographic crisis,

I make only the most fleeting reference to these questions, because my chief concern, as I have said, is to determine, if possible, what the long-term psychological effects of this age of disease may have been. The immediate horrors of great epidemics have been vividly described by eminent writers from Thucydides to Albert Camus and have been pictured on canvas by famous artists like Raphael and Delacroix.[34] At news of the approach of the disease a haunting terror seizes the population, in the Middle Ages leading on the one hand to great upsurges of repentance in the form of flagellant processions and on the other to a mad search for scapegoats, eventuating in large-scale pogroms of the Jews.[35] The most striking feature of such visitations has always been the precipitate flight from the cities, in which not only the wealthier classes but also town officials, professors and teachers, clergy, and even physicians took part.[36] The majority of the population, taking

---

superimposed on a food crisis (1315–1320) and a financial crisis (1335–1345); Robert S. Lopez, "The Trade of Medieval Europe: The South," in *Cambridge Economic History of Europe* (Cambridge, 1952), II, 338 ff.; M. Postan, "The Trade of Medieval Europe: The North," in *Cambridge Economic History of Europe,* II 191 ff.; and Lopez's review of M. Mollat's *Le Commerce maritime normand à la fin du moyen âge,* in *Speculum,* XXXII (1957), 383–389.

[34] Cf. the realistic account in Albert Camus, *La Peste* (Paris, 1947), with the contemporary account of the yellow fever epidemic in Philadelphia in 1793 in Howard W. Haggard, *Devils, Drugs and Doctors* (New York, 1929), p. 213. Recent, as yet unpublished, studies of modern epidemics by Professors James Diggory and A. Pepitone of the University of Pennsylvania bear out all the main features of earlier descriptions. Some striking plague paintings are reproduced in Raymond Crawfurd, *Plague and Pestilence in Literature and Art* (Oxford, 1914).

[35] Although the appearance of flagellantism and the beginnings of the Jewish pogroms antedated the Black Death, they reached their fullest development in 1348–1349. See the basic accounts by Karl Lechner, "Die grosse Geisselfahrt des Jahres 1349," *Historisches Jahrbuch,* V (1884), 437–462; Heinz Pfannenschmid, "Die Geissler des Jahres 1349 in Deutschland und den Niederlanden," *Die Lieder und Melodien der Geissler des Jahres 1349,* ed. Paul Runge (Leipzig, 1900), pp. 89–218; Joseph McCabe, *The History of Flagellantism* (Girard, Kans., 1946), especially pp. 33 ff.; Norman Cohn, *The Pursuit of the Millenium* (London, 1957), chap. 6. See further Hecker, *Epidemics of the Middle Ages,* pp. 32 ff.; Hoeniger, *Der Schwarze Tod;* Johannes Nohl, *The Black Death* (London, 1926); A. L. Maycock, "A Note on the Black Death," *Nineteenth Century,* XCVII (1925), 456–464. As late as 1884 in Italy physicians were suspected as agents of the rich to poison the poor, and in 1896 British officials in Bombay were charged with spreading the plague. See Melitta Schmideberg, "The Role of Psychotic Mechanisms in Cultural Development," *International Journal of Psychoanalysis,* XI (1930); 387–418; René Baehrel, "La haine de classe au temps d'épidémie," *Annales,* VII (1952), 351–360, who analyzes the popular reaction to the cholera epidemic of 1831–32; and Ilza Veith, "Plague and Politics," *Bulletin of the History of Medicine,* XXVIII (1954), 408–415.

[36] The extent of such exodus may be judged from the fact that during the yellow fever epidemic of 1878 about 60 percent of the population fled the city of Memphis (unpublished MS by James C. Diggory).

the disaster as an expression of God's wrath, devoted itself to penitential exercises, to merciful occupations, and to such good works as the
repair of churches and the founding of religious houses. On the other
hand, the horror and confusion in many places brought general demoralization and social breakdown. Criminal elements were quick to
take over, looting the deserted houses and even murdering the sick in
order to rob them of their jewels. Many, despairing of the goodness
and mercy of God, gave themselves over to riotous living, resolved, as
Thucydides says, "to get out of life the pleasures which could be had
speedily and which would satisfy their lusts, regarding their bodies
and their wealth alike as transitory." Drunkenness and sexual immorality were the order of the day. "In one house," reported an observer of the London plague of 1665, "you might hear them roaring
under the pangs of death, in the next tippling, whoring and belching
out blasphemies against God." [37]

The vivid description of the Black Death in Florence in the introduction of Boccaccio's *Decameron* is so familiar that further details
about the immediate consequences may be dispensed with. Unfortunately neither the sources nor later historians tell us much of the long-
range effects excepting that in the late nineteenth century a school of
British writers attributed to the Black Death fundamental changes in
the agrarian system and indeed in the entire social order. The English
prelate-historian, Francis Cardinal Gasquet, contended that the great
epidemic, with its admittedly high mortality among the clergy, disrupted the whole religious establishment and thereby set the scene for
the Protestant revolt. Though this thesis is undoubtedly exaggerated,
it does seem likely that the loss of clergy, especially in the higher ranks,
the consequent growth of pluralities, the inevitable appointment of
some who proved to be "clerical scamps" (Jessopp), and the vast enrichment of the Church through the legacies of the pious, all taken

---

[37] Quoted in Walter G. Bell, *The Great Plague in London in 1665* (London,
1924), p. 22. In addition to the classic accounts of Thucydides (*Peloponnesian
War*, Book II) and Boccaccio (*Decameron*, intro.), see also the notes of the great
physician, Ambroise Paré, *De la Peste* in *Oeuvres complètes* (Paris, 1841), III,
350–464; Mullett, *The Bubonic Plague*, p. 118, on the London plague of 1603;
F. P. Wilson, *The Plague in Shakespeare's London* (Oxford, 1927), chap. 5, on
the London plague of 1625. Much evidence is adduced in B. S. Gowen, *Some Psychological Aspects of Pestilence and Other Epidemics* (Winchester, Tenn., 1907);
enlarged reprint from the *American Journal of Psychology*, XVIII (January 1907),
1–60; Karl Lechner, *Das grosse Sterben in Deutschland* (Innsbruck, 1884), pp.
93 ff.; and the books of Creighton, Kowalewsky, Hecker, Nohl, Gasquet, and
Coulton, all cited above.

together played a significant role in the development of the Church in the later Middle Ages.[38]

But again, these are essentially institutional factors which may reflect but do not explain the underlying psychological forces. That unusual forces were operative in the later Middle Ages seems highly probable. Indeed, a number of eminent historians have in recent years expatiated on the peculiar character of this period.[39] I will not attempt even to summarize the various interpretations of the temper of that age which have been advanced on one side or the other. None of the commentators, so far as I know, have noted or analyzed the connection between the great and constantly recurring epidemics and the state of mind of much of Europe at that time. Yet the relationship would seem to leap to the eye. The age was marked, as all admit, by a mood of misery, depression, and anxiety, and by a general sense of impending doom.[40] Numerous writers in widely varying fields have commented

[38] On the high mortality of the clergy in England see especially Russell, *British Medieval Population*, pp. 222 ff., 367. On the general problem see Gasquet, *Great Pestilence*, pp. xvi–xvii, 203 ff.; Augustus Jessopp, *The Coming of the Friars and Other Historical Essays* (New York, 1889), pp. 245 ff.; Coulton, *The Black Death*, p. 48, and particularly his chapter on the Black Death in *Medieval Panorama* (New York, 1938); Hoeniger, *Der Schwarze Tod*, pp. 126 ff.; Anna M. Campbell, *The Black Death and Men of Learning* (New York, 1931), p. 136 ff.; A. Hamilton Thompson, "The Registers of John Gynewell, Bishop of Lincoln, for the years 1349–1350," *Archeological Journal*, LXVIII (1911), 306–360, and "The Pestilences of the 14th Century in the Diocese of York," *Archeol. Journal*, LXXI (1914), 97–154. According to Peter G. Mode, *The Influence of the Black Death on the English Monasteries* (Chicago, 1916), chaps. 2, 6, the heads of at least 120 monasteries had died and some of those who succeeded proved to be veritable gangsters. Verlinden lays great stress on the enrichment of the Church in Spain through donations and legacies.

[39] Johan Huizinga's *The Waning of the Middle Ages* (London, 1927), was, in a sense, the counterpart to Jakob Burckhardt's *The Civilization of the Renaissance in Italy* (London, 1878). Of the more recent books the following seem to me particularly significant: Rudolf Stadelmann, *Vom Geist des ausgehenden Mittelalters* (Halle, 1929); Will-Erich Peuckert, *Die grosse Wende: Das apokalyptische Saeculum und Luther* (Hamburg, 1948); Hermann Heimpel, "Das Wesen des Spätmittelalters," *Der Mensch in seiner Gegenwart* (Göttingen, 1954).

[40] Huizinga, *The Waning of the Middle Ages*, chap. 1; Stadelmann, *Vom Geist des ausgehenden Mittelalters*, pp. 7, 13; Peuckert, *Die Grosse Wende*, pp. 21, 144; Willy Andreas, *Deutschland vor der Reformation* (5th ed., Stuttgart, 1948), p. 202; Otto Benesch, *The Art of the Renaissance in Northern Europe* (Cambridge, 1945), p. 10. In a broad way, Renouard (works noted in n. 28) and Lucien Febvre ("La peste noire de 1348," *Annales*, IV [1949], 102–103) have suggested the psychological and religious repercussions of the great epidemics. Some authors speak of hysteria, paranoia, and mental disease. See Willy Hellpach, *Die geistigen Epidemien* (Frankfurt, 1905), pp. 84 ff.; Gregory Zilboorg, *A History of Medical Psychology* (New York, 1941), pp. 153 ff.; Norman Cohn, *Pursuit of the Millenium*, p. 73.

on the morbid preoccupation with death, the macabre interest in tombs, the gruesome predilection for the human corpse.[41] Among painters the favored themes were Christ's passion, the terrors of the Last Judgment, and the tortures of Hell, all depicted with ruthless realism and with an almost loving devotion to each repulsive detail.[42] Altogether characteristic was the immense popularity of the Dance of Death woodcuts and murals, which, with appropriate verses, appeared soon after the Black Death and which, it is agreed, expressed the sense of the immediacy of death and the dread of dying unshriven. Throughout the fifteenth and sixteenth centuries these pitilessly naturalistic pictures ensured man's constant awareness of his imminent fate.[43]

The origins of the Dance of Death theme have been generally traced to the Black Death and subsequent epidemics, culminating in the terror brought on by the outbreak of syphilis at the end of the fifteenth century. Is it unreasonable, then, to suppose that many of the other phenomena I have mentioned might be explained, at least in part, in the same way? We all recognize the late Middle Ages as a period of popular religious excitement or overexcitement, of pilgrimages and penitential processions, of mass preaching, of veneration of relics and

[41] See especially Frederick P. Weber, *Aspects of Death and Correlated Aspects of Life in Art, Epigram and Poetry* (London, 1918), pp. 157 ff.; Erna Döring-Hirsch, *Tod und Jenseits im Spätmittelalter* (Berlin, 1927), *passim*. See also Huizinga, *The Waning of the Middle Ages*, chap. 11; Peuckert, *Die Grosse Wende*, pp. 95 ff.; and especially Emile Mâle, *L'Art religieux de la fin du moyen âge en France* (Paris, 1908), pp. 375 ff., 423 ff. Paul Perdrizet, *La Vierge de Miséricorde* (Paris, 1908), chap. 9. Michelangelo on one occasion wrote to Vasari: "No thought is born in me which has not 'Death' engraved upon it" (quoted in Piero Misciatelli, *Savonarola* [English trans., Cambridge, 1929], p. 103).

[42] See Mâle, *L'Art religieux*, pp. 477 ff.; Millard Meiss, *Painting in Florence and Siena after the Black Death* (Princeton, 1951), especially chap. 2; Crawfurd, *Plague and Pestilence*, chap. 8. On the German painters see Joseph Lortz, *Die Reformation in Deutschland* (3rd ed., Freiburg, 1940), I, 102; Benesch, *Art of the Renaissance*, pp. 10 ff.; Arthur Burkhard, *Matthias Grünewald* (Cambridge, Mass., 1936), pp. 74 ff.; Gillo Dorfles, *Bosch* (Verona, 1953).

[43] On the artistic side see Crawfurd, *Plague and Pestilence*, chap. 7; Mâle, *L'Art religieux*, pp. 383 ff.; Curt Sachs, *The Commonwealth of Art* (New York, 1946), pp. 88 ff. See also Andreas, *Deutschland vor der Reformation*, pp. 206 ff.; Stadelmann, *Vom Geist des ausgehenden Mittelalters*, pp. 18 ff.; and the specialized studies of Gert Buchheit, *Der Totentanz* (Berlin, 1926); Henri Stegemeier, *The Dance of Death in Folksong* (Chicago, 1939); Wolfgang Stammler, *Der Totentanz* (Munich, 1948); and the particularly significant historical analysis of Hellmut Rosenfeld, *Der mittelalterliche Totentanz* (Münster, 1954), pp. 33 ff., 59 ff.

adoration of saints, of lay piety and popular mysticism.[44] It was apparently also a period of exceptional immorality and shockingly loose living, which we must take as the expression of the "devil-may-care" attitude of one part of the population. This the psychologists explain as the repression of unbearable feelings by accentuating the value of a diametrically opposed set of feelings and then behaving as though the latter were the real feelings.[45] But the most striking feature of the age was an unusually strong sense of guilt and a truly overwhelming fear of retribution, seeking expression in a passionate longing for effective intercession and in a craving for direct, personal experience of the Deity, as well as in a corresponding dissatisfaction with the Church and with the mechanization of the means of salvation as reflected, for example, in the traffic in indulgences.[46]

These attitudes, along with the great interest in astrology, the increased resort to magic, and the startling spread of witchcraft and Satanism in the fifteenth century were, according to the precepts of modern psychology, normal reactions to the sufferings to which mankind in that period was subjected.[47] It must be remembered that the

[44] The subject is too large to permit of cursory analysis, but see Stadelmann, *Vom Geist des ausgehenden Mittelalters*, chap. 3; Lortz, *Die Reformation*, I, 99 ff.; Andreas, *Deutschland vor der Reformation*, chap. 3 and pp. 191 ff.; and Heimpel, note 39 above. See also Evelyn Underhill, *Mysticism* (12th ed., London, 1930), esp. 453 ff., and "Medieval Mysticism," *Cambridge Medieval History*, VII (New York, 1932), chap. 26; Margaret Smith, *Studies in Early Mysticism in the Near and Middle East* (London, 1931), pp. 256–257. In 1880 the eminent orientalist Alfred von Kremer suggested the connection of mysticism (Sufism) with the great plague epidemics in the Middle East. See his "Über die grossen Seuchen des Orientes nach arabischen Quellen," *Sitzungsberichte der philosophisch historische Classe der kaiserlichen Akademie der Wissenschaften, Wien*, XCVI (1880), 69–156.

[45] James W. Thompson, "The Aftermath of the Black Death and the Aftermath of the Great War," *American Journal of Sociology*, XXVI (1920–1921), 565–572, on the continuing degeneration.

[46] Wallace K. Ferguson, "The Church in a Changing World: A Contribution to the Interpretation of the Renaissance," *Amer. Hist. Rev.*, LIX (1953), 1–18; review by Kurt F. Reinhardt of Friedrich W. Oedinger, *Über die Bildung der Geistlichen im späten Mittelalter* (Leiden, 1953), in *Speculum*, XXXII (1957), 391–392; Lortz, *Die Reformation*, I, 99 ff.; Andreas, *Deutschland vor der Reformation*, pp. 152–153, 169 ff.; and the eloquent pages on the Church in the mid-fourteenth century in Henri Daniel-Rops, *Cathedral and Crusade: Studies of the Medieval Church, 1050–1350* (London, 1957), pp. 593 ff. Norman Cohn, *Pursuit of the Millenium*, is devoted entirely to a study of the "revolutionary chiliastic movements" in Europe from the Crusades onward.

[47] On the triumph of astrology see Lynn Thorndike, *A History of Magic and Experimental Science* (New York, 1934), IV, 611 ff.; H. A. Strauss, *Psychologie und astrologische Symbolik* (Zurich, 1953); Mark Graubard, *Astrology and Al-*

Middle Ages, ignoring the teachings of the Greek physicians and relying entirely upon Scripture and the writings of the Church fathers, considered disease the scourge of God upon a sinful people.[48] All men, as individuals, carry within themselves a burden of unconscious guilt and a fear of retribution which apparently go back to the curbing and repression of sexual and aggressive drives in childhood and the emergence of death wishes directed against the parents. This sense of sin, which is fundamental to all religion, is naturally enhanced by the impact of vast unaccountable and uncontrollable forces threatening the existence of each and every one.[49] Whether or not there is also a primordial racial sense of guilt, as Freud argued in his *Totem and Taboo* (1913), it is perfectly clear that disaster and death threatening the entire community will bring on a mass emotional disturbance, based on a feeling of helpless exposure, disorientation, and common

chemy (New York, 1953), chaps. 4, 5. On the re-emergence of pagan superstitions, the practice of magic, and the belief in witches as a heretical sect devoted to worship of the devil and the perpetration of evil see Thorndike, *History of Magic*, IV, 274 ff.; Peuckert, *Die grosse Wende*, pp. 119 ff.; Andreas, *Deutschland vor der Reformation*, pp. 28 ff.; Joseph Hansen, *Zauberwesen, Inquisition und Hexenprozess im Mittelalter* (Munich, 1900), pp. 326 ff.; Margaret A. Murray, *The Witch-Cult in Western Europe* (Oxford, 1921), especially pp. 11 ff.; Harmanns Obendiek, *Satanismus und Dämonie in Geschichte und Gegenwart* (Berlin, 1928); Montague Summers, *The History of Witchcraft and Demonology* (2nd ed., New York, 1956), pp. 1 ff.; Zilboorg, *History of Medical Psychology*. It may be noted, for what it is worth, that in the fifteenth century witches were accused of inhibiting human fertility; possibly a reflection of popular concern over the rapidly diminishing population. It is also interesting to observe that witch trials died out in Europe concurrently with the disappearance of the plague in the eighteenth century.

48 God might, of course, act through natural phenomena such as comets, floods, droughts, or miasma. For a good discussion of this point see G. G. Coulton, *Five Centuries of Religion*, II (Cambridge, 1927), p. 394; Hirst, *Conquest of Plague*, chap. 2; Kenneth Walker, *The Story of Medicine* (New York, 1955), pp. 71 ff.; and especially Paul H. Kocher, "The Idea of God in Elizabethan Medicine," *Jour. Hist. Ideas*, XI (1950), 3–29. This explanation was generally accepted through the early modern period and undoubtedly presented a great obstacle to the development of medical and sanitational measures. See Mullett, *The Bubonic Plague*, pp. 74, 88. Recent studies on modern disasters indicate that it is still widely held, despite the discoveries of Pasteur and his successors. See Martha Wolfenstein, *Disaster: A Psychological Study* (Glencoe, Ill., 1957), pp. 199 ff.

49 The crucial problem of guilt feelings has not been much studied except by Freud and his successors. See Freud, "Thoughts for the Times on War and Death" (1915), and the succinct discussion in Ernest Jones, *What is Psychoanalysis?*, pp. 101 ff., 114. For the continuance of this feeling in modern times see Wolfenstein, *Disaster*, p. 71. Hadley Cantril, *The Invasion from Mars* (Princeton, 1940), pp. 161 ff., quotes one man as saying: "The broadcast had us all worried, but I knew it would at least scare ten years' life out of my mother-in-law."

guilt.[50] Furthermore, it is altogether plausible to suppose that children, having experienced the terror of their parents and the panic of the community, will react to succeeding crises in a similar but even more intense manner. In other words, the anxiety and fear are transmitted from one generation to another, constantly aggravated.

Now it has long been recognized by psychologists that man, when crushed by unfathomable powers, tends to regress to infantile concepts and that, like his predecessor in primitive times, he resorts to magic in his efforts to ward off evil and appease the angry deity.[51] It is generally agreed that magic and religion are closely related, both deriving from fear of unknown forces and especially death, and both reflecting an effort to ensure the preservation of the individual and the community from disease and other afflictions.[52] Death-dealing epidemics like those of the late Middle Ages were bound to produce a religious revival, the more so as the established Church was proving itself ever less able to

---

[50] A later explanation of the sense of communal guilt, as it appears among the Jews, was advanced by Freud in his *Moses and Monotheism* (London, 1939). Still another, quite different and quite persuasive, argument is presented by Theodor Reik, *Myth and Guilt: The Crime and Punishment of Mankind* (New York, 1957), especially pp. 34 ff., 146 ff. Oskar Pfister, *Das Christentum und die Angst* (Zurich, 1944) has examined the relation of anxiety to guilt feelings and the magnification of communal anxieties in the face of disaster. For concrete studies of medieval mass hysteria see Louis F. Calmeil, *De la Folie* (Paris, 1845); René Fülöp-Miller, *Leaders, Dreamers and Rebels* (New York, 1935); and especially the admirable scholarly study of Cohn, *Pursuit of the Millenium*, which stresses the analogies between individual and collective paranoia.

[51] C. G. Jung, "After the Catastrophe," *Essays on Contemporary Events* (London, 1947). See also Johann Kinkel, "Zur Frage der psychologischen Grundlagen und des Ursprungs der Religion," *Imago*, VIII (1922), 23–45, 197–241; Henry E. Sigerist, *Civilization and Disease* (Ithaca, 1943), chap. 6; Arturo Castiglioni, *Adventures of the Mind* (New York, 1946), pp. ix, 2, 11, 19; Bronislaw Malinowski, *Magic, Science and Religion* (Boston, 1948), pp. 15, 29, 116; Charles Odier, *Anxiety and Magic Thinking* (New York, 1956), pp. 38 ff.; Melitta Schmideberg, *International Journal of Psychoanalysis*, XI (1930), 387–418; Franz Alexander, "On the Psychodynamics of Regressive Phenomena in Panic States," *Psychoanalysis and the Social Sciences*, IV (1955), 104–111. Hirst, *Conquest of Plague*, has noted the reversion to magic during all great plague epidemics and reports that charms and amulets were never more prevalent among even educated Englishmen than during the epidemic of 1665. Jessopp, *Coming of the Friars*, p. 166, remarked that in his day the threat of any epidemic still brought on "wild-eyed panic" and resort to all kinds of superstitious practices.

[52] James H. Leuba, *The Psychological Origin and the Nature of Religion* (London, 1921), pp. 4, 81; George F. Moore, *The Birth and Growth of Religion* (New York, 1924), pp. 3, 8, 17; W. B. Selbie, *The Psychology of Religion* (Oxford, 1924), p. 32; Malinowski, *Magic, Science and Religion*, p. 29; Willy Hellpach, *Grundriss der Religionspsychologie* (Stuttgart, 1951), pp. 6 ff.

satisfy the yearning for more effective intercession and for a more personal relationship to God.[53] Wyclif, himself a survivor of the Black Death, is supposed to have been deeply affected by his gruelling experience, and there is nothing implausible in the suggestion that Lollardy was a reaction to the shortcomings of the Church in that great crisis.[54] In this connection it is also worth remarking that the first expression of Zwingli's reformed faith was his *Song of Prayer in Time of Plague*.[55]

Most striking, however, is the case of the greatest of the reformers, Martin Luther, who seems to me to reflect clearly the reaction of the individual to the situation I have been sketching. Luther left almost a hundred volumes of writings, thousands of letters, and very voluminous table-talk, suggesting an unusually self-analytical and self-critical personality.[56] From all this material it has long been clear that he suffered from an abnormally strong sense of sin and of the immediacy of death and damnation. Tortured by the temptations of the flesh and repeatedly in conflict with a personalized demon, he was chronically oppressed by a pathological feeling of guilt and lived in constant terror of God's

[53] In this connection the great expansion of the cult of the Virgin Mary, and even more of her mother, St. Anne, is worth noting; also the fact that among the ten or twelve most popular saints of the late fifteenth century, the so-called "plague saints" (St. Anthony, St. Sebastian, St. Roch), were particularly favored. See Huizinga, *Waning of the Middle Ages*, chap. 12; Crawfurd, *Plague and Pestilence*, chap. 8; and especially Mâle, *L'Art religieux*, pp. 157 ff., 193 ff. and Perdrizet, *La Vierge de Miséricorde, passim*.

[54] *The Last Age of the Church*, written in 1356 and first published in 1840, is a violent denunciation of the depravity revealed in the time of the Black Death. It was long believed to have been the first work of Wyclif but is now attributed to an unnamed Spiritual Franciscan. See James H. Todd, *The Last Age of the Church, by John Wycliffe* (Dublin, 1840); J. Foster Palmer, "Pestilences: Their Influence on the Destiny of Nations," *Transactions of the Royal Historical Society*, I (1884), 242–259; H. B. Workman, *John Wyclif: A Study of the English Medieval Church* (Oxford, 1926), I, 14; Robert Vaughan, *The Life and Opinions of John de Wyclife* (London, 1928), I, 238 ff.; and, on the general problem, Coulton, *The Black Death*, p. 111, and Mullett, *The Bubonic Plague*, p. 34.

[55] This very moving appeal for divine aid (1519) is reprinted in Georg Finsler, et al., *Ulrich Zwingli: Eine Auswahl aus seinen Schriften* (Zurich, 1918), pp. 17–19. See also Pfister, *Das Christentum und die Angst*, 321 ff., according to whom Calvin was terror-stricken by the plague and, unlike Luther, was unwilling to stick at his post during severe epidemics. He firmly believed that a group of thirty-four men and women witches had for three years spread the plague in Geneva and that in their case even the most extreme forms of torture were justified.

[56] Karl Holl, "Luthers Urteile über sich Selbst," *Luther*, vol. I of *Gesammelte Aufsätze zur Kirchengeschichte* (Tübingen, 1921); Heinrich Böhmer, *Road to Reformation; Martin Luther to the Year 1521* (Philadelphia, 1946), foreword; Karl A. Meissinger, *Der katholische Luther* (Munich, 1952), p. 2.

judgment. So striking were these traits that some of his biographers have questioned his sanity.[57]

Here it is interesting to recall that one of our own colleagues, the late Professor Preserved Smith, as long ago as 1913 attacked this problem in an article entitled "Luther's Early Development in the Light of Psychoanalysis."[58] Smith, who was remarkably conversant with Freudian teaching when psychoanalysis was still in its infancy, considered Luther highly neurotic—probably driven to enter the monastery by the hope of finding a refuge from temptation and an escape from damnation, and arriving at the doctrine of salvation by faith alone only after he had convinced himself of the impossibility of conquering temptation by doing penance. Smith may have overplayed his thesis, but the fact remains that his article was treated with great respect by the Danish psychiatrist, Dr. Paul J. Reiter, who later published a huge and greatly detailed study of Luther's personality. Reiter reached the conclusion, already suggested by Adolf Hausrath in 1905, that the great reformer suffered from a manic-depressive psychosis, which, frequently associated with genius, involved a constant struggle with, and victory over, enormous psychological pressures. The point in mentioning this is to suggest that Luther's trials were typical of his time. In any event, it is inconceivable that he should have evoked so great a popular response unless he had succeeded in expressing the underlying, unconscious sentiments of large numbers of people and in providing them with an acceptable solution to their religious problem.[59]

I must apologize for having raised so grim a subject on so festive an

[57] Hartmann Grisar, *Luther* (London, 1913–1917), I, 110 ff.; VI, chap. 36, discusses many of these views but Grisar himself takes a more moderate stand. The most recent Catholic biography is that of Joseph Lortz, *Die Reformation,* which is a very model of reasonableness.

[58] *Amer. Jour. Psychology,* XXIV (1913), 360–377.

[59] Adolf Hausrath, *Luthers Leben* (Berlin, 1905); Paul Reiter, *Martin Luthers Umwelt, Charakter und Psychose* (Copenhagen, 1937, 1941); Wilhelm Lange-Eichbaum, *Genie, Irrsinn und Ruhm* (4th ed., Munich, 1956), pp. 375–378. See also Walther von Loewenich, "Zehn Jahre Lutherforschung," in *Theologie und Liturgie,* ed. Liemar Hennig (Cassel, 1952), pp. 119–170; and Martin Werner, "Psychologisches zum Klostererlebnis Martin Luthers," *Schweizerische Zeitschrift für Psychologie,* VII (1948), 1–18, who follows Smith's thesis closely. The argument hinges on the harshness of Luther's upbringing and the extent of his father fixation. Smith noted that on at least one occasion Luther asserted that he had entered the monastery to escape harsh treatment at home. His father's unalterable opposition to this step may have played a part in Luther's later decision to leave the monastery. According to Roland H. Bainton, *Here I Stand: A Life of Martin Luther* (New York, 1950), pp. 288 ff., Luther's decision (in 1525) to marry was

occasion, but I could not resist the feeling that the problems presented by the later Middle Ages are exactly of the type that might be illuminated by modern psychology. I do not claim that the psychological aspects of this apocalyptic age have been entirely neglected by other students. Indeed, Millard Meiss, a historian of art, has written a most impressive study of Florentine and Sienese painting in the second half of the fourteenth century in which he has analyzed the many and varied immediate effects of the Black Death, including the bearing of that great catastrophe on the religious situation.[60] But no one, to my knowledge, has undertaken to fathom the prolonged psychological crisis provoked by the chronic, large-scale loss of life and the attendant sense of impending doom.

I would not, of course, argue that psychological doctrine, even if it were more advanced and more generally accepted than it is, would resolve all the perplexities of the historian. Better than most scholars, the historian knows that human motivation, like causation, is a complex and elusive process. In view of the fact that we cannot hope ever to have complete evidence on any historical problem, it seems unlikely that we shall ever have definite answers. But I am sure you will agree that there are still possibilities of enriching our understanding of the past and that it is our responsibility as historians to leave none of these possibilities unexplored. I call your attention to the fact that for many years now young scholars in anthropology, sociology, religion, literature, education, and other fields have gone to psychoanalytic institutes for special training, and I suggest that some of our own younger men might seek the same equipment. For of this I have no doubt, that modern psychology is bound to play an ever greater role in historical interpretation. There is already a growing readiness to recognize the

---

at least in part due to his wish to gratify his father's desire for progeny. Recent writers tend to explain away the harshness of Luther's youth, which indeed was probably less unusual and less important than Smith supposed. See Otto Scheel, *Martin Luther* (Tübingen, 1916); Böhmer, *Martin Luther;* Meissinger, *Der katholische Luther;* Robert H. Fife, *The Revolt of Martin Luther* (New York, 1957), pp. 5, 9, 99, 117 ff.; Bainton, *Here I Stand,* pp. 23, 25, 28 and chap. 21 *passim,* who insists that Luther's psychological troubles were of a strictly religious character, due to "tensions which medieval religion deliberately induced, playing alternately upon fear and hope."

[60] Meiss, *Painting in Florence and Siena after the Black Death,* while dealing with a restricted subject and a limited period, is in my opinion a masterpiece of synthesis and one of the very few books to recognize the full and varied impact of the Black Death. See also Hans Baron, *The Crisis of the Early Italian Renaissance* (Princeton, 1955), II, 479–480.

irrational factors in human development, and to lay increased emphasis on psychological forces. Perhaps the most stimulating non-Marxist interpretation of imperialism, that of the late Joseph Schumpeter, which goes back to 1918, rests squarely on a psychological base and recent treatments of such forces as totalitarianism and nationalism lay great stress on their psychological aspects.[61] Indeed, within the past year two books have appeared which have a direct bearing on my argument. One is T. D. Kendrick's *The Lisbon Earthquake,* which is devoted to a study of the effects of that disaster of 1755 upon the whole attitude and thought of the later eighteenth century. The other is Norman Cohn's *The Pursuit of the Millenium,* which reviews the chiliastic movements of the Middle Ages and comes to the conclusion that almost every major disaster, be it famine, plague, or war, produced some such movement which only analysis of their psychic content will help to explain.

Aldous Huxley, in one of his essays, discusses the failure of historians to devote sufficient attention to the great ebb and flow of population and its effect on human development. He complains that while Arnold Toynbee concerned himself so largely with challenges and responses, there is in the index of his first six volumes no entry for "population," though there are five references to Popilius Laenas and two to Porphyry of Batamaea.[62] To this I might add that the same index contains no reference whatever to pestilence, plague, epidemics, or Black Death. This, I submit, is mildly shocking and should remind us, as historians, that we cannot rest upon past achievements but must constantly seek wider horizons and deeper insights. We find ourselves in the midst of the International Geophysical Year, and we all know that scientists have high hopes of enlarging through cooperation their understanding as well as their knowledge of the universe. It is quite possible that they may throw further light on such problems as the influence of sunspots on terrestrial life and the effects of weather on the conduct of human affairs.[63] We may, for all we know, be on the threshold of a new era

[61] See, for example, Hannah Arendt, *The Origins of Totalitarianism,* and Boyd C. Shafer, *Nationalism: Myth and Reality* (New York, 1955).

[62] Aldous Huxley, *Tomorrow and Tomorrow and Tomorrow* (New York, 1956), p. 221.

[63] Fully a generation ago a Soviet scientist thought he could establish an eleven-year cycle of maximum sunspot activity and that these periods were also those of maximum mass excitability as revealed by revolutions and other social disturbances. Furthermore, his correlation of periods of maximum sunspot activity with cholera epidemics in the nineteenth century seemed to reveal a remarkable coincidence. See the summary translation of the book by A. L. Tchijevsky, "Physical

431

when the historian will have to think not merely in global, but also in cosmic, terms.

Factors of the Historical Process," as read before the American Meteorological Society, Dec. 30, 1926, and now reprinted in *Cycles*, VIII (February, 1957), 31–51. Of the many studies of climatic, nutritional, and similar influences on human affairs, see Ellsworth Huntington, *Civilization and Climate* (New Haven, 1915); *The Character of Races* (New York, 1924); *Mainsprings of Civilization* (New York, 1946); Willy Hellpach, *Geopsyche* (5th ed., Leipzig, 1939); Louis Berman, *Food and Character* (Boston, 1932); C. C. and S. M. Furnas, *Man, Bread and Destiny* (Baltimore, 1937); E. Parmalee Prentice, *Hunger and History* (New York, 1939); Josué de Castro, *The Geography of Hunger* (Boston, 1952).

23

Europe's Initial Population Explosion

1963

The use of the dramatic term "explosion" in discussions of the present-day population problem may serve to attract attention and underline the gravity of the situation, but it is obviously a misnomer. The growth of population is never actually explosive, and as for the current spectacular increase, it is really only the latest phase of a development that goes back to the mid-eighteenth century.

Prior to that time the history of European population had been one of slow and fitful growth. It then took a sudden spurt and thenceforth continued to increase at a high rate. From an estimated 140,000,000 in 1750 it rose to 188,000,000 in 1800, to 266,000,000 in 1850, and eventually to 400,000,000 in 1900. The rate of increase was not uniform for all parts of the continent, but it was everywhere strikingly high. Even in Spain, where there had been a remarkable loss of population in the seventeenth century, the population grew from 6,100,000 in 1725 to 10,400,000 in 1787 and 12,300,000 in 1833.[1]

This tremendous change in terms of European society has received far less attention from historians than it deserves. In the early nineteenth century it troubled the Reverend Thomas Malthus and precipitated a formidable controversy over the problem of overpopulation and the possible remedies therefor. But the discussion remained inconclusive until reopened in more recent times by British scholars, making use of the rather voluminous English records and directing their attention almost exclusively to their own national history. It is not unlikely that this focusing on the British scene has had the effect of distorting the issue, which after all was a general European one.

Note: Reprinted from the *American Historical Review*, LXIX (October 1963), 1–17.

[1] Albert Girard, "Le Chiffre de la population de l'Espagne dans les temps modernes," *Revue d'histoire moderne*, IV (January–February 1929), 3–17. The growth of population was equally or even more spectacular in the United States and French Canada, to say nothing of China, but this paper considers only the problem as it emerged in Europe.

The point of departure for recent attacks on the problem was the publication, in the same year, of two closely related books: G. T. Griffith's *Population Problems in the Age of Malthus* (Cambridge, Eng., 1926) and M. C. Buer's *Health, Wealth and Population in the Early Days of the Industrial Revolution* (London, 1926). To these should be added the keen corrective criticism of T. H. Marshall's essay, "The Population Problem during the Industrial Revolution." [2]

Taken together, these writings provided a coherent, comprehensive analysis. Based on the proposition that the unusual increase of the population in the late eighteenth century was due primarily to a marked decline in the death rate, they attempted to show that this decline must, in turn, have been due to an alleviation of the horrors of war, to a reduction in the number and severity of famines, to an improvement in the food supply, and finally to a falling off of disease as a result of advancing medical knowledge and better sanitation.

These conclusions were not seriously challenged until after the Second World War, when a number of demographic and sociological analyses by British and American scholars called various items of the accepted theory seriously into question. Because of the inadequacy of the statistical data some aspects of the problem can probably never be disposed of definitively. However, the very foundation of the Griffith thesis has now been badly sapped. A number of specialists have come to the conclusion that the spectacular rise in the European population may have been due not so much to a reduction in the death rate as to a significant rise in the birth rate which, according to Griffith, did not vary greatly throughout the period.[3]

From these excellent studies of fertility and mortality there has not, however, emerged any satisfactory explanation to replace the argumentation of Griffith and Buer about underlying causes. It may not be amiss, then, for a historian to join the debate, even though he must dis-

---

[2] T. H. Marshall, "The Population Problem during the Industrial Revolution," *Economic History*, I (January 1929), 429–456.

[3] Halvor Gille, "The Demographic History of the Northern Countries," *Population Studies*, III (June 1949), 3–66; K. H. Connell, "Some Unsettled Problems in English and Irish Population History," *Irish Historical Studies*, VII (September 1951), 225–234; H. J. Habakkuk, "The English Population in the Eighteenth Century," *Economic History Review*, 2nd ser., VI (December 1953), 117–133; J. T. Krause, "Changes in English Fertility and Mortality, 1781–1850," *Economic History Review*, 2nd ser., XI (August 1958), 52–70; J. T. Krause, "Some Implications of Recent Work in Historical Demography," *Comparative Studies in Society and History*, I (January 1959), 164–188; Phyllis Deane and W. A. Cole, *British Economic Growth, 1688–1959* (Cambridge, Eng., 1962), pp. 129–133.

claim at the outset any professional competence in demography or statistics.

From the strictly historical standpoint none of the previous interpretations of the initial spurt of the European population has been satisfactory. At the time it was commonly thought that the so-called "Industrial Revolution," with its high requirement for child labor, may have induced larger families.[4] This explanation could at best apply primarily to Britain, where the demographic revolution was roughly contemporaneous with industrialization. Since the rate of population increase was just as striking in completely unindustrialized countries like Russia, a less parochial explanation was clearly required. At the present time it seems more likely that industrialization saved Europe from some of the more alarming consequences of overpopulation.[5]

Griffith's theses, inspired by Malthusian doctrine, are unacceptable, for the historical evidence provides little support for the notion of a marked decline in the death rate. Take, for instance, the mortality occasioned by war. Granted that no conflict of the eighteenth or early nineteenth centuries was as deadly as the Thirty Years' War is reputed to have been, there is yet no evidence of a difference so marked as to have made a profound change in the pattern of population. It is well known that nations usually recover quickly from the manpower losses of war. If it were not so, the bloody conflicts of the French revolutionary and Napoleonic periods should have had a distinctly retarding effect on the growth of the European population.

Not much more can be said of the argument on food supply. What reason is there to suppose that Europe suffered less from famine? We know that there were severe famines in the first half of the eighteenth century and that the years 1769–1774 were positively calamitous in terms of crop failures. The early 1790's and the years immediately following the peace in 1815 were almost as bad, while at much later periods (1837–1839, 1846–1849) all Europe suffered from acute food shortages. Even in western and central Europe famine was a constant threat until the railroads provided rapid, large-scale transportation.

Griffith was convinced that the important advances in agronomy (rotation of crops, winter feeding of cattle, systematic manuring, im-

[4] Joseph J. Spengler, "Malthus's Total Population Theory," *Canadian Journal of Economics and Political Science*, XI (February 1945), 83–110.

[5] This question is well discussed in H. J. Habakkuk, "The Economic History of Modern Europe," *Journal of Economic History*, XVIII (September 1958), 486–501.

proved breeding of livestock, and so forth) as well as the practice of enclosure all made for more productive farming and greatly enhanced the food supply. But even in Britain, where agriculture was more advanced than elsewhere, these improvements did not make themselves generally felt until the mid-nineteenth century. There were many progressive landlords, on the continent as in Britain, and no doubt there was improvement in grain production, but it was too slow, and grain imports were too slight to have had a decisive bearing on the rate of population growth. Even in mid-nineteenth-century Britain the three-field system was still prevalent, ploughs and other implements were old-fashioned and inefficient, grain was still cut by sickle or scythe and threshed with the flail, and ground drainage was primitive. Of course, more land had been brought under cultivation, but the available data reflect only a modest increase in the yield of grain per acre in this period.[6]

Crucial to the argumentation of Griffith and Buer was the proposition that improved health entailed a significant reduction in the death rate. The disappearance of bubonic plague, the falling off of other diseases, the advances in medical knowledge and practice (especially in midwifery), and progress in sanitation were in turn alleged to have produced the greater health of the people.

No one would deny that the disappearance of plague in the late seventeenth and early eighteenth centuries rid the Europeans of their most mortal enemy, and so reacted favorably on the development of the population. For the repeated plague epidemics had been fearfully destructive of life, especially in the towns. In the Black Death of 1348–1349 fully a quarter of the population had been carried away, while even as late as the epidemic of 1709–1710 from one-third to one-half of the inhabitants of cities such as Copenhagen and Danzig fell victims. In Marseilles in 1720 there were 40,000 dead in a total population of 90,000. In Messina in 1743 over 60 percent of the population was carried off.[7]

---

[6] See especially James Caird, *English Agriculture in 1850–1851* (2nd ed., London, 1852), pp. 474 ff.; R. E. P. Ernle, *English Farming, Past and Present* (6th ed., Chicago, 1961), pp. 108, 135, 265, 357 ff.; G. E. and K. R. Fussell, *The English Countryman* (London, 1955), p. 126; H. W. Graf Finckenstein, *130 Jahre Strukturwandel und Krisen der intensiven europäischen Landwirtschaft* (Berlin, 1937); M. K. Bennett, "British Wheat Yield per Acre for Seven Centuries," *Economic History*, III (February 1935), 12–29.

[7] Karl F. Helleiner, "The Vital Revolution Reconsidered," *Canadian Jour. Ec. and Poli. Sci.*, XXIII (February 1957), 1–9, and more generally Hans Zinsser,

But whatever may have been the gains from the disappearance of plague, they were largely wiped out by the high mortality of other diseases, notably smallpox, typhus, cholera, measles, scarlet fever, influenza, and tuberculosis. Of these great killers smallpox flourished particularly in the eighteenth century and tuberculosis in the eighteenth and nineteenth, while the deadly Asiatic cholera was a newcomer in 1830–1832.

Smallpox, though it reached up on occasions to strike adults, even of high estate, was primarily a disease of infancy and early childhood, responsible for one-third to one-half of all deaths of children under five. In 1721 the practice of inoculating children with the disease, in order to produce a mild case and create immunity, was introduced into England. It was rather widely used by the upper classes, but quite obviously had little effect on the epidemiology of the disease.[8] There appears to have been a gradual falling off of the disease after 1780, but even the introduction of vaccination by Edward Jenner in 1798 did not entirely exorcise the smallpox threat, though vaccination was offered gratuitously to thousands of children and was made compulsory in England in 1853. Mortality remained high, especially in the epidemics of 1817–1819, 1825–1827, 1837–1840, and 1847–1849. In the last great epidemic (1871–1872), when most people had already been vaccinated, the toll was exceedingly heavy: 23,062 deaths in England and Wales, 56,826 in Prussia in 1871 and 61,109 in 1872. Small wonder that opponents of vaccination stamped it a dangerous and futile procedure.[9]

Typhus, often associated with smallpox, attacked adults and was just as lethal. Like smallpox, it began to disappear only after 1870, to be replaced in part by measles, scarlet fever, and influenza.[10]

Rats, Lice and History (New York, 1935); L. F. Hirst, *The Conquest of Plague* (London, 1953).

[8] Genevieve Miller, *The Adoption of Inoculation for Smallpox in England and France* (Philadelphia, 1957). For excellent general historical studies of smallpox, see Charles Creighton, *A History of Epidemics in Britain* (Cambridge, Eng., 1891–1894), II, chap. 4; Alfons Fischer, *Geschichte des deutschen Gesundheitswesens* (Berlin, 1933), II, 563 ff.; Jean Bourgeois-Pichat, "Evolution de la population française depuis le xviii° siècle," *Population*, VI (October–December 1951), 635–662.

[9] W. Scott Tebb, *A Century of Vaccination* (2nd ed., London, 1899), pp. 58–59; David Johnston, *A History of the Present Condition of Public Charity in France* (Edinburgh, 1829), pp. 539 ff.; and for the rest, Creighton, *Epidemics in Britain*, II, 606, and Fischer, *Deutsches Gesundheitswesen*, II, 556.

[10] See Creighton, *Epidemics in Britain*, for a detailed history of each of these diseases.

Tuberculosis, which no doubt was as old as human history, was the chief cause of premature deaths in the nineteenth century. It seems to have been widespread even in the mid-eighteenth century and continued so for well over a hundred years.[11] But it was less spectacular than the terrifying cholera, which carried off half its victims within one to three days, and which struck Europe in four great epidemics during the nineteenth century. Paris in 1832 had 7,000 dead in eighteen days. Palermo in 1836–1837 lost 24,000 out of a population of 173,000. The epidemics of 1849 and 1866 were particularly lethal, especially on the continent. Paris in three months of 1849 had 33,274 cases, of which 15,677 were fatal. Prussia in 1849 had 45,315 deaths, and in 1866, 114,-683, while Russia in 1848–1849 registered over 1,000,000 dead.[12]

Considering the terrible and continuing ravages of disease in the days before the fundamental discoveries of Louis Pasteur and Robert Koch, it is hard to see how anyone could suppose that there was an amelioration of health conditions in the eighteenth century sufficient to account for a marked decline in the death rate.

Recent studies have pretty well disposed also of the favorite Griffith-Buer theme, that advances in medical knowledge and practice served to reduce mortality, especially among young children. Doctors and hospitals were quite incompetent to deal with infectious disease. The supposed reduction in child mortality was certainly not reflected in the fact that as late as 1840 half or almost half of the children born in cities like Manchester or even Paris were still dying under the age of five.[13]

---

[11] René and Jean Dubos, *The White Plague* (Boston, 1952), pp. 6 ff.; Fischer, *Deutsches Gesundheitswesen*, II, 570 ff.; Arturo Castiglione, *History of Tuberculosis* (New York, 1933); S. R. Gloyne, *Social Aspects of Tuberculosis* (London, 1944); S. L. Cummins, *Tuberculosis in History* (Baltimore, 1949).

[12] The first great epidemic (1831–32) has of late attracted a great deal of attention. See Sergei Gessen, *Cholernye Bunty, 1830–1832* (Moscow, 1932); Louis Chevalier, ed., *Le Cholera: La première Épidémie du xix⁰ siècle* (Paris, 1958); R. E. McGrew, "The First Cholera Epidemic and Social History," *Bulletin of the History of Medicine*, XXXIV (January–February 1960), 61–73; Asa Briggs, "Cholera and Society in the Nineteenth Century," *Past and Present*, no. 19 (April 1961), pp. 76–96. For the rest, see Francesco Maggiore-Perni, *Palermo e le sue grandi epidemie* (Palermo, 1894), pp. 190, 244; Creighton, *Epidemics in Britain*, II, chap. 9; Fischer, *Deutsches Gesundheitswesen*, II, 557; Georg Sticker, *Abhandlungen aus der Seuchengeschichte und Seuchenlehre* (Giessen, 1908–1912), II, 110 ff., 158 ff.; C. Macnamara, *A History of Asiatic Cholera* (London, 1876), pp. 86 ff.

[13] Fischer, *Deutsches Gesundheitswesen*, II, 341, 369, 388 ff., and the fundamental article of Habakkuk, *Economic History Review*, 2nd ser., VI (December 1953), pp. 117–133; Thomas McKeown and R. G. Brown, "Medical Evidence

Malthus thought the cities of his day better paved and drained than before, and this observation of the matter was exploited to the full by Griffith and Buer. Actually the improvements were mostly in the better sections of the towns, and Buer felt obliged to admit that living conditions were horrible, despite some amelioration. If one reviews these conditions even in the mid-nineteenth century in any large European city—the dank cellar dwellings, the overcrowded courts, the vermin-infested rookeries, the filthy streets, the foul water supply—one can only shudder at the thought of what they may formerly have been. One can hardly persuade oneself that the improvements were such as to have effected a drop in the death rate.[14]

For Malthus "the whole train of common diseases and epidemics, wars, plague and famine" were all closely linked to "misery and vice" as positive checks to population growth. But misery and vice also included "extreme poverty, bad nursing of children, excesses of all kinds."

In this context it may be said that in Europe conditions of life among both the rural and urban lower classes—that is, of the vast majority of the population—can rarely have been as bad as they were in the early nineteenth century. Overworked, atrociously housed, undernourished, disease-ridden, the masses lived in a misery that defies the modern imagination. This situation in itself should have drastically influenced the population pattern, but two items in particular must have had a really significant bearing. First, drunkenness: this period must surely have been the golden age of inebriation, especially in the northern countries. The per capita consumption of spirits, on the increase since the sixteenth century, reached unprecedented figures. In Sweden, perhaps the worst-afflicted country, it was estimated at ten gallons of *branvin* and *akvavit* per annum. Everywhere ginshops abounded. London alone counted 447 taverns and 8,659 ginshops in 1836, some of

---

Related to English Population Changes in the Eighteenth Century," *Population Studies*, IX (November 1955)), 119–141; Richard H. Shryock, "Medicine and Society in the Nineteenth Century," *Journal of World History*, V (1959), 116–146.

[14] Diseases such as typhus and cholera were dirt diseases, carried often through contaminated water supply. Vienna secured an adequate water supply only in 1840; Hamburg in 1848; Berlin in 1852. In London there were still 250,000 cesspools in 1850; in Berlin only 9 percent of all dwellings had water closets. For contemporary accounts, see Thomas Beames, *The Rookeries of London* (London, 1851); George Godwin, *London Shadows* (London, 1854); Fischer, *Deutsches Gesundheitswesen*, II, 500 ff.; Laurence Wright, *Clean and Decent: The Unruffled History of the Bathroom and the W.C.* (New York, 1960).

which at least were visited by as many as 5,000–6,000 men, women, and children in a single day.[15]

So grave was the problem of intemperance in 1830 that European rulers welcomed emissaries of the American temperance movement and gave full support to their efforts to organize the fight against the liquor menace. To what extent drunkenness may have affected the life expectancy of its addicts, we can only conjecture. At the very least the excessive use of strong liquor is known to enhance susceptibility to respiratory infections and is often the determining factor in cirrhosis of the liver.[16]

Of even greater and more obvious bearing was what Malthus euphemistically called "bad nursing of children" and what in honesty must be termed disguised infanticide. It was certainly prevalent in the late eighteenth and nineteenth centuries and seems to have been constantly on the increase.[17]

In the cities it was common practice to confide babies to old women nurses or caretakers. The least offense of these "Angelmakers," as they were called in Berlin, was to give the children gin to keep them quiet. For the rest we have the following testimony from Benjamin Disraeli's novel *Sybil* (1845), for which he drew on a large fund of sociological data: "Laudanum and treacle, administered in the shape of some popular elixir, affords these innocents a brief taste of the sweets of existence and, keeping them quiet, prepares them for the silence of their impending grave." "Infanticide," he adds, "is practised as extensively and as legally in England as it is on the banks of the Ganges; a circumstance which apparently has not yet engaged the attention of the Society for the Propagation of the Gospel in Foreign Parts."

It was also customary in these years to send babies into the country to be nursed by peasant women. The well-to-do made their own arrangements, while the lower classes turned their offspring over to

[15] James S. Buckingham, *History and Progress of the Temperance Reformation* (London, 1854), pp. 28 ff.; Adolf Baer, *Der Alcoholismus* (Berlin, 1878), 196, 203 ff.

[16] On the liquor problem, see P. S. White and H. R. Pleasants, *The War of Four Thousand Years* (Philadelphia, 1846), pp. 240 ff.; P. T. Winskill, *The Temperance Movement and Its Workers* (London, 1891–1892), I, chap. 4; John C. Woolley and William E. Johnson, *Temperance Progress of the Century* (Philadelphia, 1905), chap. 15; Johann Bergmann, *Geschichte der anti-Alkoholbestrebungen* (Hamburg, 1907), chap. 12.

[17] Alexander von Öttingen, *Die Moralstatistik* (3rd ed., Erlangen, 1882), pp. 236 ff.

charitable nursing bureaus or left them at the foundling hospitals or orphanages that existed in all large cities. Of the operation of these foundling hospitals a good deal is known, and from this knowledge it is possible to infer the fate of thousands of babies that were sent to the provinces for care.[18]

The middle and late eighteenth century was marked by a startling rise in the rate of illegitimacy, the reasons for which have little bearing on the present argument. But so many of the unwanted babies were being abandoned, smothered, or otherwise disposed of that Napoleon in 1811 decreed that the foundling hospitals should be provided with a turntable device, so that babies could be left at these institutions without the parent being recognized or subjected to embarrassing questions. This convenient arrangement was imitated in many countries and was taken full advantage of by the mothers in question. In many cities the authorities complained that unmarried mothers from far and wide were coming to town to deposit their unwanted babies in the accommodating foundling hospitals. The statistics show that of the thousands of children thus abandoned, more than half were the offspring of married couples.

There is good reason to suppose that those in charge of these institutions did the best they could with what soon became an unmanageable problem. Very few of the children could be cared for in the hospitals themselves. The great majority was sent to peasant nurses in the provinces. In any case, most of these children died within a short time, either of malnutrition or neglect or from the long, rough journey to the country.

The figures for this traffic, available for many cities, are truly shocking. In all of France fully 127,507 children were abandoned in the year 1833. Anywhere from 20 to 30 percent of all children born were left to their fate. The figures for Paris suggest that in the years 1817–1820 the "foundlings" comprised fully 36 percent of all births. In some of the Italian hospitals the mortality (under one year of age) ran to 80 or 90 percent. In Paris the *Maison de la Couche* reported that of 4,779

---

[18] In the years 1804–1814 the average annual number of births in Paris was about 19,500. Of these newcomers, roughly 4,700 were sent to the country by the *Bureau des Nourrices,* and 4,000 were sent by the foundling hospital, *Maison de la Couche.* With the addition of children privately sent, it appears that a total of about 13,500 babies were involved (Louis Benoiston de Chateauneuf, *Recherches sur les consommations de tout genre de la ville de Paris* [Paris, 1821], p. 37).

babies admitted in 1818, 2,370 died in the first three months and another 956 within the first year.[19]

The operation of this system was well known at the time, though largely forgotten in the days of birth control. Many contemporaries denounced it as legalized infanticide, and one at least suggested that the foundling hospitals post a sign reading "Children killed at Government expense." Malthus himself, after visiting the hospitals at St. Petersburg and Moscow, lavishly endowed by the imperial family and the aristocracy, could not refrain from speaking out:

> Considering the extraordinary mortality which occurs in these institutions, and the habits of licentiousness which they have an evident tendency to create, it may perhaps be truly said that, if a person wished to check population, and were not solicitous about the means, he could not propose a more effective measure than the establishment of a sufficient number of foundling hospitals, unlimited as to their reception of children.

In the light of the available data one is almost forced to admit that the proposal, seriously advanced at the time, that unwanted babies be painlessly asphyxiated in small gas chambers, was definitely humanitarian.[20] Certainly the entire problem of infanticide in the days before widespread practice of contraception deserves further attention and study. It was undoubtedly a major factor in holding down the population, strangely enough in the very period when the tide of population was so rapidly rising.

Summing up, it would seem that in the days of the initial population explosion one can discern many forces working against a major increase and few if any operating in the opposite direction. It is obviously nec-

---

[19] Léon Lallemand, *Histoire des enfants abandonnés et délaissés* (Paris, 1885), pp. 207, 276. Among contemporary commentators, see Johnston, *Public Charity in France*, pp. 319 ff.; Frederic von Raumer, *Italy and the Italians* (London, 1840), I, 180 ff., 266; II, 80, 284; Richard Ford, *Gleanings from Spain* (London, 1846), chap. 17; and among later studies F. S. Hügel, *Die Findelhäuser und das Findelwesen Europas* (Vienna, 1863), pp. 137 ff.; Arthur Keller and C. J. Klumper, *Säuglingsfürsorge und Kinderschutz in den europäischen Staaten* (Berlin, 1912), I, 441 ff.; Joseph J. Spengler, *France Faces Depopulation* (Durham, N. C., 1938), pp. 45 ff.; Roger Mols, *Introduction à la démographie historique des villes d'Europe du xiv* au xviii* siècle* (Louvain, 1954–1956), II, 303 ff.; Krause, *Comparative Studies in Society and History*, pp. 164–188; Hélène Bergues, *La Prévention des naissances dans la famille* (Paris, 1960), pp. 17 ff.

[20] "Marcus" (pseudo.), *Essay on Populousness and on the Possibility of Limiting Populousness* (London, 1838). The quotation from Malthus is from his *Essay on the Principle of Population* (6th ed., London, 1826), p. 313.

essary, then, to discover one or more further factors to which a major influence can fairly be attributed.

If indeed the birth rate was rising, this was presumably due primarily to earlier marriage and to marriage on the part of a growing proportion of the adult population. Even slight variations would, in these matters, entail significant changes in the birth rate.[21]

Unfortunately the marriage practices of this period have not been much investigated. Under the feudal system the seigneur frequently withheld his consent to the marriage of able-bodied and intelligent young people whom he had selected for domestic service in the manor house. Likewise under the guild system the master had authority to prevent or defer the marriage of apprentices and artisans. Whether for these reasons or for others of which we have no knowledge, there appears to have been a distinct decline in the number of marriages and a rise in the age of marriage in the late seventeenth and early eighteenth centuries. Some writers have even spoken of a "crise de nuptialité" in this period. But by the mid-eighteenth century the old regime was breaking down, soon to be given the coup de grâce by the French Revolution. With the personal emancipation of the peasantry and the liquidation of the guild system, the common people were freer to marry, and evidently did so at an early age. There is, in fact, some indication that the duration of marriages was extended by as much as three years, at least in some localities.[22]

The rapid increase of the population was at the time often attributed to these changes, and before long a number of German states tried to counter the trend by laws specifically designed to restrict marriage: men were refused marriage licenses until they were thirty and received them then only if they could show that they had learned a trade and had a job waiting for them. Those who had been on relief in the preceding three years were denied a license on principle. Under these circumstances it is altogether likely that many of the young people who emigrated from Germany in these years did so chiefly in order to get married.[23]

[21] This aspect is rightly stressed by Habakkuk, *Economic History Review*, 2nd ser., VI (December 1953), 117–133.

[22] On the problem of marriage, see especially the excellent discussion in Mols, *Démographie historique*, II, 267 ff.

[23] A. S. [Alexander Schneer], Über die Zunahme der Bevölkerung in dem mittleren Europa und die Besorgnisse vor einer Überbevölkerung," *Deutsche Vierteljahrsschrift*, III (1844), 98–141; Wilhelm G. Roscher, *Die Grundlagen der Nationalökonomie* (Stuttgart, 1854), pp. 490 ff. The eminent jurist, Robert von

Marriage practices, though obviously important, seem hardly to provide a complete explanation of the population growth. To discover a further, possibly decisive factor, it is necessary to return to consideration of the food supply, recalling the proposition advanced by the physiocrats and heavily underlined by Malthus, that the number of inhabitants depends on the means of subsistence—more food brings more mouths.[24] That population tends to rise and absorb any new increment of the food supply is familiar to us from the history of underdeveloped societies. Historically it has been demonstrated by studies of the relationship between harvest conditions on the one hand and marriage and birth rates on the other. In Sweden, for example, where careful statistics were kept as long ago as the seventeenth century, the annual excess of births over deaths in the eighteenth century was only 2 per thousand after a poor crop, but 6.5 after an average harvest, and 8.4 after a bumper crop. Invariably, and as late as the mid-nineteenth century, high wheat prices have been reflected in a low marriage and to some extent in a low birth rate.[25]

The addition of an important new item to the existing crops would necessarily have the same effect as a bumper crop. Such a new item—one of the greatest importance—was the common potato, a vegetable of exceptionally high food value, providing a palatable and satisfying, albeit a monotonous diet. Ten pounds of potatoes a day would give a man 3,400 calories—more than modern nutritionists consider necessary—plus a substantial amount of non-animal protein and an abundant

Mohl, considered antimarriage laws indispensable unless the poorer classes exercised prudence in marriage. See D. V. Glass, "Malthus and the Limitation of Population Growth," in his *Introduction to Malthus* (London, 1953), pp. 25–54.

[24] Richard Cantillon, *Essai sur la nature du commerce en général* (London, 1755), argued that an increase in subsistence would positively provoke a rise in the population; Malthus wrote: "The only true criterion of a real and permanent increase in the population of any country is the increase of the means of subsistence" (*Essay*, 6th ed., p. 294).

[25] E. E. Heckscher, "Swedish Population Trends before the Industrial Revolution," *Economic History Review*, 2nd ser., II (1950), 266–277; Dorothy S. Thomas, *Social and Economic Aspects of Swedish Population Movements, 1750–1933* (New York, 1941), pp. 81 ff.; Jean Meuvret, "Les Crises de subsistance et la démographie de la France d'ancien régime," *Population*, I (October–December 1946), 643–650; F. G. Dreyfus, "Prix et population à Trèves et à Mayence au xxviie siècle," *Revue d'histoire économique et sociale*, XXXIV (1956), 241–261; C. H. Pouthas, *La Population française pendant la première moitié du xixe siècle* (Paris, 1956), p. 29; Louis Chevalier, *Démographie générale* (Paris, 1951), pp. 338–339.

supply of vitamins.[26] Furthermore, the potato could be grown on even minute patches of poor or marginal land, with the most primitive implements and with a minimum of effort. Its yield was usually abundant. The produce of a single acre (the equivalent in food value of two to four acres sown to grain) would support a family of six or even eight, as well as the traditional cow or pig, for a full year. The yield in terms of nutriment exceeded that of any other plant of the temperate zone.[27]

The qualities of the potato were such as to arouse enthusiastic admiration among agronomists and government officials. It was spoken of as "the greatest blessing that the soil produces," "the miracle of agriculture," and "the greatest gift of the New World to the Old." The eminent Polish poet, Adam Mickiewicz, writing as a young man in the hard and hungry years following the Napoleonic Wars, composed a poem entitled *Kartofla*, celebrating this humble vegetable which, while other plants died in drought and frost, lay hidden in the ground and eventually saved mankind from starvation.[28]

The history of the potato in Europe is most fully known as it touches Ireland, where in fact it became crucial in the diet of the people. It was introduced there about the year 1600 and before the end of the seventeenth century had been generally adopted by the peasantry. By the end of the eighteenth century the common man was eating little else:

> Day after day, three times a day, people ate salted, boiled potatoes, probably washing them down with milk, flavouring them, if they were fortunate, with an onion or a bit of lard, with boiled seaweed or a scrap of salted fish.[29]

Because this was so, Ireland provides a simple, laboratory case. There were in Ireland no industrial revolution and no war, but also

[26] Redcliffe N. Salaman, *The History and Social Influence of the Potato* (Cambridge, Eng., 1949), pp. 122 ff.; K. H. Connell, *The Population of Ireland, 1750–1845* (Oxford, Eng., 1950), pp. 151 ff.

[27] On its qualities, see the detailed report of Antoine Parmentier, *Examen chymique des pommes de terre* (Paris, 1773), p. 3; also Berthold Laufer, "The American Plant Migration: Part II, the Potato," *Field Museum of Natural History, Anthropological Ser.*, XXVIII (July 1938), II.

[28] *Adam Mickiewicz, Poet of Poland*, ed. Manfred Kridl (New York, 1951), pp. 242 ff.; see also Henry Phillips, *The History of Cultivated Vegetables* (2nd ed., London, 1822), II, 85 ff.; Georges Gibault, *Histoire des légumes* (Paris, 1912), pp. 243 ff.

[29] K. H. Connell, "The Potato in Ireland," *Past and Present* no. 23 (November 1962), pp. 57–71. Salaman, *History and Social Influence of the Potato*, is little short of an economic-social history of the British Isles; on Ireland, see especially chaps. 11–16.

no fundamental change in the pattern of famine or disease. The unspeakable poverty of the country should, it would seem, have militated against any considerable population increase. Yet the population did increase from 3,200,000 in 1754 to 8,175,000 in 1846, not counting some 1,750,000 who emigrated before the great potato famine of 1845–1847.[30]

It was perfectly obvious to contemporaries, as it is to modern scholars, that this Irish population could exist only because of the potato. Poverty-stricken though it might be, the Irish peasantry was noteworthy for its fine physique. Clearly people were doing very well physiologically on their potato fare. Young people rented an acre or less for a potato patch. On the strength of this they married young and had large families.

So impressive was the role of the potato in Ireland that Arthur Young, in *The Question of Scarcity Plainly Stated and Remedies Considered* (London, 1800), urged the British government, as a hedge against failure of the grain crop, to endow every country laborer who had three or more children with a half acre of land for potatoes and enough grass to feed one or two cows: "If each had his ample potato-ground and a cow, the price of wheat would be of little more consequence to them than it is to their brethren in Ireland."

Malthus at once objected to this proposed remedy for want. Young's system, he argued, would operate directly to encourage marriage and would be tantamount to a bounty on children. Potatoes tended to depress wages and living standards by making possible an increase in the population far beyond the opportunities of employment.[31]

Why should not the impact of the potato have been much the same in Britain and on the continent as in Ireland? If it made possible the support of a family on a small parcel of indifferent soil, frequently on that part of the land that lay fallow, and thereby encouraged early marriage, why should it not in large part explain the unusual rise in the population anywhere?

A definitive answer is impossible partly because the history of potato culture has not been intensively studied, and partly because the situation in other countries was rarely if ever as simple or as parlous as that of Ireland.[32] The most nearly comparable situation was that obtaining

[30] Connell, *Population of Ireland, passim.*
[31] Thomas Malthus, *Essay on the Principle of Population* (London, 1798; 2nd enlarged ed., 1803), Bk. I, chap. 2, p. 7.
[32] Salaman's lengthy and valuable study is by no means as comprehensive

in the Scottish Highlands and the Hebrides, where the potato proved to be "the most beneficial and the most popular innovation in Scottish agriculture of the eighteenth century." By 1740 the potato had become a field crop in some sections, grown in poor soil and sand drift and soon becoming the principal food of the population, much as in Ireland. In these areas also the spread of potato culture ran parallel to a marked expansion of the population.[33]

In the Scottish Lowlands, as in England, the potato met with greater resistance. Scottish peasants hesitated to make use of a plant not mentioned in the Bible, and it was feared in many places that the potato might bring on leprosy. In southern England in particular, the peasants suspected that the potato would tend to depress the standard of living to the level of that of the Irish. Nonetheless the potato, having in the early seventeenth century been a delicacy grown in the gardens of the rich, was strongly urged in the 1670's as a food for the poor. In Lancashire it was grown as a field crop before 1700. During the ensuing century it established itself, even in the south, as an important item in the peasant's and worker's diet. The lower classes continued to prefer wheat bread, but growing distress forced the acceptance of the potato which was, in fact, the only important addition to the common man's limited diet in the course of centuries.[34] Long before the end of the eighteenth century, large quantities of potatoes were being grown around London and other large cities. By and large the spread of the potato culture everywhere corresponded with the rapid increase of the population.[35]

Much less is known of the potato's history on the continent. It was introduced in Spain from South America in the late sixteenth century and quickly taken to Italy, Germany, and the Low Countries. As in England, it was cultivated by the rich in the seventeenth century and gradually adopted by the common people in the eighteenth. It appears to have been grown quite commonly in some sections of Saxony even be-

---

as the title would suggest. It is, in fact, restricted to a history of the potato in the British Isles.

[33] James E. Handley, *Scottish Farming in the Eighteenth Century* (London, 1953), chap. 8; see also Malcolm Gray, "The Highland Potato Famine of the 1840's," *Economic History Review*, 2nd ser., VII (April 1955), 357–368.

[34] G. E. Fussell, "The Change in Farm Labourers' Diet During Two Centuries," *Economic History*, I (May 1927), 268–274; Jack C. Drummond and Anne Wilbraham, *The Englishman's Food* (2nd ed., London, 1958), pp. 208 ff.

[35] Salaman, *History and Social Influence of the Potato*, chaps. 23–26 and the interesting chart on p. 538; see also Philip Miller, *The Gardener's Dictionary* (6th ed., London, 1752); Ernest Roze, *Histoire de la pomme de terre* (Paris, 1898); Gibault, *Histoire des légumes*.

fore the eighteenth century, while in some parts of Southern Germany it became common in the period after the War of the Spanish Succession. In several instances soldiers campaigning in foreign lands came to know and appreciate its qualities.

One of the greatest champions of the potato was Frederick the Great, who throughout his reign kept urging its value as food for the poor, prodding his officials to see that it was planted by the peasants, and providing excellent instructions as to its culture and preparation. He met at first with much resistance, but after the crop failures of 1770 and 1772 even the most hidebound peasantry came to accept it. They were impressed by the fact that the potato thrived in wet seasons, when the wheat crop suffered, and that the potato did well in sandy soil. They also realized that it would make an excellent salad and that it went exceptionally well with herring.

By the beginning of the nineteenth century the potato was already a major field crop in Germany, especially in Prussia, Posen, Pomerania, and Silesia. By the mid-century the per capita consumption in Prussia was nine bushels per annum, and potato production almost equaled in volume the production of all other cereals taken together.[36]

The Austrian government followed Frederick's lead and succeeded in securing the adoption of the potato in the German parts of the monarchy. Galicia, Bohemia, and Hungary became major centers of potato production.[37] In France, too, potato culture had become established in the eastern provinces, such as Lorraine, Alsace, and Burgundy. In 1770 the eminent pharmacist and chemist, Antoine Parmentier, who had become acquainted with the vegetable in Germany during the Seven

[36] See the detailed and appreciative account in Johann G. Krünitz, *Ökonomisch-technologische Encyklopedie* (Berlin, 1778–1843), pt. 35, pp. 232–412; Curt Dietrich, *Die Entwicklung des Kartoffelfeldbaues in Sachsen* (Merseburg, 1919), pp. 10 ff. The various instructions and orders of Frederick the Great are printed in Rudolph Stadelmann, *Preussens Könige in ihrer Thätigkeit für die Landescultur* (Leipzig, 1878–1887), II, nos. 144, 158, 186, 258, 294; see further Theodor Freiherr von der Goltz, *Geschichte der deutschen Landwirtschaft* (Berlin, 1902), I, 455 ff.; Hans Lichtenfelt, *Die Geschichte der Ernährung* (Berlin, 1913), p. 95; Kurt Hintze, *Geographie und Geschichte der Ernährung* (Leipzig, 1934), pp. 98 ff.; Kurt Hanefeld, *Geschichte des deutschen Nährstandes* (Leipzig, 1935), pp. 297 ff.; C. F. W. Dieterici, *Handbuch der Statistik des Preussischen Staates* (Berlin, 1861), pp. 264 ff.; Hans W. Graf Finck von Finckenstein, *Die Entwicklung der Landwirtschaft in Preussen und Deutschland* (Göttingen, 1960).

[37] See the scholarly analysis of Ignaz Hübel, "Die Einführung der Kartoffelkultur in Niederösterreich," *Unsere Heimat*, n. s., V (March 1932), 69–78; Friedrich W. von Reden, *Deutschland und das übrige Europa* (Wiesbaden, 1854), p. 151.

Years' War, won the prize offered by the Besançon Academy for an essay on the best vegetable to use as a substitute for wheat in times of food shortage. Parmentier was certainly not responsible for the introduction of the potato into France, but he proved himself an able promoter and succeeded in securing the support of Louis XVI. He tells us that in the early 1770's the markets of Paris were already full of potatoes and that they were sold raw or roasted on the streets, much like chestnuts.[38]

By 1800, then, the common people in the Netherlands as in the British Isles, Germany, and Scandinavia were eating potatoes twice a day, and even the French peasantry (passionately devoted to white wheat bread) was rapidly capitulating. In the early nineteenth century French potato production increased from 21,000,000 hectoliters in 1815 to 117,000,000 in 1840. This, be it noted, was a period when the French population was still increasing.[39]

A few words should, perhaps, be said about eastern Europe. The rate of population growth in the Russian Empire appears to have been higher than in any other continental country. The population increased from about 16,000,000 in 1745 to 37,500,000 in 1801 to 62,000,000 in 1852. Part of this increase was of course due to the substantial territorial acquisitions of Catherine the Great and Alexander I. Yet the territory of 1725 saw a rise from 14,000,000 in that year to 45,000,000 in 1858.[40] In this case the population growth seems indeed to have been due to an exceptionally high birth rate. The death rate too was high (about

[38] Parmentier, *Examen chymique des pommes de terre*, pp. 5, 186. Already in 1755 Henri-Louis Duhamel du Monceau (*Traité des cultures des terres* [Paris, 1750–1751]) had urged the value of the potato in times of want, and Turgot as well as the *philosophes* had appealed to the people to abandon their superstitions and prejudices. (See Gibault, *Histoire des légumes*, pp. 243 ff.).

[39] B. H. Slicher van Bath, *De agrarische Geschiedenis van West-Europa, 500–1850* (Utrecht, 1960), pp. 291 ff.; Paul Lindemans, *Geschiedenis van de Landbouw in België* (Antwerp, 1952), II, 182 ff. On France, see Benoiston de Chateauneuf, *Recherches sur les consommations . . . de la ville de Paris*, p. 99; Charles Dupin, *Les Forces productives et commerciales de la France* (Paris, 1827), II, 194, 208; Sébastien Charléty, *La Monarchie de Juillet* (Paris, 1921), p. 190; Henri Sée, *Histoire économique de la France* (Paris, 1948–1951), II, 181. As late as 1837, however, Stendahl (*Mémoires d'un touriste* [Paris, 1837; new ed., 2 vols., Paris, 1953]) noted that in some sections of France the peasants still looked down on those who subsisted chiefly on potatoes.

[40] There are substantial discrepancies in the figures given by various authors. See Ludwik de Tegoborski, *Études sur les forces productives de la Russie* (Paris, 1852–1855), and the English translation, *Commentaries on the Productive Forces of Russia* (London, 1855); see also the discussion in Jerome Blum, *Lord and Peasant in Russia from the Ninth to the Nineteenth Century* (Princeton, N. J., 1961), p. 278.

39.4 per 1,000 in the period 1840–1860), but the birth rate was substantially higher (49.7 per 1,000 from 1841 to 1850, and 52.4 per 1,000 from 1851 to 1860).

Information available on the culture of the potato in Russia is not sufficient to warrant any firm conclusion. Russian armies became acquainted with the vegetable in Germany during the Seven Years' War, at which time it seems to have been already well established in Poland and the Baltic Provinces. During a famine and epidemic in 1765 a board of medical advisers convinced Catherine the Great and her government of the importance of the potato as a preventive of famine and typhus. The government thereupon embarked on a systematic campaign of propaganda with the result that by 1800 the potato was widely cultivated in the Ukraine and the western *gubernias*. In many areas, however, the superstitions of the peasantry proved almost insurmountable. It was only after the crop failures of 1838–1839, when Tsar Nicholas reinforced the earlier efforts to further its adoption, that it became a key crop in central Russia also. By 1900 Russia was second only to Germany as a potato-producing country.[41]

Any conclusion to be drawn from these data must be tentative. The great upswing in the European population beginning around the middle of the eighteenth century can never be explained with any high degree of assurance or finality. It is extremely difficult to demonstrate whether it was due primarily to a decline in the death rate or to a rise in the birth rate. And beyond any such demonstration would lie the further question of the forces making for such demographic change. It is most unlikely that any single factor would account for it. Thus far the many explanations that have been advanced seem woefully inadequate. It seems altogether probable, therefore, that the introduction and general adoption of the potato played a major role. Its establishment as a field crop and as a basic food item of the general population coincided roughly with the sudden spurt of the population. Furthermore, it would appear that the areas of the most intensive potato culture such as Ireland, the Scottish Highlands, Lancashire, and western and southwestern Germany were also the areas of exceptionally rapid population increase, population pressure, and early emigration.

[41] Tegoborski, *Études,* II, 104 ff.; August von Haxthausen, *The Russian Empire* (London, 1856), II, 410, 425; and the exhaustive study of V. C. Lekhnovich, "K Istorii Kultury Kartofelia v Rossii," *Materiali po Istorii Zemledeliia SSSR,* II (1956), 248–400.

So much at least seems clear: that marriage was easier in the generations before and after 1800 than in earlier times, and that there was a much better opportunity for men and women to marry at an early age. For the fact that on a pathetically small patch of ground one could grow in potatoes from two to four times as much food as one could in terms of wheat or other grains, enough indeed to feed a family of more than average size was, I submit, a major revolutionary innovation in European life. In 1844 the eminent German agronomist, Baron August von Haxthausen, noted that the introduction of the potato "has undoubtedly produced immense effects upon Europe, in the moulding and culture of which it has probably operated more powerfully than any other material object." A few years later the equally authoritative German economist, Wilhelm Georg Roscher, declared without qualification that the adoption of the potato had resulted in a rapid growth of population.[42]

Perhaps the time has come, then, for historians to pay greater attention to the evolution of the human diet and its social consequences. As a first step, more intensive research might be initiated to test whether so startling a new departure in European history as the initial population explosion is to be attributed at least in large part to so drastic a change in the people's food as the advent of the common potato.

[42] Haxthausen, *Russian Empire,* II, 425; Roscher, *Grundlagen der National-ökonomie,* p. 438.

24

The Pattern of Urban Revolution in 1848

1966

Although the centennial celebrations of 1948 spawned many publications and brought into new relief many aspects of the European upheavals of the mid-nineteenth century, relatively little attention has been devoted to the comparative study of these revolutions. The objective of this essay is to examine the outbreaks of February and March 1848 so as to determine what, if anything, they had in common, and to raise the question whether these famous revolutions were inevitable or even beneficial.

Although there were disturbances in the countryside as well as in many cities, the events in the four great capitals, Paris, Vienna, Berlin, and London, were crucial. It is true that these government centers had been but little touched by the new industrialism and that therefore the proletariat of the factories played but a very subordinate role, especially in the early days of the revolutions. Yet the capitals were the seats of traditional industry, with a huge population of craftsmen, tradesmen, and specialized workers of all kinds.[1] London and Paris, in particular, harbored thousands of different industries without having much of a modern industrial proletariat.[2] The workers were mostly what might be termed *menu peuple* (lesser bourgeoisie).

This does not mean that the capital cities were less restless than the new factory towns. In all of them life had become unsettled and precarious, for everywhere the traditional artisan was exposed to the competition of machine industry, located chiefly in the provincial towns.

Note: From *French Society and Culture Since the Old Regime,* edited by Evelyn M. Acomb and Marvin L. Brown, Jr. Copyright © 1966 by Holt, Rinehart and Winston, Inc. Reprinted by permission of Holt, Rinehart and Winston, Inc.

[1] E. J. Hobsbawm, *Social Bandits and Primitive Rebels* (New York, 1959), chap. 7; George Rudé, "The Study of Popular Disturbances in the 'Pre-Industrial' Age," *Historical Studies: Australia and New Zealand,* X (1963), 457–469.

[2] On the multifarious London industry, see George L. Gomme, *London in the Reign of Victoria* (London, 1898), chap. 4 and app. 2, in which the *London Directory* of 1837 is analyzed. For the industries of Paris see especially Charles Dupin, *Les Forces productives et commerciales de la France* (Paris, 1827), II, 196 ff.

Wages, if they did not actually decline, remained low, while employment became steadily more uncertain. The plight of the urban workers following the economic crisis of 1846–47 is well known, and its bearing on the revolutions of 1848 has been duly stressed by Professor Labrousse and others. Basically it was inevitable that the early stages of industrialization should have brought instability and hardship, but the situation in mid-century was greatly aggravated by the fantastic growth of the European population; this growth entailed an unprecedented movement of rural workers to the cities, which for centuries had held the promise of opportunity.

In the years from 1800 to 1850 the growth of the European capitals was stupendous, with the result that at the end of the period a large proportion of the population was not native born. It consisted largely of immigrants, permanent or temporary, coming either from nearby areas, or from abroad. In the 1840s alone about 250,000 persons came into London, 46,000 of whom were Irishmen, who were particularly disliked and feared by the English workers because of their incredibly low standard of living. In addition, there were substantial numbers of Belgian and German workers.[3]

As for Paris, the researches of Louis Chevalier and others have thrown a flood of light on the nature of the population and the conditions of life. The number of inhabitants just about doubled between 1800 and 1850, due very largely to immigration. Thus, between 1831 and 1836 about 115,000 arrived, and from 1841 to 1846 another 98,000. Most of the newcomers were from the neighboring *départements*, but there were many foreigners as well. Accurate statistics are lacking, but there appear to have been upward of 50,000 Germans (mostly tailors, shoemakers, cabinetmakers) in Paris, to say nothing of large numbers of Belgian and Italian workers and sizable contingents of political refugees from many lands.[4]

[3] Adna F. Weber, *The Growth of Cities in the 19th Century* (New York, 1899), pp. 244, 283; Arthur Redford, *Labour Migration in England, 1800–1850* (London, 1926), chaps. 4, 8, 9; H. A. Shannon, "Migration and the Growth of London, 1841–1891," *Economic History Review*, V (1935), 79–86; J. H. Clapham, "Irish Immigration into Great Britain in the 19th Century," *Bulletin of the International Committee of the Historical Sciences*, V (1933), 596–604; Barbara W. Kerr, "Irish Seasonal Migration to Great Britain, 1800–1838," *Irish Historical Studies*, III (1942), 365–380; John A. Jackson, *The Irish in Britain* (Cleveland, 1963).

[4] Louis Desnoyers *et al.*, *Les Étrangers à Paris* (Paris, 1846), pp. 163 ff., 181 ff.; Georges Manco, *Les Étrangers en France* (Paris, 1932), pp. 36 ff.; Louis Chevalier, *La Formation de la population parisienne au xix⁰ siècle* (Paris, 1949), pp. 45, 48, 183; Louis Chevalier, *Classes laborieuses et classes dangereuses à Paris pendant*

The situation in Vienna and Berlin was much the same. The population of the Austrian capital numbered about 400,000. One-hundred-twenty-five-thousand had been added between 1827 and 1847. In 1845 there were some 130,000 Czech, Polish, and Italian immigrants.[5] In Berlin the population rose from 180,000 to 400,000 between 1815 and 1847, due largely to the heavy immigration from the eastern provinces.[6]

In all cities the steady influx of people created an acute housing shortage. This was less true of London than of the continental capitals, for there the government offices had long since moved from the Old City to Westminster and the well-to-do had built new homes in the West End and along the main highways to the west and northwest. The 125,000 people who still lived in the Old City were for the most part clerks, runners, cleaners, and other employees of the great banks and business houses. In the continental capitals, however, the exodus of the upper classes from the old central districts had only just begun. The new and fashionable sections of northwestern Paris were still far from complete, while the oldest part of the city was incredibly congested, "an almost impenetrable hive of tenements and shops."[7] The efforts of Rambuteau, the *préfet* of the Seine, to open up the dingiest areas by constructing larger arteries, involved the destruction of much cheap housing, little of which was replaced elsewhere. Under the circumstances, rents rose rapidly. Most immigrant workers were lucky to find even miserable quarters in the center of the town or in the workers' sections of eastern Paris. "The difficulty of finding lodgings," wrote a

---

la première moitié du xix⁰ siècle (Paris, 1958), pp. 267 ff. It is worth noting that contemporaries like Karl Gutzkow, *Pariser Briefe* (Leipzig, 1842), p. 276 and Arnold Ruge, *Zwei Jahre in Paris* (Leipzig, 1846), I, 59, 431, estimated the German population of Paris at 80,000 to 85,000 and reported that German could be heard in almost every street.

[5] Adolf Schmidl, *Wien und seine nächsten Umgebungen* (Vienna, 1847), p. 142; Friedrich Walter, *Wien: die Geschichte einer deutschen Gross-Stadt an der Grenze* (Vienna, 1944), III, 105 ff.; Ernst Fischer, *Oesterreich, 1848* (Vienna, 1946), pp. 38 ff.

[6] *Bericht über die Verwaltung der Stadt Berlin in den Jahren 1841 bis inclus. 1850* (Berlin, 1853), pp. 3–4; Karl Haenchen, "Zur revolutionären Unterwühlung Berlins vor den Märztagen," *Forschungen zur brandenburg-preussischen Geschichte*, LV (1943), 83–114; Dora Meyer, *Das öffentliche Leben in Berlin vor der Märzrevolution* (Berlin, 1912), pp. 11 ff.; Richard Dietrich, "Berlins Weg zur Industrie und Handelsstadt," *Berlin: Neun Kapitel seiner Geschichte* (Berlin, 1960), pp. 159–198.

[7] David H. Pinkney, *Napoleon III and the Rebuilding of Paris* (Princeton, 1958), p. 7.

contemporary, "is for the worker a constant ordeal and a perpetual cause of misery."[8]

In Vienna and Berlin, as in Paris, a great many immigrant workers found refuge in the lodging houses, which enjoyed a golden age at this time. In the low-grade places men and women were housed together, and it was by no means uncommon for eight or nine persons to be crowded into one room. The old Innere Stadt of Vienna, still surrounded by its seventeenth-century walls, was so hopelessly congested that some members of the aristocracy were obliged, most reluctantly, to build new "villas" beyond the Kärntner Tor, while practically all industry, with the exception of the old-established silk trade, was compelled, by government decree, to locate in the suburbs. In Berlin, too, the rapidly developing textile and metallurgical industries were concentrated in the northern areas, while the upper classes lived mostly in the western and southwestern sections. Berlin was notorious for its wretched lodging houses and workers' barracks.[9]

Considering the great instability of the changing social order, it is not surprising that many of the newcomers in the cities failed to find the hoped-for employment. Thousands were chronically out of work, reduced to living in dank cellars or unheated garrets, and often driven by desperation into robbery or other crimes. In Paris, as in most other cities, about a quarter of the population was indigent, dependent on government or private relief. The situation thus engendered was particularly dangerous because as yet in many cities the rich and poor lived cheek-by-jowl. The Paris apartment house, whose lower floors were occupied by the well-to-do while the *petite bourgeoisie* took over the upper stories and the paupers were left the crannies under the eaves, are familiar to us from Balzac's novels, but it must be remembered that, in almost every part of Paris, prosperous residential areas and pockets of slums were intermingled. There was no strictly aristocratic quarter and no strictly workingmen's quarter. Even in metropolitan London fashionable streets were often backed by abandoned

[8] Théophile Lavallée, *Histoire de Paris* (Paris, 1852), p. 205.

[9] According to Etienne Laspeyres, *Der Einfluss der Wohnung auf die Sittlichkeit* (Berlin, 1869), there were in Paris in 1848, 2,360 *chambres garnis*. Of the lodgers only 4 percent of the men and 8 percent of the women were married. On the Paris lodging houses see also Chevalier, *La Formation de la population parisienne*, p. 102, and his *Classes laborieuses*, pp. 271 ff. For Vienna see Walter, *Wien*, III, 114; Fischer, *Oesterreich*, pp. 38 ff., and for Berlin see the well-known contemporary account of Ernst Dronke, *Berlin* (Frankfurt, 1846).

"rookeries." Such existed even in the West End, in the vicinity of Buckingham Palace.[10]

Overall conditions in the crowded cities of the early or mid-nineteenth century were such as to create chronic social tension. Riots by the hungry or unemployed were all too common, as were also clashes between native and foreign workers. It is obvious that these outbreaks could and at times did assume such proportions as to threaten governments, if not the entire social order.

To combat disturbances European governments had traditionally relied upon their military forces. Napoleon's "whiff of grapeshot" was an example of the use even of artillery in breaking up a hostile demonstration. More common, however, was the employment of sabrecharging cavalry. Nicholas I of Russia, though confronted with the most formidable and urgent social problem in Europe, escaped revolution in 1848 by ruthless application of these tactics. His internal defense force, quartered throughout the country, numbered some 200,000 men and beat down any threat of insurrection. The secret police and the cossack brigades showed the world how to maintain order and vindicated Nicholas's claim to be the gendarme of Europe.[11]

But in western Europe these methods of brutal repression had by the nineteenth century become as difficult to apply as they were objectionable. To ride or shoot down unarmed citizens was hardly the answer to political or social problems, to say nothing of the fact that conscripted soldiers showed ever greater unwillingness to fire upon the people.[12] In Britain, where the problems created by the industrial revolution were most acute, the government had, before 1848, worked out a different procedure or policy. In connection with the very formidable and menacing Chartist demonstrations of 1839 and 1842 freedom of speech

[10] For Paris see Chevalier, *Classes laborieuses,* pp. 267 ff., 538 ff.; Adeline Daumard, *La Bourgeoisie parisienne de 1815 à 1848* (Paris, 1963), pp. 181 ff.; for London see Thomas Beames, *The Rookeries of London* (London, 1851); George Godwin, *London Shadows* (London, 1854); Gomme, *London in the Reign of Victoria,* p. 57. According to Dronke, the situation in Berlin was very similar.

[11] Nikolai I. Tourguenieff, *La Russie et les russes* (Paris, 1847), chap. 7; John S. Curtiss, "The Army of Nicholas I, Its Role and Character," *American Historical Review,* LXIII (1958), 880–889; A. S. Nifontov, *Russland im Jahre 1848* (Berlin, 1954).

[12] *First Report of the Commissioners to Inquire as to the Best Means of Establishing an Official Constabulary Force in the Counties of England and Wales* (London, 1839), p. 160; on the problem generally, see the excellent military analysis written in 1906 by Hermann Kriebel, *Über die Bezwingung innerer Unruhen nach den Erfahrungen der Geschichte in der ersten Hälfte des XIX Jahrhunderts* (Innsbruck, 1929).

and assembly were generally respected, but the authorities made it perfectly clear that any effort to subvert the government or the social order would be ruthlessly suppressed. Furthermore, General Charles Napier, in charge of the forces in the industrial areas of the north, by adroitly placing his troops and by bringing additional soldiery from Ireland to ensure against defection, succeeded in creating a genuine deterrent.

As for London, much greater advances had been made in the direction of public security. In 1829 the first modern civil police force had been established, consisting of selected, uniformed, trained, and well-paid constables numbering by 1848 about 5,500 men. Despite much popular hostility, the London police soon made itself respected and indeed worked out the tactics of what today are called "riot control formations," that is, the organization and employment of squad or platoon wedges to penetrate mobs, arrest leaders, and break up demonstrations, and of echelons to pry rioters away from buildings and force them to move in specified directions.[13]

CHARTIST DEMONSTRATION IN LONDON

Some insight into the problems confronting continental governments in February and March 1848 can be gained by reviewing the great Chartist demonstration and petition scheduled for April 10 in London as the culmination of a series of disturbances in Glasgow, Manchester, and even in the capital that echoed the revolutionary events on the continent in the preceding weeks.

In the councils of the Chartist movement there were some who, as in 1839, favored revolutionary action and the use of violence in the event that the great petition were again rejected by parliament. But the majority of the leaders, long since convinced of the government's determination to suppress any attempt at insurrection, still hoped to attain their ends by peaceful demonstration. The plan then was to stage a monster meeting followed by the procession of thousands of workers to the House of Commons. The great day was to be April 10, when contingents of Chartists marched from various assembly points in the

[13] For the conditions prior to 1829 see John Wade, *A Treatise on the Police and Crimes of the Metropolis* (London, 1829); for the rest see W. L. Melville Lee, *A History of Police in England* (London, 1901), chaps. 10, 12, 13; Charles Reith, *A Short History of the British Police* (London, 1948), chaps. 7, 9; Douglas G. Browne, *The Rise of Scotland Yard* (London, 1956), chaps. 8, 9; F. C. Mather, *Public Order in the Age of the Chartists* (Manchester, 1959), chaps. 3, 4.

metropolis to Kennington Common, in southwestern London. When they gathered, at about 11:00 A.M., the police were already at hand. Feargus O'Connor, the leader, was warned that while the meeting itself was permissible, the law forbade large demonstrations designed to intimidate Parliament and that therefore the crowd would be permitted to recross the river only in small groups. O'Connor, a demagogue braver in words than in deeds, at once urged his followers to accept the police ruling. There was some speech-making, but presently the whole meeting was washed out by rain. The demonstrators straggled back over Blackfriars Bridge, while the petition, with its millions of signatures, was taken to Parliament by a small delegation riding in three cabs. The day ended without even a window having been broken.

There is every reason to think that the London police could by itself have dealt with the Chartist demonstration. But the government had been unwilling to take the chance and had, with the full support of the propertied classes, made preparations far beyond anything the situation called for. The aged Duke of Wellington had been put in command of the troops, which were brought in from the surrounding areas. At the same time, a call was sent out for special constables, to which all respectable elements, from peers to business and professional men, down to clerks, railroad officials, shopkeepers, and others responded in great numbers. It is said, and was so reported in the *Times*, that no less than 150,000 of these constables were enrolled. They sandbagged and garrisoned the Bank of England, the Post-Office, India House, and other valuable properties, while the troops, which were kept out of sight as much as possible, occupied the Tower and other strong points. On the river three ships were held in readiness, with steam up, to transport troops or supplies to any threatened spot. The Chartists, as they marched to their rendezvous, could hardly fail to notice the reception that awaited them in case of serious unrest.

So much certainly was to be learned from the London experience: (1) an efficient police force was capable of dealing with even large-scale demonstrations; (2) a government acceptable to the citizenry could count on the support of huge numbers of volunteers; (3) the troops could be kept in reserve, to be used only in an emergency; (4) a clean-cut policy and adequate preparations would serve as an effective deterrent. Harriet Martineau, in her account of the Kennington Common meeting, was not far off the mark when she declared exultantly: "From that day it was a settled matter that England was safe from revolution." [14]

It is true, of course, that the British government had the advantage, in facing the Chartist threat, not only of previous experience but of the experience of the continental governments that had succumbed to revolution. Nonetheless, it will be useful to review the outbreak of insurrection in Paris, Vienna, and Berlin in the light of what could and was done in another country in what were roughly comparable circumstances. For it is probably a mistake to argue that Britain, because it had no revolution in 1848, was in some mysterious way different and therefore exempt from major social ructions. If there was a great deal of talk of revolution on the continent in the years preceding 1848, there was hardly less of such talk in England. Friedrich Engels, it will be recalled, in 1845 held that social revolution was unavoidable.

THE 1848 REVOLUTION IN PARIS

The events of February 1848 in Paris, which ended with the downfall of the Orleans Monarchy, were conscientiously analyzed by M. Crémieux more than fifty years ago.[15] They were far too complicated to be satisfactorily summarized in a brief essay. Certain features, however, should be highlighted. It is well known, for instance, that Louis Philippe and his chief minister, M. Guizot, were surprised by the insurrection by which they were overtaken. This surprise is at least understandable, for even though opposition to the régime had been mounting, it certainly did not suggest the possibility of a major upheaval. The opposition, insofar as it was organized and directed, was in the main a parliamentary opposition calling for very modest changes: liberalization of the electorate, limitation of political patronage, extension of civil liberties. It is hardly an exaggeration to describe this opposition as a family affair, the struggle of one faction against another within the same social framework. Its leaders did not plan revolution,

[14] Harriet Martineau, *History of England, 1816–1854* (Boston, 1866), IV, 571 ff. Among the many other accounts see especially Preston W. Slosson, *The Decline of the Chartist Movement* (New York, 1916), pp. 94 ff.; Julius West, *A History of the Chartist Movement* (Boston, 1920), chap. 8; Edouard Dolléans, *Le Chartisme* (rev. ed., Paris, 1944), pp. 300 ff.; Albert R. Schoyen, *The Chartist Challenge* (New York, 1958), pp. 160 ff.

[15] Albert Crémieux, *La Révolution de février* (Paris, 1912). For a more recent and much briefer account see Jean Bruhat, *Les Journées de février, 1848* (Paris, 1948).

nor even desire it. For months they had been carrying on a campaign of propaganda and agitation centering about a program of political banquets. But these methods, if they were not directly imitated from the British, were at any rate the counterpart of the great pressure campaigns conducted across the Channel by Daniel O'Connell and Richard Cobden, namely the campaigns that led to the emancipation of the Catholics, to the great Reform Act of 1832, and to the repeal of the Corn Laws in 1846. These victories over a well-entrenched ruling class were watched with the utmost interest by liberals all over the continent. When Cobden in 1847 made a tour of the continental countries he was everywhere feted by the enlightened, educated circles, all of which took heart from the British experience. Considering that in the French Chamber most of the prominent members had, by 1848, aligned themselves with the opposition, there is no reason to suppose that in the not too distant future the resistance of even Guizot and Louis Philippe would have crumbled.

Only a few words need be said in this context of the more popular opposition, that of the disfranchised writers, artists, tradesmen, and workers who, ever since their disillusionment with the July Revolution of 1830, had been organized in secret societies and some of whom, certainly, were quite prepared to rise in revolt in the name of democracy or socialism. The unemployment, want, and unrest in Paris were such that a great social uprising seemed to some, like Tocqueville, a real and immediate threat. It will be remembered that the monster opposition banquet that had been planned for the first *arrondissement* was moved to a hall in the aristocratic quarter and that, when it was prohibited by the authorities, the opposition leaders were positively relieved. Far from wanting a popular disturbance, the opposition was intent on remaining within the bounds of legality. But in actuality the popular opposition, while noisy and threatening, was so limited in numbers, so divided and weak, so unprepared as to be quite innocuous. It may be recalled that popular leaders like Louis Blanc positively dreaded an insurrection, knowing that the lower classes were bound to be defeated.[16]

[16] Percy B. St. John, *The French Revolution in 1848* (New York, 1848), pp. 60 ff.; Sébastien Charléty, *La Monarchie de Juillet* (Paris, 1921), pp. 383 ff. For the intricacies of the question of the Paris banquet see John J. Baughman, "The French Banquet Campaign of 1847–1848," *Journal of Modern History*, XXXI (1959), 1–15; Peter Amann, "Prelude to Insurrection: the Banquet of the People," *French Historical Studies*, I (1960), 436–444.

The question now arises: How well equipped and prepared was the government to deal with major disorders? It had faced a series of formidable disturbances in the years 1830–1834 and a concerted attempt at insurrection in 1839. Its security forces were briefly as follows. The regular, uniformed police force (*sergents de ville*) numbered only a few hundred men, but was reinforced by an essentially military *Garde municipale*. This body, recruited largely among army veterans, consisted of 16 companies of infantry and 5 squadrons of cavalry (a total of 3,200 men), splendidly accoutered, thoroughly drilled, and so notorious for its brutality as to be passionately hated by the population.[17]

The *Garde municipale* was roughly the equivalent of the London metropolitan police, except that it was more pronouncedly military in character. It, in turn, was expected to rely for support on the *Garde nationale* which, again, was intended to play the same role as the London special constables. The *Garde nationale* was, however, a permanent force, more or less regularly trained and exercised, for the most part uniformed and armed. It consisted of one legion for each of the 12 *arrondissements*, plus one elite cavalry legion and 4 suburban legions—all told a force of no less than 84,000 men. All able-bodied men were liable for service in the *Garde nationale*, but actually only those who paid a certain annual tax were enrolled. It was understood that the *Garde* was an essentially bourgeois formation, designed for defense of the régime. Only after it had gone into action against insurgents was the regular garrison expected to take part. This garrison consisted of some 30,000 troops, quartered in barracks scattered throughout the city.[18]

In the July Revolution of 1830 the commander of the forces, Marshal

---

[17] Charles Simond, *Les Centennales parisiennes* (Paris, 1903), pp. 31 ff.; Frances Trollope, *Paris and the Parisians in 1835* (London, 1836), I, 135: "I never saw any corps of more superb appearance"; F. S. Bamberg, *Geschichte der Februar Revolution* (Braunschweig, 1848), p. 123: "Der reitende Theil . . . war das schönste Truppen-Corps der französischen Armee." According to St. John, *The French Revolution in 1848*, 72 ff., the crowd on February 22 began to throw stones at the mounted guards whereupon "this body, detested by the Parisians as police, kept up continual charges upon the crowd until it gradually dispersed." No mercy was shown, reported this observer: "They kept galloping suddenly towards the multitude" and even used their swords. The behavior of the mounted forces in all the capitals seems to have been uniformly ruthless, which no doubt had a lot to do with roiling the populace.
[18] Edmond Téxier, *Tableau de Paris* (Paris, 1852), II, 319; Bamberg, *Geschichte der Februar Revolution*, p. 119; Paul Pichon, *Histoire et organisation des services de police en France* (Issoudun, 1949), pp. 88 ff. On the *Garde nationale* the recent study by Louis Girard, *La Garde nationale, 1814–1871* (Paris, 1964),

Marmont, had been faced by the refusal of his troops to fire on the populace. The danger of defection in the event of civil strife was a continuing one and for that very reason the government relied chiefly on the *Garde nationale* to quell the disturbances of the 1830s. It proved to be a matter of prime importance, then, that the devotion of the *Garde* to the King had weakened greatly by 1848. Ever since 1835 the upper classes had evaded service, while the legions of the poorer *arrondissements* had become seriously disgruntled. The King was certainly not ignorant of these developments. Indeed, after 1840 he did not even review the *Garde,* though to show his displeasure in this way was probably unwise. The estrangement between the ruler and the formations that were supposedly the mainstay of his régime was to be the crucial factor in the events of February 22–24, 1848.

The crowd that assembled on the Place de la Madeleine on the rainy morning of February 22 was altogether nondescript and evidently moved more by curiosity than by any set purpose. It surged aimlessly to and fro until in the later morning a group of students from the Left Bank led the way to the Chamber of Deputies, where the first minor clashes took place before the crowd was pressed back over the river to the Place de la Concorde. The King and the government clearly did not take the demonstration seriously, for preparatory measures that had been decided on were countermanded, probably from fear that action by the troops would only roil the populace and possibly from uncertainty as to the reliability of the forces. In this connection it is interesting to note that on this very first day of unrest the troops tended to stand aloof. They watched idly while the crowd broke street lanterns and overturned omnibuses, and in some cases stood inactive while barricades were being thrown across the streets.[19]

From the outset the *Garde municipale* acted with its usual energy and ruthlessness and, as might be expected, enraged the populace. It might conceivably have broken up the demonstrations by its own efforts, had it been given appropriate orders. But these were not forthcoming, so the *Garde* found itself reduced to purely defensive opera-

---

supersedes all previous works. Mrs. Trollope, *Paris and the Parisians,* I, 139, succinctly described the National Guard in 1835 as "the industrious and orderly part of the community, organised to keep in check the idle and disorderly."

[19] *Les Barricades: Scènes les plus saisissantes de la Révolution de 1848* (Paris, 1848); Crémieux, *La Révolution de février,* pp. 92 ff.; Gaston Bouniols, *Histoire de la Révolution de 1848* (Paris, 1918), pp. 35 ff. See also the strictures on the military in Max Jähns, *Das französische Heer* (Leipzig, 1873), pp. 339 ff.

tions. Since the disorders continued to spread, the King on the morning of February 23 reluctantly called out the *Garde nationale,* only to find, to his horror, that even the legions from the well-to-do sections had joined the opposition to the Guizot régime and insisted on immediate reforms. The effect of this revelation was to precipitate the rather unceremonious dismissal of Guizot.[20] Had the King then called at once on the opposition leaders, Thiers and Barrot, to form a ministry and had he, at the same time, accepted the modest reforms demanded by the opposition, the situation might well have been saved. But Louis Philippe disliked Thiers and was loath to accept changes. In the sequel he was to agree to a reform ministry but without consenting to reforms and, belatedly, to show a determination to resist that, at an earlier hour, might have stood him in good stead.

For the time being, both the *Garde* and the troops were left without adequate directives. In the growing disorder the officers lost confidence while the men became demoralized.[21] Meanwhile the center of disturbance shifted to the crowded *arrondissements,* where barricades went up by the hundreds.[22] On the evening of February 23 there took place the "massacre" of the Boulevard des Capucines, when a surging crowd of National Guards and people collided with a detachment of troops which, hard pressed, opened fire, leaving some fifty persons dead on the pavement. Only after this tragic episode, which raised the resentment of the populace to fever heat, did Louis Philippe entrust command of both the troops and the *Garde nationale* to Marshal Bugeaud,

[20] The attitude of the various *Garde* legions was analyzed in detail by Crémieux, *La Révolution de février,* chap. 4; see also Girard, *La Garde nationale,* pp. 284 ff.; Daumard, *La Bourgeoisie parisienne,* pp. 595 ff.

[21] Comte de Montalivet, *Fragments et souvenirs* (Paris, 1899–1900), II, 119; Crémieux, *La Révolution de février,* p. 164; P. Chalmin, "La crise morale de l'armée française," *L'Armée et la Seconde République* (Paris, 1955), pp. 27–76.

[22] Barricades had not played an important part in the great French Revolution, yet were positively decisive in July 1830 and prominent in other disturbances of the 1830's. In London they did not appear at all. The explanation seems to lie in the progressive paving of the city streets. In London macadamized pavement, which was quieter, was largely used, granite blocks having been introduced only in 1828. In Paris, on the other hand, the durable and relatively cheap granite blocks (at first in large sizes, six inches square by nine inches deep) were the usual thing. These blocks were, of course, the ideal material for the construction of barricades, for they were near at hand, could be easily lifted with pieces of iron railing, and provided the necessary solidity. Mrs. Trollope was undoubtedly right in remarking that if Paris streets were macadamized, real difficulties would be thrown in the way of future barricade heroes. See further S. Dupain, *Notice historique sur le pavé de Paris* (Paris, 1881), pp. 205 ff.; E. G. Love, *Pavements and Roads, Their Construction and Maintenance* (New York, 1890), p. 232.

victor of the Algerian campaigns and a soldier renowned for his tough-ness, who had been itching for a chance to put the "rabble" in its place. Bugeaud started out bright and early on the morning of February 24 in an attempt to reopen communications between the key points of the city. Yet before noon he proclaimed a cease-fire. The reasons for this *volte-face* on the part of a fire-eating commander have been the subject of much debate, but need not detain us here. The fact is that the weariness and demoralization of the troops, the almost complete de-fection of the *Garde nationale,* and above all the hundreds of barri-cades must have shown him the futility of his effort.[23] The King made a last desperate but vain attempt to rally the support of at least part of the *Garde nationale,* after which he was driven to the inevitable decision to abdicate.

In review it must be reiterated that the revolution that developed in Paris was neither planned nor desired. The outbreaks were disjointed, isolated, leaderless, and utterly without plan or coordination. The King, through poor judgment, distrust, and indecision, allowed the disturb-ances to develop to the point at which suppression became impossible. When he failed to conciliate the *Garde nationale,* he sealed the fate not only of the régime but of the dynasty.[24]

REVOLUTION IN VIENNA

The situation in Vienna was strikingly similar to that in Paris, despite the vast disparity between France and the Hapsburg Monarchy in terms of political and social development. Opposition to the Metternich system had been growing apace during the 1840s and by 1848 had reached the point at which even the old feudal estates were calling for change and, more importantly, influential officials, army officers, and intellectuals were agitating for reforms along the lines of Western liberalism. The government suffered much from the fact that the Em-peror was incompetent to rule, while the imperial family was divided on questions of policy. Certainly Prince Metternich had many enemies,

[23] Bugeaud claimed that his cease-fire was demanded by the new Thiers-Barrot cabinet, which was intent on conciliation and pacification. The best detailed nar-rative is that of Crémieux, *La Révolution de février,* pp. 210 ff.; but see also Comte Henry d'Ideville, *Le Maréchal Bugeaud* (Paris, 1882), III, 316 ff.; Maurice Andrieux, *Le Père Bugeaud* (Paris, 1951), pp. 268 ff.

[24] Crémieux, *La Révolution de février,* pp. 467 ff.; Charléty, *La Monarchie de Juillet,* p. 299, who holds that at any time during the insurrection the king could have mastered it, had he not labored under delusions which robbed him of necessary will-power.

a situation that obliged him to acquiesce in the establishment of the *Gewerbeverein* and the *Leseverein,* organizations that soon became strongholds of the liberal, reforming factions. It is rather hard to believe that, in the natural course of events, Metternich would not soon have been forced out of office and a more liberal, progressive policy adopted.[25]

Naturally the news from Paris, the reports of the ease with which Guizot and Louis Philippe had been driven out by popular demonstration, greatly reinforced the pressure on the Vienna court. A veritable whirlwind of petitions called for an end to repression and the introduction of a liberal system. Most prominent among these was the petition submitted by the 4,000 Viennese students, many of whom came from the lower classes, and all of whom suffered under the restrictions of the Metternich system. This, like other petitions, was rejected, largely because of the unwillingness of the Archduke Louis, chief of the council of state, to consider making concessions under pressure.

The Viennese government in no sense faced a threat of revolution. The loyalty of the entire population to the dynasty—even to the half-witted Emperor—was such as to astound contemporaries.[26] The opposition was, as in France, directed against the ministry, hoping that its policy of immobility or stagnation could be gotten rid of by peaceful pressure. The only real danger of upheaval lay in the workingmen of the suburbs, who like workers elsewhere in Europe were suffering, and who, by the spring of 1848, were in such ferment that the government was obliged to set up public works and open soup kitchens to alleviate the unemployment and want. But not even the workers were revolutionary in the sense of having an organization or program. The workers were desperate but knew no course of action besides wrecking the hated machines and occasionally plundering the foodshops.[27]

[25] Heinrich Friedjung, *Oesterreich von 1848 bis 1860* (Stuttgart, 1908), I, 17–18; Heinrich von Srbik, *Metternich, der Staatsmann und der Mensch* (Munich, 1925), II, 259 ff.; Veit Valentin, *Geschichte der deutschen Revolution von 1848–1849* (Berlin, 1930), I, 400 ff.; Rudolf Kiszling, *Die Revolution im Kaisertum Oesterreich, 1848–1849* (Vienna, 1948–1952), I, 35.

[26] Josef A. Ditscheiner, *Der Wiener Freiheitskampf* (Vienna, 1848), p. 4; Carl Graf Vitzthum von Eckstädt, *Berlin und Wien in den Jahren 1845–1852* (Stuttgart, 1886), p. 83 (letter of March 17, 1848): "Die Anhänglichkeit an das Kaiserhaus ist hier noch fabelhaft . . ." See also Kiszling, *Die Revolution,* I, 41.

[27] Schmidl, *Wien und seine nächsten Ungebungen,* p. 164; Karl Weiss, *Geschichte der Stadt Wien* (Vienna, 1872), II, 176 ff.; Ernst von Zenker, *Die Wiener Revolution in ihren sozialen Voraussetzungen und Beziehungen* (Vienna, 1897), pp. 96 ff.; Ludwig Brügel, *Geschichte der oesterreichischen Sozialdemokratie*

Besieged by deputations and all but buried under petitions, the government, fearing disturbances, ordered the garrison troops in readiness. These forces numbered about 14,000, mostly quartered in barracks just outside the walls. On these the government would have to rely in case of serious disorder, for the police forces were altogether inadequate. The civil police was almost exclusively a secret police, assigned to the surveillance of dangerous and subversive persons and organizations. Under its supervision was a *Militär-Polizeiwache* consisting of 1,100 to 1,200 men. On paper, at least, there stood between these police forces and the regular troops something akin to the French *Garde nationale,* namely, a *Bürgerwehr* (Citizens' Guard) that, during the French occupation in 1809 had served a useful purpose but that had since 1815 sunk to the status of a ceremonial guard, noted chiefly for the excellence of its band-music. Officially, the *Bürgerwehr* comprised 14,000 men of the upper and middle bourgeoisie, electing its own officers and serving at its own expense. Only about a third of the force was equipped with firearms.[28]

The events of March 13 in Vienna were as confused as the February days in Paris. It was a bright spring morning and many people, including elegantly-dressed ladies, assembled before the palace of the Estates of Lower Austria, because it was known that this influential body was about to proceed to the palace with yet another petition. Presently a large body of students arrived, hoping to enlist the support of the Estates for their own petition. No one knew just what to do. While waiting, some of the students began to make speeches. There was much milling about in the narrow Herrengasse and in the courtyard of the palace. Eventually, toward noon, the president of the Estates appealed to the Archduke Albert, commanding the troops, for relief from popular pressure. The soldiers had a hard time making their way to the

---

(Vienna, 1922–1925), I, 15, 23, 54; Heinrich von Srbik, "Die Wiener Revolution des Jahres 1848 in sozialgeschichtlicher Beleuchtung," *Schmollers Jahrbuch,* XLIII (1919), 19–58; Julius Marx, "Die Wirtschaftslage im deutschen Oesterreich vor dem Ausbruch der Revolution, 1848," *Vierteljahrschrift für Sozial- und Wirtschaftsgeschichte,* XXXI (1938), 242–282. Vitzthum, *Berlin und Wien,* p. 75, reported great unrest in the suburbs as early as March 5, 1848.

[28] For an excellent contemporary account see Schmidl, *Wien,* pp. 162–163. See also Weiss, *Geschichte der Stadt Wien,* II, 239 ff.; Viktor Bibl, *Die Wiener Polizei* (Vienna, 1927), pp. 313 ff.; Hugo Kerchnawe, *Die Überwindung der ersten Weltrevolution* (Innsbruck, 1932), pp. ii ff. Vitzthum, *Berlin und Wien,* p. 78, speaks of 1,000 more men having been recruited on March 12. Even if this is true, these late-comers could hardly have counted for much in the confusion of the ensuing days.

center of disturbances. Presently, tiles and other missiles were thrown at them from roofs and windows; guns went off, no one knew how or why; there were five dead. Like the much more horrible "massacre" of the Boulevard des Capucines, this episode was enough to set off a whole series of desultory clashes between the military and the people. At the same time crowds of workers from the suburbs began to invade the Inner City until the gates were closed against them. Some remained outside the walls, howling like hungry wolves. Most of them, however, returned to the suburbs to engage in an orgy of incendiarism and plunder.[29]

Franz Grillparzer, the great Austrian dramatist, was an eyewitness of the events of March 13 and pictured the initial demonstrations at the Ständehaus as a pleasant, good-natured fracas. The whole thing, he wrote in his recollections, could have been snuffed out by two battalions of soldiers, but no troops, in fact not even the police, were to be seen.[30] The military, when at last it appeared, did too much. After the first bloodshed and after the arrival of the workers from the suburbs, the situation became much more ominous. During the afternoon the demand for Metternich's dismissal became deafening. At the same time there were violent clashes between the troops and the populace, led by the students. Efforts to storm the arsenal led to considerable bloodshed, while at the Schottentor the workers actually managed to secure control of the entrance. In the elegant suburb of Wieden the mob sacked Metternich's villa and other aristocratic homes.

In the hope that order might still be restored, a group of prominent citizens in the late afternoon persuaded the Lord Mayor, Count Czapka, to call out the *Bürgerwehr*, of which he was the commanding officer, and if possible induce the military to withdraw from the city while the

[29] Ernst Violand, *Die soziale Geschichte der Revolution in Oesterreich* (Leipzig, 1850), pp. 69 ff.; Zenker, *Die Wiener Revolution*, pp. 112 ff. The fact that so many of the workers were non-Germans—Czechs, Italians, Poles, Swiss—gave rise to the theory, firmly held by Metternich, that the whole outbreak was instigated by foreign agents. See Srbik, *Metternich*, II, 280; Valentin, *Geschichte der deutschen Revolution*, I, 400 ff.; R. John Rath, *The Viennese Revolution of 1848* (Austin, 1957), p. 54. Good contemporary narratives of the events of March 13 are F. C. Schall, *Oestrreichs glorreichste Tage* (Vienna, 1848); Josef A. Ditscheiner, *Der Wiener Freiheitskampf* (Vienna, 1848). The work of Heinrich Reschauer, *Geschichte der Wiener Revolution* (Vienna, 1872), is an almost painfully detailed chronicle which, unfortunately, is undocumented.

[30] Franz Grillparzer, "Erinnerungen aus dem Jahre 1848," in August Sauer, ed., *Grillparzers sämtliche Werke*, XX, 185–211. Later historians, such as Valentin and Jacques Droz, *Les Révolutions allemandes de 1848* (Paris, 1957), p. 185, tend to agree with Grillparzer's judgment.

Bürgerwehr took over. The chronology is hopelessly confused and it is hardly worthwhile trying to fix it. Archduke Albert, the commander of the forces, who himself had been badly injured by a block of wood thrown at him from a window, did in fact evacuate the inner city. For the next several, critical days, the garrison troops stood idle and useless on the parade ground just outside the walls.[31]

The *Bürgerwehr*, meanwhile, was to play the same role as that of the Paris *Garde nationale*. A deputation of *Bürgerwehr* officers at once proceeded to the palace to demand the dismissal of Metternich (allowing the court until 9:00 P.M. to make up its mind) and the arming of the students. These were hard decisions for the court to make, for the emperor was feeble-minded and his relatives were bady divided. Several of the archdukes, led by Archduke John, had long since convinced themselves that Metternich must go and that real reforms must be undertaken. On the other hand, Archduke Louis abominated reforms and was urged by Metternich and Field Marshal Prince Windischgrätz to stand firm. The whole disturbance, argued the aged chancellor, was nothing more than a riot that could be easily mastered by the police and the troops. What led to the downfall of Louis Philippe was his eagerness to dismiss Guizot. Where a policy of concessions would lead no one knew. As for Windischgrätz, he had had years of experience dealing with serious workers' outbreaks in Prague and other Bohemian cities. He was sure that energetic action by the military could quickly suppress the disturbances. To dismiss Metternich, he held, would be nothing short of shameless cowardice.[32]

In the end, "the impotent scarecrows" (Kudlich) were unable to withstand the pressure of *Bürgerwehr*, students, and members of the Estates. In the evening Metternich was obliged to resign and permission was given for the immediate arming of the students, who alone were thought to have any influence with the rampaging workers. In the course of the night thousands of muskets were dealt out to students and citizens. These, in turn, formed patrols and managed to restore some semblance of order.

No good purpose would be served by pursuing the story further. At the end of the first day the court had surrendered to the liberal el-

---

[31] Vitzthum, *Berlin und Wien*, pp. 78 ff.; Weiss, *Geschichte der Stadt Wien*, II, 310; Friedjung, *Oesterreich*, I, 20; Kiszling, *Die Revolution*, I, 42.

[32] Srbik, *Metternich*, II, 280 ff.; Paul Müller, *Feldmarschall Fürst Windischgrätz* (Vienna, 1934), pp. 66, 88–89.

ements, if only in order to master the radicalism of the workers—that is, to put an end to an unwanted revolution for which the indecision of the court was largely to blame. A few words should, however, be said of the immediate aftermath. Like Louis Philippe in his belated appointment of Marshal Bugeaud, the Viennese court made a hopeless attempt to save the situation by naming Prince Windischgrätz civil and military governor of Vienna (noon, March 14). He was to proclaim martial law, while the government was to revoke all the concessions made under popular pressure on the preceding day. The field marshal apparently thought the situation too far gone, and his efforts to assert his authority did, in fact, prove altogether futile. The court was no longer in a position to refuse the demand for the organization of a national guard, which was to include a separate student corps (*Akademische Legion*). This new national guard was intended to comprise about 10,000 reliable citizens, but popular pressure led to the enrollment of some 30,000, in addition to the 7000 students in the special legion. Windischgrätz was, for the time being, quite helpless. On the following day (March 15) the court had to agree to a constitution, with which the first phase of this rather incredible revolution was brought to a close.[33]

REVOLUTION IN BERLIN

The story of the Berlin revolution—our last case study—provides a classic example of how *not* to deal with revolutionary situations. Berlin, like other capitals, was in a process of rapid economic transformation and was, in addition, a veritable hotbed of radical philosophical thought. Yet, politically, the population was strikingly inexperienced and apathetic. The rapidly developing liberal movement in Prussia had its stronghold not in Berlin, but in the Rhineland and in provincial cities such as Königsberg and Breslau. The famous United Diet of 1847 had revealed the wide divergence between the aspirations of the rising middle class and the outmoded, traditionalist notions of the ruler. But even then the liberals, for all their discontent, were far from advocating revolution. Like their counterparts elsewhere in Europe, they relied on agitation and pressure to bring about a constitutional régime. A sober evaluation of the evidence suggests that they were probably justified

[33] Vitzthum, *Berlin und Wien*, pp. 78 ff.; Paul Molisch, "Die Wiener akademische Legion," *Archiv für Oesterreichische Geschichte*, CX (1924), 64 ff.; Müller, *Windischgrätz*, pp. 90 ff. For details of the National Guard see Kerchnawe, *Die Überwindung der ersten Weltrevolution*, pp. 12, 17.

in their expectations. By the beginning of 1848 even so recalcitrant a prince as Frederick William IV was beginning to yield to the constitutionally-directed importunities of his ministers.[34]

Berlin is supposed to have had, in 1848, some 40,000 to 50,000 industrial workers in the textile and metallurgical trades, and certainly far more in the traditional artisan occupations. As elsewhere, the workers suffered acutely from the rapid economic changes; five-eighths of the laboring population is supposed to have been in extreme want. In the years just preceding 1848 some workers' associations had sprung up and some revolutionary groups, such as the *Zeitungshalle,* had emerged. But these were exceptional. The workers were, for the most part, illiterate and apathetic so far as politics were concerned. Class consciousness and subversive activity were practically nonexistent.[35]

It was no doubt inevitable that news of the Paris insurrection should have led to much excitement and that, somewhat later, reports of Metternich's fall should have evoked widespread enthusiasm. From March 6 on, there were many meetings, speeches, resolutions, and petitions, all advancing the familiar liberal demands. The general tone of both meetings and petitions was one of hope and good will. And rightly so, for the Prussian government, like those of the South German states, was on the verge of giving way to popular pressure. There was, to be sure, strong conservative opposition, led by Prince William of Prussia, the King's brother. But there were even stronger forces convinced that fundamental changes were inescapable and that Prussia's future position in Germany depended on leadership of the liberal movement. As early as March 12 the King, albeit reluctantly and with mental reservations, made the basic decision to accept a constitution and a responsible ministry.[36]

Had the Prussian government provided Berlin with an adequate

[34] Valentin, *Geschichte der deutschen Revolution,* I, 416–417; Rudolf Stadelmann, *Soziale und politische Geschichte der Revolution von 1848* (Munich, 1948), pp. 6 ff.; Droz, *Les Révolutions allemandes,* pp. 71–83.

[35] On economic and social conditions see Pierre Benaerts, *Les Origines de la grande industrie allemande* (Paris, 1934), chaps. 4, 16; Dora Meyer, *Das öffentliche Leben in Berlin im Jahr vor der Märzrevolution* (Berlin, 1912), chap. 2; Karl Obermann, *Die deutschen Arbeiter in der ersten bürgerlichen Revolution* (Berlin, 1950), p. 20. On the political immaturity and indifference of the population see Stadelmann, *Soziale und politische Geschichte,* p. 53; Droz, *Les Révolutions allemandes,* p. 194.

[36] On the early meetings see Valentin, *Geschichte der deutschen Revolution,* I, 416–417; Stadelmann, *Soziale und politische Geschichte,* pp. 45, 53; Ernst Kaeber, *Berlin 1848* (Berlin, 1948), chap. 2; Alfred Herrmann, *Berliner Demo-*

civil police, there is no reason to suppose that the popular meetings and processions would have gotten out of hand. But, incredible though it may seem, in this city of 400,000 there was no police to speak of, nor even anything akin to a civic or national guard. Officially there was a gendarmerie consisting of 40 sergeants and 110 men, but these gendarmes were employed almost exclusively in the law courts, markets, places of amusement, and so forth. For the preservation of public order the government relied on the garrison troops (about 12,000 in number).[37] In short, the government could deal with serious disturbances only by the methods employed in Russia, methods altogether unsuited to the conditions of a large western city. This had become clear during the so-called "Potato Revolution" of April 1847—large-scale food riots during which some barricades had been erected and severe clashes between troops and people had taken place. At that time the city authorities had petitioned for a modest constabulary, to act in the first instance. But the government had been unwilling to delegate such authority. It therefore remained dependent on the armed forces, which, because of their ruthless and brutal action, were intensely hated by the populace, and which, in turn, despised the "rabble." [38]

As popular excitement grew, the authorities brought more and more troops into the city. Clashes were almost inevitable. They began to take place on March 13 and the ensuing days, with some loss of life and much burning resentment, accompanied by insults and provocations on both sides. On March 9 the city authorities had renewed the request for formation of a civil constabulary, which was belatedly granted on March 16. Civic guard units (*Bürgerschutzkommissionen*) were hastily enrolled. There was to be a force of 1,200 men, patrolling in groups of 10 to 20, armed only with truncheons. It was, however, understood that thenceforth the military should act only if called upon

---

kraten (Berlin, 1948), pp. 114 ff. For an excellent discussion of the prospects for reform see Wilhelm Busch, *Die Berliner Märztage von 1848* (Munich, 1899), pp. 4, 10.

[37] On the police see C. Nobiling, *Die Berliner Bürgerwehr in den Tagen vom 19ten März bis 7ten April, 1848* (Berlin, 1852), pp. 5–6; Hubert von Meyerinck, "Die Tätigkeit der Truppen während der berliner Märztage des Jahres 1848," *Militär-Wochenblatt, Beiheft 4–5* (1891), 99–168; Kaeber, *Berlin, 1848*, pp. 40–41.

[38] On the Potato Revolution and the resulting antagonism between the military and the populace see especially Anon., *Die berliner Märztage, vom militärischen Standpunkte geschildert* (Berlin, 1850), pp. 11 ff.; Nobiling, *Berliner Bürgerwehr*, p. 6; Meyerinck, *Militär-Wochenblatt, Beiheft 4–5*, p. 104; Meyer, *Das öffentliche Leben*, pp. 86–90; Gordon A. Craig, *The Politics of the Prussian Army, 1640–1945* (Oxford, 1955), pp. 90 ff.

by officers of the civic guard. In a word, they were expected to play the same role as the special constables in London.[39]

Actually this improvised constabulary played but a sorry role in the Berlin uprising. The men had little more than good will. Neither the military nor the populace paid much attention to them. On the contrary, their efforts met with derision. The crowds grew increasingly restless and the troops more and more eager to beat them into submission. Hence the growing demand on the part of the people for the withdrawal of the military from the city and the formation of a real national guard, which would have been tantamount to the King's putting himself at the mercy of his subjects. This he was naturally unwilling to do, but on March 18, just as a monster demonstration at the royal palace was being organized, the King issued the famous "patent" by which he promised the early convocation of the United Diet, expressed his acceptance of constitutional government, and announced his leadership of the liberal, national movement in Germany. Since this document met most of the popular demands, it called forth general enthusiasm. Huge crowds gathered in the palace square, while the recently established civic guards stood in array before the portals of the palace. Then the sight of troops massed in the courtyard of the palace led to renewed cries for withdrawal of the soldiers. The commotion became so great that the King ordered General von Prittwitz, the commander of the troops, to clear the square. The general's cavalry squadron was so hard pressed by the crowds that infantry was sent out to relieve him. In the din and confusion two rifle shots rang out. No one was hurt, but the crowds suddenly panicked. Like the Paris populace after the massacre of the Boulevard des Capucines, the Berliners were convinced that they had been betrayed: that they had been lured to the palace by promises of reforms, only to be fallen upon by the hated military. Scattering before the advancing troops, they spread all sorts of alarming stories through the city. Everywhere barricades began to go up, and before evening fighting had broken out in many sections of the metropolis.[40]

[39] Meyerinck, *Militär-Wochenblatt, Beiheft* 4–5, pp. 101, 104, 108; Busch, *Berliner Märztage von 1848*, p. 6; Felix Rachfahl, *Deutschland, König Friedrich Wilhelm IV, und die berliner Märzrevolution* (Halle, 1901), p. 128; Karl Haenchen, "Aus dem Nachlass des Generals von Prittwitz," *Forschungen zur brandenburg-preussischen Geschichte*, XLV (1933), 99–125.

[40] These events are, of course, narrated in all histories of the German revolution. In the present context the accounts of special interest are those of Meyerinck, *Militär-Wochenblatt, Beiheft* 4–5, pp. 112 ff.; Rachfahl, *Deutschland*, pp. 133, 143;

The King and his military advisers were always convinced that the insurrection of March 18–19 was instigated and planned by foreign agents—French, Swiss, Poles, 10,000 of whom were reputed to have arrived in the city. But this comfortable theory was not supported by solid evidence. No one doubts that there were a great many foreigners, mostly workers, in Berlin, nor that many German workers had spent some years in Switzerland or Paris. Furthermore, there were certainly some confirmed revolutionaries who provided what inspiration and leadership they could. But the insurrection showed little, if any, evidence of planning or organization. All strata of the Berlin population were involved in one way or another. The students played a far less significant role here than in Vienna, but they do seem to have been instrumental in bringing workers from the suburbs to help man the barricades. But judging from the losses, the actual fighting was carried on largely by young artisans, the traditional craftsmen of the city.[41]

Prittwitz had at his disposal a total force of about 15,000, consisting of cavalry, artillery, and infantry, with which he proceeded to act with great energy. The insurgents, on the other hand, had but few muskets or munitions and had to make do with improvised weapons. Under these circumstances they could not hope adequately to defend the barricades, many of which were but lightly constructed. Instead, they hurled paving stones and tiles from the roofs or poured boiling water from the windows. The troops invaded the houses, pursued the rebels to the garrets, and there either cut them down or dragged them away captive. The advantage throughout lay with the military, and indeed by midnight of March 18 Prittwitz had established effective control over the center of the city. This is not to say that the completion of the operation would not have been an arduous business. Prittwitz seems to have hoped that he could persuade the king to go to Potsdam, after which he would have concentrated his troops outside the city for establishment of a blockade. Eventually, if necessary, he planned to snuff out the insurrection by bombardment of the disaffected quarters. The

---

Valentin, *Geschichte der deutschen Revolution*, I, 430 ff.; Kaeber, *Berlin, 1848*, pp. 55 ff.; Droz, *Les Révolutions allemandes*, pp. 198 ff.

[41] The military viewpoint is well presented in *Die Berliner Märztage*, p. 24; Busch, *Berliner Märztage von 1848*, pp. 8, 17, and Meyerinck, *Militär-Wochenblatt, Beiheft* 4–5, 106; see also Rachfahl, *Deutschland*, pp. 122, 126; Valentin, *Geschichte der deutschen Revolution*, I, 419; Herrmann, *Berliner Demokraten*, p. 121; Stadelmann, *Soziale und politische Geschichte*, pp. 46, 57, 60; and especially the careful analysis of radical activities in Haenchen, *Forschungen zur brandenburg-preussischen Geschichte*, LV (1943), 83–114.

King, however, wanted to put an end to the fighting at almost any cost. Hence his pathetic appeal "To my dear Berliners," drafted in the night, offering to discuss the situation with representatives of the people and to withdraw the troops once the barricades had been taken down.[42]

The picture at court on the morning of March 19 was one of utter confusion; the King, in a state of near collapse, was evidently unable to appreciate all the implications of his decisions or in general to provide consistent leadership. Beset on all sides by officials and deputations of citizens and, furthermore, misled by unconfirmed reports that barricades were already being dismantled, he ordered the withdrawal of the troops to their barracks except for the guards at the palace and the arsenal. Through misunderstanding even these critical places were presently abandoned. It seems likely that the King intended to leave Berlin as part of Prittwitz's plan.[43] But all arrangements for his departure were hopelessly upset when, early in the afternoon, a great procession arrived at the palace bearing the bodies of some 200 victims of the street-fighting, their wounds exposed. Eventually the crowd made its way into the courtyard of the palace. On vociferous demand of the throng the King was obliged to appear and even to doff his cap in reverence to the people's dead. Nothing, certainly, could have demonstrated more clearly the complete capitulation of the monarchy. The people, on the verge of defeat in battle, had secured not only the removal of the troops to their barracks but also the establishment of a civic guard. (The King agreed to this immediately after his humiliating appearance on the balcony.)

The *Bürgerwehr,* as the new civic guard was called, was to be organized by districts, each to have roughly 100 men. Only those who had full citizen rights (*Bürgerbrief*) were eligible for enrollment and the old traditional marksmans-guild (*Schützengilde*) was to provide the kernel of the hastily constructed force of 6000 men. Several thousand muskets were immediately supplied from the arsenal. By 6:00 P.M. on March 19 the elite *Schützengilde* and the newly recruited *Bürgerwehr* were able to take over guard duty at the palace.[44] Frederick William had placed himself entirely under the protection of his subjects. He

[42] On the morning of March 19 the outcome of the fighting was at best a draw. Most writers consider that the military had the upper hand.

[43] On preparations for the king's departure see especially Busch, *Berliner Märztage von 1848,* p. 32; Stadelmann, *Soziale und politische Geschichte,* p. 59.

[44] Nobiling, *Berliner Bürgerwehr,* pp. 1 ff.; O. Rimpler, *Die Berliner Bürgerwehr im Jahre 1848* (Brandenburg, 1883), pp. 3 ff.

was as defenseless, wrote the American minister in Berlin on March 21, "as the poorest malefactor of the prisons." Early in the morning of March 21 the entire Berlin garrison was withdrawn from the city. For the moment the revolution was triumphant.

CONCLUSION

By the mid-nineteenth century the economic and social transformation of western and much of central Europe had reached the point at which basic political changes had become imperative.

There was much pressure on the part of the propertied middle classes for such changes, as is shown most vividly by the fact that in both Paris and Vienna the national guard, designed to protect the existing régime, lent their support to the cause of reform.

Yet there was remarkably little organization or planning for revolution. The colorful heroism of a few revolutionary leaders and the occasional spectacular outbreaks of radical elements are apt to be misleading.

The proponents of liberalism and reform expected to attain their ends by peaceful organization and action. They were fascinated by the achievements of O'Connell and greatly heartened by the triumph of Cobden and the free-trade movement.

After 1846 the forces of liberalism were so formidable and insistent as to be almost irresistible.

It was the unpardonable fault of the continental princes to have failed to gauge the strength of the opposition and to have refused to accept the inevitable. This was particularly true of Louis Philippe, because the reforms called for in France were of a modest nature and the failing loyalty of the National Guard must certainly have been known to him.

Ways to avoid serious upheaval were demonstrated not only by the preventive measures taken later in London, but also by the timely concessions made by King Leopold of Belgium, through which his government secured the support of the opposition which enabled it to present a united front to efforts at radical insurrection.[45]

[45] J. Dhondt, "La Belgique en 1848," *Actes du congrès historique du centenaire de la Révolution de 1848* (Paris, 1948), pp. 115–132; Jean Bartier, "1848 en Belgique," in Francois Fejtö, ed., *Le Printemps des peuples* (Paris, 1948), I, 355–372; Georges Eckhout, "La Réforme électoral de 1848," Jean de Harveng, ed., *Histoire de la Belgique contemporaine* (Brussels, 1928–1930), I, 371 ff. Brison D. Gooch, *Belgium and the February Revolution* (The Hague, 1963).

The alternative to concession was systematic repression, as practiced in quite different forms in Britain and Russia. But prevention of insurrection called above all for vigorous action. The situation in the European capitals, with their dislocated artisan economy, widespread unemployment, fluid population, and appalling living conditions, was necessarily explosive. It was imperative, therefore, to prevent ordinary assemblages of people from degenerating into mob action and eventual revolution.

Everywhere on the continent the civil police was inadequate for the task. As of old, governments still relied on their military forces to prevent major disorders. But the use of troops for police duty, always undesirable because too drastic, had by 1848 become extremely hazardous. For even though the aristocratic officer corps might spoil for a chance to put "the rabble" in its place, the common soldier in conscript armies was understandably reluctant to shoot at unarmed citizens. In the July Revolution Marshal Marmont saw most of his forces melt away. Even in England it was sometimes thought advisable to bring troops from Ireland, lest the English troops assigned to quell disturbances in the industrial areas prove unreliable.[46]

In these circumstances it behooved governments to move promptly and energetically. In all the capitals the initial demonstrations were amorphous, aimless, unaggressive. Yet nowhere did the authorities show the required determination. Troops were left to act as best they could; higher direction was almost completely lacking.[47]

As a result, fairly innocuous aggregations of people quickly turned into bellicose mobs. Open conflict between people and troops ensued,

[46] F. C. Mather, "The Railways, the Electric Telegraph and Public Order during the Chartist Period," *History*, n.s., XXXVIII (1953), 40–53. On the July Revolution see the anonymous pamphlet, *Les Barricades immortelles de Paris* (Paris, 1830); *Mémoires du Maréchal Marmont, Duc de Raguse* (Paris, 1857) VIII, 239 ff.; and on the general problem the excellent analysis of Hermann Kriebel, *Über die Bezwingung innerer Unruhen nach den Erfahrungen der Geschichte in der ersten Hälfte des XIX. Jahrhunderts* (Innsbruck, 1929).

[47] In this connection one may appropriately quote the judgment of Michael Bakunin (surely an expert in things revolutionary) on the European insurrections of February–March, 1848: "La révolution avait pris tout le monde à l'improviste; personne n'y était préparé. Il n'y avait pas même l'ombre d'une organisation, aucun but déterminé, rien qui ressembla à un plan." (The revolution had taken the whole world by surprise; no one was prepared for it. There was not even the shadow of an organization, no fixed objective, nothing that resembled a plan.) But, he adds, the rulers and governments were so frightened that the first gust of revolutionary wind brought down a harvest of concessions. (From the first draft of Bakunin's "Manifesto to the Slavs," quoted in Josef Pfitzner, *Bakuninstudien* [Prague, 1932], p. 100.)

476

and presently military operations in the narrow, congested quarters of the city became all but impossible. Insurrection fed on itself. Radical elements were able to take advantage of a situation that they by themselves could never have created.

Thus, by ineptitude and indecision the governments provoked revolutions that were as unexpected as they were unwanted, even by the opposition. In discussing this period stress should be laid on the failure of monarchy rather than on the forces of revolution.

To explain this failure presents something of a challenge. We must attribute it chiefly, I think, to the feeling of insecurity common to almost all princes in the period after the French Revolution. Their fear of the actually ineffectual secret societies and their dread of a world conspiracy against the throne and the altar are well known. Moreover, they were apprehensive of the newly aroused people, the more so in view of the frightful barricade fighting in Paris in July 1830 and, in the 1840s, the growing threat of a desperate proletariat.

The liberal middle classes, too, bear a heavy responsibility for the disastrous revolutions that ensued. In retrospect, it seems almost incredible that the Paris national guard should have carried its dislike of the régime and its desire for reforms to the point of standing aside, allowing the insurrection to develop and opening the door to political and social upheaval that, in turn, provided the opportunity for a repressive dictatorship. In Vienna the *Bürgerwehr* played an equally dubious role, setting the stage for the radicalism of the summer of 1848 and the ensuing counterrevolution.

Finally, one may fairly ask whether the revolutions of 1848 were necessary or even desirable. The work of reform was carried through more rapidly and more smoothly in countries such as Britain, the Low Countries, Scandinavia, and even Russia, in which there were no revolutions. In the last analysis the continental revolutions, while they achieved some measure of reform, led to grave political and social conflicts, to say nothing of national antagonisms and wars that might otherwise have been avoided. In view of the period of reaction that almost everywhere followed the revolutions it would seem that these upheavals actually delayed many urgently needed changes. Without the revolutions many later tensions might have been forestalled or at least attenuated, and Europe might have escaped a veritable harvest of both internal and external strains and animosities.

Retrospective

25

The Wellspring of Our Discontents

1968

The problem of perspective is one of the historian's chronic concerns. He knows that events look different when viewed in a millennial setting from what they seem at close hand. Take the French Revolution as a striking and instructive example. Contemporaries had strong opinions as well as violent feelings about it. But no one would contend that these contemporaries could have seen the larger import of that great cataclysm. If it were so, historians would be wasting their time and effort. In actual fact historians are still groping, after the lapse of almost two centuries, for a fuller and deeper understanding of this truly drastic turn in human affairs. Indeed, the wealth of data and the refinement of argument deriving from their efforts make one wonder at times whether perhaps greater emphasis should not be given to earlier and simpler interpretations.

Half a century has now elapsed since the conclusion of the First World War and the ensuing peace settlements. This is perhaps an ideal time for reviewing this great conflict, for fifty years gives us enough perspective to see things in the light of later developments. Yet we are not so far removed that we cannot recapture the hopes, the disillusions, and the enmities of that time. There are still many men alive, including the present writer, who fought in the First World War and have, over the years, observed its effects. Assuming then that the time is ripe for review and revaluation, let us attempt to determine what the impact of those years has been on European and world history.

Some historians see the First World War as a watershed and consider the period 1914–1919 as marking a halt in the headlong advances, political and social, of the nineteenth century. They stress the destruction of material and spiritual values, the release of forces of evil, and the revamping of Europe in such a way as to court future trials and disasters.

Note: Reprinted from *The Journal of Contemporary History* (October 1968), pp. 3–17.

There is certainly much to be said in support of this interpretation. On the other hand it must be said that, viewed in perspective, the major tribulations of the world today do not by any means all flow from the First World War. The march of modern science, on which so much of our civilization depends, has continued at the accelerating tempo set long before 1914 only to culminate in the nuclear threat to society and all mankind. Similarly, the phenomenal and frightening growth of the world population, one of the most ominous features of our times, had its origins in the eighteenth century and has proceeded quite independently of the First World War tragedy and the very considerable human losses which that conflict entailed. Again, the urbanization of western society and the mounting racial tensions throughout the world were affected in only a minor way, if at all, by the events of 1914–1919. And finally, the nationalistic fervor rampant in the world today drew its inspiration from developments long anteceding the great war. No doubt that conflagration stimulated national feeling and provoked national antagonisms, but the examples of India and Egypt, to mention only two cases, will suffice to demonstrate the rapid spread of nationalist principles well before the outbreak of hostilities in Europe.

It is clear then that some of the major concerns of modern society have deep roots in the historical evolution of recent centuries. To a large extent they are the inescapable concomitants of that fundamental transformation familiarly known as the Industrial Revolution which, while it brought humanity an untold enrichment in goods and an unprecedented rise in the standard of living, entailed dislocations and tensions of such magnitude as almost to defy nonviolent solutions.

Leaving these larger considerations aside, we must apply ourselves to the analysis of the impact of the war and the repercussions of the peace settlements. In so doing, we are struck at once by the stimulus provided by the war to various forces already operative. Looking back, we can distinguish the rising tide of totalitarianism, that is, the ominous antecedents of both Fascism and Bolshevism, as well as the recrudescence of revolutionary socialism which eventuated in Bolshevism. We can recognize the impact of Nietzschean teaching and the influence of Sorel, and we can see also the significance of such movements as the Action Française and Futurism. On the other side we can note in the labor movements the revulsion against the revisionism of Bernstein, the persuasive argumentation of Luxemburg and Hilferding, and the emergence of Lenin as a dominant leader.

Taken all in all, though, it is most unlikely that any of these extremist movements would have scored an early success had there been no major upheaval. The proto-fascist movements were spectacular, but not very influential. They were certainly far from shaking the general confidence of people in democracy and the forms of constitutional government. By many they were regarded as the demonstrations of cranks. On the other side, socialism and the labor movements were becoming steadily more domesticated. Despite all the party programs and congresses, despite all the revolutionary oratory, the laboring classes were more and more taking on the trade union mentality so hateful to Marx and Lenin, and were taking advantage of universal suffrage and parliamentary institutions to move from one success to another. By 1914 socialism had lost much of its bite and was rapidly becoming a liberal progressive movement directed by sober, intelligent leaders. At the same time the middle classes were becoming converted to the principles of the welfare state, to social security, and to the sharing of the product of labor. The extremists and their programs were voted down in the party congresses, and, when in 1914 the internationalism of the socialist parties was put to the test, the representatives of those parties voted almost to a man exactly like their bourgeois associates. It is surely no exaggeration to say that without the shattering impact of the great war the revolutionary elements would not for a long time, if ever, have been able to subvert any major government, not even the Russian.

The liquidation of the war and the forging of the peace settlements, too, must be viewed in the light of the animosities, the rancor, and the vindictiveness engendered by four years of desperate fighting. All wars tend to arouse the worst of human passions, and it was inevitable that so prolonged a holocaust as the First World War should inflame hatred of all kinds. Modern war, it has often been pointed out, involves the mobilization of all the varied forces of a nation and requires the utmost exertion of the entire people. In order to bring this about, governments feel impelled to stimulate effort by fostering antipathies and revengefulness. They did this in the First World War not only by perfecting the techniques of traditional psychological warfare, but also by the falsification of documents and by atrocity propaganda cut from whole cloth.

The French, who suffered particularly high losses in men and goods and who had behind them a long history of Franco-German hostility, were most uncompromising in the hour of victory. Clemenceau, who did not spare his own countrymen in the drive to win the war, was most obdurate in his insistence on revenge. A politician who even in 1870 was one of the mayors of Paris, who saw his country prostrate while the enemy marched victoriously down the Champs Elysées, and who witnessed the horrors of the Paris Commune, Clemenceau had ever since dreamed of the day of retribution. For him nothing should be allowed to stand in the way of a drastic reduction in German power for as long a period as possible, and of guarantees of French security. He and Foch could not hope to satisfy all their desires, but they did attain many of their ends and persisted in their demand that Germany pay the costs of the war. The continuance of the "hunger blockade" of Germany, in violation of the armistice, was regarded by Clemenceau as a convenient weapon to enforce acceptance of harsh peace terms. Similarly, the creation of new states in eastern Europe was thought of as providing a system of French satellites to replace Tsarist Russia as a bulwark against German expansion. The logic of the French position is not hard to grasp, but it does not alter the fact that Clemenceau obstructed all efforts to transcend the wartime mentality so as to shape the settlements with an eye to the future rather than to the satisfaction of time-worn enmities.

Lloyd George and Orlando were cooler and less emotional in their approach to the problems of peace, though they were more exposed to political pressure at home than was Clemenceau. The British Prime Minister is often given credit for having realized, at least towards the end, that the reconstruction of Europe was going awry and that French aims and claims threatened to provoke further tensions and crises. But Lloyd George was the man of the "knock-out" blow, the man who had skilfully avoided all efforts at mediation, the man who even in December 1916, when he replaced Asquith, had called for a peace on the basis of "complete restitution, full reparation and effectual guarantees." He did nothing to disabuse his countrymen of the idea that the Germans could and would pay for everything, and in the sequel of the all-too-successful elections of December 1918, he never showed any willingness to defy the forces demanding a draconian peace. Furthermore, if the Prime Minister belatedly softened in his attitude towards the German treaty, it was only after the decision had been reached by the conference to destroy German naval power and to cripple German economic life by the surrender of the merchant fleet, of railroad rolling stock, and of valuable natural resources. In addition, the liquidation of the German colonial empire and the division of the spoils (greatly in Britain's favor) under the guise of the mandate system had already been decreed. In short, Lloyd George's conversion came only after essential British interests had been secured, when the threat of French domination of the Continent became truly ominous. Even then he was hardly ever willing to go to bat for the policy of moderation which he now advocated.

As for Woodrow Wilson, his figure still remains enigmatic, despite much excellent work that has been done of late in the study of his career and policy. In retrospect one cannot help being impressed with the depth of his understanding. Though he had a low opinion of European alliances and balance of power and secret diplomacy, though he thought as late as 1918 that the Europeans should be left to settle their specific territorial and other problems by themselves, he had a keen perception of the larger problems of peacemaking. Before the intervention of the United States in the conflict, he had exposed himself to obloquy by calling for peace without victory, by which he meant a compromise peace negotiated between equals. In his address to the Senate on January 22, 1917, he argued that

> the right state of mind, the right feeling between nations, is as necessary for a lasting peace as is the just settlement of vexed questions of territory or of racial and national allegiance . . . Victory would mean peace forced upon the loser, a victor's terms imposed upon the vanquished. It would be accepted in humiliation, under duress, at an intolerable sacrifice, and would have a sting, a resentment, a bitter memory upon which terms of peace would rest, not permanently, but only as upon quicksand.

And later, in a speech of September 27, 1918, he called for impartial justice which "must involve no discrimination between those to whom we wish to be just and those to whom we do not wish to be just." Finally, on the very eve of the armistice, Sir William Wiseman reported the President as saying in conversation (October 16, 1918): "If we humiliate the German people and drive them too far, we shall destroy all form of government, and Bolshevism will take its place. We ought not to grind them to powder or there will be nothing to build up from." He disliked, he said, the idea of settling peace terms without the ene-

485

mies being present to state their case, and thought that Germany should be a member of the League of Nations, which "should be the very centre of the Peace Settlement, the pillar upon which the house will stand."

Wilson, then, saw all the dangers of a complete victory and of a draconian peace dictated to the defeated. For that very reason he felt that an international organization to revise and rectify provisions of the treaties, as well as to forestall future conflict, was of transcendent importance. One can hardly question the sincerity of his purpose or the nobility of his vision. The question is rather whether at Paris he made full use of his great power and immense prestige to implement his program. Why, after being hailed in December 1918 by the peoples of Europe as the harbinger of a new order, did he yield step by step to the pressures of his fellow-statesmen? In the matter of the League covenant he did persist. While Lloyd George and Clemenceau argued that the settlement of concrete issues was the necessary foundation for international organization, Wilson insisted that it be taken up first and that the covenant of the League be made an integral part of the peace treaty. It is more than likely that if he had yielded on this crucial issue the sceptics and opponents of the League idea would eventually, after securing what they wanted, have scuttled the entire project. But preoccupation with the League covenant of necessity distracted the attention of the President from other more mundane matters and made it difficult for him not to reciprocate in making concessions.

If, with respect to concrete issues, Wilson lent himself to mistaken decisions, it must be remembered that until a late date he thought of leaving these matters to the Europeans and still reckoned on the Germans being brought into the discussions when a draft of the treaty was completed. It is worth noting, too, that he was by upbringing decidedly Anglophil, that he shared the common American devotion to France, and that, without looking much into the matter, he accepted the prevalent conviction that the German government, if not the German people, was responsible for the catastrophe. He himself had a very limited acquaintance with continental countries and but little knowledge of their problems. An American committee of experts (the Inquiry) had been studying important issues for some time, and in the course of the peace conference American commissioners were sent to many Central European countries to report on conditions as they developed. But the President was not the man to turn readily to others for an opinion, and, when he did so, it might often be when the fat was already in the fire. Besides, it must be confessed that the American experts and commissioners were not all immune to the wartime fever. Some of their opinions and recommendations would not in retrospect meet with much approval.

More important, however, than these considerations was the political pressure under which Wilson worked at Paris. The national elections of November 1918 had returned Republican majorities in both houses of the legislature, and Republican leaders, rightly or wrongly, interpreted this result as popular endorsement of a harsh peace. Former president Theodore Roosevelt and Senator Henry Cabot Lodge called for unconditional surrender and the stiffest possible terms. "No peace that satisfies Germany in any degree can ever satisfy us," declared Lodge in August 1918; "it cannot be a negotiated peace. It must be a dictated peace." This was only the opening shot in a steadily spreading campaign. It may well be that Wilson under-estimated the strength of the opposition, but he must have noticed that his fellow-statesmen in Paris questioned whether in fact he could speak for his country. We may assume that this made it seem to him all the more imperative to clinch the League issue, for which there was far more support in the United States than for a moderate nego-tiated peace. Actually the very fact that the President had insisted on the inclusion of the covenant in the Treaty of Versailles gave his opponents a welcome opening for attack. The battle of the amend-ments began. Some of them made good sense from the standpoint of American interests, and others, while not of crucial import, were at least reasonable and would indubitably have been accepted by the European governments in order to secure the adherence of the United States to the new organization. The dispute, it might be said, hinged less on the animosity of men such as Lodge to the President or to the League project, than on Wilson's obduracy. Before as well as after his collapse the President refused to yield even a tittle of his sacred text, probably as a matter of prestige, but also because of his unshakable belief that the sentiment of the country would support him. Having retreated from the pinnacle of his idealism, Wilson was determined to stand his ground come what may, and so the treaty, with the League covenant, was lost in the Senate. The tragedy of this outcome it would be hard to overstate, for the United States, after overcoming its isola-tionism in 1917 in order to rescue western Europe, now rejected its newly acquired leadership, eschewed all participation in world organization, and declined all responsibility for collective action on behalf of peace. Who would now deny that the United States, by the Senate's final rejection of the Versailles Treaty and its desertion of the League, underlined all the shortcomings of the peace settlements, and assumed a heavy responsibility for the weakness and ineffectuality of the world organization, that is for the return of international anarchy in more aggravated form than ever?

The Treaty of Versailles violated the spirit and in some respects the letter of Wilson's Fourteen Points, on which the surrender of Germany and the armistice were based. This was presumably of little concern to Clemenceau and Lloyd George, who had never endorsed the Wilsonian program and who resented the President's high-handed assumption of the role of sole negotiator for the Allied powers. This violation of solemn agreements, however, undermined Wilson's position and cost him the support of many who had looked upon him as the harbinger of a new age and a more just order. Increasingly, as the weeks went by, the President was impelled to yield on vital items of the settlement, until in the end the sum total of the treaty was a punitive document indeed, and one which was imposed on the Germans on a take-it-or-leave-it basis.

This is hardly the place to attempt a summary of the hundreds of articles by which the defeated enemy, charged with sole responsibility for the outbreak of the war (article 231), was shorn of substantial territories, obliged to assume heavy servitudes, disarmed except for a paltry 100,000 man army for domestic security, and burdened with a preposterous but purposely undefined bill for reparations, the effect of which was intended to be the long-term debility of the country. It will long remain a mystery how, in the circumstances, the new German republic was able to survive and successfully repel the rising forces of desperation and revolt. Looking back, one can hardly escape the conclusion that the entire reparations program was an international calamity of the first order. Not only Keynes but also other experts foresaw the disastrous consequences for the victors as well as the vanquished. Despite successive adjustments, such as the Dawes and Young Plans, the issue had not been fully disposed of when the great depression broke over the Western world. No doubt the economic tribulations and financial confusion engendered by the reparations servative forces. While on the left the Bolshevik program of no annexations and no indemnities made a genuine appeal and strengthened the demand for a new order along Wilsonian lines, on the right there was an ever more insistent demand for drastic action and harsh terms, to say nothing of military intervention to crush Bolshevism in its infancy.

As for the statesmen, it would appear that initially they believed that so extreme and radical a movement as Bolshevism could not long maintain itself; that in fact a strict quarantine would suffice to strangle it. But when, in the winter of 1918–19, the whole of central and eastern Europe sank into chaos, and the Bolsheviks, though hard pressed at home, launched an aggressive propaganda appeal to all peoples to rise against the upper classes, the threat of subversion became formidable and immediate. It is well known that Lenin's great hope and expectation was that defeated and hungry Germany would revolt and carry much of the Continent with it. The German provisional government itself raised the specter of a German-Russian alliance in the hope of securing more favorable treatment, but in reality proved itself uncompromisingly hostile to Spartacism and other radical movements. The Germans could certainly have done their former enemies no greater favor than to stamp out the forces of social subversion and stand guard against the Bolshevik advance in the Baltic area. Nonetheless, the situation in the spring of 1919 was touch and go, as demonstrated by the establishment of Communist régimes in Bavaria and Hungary.

Conservatives, such as Winston Churchill, persistently urged the destruction of the Bolshevik régime by military force as the only safeguard against the triumph of Communism in much of Europe. But none of the leading statesmen, least of all Wilson, would countenance such drastic action, chiefly from fear lest the working classes rise in revolt against their governments, but also because of the impossibility of finding enough troops for so formidable an operation. A limited intervention, chiefly of a defensive nature, had already taken place in 1918. But even this met with vigorous opposition from the war-weary peoples, who made it clear that they would not allow a new war, for whatever purposes, to be foisted upon them. Mutinous outbreaks among the British and French troops in Russia made it equally clear that large-scale military action was entirely out of the question.

Efforts were made by the peace conference to find a solution in conjunction with exiled Russian statesmen such as Sazonov, but these

problem played a significant role in undermining the postwar order.

To the material items of the settlement must be added the moral obloquy and shock to German self-respect involved in the so-called war-guilt clause and the sense of betrayal and outrage provoked by the violations of the Fourteen Points and the prolongation of the hunger blockade. Psychologically the scene was set for the stab-in-the-back agitation, the great war-guilt debate, and the emergence of Nazism. In addition the excesses of the peace treaty contributed mightily to the growing tensions of the ensuing twenty years. They help to explain the rising uncertainty as to the justice of the treatment meted out to the defeated in 1919 and the steadily mounting feeling that concessions should be made to rectify acknowledged injustices. This sense of guilt on the part of the erstwhile victors was of course an integral part of the policy of appeasement, and this policy in its turn served only to strengthen Hitler's hand and to encourage him to press further and further along the road that led to the Second World War.

The peace settlements (the secondary treaties as well as the Versailles Treaty) were designed, in the constructive sense, to ensure the triumph of nationalism and democracy. All peoples were to be accorded the right of self-determination and were to be supported in establishing popular, representative government. The defeated Germans, to be sure, especially those of the former Hapsburg Monarchy, were considered an exception. Clemenceau was adamant in his refusal to see Germany enlarged by the addition of the German provinces of Austria. Elsewhere, however, the principle of nationalism was given full expression and high hopes were placed on a world made safe for democracy. In retrospect it is plain that much of this program and policy was pursued uncritically. Experience has taught how far most of the Continent was from being prepared for democratic government. Furthermore, it might be argued that the new nations, although they have proved durable, by disrupting the eastern empires sapped the stability of the entire area and destroyed a well-established balance of power. None of the succession states, not even Poland, was strong enough politically or economically or militarily to withstand the pressures of Nazi Germany or Soviet Russia. No doubt many people in these states have asked themselves whether the game was worth the candle—whether a factitious independence ending in foreign domination and reduction to satellite status was preferable to the pre-1914 régime.

In this context it must be remembered that this disruption of central and eastern Europe was not foreordained. Nationalism had been a potent and effective instrument for unifying the numerous small states of the area in the nineteenth century, and there had been a recrudescence of nationalist ardor in the immediate prewar period, due in part to conflicting imperialist claims but even more to the opposition of conservative forces to the growing internationalism of both capital and labor. The effect of the war was to arrest the trend towards international cooperation and European unity and at the same time to raise the issue of weakening the enemy by fostering centrifugal forces within its boundaries. Both sides resorted to these tactics, but the Allied powers had by far the most to offer, and it was their policy that eventually produced the breakup of the Hapsburg Monarchy and the emergence of the new states. It is often said that they had relatively little to do with this business; that the new states had already proclaimed their independence and set up their governments before the Paris peace conference even met. But this is surely only a half-truth. The national movements in central and eastern Europe had before the war been modest and limited in their aspirations. Their aim was to secure greater autonomy and increased cultural freedom. Only a few extremists talked of independence, which most of the leaders recognized as impracticable, if only for economic reasons. And so the situation remained during most of the war, the French government in particular favoring the preservation of the Hapsburg Monarchy as an important factor in the balance of power. Only after efforts to secure the defection of the Vienna government had failed and after Wilson had proclaimed the Fourteen Points did the Allied governments abandon the policy of sustaining the Austrian Empire in favor of the various national committees, which were then encouraged to set their sights on full independence.

The defection of Russia and France's need for new friends and supporters in the east may well have influenced Clemenceau to change his mind in favor of Poland, Czechoslovakia, and the other succession states, but Wilson's policy was probably the decisive force. The President was positively obsessed with the principle of self-determination, without having much notion of the difficulties in the way of its realization. It was in this respect that his ignorance of European conditions bore its bitterest fruit. Had he learned sooner that there were three million Germans in Bohemia, he might have been less hasty in

accepting and backing the new Czechoslovak state. By 1919 it was too late. When he finally stood out against the Italian claims in the Adriatic, he cut a sorry figure. In any event, as we look back from the vantage point of fifty years and review the countless trials and tribulations which these new states have had to endure, to say nothing of the international tensions occasioned by their very existence, we are certainly justified in asking whether the peace conference's role in the fragmentation of much of Europe was a blessing or a misfortune.

Many issues raised by the war and the peace must be passed over in a summary essay of this kind, but the Russian problem was of such overriding importance as to deserve special consideration and emphasis. The charge often levelled against the peacemakers, that they failed to understand the Russian problem and to come to grips with it, is hardly tenable. Numerous recent studies, based on the official records, have highlighted the fact that, on the contrary, the statesmen at Paris were all too conscious of the problem and wrestled with it as best they could. It is hardly an exaggeration to say that the specter of Bolshevism and social revolution hovered in the background of the peace conference from beginning to end and that, furthermore, many different moves were made in the effort to exorcize it.

It stands to reason that the Bolshevik seizure of power in November 1917 came as a surprise, for, despite the chaotic situation in Russia in the summer of 1917, it seemed unlikely that a small minority group should be able to outmaneuver much stronger parties such as the Social Revolutionaries, should establish control of a major European state, proclaim a Communist régime which theretofore had been of only theoretical interest, and presently desert Russia's western allies in the hour of their greatest need. Naturally the Bolshevik Revolution profoundly changed the complexion of the war and at the same time loosed forces which had hitherto been dormant. Labor everywhere could hardly avoid the fascination of an experiment which promised so much of what the working classes had been striving for. During the year 1918 the lower classes in all countries were becoming war-weary and restless. It was a question how long they could be counted on to support the struggle. At the same time the propertied classes were profoundly disturbed and soon apprehensive of possible social upheaval. In the larger sense the Bolshevik victory, while it tended to divide and so to weaken the forces of labor, provoked a recrudescence of co

proved fruitless. Like most emigré groups, the Russian group was rent by dissension, and none of its leaders was willing or able to commit himself to such a democratic program as the Allies required. Similarly, moves made to deal directly with the Bolsheviks ran into countless difficulties, and the Allies saw no alternative to the program of financial and military support of the various counterrevolutionary generals. Of these, it is clear, none had much popular support or much chance of success. The Paris peacemakers desired nothing more ardently than the destruction of the Bolshevik régime. Their action against the Communist rule of Bela Kun in Hungary shows that they would shrink from no course that was feasible and promising. However, in the case of Russia there was no such possibility. Nothing they could do was really effective. In the end all they achieved was the distrust and enmity of the Bolsheviks, which was to color all international relations for decades to come and which, more than anything else, provided the foundation for the division of Europe and later the world into opposing ideological camps.

Many of the peace terms so passionately formulated at Paris were soon obliterated and others were presently serving purposes diametrically opposed to those intended by the framers. The reparations program proved a dismal failure, the Rhineland occupation was abandoned before its term, the disarmament of Germany, which was to be the prelude to general disarmament, was never susceptible of enforcement and soon lost its *raison d'être*. Furthermore, Germany, deprived of so many capital goods, was able to start afresh and with the support of former enemies to build an ultramodern industrial plant. Shorn of its colonies, Germany was spared the agony and expense attending the gradual liquidation of European imperialism. The triumph of nationalism in the Danube Basin served among other things to facilitate the resumption of the traditional *Drang nach Osten*. The German professional army provided the officer corps for the vast expansion and high standards of the great military machine that was to stage the blitzkriegs of 1939–1941. All told, it would seem in retrospect that much of the effort of 1919 to break the power of Germany for at least a generation actually accrued to the benefit of that country in an even shorter time. Apparently a Carthaginian peace, if it falls short of the actual destruction of the enemy, is about the least profitable settlement imaginable.

Over the long term the greatest contribution of the war and the peace seems to have been the launching of the League of Nations. This can be said even with full realization of the weaknesses of that institution, for we can easily see that the League marked an important departure in the conduct of international relations. Had the three great powers—isolationist United States, defeated Germany, and outlawed Russia—been present at its councils from the very beginning, it might well have progressed instead of gradually failing and ultimately disintegrating. It is one more irony of history that, in the 1930s when the decay of the international order was already well advanced, Russia was admitted and the United States, though still only an "observer," began to show a greater readiness to cooperate—too late, too late. However, the eclipse of the League was to be shortlived, for the second great world conflict underlined even more heavily the overriding need for international organization and action. This is the most eloquent testimony to the achievement, however partial, of the original effort. The United Nations, too, has its weaknesses and its frustrations, yet it marks a further advance towards effective international authority, without which modern society cannot hope long to survive.

Beyond these particulars there are still imponderable and immeasurable effects of the war and the peace which cannot be left out of account. Even the appalling human losses and the vast destruction of hard-won goods were probably of less account than the impact of fratricidal war on the European community and the ensuing division of western society by ideological antagonisms as well as by the distrust and animosity that flourish in times of conflict. How shall we evaluate the revival of ruthlessness and violence, the disillusionment about progress, the profound spiritual deflation which were the legacy of the war and the peace? Nor were these effects confined to Europe itself. They reached out to all corners of the earth, destroyed the image of Europe as the vanguard of modern civilization, and prepared the backlash against imperialism with which we are all familiar. The massacres on the battlefields of Europe were witnessed by hundreds of thousands of non-European troops and laborers, who no doubt contributed to the loss of respect for the white peoples which soon seized on the peoples of Asia and Africa. From the extreme nationalism fostered by the warring powers, non-Europeans were to draw the inspiration for their new, often immature and sometimes preposterous nationalisms. To be sure, the time had not yet come to challenge European rule with any real chance of success, but the seed had been planted and by 1939 had already germinated. It took only another severe shock to the European order to destroy the primacy of that continent and encompass the liquidation of imperialism, the hallmark of European ascendancy. Whatever the reservations one might wish to make, the conclusion is incontestable that the First World War and more particularly the crucial years 1917–1919 marked a major turning point in European and world affairs and, furthermore, that they helped substantially to undermine the foundations on which our civilization now so precariously stands.

Chronological List of William L. Langer's Publications

Note: This bibliography does not include book reviews or brief topical articles.

1919

With "E" of the First Gas, with Robert B. MacMullin. Brooklyn: 1919. Republished with a new introduction by Langer and without the chapter by MacMullin under the title *Gas and Flame in World War I*. New York: Alfred A. Knopf, 1965.

1925

"The Franco-Russian Alliance, 1890–1894," in two parts, *Slavonic Review*, III, no. 9 (March 1925), 554–575, and IV, no. 10 (June 1925), 83–100.
"The European Powers and the French Occupation of Tunis, 1878–1881," in two parts, *American Historical Review*, XXXI (October 1925), 55–78, and XXXV (January 1926), 251–265.

1926

"Der Russisch-Japanische Krieg," *Europäische Gespräche*, IV, no. 6 (June 1926), 279–322. The English original, "The Origin of the Russo-Japanese War," is published for the first time in this collection.
"Fascism on the Offensive," *Foreign Notes*, II, no. 10 (September 1926), 1. [A publication of the Chicago Council on Foreign Relations.]
"International Relations," chap. 33 in A. C. Flick, *Modern World History, 1776–1926*. New York: Alfred A. Knopf, 1926, pp. 503–528. [Authorship not specified in publication.]

1928

"Russia, the Straits Question, and the Origins of the Balkan League, 1908–1912," *Political Science Quarterly*, XLIII, no. 3 (September 1928), 321–363.

1929

The Franco-Russian Alliance, 1890–1894. Cambridge, Mass.: Harvard University Press, 1929.
"Russia, The Straits Question, and the European Powers, 1904–1908," *English Historical Review*, XLIV (January 1929), 59–85.

"The 1908 Prelude to the World War," *Foreign Affairs*, VII, no. 4 (July 1929), 635–649.
"Recent Books on the History of the Near East," *Journal of Modern History*, I, no. 3 (September 1929), 420–441.

1931

European Alliances and Alignments, 1871–1890. New York: Alfred A. Knopf, 1931. Second edition with supplementary bibliography, 1950. Paper back, New York: Vintage Books, 1964.
"History and Nationalism as Portrayed by Sidney B. Fay," in *Methods in the Social Sciences: A Case Book,* ed. Stuart A. Rice. Chicago: University of Chicago Press, 1931, pp. 383–394.

1932

"The Rise of the Ottoman Turks and Its Historical Background," with Robert P. Blake. *American Historical Review*, XXXVII, no. 3 (April 1932), 468–505.

1933

Foreign Affairs Bibliography, 1919–1932, with Hamilton Fish Armstrong. New York: Harper and Brothers, 1933.

1934

The Rise of Modern Europe (Editor) 20 vols. New York: Harper and Brothers, 1934 and thereafter.

1935

The Diplomacy of Imperialism, 2 vols. New York: Alfred A. Knopf, 1935. Second edition with supplementary bibliography, 1951.
"A Critique of Imperialism. 'Imperialism: A Study," by J. A. Hobson, London, 1902," *Foreign Affairs*, XIV, no. 1 (October 1935), 102–119.

1936

"The Struggle for the Nile," *Foreign Affairs*, XIV, no. 2 (January 1936), 259–273.
"Alliance System and League. Are both moving in the same direction?" *Polity* (February 1936), pp. 10–11.

1937

"The Revival of Imperialism," *Harvard Guardian* (March 1937), pp. 3–7.
"Struggle for Control of the Mediterranean," *Harvard Alumni Bulletin* (Dec. 3, 1937), pp. 300–302.
"Tribulations of Empire," *Foreign Affairs*, XV, no. 4 (July 1937), 646–659.

1938

"When German Dreams Come True," *Yale Review*, XXVII, no. 4 (June 1938), 678–698.

1940

An Encyclopedia of World History (Editor). Boston: Houghton Mifflin, 1940. Other editions 1948, 1952, 1968.

1941

"The Faith of Woodrow Wilson," *New York Times Magazine* (May 4, 1941), p. 5.

1947

Our Vichy Gamble. New York: Alfred A. Knopf, 1947. Paper back, New York: W. W. Norton, 1966.
"Political Problems of a Coalition," *Foreign Affairs*, XXVI, no. 1 (October 1947), 73–89.

1948

"The American Attitude Toward Europe: An Historical Approach," Three lectures delivered in 1948, published for the first time in this collection.
"Scholarship and the Intelligence Problem," *Proceedings of the American Philosophical Society*, XCII, no. 1 (March 1948), 43–46.
"The Mechanism of American Foreign Policy," *International Affairs*, XXIV, no. 3 (July 1948), 319–328.

1952

The Challenge to Isolation, 1937–1940, with S. Everett Gleason. New York: Harper, 1952. Paperback in two volumes, New York: Harper and Row, 1964.
"American Objectives," *Naval War College Review*, V, no. 1 (September 1952), 14–30.

1953

The Undeclared War, 1940–1941, with S. Everett Gleason. New York: Harper, 1953.
"Preface," in *Essays in honor of Conyers Read*, ed. Norton Downs. Chicago: University of Chicago Press, 1953, pp. vii–xiv.
"The Historian and the Present," *Vital Speeches of the Day*, XIX, no. 10 (March 1953), 312–314.

1956

"Die Innenseite der amerikanischen Aussenpolitik," *Geschichte und Politik*, no. 23 (1956), pp. 1–25.
"Woodrow Wilson: His Education in World Affairs," *Confluence*, V, no. 3 (Autumn 1956), 183–194.

1957

"From Isolation to Mediation" and "Peace and the New World Order," in *Woodrow Wilson and the World of Today*, ed. Arthur P. Dudden. Philadelphia: University of Pennsylvania Press, 1957, pp. 22–46, 67–96.

1958

"The Next Assignment," *American Historical Review,* LXIII, no. 2 (January 1958), 283–304. Also published in *American Imago,* XV, no. 3 (1958), 235–266.

1960

"Conyers Read (1881–1959)," *Yearbook of the American Philosophical Society.* Philadelphia: 1960, pp. 172–176.

1961

"Bismarck as a Dramatist," in *Studies in Diplomatic History and Historiography,* ed. A. O. Sarkissian. London: Longmans, Green, and Co., 1961, pp. 199–216.

1962

"Red Rag and Gallic Bull: The French Decision for War, 1870," in *Europa und Übersee: Festschrift für Egmont Zechlin.* Hamburg [1962], pp. 135–154.

"The Role of the United States in the World," *Bulletin of the National Association of Secondary School Principals,* XLVI, no. 274 (May 1962), 121–130.

"Farewell to Empire," *Foreign Affairs,* XLI, no. 1 (October 1962), 115–130.

1963

"Europe's Initial Population Explosion," *American Historical Review,* LXIX, no. 1 (October 1963), 1–17.

1964

"Foreword," in Halvdan Koht, *Driving Forces in History.* Cambridge, Mass.: Harvard University Press, 1964, pp. v–vi.

"The Black Death," *Scientific American,* CCX, no. 2 (February 1964), 114–121.

1965

"Population in the Perspective of History," *Harvard Public Health Alumni Bulletin,* XXII, no. 1 (January 1965), Supplement, 5–7.

1966

"The Pattern of Urban Revolution in 1848," in *French Society and Culture Since the Old Regime,* ed. Evelyn M. Acomb and Marvin L. Brown, Jr. New York: Holt, Rinehart and Winston, 1966, pp. 89–118.

1968

"The Well-Spring of our Discontents," *Journal of Contemporary History,* III, no. 4 (October 1968), 3–17.

Index

501

Index

Ašikpašazāde, 363, 390, 396
Asquith, Herbert Henry, 83, 484
Assab, 224
Assim Bey, 105, 109, 112, 117–121
Aswan, 188
Aswan Dam, 188, 191; enlargement of, 191, 192. *See also* Nile River
Atbara, 188, 190
Atlantic Charter, 323–324, 325
Atomic bomb, as deterrent, 338–339
Austria: relation to Russia and the Near East, 46, 48, 115, 120; proposed agreement with Russia, 57–59, 61–62, 79–81; annexation of Bosnia-Herzegovina, 63–64, 75, 76, 79, 81; and Serbia, 78–80, 87–88, 98, 108; supported by Germany, 84–85; and Rumania, 96; proposed Balkan League against, 103, 126; and Italy, 203; and *Anschluss*, 207, 227; target of Pan-Germanism, 229–233; in World War I, 490
Austria-Hungary: as naval power, 217; obstacle to German expansion, 235
Austro-Russian Agreement (1897), 49, 99
Azores, the, 216

Babinger, Franz, 361n, 364, 365, 394
Baghdad railway, 51, 113
Bahr-el-Jebel, 190, 192
Baker, Sir Samuel, 188
Balearics, 215, 216, 220, 224–225
Balfour, Arthur James, 27
Balkan Entente, 204, 206
Balkan War, 127
Balkans: Charykov's plan for, 93–95, 110; rivalries in, 95–96, 127; Russia and, 100–120; Hartwig's plan for, 103; proposed league of, 105–107, 120; linked to Straits problem, 110; Italian alliances in, 203; Hitler's plan for, 237, 240–241; Soviet policy toward, 325; nomads in, 373. *See also* Bosnia, Herzegovina
Bancroft, George, 289
Bandung Conference, 254
Barlow, Joel, 288
Barrère, Camille, 215, 218
Barrot, Odilon, 463
Barthold, W. W., 371
Barthou, Jean Louis, 204, 205, 241–242
Bavaria, 492
Bayezid II, 363
Bedr-ed-din, Sheikh, 391

Bektash, Hājjī, 390–391; Order of, 391–392
Belgium, 17; and German colonies, 211; and the Congo, 249–250
Benckendorff, 55, 56, 119
Benedetti, Count: on Hohenzollern candidacy to Spanish throne, 129, 132, 135, 138; supposed insolence of, 141–142, 149, 158; on Prussian refusal of guarantees, 151, 154, 157
Beneš, Eduard, 202, 235
Berchtesgaden, 63, 91
Bergson, Henri, 406
Berlin: revolution of 1848 in, 452, 469–475; immigration to, 454; housing in, 455; lack of police in, 471
Berlin, Treaty of, 62, 73, 79
Berlin-Baghdad railway, 231, 238
Bernstein, Eduard, 482
Bessarabia, 202
Bezobrazov, Alexander, 35, 36, 43, 44; project for Korea, 14–15; and the Boxer rising, 18; attack on April Convention, 29–30; plan for Manchuria, 30–34, 38n
Biography, application of psychoanalysis to, 412–414
Birth rate, European: causes of rise in, 443, 450–451; and marriage customs, 443, 451; and introduction of new crops, 444–450. *See also* Population
Bismarck, Otto von, 46, 157, 214; and Triple Alliance, 76–77, 85, 200; on the Ems dispatch, 128–129, 147; and events preceding Ems, 130–137; confusion of dates by, 134–135; dinner party of, 137–140; and legend of Ems, 141–142; basic purpose of, 143–144, 151; memoirs of quoted, 144–146; opposed to Pan-Germanism, 229, 230, 232, 241; on imperialism, 247
Bissagos Islands, 225
Bithynia, 384, 396
Bizerta, 214, 224
Black Death: psychological effects of, 418, 421–422; mortality rates of, 419, 436; long-term effects of, 422–430. *See also* Epidemics; Middle Ages
Black Sea, as Russian base, 52, 56, 58, 78
Blue Nile, 188, 189, 190–191; proposed dam on, 191
Boak, Arthur, 417
Boccaccio, Giovanni, 422
Bohemia, 232, 233, 239, 240
Bokhara, 253

502

Index

Uruj 'ibn 'Adil, chronicle of, 364

Vambéry, Armin, 368
Vandenberg, Arthur H., 309
Vannovski, Colonel, 29
Vasil'ievski, V. G., 385
Venizelos, Eleutherios, 105, 109
Versailles, Treaty of, 201, 204, 303; Wilson and, 354–356, 486–487; Senate rejection of, 488; punitive aspects of, 488; effects of, 488–489, 493
Vesnic, M., 82
Victor Emmanuel, king of Italy, 220
Victoria, Lake, 189, 190
Vienna: revolution of 1848 in, 452, 464–469; immigration to, 454; housing in, 455
Vienna School League, 231
Vitzthum, Count, 160
Vladivostok, 11; acquired by Russia, 5
Vonliarliarski, V. M., 14–15
Vorontsev-Dashkov, I. I., 14–15

Waeber, 32
Wagner, Richard, 401
Wakatsuki, Baron, 177–178
Wallace, Sir Donald MacKenzie, 55
Wallace, Henry, 311
War, linked to changes in population, 434, 435
War of 1812, 279–280, 288
Washington, George, 274, 283; on European involvement, 275, 276–278
Weber, Alfred, 403
Webster, Daniel, 283, 292
Webster, Noah, 288, 289
Welles, Sumner, 315, 320, 322
Werther, Baron von, 134, 135, 136, 138, 157, 161
West, American. See Frontier
Western Germany, rearmament of, 342
Westernization of world, tendency toward, 255–256, 257; contribution of, 258–259
White, J. G., Engineering Corporation, 196
White Nile, 188, 189, 190; dam on, 192
Whitman, Walt, 289
Wilenski, R. H., 406
Wilhelm II, Kaiser, 73–74, 129, 298; on Hohenzollern candidacy for Spanish throne, 132, 137, 138, 141, 151–152, 161

Wilson, Woodrow, 263–266; and neutrality, 299–300; and the League, 302–303, 353, 486–487; changing reputation of, 348–349; changes in outlook of, 350–352; Fourteen Points of, 353–354, 488, 490; at peace conference, 354–356; errors of in estimating public opinion, 356–357; attitude toward peace settlement, 485–488; on self-determination, 490
Windischgrätz, Field Marshal Prince, 468, 469
Winslow, Edward, 269
Wiseman, Sir William, 485
Withoft, Admiral, 39
Witte, Count, 6, 91; policy toward China, 8–11, 16–17; on Korea, 9, 24; declining influence of, 13; and the Bezobrazov project, 15, 19, 29–30, 32–33; and Boxer rising, 18–19; on Manchuria, 21, 23; resignation of, 37; consequences of policy of, 43–44; and the Nelidov plan, 49; and proposed English alliance, 54–55
Wittek, Paul, 363
Woodward, Sir Llewelyn, 400
World War I: parallels with crisis of 1908, 76; situation in Mediterranean, 219–220; stage in breakdown of imperialism, 251; American intervention in, 300–301; efforts of Wilson to intervene in, 350–352; in retrospect, 481–495; problems raised by peace settlement, 484–491; and the Russian problem, 491–493; final effect on Germany, 493; League a result of, 493–494; legacy of, 494–495
World War II, and breakdown of imperialism, 251–252
Wyclif, John, 428

Xenoi Tekmoreioi, 396

Yaḥši Faḳih, 363
Yaḥyā ben Khalîl, 393
Yalta Conference, 325–327
Yalu Concession, 14
Yalu River, 31, 32, 35, 41
Yamagata, 7
Yangtze agreement, 20
Yayā, the, 397
Yemen, 186, 223
Yenišehir, 387
Yinanç, Mükrimin Halil, 364
Yongampo, 35
Young, Arthur, 446

516